THE LAW OF PUBLIC ORDER
AND PROTEST

THE LAW OF PUBLIC ORDER AND PROTEST

By

HIS HONOUR JUDGE PETER THORNTON QC

Senior Circuit Judge, Central Criminal Court

RUTH BRANDER

Barrister, Doughty Street Chambers

RICHARD THOMAS

Barrister, Doughty Street Chambers

DAVID RHODES

Barrister, Doughty Street Chambers

MIKE SCHWARZ

Partner and member of Bindmans LLP
Visiting lecturer at Westminster University

EDWARD REES QC

Barrister, Doughty Street Chambers

OXFORD
UNIVERSITY PRESS

OXFORD

UNIVERSITY PRESS

Great Clarendon Street, Oxford OX2 6DP

Oxford University Press is a department of the University of Oxford.
It furthers the University's objective of excellence in research, scholarship,
and education by publishing worldwide in

Oxford New York

Auckland Cape Town Dar es Salaam Hong Kong Karachi
Kuala Lumpur Madrid Melbourne Mexico City Nairobi
New Delhi Shanghai Taipei Toronto

With offices in

Argentina Austria Brazil Chile Czech Republic France Greece
Guatemala Hungary Italy Japan Poland Portugal Singapore
South Korea Switzerland Thailand Turkey Ukraine Vietnam

Oxford is a registered trade mark of Oxford University Press
in the UK and in certain other countries

Published in the United States
by Oxford University Press Inc., New York

British Library Cataloguing in Publication Data

Data available

Library of Congress Cataloging-in-Publication Data

The law of public order and protest / Peter Thornton ... [et al.].

p. cm.

ISBN 978-0-19-956614-3 (hardback)
1. Breach of the peace–Great Britain. 2. Offenses against public safety–Great
Britain. 3. Civil rights–Great Britain. I. Thornton, Peter, 1946–
KD8035.L39 2010
345.41'0243–dc22

2010003767

Typeset by Glyph International, Bangalore, India
Printed in Great Britain
on acid-free paper by
CPI Anthony Rowe
ISBN 978-0-19-956614-3

1 3 5 7 9 10 8 6 4 2

PREFACE

The object of this book is to provide a comprehensive account of public order law. The emphasis is upon public order law in the context of protest, but not to the exclusion of other relevant aspects of the subject.

The law of public order is often made to reflect its time. The Public Order Act 1936 was born out of the fascist marches of the 1930s. The Public Order Act 1986, still the bedrock of the modern law, came after the Southall riots of 1979 and the Brixton disorders of 1981, events fuelled by a blend of race and inner city discontent. More recently the Serious Organised Crime and Police Act 2005 tried, but failed, to bring an end to what some MPs called 'unsightly' camps of protestors, outside the home of democracy in Parliament Square.

Just as protest itself has moved on from the miners' strike and secondary picketing at factories in the 1970s and 1980s to environmental issues such as GM crops; nuclear power stations; and airport runways; protest against war and conflict has always brought people to the streets. Once it was the Vietnam war, now it is Iraq, Afghanistan, and Palestine, Burma, and Sri Lanka, to name but a few. Protest may often seem a symbol of somebody else's problems far away: a lone protestor and a tank in Tiananmen Square; monks in Tibet; students in Tehran; even the refusal of Rosa Parks to give up her seat on the bus in Montgomery, Alabama. But sometimes it happens in your own backyard, often a local issue of burning concern—an ugly skyscraper; a mobile telephone cell mast; a village bypass. Then you hear, in Surrey or Cheshire, 'I never thought I'd join the great unwashed.' In short, protest may be international or local, on big issues or small. But as long as it is peaceful, it forms an important role, described by a senior judge as 'the lifeblood of democracy'.[1]

It is not always peaceful, though. Disorder has taken place not just in London, but in Southall and Brixton, and in Trafalgar Square against the poll tax in 1990. In Bradford in 2001 race protest became violent and widespread, and was prosecuted as riot, with heavy deterrent sentences. There has been police violence too. It may be rare but it is not new. It is always shocking. For example, in 1979 Blair Peach, a teacher, was killed by still unidentified police officers on his way home from a demonstration in Southall. Exactly thirty years later in 2009 a newspaper seller, not a protestor, was pushed over and baton struck by a police officer. He was on his way home too, trying to avoid police no-go zones to control protests at the G20 summit in London.[2] Minutes later he collapsed and later died, apparently of a heart attack.

---

[1] Lord Steyn in *R v Home Secretary of State, ex p Simms* [2000] 2 AC 115, 126.
[2] See <http://www.guardian.co.uk> video footage.

But despite some violence and discontent, and the ever present threat of public terrorism, the theme of liberty still runs strong and deep. And for good reason. Whatever view you hold about the purpose or effect of demonstrating, public protest is at the heart of any reasonably free and open democracy. It is the outward and visible sign of serious complaint, usually by those who have no more power than the right to vote every few years. What I wrote twenty years ago still holds good today: 'The right to peaceful protest is a traditional and legitimate expression of a point of view. Peaceful protest is public, open and visible. It is designed to inform, persuade and cajole. It may be a nuisance; it may even be intended to be. It is often noisy and inconvenient. But it is a legitimate form of public expression, protected by the European Convention on Human Rights.' That Convention has now become embodied in the Human Rights Act 1998.

Freedom of expression in public has long been enshrined in English law—not in statute but by statements of the judges. Lord Denning said in 1976 in *Hubbard v Pitt* that 'The right to demonstrate and the right to protest on matters of public concern . . . are rights which it is in the public interest that individuals should possess; and, indeed, that they should exercise without impediment so long as no wrongful act is done.'[3] He referred to 'the undoubted right of Englishmen' to meet together, to go in procession, to demonstrate, and to protest on matters of public concern.[4] Lord Justice Sedley stated in *Redmond-Bate v DPP*[5] that 'Free speech includes not only the inoffensive but the irritating, the contentious, the eccentric, the heretical, the unwelcome and the provocative provided it does not tend to provoke violence. Freedom only to speak inoffensively is not worth having. What Speakers' Corner (where the law applies as fully as anywhere else) demonstrates is the tolerance which is both extended by the law to opinion of every kind and expected by the law in the conduct of those who disagree, even strongly, with what they hear.'

But the common law cases started from a negative standpoint. Protest was lawful only when it infringed no other law. Since then the Human Rights Act 1998 has incorporated into English law the European Convention on Human Rights. And freedom of expression and freedom of assembly, Articles 10 and 11 of the Convention, have taken their place in the front row. They are positive rights, and although they are not absolute rights, any violation of them must be justified by the State. Decisions of the European Court of Human Rights have frequently repeated the value of these rights. For example in *Handyside v UK*[6] the Court recognized that 'Freedom of expression constitutes one of the essential foundations of . . . a [democratic] society, one of the basic conditions for its progress and for the development of every man.' The State now has a positive duty to safeguard Article 10 and 11 rights. While Convention rights are not 'a trump card', the courts are obliged to ensure that the exercise of them is 'practical and effective', not merely 'theoretical and illusory'.[7]

---

[3] [1976] QB 142, 178.
[4] See also *Kent v Metropolitan Police Commissioner*, The Times, 15 May 1981.
[5] [2000] HRLR 249; [1999] EWHC Admin 732.
[6] (1976) 1 EHRR 737, para 49.
[7] *Artico v Italy* (1981) 3 EHRR 1, para 33.

This is a big change: from a negative standpoint to a positive assertion of rights. The change means that any interference with the right of expression or assembly by way of protest must be 'prescribed by law', justified by the State, and be 'proportionate' in terms of restriction. Even protest causing disruption may be tolerated, and therefore not prosecuted; so long as the disruption is peaceful; does not put the safety of the public at risk; is of modest duration; and does not interfere substantially with the rights of others.[8] The new approach is illustrated by a decision about Parliament Square. Westminster City Council tried to remove by way of injunction Brian Haw's encampment there as an obstruction of the highway. The finding against the Council included the 'significant consideration' that Haw was exercising his right to freedom of expression on a political issue, and directly in front of Parliament which he wished to influence over its policy towards Iraq.[9]

But there have been many other developments in the law of public order in recent times. Since I wrote *Public Order Law* in 1987, shortly after the 1986 Act came into force, much has changed. The main public order offences have remained the same both in the Act and elsewhere. Riot, violent disorder, and affray in the 1986 Act and lesser offences elsewhere such as obstruction of the highway and obstructing a police officer in the execution of his duty are still widely used, alongside old common law breach of the peace powers.

But a remarkable number of new measures have been created or approved. *Justice* has described them as 'a bewildering array of [overlapping] powers and offences', decreasing the foreseeability and predictability of the law. They include 'kettling'. The House of Lords decided in *Austin v Metropolitan Police Commissioner*[10] that the police could 'in very exceptional circumstances' cordon off a group of protestors for hours on end, without food, drink, or toilets, in order to prevent an imminent breach of the peace.

Other offences and powers not designed to inhibit protest have been used by the police: for example, dispersal under the Anti-social Behaviour Act 2003 (ss 30–6), and the use of the Protection from Harassment Act 1997, originally designed to catch stalkers. The Human Rights Joint Committee of the House of Commons has recommended the repeal of the 'insulting words' element of the offence of harassment, alarm, or distress, contrary to s 5 of the Public Order Act 1986, which has been used inappropriately, for example against a protestor with a sign, 'Scientology is not a religion, it is a dangerous cult' and a student in Oxford who called a police horse 'gay'. There are new powers under the Police Reform Act 2002 for Police Community Support Officers and new powers to stop vehicles (s 59). Trespassers (and unauthorized campers) may now be prosecuted in a number of specific circumstances (Criminal Justice and Public Order Act 1994, ss 61, 68, 69, 77; Serious Organised Crime and Police Act 2005, s 128).

And terrorism has brought its cost. Five Acts of Parliament dealing with terrorism have been passed this last decade alone. Within them there are controversial measures affecting everyday activity, which are used at demonstrations against protestors and journalists. These include wide stop and search powers without the need for the police to have any

---

[8] Although there is some conflict of European authority: see Ch 10.
[9] *Westminster City Council v Haw* [2002] EWHC 2073, QB, Gray J, see 3.122 et seq and 4.46.
[10] [2009] 1 AC 564.

reasonable suspicion (Terrorism Act 2000, ss 44–47), for example against a protestor and a journalist outside an arms fair at the Excel Centre in Docklands.[11] These sections also give further powers to stop vehicles. There are powers which are perceived to criminalize photographing and filming of police officers (Counter-Terrorism Act 2008, s 76). At the same time the police have been criticized for collecting their own data on individuals who have acted lawfully.[12]

The 'designated area' provisions are designed to curb protests in Parliament Square and opposite Downing Street by requiring at least twenty-four hours' notice (Serious Organised Crime and Police Act 2005, ss 132–8). Gordon Brown's promise in 2007 to repeal them remains unfulfilled. When the Home Office was asked to state what alternative laws were available should the Parliament Square powers be repealed, it itemized twenty-two separate available powers and offences without it being 'an exhaustive list'.

This may all be a far cry from the sweeping powers given to local police in Zimbabwe to ban political rallies and prosecute for criticizing the president (Public Order and Security Act 2002, ss 16, 26, and 27). But there is a trend, driven by political will, and reflected in other areas of the criminal law, to keep making more law without codification or apparent thought for the adequacy of existing powers. With this backdrop of increasing laws and perhaps increasing uncertainty as to what the law exactly is, we have ventured to guide the lawyer, student, and citizen through the maze. If the emphasis lies inevitably with the criminal law and police powers, civil law aspects are not ignored.

I would like to thank the team of authors for their hard work and dedication to this project. Special thanks must go to Faye Judges who as publishing editor has born the brunt of tardy text, along with Emma Barber at OUP. It has been a pleasure to work with them. Thanks also to Anna Edmundson, Alison Pickup, Gemma Hobcraft, Sarah Hemmingway, David Wood, and Bridget Palmer for their valued legal research.

The law is stated, with best endeavours at accuracy, as at 15 January 2010. At this time s 290(2) of the Criminal Justice Act 2003, which will extend the power of magistrates to sentence for a single offence which carries imprisonment from six months to fifty-one weeks, is not yet in force. Nor are various provisions of the Policing and Crime Act 2009 which received Royal Assent on 12 November 2009.

PETER THORNTON
Central Criminal Court
Old Bailey
15 January 2010

---

[11] The *Gillan* case [2006] 2 AC 307, and despite police guidance that the power 'must never be used as a public order tactic' (National Policing Improvement Agency). Cf., however, the decision of the European Court of Human Rights, at 6.87 et seq.

[12] For the limits on collection and storage, see *Wood v Metropolitan Police Commissioner* in the Court of Appeal, at 10.48 et seq.

CONTENTS—SUMMARY

Preface   v
Table of Cases   xxv
Table of Statutes   xlvii
Table of Secondary Legislation   lxii
Table of International Legislation   lxiv

1. The Public Order Act 1986: Offences   1
2. Other Public Order Offences   51
3. Processions, Assemblies, and Meetings   99
4. Use of the Highway   145
5. Trespass to Land   179
6. Police Powers Before Arrest   223
7. Arrest, Detention, and Bail   277
8. Defences of Excuse and Justification   319
9. Punishment, Appeals, and Restrictive Orders   355
10. Human Rights   397

Index   449

DETAILED CONTENTS

Preface   v
Table of Cases   xxv
Table of Statutes   xlvii
Table of Secondary Legislation   lxii
Table of International Legislation   lxiv

1. The Public Order Act 1986: Offences

  A. Introduction   1.01

  B. Riot: Public Order Act 1986, s 1   1.05
      Historical development   1.05
      The definition of riot under the Public Order Act 1986, s 1   1.15
      Jurisdiction   1.16
      Essential elements of the offence   1.19
        Twelve or more persons   1.20
        Present together   1.22
        Using or threatening unlawful violence   1.25
        For a common purpose   1.32
        A person of reasonable firmness present at the scene   1.36
        Mental element *(mens rea)*   1.37
        Intoxicated rioters   1.42
        Sentencing   1.46
        Compensation for Riot Damage   1.53

  C. Violent Disorder: Public Order Act 1986, s 2   1.56
      Historical development   1.56
      The definition of violent disorder under the Public Order Act 1986, s 2   1.59
      Jurisdiction   1.62
      Essential elements of the offence   1.63
        Three or more persons present together   1.65
        Using or threatening unlawful violence   1.71
        Cumulative effect   1.74
        Person of reasonable firmness present at the scene   1.76
        Mental element *(mens rea)*   1.78
        Alternative verdicts   1.80
        Sentencing   1.82

  D. Affray: Public Order Act 1986, s 3   1.89
      Historical development   1.89
      The definition of affray under the Public Order Act 1986, s 3   1.93
      Jurisdiction   1.95
      Essential elements of the offence   1.96
        Uses or threatens   1.98

Unlawful violence	1.103
Towards another	1.104
A person of reasonable firmness present at the scene	1.108
Mental element *(mens rea)*	1.119
Cumulative effect	1.121
Public or private place	1.122
Alternative verdicts	1.123
Sentencing	1.124
E. Fear or Provocation of Violence: Public Order Act 1986, s 4	1.128
Historical development	1.128
Definition under the Public Order Act 1986, s 4	1.133
Jurisdiction	1.135
Essential elements of the offence	1.136
Uses towards another	1.137
Threatening, abusive, or insulting	1.143
Distribute or display	1.150
Mental element *(mens rea)*	1.154
Public or private place	1.166
F. Harassment, Alarm, or Distress: s 5	1.171
Historical development	1.171
Definition under the Public Order Act 1986, s 5	1.174
Jurisdiction	1.177
Essential elements of the offence	1.178
Threatening, abusive, or insulting words or behaviour	1.180
Disorderly behaviour	1.181
Within the sight or hearing	1.184
Harassment, alarm, or distress	1.186
Mental element *(mens rea)*	1.191
Public or private place	1.193
Specific defences	1.195
Sentencing	1.203
G. Intentional Harassment, Alarm, or Distress: Public Order Act 1986, s 4A	1.206
Historical development	1.206
Definition under the Public Order Act 1986, s 4A	1.207
Jurisdiction	1.208
Proportionality	1.209
Essential elements of the offence	1.210
Causation	1.211
Mental element *(mens rea)*	1.214
Intoxication	1.217
Public or private	1.218
Special defences	1.220
Police powers	1.224
Sentencing	1.227
2. Other Public Order Offences	
A. Overview	2.01

B. Assault on or Obstruction of a Constable in the Execution of his Duty	2.02
Assaulting a constable in the execution of his duty	2.03
Elements of the offence	2.04
Constable	2.05
Execution of duty	2.06
Self-defence	2.07
Mistaken self-defence	2.10
Sentencing	2.11
Resisting or wilfully obstructing a constable	2.12
Obstructs	2.13
Wilfully	2.18
Constable	2.20
Execution of his duty	2.21
What takes an officer outside of his duty?	2.31
C. Prohibition of Political Uniforms	2.37
D. Prohibition of Quasi-Military Organizations	2.42
Interpretation	2.44
Usurpation	2.45
Reasonable apprehension	2.46
Procedure	2.47
Defence	2.48
Powers of the High Court	2.49
E. Bomb Hoaxes	2.51
Sentencing	2.52
F. Racial and Religious Hatred	2.56
Stirring up racial and religious hatred (or on grounds of sexual orientation)	2.57
Racial hatred	2.60
Religious hatred	2.62
Actus reus	2.65
Mens rea	2.66
Words, behaviour, written material stirring up racial and religious hatred (s 18 racial hatred/s 29B religious hatred)	2.67
Publishing or distributing written material stirring up racial or religious hatred	2.69
Public performance of a play stirring up racial or religious hatred	2.73
Distributing, showing, or playing a recording stirring up racial or religious hatred	2.75
Broadcasting a programme stirring up racial or religious hatred	2.78
Possession of written material or recording stirring up racial or religious hatred	2.80
Defences	2.82
Liability of corporations	2.83
Sentence	2.84
Forfeiture	2.87
Racially or religiously aggravated offences	2.88
The Test (s 28)	2.89
Racial or religious groups	2.90
Hostility	2.93
Sentencing	2.97

G. Public Nuisance   2.99
    Definition   2.101
    Public nuisance vs private nuisance   2.106
    Mens rea   2.108
    Vicarious liability   2.109
    Defences   2.110
    Sentence   2.111

H. Criminal Damage   2.112
    Criminal damage   2.113
    Aggravated criminal damage; arson; threats to damage property,
        possession with intent to destroy or damage property   2.120

I. Animal Research Facilities   2.125
    The legislative intent   2.126
    Interference in contractual relations so as to harm animal research organization   2.131
    Intimidation of persons connected with animal research organization   2.132
    Criticism of the legislation   2.133
    Sentence   2.136
        R v Diane Jamieson   2.140
        R v Joseph Harris   2.141
        R v Suzanne Jaggers   2.142
        AG's Reference (No 113 of 2007)   2.143
        R v Susanne Taylor; R v Theresa Portwine; R v Mark Taylor   2.144
        R v Greg Avery; R v Natasha Avery; R v Heather Nicholson;
        R v Daniel Wadham; R v Gerrah Selby; and *R v Daniel Amos*   2.145

J.   Contamination or Interfering with Goods   2.146
    Contamination of or interference with goods   2.147
    Threatening to contaminate or interfere with goods, or claiming to have done so   2.149
    Possession of articles with a view to contaminating or interfering in goods   2.151
    Sentence   2.152

K. Intimidation, including Watching and Besetting   2.154
    Origin of the offence   2.155
    The offence   2.158
    Elements of the offence   2.159
        With a view to compelling any other person   2.159
        Wrongfully and without legal authority   2.161
        Intimidates   2.162
        Persistently follows   2.163
        Hiding tools   2.164
        Watching or besetting   2.165
    Penalties   2.167

L. Drunk and Disorderly   2.168
    Drunk and disorderly   2.170
    Drunk in a public place   2.173
    Drunk and disorderly person failing to leave   2.175
    Alcohol consumption in a designated place   2.176
    Drunk on an aircraft   2.177

M. Football Related Disorder 2.178
N. Taking a Photograph of a Police Officer 2.183

3. **Processions, Assemblies, and Meetings**
A. Overview 3.01
A right to assemble or process? 3.02
B. Processions 3.07
Procession 3.08
Public place 3.10
Advance notice of processions (s 11) 3.12
Background 3.13
Advance notice provision (s 11(1)) 3.15
Exception 1: 'commonly or customarily held' (s 11(2)) 3.16
Exception 2: 'not reasonably practicable' (s 11(1)) 3.20
Processions without a determined route 3.21
Nature and delivery of notice to the police 3.22
Failure to comply: prosecution 3.24
Conditions imposed on public processions (s 12) 3.28
Background 3.29
Imposing conditions 3.31
Failure to comply with conditions: prosecution 3.37
Banning processions (s 13) 3.38
Procedure outside London 3.40
Procedure in London 3.42
Failure to comply with a ban: prosecution 3.46
Judicial review 3.47
C. Assemblies 3.53
Background 3.53
Definition of 'public assembly' 3.56
No advance notice requirement 3.64
Police controls over public assemblies (s 14) 3.65
Imposing conditions 3.66
Conditions 3.71
Failure to comply with conditions: prosecution 3.73
No power to prohibit assemblies 3.74
D. Meetings 3.76
Definition of public meeting 3.80
Control of public meetings 3.84
Attempts to break up public meetings 3.87
Police powers to attend meetings 3.88
Election meetings 3.90
E. Parliament Square 3.94
Background 3.95
The legislation 3.100
Designated area 3.101
Written notice 3.103

Authorization		3.107
Offences		3.112
Human rights compliance		3.117
The Brian Haw litigation		3.122
The future		3.126
F.	Other Specific Areas	3.130
	Trafalgar Square and Parliament Square Garden	3.130
	Royal Parks (including Hyde Park) and other Open Spaces	3.135
G.	Other Offences Specific to Location	3.137
	Nuclear bases	3.137
	NHS facilities	3.138
	At a person's home	3.142
	Police directions to stop the harassment of a person in his home (Criminal Justice and Police Act 2001, s 42)	3.143
	Offence of harassment of a person in his home (Criminal Justice and Police Act 2001, s 42A)	3.148
H.	By-laws	3.152
	Criminal proceedings	3.156
	Private law	3.161

4. Use of the Highway

A.	Introduction	4.01
B.	Definition of the Highway	4.03
C.	Use of the Highway	4.05
D.	Obstruction of the Highway	4.19
	Essential elements of the offence	4.20
	Obstruction	4.23
	Wilfulness	4.29
	Without lawful authority or excuse (reasonableness)	4.33
	Reasonableness and human rights	4.38
	Power to order offender to remove obstruction	4.49
E.	Picketing	4.51
	Picketing in the employment law context	4.53
	Picketing and breach of the peace	4.61
	Consumer picketing	4.68
F.	Police Road Blocks	4.72
	At common law	4.73
	Police and Criminal Evidence Act 1984	4.77
	Terrorism Act 2000	4.80
	Criminal Justice and Public Order Act 1994	4.92
G.	By-laws	4.94
H.	Street-based Prostitution	4.103
	Loitering or soliciting	4.108
	Jurisdiction and penalty	4.109

Essential elements 4.110
   Common prostitute 4.111
   Loiter or solicit 4.115
   Street or public place 4.119
   For the purpose of prostitution 4.124
Kerb crawling 4.125
   Jurisdiction and penalty 4.126
   Who can commit the offence? 4.127
   Essential elements 4.128
     Solicits 4.129
     Persistently 4.131
     Likely to cause annoyance or nuisance 4.132
     Street or public place 4.136
     From or in the immediate vicinity of a motor vehicle 4.138
     For the purpose of prostitution 4.141
Persistent soliciting 4.142
   Jurisdiction and penalty 4.143
   Who can commit the offence? 4.144
   Essential elements 4.145

5. Trespass to Land

A. Introduction 5.01

B. Civil Law of Trespass to Land 5.06
The scope of the tort of trespass to land 5.06
Defences to tort of trespass 5.11
   Necessity 5.11
   Human rights 5.13
Who can sue for trespass? 5.16
Remedies against trespassers 5.18
   Orders for possession 5.18
   Interim possession orders 5.23
   Injunctions 5.30
   Self-help or abatement 5.34
   The role of the police in ejecting trespassers 5.38
   Damages 5.40

C. Criminal Law 5.41
Development of the criminal law of trespass 5.41

Criminal Justice and Public Order Act 1994, Part V 5.47
   Aggravated trespass 5.47
     Trespass on land 5.55
     Act additional to mere act of trespass 5.57
     Intention to intimidate, obstruct, or disrupt 5.58
     Lawful activity 5.59
     Defences 5.63
   Powers to remove persons committing or participating in aggravated trespass 5.66
   Powers to remove trespassers present on land for purpose of residing there 5.74
     Directions to leave the land 5.74

Definitions   5.78
Offence of failing to leave or re-entering after direction   5.84
Defences   5.86
Human rights considerations   5.87
Power to seize and remove vehicles   5.90
Powers to remove trespassers with caravans   5.91
Definitions   5.93
Offence of failing to leave or re-entering after a direction   5.95
Defence   5.96
Powers to seize and remove vehicles   5.97
Powers to remove those preparing for or attending raves   5.98
Directions to leave the land   5.98
Definitions   5.99
Definitions   5.102
First rave offence: failing to leave or re-entering after direction (s 63(6)) 5.104
Statutory defences   5.105
Second rave offence: preparing for/attending a rave within twenty-four hours
    of direction (s 63(7A))   5.107
Third rave offence: proceeding to a rave contrary to direction (s 65)   5.108
Powers to seize and remove vehicles and sound equipment   5.109
Forfeiture of sound equipment   5.110
Unauthorized campers: powers of removal   5.113
Directions to leave: residing in a vehicle   5.114
Statutory defence   5.119
Application to the magistrates' court: Criminal Justice and
    Public Order Act 1994, s 78   5.120
Guidance on use of powers under ss 77 and 78   5.125

Public Order Act 1986, ss 14A–C   5.126
Trespassory assemblies   5.126
The circumstances in which a ban may be imposed   5.129

Serious and Organised Crime and Police Act 2005, s 128   5.140
Trespass on a protected site   5.140

Other offences involving trespass   5.149
By-laws   5.149
Being in a prohibited place for a purpose prejudicial to the
    safety or interests of the State   5.152
Offences under the Vagrancy Act 1824   5.155
Failure to leave an exclusion zone   5.158
Violence for securing entry   5.159
Trespass during currency of interim possession order   5.160
Adverse occupation of residential premises   5.161
Trespassing with a weapon of offence   5.165
Trespassing on premises of foreign missions, etc   5.167
Obstruction of enforcement officers or court officers executing
    High Court or county court process   5.170
Trespassing on licensed aerodromes   5.176

Trespassing on a railway	5.177
Poaching	5.178
Burglary	5.179
Trespass with intent to commit a sexual offence	5.181

6. Police Powers Before Arrest

A. The Nature of Policing	6.01
Information gathering	6.01
Responding to protest	6.06
Police community support officers and accredited persons	6.08
Private security companies	6.16
B. Contact with the Police Short of Arrest	6.18
C. Establishing Identity	6.26
Name, address, date of birth, and personal details	6.27
Disguises	6.33
An inspector's 'authorization'	6.34
A constable's power	6.40
The power and the European Convention on Human Rights	6.42
Fingerprints	6.43
Photographs and filming	6.44
Photographs: following exercise of other police powers	6.44
Photographs: overt surveillance	6.45
D. Control of Movement	6.55
Directions to leave and alcohol-related disorder	6.57
Dispersal of groups and anti-social behaviour	6.60
A superintendent's 'authorization'	6.60
A constable's 'direction'	6.64
'Removal' of children to their home	6.67
Police cordons	6.69
E. Stop and Search: Before Arrest	6.72
Police and Criminal Evidence Act 1984, s 1	6.73
Criminal Justice and Public Order Act 1994, s 60	6.82
An inspector's 'authorization'	6.82
A constable's powers	6.85
Terrorism Act 2000, s 44	6.87
The commander or assistant chief constable's 'authorization'	6.90
The constable's power	6.97
Code A and the conduct of the search	6.102
Searches and the European Convention on Human Rights	6.112
Road traffic stops	6.118
Stop and seizure of vehicles	6.118
Road checks	6.119
A superintendent's 'authorization'	6.120
The constable's power	6.121
Road stops	6.122

F. Breach of the Peace	6.125
What is a breach of the peace?	6.129
Definition	6.129
Breach of the peace and the criminal law	6.139
Who may take action?	6.141
When may action be taken?	6.142
What action may be taken?	6.153
Arrest	6.156
Limits on pickets	6.160
Police powers and private property	6.161
The application of human rights principles	6.162
Against whom may action be taken?	6.168
G. The Use of Force by the Police	6.174
Sources of power to use force	6.175
What is 'reasonable' force?	6.181
The European Convention	6.184
Equipment	6.195
Policing protests	6.201
H. Conclusion	6.205
7. Arrest, Detention, and Bail	
A. Arrest	7.01
What is an arrest?	7.01
The police's power of arrest	7.02
The arresting officer's own suspicion: *Castorina 1*	7.07
Reasonable grounds for the officer's suspicion: *Castorina 2*	7.08
The discretion to arrest: *Castorina 3*	7.18
The reasons for arrest: s 24(5)	7.19
The 'necessity' test: s 24(4)	7.22
Wednesbury and Wednesbury Plus	7.27
The citizen's power of arrest	7.33
Information to be given on arrest	7.38
Search of a person after arrest	7.45
Entry and search of property on arrest	7.49
After arrest: street bail or police station	7.54
The implications of failing to make a lawful arrest	7.60
B. Detention at the Police Station	7.65
The role of the custody officer	7.66
Collecting personal information	7.72
A detainee's rights	7.78
Consultation of the Codes	7.78
Legal advice	7.79
The right to have someone informed when arrested	7.83
Special groups	7.85
Conditions during detention	7.89

Police detention and charge	7.94
The decision to detain	7.95
Further investigations	7.99
Is there sufficient evidence to charge?	7.103
The decision to charge	7.105
C. Bail Conditions and Remands in Custody After Charge	7.109
Introduction	7.109
The European Convention	7.112
PACE and the Bail Act	7.121
Granting bail (with or without conditions)	7.122
Bail conditions from the police station (Bail Act 1976, s 3A)	7.122
Bail conditions from the court (Bail Act 1976, s 3)	7.126
Implications of breaching bail	7.131
Breach of street bail	7.131
Breach of bail from the police station to return to the police station	7.132
Breach of bail to attend court (Bail Act, s 7)	7.134
Impact on sentencing of commission of offence while on bail	7.139
Refusing bail	7.140
The police's power to refuse bail	7.141
The courts' power to refuse bail	7.144
The courts' approach	7.144
Defendants charged with non-imprisonable offences (Part II of Schedule 1)	7.148
Defendants charged with imprisonable summary offences (Part IA of Schedule 1)	7.150
Defendants charged with imprisonable non-summary offences (Part I of Schedule 1)	7.152
Reviews and challenges to bail decisions	7.155
Records of decisions	7.155
Varying bail conditions following street bail	7.157
Defence applications to vary bail conditions from the police station	7.159
Prosecution applications for reconsideration of bail decision by the police or magistrates	7.160
Applications to vary bail conditions after first court hearing	7.161
Appeals against bail conditions, from a magistrates' court to the Crown Court	7.162
Renewed applications for bail to the same court	7.163
Appeals against refusals of bail by a magistrates' court to the Crown Court	7.164
Appeals to the High Court	7.165
8. Defences of Excuse and Justification	
A. Introduction	8.01
B. General Principles	8.03
Reasonableness	8.05
General	8.05
Subjective belief in the circumstances	8.11
Relevance of the actual circumstances	8.15
Burden of proof	8.24

C. The Prevention of Crime   8.33
   The use of 'force'   8.36
   'The prevention of crime'   8.56
   'Such force as is reasonable in the circumstances'   8.64
     The Criminal Justice and Immigration Act 2008   8.64
     Subjective belief   8.66
     The role of the democratic process: Lord Hoffmann   8.71
   Remoteness   8.86

D. The Protection of Property   8.89
   The common law   8.89
   Lawful excuse: Criminal Damage Act 1971, s 5   8.91
   The meaning of property   8.95
   The meaning of 'damage'   8.99
   Belief in consent   8.103
   Subjective belief   8.106
   Remoteness: 'in order to protect' and 'immediate need'   8.110

E. Necessity/Duress of Circumstances   8.124
   A single defence?   8.124
   Duress of circumstances: definition   8.136
   Persons for whom the defendant has responsibility   8.140
     Compulsion   8.147
   Mixed test: subjective but reasonable belief   8.148
     Subjective belief   8.148
     Reasonable belief   8.152
   Death or serious injury   8.158

F. Acting in the Public Interest   8.161

9. Punishment, Appeals, and Restrictive Orders

A. Sentencing Principles in Protest Cases   9.01
   Conditional discharge: *R v Jones (Margaret)*   9.03
   Fines   9.13
   Community penalty   9.14
   Mitigation   9.19

B. Binding Over   9.20
   Binding over to keep the peace   9.20
     Introduction   9.20
     Preventative justice   9.23
     Bind over: how it works   9.24
     To be of good behaviour?   9.26
     Procedural requirements   9.31
     Refusal to be bound over   9.38
     Failure to comply and forfeiture   9.40
   Binding over to come up for judgment   9.42

C. Alternatives to Conviction   9.47
   Cautions   9.47
   Simple cautions   9.49

Criteria for a simple caution	9.51
Adminstering the caution	9.56
Consequences of a caution	9.57
Conditional cautions	9.59
Offences that may be conditionally cautioned	9.61
Statutory criteria for a conditional caution	9.63
Conditions	9.65
Effect of a conditional caution	9.68
Failure to comply with conditions	9.69
Juveniles: warnings and reprimands	9.70
Fixed penalty notices	9.73
Penalty offences	9.74
Giving the notice	9.75
Penalty notices	9.77
Effect of the penalty notice	9.80
D. Appeals	9.82
General	9.82
Appeals from the magistrates' court to the Crown Court	9.83
Appeals against conviction	9.83
Appeals against sentence	9.90
Appeals against binding over	9.94
Appeals by way of case stated: from the magistrates' court and Crown Court to the Divisional Court	9.95
The magistrates' court	9.95
The Crown Court	9.103
Judicial review	9.105
General	9.105
The Crown Court: trial on indictment	9.110
The magistrates' court and Crown Court appeals	9.113
Procedure	9.115
Appeals from the Crown Court to the Court of Appeal	9.117
Interlocutory appeals	9.117
Appeals against conviction	9.120
Appeals against sentence by the defendant	9.130
Appeals against sentence by the prosecution	9.134
Attorney General's Reference on a point of law following acquittal	9.138
Prosecution appeals against rulings	9.140
Prosecution applications for retrials for serious offences	9.149
Referrals by the Criminal Cases Review Commission	9.153
Appeals from the Court of Appeal and Divisional Court to the Supreme Court	9.157
Petitions to the European Court of Human Rights	9.159
E. Injunctions	9.166
Injunctions in Protest Cases	9.170
F. Anti-social Behaviour Orders (ASBOs)	9.178
G. Football Banning Orders	9.183

10. Human Rights

A. Introduction   10.01

B. Articles 10 and 11   10.13
   Introduction to Articles 10 and 11   10.15
      Assembly for the purpose of imparting information and ideas   10.22
   Positive and negative obligations   10.28
      Direct and indirect obstacles to freedom of assembly   10.28
      Securing effective enjoyment of the rights to freedom
         of expression and assembly   10.31
      Duty to protect against counter-demonstrators   10.34
      Obligations on the state; no excessive burdens on demonstrators   10.36
      Demonstrators vs counter-demonstrators: the balance to be struck   10.37
   The scope of Articles 10 and 11   10.39
      Activity which shocks, offends, or disturbs   10.39
      The application of Articles 10 and 11 in English cases: is protection
         from insult a 'legitimate aim'?   10.41
      Disruptive activity (including disruption to traffic)   10.56
      Violent activity   10.67
      Illegality   10.71
      Private property   10.72
   Limitations on the right to protest   10.77
   'Prescribed by law': the requirement of legality   10.78
      Accessible   10.81
      Not arbitrary, not uncertain   10.82
   Legitimate aims   10.98
   Necessary in a democratic society   10.101
      Prior authorization   10.111

C. Article 9: Freedom of Thought, Conscience, and Religion   10.122
   Manifesting a belief   10.126
   Article 9: and Articles 10 and 11   10.131
      Preacher cases   10.139

D. Article 8: Right to Respect for Private and Family Life   10.144

E. Article 5: Right to Liberty and Security   10.150
   'Kettling': deprivation of liberty vs restriction of movement   10.158

F. Article 6: Right to a Fair Trial   10.162
   Statutory defences and reverse burdens of proof   10.163
   Legal assistance   10.167
   Disclosure   10.174

G. Article 2: Right to Life   10.180

H. Article 3: Prohibition of Torture   10.184

Index   449

TABLE OF CASES

A (a Juvenile) v R [1978] Crim LR 689 . . . . 8.100
A (Children), Re [2000] 4 All ER 961 . . . . 8.130
A (Conjoined Twins), In re [2001] Fam 147 . . . . 8.128, 8.147
A Local Authority v B [2009] 1 FLR 289 . . . . 7.86
A v Secretary of State for the Home Department [2004] UKHL 56; [2005] 2 AC 68 . . . . 8.91
Abbott v Commissioner of the Police for the Metropolis, Claim No CO/6790/2009 . . . . 6.166
Adali v Turkey, Application No 38187/97, 31 March 2005 . . . . 10.101
Agnew v Munrow (1891) 28 SLR 335 . . . . 2.160
Ahmad v United Kingdom (1981) 4 EHRR 126 . . . . 10.130
Ahmed v Shafique Arora [2009] EWHC 618, QB 7.11
Akhurst v DPP [2009] EWHC 806 (Admin) 5.156
Aksoy v Turkey (1997) 23 EHRR 553 . . . . 10.185
Al Fayed v Commissioner of Police of the Metropolis (2004) 148 SJLB 1405, CA;
    [2004] EWCA Civ 1579 . . . . 7.10, 7.27, 7.30, 7.68, 7.96
Albert v Lavin [1982] AC 456 . . . . 2.36, 6.141, 6.142, 6.153, 6.168, 8.28, 10.38
Aldemir v Turkey, Application No 32124/02, 18 December 2007 . . . . 10.28
Alderson v Booth [1969] 2 QB 216 . . . . 7.01
Allaham v Greece (2009) 49 EHRR 10 . . . . 6.188
American Cyanamid v Ethicon [1975] AC 367 . . . . 5.32, 9.168
Amuur v France (1996) 22 EHRR 533 . . . . 10.154
Anderson v United Kingdom [1998] EHRLR 218 . . . . 10.25, 10.75
Andersson v Sweden, Application No 12781/87, 13 December 1987 . . . . 10.60, 10.71, 10.98
Andreou v Turkey (2009) Application No 00045653/99, 27 October 2009 . . . . 6.186
Anisimic Ltd v Foreign Compensation Commission [1979] AC 147 . . . . 3.157
Ansell v Swift [1987] Crim LR 194 . . . . 2.10
Appleby v United Kingdom (2003) 37 EHRR 783 . . . . 5.13, 10.18, 10.22, 10.33,
                                                                        10.72, 10.74, 10.75, 10.76
Aquilina v Malta (2000) 29 EHRR 185 . . . . 7.163
Armhouse Lee Ltd v Chappell, The Times, 7 August 1996, DC 4.111, 4.124
Arrowsmith v Jenkins [1963] 2 QB 561 . . . . 2.18, 3.27, 4.30
Arrowsmith v United Kingdom (1978) 3 EHRR 218 . . . . 10.124, 10.127
Asher v Whitlock (1865) LR 1 QB 1 . . . . 5.17
Ashingdane v United Kingdom (1985) 7 EHRR 528 . . . . 4.101, 10.154
Ashughyan v Armenia, Application No 33268/03, 17 July 2008 . . . . 10.98
Assenov v Bulgaria (1998) 28 EHRR 652 . . . . 10.185
Associated Provincial Picture Houses Ltd v Wednesbury Corporation
    [1948] 1 KB 223 . . . . 3.49, 3.52, 5.21, 7.03, 7.05, 7.06, 7.18, 7.27, 7.30,
                                        7.129, 7.165, 9.108, 10.18, 10.23, 10.67, 10.134, 10.135
Atkin v DPP (1989) 89 Cr App R 199, DC 1.138, 1.167
Attorney-General for Northern Ireland's Reference (No 1 of 1975) [1976] 2 All ER 937 . . . . . . 8.80
Attorney-General v O'Brien [1936] ITLR 101 . . . . 2.166
Attorney-General v PYA Quarries Ltd [1957] 2 QB 169 . . . . 2.106
Attorney-General v Whelan [1934] IR 518 . . . . 8.26
Attorney-General's Reference (No 113 of 2007) [2008] EWCA Crim 22 . . . . 2.143
Attorney-General's Reference (No 19 of 2005) [2006] EWCA Crim 785 . . . . 9.136
Attorney-General's Reference (No 2 of 1983) [1984] QB 456, CA 6.179

Attorney-General's Reference (No 4 of 1989) [1990] 1 WLR 41 . . . . .9.134
Attorney-General's Reference (No 4 of 2002) [2004] UKHL 43 . . . . .10.165
Attorney-General's Reference (No 4 of 2004) [2005] 2 Cr App R 26, CA 2.90
Austin and another v Commissioner of Police of the Metropolis
    [2009] UKHL 5 . . . . .4.73, 4.74, 6.69, 6.81, 6.114, 7.33
Austin and Saxby v Commissioner of Police for the Metropolis
    [2005] EWHC 480 . . . . .3.32, 3.36, 3.63, 3.74, 3.75,
Austin and Saxby v Commissioner of Police for the Metropolis [2007]
    EWCA Civ 989; [2008] 2 WLR 415, CA 4.67, 6.56, 6.140
Austin v Commissioner of Police of the Metropolis
    [2008] QB 660, CA 6.152, 6.170, 6.172, 6.173
Austin v Commissioner of Police of the Metropolis
    [2009] 1 AC 564, HL 6.163, 6.166, 6.169
Austin v Metropolitan Police Commissioner
    [2009] 2 WLR 381 . . . . .10.155, 10.158, 10.160, 10.161
Austin v United Kingdom, Application No 39692/09 . . . . .6.166
Averill v United Kingdom (2001) 31 EHRR 36 . . . . .7.79

B (a Minor) v DPP [2002] AC 428 . . . . 8.11, 8.155
B v Chief Constable of Avon and Somerset Constabulary [2001] 1 WLR 340 . . . . .9.189
B v DPP (2008) 172 JP 449, DC 6.107
B v France, Application No 10179/82; (1987) 52 DR 111 . . . . .6.115
Baczkowski and others v Poland, Application No 1543/06, 3 May 2007 . . . . . . 10.30, 10.31, 10.101
Bailey v Williamson (1873) LR 8 QB 118 . . . . .3.136
Baker v CPS (2009) 173 JP 215, DC 7.51
Baker v Oxford [1990] RTR 315, DC 7.25
Balcik v Turkey, Application No 25/02, 29 November 2007 . . . . .6.188, 6.189, 6.194,
                                                    10.30, 10.58, 10.61, 10.121, 10.188, 10.189
Barthold v Germany (1985) 7 EHRR 383 . . . . .10.78
Baseley v Clarkson (1682) 3 Lev 37 . . . . .5.07
Bayer v DPP [2003] EWHC 2567 (Admin) 8.28, 8.35, 8.42, 8.53, 8.89, 8.90
Beard v Wood [1980] RTR 454, QB 6.124
Beatty v Gillbanks (1882) 9 QBD 308 . . . . 3.82, 10.38, 10.140
Bedfordshire Police Authority v Constable [2009] EWCA Civ 64 . . . . .1.55
Bedfordshire Police Authority v David Constable [2008] EWHC 1375 (Comm) 1.55
Behrendt v Burridge (1976) 63 Cr App R 202 . . . . 4.118, 4.122
Bentley v Brudzinski (1982) 75 Cr App R 217 . . . . .2.08
Bezicheri v Italy (1990) 12 EHRR 210 . . . . .7.163
BH and MB v United Kingdom (18 July 1986) Application No 11991/86 . . . . .10.129
Bibby v Chief Constable of Essex Police (2000) 164 JP 297, CA 6.136, 6.157
Birch v DPP (1999) unreported, CO 2381/99, 10 December 1999 . . . . .4.36
Black v United Kingdom, Application No 40713/09 . . . . .6.166
Blackburn v Bowering [1994] 1 WLR 1324 . . . . .2.10
Blake v DPP [1993] Crim LR 586 . . . . 8.37, 8.104, 8.111
Blum and others v DPP (2007) UKHRR 233 . . . . 6.171, 10.111, 10.113, 10.114,
                                                    10.115, 10.116, 10.117
Blum, Stephen, Aqil Shaer, Maya Evans and Milan Rai v DPP, CPS and SSHD
    [2006] EWHC 3209 (Admin) 3.103, 3.117
Boddington v British Transport Police (1998) 2 WLR 639 . . . . .3.157
Boddington v British Transport Police [1999] 2 AC 143, HL 5.151, 6.162
Bogdanov Kandshov v Bulgaria, Application No 68294/01, 6 November 2008 . . . . .10.22
Bonner v DPP [2005] ACD 56, DC 6.107

Bonsall [1985] Crim LR 150 . . . . .2.159
Bouessel du Bourg v France (1993) 16 EHRR CD 49 . . . . .10.129
Boyland & Son v Persons unknown (2007) HLR 24 . . . . .5.22
Bracegirdle v Oxley [1947] KB 349 . . . . .9.96
Braintree District Council v Thompson [2005] EWCA Civ 178 . . . . .9.96
Brazil v Chief Constable of Surrey [1983] 1 WLR 1155, QB .7.46
Brennan v United Kingdom (2002) 34 EHRR 670 . . . . .7.82
Bridge v Campbell (1947) 177 JP 444 . . . . .4.116
British Airports Authority v Ashton [1983] 3 All ER 6 . . . . .2.165
Broadwith v Chief Constable of Thames Valley Police Authority [2000] All ER (D) 225 . . . . . . .3.61
Brogan v United Kingdom (1989) 11 EHRR 117 . . . . .7.113
Bronda v Italy (1998) 33 EHRR 81 . . . . .10.84
Broome v DPP [1974] AC 587 (Hunt v Broome) 2.165, 4.52, 4.56
Bruggemann and Scheuten v Germany (1977) 3 EHRR 244 . . . . 10.146, 10.147
Brutus v Cozens [1973] AC 854 . . . . .1.145, 1.146, 1.147, 1.148, 1.180
Bryan v Robinson [1960] 1 WLR 506 . . . . .1.148
Buckley v Chief Constable of Thames Valley Police [2009] EWCA Civ 356 . . . . 7.09, 7.13, 7.17
Bugg v Director of Public Prosecutions [1993] QB 473 . . . . .3/159
Bukta v Hungary, Application No 25691/04, 17 July 2007 . . . . . 3.20, 3.103, 10.57, 10.115, 10.116
Bullard v R [1957] AC 635, HL 8.32
Burden v Rigler [1911] 1 KB 337 . . . . .3.82
Burnley BC v England (1977) 76 LGR 393 . . . . .3.161
Burris v Azadani [1995] 1 WLR 1372 . . . . 9.171, 9.173
Burton v Winters [1993] 1 WLR 1077 . . . . 5.11, 5.34, 5.35
Buscarini v San Marino (2000) 30 EHRR 208 . . . . .10.124
Button v DPP [1966] AC 591 . . . . .1.90

C v United Kingdom (1983) 37 DR 142 (Application No 10358/83) 10.128
Campbell v MGN Ltd [2004] 2 AC 457 . . . . .10.148
Capon v DPP, Independent, 23 March 1998 . . . . .5.71
Carroll v DPP [2009] EWHC 554 (Admin) 2.170
Carter v Crown Prosecution Service [2009] EWHC 2197 (Admin) 6.60
Castells v Spain, 23 April 1992, Series A No 236 . . . . .10.105
Castorina v Chief Constable of Surrey (1988) 138 NLJ Rep 180, CA 7.03, 7.05, 7.06, 7.07, 7.13, 7.18, 7.24, 7.27
Central Criminal Court, ex parte Boulding [1984] QB 813 . . . . .9.34
Chamberlain v Lindon [1998] 1 WLR 1251 . . . . .8.122
Chambers and Edwards v DPP [1995] Crim LR 896 . . . . 1.181, 1.186
Chapman v DPP (1989) 89 Cr App R 190, DC 7.07
Chappell v DPP (1988) 89 Cr App R 82 . . . . .1.153
Chappell v United Kingdom, Application No 12587/86, 14 December 1991,
    53 DR 241 . . . . .10.133
Chassagnou v France (1999) 29 EHRR 615 . . . . 10.17, 10.23, 10.102
Chief Constable of Hertfordshire v Van Colle; Smith v Chief Constable
    of Sussex [2008] 3 WLR 593 . . . . .10.181
Chief Constable of West Yorkshire v Armstrong [2008] EWCA Civ 1582 . . . . .7.07, 7.08, 7.09, 7.13
Chisholm v Doulton (1889) 22 QBD 736 . . . . .2.109
Chorherr v Austria (1993) 17 EHRR 358 . . . . 10.53, 10.92
Christian Democratic People's Party v Moldova, Application No 28793/02,
    14 May 2006 . . . . 10.17, 10.101
Christians against Racism and Fascism v United Kingdom (1980) 21 DR 138 . . . . 3.45, 6.171
Christie v Leachinsky [1947] AC 573, HL 7.40, 7.61

CIN Properties Ltd v Rawlins [1995] 2 EGLR 130 . . . . 10.75
Ciraklar v Turkey, Application No 19601/92; 80-A/B(E) DR 46, 19 January 1995 . . . 10.67, 10.113
Cisse v France, Application No 51346/99, 9 April 2002 . . . . 10.67, 10.71
Clarke v Chief Constable of North Wales [2000] PoLR 83; [2000]
    All ER (D) 477 . . . . 7.12, 7.40, 7.43, 7.61, 7.101
Clements v DPP [2005] EWHC 1279 . . . . 7.17
Cleveland Police v McGrogan [2002] 1 FLR 707, CA 6.144, 6.153, 6.158, 6.159
    Clooth v Belgium (1992) 14 EHRR 717 . . . . 7.113, 7.114, 7.115
Coffin v Smith (1980) 71 Cr App R 221 . . . . 2.24, 2.29, 2.30, 5.39
Coles v Chief Constable of South Yorkshire Police, 12 October 1998, CA 6.183
Collins v Wilcock [1984] 1 WLR 1172 . . . . 2.33, 6.175
Commission for Racial Equality v Dutton [1989] QB 783 . . . . 2.91
Connolly v DPP [2007] HRLR 17
Connor v Kent [1891] 2 QB 545 . . . . 2.162
Connors v United Kingdom (2005) 40 EHRR 9 . . . . 6.193, 10.145
Consolidated Criminal Practice Direction 2002, ... 9.87
Coudrat v Commissioners for Customs and Excise [2005] STC 1006 . . . . 7.14
Cox v Riley (1986) 83 Cr App R 54 . . . . 8.101
CPS v North West Surrey Magistrates Court [2009] 5.49
Cresswell v DPP [2006] EWCA 3379 . . . . 8.90, 8.97
CS v Germany, Application No 13858/88, 6 March 1989 . . . . 10.60, 10.67, 10.84
Cumming v Chief Constable of Northumbria [2003] All ER (D) 305 (Dec);
    [2004] PoLR 61, CA 6.81, 7.15, 7.16, 7.29
Currie v DPP (1994) 171 JP 233 . . . . 9.80, 8.97
Customs & Excise Commissioners v City of London Magistrates' Court
    [2000] 1 WLR 2020 . . . . 6.139

Daiichi UK Ltd v Stop Huntingdon Animal Cruelty [2003] EWHC 2337 . . . . 9.170
Dale v Smith [1967] 1 WLR 700 . . . . 4.131
Dallison v Caffrey [1965] 1 QB 348, CA 7.37
Daniel v Morrison (1980) 70 Cr App R 142 . . . . 4.76
Darroch v DPP (1990) 91 Cr App R 378 . . . . 4.130, 4.146
Davis v Lisle [1936] 2 KB 434 . . . . 3.79
Dehal v DPP [2005] EWHC 2154 (Admin) 1.209, 1.223, 4.43, 10.41,
    10.42, 10.48, 10.53
Dennis v Ministry of Defence [2003] EWHC 793, QB 8.166, 8.167
Despard v Wilcox (1910) 102 LT 103 . . . . 2.27
Dhesi v Chief Constable of the West Midlands Police [2000] PoLR 120, CA 7.38
Dibble v Ingleton [1972] 1 QB 480 . . . . 2.16
Director of Public Prosecutions for Northern Ireland v Lynch [1975] AC 653 . . . . 8.26
Djavit An v Turkey (2005) 40 EHRR 45 . . . . 6.205
Djavit An v Turkey, Application No 20652/92, [2003] Reports of Judgments
    and Decision, 2003-III, p 233 . . . . 10.17, 10.23, 10.101
Doe d Hughes v Dyeball (1829) Mood & M 346 . . . . 5.17
Doherty v Birmingham City Council [2008] 3 WLR 636 . . . . 5.22
Donnelly v Jackman [1970] 1 WLR 562 . . . . 2.34
DPP v Avery [2002] 1 Cr App R 31, DC 6.41, 6.42
DPP v Baillie [1995] Crim LR 426 . . . . 3.37
DPP v Barnard [2000] Crim LR 371 . . . . 5.54
DPP v Beyer [2004] 1 Cr App R 38 . . . . 8.109
DPP v Brian Haw [2007] EWHC 1931 (Admin); (2008) 1 WLR 379 . . . . 3.124
DPP v Bull [1995] 1 Cr App R 413 . . . . 4.113

DPP v Clarke (1991) 94 Cr App R 359 . . . . 1.192, 1.199
DPP v Fidler and another [1992] 1 WLR 91 . . . . 2.157, 2.159
DPP v Harris [1995] 1 Cr App R 170 . . . . 8.136
DPP v Hawkins [1988] 1 WLR 1166, QB 7.39
DPP v Howard [2008] 4 Archbold News 3, DC 2.94
DPP v Hutchinson [1990] 3 WLR 196 . . . . 5.149
DPP v Inegbu [2008] EWHC 3242 (Admin); [2008] All ER (D) 269 . . . . 3.154
DPP v Jones (Margaret) and another [1999] 2 AC 240 . . . . 4.04, 4.09, 4.12, 4.27, 4.39, 4.48,
4.51, 5.10, 5.56, 5.136, 9.03, 9.04,
9.05, 9.06, 10.05, 10.06, 10.08
DPP v Jones [2002] EWHC 110 . . . . 3.59
DPP v Lal [2000] Crim LR 756 . . . . 2.95
DPP v Lawrence [2008] 1 Cr App R 10, DC 7.44
DPP v M [2004] 1 WLR 2758 . . . . 2.90
DPP v Majewski; R v Majewski [1977] AC 443 . . . . 1.43
DPP v Morgan [1976] AC 182 . . . . 8.67, 8.68, 8.156
DPP v Morrison (2003) 167 JP 577, DC 6.70
DPP v Orum [1989] 1 WLR 88 . . . . 1.185
DPP v Ramos [2000] Crim LR 768 . . . . 1.164, 1.165
DPP v Roffey [1959] Crim LR 283 . . . . 3.59
DPP v Stoke on Trent Magistrates' Court [2003] 3 All ER 2.179
DPP v Stonehouse [1978] AC 55 . . . . 8.118, 8.119, 8.120, 8.121
DPP v Tilly [2002] Crim LR 128 . . . . 5.62
DPP v Todd [1996] Crim LR 344, DC 7.14
DPP v Weeks, unreported, 14 June 2000, CO/3957/99 . . . . 1.216
DPP v Wilson [1991] RTR 284, DC 7.10
Duncan v Jones [1936] 1 KB 218 . . . . 3.04, 3.05, 3.82, 6.154, 10.03, 10.04, 10.140

E (a child) v Chief Constable of the Royal Ulster Constabulary
    [2009] 1 AC 536, HLNI 6.190, 6.192
E v Chief Constable of the Royal Ulster Constabulary [2008] 2 WLR 1208 . . . . 10.183, 10.190
Eaton v Cobb [1950] 1 All ER 1016 . . . . 2.18, 4.30, 4.31
Edwards v United Kingdom (1992) 15 EHRR 417 . . . . 10.175
Edwards v United Kingdom (2000) 30 EHRR 121 . . . . 10.175
Elkins v Cartlidge [1947] 1 All ER 829 . . . . 4.123
Elsey v Smith [1983] IRLR 292 . . . . 2.163
Emerson Developments Ltd v Avery [2004] EWHC 194 . . . . 9.170
Engel v Netherlands (No 1) (1979–80) 1 EHRR 647 . . . . 6.115, 10.154, 10.156
Ergi v Turkey (2001) 32 EHRR 18 . . . . 6.186
Essen v DPP [2005] EWHC 1077 . . . . 9.101
Ettridge v Morrell, unreported, 1 January 1987 (CA) 3.92
Ezelin v France (19991) 14 EHRR 362 . . . . 3.119, 4.44, 6.171, 10.07, 10.17,
10.18, 10.67, 10.77, 10.82, 10.109, 10.113

F (Mental Patient: Sterilisation), In re [1990] 2 AC 1 . . . . 8.131
F v Austria (1992) 15 EHRR CD68 . . . . 10.106
F v Switzerland (1987) 10 EHRR 411 . . . . 4.101
Fawcett Properties Ltd v Buckinghamshire County Court [1964] AC 636 . . . . 3.161
Feldek v Slovakia No 29032/95, ECHR 200-VIII 10.19
Ferguson v Carnochan (1889) 16 R (J) 93 . . . . 6.139
Fielden v Cox (1906) 22 TLR 411 . . . . 4.15
Finucan v United Kingdom (2003) 37 EHRR 656 . . . . 10.181

Fitt v United Kingdom (2000) 30 EHRR 480. . . . . .10.176
Fleming and Robinson [1989] Crim LR 658; (1989) 153 JP 517 . . . . .1.67
Flockhart v Robinson [1950] 2 KB 498. . . . . .3.09, 3.19, 3.20, 3.25
Foulkes v Chief Constable of Merseyside [1998] 3 All ER 705. . . . . 5.38, 6.136, 6.157
Fowler v Kibble [1922] 1 Ch 140 and [1922] 1 Ch 487, CA 2.164
Fox, Campbell and Hartley v United Kingdom (1991)
    13 EHRR 157 . . . . .7.08, 7.09, 7.17, 7.40, 7.41, 7.42
Foy v Chief Constable of Kent, unreported, 20 March 1984 . . . . .4.64
Friedl v Austria, Application No 15225/89, 30 November 1992 . . . . .10.60
Fuentes Bobo v Spain, Application No 39293/98, judgment of 29 February 2000 . . . . .10.32

G and E v Norway, Application Nos 9278/81 and 9415/81, 3 October 1983. . . . . .10.60
G v Germany (1989) 60 DR 256 . . . . 4.45, 10.67
G v The Federal Republic of Germany, Application No 13079/87,
    6 March 1989. . . . . 10.61, 10.113
Galstyan v Armenia, Application No 26986/03, 15 November 2007. . . . . .10.57
Galstyan v Armenia, Application No 26986/03, 18 October 2007 .10.60
Gaweda v Poland (2002) 12 EHRC 486 . . . . .3.160
Gayford v Trouler [1898] 1 QB 316 . . . . .8.100
Gelberg v Miller [1961] 1 All ER 291 . . . . .4.76
Ghani v Jones [1970] 1 QB 693, CA. 6.70, 6.72
Gibson v Lawson [1891] 2 QB 545. . . . . 2.162, 3.70
Gillan and Quinton v United Kingdom, Application No 4158/05. . . . . 6.113, 6.114
Gillick v West Norfolk and Wisbech Area HA [1986] 1 AC 142 .8.131
Giuliani and Gaggio v Italy, Application No 23458/02, 25 August 2009 . . . . 6.185, 6.186
Gldani Congregation of Jehovah's Witnesses v Georgia, Application No 71156/01,
    3 May 2007 . . . . .10.184
Glynn v Simmonds [1952] 2 All ER 57. . . . . .4.123
Goral v Poland, Application No 38654/97 . . . . .7.113
Gough v Chief Constable of Derbyshire [2002] QB 1213. . . . . .9.189
Govell v United Kingdom, Application No 27237/95, 26 February 1995 . . . . .10.81
Granger v United Kingdom (1990) 12 EHRR 469 . . . . .10.168
Gray v DPP, unreported, 1999, CO/5069/98 . . . . .1.118
Great Central Railway Co v Bates [1921] 3 KB 578. . . . . .3.79
Green v DPP (1991) 155 JP 816. . . . . .2.13
Groppera Radio AG v Switzerland (199) 12 EHRR 321 . . . . .10.22
GS v Austria, Application No 14923/89, 30 November 1992 . . . . .10.60
Guenat v Switzerland (1995) 81 DR 130 . . . . .10.159
Gulec v Turkey (1999) 28 EHRR 121. . . . . 6.186, 10.180
Guneri v Turkey, Application No 42853/98, 12 July 2005. . . . . .10.28
Guzzardi v Italy (1981) 3 EHRR 333 . . . . .6.114, 7.116, 10.154, 10.155
Gypsy Council of Great Britain v United Kingdom, Application
    No 00066336/01, 14 May 2002. . . . . 5.139, 10.145

Hadjisava [2004] EWCA Crim 1316 . . . . .1.67
Hague v Committee for Industrial Organisation, 307 US 496 (1939) 10.09
Halford v United Kingdom (1997) 24 EHRR 523 . . . . .10.148
Hall v Davis (1825) 2 C & P 33 . . . . .5.38
Hall, Christopher David and others v Save Newchurch Guinea Pigs (Campaign)
    and sixteen others [2005] EWHC 372, QB. 9.172
Hammond v DPP [2004] EWHC 69 (Admin), The Times,
    28 January 2004. . . . . 1.202, 4.43, 10.50, 10.52, 10.139

Hampshire Waste Services Ltd v Intending Trespassers upon Chineham
    Incinerator [2004] Env LR 5.33
Handyside v United Kingdom (1979–80) 1 EHRR 737 . . . . 4.40, 6.135, 10.20, 10.39,
    10.103, 10.106
Hannover v Germany (2005) 40 EHRR 1. . . . . 10.148
Hanway v Boultbee (1830) 1 M and Rob 15 . . . . 8.42
Hardman v Chief Constable of Avon and Somerset Constabulary
    [1986] Crim LR 330. . . . . 2.116, 8.100
Harrison v Duke of Rutland [1893] 1 QB 142 . . . . 4.06, 4.07, 4.14
Harrow Crown Court, ex parte Dave [1994] 1 WLR 98 . . . . .9.86
Hashman and Harrup v United Kingdom (2000)
    30 EHRR 241 . . . . 6.146, 9.27, 9.29, 9.36,
    10.62, 10.85, 10.89
Hayes v Stevenson (1860) 25 JP 39. . . . . 5.156
Heathrow Airport and others v Garman and six others [2007]
    EWHC 1957, QB 5.31, 5.45, 10.96
Hellewell v Chief Constable of Derbyshire [1995] 1 WLR 804, QB .7.74
Hemmings v Stoke Poges Golf Club [1920] 1 KB 720. . . . . 5.34, 5.38
Hickman v Maisey [1900] 1 QB 752 . . . . 4.07
Hill and Hall (1988) 89 Cr App R 74 . . . . 8.31, 8.112, 8.115, 8.117,
    8.118, 8.120, 8.121, 8.123
Hillen v ICI (Alkali) Ltd [1936] AC 65, HL 5.06
Hills v Ellis [1983] QB 680. . . . . 2.19
Hinchcliffe v Sheldon [1955] 1 WLR 1207. . . . . 2.13
Hirst and Agu v Chief Constable of West Yorkshire (1987)
    85 Cr App R 143 . . . . 4.22, 4.24, 4.25, 4.27, 4.29,
    4.31, 4.33, 4.36, 4.38, 4.70
HL v United Kingdom (2004) 81 BMLR 131. . . . . 10.161
HL v United Kingdom (2005) 40 EHRR 32. . . . . 6.113, 6.114
HM v Switzerland (2002) 38 EHRR 314 . . . . 10.159
Holgate-Mohammed v Duke [1984] AC 437 . . . . .7.32
Horton v Mead [1913] 1 KB 154 . . . . 4.117
Hough v Chief Constable Staffordshire Plice [2001] All ER (D) 63 (Jan);
    [2001] PoLR 6 . . . . 7.10, 7.11, 7.13
Hubbard v Pitt [1976] QB 142. . . . . 3.01, 3.05, 4.28, 4.52, 4.68, 4.69, 4.70, 4.71
Hughes v Holley (1988) 86 Cr App R 130 . . . . .9.26
Humphries v Connor (1864) 17 ICLR 1. . . . . 6.133, 6.154
Huntingdon Life Sciences v Stop Huntingdon Animal Cruelty [2007] EWHC 522 . . . . .9.175
Huohvanainen v Finland (2008) 47 EHRR 44 . . . . .6.186
Hurman v State of Mauritius [2006] 1 WLR 857, PC. 7.147
Hutchinson v Newbury Magistrates' Court (2000) 12 ILR 499; The Independent,
    20 November 2000, judgment 9 October 2000. . . . . 8.43, 10.22
Hutt v Commissioner of the Police of the Metropolis [2004] PoLR 13, CA 7.62

I v DPP; M v DPP; H v DPP [2002] 1 AC 285, HL 1.73, 1.99, 1.105
IA v France 1998-VII RJD 2951. . . . . .7.113
ILCC, ex parte London Borough of Lambeth [2000] Crim LR 303. .9.86
Incal v Turkey (2000) 29 EHRR 449. . . . . 10.55, 10.131
Inner London Crown Court, ex p Benjamin (1986) 85 Cr App R 267. . . . . .9.25
Ireland v United Kingdom (1979–80) 2 EHRR 25 . . . . 6.187, 10.186
Iveagh v Martin [1961] 1 QB 232. . . . . .4.05
Iwanczuk v Poland (2004) 38 EHRR 8 . . . . .7.117

Jaggard v Dickinson [1981] QB 527 . . . . 8.108
James v Chief Constable of South Wales, 16 April 1991, CA, Independent, 28 April 1991 . . . . . 7.12
Järvinen v Finland, Application No 30408/96 . . . . 6.115
Jasper v United Kingdom (2000) 30 EHRR 411 . . . . 10.176
Jespers v Belgium, Application No 8403/78, 15 October 1980 . . . . 10.175
JK v Netherlands, Application No 15928/89, 13 May 1992 . . . . 10.60
John Lewis & Co v Tims [1952] AC 676, HL 7.37
Johnson v DPP [1994] Crim LR 673 . . . . 8.110, 8.115
Johnson v DPP [2008] EWHC 509 (Admin) 2.93
Johnson v Phillips [1975] 3 All ER 682 . . . . 4.34, 4.76
Jones v Carnegie 2004 JC 136 . . . . 6.139
Jones v DPP [2007] 1 AC 136 . . . . 10.168
Jordan v United Kingdom (2003) 37 EHRR 52 . . . . 10.173, 10.179, 10.181
Joyce v Hertfordshire Constabulary (1985) 80 Cr App R 298, DC 6.168, 7.10

K v Netherlands, Application No 15928/89, 13 May 1992 . . . . 10.124
Kamara v DPP [1974] AC 104 . . . . 1.56, 5.42, 5.167
Karabulut v Turkey, Application No 16999/04, 27 January 2009 . . . . 6.187, 6.188, 6.189, 6.194
Karaduman v Turkey (1993) 74 DR 93 . . . . 10.130
Karman v Russia No 29372/02, 14 December 2006 . . . . 10.19
Kavanagh v Hiscock [1974] QB 600, DC 6.160
Kay (FC) v Commissioner of Police for the Metropolis [2008] 1 WLR 2723 . . . . 3.09, 3.18
Kay v Hibbert [1977] Crim LR 226 . . . . 2.32
Kay v Lambeth LBC [2006] 2 AC 465 . . . . 5.21
Kenlin and another v Gardiner and another [1967] 2 QB 510 . . . . 2.10, 2.33, 6.176, 7.01
Kennaway v Thompson [1981] 1 QB 88 . . . . 8.166
Kennedy v Cowie (1909) 47 SLR 209 . . . . 2.162
Kent v Metropolitan Police Commissioner, The Times,
    15 May 1981 . . . . 3.05, 3.08, 3.38, 3.44, 3.50
Kerr v DPP [1995] Crim LR 394 . . . . 2.08, 2.37
Key Tabernacle v Secretary of State for Defence [2008] EWHC 416 (Admin) 3.160
Khudobin v Russia (2009) 48 EHRR 22 . . . . 7.144
Kilic v Turkey (2001) 33 EHRR 1357 . . . . 10.181
King v Hodges [1974] Crim LR 424, DC 6.154
King-Ansell v Police [1979] 2 NZLR 531 . . . . 2.91
Kingston-upon-Thames Crown Court, ex parte Guarino [1986] Crim LR 325 . . . . 9.25
Kjeldsen, Busk Madsen and Pedersen v Denmark (1976) 1 EHRR 711 . . . . 10.130
Knight v Fryer [1976] Crim LR 322 . . . . 4.124
Kokkinakis v Greece (1993) 17 EHRR 397 . . . . 10.123, 10.126, 10.138
Kuijper v Netherlands, Application No 64848/01, 3 March 2005 . . . . 10.84
Kurnaz and others v Turkey, Application No 36672/97, 24 July 1997 . . . . 6.187
Kuznetsov, Sergey v Russia, Application No 10877.04,
    23 October 2008 . . . . 10.07, 10.18, 10.19, 10.23, 10.25, 10.57,
                                                        10.61, 10.63, 10.101, 10.109, 10.117
Kynoch Ltd v Rowlands [1912] 1 Ch 527 . . . . 5.06

L v CPS [2008] 1 Cr App R 8 . . . . 5.156
Laidlaw v Atkinson, The Times, 2 August 1986 . . . . 7.136
Lamy v Belgium (1989) 11 EHRR 529 . . . . 7.144
Lanham v Rickwood (1984) 148 JP 573 . . . . 2.171
Larissis and others v Greece, judgment of 24 February 1998,
    Reports 1998-I, p. 377 . . . . 10.84

Lavender v Betts [1942] 2 All ER 72 . . . . 5.06
League Against Cruel Sports Ltd v Scott [1986] QB 240 . . . . 5.06
Ledger v DPP [1991] Crim LR 439 . . . . 2.16
Letellier v France (1992) 14 EHRR 83 . . . . 7.113, 7.144
Lewis v Cattle [1938] 2 KB 454 . . . . 2.05
Lewis v Chief Constable of the South Wales Constabulary [1991] 1 All ER 206, CA 7.43, 7.60
Lewis v Cox [1985] 1 QB 405. . . . . 2.18, 2.19
Lewis, ex parte (1888) 21 QBD 191 . . . . 3.76, 3.131, 4.04, 4.51
Lincoln Crown Court, ex p Jude [1998] 1 WLR 24. . . . . 9.25, 9.34
Lindley v Rutter [1981] QB 128, DC. 7.46
Lingens v Austria (1986) 8 EHRR 407 . . . . 10.22
Llandudno Urban District Council v Woods [1899] 2 Ch 705 . . . . 4.15
Lloyd v DPP [1992] 1 All ER 982. . . . . 8.116
Loade v DPP [1990] 1 QB 1052. . . . . 9.101
Lobo Machado v Portugal (1996) 23 EHRR 79 . . . . 10.174
Lockwood [2002] EWCA Crim 60. . . . . 8.158
Lodwick v Sanders [1985] 1 WLR 382, DC 6.124
Lord Advocate's Reference (No 1 of 2000). 8.146
Lowenthal and O'Shea v United Kingdom, Application No 41008/09 . . . . 6.166
Lucas v United Kingdom, Application No 39013/02,
    18 March 2003. . . . . 6.139, 10.59, 10.61, 10.91, 10.98
Ludlow and others v Burgess 75 Cr App R 227 . . . . 2.33
Lunt v DPP [1993] Crim LR 535 . . . . 2.17
Lyons v Wilkins [1896] 1 Ch 811 . . . . 2.160, 2.165

M'Cusker v Smith [1918] 2 IR 432. . . . . 2.165
    Mace v Philcox (1864) 15 CBNS 600 . . . . 5.06
Makhmudov v Russia, Application No 35082/04, 26 July 2007 . . . . 10.07
Malone v United Kingdom (1984) 7 EHRR 14. . . . . 10.85
Managers of the Metropolitan Asylum District v Hill (1881) LR 6 AC 193 . . . . 2.110
Manchester Airport v Dutton [1999] 3 WLR 524, CA 5.16
Mandla v Dowell Lee [1983] 2 AC 548. . . . . 2.90
Mannall v Fisher (1859) 5 CBNS 856. . . . . 5.09
Mapstead v DPP [1996] Crim LR 111 . . . . 2.34
Markt Intern Verlag GmbH & Klaus Beerman v Germany (1989) 12 EHRR 161 . . . . 10.22
Marlow Justices, ex parte O'Sullivan [1984] QB 381, DC. 9.41
Marper v United Kingdom, Application Nos 30562/04 and 30566/04,
    4 December 2008. . . . . 10.146
Marsh v Alabama 326 US 501, 66 S Ct 276, 90 L Ed 265 (1946) 10.73
Marshall v Tinnelly (1937) 81 SJ 902 . . . . 3.78
Masterson v Holden [1986] 1 WLR 1017. . . . . 1.149
Matznetter v Austria (1979–80) 1 EHRR 198. . . . . 7.114
MB v DPP (2007) 171 JP 10, DC. 6.65
McBride v United Kingdom, Application No 27786/95, 5 July 2001 . . . . 10.91
McCann v United Kingdom (1995) 21 EHRR 97. . . . . 6.186
McCann v United Kingdom [2008] 2 FLR 899, ECHR 5.22
McCarrick v Oxford [1983] RTR 117, CA 7.13
McConnell v Chief Constable of Greater Manchester [1990] 1 165, WLR 364, CA 6.161
McDonald v Procurator Fiscal (2003) SLT 467. . . . . 7.116
McE v Prison Service of Northern Ireland [2009] 2 WLR 782, HL 7.82
McLeod v Metropolitan Police Commissioner [1994] 4 All ER 553, CA 6.140, 6.161
McMichael v United Kingdom (1995) 20 EHRR 205. . . . . 10.179

McMillan v Crown Proseuction Service (2008) 172 JP 485, DC 6.175
McPhail v Persons unknown [1973] Ch 447 . . . . 5.20
McQuade v Chief Constable of Humberside [2002] 1 WLR 1347, CA 6.161
McVicar v United Kingdom (2002) 35 EHRR 584 . . . . 10.171
Mepstead v DPP [1996] COD 13, QB 6.175
Mercer v Chief Constable of the Lancashire Constabulary [1991] 1 WLR 267, CA 7.95
Meredith, ex parte (1973) 57 Cr App R 451 . . . . 9.112
Miller v Jackson [1977] 1 QB 966 . . . . 8.166
Milner v Maclean (1825) 2 C & P 17 . . . . 8.47
Minto v Police [1987] 1 NZLR 374 . . . . 6.148
Moase, Daniel v City of Westminster Magistrates' Court, unreported,
    27 June 2008 . . . . 3.121, 10.114
Moles, In re [1981] Crim LR 170 . . . . 7.120, 7.163
Molnar v Hungary, Application No 10346/05, 7 October 2008 . . . . 10.120
Monsanto plc v Tilly [2000] Env LR 313, CA 5.12, 5.16, 8.167, 9.175
Moore v Green [1983] QB 667 . . . . 2.19
Moratilla v Spain (1992) 72 DR 256 . . . . 10.129
Morphitis v Salmon [1990] Crim LR 48 . . . . 8.100
Moss v McLachlan [1985] IRLR 76 . . . . 4.64, 4.65, 4.66, 4.76, 6.132, 6.148, 6.151
Mossop v DPP [2003] EWHC 1261 (Admin) 7.14
MS v Sweden (1997) EHRR 313 . . . . 6.05
Muller v Austria (1988) 13 EHRR 51 . . . . 10.22
Murray v Ministry of Defence [1988] 1 WLR 692, HL 6.115
Murray v United Kingdom (1994) 19 EHRR 193 . . . . 6.53

N v United Kingdom (2008) 47 EHRR 885 . . . . 10.159
Nagy v Weston [1965] 1 WLR 280 . . . . 4.24, 4.35, 4.36, 4.39
National Provincial Bank v Ainsworth [1965] 2 All ER 472, HL 5.16
Neale v RJME (a minor) (1984) 80 Cr App R 20 . . . . 2.171
Nelder v DPP, The Times, 11 June 1998 . . . . 5.53, 5.54, 5.61
Neumeister v Austria (1979–80) 1 EHRR 91 . . . . 7.113, 7.116, 7.144, 7.155
Newman v Francis (1953) 51 LGR 158 . . . . 3.160
News Group Newspapers Ltd v Society of Graphical and Allied Trades
    1982 (No 2) [1987] ICR 181 . . . . 2.162, 3.05, 3.70
Nicol and Selvanayagam v DPP (1996) 160 JP 155, DC 6.136
Nicol and Selvanayagam v United Kingdom, Application No 32213/96,
    11 January 2001 . . . . 10.91
Nielsen v Denmark (1988) 11 EHRR 175 . . . . 10.159
Niemitz v Germany (1992) 16 EHRR 97 . . . . 10.145
Nikolova v Bulgaria (2001) 31 EHRR 3 . . . . 7.113, 7.144
Norwood v DPP [2003] EWHC 1564 (Admin);
    [2003] Crim LR 888 . . . . 1.202, 4.43, 10.51, 10.52
Norwood v United Kingdom, Application No 23131/03,
    16 November 2004 . . . . 10.143
Nurettin Aldemir and others v Turkey, Applications Nos 32124/02, 32126/02,
    32129/02, 32133/02, 32137/02, 32138/02,
    18 December 2007 . . . . 10.58, 10.61, 10.63, 10.71

O (A Juvenile) v DPP (1999) 163 JP 725, QB 2.35
O'Halloran and Francis v United Kingdom (2008) 46 EHRR 21 . . . . 6.29
O'Hara v Chief Constable of the Royal Ulster Constabulary
    [1997] AC 286, HL 7.07, 7.08, 7.09, 7.10, 7.11

O'Kelly v Harvey (1883) 14 LR Ir 105 . . . . 4.67, 6.134
O'Loughlin v Chief Constable of Essex [1998] 1 WLR 374, CA 6.176, 7.51
O'Moran v DPP [1975] QB 864 . . . . 2.39
Öllinger v Austria, Application No 76900/01, 29 June 2006 . . . . 10.17, 10.37, 10.142
Osman v DPP (1999) 163 JP 725, QB 6.25, 6.107, 6108
Osman v United Kingdom (2000) 29 EHRR 245; [1999] 1 FLR 193, ECHR. 6.186, 10.181
Ostler v Elliot [1980] Crim LR 584 . . . . 2.18
Ouranio Toxo v Greece, Application No 74989/01, ECHR 2005-X 10.101
Oxford University and others v Broughton and others [2006] EWHC 1233;
     [2006] EWCA Civ 1310. . . . . 9.171
Oxford University and others v Broughton and others [2008] EWHC 75, QB 9.171
Oya Ataman v Turkey, No 74552/01,
     5 December 2006. . . . . 10.28, 10.57, 10.58, 10.61, 10.63, 10.71
Özgür Gündem v Turkey, Application No 23144/93, ECHR 2000-III,
     judgment of 16 March 2000 . . . . 10.32

Palmer v R [1971] AC 814; [1971] 1 All ER 1077. . . . . 8.65, 8.81
Palmer v The Queen [1971] AC 814, PC 6.179, 6.181
Pannell v Mill (1846) 3 CB 625 . . . . 5.09
Panovits v Cyprus, Application No 4268/04, 11 December 2008 . . . . 7.79
Papworth v Coventry [1967] 1 WLR 66 . . . . 3.96
para I.13. . . . . 7.138
Parkin v Norman [1983] QB 92 . . . . 1.148, 4.133
Patyi and others v Hungary, Application No 5529/05,
     7 October 2008 . . . . 10.57, 10.98, 10.106
Paul v Chief Constable of Humberside Police [2004] All ER (D) 333 (Mar);
     [2004] PoLR 179, CA. 7.30, 7.32
Paul v DPP (1990) 90 Cr App R 173 . . . . 4.133, 4.134
Peck v United Kingdom (2003) 36 EHRR 41 . . . . 10.148
Pendragon v United Kingdom [1999] EHRLR 223 . . . . 3.131, 10.133, 10.137
Pepper v Hart [1993] AC 593. . . . . 3.122
Percy v DPP [1995] 1 WLR 1382, DC. 6.129, 6.130
Percy v DPP [2001] EWHC 1125 (Admin); [2002] Crim LR 835;
     (2002) 166 JP 93 . . . . 1.201, 2.96, 4.43, 10.22, 10.44, 10.48, 10.53
Percy v Hall [1997] QB 924 . . . . 3.160, 3.161, 7.14
Perry v Clissold [1907] AC 73. . . . . 5.17
Piddington v Bates [1961] 1 WLR 162 . . . . 2.165, 4.62, 4.63, 4.66, 6.160
Piermont v France (1995) 20 EHRR 301 . . . . 10.19, 10.99, 10.105
Pine v Law Society [2002] UKHRR 81. . . . . 10.172
Plattform "Ärzte für das Leben" v Austria (1988)
     13 EHRR 204 . . . . 10.31, 10.34, 10.35, 10.113
Police v Reid [1987] Crim LR 702 . . . . 3.70
Pollard v The Chief Constable of West Yorkshire Police [1999] PIQR P219. . . . . 6.183
Porter v Commissioner of Police of the Metropolis, unreported,
     20 October 1999, CA. 5.38, 5.39, 6.161

Quaranta v Switzerland, Application No 11932/86. . . . . 10.168

R (on the application of Ajaib) v Birmingham Magistrates' Court
     [2009] EWHC 2127 . . . . 7.120
R (on the application of Begum) v Governors of Denbigh High School
     [2007] 1 AC 100 . . . . 10.130

R (on the application of Boughton) v HM Treasury [2006] EWCA Civ 504,
    4 May 2006 . . . . 10.129
R (on the application of C) v Chief Constable of A [2006]
    EWHC 2352 (Admin) 7.20, 7.31, 7.102
R (on the application of Campaign for Nuclear Disarmament) v Prime Minister of the
    UK [2003] 3 LRC 335 . . . . 8.85
R (on the application of Countryside Alliance) v Attorney-General [2008]
    1 AC 719; [2007] 3 WLR 922 . . . . 10.07, 10.19, 10.25, 10.107, 10.147
R (on the application of CPS) v Chorley Justices [2002]
    166 JP 764, HC 7.117, 7.118, 7.123, 7.126, 7.129
R (on the application of Daly) v Secretary of State for the Home
    Department [2001] 2 AC 532. . . . . 9.109
R (on the application of DPP) v Humphrey [2005] EWHC 822 (Admin) 1.180
R (on the application of Drohan) v Waterford JJ (1990) 2 IR 309 . . . . 9.98
R (on the application of E, T and Morris) v Chief Constable of Kent Police,
    Claim No CO/10579/2008 . . . . 6.81
R (on the application of Ellis) v Chief Constbale of Essex Police [2003]
    EWHC 1321 (Admin) 7.74
R (on the application of Ellison) v Teeside Magistrates' Court (2001) 165 JP 355, DC. 7.135
R (on the application of European Roma Rights Centre) v Immigration
    Officer at Prague Airport (United Nations High Commissioner for
    Refugees intervening) [2005] 2 AC 1, HL 6.98
R (on the application of Faisaltex Ltd) v Preston Crown Court [2009] 1 Cr App R 37 . . . . 7.81
R (on the application of Fergus) v Southampton Crown Court [2008]
    EWHC 3273 (Admin) 7.144, 7.155, 7.156
R (on the application of Fullard) v Woking Magistrates' Court [2005]
    EWHC 2922 . . . . 2.32
R (on the application of Fuller) v Chief Constable of Dorset Police [2003]
    1 QB 480 . . . . 5.73, 5.77, 5.88, 5.90
R (on the application of G) v Chief Constable of West Yorkshire [2008]
    1 WLR 550, CA. 7.96, 7.103
R (on the application of Gillan) v Commissioner of Police of the Metropolis
    [2006] 2 AC 307, HL; [2006] 4 All ER 1041 . . . . 4.84, 6.87, 6.90, 6.91, 6.95,
                                                6.113, 10.79, 10.81, 10.87, 10.148, 10.157
R (on the application of Hauschildt) v Highbury Corner Magistrates' Court
    [2009] Crim LR 512. . . . . 7.165
R (on the application of Haw) v Secretary of State for he Home Department
    [2006] QB 359; [2006] EWCA Civ 532. . . . . 3.122
R (on the application of Hussain) v Derby Magistrates' Court [2001]
    1 WLR 2454, DC. 7.135
R (on the application of Laporte) v Chief Constable of Gloucestershire
    [2007] 2 AC 105 . . . . 3.02, 3.160, 4.61, 4.63, 4.65, 4.67, 4.75,
                                        5.31, 6.03, 6.28, 6.56, 6.81, 6.114, 6.125, 6.129,
                                        6.131, 6.136, 6.139, 6.140, 6.141, 6.142, 6.146,
                                        6.147, 6.149, 6.150, 6.151, 6.153, 6.154, 6.160, 6.167,
                                        6.168, 6.169, 6.170, 6.171, 6.173, 7.33, 10.03, 10.38, 10.80
R (on the application of Louis Brehony) v Chief Constable of Greater Manchester
    [2005] EWHC 640 . . . . 3.72
R (on the application of M) v Commissioner of Police of the Metropolis
    [2001] PoLR 264, DC 7.82
R (on the application of M) v Isleworth Crown Court [2005] EWHC 363 (Admin) 7.165
R (on the application of McCann) v Manchester Crown Court [2001] 1 WLR 1084 . . . . 9.189

R (on the application of Nikonovs) v Governor of Brixton Prison
  [2006] 1 WLR 1518, DC..7.143
R (on the application of P) v Liverpool City Magistrates (2006) 170 JP 453................9.113
R (on the application of Parminder Singh and another) v Chief Constable
  of the West Midlands Police [2006] 1 WLR 3374......................10.68, 10.141
R (on the application of Pro-Life Alliance) v BBC [2003] 1 AC 185....................10.32
R (on the application of R) v DPP [2006] EWHC 1375 (Admin)................1.187, 1.188
R (on the application of R) v Durham Constabulary [2005] 1 WLR 1184............9.51, 9.64
R (on the application of Rottman) v Commissioner of Police of the Metropolis
  [2002] 2 AC 692, HL..7.45
R (on the application of Samaroo) v Secretary of State for the Home Department
  [2001] EWCA Civ 1139..3.72
R (on the application of Securiplan plc, Ullmann Sabrewatch Ltd and Lucas)
  v Security Industry Authority and Hutchins (interested party)
  [2009] 2 All ER 211, DC..6.17
R (on the application of Shergill) v Harrow Crown Court [2005] EWHC 648 (Admin)......7.155
R (on the application of Singh) v Chief Constable of the West Midlands Police
  [2006] 1 WLR 3374, CA..6.66
R (on the application of Thomas) v Greenwich Magistrates' Court [2009]
  Crim LR 800, DC..7.120, 7.135
R (on the application of Torres) v Commissioner of Police of the Metropolis
  [2007] EWHC 3212 (Admin)................................7.102, 7.122
R (on the application of Vickers) v West London Magistrates' Court
  (2003) 167 JP 473, QB..7.135
R (on the application of W) v Commissioner of Police of the Metropolis
  [2007] QB 399, CA..6.62, 6.68
R (on the application of Watson) v Dartford Magistrates' Court [2005]
  EWHC 905 (Admin)..9.101
R (on the application of Wiggins) v Harrow Crown Court [2005]
  EWHC 882 (Admin)................................7.145, 7.149, 7.151, 7.153
R (on the application of Williamson) v Secretary of State for Education
  [2005] 2 AC 246..10.124
R v Abdul-Hussain [1999] Crim LR 570................................8.128, 8.138
R v Abraham [1973] 1 WLR 1270..8.27
R v Abu Hamza [2006] QB 659..2.85
R v Afzal [1993] Crim LR 791..1.161
R v Alladice (1988) 87 Cr App R 380, CA..7.81
R v Ambrose (1973) 58 Cr App R 539, CA..1.148
R v Arbery and Mobley [2008] EWCA Crim 702................................9.186
R v Ashford and Smith [1988] Crim LR 682................................8.112
R v Ashley [2004] 1 WLR 2057, CA..7.135
R v Ayliffe et al, Cardiff CC, September 2005................8.16, 8.55, 8.86
R v Ayodeji [2001] 1 Cr App R (S) 370..2.177
R v Ayu [1958] 1 WLR 1264..9.44
R v Babbs [2007] EWCA Crim 2737..2.93
R v Backshall [1998] 1 WLR 1506..8.136
R v Badham [1987] Crim LR 202, CC..7.52
R v Baker (1911) 7 Cr App R 89..2.162
R v Baker and Wilkins [1997] Crim LR 497, CA................8.68, 8.70, 8.95
R v Beaumont [2008] EWHC 523 (Admin)................................9.186
R v Beckford (Junior) (1992) 94 Cr App R 43, CA................................7.52
R v Beckford [1988] AC 130..8.68

R v Bird [1985] 1 WLR 816, CA. 6.179
R v Birdwood, unreported, 11 April 1995. . . . . .2.82
R v Blackwood [2002] EWCA Crim 3102 . . . . .1.41
R v Blake [2004] EWCA Crim 1238. . . . . .8.154
R v Blinkhorn [2006] EWCA Crim 1416 . . . . 1.114–1.117
R v Bourne [1939] 1 KB 687 . . . . .8.131
R v Bournemouth Magistrates' Court, ex parte Cross, Griffin and Pamment
   (1989) 89 Cr App R 90, DC. 7.126, 7.127, 7.128
R v Boyle [1993] Crim LR 40, CA 7.138
R v Braxton [2005] 1 Cr App R (S) 167 . . . . .9.181
R v Bridger [2006] EWCA Crim 3169 . . . . .2.97
R v Britton [1967] 2 QB 51 . . . . .2.72
R v Brodie [2000] Crim LR 775, CA 1.73, 1.74
R v Bronson [2004] EWCA Crim 903 . . . . .8.154
R v Brown [2003] EWCA Crim 2637. . . . . .8.158
R v Brown 174 ER 522. . . . . .6.141
R v Bull, Farrelly and Fox [2009] NIQB 2, QBD 7.23, 7.25, 7.31
R v Caird and others (1970) 54 Cr App R 499. . . . . 1.09, 1.34, 1.46
R v Cairns [1999] 2 Cr App R 137 . . . . .8.149
R v Cameron [1973] Crim LR 520 . . . . .8.27
R v Carlisle CC, ex parte Marcus-Moore, The Times, 26 October 1981. . . . . .9.114
R v CCRC, ex parte Pearson [2000] 1 Cr App R 141. . . . . .9.154
R v CF [2007] 1 WLR 1021 . . . . .1.170
R v Chalkley [1998] QB 848, CA. 7.32
R v Challinor (1984) 80 Cr App R 253 . . . . .8.120
R v Chapman [2002] EWCA Crim 2346 . . . . .1.84
R v Charnley (1937) 81 Sol Jo 108 . . . . .2.39
R v Chichester CC, ex parte Abodunrin (1984) 79 Cr App R 293 . . . . .9.112
R v Chief Constable of Devon and Cornwall, ex parte Central Electrical
   Generating Board [1982] 1 QB 458 . . . . .5.38, 5.39, 6.129, 8.49
R v Chief Constable of Sussex, ex parte International Traders Ferry [1999]
   2 AC 418, HL 6.154, 6.192
R v Chief Constable, ex parte ITF Ltd [1999] 2 AC 418 . . . . .10.65
R v Christopher Bristol [2007] EWCA Crim 3214; (2008) 172 JP 161, CA 2.35, 6.106
R v Church [2000] 4 Archbold News 3, CA 1.73
R v Churchill [1989] Crim LR 226, CA 7.45
R v Clegg [1995] 1 AC 482, HL. 6.183
R v Cole [1994] Crim LR 582. . . . . .8.128
R v Colin Chisam (1963) 47 Cr App R 130, CA 6.179
R v Collins [1972] 2 All ER 1105 . . . . .5.55
R v Commissioner of the Metropolitan Police ex p Porter 5.39
R v Conway [1989] QB 290. . . . . 8.128, 8.136, 8.154
R v Conway, 70 Cr App R 4 . . . . .9.155
R v Cooper [1969] 1 QB 267 . . . . .9.123
R v County of London Quarter Sessions Appeals Committee,
   ex parte Metropolitan Police Commissioner [1948] 1 KB 670. . . . . .6.139
R v Crown Court at Winchester, ex parte Lewington [1982] 1 WLR 1277. . . . . .9.98
R v Cruickshank [2001] 2 Cr App R (S) 278. . . . . .2.153
R v David (1939) 27 Cr App R 50. . . . . .9.44
R v Davis (1986) 8 Cr App R (S) 64 . . . . .7.138
R v Davis [1993] 1 WLR 613 . . . . 10.175, 10.176
R v Davison [1992] Crim LR 31, CA 1.109, 1.111, 1.112, 1.116, 1.117

R v De Munck [1918] 1 KB 635 . . . . 4.111
R v Dean Boness and others [2005] EWCA Crim 2395; [2006] 1 Cr App R (S) 120 . . . . 9.18, 9.180
R v Denton [1981] 1 WLR 1446 . . . . 8.103
R v Dial [2005] 1 WLR 1660 . . . . 9.125
R v Diane Jamieson, unreported, 22 May 2008 . . . . 2.140
R v Dixon [1993] Crim LR 579 . . . . 1.101, 1.102
R v Dorking JJ, ex parte Harrington [1984] AC 743 . . . . 9.113
R v DPP, ex parte Lee [1999] 1 WLR 1950, QB 7.144
R v DPP, ex parte Percy [2002] 1 AC 800 . . . . 10.127
R v Drane [2008] EWCA Crim 1746 . . . . 8.68
R v Duffy [1967] 1 QB 63, CA 6.179, 8.52
R v Dunbar (1987) 9 Cr App R (S) 393 . . . . 2.53
R v Dunlop [2006] EWCA 1354 . . . . 9.151
R v Edwards (1983) 5 Cr App R (S) 145 . . . . 2.86
R v Edwards and Roberts (1978) 67 Cr App R 228 . . . . 2.40, 3.11
R v El-Faisal (Abdullah Ibrahim) (Reasons for Dismissal of Appeal)
    [2004] EWCA Crim 456 . . . . 2.85
R v Elliot (Gregory) [2007] EWCA Crim 1002 . . . . 9.186
R v Elliot [2007] 2 Cr App R (S) 430 . . . . 9.186
R v Evans and others, The Times, 2 July 1969 . . . . 2.46
R v Fancy [1980] Crim LR 171 . . . . 8.100
R v Fennelly [1989] Crim LR 142 . . . . 6.107
R v Fiak [2005] EWCA Crim 2381, CA 2.115, 7.01, 8.100
R v G [2004] 1 AC 1034 . . . . 2.117
R v Gent (1989) 89 Cr App R 247 . . . . 8.120
R v George [2007] EWCA Crim 2722 . . . . 9.125
R v Gordon (Note) (1987) 92 Cr App R 50 . . . . 8.120
R v Graham (1888) 16 Box CC 420 . . . . 10.05
R v Graham [1982] 1 WLR 294 . . . . 8.153, 8.154
R v Grant [2006] QB 60 . . . . 7.82
R v Gray [1999] 1 Cr App R (S) 50 . . . . 2.86
R v Greenall [2005] 2 Cr App R (S) 276 . . . . 1.88
R v Greg Avery; R v Natasha Avery; R v Heather Nicholson; R v
    Daniel Wadham; R v Gerrah Selby; R v Daniel Amos, unreported,
    21 January 2009 . . . . 2.145
R v H and C [2004] 2 AC 134 . . . . 10.175, 10.176
R v Hamilton [1986] Crim LR 187 . . . . 7.42
R v Harris [2005] 2 Cr App R (S) 649 . . . . 2.55
R v Harris [2006] 1 Cr App R 55 . . . . 9.125
R v Harrison [1997] 2 Cr App R (S) 174 . . . . 2.55
R v Hasan (Z) [2005] UKHL 22; [2005] 2 AC 467 . . . . 8.26, 8.128
R v Havering Magistrates' Court, ex parte DPP [2001] 1 WLR 805, DC 7.120, 7.135
R v Hendon Justices, ex parte Gorchein [1973] 1 WLR 1502 . . . . 9.31
R v Henn [1981] AC 850 . . . . 9.161
R v Hewke et al, Maidstone CC, September 2008 . . . . 8.16
R v Hibbert (1995) 99 CCC (3d) 193 . . . . 8.26
R v Higgins [1952] 1 KB 7 . . . . 2.111
R v Hillingdon LBC, ex parte McDOnagh [1998] 31 HLR 531 . . . . 5.125
R v Home Secretary, ex parte Simm [2000] 2 AC 115 . . . . 10.83
R v Horseferry Road Magistrates' Court, ex parte Bennett [1994] 1 AC 42, HL 7.63
R v Horseferry Road Stipendiary, ex parte Siadatan (DC) [1991] 1 QB 260 . . . . 1.162, 1.163
R v Hourigan (2003) 147 SJLB 901; [2003] EWCA Crim 2306 . . . . 7.138

R v How [1993] Crim LR 201, CA. 7.138
R v Howe [1987] AC 417. . . . . 8.128, 8.154
R v Howell [1982] 1 QB 416 . . . . 4.63, 6.129, 6.154, 6.156, 6.158, 9.26
R v Hughes [2006] 1 Cr App R (S) 632 . . . . .9.188
R v Hunt (1977) 66 Cr App R 105 . . . . 8.111, 8.112, 8.114, 8.117, 8.123
R v Huyton JJ, ex parte Roberts [1988] COD 43 . . . . .9.114
R v Ibrahim [2009] 1 WLR 578, CA. 6.28
R v Inner London CC, ex parte Benjamin (1987) 85 Cr App R 267. . . . . .9.111
R v Inwood [1973] 1 WLR 647 . . . . .7.01
R v Isleworth Crown Court, ex p Clarke [1998] 1 Cr App R 257. . . . . .7.160
R v James [2008] EWCA Crim 1869 . . . . .7.81
R v Jefferson [1994] 1 All ER 270 . . . . .1.35
R v Jones (1974) 59 Cr App R 120 . . . . 1.23, 2.162, 3.70
R v Jones [2003] EWCA Crim 894 . . . . .8.06, 8.31, 8.107, 8.116
R v Jones [2004] EWCA Crim 2637; [2004] 3 WLR 1362, CA. .8.106
R v Jones [2005] QB 259 . . . . .8.99
R v Jones and Milling [2007] 1 AC 136. . . . . 8.44, 8.46, 8.57, 8.58, 8.59, 8.69,
                                                                      8.70, 8.73, 8.86, 8.117, 8.167
R v Jones and others [2006] EWCA Crim 2942 . . . . 9.14, 9.17, 9.18
R v Jones and others [2006] UKHL 16 . . . . .9.17
R v Jones; Ayliffe v DPP [2007] 1 AC 136. . . . . 5.54, 5.60
R v Jones; R v Smith [1976] 1 WLR 672. . . . . .5.55
R v Jordan and Tyndall [1963] Crim LR 124. . . . . .2.46
R v Joseph Harris [2006] EWCA Crim 3303. . . . . .2.141
R v K [2001] 3 WLR 471 . . . . 8.11, 8.155
R v Kelleher [2003] EWCA Crim 2486 . . . . 8.95, 8.120
R v Kelly [2001] 1 Cr App R (S) 341 . . . . .2.97
R v Kelly and Donnelly [2001] 2 Cr App R (S) 73. . . . . .2.97
R v Keys and others (1986) 8 Cr App R (S) 444. . . . . .1.125
R v Khan [1995] Crim LR 78 . . . . .8.27
R v Kimber 77 Cr App R 225 . . . . .8.28
R v Kirby [2006] 1 Cr App R (S) 151 . . . . .9.181
R v Kirk [2000] 1 WLR 567, CA 7.42
R v Lamb [2006] 2 Cr App R (S) 84 . . . . .9.181
R v Leeds CC, ex parte Maloney (1998) 31 HLR 552 . . . . .5.125
R v Legal Services Commission, ex parte Jarrett [2002] ACD 25 . . . . .10.172
R v Lemon [2002] EWCA Crim 1661 . . . . .1.69
R v Lincolnshire CC and Wealden DC, ex parte Atkinson, Wales and Stratford
     (1995) 8 Admin 529. . . . . .5.125
R v Liverpool City Justices, ex parte DPP [1993] QB 233 . . . . 7.120, 7.135
R v Lobell [1957] 1 QB 547 . . . . .8.27
R v Lowe [1986] Crim LR 49 . . . . .7.43
R v Lyons and Wilkins (1899) 1 Ch 255 . . . . .2.159
R v M [2003] EWCA Crim 1170 . . . . .8.154
R v Mabee (Craig) [2007] EWCA Crim 3230. . . . . .9.186
R v Mahroof (1988) 88 Cr App R 317 . . . . 1.67, 1.80
R v Maidstone CC, ex parte Gill (1987) 84 Cr App R 96. . . . . .9.111
R v Malik [1968] 1 All ER 582 . . . . .2.56
R v Mann [2002] EWCA Crim 3045 . . . . .1.119
R v Mansfield Justices, ex parte Sharkey [1985] QB 613 . . . . .7.120, 7.126, 7.127, 7.129
R v Martin (Colin) [1989] 1 All ER 652. . . . . .8.128, 8.137, 8.139, 8.148, 8.154, 8.160
R v Martin (DP) [2000] 2 Cr App R 42. . . . . .8.64

R v Maxwell and Clanchy (1909) 2 Cr App R 26 . . . . 2.05
R v Mbagwu and Munnings [2007] EWCA Crim 1068 . . . . 1.69, 1.81
R v McFarlane (1994) 99 Cr App R 8 . . . . 4.112
R v McGarry (1945) 30 Cr App R 187 . . . . 9.45
R v McGrath [2005] 2 Cr App R (S) 52 . . . . 9.180
R v McGregor [1945] 2 All ER 180 . . . . 9.41
R v McInnes (1971) 55 Cr App R 551 . . . . 2.07, 8.65
R v McKenzie [1892] 2 QB 519 . . . . 2.159
R v Mechan [2004] EWCA Crim 388 . . . . 1.66, 1.72
R v Middlesex Crown Court, ex parte Khan (1997) 161 JP 240 . . . . 9.33
R v Miell [2008] 1 WLR 627 . . . . 9.151
R v Mildenhall Magistrates' Court, ex parte Forest Heath District Council
    (1997) 161 JP 401 . . . . 9.99
R v Mitchell [2004] Crim LR 139 . . . . 8.116
R v Morris [1951] 1 KB 384 . . . . 2.111
R v Morris-Lowe [1985] 1 All ER 400 . . . . 4.114
R v Morrison [2001] 1 Cr App R (S) 5, CA 2.98
R v Morrison [2006] 1 Cr App R (S) 488 . . . . 9.181
R v Mullen [2000] QB 520, CA 7.63, 9.124
R v Muranyi (1986) 8 Cr App R (S) 176 . . . . 1.48
R v Najeeb and others [2003] 2 Cr App R (S) 69 . . . . 1.49–1.52
R v Naylor [1979] Crim LR 532 . . . . 7.47
R v Nottingham Justices, ex parte Davies [1981] QB 38, DC 7.163
R v O'Brien [2004] EWCA Crim 2900 . . . . 8.27
R v Oatridge (1992) 94 Cr App R 367 . . . . 8.68
R v Olden [2007] EWCA Crim 726, CA 7.07, 7.12
R v Olditch and Pritchard, Bristol CC, April 2007 . . . . 8.16, 8.32, 8.55, 8.59, 8.123
R v Ong [2001] 1 Cr App R (S) 404 . . . . 2.104
R v Palmer [1971] AC 814 . . . . 2.07
R v Paul Michael Judge [2009] 1 Cr App R (S) 439 . . . . 2.51
R v Pells, AG's Ref (No 92 of 2003), The Times, 21 April 2004, CA 2.97
R v Pendleton [2002] 1 WLR 72 . . . . 9.125
R v Perrins [1995] Crim LR 432 . . . . 1.81
R v Philipson [2008] 2 Cr App R (S) 110 . . . . 2.55
R v Pilgrim (1983) 5 Cr App R (S) 140 . . . . 1.48
R v Plavecz [2002] Crim LR 837 . . . . 1.117
R v Plymouth JJ, ex parte Rogers [1982] QB 863 . . . . 9.161
R v Pommell [1995] 2 Cr App R 607 . . . . 8.31, 9.111, 8.136
R v Povey (2009) 1 Cr App R (S) 42 . . . . 7.139
R v Prebble and others (1858) 1 F&F 325 . . . . 3.79, 5.39
R v Quayle [2005] EWCA Crim 1415 . . . . 8.126, 8.132, 8.158, 8.159
R v Rafferty [2004] EWCA Crim 968 . . . . 1.118
R v Rahman [2008] UKHL 45 . . . . 1.35
R v Rees, McElroy, Carroll, Killick and Morris [2006] 1 Cr App R (S) 20 . . . . 1.87, 2.178
R v Relf (1979) 1 Cr App R (S) 111 . . . . 2.86
R v Renouf [1986] 2 All ER 449 . . . . 8.28, 8.35, 8.38
R v Richards and Leeming (1985) 81 Cr App R 125 . . . . 3.79
R v Rimmington and Goldstein [2006] 1 AC 459 . . . . 2.99, 2.100, 2.101, 2.106,
                                                                              2.107, 2.108, 2.109
R v Robinson [1970] 3 All ER 369 . . . . 8.47
R v Robinson [1993] Crim LR 581 . . . . 1.100, 1.102
R v Rochford JJ, ex parte Buck (1979) 68 Cr App R 114 . . . . 9.101

R v Rogers [2007] 1 AC 62, HL 2.90, 2.95
R v Rose (1847) 2 Cox 329 . . . . .8.42
R v Rothwell and Barton [1993] Crim LR 626, CA 1.30, 1.72, 1.103, 1.161, 8.35
R v Rowland, 14 February 1991, CA 7.135
R v Rozburgh (1871) 12 Cox CC 8 . . . . .5.39
R v Ruffell (1991) 13 Cr App R (S) 204 . . . . .2.104
R v S (DM) [2001] Crim LR 986 . . . . .8.128
R v Safi [2004] 1 Cr App R 157 . . . . .8.13, 8.128, 8.147, 8.148, 8.150,
                                                                                 8.153, 8.155, 8.156, 8.157
R v Saleem, Nuhid and Javed [2008] 2 Cr App R (S) 12 . . . . .2.85
R v Samuel [1988] QB 615, CA 7.81
R v Sanchez [1996] Crim LR 572 . . . . 1.111, 1.113
R v Saunders [2000] 1 Cr App R (S) 71, CA 2.97
R v Scott (2008) 172 JP 149, CA 7.136
R v Secretary of State for the Home Department, ex parte Amin
     [2004] 1 AC 653 . . . . 10.173, 10.182
R v Secretary of State for the Home Department, ex parte Daly [2001] AC 532 . . . . .3.52
R v Secretary of State for the Home Department, ex parte Simms [2000] 2 AC 115 . . . . .4.40
R v Self [1992] 1 WLR 657, CA 7.35
R v Senior [1899] 1 QB 283 . . . . .2.18
R v Sharp and Johnson [1957] 1 QB 522 . . . . .1.89
R v Shayler [2001] 1 WLR 2206 .8.128, 8.129, 8.136, 8.142, 8.164, 8.168
R v Shayler [2003] 1 AC 247 . . . . .10.103
R v Shorrock [1994] QB 279 . . . . .2.104, 2.106, 2.108, 2.109
R v Smalley [1985] AC 622 . . . . 9.110, 9.111
R v Smith (Paul Roger) [2003] EWCA Crim 2480 . . . . .9.186
R v Smith [1997] 1 Cr App R 14 . . . . .1.94
R v Smith [2004] 1 Cr App R (S) 341 . . . . .9.188
R v Southwark CC, ex parte Tawfick, The Times, 1 December 1994 . . . . .9.112
R v Spratling [1911] 1 KB 77 . . . . .9.42
R v St Pancras Assessment Committee (1877) 2 QBD 581 . . . . .5.16
R v Stanley [1993] Crim LR 618 . . . . .1.81
R v Stephens (1866) LR 1 QB 702 . . . . .2.109
R v Stewart [1896] 1 QB 300 . . . . .3.156
R v Stratford Justices, ex parte Imbert [1999] 2 Cr App R 276 . . . . 10.177, 10.178
R v Suzanne Jaggers, unreported, 5 February 2008 . . . . .2.142
R v Suzanne Taylor; R v Theresa Portwine; R v Mark Taylor, unreported,
     6 March 2007 . . . . .2.144
R v Swindon Crown Court, ex parte Murray (1998) 162 JP 36 . . . . .9.92
R v Tacey (1821) Russ & Ry 452 . . . . .8.100
R v Thind [1999] Crim LR 842 . . . . 1.101, 1.107, 1.113
R v Thompson [1984] 1 WLR 962 . . . . .8.120
R v True [2003] EWCA Crim 2255 . . . . .8.82
R v Vantandillo (1815) 4 M&S 73 . . . . .2.104
R v W and F [2007] 1 WLR 339 . . . . 9.180, 9.181
R v Walker (1934) 24 Cr App R 117 . . . . .2.18
R v Wall (1907) 21 Cox CC 401 . . . . .2.163
R v Wang [2005] 2 Cr App R 8 . . . . 8.76, 8.121
R v Waterfield and Lynn [1964] 1 QB 164 . . . . 2.27, 2.29, 2.30
R v Waugh, The Times, 1 October 1986 . . . . .2.17
R v Webb [1964] 1 QB 357 . . . . .4.111
R v Webb, The Times, 19 June 1995 . . . . .2.51

R v Wheeler [1967] 3 All ER 829 . . . . 8.27
R v White (Anthony) [2001] 1 WLR 1352 . . . . 2.90, 2.95
R v White and Ward (1757) 1 Bur 333 . . . . .2.104
R v Whiteley (1991) 93 Cr App R 25 . . . . 8.100, 8.101
R v Willer (1986) 83 Cr App R 225 . . . . .8.136
R v Williams (Gladstone) (1984) 78 Cr App R 276 . . . . 2.10, 8.28, 8.68
R v Williams [1982] 1 WLR 1398 . . . . 9.44, 9.46
R v Wilson [1955] 1 WLR 493, CA 7.61
R v Woking Justices, ex parte Gossage [1973] QB 448 . . . . .9.32
R v Wood (1937) 81 Sol Jo 108 . . . . .2.39
R v Woodrow (1959) 43 Cr App R 105 . . . . .1.23
R v Worton (1989) 154 JP 201 . . . . 1.67, 1.80
R v Wright [2000] Crim LR 510 . . . . .8.141
Rai, Allmond and "Negotiate Now" v United Kingdom (1995)
    19 EHRR CD 93 . . . . 3.131, 4.101, 10.18, 10.86, 10.134, 10.136
Raissi v Commissioner of the Metropolis [2009] 2 WLR 1243 . . . . 7.05, 7.09, 7.11, 7.12, 7.17
Randall (1986) 8 Cr App R (S) 433 . . . . .9.36
Raninen v Finland (1998) 26 EHRR 563 . . . . 6.187, 6.188, 6.189, 6.193, 10.187
Rankin v Murray 2004 SLR 1164 . . . . .2.41
Rassemblement Jurassien v Switzerland, No 8191/78, Commission
    decision of 10 October 1978, DR 17 . . . . 3.119, 10.07, 10.18, 10.23, 10.25, 10.106
RD v Poland (2004) 39 EHRR 240 . . . . .10.168
Redmond-Bate v Director of Public Prosecutions (1999)
    163 JP 789 . . . . 4.63, 6.135, 6.154, 6.168, 10.03, 10.39, 10.139, 10.140
Reed v Wastie [1972] Crim LR 221, DC 6.183
Remice v HMP Belmarsh [2007] Crim LR 796 . . . . .7.165
Reynolds v Commissioner of Police of the Metropolis [1985] QB 881, CA 7.17
Reynolds v Times Newspapers Ltd [2001] 2 AC 127 . . . . .10.101
Reyntens v Belgium, Application No 16810/90; 73 DR 136 . . . . .6.115
Ribitsch v Austria (1996) 21 EHRR 573 . . . . .10.187
Rice v Connolly [1966] 2 QB 414 . . . . 2.13, 2.15, 2.23, 6.19, 6.53
Ricketts v Cox (1982) 74 Cr App R 298, DC 6.21
Riley v DPP (1989) 91 Cr App R 14 . . . . .2.36
RIVAS v France [2005] Crim LR 305, Application 59584/00 . . . . 6.188, 6.189
RL and M-J D v France [2005] Crim LR 307, Application No 44568/98 . . . . 6.188, 6.189
Roberts v Chief Constable of Kent [2008] EWCA Civ 1588 . . . . .6.183
Roe v Kingerlee [1986] Crim LR 735 . . . . 2.115, 8.100
Rogers, Blake, Wynn, Ross and Nicholls v DPP, unreported,
    22 July 1999, CO/4041/98 . . . . .1.212
Rookes v Barnard [1964] 1 AC 1129 . . . . 2.162, 3.70
Rowe and Davis v United Kingdom (2000) 30 EHRR 1 . . . . 10.175, 10.176
Rukwira v DPP [1993] Crim LR 882 . . . . .1.167
RWE Npower v Rev Malcolm Carrol [2007] EWHC 947 . . . . .9.175

S and Marper v United Kingdom (2009) 48 EHRR 50 . . . . 6.05, 6.53, 7.77
S v DPP [2008] EWHC 438 (Admin) 1.213, 1.215
S v Switzerland (1992) 13 EHRR 670 . . . . .7.82
Salduz v Turkey (2009) 49 EHRR 19 . . . . .7.79
Salman v Turkey (GC) Application No 21986/93; ECHR 2000-VII 10.188
Samuels v Commissioner of Police for the Metropolis, 3 March 1999, CA 6.21, 7.16
Samuels v Stubbs [1972] 4 SASR 200 . . . . .8.100
Sandbach Justices, ex parte Williams [1935] 2 KB 192 . . . . .9.34

Saunders v Holborn District Board of Works [1895] 1 QB 64 . . . . 2.110
Savage v South Essex Partnership NHS Trust [2009] 2 WLR 115 . . . . 10.181
Saya and others v Turkey, Application No 4327/02, 7 October 2008 . . . . 10.188, 10.189
Schiefer v Germany, Application No 13389/89, 6 March 1989 . . . . 10.60
Schmid v Austria, Application No 10670/83; (1985) 44 DR 195 . . . . 7.116
Schmidberger v Republik Österreich, Case C-112/00 ECJ, 12 June 2003 . . . . 10.65
Secretary of State for Defence and Ministry of Defence v Percy
    [1999] 1 All ER 732 . . . . 3.161, 5.149
Secretary of State for the Home Department v JJ [2008]
    1 AC 385, HL 7.116, 10.155, 10.156
Secretary of State for the Home Department v MB [2008] 2 AC 307, HL 10.156
Sedleigh-Denfield v O'Callaghan [1940] AC 880 . . . . 5.34
SEGI v IS States of the EU, Application Nos 6422/02 and 9916/02,
    Decision 23 May 2002 . . . . 10.27
Sekfali and others v DPP [2006] EWHC 894 (Admin) 2.14, 6.21
Selmouni v France (2000) 29 EHRR 403 . . . . 6.187
Selvanayagam v United Kingdom, Application No 57981/00, 12 December 2002 . . . . 10.96
Shabaan Bin Hussien v Chon Fook Kam [1970] AC 942. . . . . 7.01, 7.07
Shaw v Hamilton [1982] 1 WLR 1308 . . . . 9.37, 9.94
Sheldon v Bromfield Justices [1964] 2 QB 573 . . . . 9.25, 9.31
Sheldrake v DPP [2004] UKHL 43; [2005] 1 AC 264. . . . . 1.45, 1.197, 1.198, 1.199,
                                                                                                 5.105, 10.163, 10.165
Sherras v De Rutzen [1895] 1 QB 918 . . . . 2.109
Shishkov v Bulgaria ECHR-2003-I. 7.145
Siddiqui v Swain [1979] RTR 454, DC. 7.07
Sidiropoulos v Greece (1998) 27 EHRR 633. . . . . 10.98
Sierny v Director of Public Prosecutions (2006) 170 JP 697, DC. 6.63
Silverton v Gravett, unreported, 19 October 2001. . . . . 9.175
Sivalingham v DPP [1975] CLY 2037. . . . . 9.98
Six Carpenters' Case (1610) 8 Co Rep 146a 5.06
Smith v Donnelly [2001] SCCR 800; 2002 JC 65. . . . . 6.139, 10.59
Smith v Hughes [1960] 1 WLR 830 . . . . 4.121, 4.122
Smith v Thomasson (1890) 62 LT 68 . . . . 2.163
Smithkline Beecham plc and eleven others v Greg Avery (representing SHAC)
    and Robin Webb (representing ALF) [2007] EWHC 948, QB 9.175, 9.177
Societatea de Vanatoare "Mistretful" v Romania, Application No 33346/96,
    Decision 4 April 1999. . . . . 10.27
Soering v United Kingdom (1989) 11 EHRR 439. . . . . 10.159
Southard v DPP [2006] EWHC 3449 (Admin) 1.180, 1.186, 1.189
Southwark London Borough Council v Williams [1971] 1 Ch 734 . . . . 5.12, 8.147
Spicer v Holt [1977] AC 987, HL. 7.01
Stacey v Sherrin (1913) 29 TLR 555 . . . . 5.11
Staden v Tarjani (1980) 78 LGR 614. . . . . 3.160
Stafford v DPP [1974] AC 878 . . . . 9.123, 9.125
Stankov v Bulgaria [2001] ECHR 29225/95, 2 October 2001. . . . . 4.41, 10.70, 10.104, 10.113
Stanley v Benning, 14 July 1998, CA 7.35
Steel and Morris v United Kingdom (2005) 41 EHRR 22 . . . . 10.169, 10.173
Steel and others v United Kingdom (1999) 28 EHRR 603;
    (1998) 5 BHRC 339 . . . . 6.129, 6.130, 6.138, 6.139, 6.157, 9.39,
                                                                  10.07, 10.22, 10.25, 10.38, 10.57, 10.90, 10.91
Steel v Goacher (1983) 147 JP 83, DC 6.123
Stögmüller v Austria (1979–80) 1 EHRR 155. . . . . 7.113, 7.116

Stoke-on-Trent Council v W&J Wass Ltd [1988] 1 WLR 1406 . . . . 5.08
Storck v Germany (2006) 43 EHRR 6 . . . . 6.193
Subramaniam v Public Prosecutor [1956] 1 WLR 965 . . . . 8.157
Sunday Times v United Kingdom (No 1) (1979–80)
    2 EHRR 245 . . . . 10.78, 10.81, 10.84, 10.103, 10.108
Sunday Times v United Kingdom (No 2) (1992)
    14 EHRR 229 . . . . 1.200, 4.42, 5.31, 10.20, 10.108, 10.112
Sürek v Turkey (No 1) (GC) No 26682/95, ECHR 1999-I 10.19
Swales v Cox [1981] QB 849 . . . . 8.48
Swindon Crown Court, ex p Pawitter Singh [1984] 1 WLR 449 . . . . 9.25

T v United Kingdom (1982) Application No 8231/78, 49 DR 5 . . . . 10.22
Tabernacle v Secretary of State for Defence [2009] EWHC Civ 23,
    The Times, 25 February 2009 . . . . 4.100, 5.149, 10.22
Talbot v DPP [2000] 1 WLR 1102 . . . . 5.156
Tarariyeva v Russia (2009) 48 EHRR 26 . . . . 6.189
Taylor v Chief Constable of Thames Valley [2004] 1 WLR 3155, CA 7.41, 7.42
Taylor v DPP (2006) 170 JP 485 . . . . 1.184
Taylor v DPP [1973] AC 964 . . . . 1.90
Thomas and others v National Union of Mineworkers (South Wales Area)
    and others [1986] 1 Ch 20; [1985] 2 WLR 1081 . . . . 2.161, 2.165, 3.70
Thomas v Baptiste [2006] AC 1, PC 10.15
Thomas v Marsh and Nest (1833) 5 C & P 596 . . . . 5.38
Thomas v Sawkins [1935] 2 KB 249 . . . . 3.88
Thorgeir Thorgeirson Islande v Iceland (1992) 14 EHRR 843 . . . . 10.22
Todd v DPP [1996] Crim LR 344 . . . . 2.157
Tomasi v France (1993) 15 EHRR 1 . . . . 7.144, 7.155
Tomlinson v Commissioner of Police of the Metropolis [2006]
    EWHC 2810, QB 6.181, 6.183
Toth v Austria (1992) 14 EHRR 551 . . . . 7.114
Trustees, Executors and Agency Co Ltd v Short (1888) 13 App Cas 703, PC 5.16
Tucker v DPP [2007] EWHC 3019 (Admin) 3.121, 10.114
Turner v Thorne and Thorne (1959) 21 DLR (2d) 29 . . . . 5.07
Tweed v Parades Commission for Northern Ireland [2007] 1 AC 650 . . . . 10.179
Tynan v Balmer [1967] 1 QB 91 . . . . 4.59

V v The Netherlands (1984) 39 DR 267 (Application No 10678/83) 10.129
Valentine v DPP [1997] COD 339 . . . . 1.163
Valentine v Lilley [1983] QB 92; [1982] 2 All ER 583 . . . . 4.133
Vasileva v Denmark (2005) 40 EHRR 27 . . . . 6.115
Vatan v Russia, Application No 47978/99, Decision 7 October 2004 . . . . 10.27
Vaudelle v France (2003) 37 EHRR 397 . . . . 10.168
Veater v G and others [1981] 1 WLR 567 . . . . 9.23, 9.24
Vereniging Rechtswinkels Utrecht v Netherlands, Application No 11308/84,
    13 March 1986 . . . . 10.124

Waite v Taylor (1985) 149 JP 551 . . . . 4.26, 4.27
Wallis v Hands [1893] 2 Ch 75 . . . . 5.16
Ward Lock and Co Ltd v The Operative Printers' Society (1906) 22 TLR 327 . . . . 2.165
Wemhoff v Germany (1979–80) 1 EHRR 55 . . . . 7.113, 7.144
Westminster City Council v Haw [2002] EWHC 2073, QB 3.99, 4.46, 4.48, 9.175
Westripp v Baldock [1939] 1 All ER 279 . . . . 5.06

Whalley v Lancashire and Yorkshire Railway Co (1884) 13 QBD 131 . . . . .5.06
Wheeler v Whiting (1840) 9 C & P 262 . . . . .5.38
Whelan v Leonard [1917] 2 IR 323. . . . . .5.09
Wilkins v Lyons [1899] 1 Ch At 272. . . . . .2.157
Williamson v Chief Constable of West Midlands [2004]
    1 WLR 14, CA 6.139, 6.140, 6.158, 6.159
Wills v Bowley [1983] 1 AC 57, HL 7.25
Wilmott v Atack [1977] QB 498 . . . . .2.18
Winder v DPP [1996] 160 JP 713 . . . . .5.58
Winn v DPP (1992) 156 JP 881 . . . . 1.136, 1.159
Winter v Barlow [1980] RTR 209, DC. 6.123
Winzar v Chief Constable of Kent (1983) The Times, 28 March 1983. . . . . .2.173
Wise v Dunning [1902] 1 KB 167 . . . . 6.130, 6.133, 10.38
WM and HO v Germany, Application No 13235/87, 6 March 1989. .10.60
Wong v Parkside Health NHS Trust [2001] EWCA Civ 1721 . . . . .9.170
Wood v Commissioner of Police for the Metropolis [2009] EWCA Civ 414;
    [2009] HRLR 25, 21 May 2009 . . . . 6.03, 6.05, 6.45, 6.54, 6.201, 7.77,
                                                                          10.145, 10.148, 10.149
Wood v DPP [2008] EWHC 1956 (Admin); The Times, 23 May 2008. . . . . 2.35, 6.176, 7.01
Woodford v Smith [1970] 1 All ER 1091 . . . . .3.78
Wooding v Oxley (1839) 9 C & P 1 . . . . .3.89
Woolmington v DPP [1935] AC 462 . . . . .8.27

X v Austria, Application No 8278/78; (1979) 18 DR 154 . . . . .6.115
X v Denmark (1976) 5 DR 157 . . . . .10.130
X v Federal Republic of Germany Application No 8819/79; (1981) 24 DR 158. . . . . . 6.115, 10.159
X v Switzerland, Application No 7865/77, 27 February 1979 . . . . .10.125
X v United Kingdom (1984) 6 EHRR 136 . . . . .10.172

Yagci and Sargan v Turkey (1995) 20 EHRR 505 . . . . .7.115
Yarl's Wood Immigration Ltd; GSL UK Ltd; Creechurch Dedicated Ltd
    v Bedfordshire Police Authority [2008] EWHC 2207 (Comm). .1.55
Young, James and Webster v United Kingdom (1981) 4 EHRR 38 . . . . .10.25

Z v United Kingdom (2002) 34 EHRR 3 . . . . .10.184
Ziliberberg v Moldova, Application No 61821/00
    of 4 May 2004 . . . . 3.119, 3.120, 4.101, 6.171, 10.07, 10.25,
                                                                    10.67, 10.71, 10.111, 10.112, 10.113, 10.114

TABLE OF STATUTES

Access to Justice Act 1999
  Sch 3 . . . . 10.168
Administration of Justice Act 1960
  s 1(1)(a) 9.157
Ancient Monuments and Archaeological
  Areas Act 1979 . . . . 5.81
  s 19 . . . . 3.154
Animals (Scientific Procedures)
  Act 1986 . . . . 2.131, 2.132
Anti-social Behaviour Act 2003 . . . . . 5.45, 5.49
  s 30 . . . . 6.13, 10.68
    (1) 6.60
    (3) 6.65
    (4) 6.64, 10.68
    (5) 6.63
    (6) 6.67
    (7) 10.68
  ss 30–36 . . . . 6.60
  s 31(1) 6.63
    (2)(3) 6.63
  s 32 . . . . 6.64
  s 32(2) 6.11, 6.64
    (6) 6.67
  s 33(3) 6.13
  s 34 . . . . 6.60
  s 36 . . . . 6.62
  s 57 . . . . 3.56, 5.131
  s 58 . . . . 5.103, 5.107
  s 59 . . . . 5.49
  ss 60–64 . . . . 5.91
  s 92 . . . . 6.44
  s 94(1) 6.33
Anti-terrorism, Crime and Security Act 2001
  s 39 . . . . 2.88
  s 40 . . . . 2.84
  s 90 . . . . 7.73
  s 92 . . . . 7.74
  Sch 7 . . . . 6.82
  Sch 8 . . . . 6.82
Bail Act 1976 . . . . 6.140, 7.5, 7.121,
                          7.129, 7.135
  s 1 . . . . 6.159
    (1)(b) 7.121
    (6) 7.121
  s 3 . . . . 7.121, 7.122, 7.126
    (6) 7.126
    (8)(a)(b) 7.161, 7.162

  s 3A 7.121, 7.122
    (2) 7.124
    (4) 7.159
    (5) 7.123
  s 4 . . . . 7.121, 7.122, 7.144
    (1) 7.163
    (5) 7.126
  s 5 . . . . 7.121, 7.155
    (6A) 7.164
  s 5A 7.121, 7.155
  s 5B 7.121, 7.160
    (1) 7.162
  s 6 . . . . 7.121, 7.133
    (1) 7.136
    (2) 7.136
    (7) 7.138
  s 7 . . . . 7.117, 7.121, 7.134,
                   7.145, 7.149, 7.151
    (1) 7.137
    (2) 7.137
    (3) 7.135
    (4) 7.135
    (5) 7.135
  Sch 1 . . . . 7.122, 7.146
  Pt I 7.145
    para 1(1) 7.152
    para 1(2) 7.150
    para 2(1) 7.126, 7.142
    para 2A 7.145
    para 3 . . . . 7.154
    para 5 . . . . 7.154
    para 6 . . . . 7.145
    para 8 . . . . 7.126
    para 9 . . . . 7.147
  Pt IA 7.150
    para 1 . . . . 7.150
    para 2 . . . . 7.151
    para 3 . . . . 7.151
    para 4 . . . . 7.151
    para 5 . . . . 7.151
    para 7 . . . . 7.151
  Pt II 7.148
    para 1 . . . . 7.148
    para 2 . . . . 7.149
    para 3 . . . . 7.149
    para 5 . . . . 7.149
  Pt IIA, paras 1–3 . . . . 7.163

Bail (Amendment) Act 1993
  s 1(1) 7.160
    (4) 7.160
    (5) 7.160
    (7) 7.160
British Transport Commission Act 1949
  s 55 .... 5.177, 9.74
  s 56 .... 9.74
Children and Young Persons Act 1933
  s 34 .... 7.86
  s 50 .... 7.86
Civil Aviation Act 1982
  s 39 .... 5.176
Commissioners for Revenue and Customs
  Act 2005
  s 32 .... 2.05
Commons Act 1899
  s 1 .... 3.154
  s 10 .... 3.154
Commons Registration Act 1965
  s 22 .... 5.78
    (1) 5.78
    (1A) 5.78
Communications Act 2003
  s 127(1) 2.142
  Sch 17, para 2 .... 5.153
Computer Misuse Act 1990
  s 3(6) 8.102
Conspiracy and Protection of Property Act
  1875 .... 2.157, 3.33, 3.70
  s 7 .... 2.155, 3.69
Constitutional Reform Act 2005
  s 40 .... 9.157
Control of Pollution Act 1974
  s 62(1) 3.110
Coroners Act 1988
  s 8 .... 10.192
Counter-Terrorism Act 2008
  s 75 .... 6.89
Countryside Act 1968
  s 41 .... 3.154
Countryside and Rights of Way
  Act 2000 .... 5.145
  Pt II 5.50, 5.81
  s 1 .... 5.145
  s 2 .... 5.145
    (1) 5.09, 5.145
  s 16 .... 5.145
  s 48(4) 5.50
County Courts Act 1984 .... 5.172
  s 38(1) 9.166
Courts Act 2003 .... 5.170, 5.172
Crime and Disorder Act 1998 .... 2.97,
       4.109, 4.126, 4.143, 9.178

s 1 .... 6.11, 6.30, 6.62, 9.178
  (1)(a) 9.178
  (b) 9.178
  (4) 9.178
s 1C 9.178
  (2) 5.158
  (a) 9.18, 9.178
  (b) 9.18, 9.178
s 25 .... 6.82
s 26 .... 6.41
s 28 .... 2.94
  (1)(b) 10.51
  (2) 2.89
  (3) 2.89
  (4) 2.90
  (5) 2.92
s 29 .... 2.88
s 30 .... 2.88, 2.113
s 31 .... 2.88
s 31(1)(a) 1.135
  (b) 1.208
  (c) 1.177, 10.51
  (4) 1.135, 1.177
s 32 .... 2.88
s 46 .... 7.125
s 65 .... 9.70
  (1) 9.71
s 66 .... 9.70
Crime (International Co-operation)
  Act 2003
  s 84 .... 2.05
Criminal Appeal Act 1968 .... 9.121
  s 1(1) 9.120
  (2) 9.120
  s 2 .... 9.122
  s 3 .... 9.128
  s 7 .... 9.126
  ss 12–15 .... 9.82
  s 19 .... 9.129
  s 23 .... 9.125
  s 29 .... 9.127
  s 33 .... 9.157
  s 50(1) 9.37, 9.46
Criminal Appeal Act 1995
  s 9 .... 9.153
  (2) 9.153
  s 11 .... 9.85, 9.153
  s 13 .... 9.154
  s 14 .... 9.154
  s 16C 9.156
  ss 17–21 .... 9.153
Criminal Damage Act 1971 .... 2.112, 2.116,
        8.25, 8.93, 8.102
  s 1(1) 2.113, 2.120, 8.92, 9.74

(2) 2.120
(3) 2.120
s 2 . . . . 8.92
(a) 2.122
(b) 2.122
s 3 . . . . 8.92
(a) 2.123
(b) 2.123
(6) 8.102
s 4(1) 2.119
(2) 2.121, 2.124
s 5 . . . . 2.118, 8.04, 8.11, 8.13, 8.41,
8.45, 8.53, 8.91, 8.94,
8.97, 8.106, 8.110
(1) 8.92
(2) . . . 6.180, 8.06, 8.89, 8.90, 8.91, 8.99
(a) 8.103, 8.104, 8.107
(b) 8.107
(3) 8.108, 8.109
s 10 . . . . 8.97
(1) 2.116, 8.96
(5) 8.102
Criminal Justice Act 1948
s 37(1)(d) 9.116
Criminal Justice Act 1967
s 3 . . . . 3.86
s 91 . . . . 1.176, 9.74
(1) 2.170
Criminal Justice Act 1972
s 72 . . . . 9.138
Criminal Justice Act 1982
s 37(2) 1.203
s 60(1)(b) 7.164
(3) 7.164
Criminal Justice Act 1987
s 7(1) 9.118
s 9(11) 9.117, 9.118
s 35(1) 9.120
Criminal Justice Act 1988 . . . . 8.62
s 4(2) 7.54
s 33 . . . . 6.74
s 36 . . . . 9.134
s 39 . . . . 2.03
s 139 . . . . 6.74
s 147 . . . . 7.48
s 154 . . . . 7.163
Sch 3 . . . . 9.137
Criminal Justice Act 1991
s 24(4) 2.52
Criminal Justice Act 2003 . . . 2.47, 8.22, 8.157
Pt 3 . . . . 9.59
Pt 9 . . . . 9.140, 9.145
Pt 10 . . . . 9.149
s 4 . . . . 7.55, 7.57, 7.59, 7.131

(4) 7.26
(7) 7.55
s 9 . . . . 7.75
s 10(1)–(2) 7.75
s 14 . . . . 7.145
s 15 . . . . 7.145
s 16 . . . . 7.162
(1) 7.162
(3) 7.162
s 17(2) 7.165
(3) 7.165
(6)(b) 7.165
s 22(1) 9.63
(2) 9.60
(3) 9.65
(3A) 9.65
ss 22–27 . . . . 9.59
s 23 . . . . 9.63
s 24(1) 9.69
(2) 9.64, 9.69
s 24A(1) 9.69
s 25 . . . . 9.59
s 28 . . . . 7.103, 7.104, 7.105, 7.159
s 29 . . . . 7.107
(4) 7.107
s 41 . . . . 7.54
s 57(2) 9.141
(4) 9.140
s 58 . . . . 9.140
(8) 9.142
(10) 9.142
s 59 . . . . 9.143
s 61 . . . . 9.144
s 62 . . . . 9.146
s 63 . . . . 9.147
ss 75–97 . . . . 9.149
s 78 . . . . 9.151
s 79 . . . . 9.151, 9.152
s 143(3) 7.139
s 144 . . . . 9.09
s 145 . . . . 2.88, 2.98
(2)(a) 2.98
s 146 . . . . 2.88, 2.98
s 154(1) 2.136
s 225(1)(a) 1.47
s 250 . . . . 5.158
Sch 2, para 1 . . . . 7.104, 7.159
para 2 . . . . 7.103, 7.104
para 3 . . . . 7.104, 7.105, 7.132
para 6 . . . . 7.159
Sch 4, Pt 1 . . . . 9.146
Sch 5 . . . . 9.149
Sch 15 . . . . 1.47, 1.83, 1.124
Sch 32, Pt 2, para 146 . . . . 5.157

Criminal Justice Act 2008. . . . . 3.138
  s 119 .3.138, 3.140
    (2) 3.138
    (3) 3.139
    (4) 3.138
  s 120 . . . . 3.141
  s 120(2) 3.140
    (3) 3.140
  s 120(5)–(6) 3.140
  s 121 . . . . 3.141
    (4) 3.141
Criminal Justice and Immigration
    Act 2008 . . . . 1.47, 1.124, 8.64
  s 42 . . . . 9.156
  s 49 . . . . 9.68
  s 74 . . . . 2.58, 2.62, 2.68
  s 75 . . . . 3.137
  s 76 . . . . 1.30, 1.103, 2.07, 5.65,
                6.182, 8.64, 8.65
    (3) 8.66
    (7) 8.65
    (b) 6.181
    (9) 8.64
    (10) 6.179
  s 146(2) 8.64
  Sch 8 . . . . 9.130
  Sch 10 . . . . 9.68
  Sch 12, para 6. . . . . 7.150
  Sch 16 . . . . 2.58, 2.62, 2.68
  Sch 17 . . . . 3.137
    para 3 . . . . 3.137
  Sch 27, para 27(1)–(2) 8.64
Criminal Justice and Police
    Act 2001 . . . . 3.142, 9.74, 9.76
  Pt 1, Ch 1. . . . . 6.11, 6.44
  s 1 . . . . 5.177
    (1) 9.74
    (2) 9.74
  s 2(1) 9.75
    (2) 9.75
    (3) 9.75
    (4) 9.77
  s 3(2) 9.79
    (3) 9.78
    (4) 9.78
  s 4 . . . . 9.80
  s 5 . . . . 9.78, 9.80
  s 8 . . . . 9.81
  s 12 . . . . 9.74
    (2) 2.176
    (4) 2.176
  s 13 . . . . 2.176
  s 14 . . . . 2.176
  s 42 . . . . . .2.129, 2.157, 3.143, 3.148, 6.56

    (1) 1.224
    (a) 3.149
    (b) 3.143, 3.149
    (c) 3.143
    (3) 3.144
    (4) 3.143
    (b) 3.146, 3.147
    (7) .1.225, 3.146
    (7A) 3.147
  s 42A 2.157, 3.148, 3.149, 10.54
    (1)(a) 3.149, 3.151
    (b) 3.151
    (c) 3.151
    (d) .3.149, 3.151
    (4) 3.149
    (5)–(6) 3.149
  s 43 . . . . 1.153
  s 78 . . . . 7.75
  s 82 . . . . 7.76
Criminal Justice and Public Order
    Act 1994 . . . . 5.03
  Pt II 7.160
  Pt V 5.03, 5.23, 5.43, 5.44, 5.47, 5.63
  Pt X 7.02
  s 27 . . . . 7.159
    (1)(b) 7.122
    (3) 7.122
  s 28(3) 7.142
  s 29 . . . . 7.132
  s 30 . . . . 7.160
  ss 34–38 . . . . 7.100
  s 48 . . . . 9.59
  s 49 . . . . 9.58
  s 55(2) 7.75
    (3) 7.75
  s 56 . . . . 7.76
  s 59 . . . . 7.46
  s 60 . . . . 4.92, 4.93, 6.82, 6.84
    (1) 6.35, 6.38, 6.83
    (3) 6.38
    (4) 6.85
    (5) 6.86
    (6) 6.86
    (8) 6.86
    (9) 6.84
    (9ZA). 6.84
    (10) 6.112
    (10A) 6.112
    (11) 6.82
  s 60A 6.41, 6.86
  s 60AA . . . 6.33, 6.36, 6.37, 6.39, 6.41, 6.42
    (1)(a) 6.35, 6.42
    (b) 6.42
    (b) 6.36

(2)(a) 6.40
(2)(b) 6.41
(3) 6.36, 6.38, 6.42
(4) 6.38
(6) 6.37
(7) 6.41
s 61 . . . . 5.44, 5.49, 5.74, 5.78, 5.79,
5.83, 5.88, 5.90, 5.92,
5.93, 5.102, 5.115, 10.163
(1) 5.74, 5.75, 5.77, 5.84
(2) 5.75
(3) 5.76
(4) 5.84, 5.88, 5.89
(6) 5.73, 5.86
(a) 5.105
(6A) 6.43, 7.19
(7) 5.78
(b) 5.79
(9) 5.78, 5.80, 5.83
(9)(b) 5.50
s 62 . . . . 5.90
s 62A 5.92, 5.95
(1) 5.92, 5.97
(2) 5.91, 5.92
(3) 5.92
(5) 5.94
(6) 5.94
ss 62A–62C 5.93
ss 62A–62D 5.93
ss 62A–62E 5.91
s 62B 5.95
(5) 5.96
s 62C 5.97
s 62D 5.93
s 62E 5.93, 5.95
s 63 . . . . 5.98, 5.99, 5.100, 5.101,
5.102, 5.103, 5.106,
5.110, 5.111, 10.163
(1) 5.99, 5.103, 5.107
(1A) 5.103, 5.107
(2) 5.98, 5.104, 5.107, 5.108
(3) 5.100
(4) 5.100
(5) 5.106
(6) 5.104, 5.105
(7) 5.105
(7A) 5.106, 5.107
(7B) 5.107
(9) 5.106
(10) 5.102, 5.106, 5.109
ss 63–66 . . . . 5.103
s 64 . . . . 5.101
(4) 5.101, 5.109, 5.112
s 64A 6.44

(1B) 7.19
s 65 . . . . 5.108
s 65(4) 5.108
s 66 . . . . 5.110
(3) 5.110
(5) 5.111
(7) 5.111
(8) 5.111
s 67 . . . . 5.90, 5.97, 5.112
s 68 . . . . 5.49, 5.50, 5.55, 5.63, 5.66
s 68(1) 5.47, 5.53, 5.54, 5.56,
5.57, 5.59, 5.60, 5.61,
5.62, 5.63, 5.71, 5.73
(a)–(c) 5.57
(2) 5.54, 5.59, 5.60, 5.61, 5.69
(5) 5.49, 5.50, 5.56
s 69 . . . . 5.66, 5.73, 6.56, 10.163
(1) 5.66, 5.67, 5.68, 5.71, 5.87
(2) 5.67
(3) 5.68, 5.71
(4) 5.72, 5.73
(a) 5.73, 5.105
s 69(4) 5.63
s 70 . . . . 4.10, 5.126, 5.128
s 71 . . . . 5.126, 5.128
s 73 . . . . 5.161
s 75 . . . . 5.19
(1) 5.29
(2) 5.29
s 76 . . . . 5.19, 5.26, 5.28
(1) 5.26
(2) 5.26
(4) 5.27
(6) 5.26
s 77 . . . . 5.113, 5.120, 5.125, 10.163
(1) 5.116, 5.117, 5.118
(2) 5.116
(3) 5.113, 5.117, 5.119
(4) 5.118
(5) 5.119
(6) 5.115
s 78 . . . . 5.120, 5.123, 5.125
(1) 5.120, 5.121, 5.124
(2) 5.120
(3) 5.120
(4) 5.124
(5) 5.121, 5.122
(6) 5.121
s 79 . . . . 5.116
(2) 5.122
(3) 5.117
(4) 5.117, 5.123
s 154 . . . . 1.206, 1.207
s 166 . . . . 2.180

Criminal Justice and Public Order (*cont.*)
(2) 2.180
(3) 2.180
s 168(2) 7.75
Sch 3 . . . . 7.159
Sch 10 . . . . 9.58
para 58(a). 7.75
Criminal Law Act 1967
s 2(6) 8.48
s 3 . . . . 1.30, 5.65, 6.177, 6.182,
6.183, 8.27. 8.04, 8.09, 8.13,
8.17, 8.37, 8.38, 8.43, 8.44,
8.45, 8.53, 8.57, 8.58, 8.59, 8.63,
8.64, 8.70, 8.73, 8.77, 8.160, 9.05
(1) . . . 1.72, 1.103, 8.28, 8.33, 8.65, 8.80
(2) 8.34, 8.51
s 6(3) 1.80, 1.123, 8.65, 8.80
s 10(2) 1.20
Criminal Law Act 1977 . . . . 2.51, 5.42
s 1 . . . . 5.42, 5.167
s 1(1)(a) 8.93
s 6(1) 5.37
(1A) 5.37
(2) 5.37
ss 6–10 . . . . 5.42, 5.164
s 7 . . . . 5.161
(2) 5.162
(3) 5.162
(4) 5.161
(5) 5.163
s 8 . . . . 5.165
s 9 . . . . 5.168, 5.169
(3) 5.169
(4) 5.168
(6) 5.168
s 10 . . . . 5.170, 5.175
(2) 5.171
(3) 5.173
(4) 5.175
(5) 5.174
(6) 5.172
s 12 . . . . 5.24, 5.37
(1)(a) 5.161, 5.165
(8) 5.164
s 12A 5.37, 5.161
(9) 5.162
s 51 . . . . 2.51
(1)(a) 2.51
(3) 2.51
(4) 2.52
Criminal Procedure and Investigations Act
1996. . . . . 7.99
s 3(1)(a) 10.175
s 29(1) 9.118

Cycle Tracks Act 1984. . . . . . . 5.50, 5.51, 5.81
Dangerous Dogs Act 1991 . . . . 2.99
Deer Act 1991
s 1 . . . . 5.178
Environmental Protection Act 1990 . . . . . 2.99
s 87 . . . . 9.74
Explosive Substances Act 1883 . . . . 2.51
Explosives Act 1875
s 80 . . . . 9.74
Extradition Act 2003 . . . . 7.02
Firearms Act 1968
s 20(1) 5.166
(2) 5.166
Fireworks Act 2003. . . . . 9.74
Football (Disorder) Act 2000 . . . . 9.183
Football (Offences) Act 1991 . . . . 2.179, 9.185
s 1(2) 2.178
s 2 . . . . 2.179
s 3 . . . . 2.179
s 3(2)(a) 2.179
(b) 2.179
s 4 . . . . 2.179
Football (Spectators) Act 1989 . . . 2.181, 9.183
s 14(4) 9.183
(8) 9.185
s 14A 9.184, 9.185
(2) 9.188
s 14B 9.187, 9.189
(4)(b) 9.188
s 14E(2B). 9.183
(3) 9.183
s 21C 7.121
s 23 . . . . 9.90
Sch 1 . . . . 9.185
Forcible Entry Act 1429 . . . . 8.47
Game Act 1831
s 30 . . . . 5.178
Geneva Conventions Act 1957 . . . . 8.62
Geneva Conventions (Amendment)
Act 1995 . . . . 8.62
Genocide Act 1969. . . . . 8.62
Greater London Authority Act 1999 . . . . . 3.95
s 380 . . . . 3.133, 3.134
s 383 . . . . 3.130
s 384 . . . . 3.132
Highways Act 1835
s 5 . . . . 4.03
s 72 . . . . 4.30
Highways Act 1980 . . . . 5.50, 5.51, 5.81
s 35 . . . . 10.72
s 137 . . . . 4.02, 4.18, 4.19, 4.30, 4.50, 4.54
(1) 4.19
s 137ZA. 4.50
s 328(1) 4.03

(2) 4.03
s 329(1) 5.51
Housing Act 1980
 s 89 . . . . 5.22
Human Rights Act 1998. . . . . . . 1.45, 1.149,
        1.221, 3.01, 3.03, 3.05, 3.52, 3.150,
        6.154, 7.08, 7.129, 9.159, 10.01,
        10.03, 10.177
 s 1 . . . . 10.154
 s 3 . . . . 1.45, 3.117, 3.118, 10.42
 s 6 . . . . 3.160
 s 6(1) 3.117
 s 12 . . . . 10.21
 s 13 . . . . 10.140, 10.141
  (1) 10.123
 Sch 1 . . . .1.01, 1.197, 1.200, 1.209, 10.154
Industrial Relations Act 1971
 s 134 . . . . 4.56
International Criminal Court
        Act 2001 . . . . . . 8.59, 8.60, 8.61, 10.168
 s 51 . . . . 8.60
 Sch 8, s 2 . . . . 8.61
Interpretation Act 1978 . . . . 5.49
 s 5 . . . . 1.151
 s 7 . . . . 3.106
 Sch 1 . . . . 1.151, 7.34
Justices of the Peace Act 1361 . . . . 6.127, 9.20,
        9.25, 9.36, 10.89
Justices of the Peace Act 1968 . . . . 9.25
 s 1(7) 9.20, 9.30
Knives Act 1997
 s 8 . . . . 6.82
  (8) 6.112
Land Registration Act 2002
 Pt 9 . . . . 5.18
Licensing Act 1872. . . . . 2.173
 s 12 . . . . 2.173, 9.74
Licensing Act 1902. . . . . 2.173
 s 8 . . . . 2.173
Licensing Act 2003. . . . . 5.106
 s 1(1)(c) 5.106
 s 136 . . . . 5.106
 s 140(1) 2.175
 s 143 . . . . 2.175
  (2) 2.175
Local Government Act 1972. . . . . 4.94
 s 235 . . . . 3.153, 4.95
 s 237 . . . . 3.156, 4.97
Local Government Finance Act 1988
Sch 5, paras 3–8 . . . . 5.81
Magistrates' Courts Act 1980
 s 1 . . . . 7.02, 7.107
 s 1A 9.83
 s 5 . . . . 7.121

s 10 . . . . 7.121
s 15 . . . . 7.121
s 17 . . . . 2.114, 7.34
s 18 . . . . 7.121
s 22 . . . . 2.114, 7.34
s 43B 7.159
s 55 . . . . 7.121
  (1) 5.121
  (2) 5.121
  (3) 5.121
s 108(1) 9.90
  (b) 9.83
  (3) 9.90
s 111(1) 9.95
  (2) 9.101
  (4) 9.98
  (5) 9.99
s 113 . . . . 9.88
s 115 . . . . 6.127, 9.25, 9.31, 9.41
  (1) 6.158
  (3) 9.38
s 117 . . . . 7.137
s 120 . . . . 9.41
s 127 . . . . 7.102
s 128 . . . . 4.121
s 129(1) 7.137
  (3) 7.137
s 145 . . . . 3.157
Sch 1 . . . . 7.34
  para 29. 2.114
Sch 2 . . . . 2.114
Magistrates' Courts (Appeals from Binding
        Over Orders) Act 1956
 s 1(1) 9.37, 9.94
Malicious Communications Act 1988. . . 1.153
 s 1 . . . . 1.153
Malicious Damage Act 1861. . . . . 9.14
Medway Ports Authority Act 1973
 s 21 . . . . 4.96
Merchant Shipping and Maritime Security
        Act 1997 . . . . 8.62
Metropolitan Police Act 1839
 s 52 . . . . 3.95
 s 54(13) 1.149
 s 64 . . . . 3.95
Military Lands Act 1892
 Pt II 3.159
National Parks and Access to the
        Countryside Act 1949
 s 60 . . . . 5.09
 s 90 . . . . 3.154
New Roads and Street Works Act 1991 . . . 4.03
Night Poaching Act 1828
 s 1 . . . . 5.178

Noise and Statutory Nuisance Act 1993
  s 8 .... 3.110
Nuclear Installations Act 1965 .... 5.141
Nuclear Material (Offences) Act 1983. . . 3,137
  s 1A 3.137
Occupiers Liability Act 1957 .... 3.10
Offences Against the Person Act 1861 .... 1.04
  s 28 .... 2.03
  s 20 .... 2.03, 2.88, 8.28
  s 42 .... 2.03
  s 47 .... 1.165, 2.03, 2.88
Official Secrets Act 1911............. 5.153
  s 1 .... 5.41, 5.152, 5.154
  s 3 .... 5.152
Official Secrets Act 1989. . 8.162, 8.162, 8.164
  s 1 .... 8.142
  s 4 .... 8.142
Parliament Square (Improvement)
  Act 1949 .... 3.132
Police Act 1964
  s 51 .... 3.79
Police Act 1996
  s 39A 6.204
  s 89 .... 2.02, 2.03, 2.04, 2.12
  (2) 2.14, 6.55, 6.154
Police and Criminal Evidence
  Act 1984 .... 2.35, 6.41, 6.159, 7.06
  Pt III 7.02, 7.03, 7.121
  Pt IV 7.65, 7.94, 7.121, 7.122
  Pt V 7.65
  s 1 .... 4.79, 4.82, 6.73, 6.176, 7.46
  (1) 6.73
  (2) 6.74
  (3) 6.76
  (4) 6.73
  (5) 6.73
  (6) 6.75
  (7)(a) 6.74
  (b) 6.74
  (8) 6.74
  (8A) 6.74
  (8B) 6.74
  (9) 6.74
  s 2 .... 6.103, 6.176
  (2)(3) 6.41, 6.106
  (2)–(5) 6.108
  (8) 6.109
  (9)(a) 4.82, 6.110
  s 3 .... 6.41, 6.103
  (1) 6.111
  (3) 6.111
  (7) 6.112
  s 4 .... 4.34, 4.82, 6.13, 6.119
  (1) 4.77

  (2) 6.121, 6.122
  (3) 6.120
  (5) 4.77, 6.120
  (6) 4.77
  (11)(a) 6.120
  (12) 4.78, 6.120
  (15) 6.121
  s 17 .... 6.13, 6.176, 7.51
  (6) 6.161
  s 18 .... 7.20, 7.52, 7.54
  s 24 .... 6.176, 7.03, 7.04, 7.28, 7.31, 7.32
  (1)–(3) 7.04
  (2) 7.35
  (4) 7.06, 7.13, 7.18, 7.22, 7.25
  (5) 7.06, 7.13, 7.18, 7.19, 7.22, 7.31
  (a)(b) 7.19
  (c)(i)(ii) 7.19
  (iii)....................... 7.19
  (iv) 7.21
  (v) 7.19
  (d) 7.21
  (e) 7.19
  (f) 7.19
  s 24A 7.33, 7.34
  (5) 7.34
  s 26 .... 7.135
  s 27(4) 7.75
  s 28 .... 7.38
  (1) 7.38
  (3) 7.38
  (5) 7.39
  s 30 .... 7.121
  (1) 7.54
  (1A) 7.54
  (7)(7A)..................... 7.26
  (10) 7.54
  (10A) 7.54
  s 30A 7.121
  (3A) 7.55
  (3B) 7.55
  s 30B 7.55, 7.155
  s 30C(3)...................7.57, 7.58
  (4) 7.55, 7.58
  s 30CA...................... 7.158
  (1) 7.157
  (2) 7.157
  s 30CB...................... 7.158
  s 30D....................... 7.131
  s 32 .... 6.12, 6.176, 7.20, 7.45,
                     7.46, 7.47, 7.52
  (1) 7.45
  (2)(a)(i) 7.45
  (b) 7.52
  (3) 7.45

(4) 7.46
(5) 7.45
(7) 7.52
(8) 7.47
(9) 7.47
s 34 . . . . 7.121
(1) 7.94
(2) 7.95, 7.102, 7.108
(5) 7.122
s 34(5) 6.159, 7.102, 7.108
s 36 . . . . 6.176
(3) 7.66
(5) 7.66
s 37 . . . . 6.176, 7.102, 7.121, 7.122
(1) 7.96
(2) 7.96
(7) 7.103, 7.104
    (a) 7.104
    (b) 7.104
    (c) 7.104, 7.108
    (d) 7.104
(7A) 7.104
(10) 7.97
(15) 7.86
s 37A 7.105
(3) 7.105
s 37B 7.104
s 37C 7.132
s 37CA 7.132
s 38 . . . . 7,121, 7.122, 7.132, 7.141
(2A) 7.142
(3) 7.155
s 39 . . . . 6.159
(1)(a) 7.66
(b) 7.66
s 40 . . . . 7.97
(10) 7.122
s 40(12) 7.97
ss 41–44 . . . . 7.98
s 46 . . . . 7.121
(2) 7.143
s 46A 7.132
s 47 . . . . 7.121
(1) 7.122
(1A) 7.122, 7.126
(1E) 7.159
(3A) 7.125
s 47(3) 7.102
s 54 . . . . 6.176, 7.70
(6A) 7.48
s 54A 7.73
(5) 7.73
s 55 . . . . 7.70
s 56 . . . . 7.83

s 57 . . . . 7.86
s 61 . . . . 7.75
(4),(6) 7.75
s 61A 7.75
s 62 . . . . 7.75
(10) 7.75
s 63 . . . . 7.75
s 63A 7.76
s 64A 6.59, 7.74
(1) 7.74
(1A) 6.13, 7.76
(4) 7.74
(6) 7.74
s 65 . . . . 7.75
(1) 7.70
s 66 . . . . 6.14, 10.87
s 67 . . . . 6.14
s 67(9) 6.14
(9A) 6.14
(10) 6.14
s 76 . . . . 7.63
s 78 . . . . 7.63
s 117 . . . . 6.176, 6.183, 7.47, 7.75
Sch 2 . . . . 7.135
Police and Justice Act 2006
s 7(2) 6.10
s 10 . . . . 7.122
s 11 . . . . 7.103
s 17 . . . . 9.65
Sch 6(1), para 1 . . . . 7.122
Sch 6(2), para 2 . . . . 7.55
Sch 6(3) 7.122
para 8 . . . . 7.132
Sch 6, para 10 . . . . 7.157
Sch 14 . . . . 8.102
Police Reform Act 2002 . . . . 7.33
Pt II 7.64
Pt IV, Ch 1 . . . . 6.09
s 35(1) 9.117
s 38(1)(2) 6.09
(4) 6.09
(5) 6.10
(5A) 6.10
(6) 6.10
(7) 6.10
(8) 6.178, 7.75
(9) 6.178
s 38A 6.10
s 40 . . . . 6.15
s 41 . . . . 6.15, 7.65
s 42 . . . . 6.09
s 46 . . . . 2.12
s 50 . . . . 6.12, 6.30, 6.62
s 59 . . . . 6.13

Police Reform Act 2002 (*cont.*)
    (1) 6.118
    (3) 6.118
    (4) 6.118
    (5) 6.118
    (6) 6.118
  s 107(1) 6.14
  Sch 1, Pt 1, para 2 . . . . 6.178
  Sch 4 . . . . 9.76
  Pt I 2.12, 6.10, 6.12
    para 1 . . . . 6.11, 6.12, 6.44
    para 1A 6.12
      (5) 6.12
    para 2(3) 6.12, 6.44
    para 2(4) 6.12
    para 2(6) 6.11
    para 2A 6.12
    para 3 . . . . 6.11, 6.12
    para 3A 6.11, 6.12
    para 4 . . . . 6.178
    para 4A 6.13
    para 4ZA, ZB 6.178
    para 8 . . . . 6.13
    para 9 . . . . 6.13
    para 13 . . . . 6.13
    para 14 . . . . 6.13
    para 15 . . . . 6.13
    para 15ZA 6.13
    para 29 . . . . 7.75
  Sch 7, para 9(7) 6.14
  Sch 8 . . . . 7.65
Powers of Criminal Courts (Sentencing)
  Act 2000
  s 13(6) 9.03
    (7) 9.03
    (8)(a) 9.42
  s 89 . . . . 9.38
  s 108 . . . . 9.38
  s 139(1) 9.40
    (2) 9.40
    (4) 9.40
  s 153 . . . . 2.88
  s 155(1) 9.130
Prevention of Terrorism Act 2005 . . . . . . 7.116
Private Security Industry Act 2001
  s 1 . . . . 6.17
    (2)(a) 6.17
  s 3 . . . . 6.17
    (1) 6.17
    (3) 6.17
  s 5(1) 6.17
  s 12 . . . . 6.17
  ss 14–18 . . . . 6.17
  Sch 2 . . . . 6.17

  Pt 1, para 2(1) 6.17
Proceeds of Crime Act 2002 . . . . 9.132
  s 50 . . . . 9.132
  s 11(3) 9.132
Prosecution of Offences Act 1985
  s 16(3) 9.90
  s 18(1)(b) 9.89
Protection of Animals Act 1911
  s 2 . . . . 9.90
Protection from Harassment
  Act 1997 . . . . . 3.150, 5.45, 10.94, 10.96
  s 1(1A) 9.166
  s 2 . . . . 2.88, 9.177, 10.96
  s 3 . . . . 9.166, 9.170
    (9) 9.170
  s 3A 9.166
  s 4 . . . . 2.88, 10.96
Public Assemblies Act 1979 . . . . 3.27
  s 3 . . . . 4.104
  s 4 . . . . 5.155, 5.156, 5.157
Public Health Act 1981
  s 75 . . . . 3.154
Public Meeting Act 1908 . . . . 3.80
  s 1 . . . . 3.87
    (1) 3.87
    (2) 3.87
Public Order Act 1936 . . . . 2.40, 3.08,
                     3.32, 3.44, 3.50
  s 1 . . . . 3.86
  s 1(1) 2.37, 3.29, 3.81
    (2) 2.38
  s 2 . . . . . . 2.42, 2.48, 2.49, 2.50, 3.85, 3.86
    (1) 2.43
      (a) 2.44
      (b) 2.44
    (2) 2.47
    (4) 2.47
    (5) 2.49
    (6) 2.48, 3.85
  s 3(1) 3.51
  s 5 . . . . 1.128, 1.129, 1.130, 1.131,
         1.144, 1.148, 1.162, 1.171, 2.155
  s 5A(6) 2.72
  s 7(1) 2.47
    (2) 2.38
  s 9 . . . . 3.81, 3.82
  s 32 . . . . 4.133
Public Order Act 1986 . . . . . . 1.02, 1.03, 1.04,
         1.14, 1.20, 1.28, 1.30, 1.38, 1.56,
       1.125, 1.143, 1.144, 1.149, 1.171,
       1.181, 2.01, 2.37, 2.56, 2.72, 2.148,
       2.156, 3.01, 3.02, 3.12, 3.13, 3.24,
       3.27, 3.28, 3.30, 3.32, 3.36, 3.40,
       3.44, 3.46, 3.47, 3.53, 3.54, 3.57,

3.68, 3.77, 3.80, 3.83, 3.97, 3.108,
3.109, 3.111, 3.113, 3.129, 4.60,
5.42, 6.150, 9.171
Pt I 1.25, 3.143
Pt II 3.06, 3.07
Pt III 2.57
s 1 . . . . 1.01, 1.05, 1.15, 1.53, 1.60
  (1) . . . 1.22, 1.27, 1.29, 1.30, 1.35, 1.109
  (2) 1.22
  (3) 1.32
  (5) 1.24, 1.109
  (6) 1.16
s 2 . . . . 1.01, 1.56, 1.59, 1.61, 1.63
  (1) 1.74
  (2) 1.75
  (3) 1.75
  (4) 1.64
  (5) 1.82
s 3 . . . . 1.01, 1.89, 1.93, 3.29
  (1) 1.94, 1.99, 1.105, 1.106
  (2) 1.121
  (3) 1.100, 1.102
  (4) 1.107
  (5) 1.122
  (7) 1.124
s 4 . . . . 1.01, 1.24, 1.80, 1.81, 1.122,
    1.123, 1.128, 1.131, 1.132, 1.133,
    1.135, 1.141, 1.149, 1.154, 1.165,
    1.166, 1.171, 1.178, 1.180, 1.187,
    1.192, 1.194, 1.206, 1.218, 2.88,
    4.43, 9.61, 9.185
  (1) 1.102, 1.135, 1.137, 1.155
    (a) 1.139, 1.155
    (b) 1.150, 1.155, 1.164
  (2) 1.152, 1.166
  (4) 1.135
s 4A 1.187, 1.206, 1.207, 1.208,
    1.209, 1.210, 1.211, 1.217, 1.218,
    1.220, 1.227, 2.88, 5.132, 9.61,
    10.41
  (1) 1.211, 1.214
  (2) 1.218
  (3)(a) 1.219
  (5) 1.208, 1.227
s 5 . . . . 1.01, 1.24, 1.171, 1.173,
    1.174, 1.176, 1.177, 1.180, 1.185,
    1.191, 1.192, 1.195, 1.198, 1.201,
    1.204, 1.206, 1.209, 1.210, 1.211,
    1.221, 1.222, 2.88, 2.96, 4.43,
    6.161, 7.105, 7.148, 9.61, 9.74,
    9.185, 10.40, 10.41, 10.44, 10.49,
    10.50, 10.51, 10.52, 10.54
  (1) 1.178
  (2) 1.193

  (3) 1.195, 1.202, 2.96, 10.51
    (a) 1.198, 1.199
    (b) 1.198, 1.199
    (c) 1.199, 10.50
  (6) 1.177, 1.203
s 6(1) 1.37
s 6(2) 1.78, 1.119
  (3) 1.154, 1.156
  (4) 1.191
s 6(5) 1.42, 1.45, 1.79, 1.120
s 6(6) 1.42, 1.120
s 6(7) 1.40
s 7(1) 1.17
s 7(3) 1.80, 1.123
s 8 . . . 1.25, 1.27, 1.71, 1.104, 1.160, 1.169
    (a) 1.98, 1.104
s 9(1) 3.58
s 9(2) 1.02
    (d) 1.128
s 10(1) 1.53
s 11 . . . . 3.12, 3.113
  (1) 3.15, 3.20, 3.21
  (2) 3.16
  (3) 3.22
  (4) 3.23
    (b) 3.23
  (5)(b) 3.23
  (6) 3.23
  (8) 3.26
  (9) 3.26
  (10) 3.24
s 12 . . . . 3.28, 3.31, 3.36, 3.38, 6.140
  (1) 3.34, 3.35
  (2)–(3) 3.34
  (4) 3.37
  (5) 3.37
  (6) 3.37
  (9) 3.37
  (10) 3.37
ss 12–14A 3.34
s 13 . . . . 3.38
  (2) 3.40
  (4) 3.42
  (5) 3.42
  (7) 3.46
  (8) 3.46
  (9) 3.46
  (11) 3.46
  (12) 3.46
  (13) 3.46
s 14 . . . . 3.37, 3.59, 3.60, 3.61, 3.65,
    3.73, 3.74, 3.75, 3.97, 3.122, 4.101,
    5.128, 5.131, 6.140
  (1) 3.37

Public Order Act 1986 (*cont.*)
  (a) 3.66, 3.72
  (b) 3.66
  (4) 3.73
  (5) 3.73
  (6) 3.73
  (8) 3.73
  (9) 3.73
  (10) 3.73
  s 14A 4.09, 4.10, 5.129, 5.133,
              5.134, 5.139, 10.132, 10.133
  (1) 5.129
  (2) 5.129
  (4) 5.129
  (5) 4.10, 5.126
  (6) 5.132
  (7) 5.134
  (8) 5.134
  (9) 4.10, 5.126, 5.130, 5.131
  ss 14A–14C 5.126–5.128, 5.131,
              5.138, 5.139
  s 14B 5.133
  (1) 5.135
  (2) 4.09, 5.135
  (3) 5.135
  (5) 5.135
  (6) 5.135
  (7) 5.135
  s 14C 5.133
  (3) 5.133
  s 15 . . . . 3.34, 3.39, 3.67
  s 16 . . . . 2.40, 2.90, 2.129, 3.10,
              3.56, 3.83, 5.131, 6.62
  s 17 . . . . 2.60
  ss 18–23 . . . . 2.57
  s 18 . . . . 2.67, 2.68, 2.87
  s 18(1)(a) 2.66, 2.67
  s 18(1)(b) 2.67
  (2) 2.68
  (4) 2.68
  (5) 2.67
  s 19 . . . . 2.87
  s 19(1)(a) 2.69
  (b) 2.69
  (2) 2.71
  (3) 2.72
  s 20 . . . . 2.87
  s 20(1)(a) 2.73
  (b) 2.73
  (2) 2.74
  (3) 2.73
  (4) 2.73
  (5) 2.73
  s 21(1)(a) 2.75

  (b) 2.75
  (3) 2.77
  s 22(1)–(2) 2.78
  s 23 . . . . 2.87
  s 23(1) 2.80
  (3) 2.80
  s 25 . . . . .2.81, 2.87
  s 26 . . . . 2.82
  s 27(3) 2.57
  s 28 . . . . 2.83
  s 28(3)–(6) 2.79
  s 29A 2.62
  s 29B 2.66, 2.67, 2.68, 2.87
  (2) 2.68
  (4) 2.68
  s 29B(3) 2.57
  s 29C 2.70, 2.87
  (2) 2.72
  s 29D 2.73
  s 29D(2) 2.73
  (3) 2.73
  (4) 2.73
  s 29E 2.87
  s 29F 2.78
  s 29G 2.80, 2.87
  s 29H 2.81
  s 29I 2.87
  s 29J 2.64
  s 29K 2.82
  s 29M 2.83
  s 29N 2.68
  s 34 . . . . 5.44
  ss 34–39 . . . . 5.74
  s 38 . . . . 2.146
  (1) .2.147, 2.149
  (2) 2.149
  (3) 2.151
  (4) .2.146, 2.152
  (5) 2.148
  (6) 2.150
  s 40 . . . . 2.156
  (4) 3.140
  s 280(2)–(3) 5.135
  Sch 2, para 1 . . . . 2.156
Race Relations Act 1965 . . . . 2.72
  s 3(1) 2.90
  s 6 . . . . 2.56
Race Relations Act 1976
  s 41(1)(a) 6.101
  s 42 . . . . 6.101
Racial and Religious Hatred
  Act 2006 . . . . 2.57
Railways Act 2005 . . . . 3.154
Regulation of Investigatory Powers Act 2000

Pt II 7.82
s 58(6) 7.81
s 76 . . . . 2.05
Rehabilitation of Offenders
    Act 1974 . . . . 9.58, 9.68
Representation of the People
    Act 1983 . . . . 3.80, 3.90
s 95 . . . . 3.90
s 96 . . . . 3.90
s 97 . . . . 3.87
  (1) 3.93
  (2) 3.93
Sch 5 . . . . 3.90
Riot Act 1714. . . . . 1.05, 1.10
s 2 . . . . 1.20
s 3 . . . . 1.20
Riot (Damages) Act 1886 . . . . 1.53, 1.55
Road Traffic Act 1972. . . . . 8.28
Road Traffic Act 1988 . . 2.17, 4.140, 5.51, 9.61
Pt VII. 6.29, 6.124
s 2 . . . . 4.140
s 3 . . . . 6.118
s 5(1) 10.163
  (b) 1.198
s 5(2) 1.198
s 34 . . . . 6.118
s 163 . . . . 6.13, 6.121, 6.124
  (1)(2) 6.122
  (3) 6.122
s 164 . . . . 6.29
s 165 . . . . 6.29
s 168 . . . . 6.29
s 170 . . . . 6.29
s 172 . . . . 6.29
s 185(1)(c) 4.140
Road Traffic Act 1991
s 82 . . . . 4.03
Road Traffic (Consequential Provisions) Act
    1988
s 4 . . . . 4.140
Sch 4, para 29. . . . . 4.140
Road Traffic Offences Act 1988. . . . . 9.61
Road Traffic Regulation Act 1984
s 142 . . . . 4.03
Roads (Scotland) Act 1984 . . . . 3.10, 5.81
Serious Crime Act 2007 . . . . 3.116
ss 44–46. . . . . 3.116
s 63(2) 3.116
s 87 . . . . 6.82
Sch 6, Pt 2, para 64(1)(2) 3.116
Serious Organised Crime and
    Police Act 2005. . . . . 2.125, 2.130,
             2.137, 3.98, 3.111, 3.113, 3.142,
             5.46, 10.11, 10.96, 10.114

Pt 4 . . . . 9.166
s 110 . . . . 7.04, 7.06, 7.33
s 112 . . . . 5.158
  (5) 5.158
s 115 . . . . 6.74
s 117 . . . . 6.43
s 118 . . . . 7.75
s 121(1)(2) 7.66
s 125 . . . . 10.11
  (2) 10.94, 10.95
s 126 . . . . 3.148, 10.11, 10.54
s 127(1)(2) 3.143
s 128 . . . . 5.01, 5.46, 5.140, 5.141,
        5.142, 5.143, 5.144, 5.145, 5.146
  (1A) 5.141
  (2) 5.142
  (3) 5.142
  (4) 5.146
  (5) 5.147
  (6) 5.147
  (7) 5.144
  (8)(a) 5.141
  (8)(b) 5.142
  (9) 5.142
ss 128–131. 10.11
s 131(1) 5.145
  (2) 5.146
  (3)(4) 5.146
s 132 . . . . 3.103, 3.112, 3.122
  (1) 3.113
    (a) 3.117, 3.118, 3.121, 10.111
    (b) 3.117, 3.118, 3.121
    (c) 3.122
  (3) 3.113
  (4) 3.113
  (6) 3.113, 3.122
  (7)(b) 3.114
ss 132–137. . . . . 3.100, 5.46, 5.142
ss 132–138. . . . . 3.94, 3.122, 3.128,
         3.129, 5.142, 10.11, 10.119
s 133 . . . . 3.100
  (1) 3.103
  (2) 3.103
  (3) 3.105
  (4) 3.105
  (5) 3.106
  (6) 3.106
s 134(2) 3.112, 10.111
s 134(3) 3.107
  (a)–(g) 3.115
  (7)(a) 3.114
  (8) 3.114
s 135(1) 3.115
  (3) 3.115

Serious Organised Crime and
    Police Act 2005 (*cont.*)
  s 136(1) 3.112
    (2) 3.112
    (3) 3.114, 3.115
    (4) 3.116
  s 137 . . . . 3.110
  s 138 . . . . 3.100, 5.142
  s 145 . . . . 2.131, 2.140, 2.141, 2.143,
                2.144, 3.68, 9.179,
                9.182
    (1) 2.131
    (2) 2.131
    (3) 2.131
    (4) 2.131
    (6) 2.131
    (7) 2.131
  s 146 . . . . 2.132
    (2) 2.132
  s 147 . . . . 2.130, 2.136
  s 148 . . . . 2.131, 2.132
  s 149 . . . . 2.130
  s 175 . . . . 2.136, 5.147, 5.158
  s 178 . . . . 3.122
  Sch 8, Pt 1
    para 2 . . . . 6.12
    para 4 . . . . 6.12
    para 6 . . . . 6.12
    para 12 . . . . 6.13
  Sch 9, para 4 . . . . 6.178
Sexual Offences Act 1956
  s 32 . . . . 4.117, 4.131
Sexual Offences Act 1985 . . . . 4.106
  s 1 . . . . 4.125, 4.144, 4.145, 4.147
    (2) 4.126
    (3) 4.140
  s 2 . . . . 4.144, 4.146, 4.147
    (1) 4.142
    (2) 4.143
  s 4(4) 4.136
Sexual Offences Act 2003 . . . . 4.106,
                4.113, 4.127
  Pt 1 . . . . 5.181
  s 1 . . . . 5.181
  s 3 . . . . 5.181
  s 56 . . . . 4.108, 4.113, 4.127, 4.144
  s 63 . . . . 5.179, 5.181
  s 66 . . . . 5.181
  s 67 . . . . 5.181
  Sch 1 . . . . 4.108, 4.113
  para 4 . . . . 4.127, 4.144
Sporting Events (Control of Alcohol etc)
    Act 1985 . . . . 2.182, 9.185
Statute Law Repeals Act 2008 . . . . 2.42

Street Offences Act 1959 . 4.104, 4.105, 4.106
  s 1 . . . . 4.108, 4.109
    (1) 4.113, 4.115
    (b) 4.139
    (2) 4.109
    (4) 4.119, 4.123, 4.137
Supreme Court Act 1981
  s 28 . . . . 9.103
  s 28A(3) 9.96
  s 29(3) 7.165
  s 31 . . . . 7.165
  s 37 . . . . 9.166
    (1) 9.172
  s 43 . . . . 9.113
  s 48 . . . . 9.83
    (4) 9.92
  s 79(3) 9.86
  s 81(1) 9.88
    (a) 7.164
    (d) 9.102
    (e) 9.116
    (g) 7.164
    (1J) 7.164
    (4) 7.137
  s 113 . . . . 9.98
Terrorism Act 2000 . . . . 6.13, 6.96
  s 1 . . . . 6.71, 6.89
  s 11 . . . . 10.163
    (2) 10.165
  s 13 . . . . 2.41
  s 32 . . . . 6.71
  s 33(2) 6.71
  s 33(4)(b) 6.71
  s 34 . . . . 6.89
  s 35 . . . . 6.71
  s 36 . . . . 6.13
    (1) 6.71
    (2)(3) 6.71
  s 40 . . . . 7.03
  s 41 . . . . 7.98
  s 44 . . . . 4.80, 4.82, 4.83, 4.84, 4.86,
           4.92, 6.13, 6.87, 6.95, 6.97, 6.99,
           6.100, 6.102, 6.103, 6.110, 6.113,
           6.114, 6.176, 10.81
    (1) 6.93
    (2) 6.93
    (3) 4.81, 4.86
    (4) 6.88
  s 45 . . . . 4.80, 6.103, 10.87
    (1) 4.82
    (a) 6.94
    (b) 6.95
    (2) 4.82, 6.94
    (3) 4.82, 6.110

(4) 6.112
(4)–(6) 4.83
(5)–(6) 6.112
s 46 . . . . 6.88, 6.92
s 47 . . . . 4.83
(1) 6.94
s 48 . . . . 4.88
(1) 4.88
(2) 4.88
s 49(1) 4.88
(2) 4.88
s 50 . . . . 4.89
s 50(1) 4.89
(2) 4.89
(3) 4.89
s 51 . . . . 4.90, 4.91
(1) 4.91
(2) 4.91
(3) 4.90
(4) 4.90
(5) 4.91
(6) 4.91
s 60 . . . . 6.95
s 114 . . . . 6.176
Sch 7 . . . . 6.31
Sch 8 . . . . 7.98
Terrorism Act 2005. . . . . 10.11
Terrorism Act 2006. . . . . 5.01, 5.46, 5.140
Theatres Act 1968
s 18 . . . . 2.73
Theft Act 1968
s 9 . . . . 5.41, 5.55, 5.179
(1)(a) 5.179
(b) 5.179
(3) 5.180
(4) 5.180
Sch 1, para 2(1) 5.178
Trade Union and Labour Relations
(Consolidation) Act 1992. . . . . . . 2.156
Pt 4 . . . . 2.131
s 220 . . . . 2.165, 3.113, 3.145, 4.34,
4.53, 4.56, 4.60, 4.68, 6.160

(1) 4.54, 4.55
(a) 4.54
s 241 . . . . .2.154, 2.158
(1)(b) 2.163
(e) 2.163
s 300(1) 2.156
s 421 . . . . 2.165
Sch 1 . . . . 2.156
Trafalgar Square Act 1844
s 2 . . . . 3.130
Traffic Management Act 2004
s 10(1) 2.05
Transport Act 2000. . . . . 3.154
UK Borders Act 2007
s 22 . . . . 2.05
s 23 . . . . 2.05
Unlawful Drilling Act 1819 . . . . 2.42
Vagrancy Act 1824 . . . . 5.155
Valuation and Rating (Scotland) Act 1956
s 7(2) 5.81
Violent Crime Reduction Act
2006. . . . . .9.183, 9.185
s 27 .6.44, 6.57
(1) 6.57
(2) 6.58
(3) 6.59
(4) 6.59
(5) 6.59
(6) 6.59
(7) 6.59
s 52(1) 9.183
s 65 . . . . 9.183
Sch 3 . . . . 9.183
Sch 5 . . . . 9.183
War Crimes Act 1991 . . . . 8.62
Wildlife and Countryside Act 1981
Pt III 5.50, 5.50, 5.81
s 66 . . . . 5.50
Wireless Telegraphy Act 2006
s 47 . . . . 2.51

TABLE OF SECONDARY LEGISLATION

Air Navigation Order 2000 (SI 2000/1562)
    art 57(1) 2.177
    art 65(1) 2.177
    art 122(6) 2.177
    Sch 12, Part B. 2.177
Civil Procedure Rules 1998
    (SI 1998/3132). 9.115
    19.6(4)(b) 9.177
    Pt 23 . . . . 9.168
    Pt 25 . . . . 9.168
    PD 40B, para 9.1 . . . . 9.169
    para 9.3 . . . . 9.169
    Pt 52 . . . . 9.100
    Pt 54 . . . . 7.165, 9.115
    Pt 55 . . . . 5.19
    r 55(III) 5.24
    55.21 . . . . 5.24
    55.22(6) 5.25
    55.25 . . . . 5.24, 5.25
    55.25(3) 5.25
    55.25(4) 5.25
    55.26 . . . . 5.25
    55.28 . . . . 5.25
    63.2(6) 9.84
    Pt 64 . . . . 9.100
    64.7 . . . . 9.104
    Pts 65–70 . . . . 9.121
    Pt 67 . . . . 9.144
    Pt 70 . . . . 9.137, 9.139
    Pt 74 . . . . 9.121
    78(1)–(2) 9.89
Criminal Defence Service (General)
    (No 2) Regulations 2001
    (SI 2001/1437). 9.87
Criminal Justice Act 1988 (Review of
    Sentencing) Order 2006
    (SI 2006/1116)
    Sch 1 . . . . 9.135
Criminal Justice Act 2003 (Commencement
    No 14 and Transitional Provision) Order
    2006 (SI 2006/3217) 7.145
Criminal Justice Act 2003 (Commencement
    No 16) Order 2007
    (SI 2007/1999). 7.107
Criminal Justice Act 2003 (Commencement
    No 21) Order 2008
    (SI 2008/1424). 7.107

Criminal Justice Act 2003 (Conditional
    Cautioning Code of Practice)
    Order 2004 (SI 2004/1683) 9.59
Criminal Justice and Immigration Act 2008
    (Commencement No 2 and Transitional
    Savings Provision) Order 2008
    (SI 2008/1586). 8.64
Criminal Justice and Immigration Act 2008
    (Commencement No 6 and
    Transitional Provisions) Order 2009
    (SI 2009/140). 9.59
Criminal Justice and Immigration Act 2008
    (Commencement No 5) Order 2008
    (SI 2008/3260). 3.138, 3.140, 9.68
Criminal Procedure Rules 2005 (SI 2005/384)
    Pt 19 . . . . 7.111
    r 19 . . . . 7.155
    r 19.1 . . . . 7.159
    r 19.2 . . . . 7.160
    r 19.10 . . . . 7.164
    rr 19.10–19.12 . . . . 7.155
    r 19.16 . . . . 7.160
    r 19.17 . . . . 7.160
    r 19.18 . . . . 7.164
    r 19.25 . . . . 7.127
    Pt 63 . . . . 9.84
    r 68.4 . . . . 9.120
Criminal Procedure (Amendment) Rules 2008
    (SI 2008/2076). 9.84
Electronic Commerce Directive (Racial and
    Religious Hatred Act 2006) Regulations
    2007 (SI 2007/2497) 2.57
Football (Offences) (Designation of
    Football Matches) Order 2004
    (SI 2004/2410). 2.178
Football Spectators (Prescription) Order 2004
    (SI 2004/2409). 2.181, 9.183
Football Spectators (Prescription)
    (Amendment) Order 2006
    (SI 2006/71). 9.183
Football Spectators (Seating) Order 2006
    (SI 2006/1661). 2.181
Legal Aid in Criminal and Care Proceedings
    (General) Regulations 1989
    (SI 1989/344). 9.87
Official Secrets (Prohibited Place)
    Order 1955 (SI 1955/1497) 5.153

Official Secrets (Prohibited Places)
Order 1994 (SI 1994/968) 5.153
Penalties for Disorderly Behaviour (Amount
of Penalty) Order 2002
(SI 2002/1837). 2.168, 5.177
Penalties for Disorderly Behaviour (Amount
of Penalty) Order 2009
(SI 2009/83). 1.204
art 2 . . . . 5.177
Sch, Pt 2. 5.177
Police and Criminal Evidence Act 1984
(Codes of Practice) (Revisions to
Code A) (No 2) Order 2008
(SI 2008/3146). 6.23
Police (Property) Regulations 1997
(SI 1997/1908). 6.41, 6.86
Police Reform Act 2002 (Standard Powers
and Duties of Community Support
Officers) Order 2007
(SI 2007/3202). 6.10
Police (Retention and Disposal of Items
Seized) Regulations 2002
(SI 2002/1372). 6.41, 6.86
Police (Retention and Disposal of
Vehicles) Regulations 1995
(SI 1996/723). 5.90, 5.112
Roads (Northern Ireland) Order 1993
(SI 1993/3160 (NI 15)) 5.49
Royal and Other Parks and Gardens
Regulations 1977 (SI 1977/217). . . 3.135
Royal Parks and Other Open Spaces
Regulations 1997 (SI 1997/1639). . 3.135
Royal Parks and Other Open Spaces
(Amendment) Regulations 2004
(SI 2004/1308). 3.135

Serious Organised Crime and Police Act 2005
(Commencement No 1), Transitional
and Transitory Provisions) Order 2005
(SI 2005/1521). 3.122
art 3(1)(m) 3.143
Serious Organised Crime and Police Act
2005 (Designated Area) Order 2005
(SI 2005/1537). 3.101
Serious Organised Crime and Police Act 2005
(Designated Sites) Order 2005
(SI 2005/3447). 5.143
Serious Organised Crime and Police
Act 2005 (Designated Sites under
Section 128) Order 2007
(SI 2007/930). 5.143
Serious Organised Crime and Police Act 2005
(Designated Sites under Section 128)
(Amendment) Order 2007
(SI 2007/1387). 5.143
The British Transport Police (Transitional
and Consequential Provisions)
Order 2004 (SI 2004/1573) 6.82
Ticket Touting (Designation of Football
Matches) Order 2007
(SI 2007/790). 2.180
Trafalgar Square Regulations 1952
(SI 1952/776). 3.135
Violent Crime Reduction Act 2006
(Commencement No 2) Order 2007
(SI 2007/858). 9.183
PTR 2005
Pt 66 . . . . 9.119

TABLE OF INTERNATIONAL LEGISLATION

American Declaration of the Rights
and Duties of Man 1948. . . . . 3.06
Charter of Paris 1990 . . . . 10.08
EC Treaty. 10.65, 10.66
European Convention for the Protection
of Human Rights and
Fundamental Freedoms
1953. . . . . 1.01, 2.105, 7.08, 7.111,
8.01, 9.160–9.165, 9.189,
10.01 et seq
Art 2. . . . . 6.164, 6.185, 6.186, 6.191,
10.01, 10.15, 10.173, 10.179,
10.180, 10.181, 10.185
(1) 6.185
(2) 6.185, 10.180
Art 3. . . . 6.187, 6.188, 6.189, 6.190, 6.191,
6.193, 6.194, 10.01, 10.183,
10.184, 10.165, 10.186,
0.187, 10.188, 10.189, 10.190
Art 5. . . . . 3.32, 3.36, 3.75, 4.74, 4.87,
6.114, 6.115, 6.163, 6.164, 7.03,
7.06, 7.29, 7.30, 7.40, 7.112, 7.116,
7.117, 7.120, 7.123, 7.144, 9.39,
10.150, 10.153, 10.154, 10.159
(1) 6.95, 6.139, 6.165, 10.150,
10.158, 10.159
(a)–(e) 10.158
(b) 4.87, 6.115
(c) 6.158, 7.11, 7.96
(2) 7.40
(3) 7.116, 7.144, 7.163, 10.151
(4) 10.152
(5) 10.153
Art 6. . . . . 5.88, 6.29, 7.112, 10.01,
10.162, 10.163, 10.165, 10.169
(1) 10.169, 10.172, 10.177, 10.178
(2) 1.197, 1.221, 5.73, 10.163
(3) 7.120
(a) 10.177, 10.178
(b) 10.177, 10.178
(c) 7.82, 10.168
Art 7(1) 2.100
Art 8. . . . . 4.87, 5.15, 5.21, 5.89, 5.139,
6.49, 6.50, 6.52, 6.70, 6.116, 6.161,
6.193, 7.77, 7.118, 10.01, 10.144,
10.145, 10.146, 10.147, 10.148,
10.149, 10.150, 10.179
(1) 6.50, 6.51, 6.95, 10.148

(2) 4.87, 5.89, 6.51, 6.53,
6.116, 6.193, 10.148
Arts 8–11 . . . . 7.119
Arts 8–12 . . . . 10.101
Art 9. . . . . 1.202, 2.64, 10.01, 10.17,
10.19, 10.26, 10.122, 10.123,
10.124, 10.125, 10.126, 10.127,
10.128, 10.131, 10.132, 10.133,
10.139, 10.140, 10.141, 10.142,
10.150
(1) 10.130
Art 10. . . . . 1.200, 1.201, 1.202, 2.64,
2.96, 2.133, 2.134, 2.139, 3.75,
3.100, 3.117, 3.118, 3.120, 4.40,
4.43, 4.47, 4.87, 4.100, 5.04, 5.13,
5.31, 5.32, 6.49, 6.66, 6.117, 6.147,
6.167, 6.172, 7.110, 7.118, 8.162,
9.29, 9.180, 10.01, 10.02, 10.13,
10.15, 10.17, 10.18, 10.20, 10.21,
10.22, 10.26, 10.28, 10.31, 10.38,
10.39, 10.41, 10.41, 10.44, 10.48,
10.49, 10.50, 10.51, 10.52, 10.53,
10.55, 10.57, 10.59, 10.60, 10.62,
10.65, 10.67, 10.72, 10.73, 10.74,
10.75, 10.77, 10.89, 10.105, 10.114,
10.123, 10.131, 10.132, 10.133,
10.139, 10.140, 10.141, 10.142,
10.150, 10.173
(1) 1.200, 1.209, 1.222, 9.29,
10.22, 10.39, 10.59
(2) 1.200, 3.160, 5.32, 6.117,
6.138, 6.167, 9.27, 9.29, 10.20,
10.39, 10.59, 10.98, 10.103
Art 11. . . . . 2.64, 2.139, 3.03, 3.75,
3.117, 3.118, 3.120, 3.150, 4.40,
4.87, 4.100, 5.04, 5.13, 5.32, 5.139,
6.49, 6.66, 6.117, 6.147, 6.167,
6.172, 6.194, 6.205, 7.110, 7.118,
9.180, 10.01, 10.02, 10.14, 10.15,
10.17, 10.18, 10.23, 10.25, 10.26,
10.28, 10.30, 10.31, 10.34, 10.37,
10.38, 10.39, 10.57, 10.58, 10.59,
10.60, 10.62, 10.65, 10.67, 10.71,
10.72, 10.74, 10.75, 10.77, 10.80,
10.98, 10.105, 10.114, 10.115,
10.121, 10.123, 10.131, 10.132,
10.133, 10.150
(1) 3.119, 10.59, 10.112

(2) 3.160, 5.32, 6.117,
                              6.167, 10.59, 10.98
Art 14. . . . . 5.139, 10.132, 10.133
Art 17. . . . . 10.34, 10.51, 10.143
Art 34. . . . . 10.27
Protocol 1, Art 1 . . . 5.90, 6.161, 10.73, 10.128
Protocol 4, Art 2. . . . . .6.114, 10.154
International Covenant on Civil and
   Political Rights 1966. . . . . 3.06
Rome Statute of the International Criminal
   Court 1998 . . . . 8.60

Treaty on European Union 1992
   Art F.2 . . . . 10.66
Treaty of Rome 1957
   Art 35. . . . . 9.164
   Art 234. . . . . 9.161
United Nations Charter 1945. . . . . 10.08
Chapter VIII 10.08
Universal Declaration of Human
   Rights 1948 . . . . 3.06

1

THE PUBLIC ORDER ACT 1986: OFFENCES

A. Introduction	1.01	E. Fear or Provocation of Violence:	
B. Riot: Public Order Act 1986, s 1	1.05	Public Order Act 1986, s 4	1.128
Historical development	1.05	Historical development	1.128
The definition of riot under the		Definition under the Public	
Public Order Act 1986, s 1	1.15	Order Act 1986, s 4	1.133
Jurisdiction	1.16	Jurisdiction	1.135
Essential elements of the offence	1.19	Essential elements of the offence	1.136
Compensation for Riot Damage	1.53	F. Harassment, Alarm, or Distress: s 5	1.171
C. Violent Disorder:		Historical development	1.171
Public Order Act 1986, s 2	1.56	Definition under the Public	
Historical development	1.56	Order Act 1986, s 5	1.174
The definition of violent disorder		Jurisdiction	1.177
under the Public Order Act		Essential elements of the offence	1.178
1986, s 2	1.59	G. Intentional Harassment,	
Jurisdiction	1.62	Alarm, or Distress:	
Essential elements of the offence	1.63	Public Order Act 1986, s 4A	1.206
D. Affray: Public Order Act 1986, s 3	1.89	Historical development	1.206
Historical development	1.89	Definition under the Public	
The definition of affray under the		Order Act 1986, s 4A	1.207
Public Order Act 1986, s 3	1.93	Jurisdiction	1.208
Jurisdiction	1.95	Proportionality	1.209
Essential elements of the offence	1.96	Essential elements of the offence	1.210

A. Introduction

This chapter examines the main criminal offences under the Public Order Act 1986—those **1.01** of riot (s 1), violent disorder (s 2), affray (s 3), causing fear or provocation of violence (s 4), and causing harassment, alarm, or distress (s 5). It will look at the origins of the Act, the essential elements of the offences, defences and sentencing. It will also look at aspects of the Act's compatibility with the European Convention on Human Rights.[1]

---

[1] European Convention for the Protection of Human Rights and Fundamental Freedoms (1953) (Cmd 8969) as scheduled by the Human Rights Act 1998, Sch 1.

1.02   The Public Order Act 1986 abolished the common law offences of riot, rout, unlawful assembly, and affray (s 9(1)). It also replaced offences under the Public Order Act 1936 (s 9(2)). The 1986 Act was passed amid the tumult of industrial unrest and social discord in the inner cities which characterized the early 1980s. It was an attempt to clarify and rationalize, but not to codify, the law of public order.

1.03   Today, the Act is widely used, not only for the large-scale disorder which existed at the time of its inception, but also to deal with the low-level disorder and 'anti-social' behaviour which is the target of a range of recent government initiatives. In 2008/2009, there were over 37,700 reported public order offences, of which only three were riot and 1,020 violent disorder.[2]

1.04   Two important concepts are important to grasp at the outset. Firstly, although the 1986 Act deals with episodes of violence, it focuses less upon individual victims of violence (for whom the Offences Against the Person Act 1861 deals with various offences of assault), and more upon the wider public who may be caused to fear for their own personal safety by scenes of disorder. Hence, the 'victim' of the offences under the Act is not the person who is assaulted, but the hypothetical 'person of reasonable firmness present at the scene'. Secondly, although the Act is concerned with 'public' order, many of the offences can be committed in private.

B. Riot: Public Order Act 1986, s 1

Historical development

1.05   Historically, serious riots such as the Sacheverell Riots of 1710 (which led directly to the passing of the Riot Act 1714), were prosecuted as high treason and met with the death penalty. The Chartists led by John Frost at the Newport Rising of 1839 were convicted of high treason and sentenced to be hanged, drawn, and quartered. Ultimately the Prime Minister, Lord Melbourne, commuted their sentences to transportation to Tasmania.

1.06   At common law the offence of riot (or riotous assembly) was defined by Hawk PC, bk 1, ch 65, s 1, as

> a tumultuous disturbance of the peace, by three persons, or more, assembling together of their own authority, with an intent mutually to assist one another, against any who shall oppose them, in the execution of some enterprise of a private nature, and afterwards actually executing the same in a violent and turbulent manner, to the terror of the people, whether the act intended were of itself lawful or unlawful.

1.07   Thus, in the common law we can see the origins of the modern offence. At common law, there were five essential elements of riot

(a) the presence and participation of at least three persons;

---

[2] Walker et al, *Home Office Statistical Bulletin: Crime in England and Wales 2008/09* (July 2009). Curiously, however, aside from riot and violent disorder, the vast majority of those recorded offences are described by the Home Office as 'Other offences against the State and public order'.

(b) a common purpose, whether lawful or unlawful;

(c) the execution or inception of the common purpose;

(d) an intent to help one another by force if necessary against any opposition to the execution of the common purpose; and

(e) the use or threat of force in executing the common purpose which is such as to terrify at least one person of reasonable firmness.

The penalty at common law was life imprisonment. **1.08**

The Law Commission Report, *Offences Relating to Public Order*,[3] recommended a number **1.09** of changes to the common law. Firstly, the Law Commission proposed a new offence of violent disorder as a middle ground between riot and affray. Violent disorder, as we will see later in this chapter, was designed to replace the common law offence of unlawful assembly and deal with incidents involving at least three people. The Law Commission queried whether, given that the new offence of violent disorder penalized acts of group violence with a maximum sentence of five years' imprisonment, the law of public order could effectively operate without any offence of riot.[4] Their answer was 'no', citing the case of *Caird*,[5] that riot is an offence 'which derives its great gravity from the simple fact that the persons concerned were acting in numbers and using those numbers to achieve their purpose'.

Therefore, secondly, the Law Commission proposed a substantial increase in the number **1.10** of participants required in order to form a riot, from three to twelve. The Commission conceded that any number is to some extent arbitrary. However, twelve has some historical basis, since under the Riot Act 1714 (repealed in 1967), if twelve persons were still assembled one hour after the order for dispersal ('the reading of the Riot Act'), they were guilty of a felony.

Thirdly, to reflect the extreme gravity of the offence, marked by the substantial increase in **1.11** the number of participants and the contrast with violent disorder, the maximum penalty for riot would remain significantly higher than for other public order offences, at ten years' imprisonment (though no longer life imprisonment, as under the common law). Treason and Tasmania were no longer an option.

Fourthly, the Law Commission recommended that the element of 'common purpose' be **1.12** retained but attempted to clarify it.

It will be noted that, fifthly, the mental element of the offence also changed, see below. **1.13**

With that brief, historical context in mind, we now turn to the modern offence of riot **1.14** under the Public Order Act 1986.

---

[3] Law Com 123, 24 October 1983, Cmnd 9510.
[4] Ibid, p 9, para 2.10.
[5] (1970) 54 Cr App R 499, 505.

The definition of riot under the Public Order Act 1986, s 1

1.15 Riot is the most serious offence under the 1986 Act. The elements of the offence are defined in s 1 as follows:

(1) Where 12 or more persons who are present together use or threaten unlawful violence for a common purpose and the conduct of them (taken together) is such as would cause a person of reasonable firmness present at the scene to fear for his personal safety, each of the persons using unlawful violence for the common purpose is guilty of riot.

(2) It is immaterial whether or not the 12 or more use or threaten unlawful violence simultaneously.

(3) The common purpose may be inferred from conduct.

(4) No person of reasonable firmness need actually be, or be likely to be, present at the scene.

(5) Riot may be committed in private as well as in public places.

(6) A person guilty of riot is liable on conviction on indictment to imprisonment for a term not exceeding ten years or a fine or both.

Jurisdiction

1.16 The offence of riot is triable only on indictment (s 1(6)), which means that it may only be tried in the Crown Court by judge and jury.

1.17 The offence of riot is reserved for exceptionally grave cases, as reflected by its maximum sentence of ten years and the fact that the consent of the Director of Public Prosecutions (DPP) is necessary before a prosecution can be instituted.[6]

1.18 The Crown Prosecution Service's *Charging Standards* outline the kind of disorder which might appropriately be charged as riot: 'the normal forces of law and order have broken down; due to the intensity of the attacks on police and other civilian authorities, normal access by emergency services is impeded by mob activity; due to the scale and ferocity of the disorder, severe disruption and fear is caused to members of the public; violence carries with it the potential for a significant impact upon a significant number of non-participants for a significant length of time; organised or spontaneous large scale acts of violence on people and/or property'.[7]

Essential elements of the offence

1.19 There are six essential elements of the offence of riot:

- twelve or more persons
- present together
- using or threatening unlawful violence
- for a common purpose (use of violence in furtherance thereof)
- a person of reasonable firmness
- mental element.

---

[6] Section 7(1). No prosecution for an offence of riot or incitement to riot may be instituted except by or with the consent of the DPP.

[7] See <http://www.cps.gov.uk/legal/p_to_r/public_order_offences/index.html#_Charging_Standard>.

Twelve or more persons

The 1986 Act significantly increased the requisite quorum for a riot from three to twelve **1.20** people. The Law Commission conceded that selecting any number was an arbitrary exercise, though twelve has some historical origin in the Riot Act 1714.[8] It has also been noted that twelve is something of a magic number in criminal law,[9] as it is the number required for a jury in a criminal trial. That said, in raising the number from three to twelve, the 1986 Act ensured that this offence was reserved for incidents beyond the scope of the average pub brawl.

The gravamen of riot, therefore, is the presence of large numbers. In reality, and given **1.21** that the consent of the DPP is required, the offence will only be charged where there are significantly more than twelve participants, so it will rarely be necessary to conduct a head count.[10]

Present together

The twelve or more persons must be present together (see s 1(1)), though it is immaterial **1.22** whether or not the twelve or more use or threaten unlawful violence *simultaneously* (s 1(2)). This suggests that their presence and activity should normally be proximate in time and place. Where separate incidents spring up over a period of time, for example over a period of days during repeated inner city tension in one broad locality, it is better practice to charge them as separate offences.[11]

Riot, as with other public order offences, such as affray can be a continuing offence, but it **1.23** is a question of fact and degree. Thus, it was held to be a single offence (of affray) where the accused were milling about, armed, and threatening violence over a period of four hours and across a radius of a quarter of a mile.[12] However, where the ingredients of an offence cease to exist for a period of time, the offence is over. Should those ingredients come into existence again, a second offence occurs. So, where the offenders travelled by coach to a number of different sites, causing terror at each, but were peaceful during transit between sites, then there were a number of separate offences rather than one continuous offence.[13]

---

[8] Riot Act 1714 (Long title: 'An act for preventing tumults and riotous assemblies, and for the more speedy and effectual punishing of the rioters'). Section 2 provided for a proclamation to be made 'in a loud voice' for a crowd to 'disperse themselves and peaceably to depart to their habitations'. This was the 'reading of the Riot Act'. Section 3 then provided 'That if such persons so unlawfully, riotously, and tumultuously assembled, or *twelve or more of them*, after proclamation made in manner aforesaid, shall continue together and not disperse themselves within one hour', then the justices of the peace, sheriffs, etc were empowered to 'seize and apprehend' such persons. Indeed the Act (as originally enacted) went so as to declare those lawmen involved in seizing and apprehending rioters, 'shall be free, discharged and indemnified, as well against the King's Majesty, his heirs and successors, as against all and every other person and persons, of, for, or concerning the killing, maiming, or hurting of any such person or persons so unlawfully, riotously and tumultuously assembled, that shall happen to be so killed, maimed or hurt, as aforesaid'. The Riot Act 1714 was repealed by the Criminal Law Act 1967, s 10(2).
[9] See Peter Thornton, *Public Order Law* (1987) p 9.
[10] David Ormerod (ed), *Smith and Hogan Criminal Law* (2008, 12th edn) p 1065.
[11] Thornton, *Public Order Law*, p 9.
[12] *Woodrow* (1959) 43 Cr App R 105.
[13] *Jones* (1974) 59 Cr App R 120.

1.24   Riot can be committed in a private place (s 1(5)). In contrast with offences under ss 4 and 5 of the Act, 'private place' in the context of riot is not restricted in any way, for example, by excluding dwellings. However, given the large numbers required to form a riot, it is likely that those offences charged will be in a public place—but this is not an essential element.

Using or threatening unlawful violence

1.25   'Violence' under the Public Order Act 1986 has a deliberately wider definition than offences of violence in other parts of the criminal law, such as offences against the person. Section 8 in Part I of the Act explains the interpretation of the term:

> 'violence' means any violent conduct, so that—
> (a)   except in the context of affray [see below], it includes violent conduct towards *property* as well as violent conduct towards persons, and
> (b)   it is *not restricted to conduct causing or intended to cause injury or damage* but includes any other violent conduct (for example, throwing at or towards a person a missile of a kind capable of causing injury which does not hit or falls short).

1.26   Firstly then, riot as a public order offence is distinguished from offences against the person in that it can be committed where the violent conduct is aimed at property. It encompasses the fear caused by scenes of disorder where missiles are thrown at police cars or shops are smashed up and ransacked. It perhaps obviates the need for separate charges of criminal damage.

1.27   Secondly, riot is distinguishable from offences against the person in that there is no need for the prosecution to establish that the violent conduct caused, or was even intended to cause, injury or damage. This is because the Act is concerned not with the victim of a violent assault, but with the impact of violent conduct on the hypothetical bystander— the 'person of reasonable firmness present at the scene' who would be caused to fear for their own personal safety (s 1(1)). Hence, violent conduct under s 8 of the 1986 Act also includes throwing missiles, brandishing weapons, and the punch that missed its target.

1.28   Equally, and for the same reason, the Act goes beyond the actual use of violence to encompass the threat of violence. The offence concerns twelve or more persons 'using or threatening' unlawful violence for a common purpose. Brandishing weapons, waving fists, and shouting threats could cause the bystander to fear for his personal safety just as much as the actual application of force.

1.29   However, for there to be a riot at least one of the twelve must actually use unlawful violence and only those actually using unlawful violence are guilty of the offence (s 1(1)). Thus, riot has a precondition of at least twelve persons using or threatening unlawful violence for a common purpose such as would cause a reasonable bystander to fear for his personal safety—but only those persons who actually use unlawful violence will be guilty of riot. That said, this raises interesting issues of secondary liability (see below the section on 'common purpose').

The violence must be *unlawful* violence (see s 1(1)). This preserves the general defences of   **1.30**
accident, self-defence,[14] defence of another, and the prevention of crime.[15] This was confirmed in *R v Rothwell and Barton*[16] and is now settled law. Thus, once a defence such as
self-defence has been raised (the evidential burden), there can be no conviction unless the
prosecution can disprove self-defence to the criminal standard of proof—ie so that the jury
are sure it was not self-defence.

However, one can envisage problems in a case where the defendants assert that they were   **1.31**
acting in pre-emptive self-defence—for example where twelve or more football supporters
attacked a gang of rival supporters because they feared imminent attack. Yet, as with any
defence of self-defence, the use of force must be reasonable and proportionate. It would be
difficult to maintain such a defence where a pre-emptive strike to ward off attack developed
into a sustained pitched battle.

For a common purpose

There is no definition of common purpose in the Act, nor any clear definition elsewhere. It   **1.32**
was the element of 'common purpose' which prompted Lord Scarman to refer to the 'great
forensic confusion' which prevailed when juries had the task of deciding whether this element of the common law offence of riot had been proved.[17] The 1986 Act retained the
concept, but failed to provide any definition or clarification other than to say that 'common
purpose may be inferred from conduct' (s 1(3)). That is statutory language for 'you know
it when you see it'.

The concept of 'common purpose', together with the weight of numbers, is what distin-   **1.33**
guishes riot from violent disorder and other public order offences. The Law Commission
rejected an earlier proposal that common purpose should be replaced by a concept of
'engaging in an unlawful course of conduct'. They said that common purpose more accu-
rately reflected the idea of concerted action on the part of a number of people.[18] The Law
Commission concluded:

> Persons who engage in acts of public disorder vary in the range of their conduct from
> those who, as we put it, incite or lead a riot to those whom we have described as casual partici-
> pants. The latter include individuals who, observing that disorder is taking place, take the
> opportunity to add their own acts of aimless violence or disorder, without any particular
> purpose in mind. But the effect of omitting the element of common purpose in our Working
> Paper proposal was, we think, to cause the casual participant, the pure opportunist who
> has shared no purpose with anyone but has merely added his own act of violence to those
> of others, to be guilty of riot. There is, of course, no reason why an intention to achieve

---

[14] The general defence of self-defence now has a statutory footing in the Criminal Justice and Immigration
Act 2008, s 76—though this adds little or nothing to what had always been the law of self-defence.
[15] See the provisions of the Criminal Law Act 1967, s 3, and the discussion on defences in Ch 8.
[16] [1993] Crim LR 626—where it was held that the word 'unlawful' is intended to ensure that the general
defences of self-defence, reasonable defence of a friend, or an attempt to stop a breach of the peace etc remain
good defences to the statutory offences under the Public Order Act 1986. Had Parliament intended to exclude
those defences, it would have done so expressly.
[17] Lord Scarman, *The Brixton Disorders* (1981) Cmnd 8427, para 7.39.
[18] Law Com 123, para 6.11.

a common purpose, such as an attack on the police, may not be formed upon the instant of joining in: premeditation is no more required for such an intention than for an intent to do grievous bodily harm. If, however, the particular gravity of riot as an offence were to be based simply on committing an act of violence at the same time as other people commit similar acts, then the importance of the offence would lie, not in the common purpose of the defendant shared with others, but in the cumulative damage and injury caused by the common acts. In our present view, however, it is the possession of a common purpose by a number of people which constitutes the particular danger of riot. Of course, in many instances the course of conduct of the rioters taken as a whole will be strongly indicative of what the common purpose is; but the course of conduct must essentially remain no more than evidence, usually the strongest evidence, of what the conduct is aimed to achieve. We therefore conclude that the possession of a common purpose should be an integral part of any new offences of riot.

1.34 Common purpose is more than mere motive. There is no requirement that the twelve or more persons have come together pursuant to any agreement, or that each should have agreed with the other eleven. It is sufficient that they assembled by chance, one by one, but at the point at which violence is offered they are present together directing the violence for a common purpose. Moreover, that common purpose may be either lawful or unlawful, so long as the violence itself is unlawful and offered for a common purpose. In *Caird*[19] a group of students gathered outside a hotel in Cambridge where a Greek-themed dinner was being held for the great and good of the city in celebration of 'Greek week'. The common purpose of the students was to disrupt the dinner in protest of the policies of the then military, authoritarian Greek government. In order to gain entry to the hotel and wreck the dinner, they engaged in violence with the police and guests and damaged hotel property. The common purpose (to disrupt the dinner) was lawful. The violence used in pursuit of that common purpose was unlawful.

1.35 The definition of riot poses an interesting question of secondary liability. According to s 1(1) where twelve or more people with a common purpose threaten unlawful violence but only one actually uses it, there is a riot but only one principal rioter. The section states that only the person *using* unlawful violence is guilty of riot. However, since the remaining eleven or more are present together with a common purpose to threaten unlawful violence, they *may* be regarded as encouraging the principal. Thus they would be guilty as secondary parties.[20] Professor Ormerod asks us to suppose that all twelve had agreed—'Threats, yes, but actual violence, no.' If D, for the common purpose, then uses violence, D commits riot but the rest are not necessarily guilty of riot by their mere use of threats (unless they encouraged D). And if D goes beyond the scope of the concerted action and produces a weapon the rest did not know about, they will certainly not be guilty of riot.[21]

---

[19] *R v Caird and others* (1970) 54 Cr App R 499.
[20] *Jefferson* [1994] 1 All ER 270 and see generally Ormerod (ed), *Smith and Hogan Criminal Law*. See also *Rahman* [2008] UKHL 45 on joint enterprise.
[21] Ormerod (ed), *Smith and Hogan Criminal Law*, p 1065.

A person of reasonable firmness present at the scene

The element of 'a person of reasonable firmness present at the scene' is common to the **1.36** offences of riot, violent disorder, and affray. It is an important concept to understand. It is discussed fully in the section dealing with affray.[22]

Mental element (mens rea)

A person is guilty of riot only if he *intends to use violence* or *is aware that his conduct may be* **1.37** *violent* (Public Order Act 1986, s 6(1)).

'Awareness' applies to riot, violent disorder, and affray but is a word rarely used elsewhere **1.38** in the criminal law. The Act (on the recommendation of the Law Commission) sought to avoid the ambiguity and confusion caused by the term 'recklessness'. In effect, 'awareness' means a kind of recklessness. The defendant must foresee the risk that a particular kind of harm may be done or violence may occur and yet goes on and takes that risk. For example, he throws a bottle into a crowd of police officers not caring whether the missile fell short or not, but knowing there was some risk of harm.

The difference is that, unlike recklessness, there is no objective element. Awareness does **1.39** not cover the situation in which it would be obvious to the reasonable man that there was a risk, but the defendant had not turned his mind to it. Awareness is a purely subjective concept. In reality, however, in the context of public order offences such as riot, this subtlety will rarely be of practical importance.

An additional mental element is that the person must also share a 'common purpose' with **1.40** the other eleven or more participants. This additional element is one for which proof is required in respect not merely of the defendant but of the other eleven persons.[23] Again, this can be inferred from conduct.

A direction as to the mental element of the offence should normally be given to the jury, **1.41** and care must be taken to distinguish between principal offenders and aiders and abettors in that direction.[24]

Intoxicated rioters

The Act makes special provision for the possibility of a plea of intoxication. Section 6(5) **1.42** and (6) provide as follows:

> (5) For the purposes of this section a person whose awareness is impaired by intoxication shall be taken to be aware of that of which he would be aware if not intoxicated, unless he shows either that his intoxication was not self-induced or that it was caused solely by the taking or administration of a substance in the course of medical treatment.
> (6) In subsection (5) 'intoxication' means any intoxication, whether caused by drink, drugs or other means, or by a combination of means.

Thus, as with other offences where the required mental element is recklessness, 'self- **1.43** induced' intoxication provides no defence. He will be treated as unimpaired, as aware

---

[22] See 1.108 et seq.
[23] See Public Order Act 1986, s 6(7) and also Law Com 123, para 6.28.
[24] *Blackwood* [2002] EWCA Crim 3102.

of that which he would have been aware of had he not been intoxicated.[25] Therefore, care should be taken in drafting the indictment, for if it alleges only that the defendant intended to use violence (rather than merely being aware that his conduct may be violent), this would be alleging a crime of specific intent to which a plea of self-induced intoxication may apply.

1.44 However, there is a curiosity here. In riot, unlike violent disorder and affray, there is an additional mental element of sharing a 'common purpose' with eleven or more others. That must be akin to specific intent—one cannot form a common purpose with others recklessly. Indeed, the Law Commission envisaged such a possibility:

> The element of common purpose in the proposed offence of riot, amounts in substance to a further mental element of intent. We would therefore expect that, if there was sufficient evidence to indicate that a defendant accused of riot was too intoxicated to have the common purpose, he could not be found guilty of riot. Nevertheless, if his intoxication was self-induced, he could be convicted as an alternative of violent disorder.[26]

1.45 There remains a defence of 'involuntary intoxication'—that is the rioter who had his drink 'spiked' or his intoxication was a side effect of prescription medication. Section 6(5) of the Act purports to place a reverse burden on the defendant—'shall be taken to be aware of that of which he would be aware if not intoxicated, *unless he shows* . . . that his intoxication was not self-induced'. However, since the advent of the Human Rights Act 1998, the courts have begun to 'read down' such reverse burdens,[27] where they apply to an essential element of the offence, such as *mens rea*. Accordingly, it is likely that the burden on the defendant is only to raise the issue (an evidential burden) rather than proving it to the balance of probabilities (a legal burden).[28]

Sentencing

1.46 Riot is indictable only and punishable with a maximum of ten years' imprisonment, or an unlimited fine, or both: s 1(6) Public Order Act 1986.

1.47 Riot is a serious specified offence (Criminal Justice Act 2003, s 225(1)(a) and Schedule 15). As a result, the 'dangerous offenders' provisions of the Criminal Justice Act 2003 apply, as amended on 14 July 2008 by the Criminal and Immigration Act 2008. In short, it is open to the court to pass a sentence of imprisonment for public protection or an extended sentence.[29]

---

[25] The general principle is defined in *DPP v Majewski; R v Majewski* [1977] AC 443.

[26] Law Com 123, para 6.28.

[27] Human Rights Act 1998, s 3.

[28] For the general principles of reverse burdens post-Human Rights Act 1998, see *Sheldrake v DPP* [2004] UKHL 43.

[29] A full examination of the complex provisions relating to dangerous offenders is beyond the scope of this work. A useful introductory guide is provided on the website of the Sentencing Guidelines Council: <http://www.sentencing-guidelines.gov.uk/docs/Dangerous%20Offenders%20–%20Guide%20for%20Sentencers%20and%20Practitioners.pdf>.

General guidance on the gravity of public order offences, including riot, is to be found in **1.48** *Caird*[30] in which Sachs LJ said:

> Where there is wanton and vicious violence of gross degree the court is not concerned with whether it originates from gang rivalry or from political motives. It is the degree of mob violence that matters and the extent to which the public peace is being broken . . .

> In the view of this court, it is a wholly wrong approach to take the acts of any individual participator in isolation. They were not committed in isolation and, as already indicated, it is that very fact that constitutes the gravity of the offence.[31]

The guideline sentencing authority for cases of riot is *R v Najeeb and others*.[32] That case **1.49** arose out of race riots in Bradford in 2001. A few weeks before there had been similar disturbances in Oldham and Burnley. In Bradford, the leader of the British National Party made a speech which caused such concern in the community that a World Inner City Festival scheduled to take place in the city had to be cancelled. Following the speech, supporters of the Anti-Nazi League gathered in the city square to confront a planned assembly of the National Front Party. The Asian community were concerned about the need to defend themselves against attack from right-wing extremists. Scuffles broke out and then developed into serious disorder between vast numbers of Asian and white groups. An Asian man was stabbed, which then sparked further widespread disorder throughout the city over a prolonged period. The police were the target of the violence. Barricades were built using stolen cars set alight. The police were attacked with missiles from stones to petrol bombs and from metal poles to a crossbow. Public houses, garages, and shops were looted and gutted by fire. In the result, two police officers were stabbed and over 300 officers were injured whilst the city sustained criminal damage estimated at £27 million.

Over a hundred defendants either pleaded guilty or were found guilty of riot and received **1.50** sentences ranging from four to six and a half years' imprisonment. Juvenile defendants received between six and eighteen months' detention. One defendant convicted of throwing petrol bombs was sentenced to eight and a half years' imprisonment.

Giving guidance as to sentence in *Najeeb and others*, Lord Justice Rose outlined certain factors to be considered. Those included **1.51**

- whether the riot was premeditated and planned or spontaneous;
- the local conditions involved;
- the numbers of people involved;
- the duration of the disorder;
- whether the police (or other public servants) were targeted;
- the extent of injuries sustained; and
- the extent and value of damage caused.

---

[30] (1970) 54 Cr App R 499. But see also *Pilgrim* (1983) 5 Cr App R (S) 140 and *Muranyi* (1986) 8 Cr App R (S) 176.
[31] *Caird*, 506–8.
[32] [2003] 2 Cr App R (S) 69.

1.52 The Court of Appeal in *Najeeb and others* held that deterrent sentences were called for in such cases and the offender's previous good character and personal mitigation were of comparatively little weight. The Court then provided the following guideline sentences following conviction after a trial:

Circumstances	Guideline sentence
1. Ringleader	Sentence near maximum of 10 years after trial
2. Active and persistent participant (threw petrol bomb, used weapon, drove at police)	8–9 years after trial
3. Participation over lengthy period (threw missiles such as knives/poles/gas cylinders) or set fire to cars	6–7 years after trial
4. Present for a significant period and repeated throwing of missiles (bricks/stones)	5 years after trial

Compensation for Riot damage

1.53 The Riot (Damages) Act (RDA) 1886 provides for compensation to be paid out of the 'local police fund' for damage or loss relating to houses, shops, or buildings, or their contents, provided the damage was done by 'persons riotously and tumultuously assembled together'. Section 10(1) of the Public Order Act 1986 confirms that the term 'riotously' in the 1886 Act is to be construed in accordance with the definition of riot in s 1 of the 1986 Act.

1.54 The fact that compensation claims are paid out of the local police authority fund is clearly a source of concern to the police. In July 2003, the Home Office published a consultation paper[33] assessing the options of repealing or amending that legislation. The consultation paper stated that the nature of policing has changed in the 120 years since the Act and that most criminal damage to property is nowadays covered by insurance. It argued that it was unreasonable for the police to be burdened with liability for riot damage and the 1886 Act undermined public confidence in the police because its provisions implicitly assumed that riots are the product of a culpable failure to provide adequate policing.

1.55 Nevertheless, the Riot (Damages) Act 1886 remains on the statute books and continues to cause consternation to police authorities and their insurers. For a discussion of those issues (which are beyond the scope of this book) see the litigation which ensued as a result of rioting at the Yarl's Wood Detention Centre in February 2002.[34]

---

[33] Home Office Consultation Paper, *Riot (Damages) Act 1886: Consultation on Options for Review* (July 2003).

[34] *Bedfordshire Police Authority v Constable* [2009] EWCA Civ 64; *Yarl's Wood Immigration Ltd; GSL UK Ltd; Creechurch Dedicated Ltd v Bedfordshire Police Authority* [2008] EWHC 2207 (Comm); *Bedfordshire Police Authority v David Constable* [2008] EWHC 1375 (Comm). Amongst the issues raised was whether the private company with public law powers to run an immigration detention centre could make a compensation claim under the RDA 1886 against a police authority. The High Court held that it did not qualify under the RDA 1886 and could not make a claim. Furthermore, the Court of Appeal held that a police authority was entitled to be indemnified by its excess insurers in respect of claims made under that Act.

C. Violent Disorder: Public Order Act 1986, s 2

Historical development

The offence of violent disorder was a new offence introduced by the Public Order Act **1.56**
1986, on the recommendation of the Law Commission. It replaced the common law
offence of 'unlawful assembly', which appears to have been so ill-defined that even as late as
the 1970s judges and commentators could not agree on its precise definition.[35] At common
law, it seems to have consisted of three or more persons gathered together for a common
purpose of either committing a crime of violence or to achieve some other object in a manner which would cause a reasonable man to fear a breach of the peace. That definition was
so close to the common law offence of riot, that unlawful assembly was characterized by
Lord Hailsham as 'only an inchoate riot'.[36]

However, when the Law Commission proposed that the numbers required for the offence **1.57**
of riot be raised from three persons to twelve, there was then a vast gulf between riot and
affray. The Law Commission decided there was a need for an offence to cover the middle
ground. Affray can be committed alone and it cannot be committed against property. The
new offence of violent disorder would deal with both violence against property and offences
where there was a weight of numbers (short of riot) acting in combination to either use *or*
threaten violence.

In 1983, the Law Commission was persuaded by representations from, among others, the **1.58**
Police and the Society of Justices' Clerks to recommend that the offence be made triable
either way, rather than indictable only as originally proposed, because it was felt that some
less serious forms of the offence could be dealt with expeditiously in the magistrates' court.[37]
Today, twenty-five years on, the CPS Charging Standard states, 'it is difficult to see circumstances in which it would be appropriate to represent that charges brought under section 2
would be suitable for summary disposition'.[38]

The definition of violent disorder under the Public Order Act 1986, s 2

The offence is defined in s 2 of the Public Order Act 1986 as follows: **1.59**

(1) Where 3 or more persons who are present together use or threaten unlawful violence and
the conduct of them (taken together) is such as would cause a person of reasonable firmness present at the scene to fear for his personal safety, each of the persons using or
threatening unlawful violence is guilty of violent disorder.
(2) It is immaterial whether or not the 3 or more use or threaten unlawful violence
simultaneously.
(3) No person of reasonable firmness need actually be, or be likely to be, present at the
scene.
(4) Violent disorder may be committed in private as well as in public places.

---

[35] Law Com 123, para 5.2.
[36] *Kamara v DPP* [1974] AC 104, 116.
[37] Law Com 123, para 5.6.
[38] See <http://www.cps.gov.uk/legal/p_to_r/public_order_offences/_Violent>.

1.60   The CPS Charging Standards suggest: 'This offence should only be charged in relation to instances of serious disorder falling short of those elements required to establish an offence under s 1. Planning may be an important ingredient in a case of violent disorder but regard should be had for the potential of minor incidents to flare up into serious disorder sufficient to meet the requirements of this section.'[39]

1.61   The Charging Standard then gives examples of the type of conduct which may be appropriate for a s 2 offence, which include: 'fighting between three or more people involving the use of weapons, between rival groups in a place to which members of the public have access (for example a town centre or a crowded bar) causing severe disruption and/or fear to members of the public; an outbreak of violence which carries with it the potential for significant impact on a moderate scale on non-participants; serious disorder at a public event where missiles are thrown and other violence is used against and directed towards the police and other civil authorities'.[40]

Jurisdiction

1.62   The offence of violent disorder is triable either way—which means that it can be tried either summarily in the magistrates' court or on indictment in the Crown Court by a judge and jury. It is punishable on indictment with a maximum penalty of five years' imprisonment and/or an unlimited fine, or on summary conviction, with six months' imprisonment and/or the statutory maximum fine: s 2(5) Public Order Act 1986.

Essential elements of the offence

1.63   As can be seen from s 2 there are five essential elements of the offence:

- three or more persons present together
- using or threatening unlawful violence
- cumulative effect of conduct would cause fear
- the (hypothetical) person of reasonable firmness present at the scene
- mental element (*mens rea*).

1.64   The essential elements feature some of the same elements and concepts already explored in discussion of the offence of riot and (in due course) in relation to affray. Please see those sections where the principles are the same. The differences are examined below. It should be noted, that as with the other 'public' order offences of riot and affray, violent disorder can be committed in a private place (s 2(4)).

Three or more persons present together

1.65   The essence of the offence of violent disorder is that it involves an element of what the Law Commission termed 'combination'—the gravity of the offence deriving from the increased fear caused by scenes of combined numbers of persons using or threatening unlawful violence.

---

[39] See <http://www.cps.gov.uk/legal/p_to_r/public_order_offences/_Violent>.
[40] Ibid.

It is an essential element of the offence, therefore, that at least three people used or threat- **1.66**
ened unlawful violence. This is important because where there are *only* three persons (the
three defendants) alleged to have been involved in the incident and one of them is acquitted, then the others must also be acquitted. In *Mechan*,[41] the court held that if the jury
acquitted a defendant, on the grounds of self-defence, that person could no longer be one
of the three required.

Therefore, the prosecution should exercise great care when drafting the indictment. If, on **1.67**
the facts of the case, there are potentially more than three persons involved in the disorder,
including people not named on the indictment, then the indictment should allege 'together
with persons unknown'. If there are only three involved in the incident, it may be prudent
to add an alternative count of affray.[42] It is essential that the defence know what it is they
have to meet.[43]

However, some commentators have questioned whether it must always follow that if one **1.68**
of the three is acquitted of violent disorder, the other two must also be acquitted. It is con-
ceivable, argues Professor Ormerod, that the third person still used unlawful violence but
was acquitted on some other ground, such as involuntary intoxication or duress.[44]

Indeed, this point often arises where there are issues of identification. It may be the case that **1.69**
the jury are sure that three or more persons were using or threatening unlawful violence,
but cannot be sure of the identity of the participants, other than the defendant. The Court
of Appeal held in the case of *Lemon*[45] that this would be a perfectly proper conviction. It is
certainly not the case, therefore, that violent disorder requires the *conviction* of three persons or none at all.[46]

Unlike riot, there is no requirement of a 'common purpose' or that the three should be act- **1.70**
ing in concert—so long as they are 'present together', proximate in time and place. Thus, it
could be a pub brawl involving two-against-one—certainly no common purpose between
the three there. It is only necessary that their conduct, taken together, is such as would cause
a person of reasonable firmness present at the scene to fear for his own personal safety.

Using or threatening unlawful violence

The definition of 'violence' as applicable to violent disorder is provided in s 8 of the **1.71**
Public Order Act 1986 (see full discussion in the section on riot above at 1.25). That is a
wider definition than applies in offences against the person. It includes violent conduct
against property as well as persons. It is not restricted to conduct causing or intended to

---

[41] [2004] EWCA Crim 388.
[42] *Hadjisava* [2004] EWCA Crim 1316.
[43] *Mahroof* (1989) 88 Cr App R 317; cf *Fleming and Robinson* [1989] Crim LR 658, (1989) 153 JP 517 and also *Worton* (1989) 154 JP 201.
[44] Ormerod (ed), *Smith and Hogan Criminal Law*, p 1067.
[45] [2002] EWCA Crim 1661.
[46] See also *R v Mbagwu and Munnings* [2007] EWCA Crim 1068 per Hughes LJ at para 15 'a jury may be perfectly satisfied that there were at least three people participating without being able to say to the criminal standard who most of them were. Provided that a jury is satisfied that there was unlawful violence offered by at least three people and that a particular defendant was one of them, that defendant is to be convicted, even if he is the only one who can be identified.'

cause injury or damage but includes any other violent conduct (for example, throwing at or towards a person a missile of a kind capable of causing injury which does not hit or falls short).

1.72 As with riot and affray, the violence used or threatened by each of at least three participants must be *unlawful* violence. This preserves the defences of self-defence,[47] reasonable defence of another, and prevention of crime.[48] Where there are only three alleged participants and one is using lawful self-defence, then no offence of violent disorder is committed.[49]

1.73 Unlike riot, however, violent disorder can be committed by the mere *threat* of unlawful violence alone. It does not require the actual use of unlawful violence. In *Brodie*[50] it was held that there was a *prima facie* case where B was a member of a group which followed or 'stalked' a man for three-quarters of a mile along a footpath in the middle of the night because this air of considerable implicit menace amounted to a threat.[51] Likewise in *Church*,[52] running with a group of people, some of whom were armed and committed assaults, raised a *prima facie* case of threatening unlawful violence.

Cumulative effect

1.74 So there must be at least three persons using or threatening unlawful violence. The distinctions in the role of each participant or the level of violent conduct each uses or threatens is immaterial, since s 2(1) makes clear that it is the cumulative effect of their conduct '*taken together*' which must be assessed. In *Brodie* (above) it was the cumulative effect of a stalking group of men, some armed with weapons some unarmed: because their conduct had an air of considerable implicit menace such that it amounted to a threat of violence such as would cause a person of reasonable firmness present at the scene to fear for his personal safety.

1.75 Section 2(2) states it is also immaterial whether or not the three or more use or threaten unlawful violence *simultaneously*. Nevertheless, there must be a sufficient nexus between at least three persons offering unlawful violence, such that there exists a quorum of three and their conduct taken together can be assessed.

Person of reasonable firmness present at the scene

1.76 As with riot and affray, for the offence of violent disorder to be made out, the violence used or threatened by at least three persons must be such as would cause a person of reasonable firmness present at the scene to fear for his personal safety.

1.77 The concept of this person is discussed fully in the section dealing with affray (below). It is sufficient here to say that this person is a *hypothetical* bystander. As s 2(3) states 'no person of reasonable firmness need actually be, or be likely to be, present at the scene'.

---

[47] *R v Rothwell and Barton* [1993] Crim LR 626, CA.
[48] See Criminal Law Act 1967, s 3(1).
[49] See *Mechan* [2004] EWCA Crim 388 above.
[50] [2000] Crim LR 775, CA.
[51] See also *I v DPP*; *M v DPP*; *H v DPP* [2000] 1 Cr App R 251—an 'aura of menace' could amount to a threat of unlawful violence.
[52] [2000] 4 Archbold News 3, CA.

Where no bystander is actually present, it is for the jury to assess the question hypothetically. In most cases, however, a bystander will give evidence as to the fear he was caused.

Mental element (mens rea)

The mental element for violent disorder is set out at s 6(2): 'A person is guilty of violent **1.78** disorder or affray only if he intends to use or threaten violence or is aware that his conduct may be violent or threaten violence.' As with riot the mental element is either intent or awareness (see the section on riot above at 1.37 et seq for full discussion). Of course, the difference between riot and violent disorder is that the latter offence can be committed by threats of violence alone. Thus, the least mental element required by the offender in violent disorder is the awareness that his conduct may be threatening.

As with other public order offences, self-induced intoxication provides no defence **1.79** (s 6(5))—see the discussion above in the section on riot at 1.42 et seq.

Alternative verdicts

Where the case is tried on indictment, s 7(3) of the 1986 Act makes provision for an **1.80** alternative verdict of guilty to s 4 of the Public Order Act 1986 (of threatening, abusive, or insulting words or behaviour) in the event that the jury acquit a defendant of violent disorder.[53] Section 7(3) provides:

> If on the trial on indictment of a person charged with violent disorder or affray the jury find him not guilty of the offence charged, they may (without prejudice to section 6(3) of the Criminal Law Act 1967) find him guilty of an offence under section 4.

Where a judge decides to leave s 4 to the jury as an alternative verdict, defence counsel **1.81** should be given an opportunity to address the jury.[54] In *Mbagwu*[55] it was said to be improper to leave s 4 to the jury as an alternative verdict after they had been in retirement for over a day and had already acquitted eight other defendants.

Sentencing

The maximum penalty after trial on indictment is five years' imprisonment and/or an **1.82** unlimited fine, or on summary conviction, with six months' imprisonment and/or the statutory maximum fine.[56] Violent disorder is a specified offence in Schedule 15 of the Criminal Justice Act 2003. As such the 'dangerous offenders' provisions of the Criminal Justice Act 2003 apply, as amended on 14 July 2008 by the Criminal and Immigration Act 2008. In short, if the criteria are satisfied, it is open to the court to pass an extended sentence for violent disorder.[57]

---

[53] For examples of the operation of s 7(3) see *Mahroof* (1988) 88 Cr App R 317. See also *Worton* (1989) 154 JP 201.
[54] *Perrins* [1995] Crim LR 432; *Stanley* [1993] Crim LR 618.
[55] [2007] EWCA 1068.
[56] Public Order Act 1986, s 2(5).
[57] A full examination of the complex provisions relating to dangerous offenders is beyond the scope of this work. A useful introductory guide is provided on the website of the Sentencing Guidelines Council: <http://www.sentencing-guidelines.gov.uk/docs/Dangerous%20Offenders%20–%20Guide%20for%20 Sentencers%20and%20Practitioners.pdf>.

1.83   Though the maximum sentence is five years, the courts will regularly look to impose deterrent sentences, which means a starting point of three years, even on a guilty plea, in serious cases.

1.84   An important sentencing authority for violent disorder is *R v Chapman*,[58] in which the Court of Appeal (Judge LJ as he then was, now Lord Chief Justice Judge) approved the use of deterrent sentences, taking into account not only the specific acts of the individual offender, but the wider picture of mass disorder causing fear to the public.

1.85   The background to Chapman's case was a series of riots and mass violence which erupted in Bradford in July 2001. The first episode of violence that summer was a full-scale riot lasting some twelve hours. Chapman was not involved in that. His only involvement was in a much smaller, though still significant, episode of rioting (a copycat riot) two days later. His involvement was opportunist, not having a common purpose with the others and he engaged in throwing numerous stones at the police. He was 20 years old and of previous good character. He pleaded guilty and was sentenced to three years' detention.[59]

1.86   Nevertheless, the Court of Appeal upheld the sentence and endorsed the approach of the resident judge of Bradford. It seems that in the context of mass disorder in the city that year, the judges at Bradford Crown Court had a meeting and resolved to send out a message to the city. They determined that, subject always to the individual and specific mitigation available to any defendant, they would meet any conviction for public order offences with deterrent sentences, taking into account not only the acts committed by the individuals but the wider context of disorder in the city that summer. It is an authority which merits reading because it raises questions about the legitimacy of deterrence as a general principle of sentencing.

1.87   That deterrence approach was endorsed in *R v Rees and others*[60] in the context of football hooliganism in which the then Lord Chief Justice, Lord Woolf said:

> Offences of violent disorder might take various forms. They might be extremely serious or little more than an affray. It was important that courts should pitch their sentences at the appropriate level to reflect the seriousness of the particular incident of violent disorder which they were considering. Offences of violent disorder often involved young men who had otherwise been of exemplary character. The court must have regard to their personal characteristics, but the court must also have regard to the effect of offences of violent disorder on the public who might be caused real anxiety and distress. *A feature of the offence was that it was not the individual conduct of one offender that was important, but the nature of the offending as a whole. An individual offender would want to be punished only for precisely what he had done. However from the point of view of the public, it was the collective effect of the violent disorder which was significant.* When it was the habit of young men and women to drink excessively and then behave out of character it was important to send a message that there were very real dangers involved in that sort of binge drinking. It might cause a person to behave in a way

---

[58]   [2002] EWCA Crim 2346.

[59]   That was rather a harsh sentence. Assuming he received the full one-third credit for his guilty plea, that means the sentencing judge took the view that had he been convicted after a contested trial, he would have been sentenced to four and a half years—almost the maximum sentence.

[60]   [2006] 1 Cr App R (S) 20.

which was out of character. While the courts wished to be sympathetic towards offenders, they must bear in mind the consequences of the offence as a whole on the public. The problem was that when drinking at this level took place, what started as an exhibition of high spirits descended into conduct which was criminal . . . *A heavy sentence was justified because of the need to protect the public. There was a real deterrent element in the sentence.* Deterrent sentences did not always achieve the object which they were designed to achieve. The courts must do what they could to try to stop behaviour of this nature . . . (emphasis added).

In *Greenall*,[61] sentences of four years' imprisonment were upheld for the organizers of a conspiracy to cause violent disorder, and sentences of two years were upheld for those who took part, when rival football supporters arranged to fight each other at a railway station. Some of the gang were armed with bottles, fighting continued for several minutes and three participants were knocked unconscious.[62] **1.88**

D. Affray: Public Order Act 1986, s 3

Historical development

The word 'affray' derives from the French 'effrayer'—to frighten. Though the offence has ancient, common law origins it was for more than a century regarded as obsolete, until it was revived in the 1950s.[63] Today, it is perhaps the most widely used of the indictable public order offences. **1.89**

At common law, the offence was once defined as follows:[64] **1.90**

(1) Unlawful fighting or unlawful violence used by one or more persons against another or others; or an unlawful display of force by one or more persons without actual violence;
(2) in a public place or, if in private premises, in the presence of at least one innocent person who was terrified; and
(3) in such a manner that a bystander of reasonably firm character might reasonably be expected to be terrified.

As already stated, the common law offence of affray was rarely used until relatively modern times. That might have been because other offences against the person could deal with 'unlawful fighting'. Indeed, in representations to the Law Commission, several commentators such as the National Council for Civil Liberties (now Liberty), the Haldane Society, and various trade unions were opposed to a new offence of affray on the basis that assault and offences against the person were sufficient. They argued that affray required less proof of actual fighting and intent than these other offences. In essence, they said that the offence of affray undermined the evidential safeguards and thresholds provided by more serious offences against the person.[65] **1.91**

---

[61] [2005] 2 Cr App R (S) 276.
[62] For further examples of sentences for violent disorder see *Current Sentencing Practice* at B 3-1 or *Blackstones Criminal Practice 2009* at B11.33 and *Banks on Sentence* (4th edn) pp 1277–81.
[63] *R v Sharp and Johnson* [1957] 1 QB 522 was the first reported case for over a hundred years.
[64] Definition from Smith and Hogan, *Criminal Law* (1978, 4th edn) p 757, based on two House of Lords decisions *Button v DPP* [1966] AC 591 and *Taylor v DPP* [1973] AC 964.
[65] Law Com 123, para 3.4.

1.92 Yet, in recommending the new statutory offence of affray, the Law Commission was at pains to explain that if the common law offence of affray were abolished without a replacement, this would leave a significant gap in the law.[66] In their view, an offence was needed which dealt with acts of violence which caused alarm to the public. The identity of the victim and the extent of his injuries were immaterial because affray is essentially an offence against public order, not the person.

The definition of affray under the Public Order Act 1986, s 3

1.93 Affray is defined in s 3 of the Public Order Act as follows:

> (1) A person is guilty of affray if he uses or threatens unlawful violence towards another and his conduct is such as would cause a person of reasonable firmness present at the scene to fear for his personal safety.
> (2) Where 2 or more persons use or threaten the unlawful violence, it is the conduct of them taken together that must be considered for the purposes of subsection (1).
> (3) For the purposes of this section a threat cannot be made by the use of words alone.
> (4) No person of reasonable firmness need actually be, or be likely to be, present at the scene.
> (5) Affray may be committed in private as well as in public places.

1.94 Lord Bingham described the nature of affray as follows:[67]

> It typically involves a group of people who may well be shouting, struggling, threatening, waving weapons, throwing objects, exchanging and threatening blows and so on. Again, typically it involves a continuous course of conduct, the criminal character of which depends on the general nature and effect of the conduct as a whole and not on particular incidents and events which may take place in the course of it. Where reliance is placed on such a continuous course of conduct it is not necessary for the Crown to identify and prove particular incidents. To require such proof would deprive section 3(1) of the 1986 Act of its intended effect, and deprive law-abiding citizens of the protection which this provision intends that they should enjoy. It would be asking the impossible to require a jury of 12 men and women to be satisfied beyond reasonable doubt that each or any incident in an indiscriminate mêlée such as constitutes the typical affray was proved to the requisite standard.

Jurisdiction

1.95 The offence of affray is triable either way—which means it may either be tried on indictment at the Crown Court before judge and jury or tried summarily at the magistrates' court. That decision will depend on the circumstances and seriousness of the case and, potentially, the wishes of the defendant.[68]

Essential elements of the offence

1.96 There are five essential elements of the offence of affray:

- use or threat of unlawful violence

---

[66] Ibid, para 3.3.
[67] *Smith* [1997] 1 Cr App R 14 at 17.
[68] The magistrates' court will only accept jurisdiction to try the case summarily if they conclude that their sentencing powers (up to six months' imprisonment for a single offence) are sufficient in the circumstances of that particular case. Otherwise, the magistrates will decline jurisdiction and commit the case for trial by jury at the Crown Court. However, in the event that the magistrates do accept jurisdiction, a defendant may nevertheless elect trial by jury.

- towards another
- conduct such as would cause fear
- the (hypothetical) person of reasonable firmness present at the scene
- mental element (*mens rea*).

Some of those elements have already been discussed in relation to riot and violent disorder. **1.97**
The reader is referred to those sections for a fuller examination of the issues. Where affray
presents different issues to other public order offences, these will be discussed below.
Sometimes it is necessary to break down those essential elements for the purposes of
discussion.

Uses or threatens

Like violent disorder but unlike riot, affray can be committed by the mere *threat* of unlaw- **1.98**
ful violence. Unlike both of them, for the offence of affray the use or threat of unlawful
violence cannot be directed towards *property*.[69]

In *I v DPP; M v DPP; H v DPP*;[70] the House of Lords held that, as a matter of law, the mere **1.99**
carrying of a dangerous weapon such as a petrol bomb, without more, *can* constitute a
threat of violence within the meaning of s 3(1). Whether it does so in any particular case is
a matter for the tribunal of fact.

Though threats of unlawful violence are sufficient, 'a threat cannot be made by the use of **1.100**
words alone' (s 3(3)). The fact that the experience was frightening does not make aggressive
words sufficient: *Robinson*.[71] For it to be a threat, therefore, there must also be some other
physical element of menace, such as aggressive body language or waving fists or the presence of an aggressive dog.

In *Dixon*,[72] the Court of Appeal held that setting a dog on police officers shouting 'go on, **1.101**
go on' was sufficient. Professor Ormerod comments that this case suggests that merely
saying 'I am going to set the dog on you' would not amount to an offence, but 'Seize
him Fido' would be—where Fido was a pit bull terrier whose performance would alarm a
bystander![73]

The cases of *Robinson* and *Dixon* are not easily distinguishable. The late Professor Sir John **1.102**
Smith QC, in his original commentary to *Dixon*,[74] tried to find a way through:

> It is submitted that setting a dog on another would be an assault, and, if the dog bit the other,
> a battery . . . An unresponsive dog would be a bit like an unloaded gun. The order to attack
> would be as ineffective as pulling the trigger but both acts might produce that apprehension
> of immediate violence which amounts to the *actus reus* of assault. Affray is not quite so clear.
> Pointing a gun or pulling trigger is clearly a sufficient act to amount to a threat of unlawful
> violence and amount to an affray; but if a man accompanied by a dog says to the animal,
> 'Seize him,' causing P to fear for his personal safety, can it really be said that this threat is not

---

[69] See s 8(a).
[70] [2002] 1 AC 285, 294, HL.
[71] [1993] Crim LR 581.
[72] [1993] Crim LR 579, CA.
[73] See Ormerod (ed), *Smith and Hogan Criminal Law*, p 1070. See also *Thind* [1999] Crim LR 842.
[74] [1993] Crim LR 579, 580–1.

'made by words alone'? And, so far as the answer to this question is concerned, does it make any difference that the dog is in an excitable state? The only thing the defendant has done is say those words. The presence of the dog is a circumstance that gives substance to the frightening effect of the words, it is not a thing done by its owner. However aggressive the tone and manner of uttering the words, they are still words alone: *Robinson.*

Possibly the solution is that 'the use of words alone' in s.3(3) is to be narrowly construed. The subsection is probably intended to prevent a mere threat to use force from constituting an affray—if it were otherwise, affray would swallow the lesser offence under s.4(1) of the Act. If that is the purpose of the subsection, it might be limited to that case. So, 'I am going to set the dog on you' would not be an offence, but 'Seize him Fido' would. The latter is not a mere threat to use violence, but the use or, Fido being unresponsive, attempted use, of violence. If this is right, it is arguable that the words of one accomplice to another, 'Hit him, Bill,' amount to more than 'words alone'; but it may be that a distinction can properly be taken between an intervening human act (which for some purposes breaks the chain of causation) and the operation of an instrument, animate (e.g. the dog) or inanimate (e.g. the gun).

Unlawful violence

1.103   As with riot and violent disorder, for the offence of affray to be committed the violence used or threatened must be *unlawful* violence. This preserves the defences of self-defence,[75] reasonable defence of another, and prevention of crime.[76]

Towards another

1.104   Unlike riot and violent disorder, affray *cannot* be committed against *property* (see s 8(a)). The violent conduct must be directed 'towards another'. That said, the definition of violent conduct in s 8 is wide so that it is not restricted to conduct causing or intended to cause injury or damage but includes any other violent conduct, such as throwing a punch or a missile which misses its target.

1.105   There must be 'another' person present at the scene towards whom the violent conduct is directed: see the House of Lords decision in *I v DPP; M v DPP; H v DPP.*[77] The facts of that case were as follows: In response to an anonymous telephone call the police arrived outside a block of residential flats where a large group of Asian youths had gathered. Some of the group were carrying primed petrol bombs, none of which were lit or brandished, and there was no fighting or shouting. When the group saw the police officers they dispersed immediately. The officers chased some of the group and arrested the three defendants, each of whom had thrown away a petrol bomb he had been carrying. In interview, one of the defendants stated that the group would have fought with a rival gang whose arrival they awaited and against whom the bombs were intended to be used. The defendants were charged with affray. The stipendiary magistrate found that, although the police thought that petrol bombs were being carried and one officer considered that there could be a disturbance, there had been no show or threat of violence and no member of the public had been at the scene. Nevertheless, the defendants were convicted and each appealed by way of case stated on the ground that his conduct had not amounted to 'a threat of unlawful

---

[75]   *R v Rothwell and Barton* [1993] Crim LR 626, CA. See also the statutory definition of self-defence in the Criminal Justice and Immigration Act 2008, s 76.

[76]   See Criminal Law Act 1967, s 3(1).

[77]   *I v DPP; M v DPP; H v DPP* [2002] 1 AC 285, HL.

violence towards another' within the meaning of s 3(1) of the 1986 Act. The Divisional Court, dismissing the appeals, concluded that overt carrying of the petrol bombs could constitute a threat of unlawful violence and did so in the circumstances since such a threat was directed to anyone in the vicinity including the police officers on their arrival at the scene.

The House of Lords allowed the appeals and quashed the convictions. Lord Hutton giving **1.106** the unanimous opinion of the House said that although the carrying of petrol bombs which were neither brandished nor waved might constitute a threat of unlawful violence for the purposes of an affray, in order to constitute that offence s 3(1) required such a threat to be directed 'towards another' person present at the scene; and that, accordingly, since the magistrate had found that only the police officers were present and, by implication, that the youths directed no threat towards them, the Divisional Court could not properly conclude that the defendants' conduct fell within s 3(1) of the Act.

However, whilst there must be 'another' person present at the scene towards whom the **1.107** violent conduct is directed, this should not be confused with the person of reasonable firmness who would be caused to fear for his personal safety as a result of the conduct[78]—who need not be, or be likely to be, present at the scene (s 3(4)). Again, the Act focuses on the innocent bystander, not the victim of the assault. It is to that issue we now turn.

A person of reasonable firmness present at the scene

The element of the person of reasonable firmness present at the scene is common to riot, **1.108** violent disorder, and affray. It is a concept which has caused much confusion. It is best and most starkly illustrated in dealing with affray.

Firstly, this person is a *hypothetical* being. Despite the reference in the words 'present at the **1.109** scene' in s 1(1), it is made clear in s 1(5) that 'no person of reasonable firmness need actually be, or be likely to be, present at the scene'.[79] Perhaps the key word in understanding the hypothetical nature of this person in s 1(1) is 'would'. Thus the violent conduct must be 'such as *would* cause a person of reasonable firmness present at the scene to fear for his personal safety'.

Secondly, the hypothetical reasonable bystander connotes an *objective* standard. Given that **1.110** no such bystander need be present, it is a matter of fact and degree for the tribunal of fact to assess whether, had there been such a bystander present at the scene, he would have been caused to fear for his personal safety.

Thirdly, this concept makes clear that riot, violent disorder, and affray are public order **1.111** offences aimed at protecting the bystander. There are other offences which protect the person at whom the violence is aimed. In *Davison*,[80] which was an affray case, police officers entered a house where there was a domestic argument ensuing. D picked up a knife and 'swiped' at a police officer, J. The appellant contended that the judge should have stopped

---

[78] *Thind* [1999] Crim LR 842.
[79] See also *R v Davison* [1992] Crim LR 31, CA.
[80] Ibid.

the trial as there was no case to answer—the conduct only ever having been directed at J. The appeal was dismissed. There was a case to answer and the judge had clearly directed the jury that they must be sure that the conduct, albeit directed at J, was such as would cause a hypothetical person present at the scene to fear for his personal safety. The case makes clear that the question for the jury is not whether a person of reasonable firmness in J's shoes would have been in fear, but whether the hypothetical bystander present in the room and witnessing D's conduct towards J, would have so feared for his own safety.[81]

1.112   In Professor Sir John Smith's commentary to *Davison*, he explains that the offence of affray envisages three persons: (i) the person using or threatening unlawful violence; (ii) the person towards whom the violence is directed; and (iii) a person of reasonable firmness who need not actually be, or likely to be, present at the scene who is caused to fear for *his own* personal safety.

1.113   Therefore, the person towards whom the violence is directed cannot also be the person of reasonable firmness present at the scene: *Sanchez*,[82] *Thind*.[83] The question then arises what is the position where a person of reasonable firmness witnesses what is clearly a 'one-on-one' fight with no threat to bystanders? The answer appears to be that this is not an affray—but it depends on the circumstances.

1.114   In *Blinkhorn*,[84] the appellant was attacked by his girlfriend who suspected him of infidelity. She walked into premises and slashed him across the face with a razor and then walked out. The appellant chased her out into the street, pushed her to the ground, knelt on her back and bashed her head against the pavement repeatedly. A bystander, S, got out of his car and went to help the woman. The appellant got up and walked away. S gave evidence that he was not in fear for his own safety as it was clear to him that this was a one-on-one fight and the appellant was not aggressive towards anyone else. He said that had he been in fear of his own safety, he would not have got out of his car but would simply have called the police from his mobile phone. The Court of Appeal quashed the conviction holding, on the facts, that this did not amount to an affray because an essential element was absent.

1.115   S, an actual bystander feared for the woman, not for himself. He or any other bystander would have had ample opportunity to distance themselves from the violence, if necessary. Otherwise the fearsome, hypothetical bystander was a lawyer's construct of no substance at all on the facts of the case.

1.116   The Court of Appeal in *Blinkhorn* approved Professor John Smith's commentary in *Davison* that affray is a public order offence and should not be used to supplement offences against the person:

> [Affray] is designed for the protection of the bystander. It is a public order offence. There are other offences for the protection of the person at whom the violence is aimed.

---

[81] In *Sanchez* (1996) 160 JP 321 the Divisional Court expressly approved the approach of Professor Sir John Smith in his commentary to *Davison* cited above.
[82] [1996] Crim LR 572.
[83] [1999] Crim LR 842.
[84] [2006] EWCA Crim 1416.

The definition of affray is very wide and the court agreed with defence counsel's submissions [in *Davison*] that care has to be taken to avoid extending it so widely that it would cover every offence of common assault. A common assault may be very trivial, so that it would not cause anyone to fear for his 'personal safety'.[85]

Yet *Davison* itself was a case where there was no bystander and it was clearly a one-to-one situation between D and the police officer J (see above). Why was this an affray, where *Blinkhorn* was not? The answer seems to depend on the facts of each case. Professor Smith's commentary provides the clue to the distinction. The person of reasonable firmness present at a fight taking place in a small room, with a man waving a knife around (as in *Davison*), might well be put in fear for his own personal safety (fearing he might be next). Whereas, the same person observing the same conduct in an open space would not (especially where the bystander had the opportunity to put further distance between himself and the fight, as in *Blinkhorn*).[86] **1.117**

In a trial on indictment, the judge is not required to direct the jury as to the attributes of the hypothetical person, or to give examples of reasonable firmness. *Rafferty*[87] was an affray case in which there was evidence from an actual bystander, a drunken former licensee, who was not particularly concerned about the violence he witnessed. The appellant contended that the jury should have been directed to regard this man as the yardstick by which to assess whether a reasonable bystander was put in fear. The Court of Appeal rejected that submission, doubting whether that witness was a particularly good example as a person of reasonable firmness, given his occupation and his condition at the time and his occupation, whether that witness was a particularly good example of a person of reasonable firmness. It is for the jury (or tribunal of fact) to assess the qualities of the reasonable person, perhaps envisaging themselves in the shoes of the bystander. However, as Lord Justice Sedley commented in *Gray*,[88] the bystander, though hypothetical, is not necessarily hypothetically a white person. **1.118**

Mental element (mens rea)

The mental element for affray is set out at s 6(2): 'A person is guilty of violent disorder or affray only if he intends to use or threaten violence or is aware that his conduct may be violent or threaten violence.' As with riot and violent disorder the mental element is either intent or awareness (see the section on riot above at 1.37 et seq for full discussion). Of course, the difference is that affray can be committed by threats of unlawful violence alone. Thus, the least mental element required by the offender in affray is the awareness that his conduct may be threatening.[89] **1.119**

As with other public order offences with the required mental element of 'awareness', the issue of an intoxicated defendant is provided for in s 6(5) and (6). **1.120**

---

[85] *Davison* [1992] Crim LR 31.
[86] See also *R v Plavecz* [2002] Crim LR 837.
[87] [2004] EWCA Crim 968.
[88] *Gray v DPP*, unreported, 1999, CO/5069/98.
[89] A direction as to the requisite mental element should normally be given to the jury: *Mann* [2002] EWCA Crim 3045.

Cumulative effect

1.121 As with violent disorder, it is the cumulative effect of the violent conduct on the hypotheti-cal bystander which is to be assessed. Of course, affray can be committed by a single offender, but where two or more persons use or threaten the unlawful violence, it is the conduct of them *taken together* that must be considered (s 3(2)).

Public or private place

1.122 Section 3(5) states: 'Affray may be committed in private as well as in public places.' There is no 'dwelling' exception, in contrast with offences under s 4 and s 5 (see discussion below in relation to s 4).

Alternative verdicts

1.123 Where the case is tried on indictment, the Act makes provision for an alternative verdict of guilty to s 4 of the Public Order Act 1986 (threatening, abusive, or insulting words or behaviour) in the event that the jury acquit a defendant of affray. Section 7(3) provides:

> If on the trial on indictment of a person charged with violent disorder or affray the jury find him not guilty of the offence charged, they may (without prejudice to section 6(3) of the Criminal Law Act 1967) find him guilty of an offence under section 4.

Sentencing

1.124 A person guilty of affray is liable on conviction on indictment to imprisonment for a term not exceeding three years or a fine or both, or on summary conviction to imprisonment for a term not exceeding six months or a fine not exceeding the statutory maximum or both.[90] Affray is a specified offence in Schedule 15 of the Criminal Justice Act 2003. As such the 'dangerous offenders' provisions of the Criminal Justice Act 2003 apply, as amended on 14 July 2008 by the Criminal and Immigration Act 2008. In short, it is open to the court to pass an extended sentence for affray.[91]

1.125 There is no modern guideline sentencing authority for affray. Guidance in respect of factors to be considered can be found in *R v Keys and others*[92] though that case was decided under the common law, before the 1986 Act came into effect. In *Keys*, it was said that in cases of very serious affray where it is plain that there was some measure of preparation, some measure of central organization and direction, those who are proved to be organizers and ringleaders can expect heavy custodial sentences. If an offender is convicted of other offences such as wounding or if he has shown to have manufactured, thrown, or been in possession of petrol bombs, different considerations will apply to those set out below. For organizers or ringleaders sentences will be towards the top end of the sentencing bracket

---

[90] Public Order Act 1986, s 3(7).
[91] A full examination of the complex provisions relating to dangerous offenders is beyond the scope of this work. A useful introductory guide is provided on the website of the Sentencing Guidelines Council: <http://www.sentencing-guidelines.gov.uk/docs/Dangerous%20Offenders%20-%20Guide%20for%20 Sentencers%20and%20Practitioners.pdf>.
[92] (1986) 8 Cr App R (S) 444.

(of three years),[93] apart from any sentences imposed upon them for other specific offences arising from the incident. In a prolonged and vicious attack upon the police, any participant, however slight his involvement, can expect a sentence of at least eighteen months to two years. The carrying of weapons and/or throwing of missiles ought properly to be reflected in an increase in that minimum.

In relation to cases of affray dealt with in the magistrates' court, the Sentencing Guidelines **1.126** Council[94] publishes *Magistrates' Court Sentencing Guidelines*.[95] These identify three starting points (for a first time offender pleading not guilty) according to the nature of the activity, each starting point having a defined range, which is adjusted according to the non-exhaustive list of aggravating and mitigating features. Offender mitigation is considered after the court has reached a provisional sentence based on its assessment of offence seriousness.

At the lowest level—a brief offence involving low-level violence and where no substantial **1.127** fear was created—the starting point will be a low-level community order, with a sentencing range from a fine to a medium level community order. The next level up deals with offences where there was a degree of fighting or violence that caused substantial fear. Such offences will attract sentences starting at a high level community order, with a sentencing range being a medium level community order to twelve weeks' custody. The higher level concerns fights involving a weapons and/or throwing objects or conduct causing risk of serious injury. Such offences will attract a starting point of eighteen weeks' custody, with a sentencing range of twelve weeks' custody to committal to the Crown Court. Aggravating factors are identified as follows: those indicating higher culpability are group action, threats, lengthy incident; those indicating greater degree of harm are vulnerable person(s) present, injuries caused, damage to property. Mitigating factors indicating lower culpability are as follows: did not start the trouble, provocation, stopped as soon as police arrived.

E. Fear or Provocation of Violence: Public Order Act 1986, s 4

Historical development

The Public Order Act 1986 (s 9(2)(d)) abolished the offence of threatening behaviour **1.128** (conduct conducive to breaches of the peace) under s 5 of the old Public Order Act 1936. It replaced it with a revised and extended offence of causing fear or provocation of violence under the new s 4. The new offence retained much of the old language of threatening, abusive, or insulting words or behaviour. However, it jettisoned the concept of a 'breach of the peace', replacing it with the notion of fear or provocation of violence. It also extended the reach of the offence into private places, though not dwellings.

---

[93] In *Keys*, it was suggested that sentence in the range of seven years' imprisonment and upwards were appropriate for organizers or ringleaders. Of course that case was decided under the common law, before the 1986 Act came into force and with it the maximum sentence of three years.

[94] See <http://www.sentencing-guidelines.gov.uk/>.

[95] Effective as of 4 August 2008.

1.129   The old offence under s 5 of the Public Order Act 1936 had been one of the most frequently used of all public order offences. It was also one of the most reviled. It was described by one commentator as 'a form of dragnet provision against those whose behaviour is considered by the police and the courts as worthy of punishment'.[96] In the 1984–5 miners' strike the charge was laid against some 4,000 striking miners, often for little more than shouting 'scab'.

1.130   Indeed, in submissions on the draft 1936 Bill, the National Council for Civil Liberties (now Liberty) had warned against the catch-all nature of similar offences (the predecessor to the now repealed s 5) and presciently called for its total abolition:

> The Council's experience is that a strained interpretation is frequently put on this offence by magistrates. For example, an unemployed man was fined some years ago for using the words: 'Give us bread'. The Council considers, therefore, that any extension of this vague and elastic offence is dangerous and they would, indeed, welcome its total repeal.

1.131   The Law Commission thus recommended the repeal of s 5 of the 1936 Act and the abolition of the common law offence of unlawful assembly. It proposed dividing up unlawful assembly into the new offences of violent disorder (for very serious incidents) and the new s 4 (for more minor incidents).[97]

1.132   For the Law Commission, the essence of s 4 was to penalize the use of *threats* rather than the use of actual violence.[98] However, the Commissioners did not want to restrict the offence to situations where a defendant's behaviour caused a person to fear violence to himself. They also sought to include instances where a person was caused to fear immediate unlawful violence would be used against him *or another*.

Definition under the Public Order Act 1986, s 4

1.133   The summary only offence of causing fear or provocation of violence is defined in s 4 of the Public Order Act 1986 as follows:

(1)   A person is guilty of an offence if he—
  (a)   uses towards another person threatening, abusive or insulting words or behaviour, or
  (b)   distributes or displays to another person any writing, sign or other visible representation which is threatening, abusive or insulting,
  with intent to cause that person to believe that immediate unlawful violence will be used against him or another by any person, or to provoke the immediate use of unlawful violence by that person or another, or whereby that person is likely to believe that such violence will be used or it is likely that such violence will be provoked.

(2)   An offence under this section may be committed in a public or a private place, except that no offence is committed where the words or behaviour are used, or the writing, sign or other visible representation is distributed or displayed, by a person inside a dwelling and the other person is also inside that or another dwelling.

(3)   . . .

---

[96]   A Dickey [1971] Crim LR 265.
[97]   Law Com 123, paras 5.40–41.
[98]   Ibid, para 5.40.

(4) A person guilty of an offence under this section is liable on summary conviction to imprisonment for a term not exceeding 6 months or a fine not exceeding level 5 on the standard scale or both.

The CPS Charging Standards describe the following types of conduct as examples which may at least be capable of amounting to threatening, abusive, or insulting words or behaviour: **1.134**

- threats made towards innocent bystanders or individuals carrying out public service duties;

- the throwing of missiles by a person taking part in a demonstration or other public gathering where no injury is caused;

- scuffles or incidents of violence or threats of violence committed in the context of a brawl (such as in or in the vicinity of a public house);

- incidents which do not justify a charge of assault where an individual is picked on by a gang.[99]

Jurisdiction

The offence under s 4(1) is, by virtue of s 4(4) triable summarily only—which means it may only be tried in the magistrates' court. The racially aggravated form of the offence is triable either way (Crime and Disorder Act 1998, s 31(1)(a) and (4)—see Chapter 2 at 2.88 et seq). If, on trial on indictment, the jury find the defendant not guilty of the offences of violent disorder, affray, or the racially aggravated form of the s 4 offence, they may find him guilty of the basic offence of s 4 of the Public Order Act 1986. **1.135**

Essential elements of the offence

The section creates one offence but a variety of different ways in which it can be committed.[100] Therefore, care must be taken in formulating the charge so that the defendant knows how the prosecution case is being put. However, it is possible to discern a number of essential elements: **1.136**

- uses towards another person
- threatening, abusive, or insulting
- words or behaviour
- distribution or display (alternative form)
- mental element (*mens rea*).

Uses towards another

The threat must be direct, not indirect, because threatening words or behaviour must be used *towards another* (s 4(1)). That means that the prosecution must, firstly, specify who that other person was and, secondly, prove that the conduct was in the presence of that other person and directed towards that other person. **1.137**

---

[99] See <http://www.cps.gov.uk/legal/p_to_r/public_order_offences/#_Section_4>.
[100] *Winn v DPP* (1992) 156 JP 881.

1.138 In *Atkin v DPP*,[101] two Customs and Excise officers, accompanied by a bailiff, went to the defendant's farm to recover outstanding value added tax. The two officers conducted their business in the farmhouse while the bailiff waited in a car which was parked in the farmyard, such that the bailiff was unable to hear any of the conversation inside the farmhouse. When the officers ascertained from the defendant that he was unable to pay the outstanding VAT, they informed him that the bailiff would have to enter the farmhouse to distrain on his goods. The defendant replied: 'If the bailiff gets out of the car he's a dead un.' No threats were made to the two officers. One of the officers left the farmhouse and told the bailiff that the defendant had threatened him. The bailiff did not get out of the car as he felt threatened and all three then left the farm. The justices were of opinion that threatening words were used in the farmhouse. The defendant did not want the bailiff to enter his house and therefore the defendant must have intended the officers to convey the threat to the bailiff in a bid to keep him out. The justices then convicted the defendant of having used threatening words towards the bailiff with intent to cause him to believe that immediate unlawful violence would be used against him.

1.139 The Court of Appeal allowed the appeal and quashed the conviction. Taylor LJ said that 'the phrase "uses towards another person" means, in the context of section 4(1)(a) "uses in the presence of and in the direction of another person directly." I do not think, looking at the section as a whole, the words can bear the meaning "concerning another person" or "in regard to another person."'

1.140 Thus the threat cannot be carried out indirectly or carried vicariously by another to its intended recipient.

1.141 As a result, s 4 is the only offence in the calendar of public order offences which requires the conduct to be directed towards a specific 'victim'. This may be contrasted with riot, violent disorder, and affray where, whomever is the subject of violence, the offence is concerned with the effect of violent conduct on the hypothetical bystander—the person of reasonable firmness present at the scene.

1.142 However, whilst the prosecution must prove that the threatening words or behaviour were issued in the presence and hearing of another, it is not always necessary for that other person to be called to give evidence. In *Swanston v DPP*,[102] it was held that it would be open to the prosecution to rely solely on the evidence of a bystander and to invite the inference that the victim did perceive what was said and done by the appellant.

Threatening, abusive, or insulting

1.143 The concepts of 'threatening, abusive or insulting' have been the subject of many criminal appeals. Whether the conduct complained of attains those qualities seems to be governed by an objective test. As Professor Ormerod has pointed out, this is an element of the *actus reus*. And yet, as a matter of common sense, one would think that surely those terms connote a mental element. The Act, however, assumes that the conduct (or material) may be threatening, abusive or insulting even though there is no evidence that the actor (or author)

---

[101] (1989) 89 Cr App R 199, DC.
[102] The Times, 23 January 1997, (1997) 161 JP 203.

intended it to have, or was even aware that it might have, that quality. The effect, concludes Professor Ormerod, is that the Act creates 'extremely harsh offences'.[103]

The terms 'threatening, abusive or insulting' were retained from the repealed offence under **1.144** s 5 of the Public Order Act 1936. As a result, some of the cases dealing with those words pre-date the 1986 Act. This is important because what might objectively have been 'threatening, abusive or insulting' in 1939 may no longer be so in 2009.

The terms 'threatening, abusive or insulting' are to be given their ordinary meaning and the **1.145** courts have said that it is not helpful to turn to dictionary definitions because 'an ordinary sensible man knows an insult when he sees it or hears it'.[104]

Thus, whether the conduct is 'threatening, abusive or insulting' is a question for the tribu- **1.146** nal of fact. It is not a matter of law. As Lord Reid explained in *Brutus v Cozens*:[105]

> Vigorous and it may be distasteful or unmannerly speech or behaviour is permitted so long as it does not go beyond any of these limits. It must not be threatening. It must not be abusive. It must not be insulting. I see no reason why any of these should be construed as having a specially wide or specially narrow meaning. They are easily recognisable by the ordinary man.[106]

The famous case of *Brutus v Cozens* concerned anti-apartheid protesters at the Wimbledon **1.147** lawn tennis championships in 1971. During a doubles tennis match, the appellant stepped onto the court. He began trying to distribute leaflets about the evils of the apartheid government in South Africa. He attempted to give one to a player, who was South African, and then sat down on the court and blew a whistle. With that more people from the crowd invaded the court, some bearing banners and placards protesting against apartheid. Play was disrupted for a few minutes until the police arrived and arrested the protesters. The prosecution's case was that the conduct was 'insulting' to the crowd of spectators. The justices found, as a matter of fact, that the behaviour was not 'insulting'. On appeal by the prosecution, the Divisional Court held that 'insulting' behaviour was that which affronted other people and evidenced a disrespect or contempt for their rights. On that basis, given the findings of the justices, insulting behaviour had been established and it was remitted back to the magistrates' court. The House of Lords held the Divisional Court was wrong. The justices' decision was one of fact, not law, just as would be the decision of a jury. The finding of fact that this was not insulting was not an unreasonable one.

A number of early cases can illustrate the ambit of the terms, but it must be stressed that it **1.148** is a question of fact for the tribunal. In *Bryan v Robinson*,[107] it was said that words or behaviour might be annoying without being insulting. That case simply involved a woman touting for business outside a café. In *R v Ambrose*,[108] it was said that words which are rude and offensive are not necessarily insulting. The Court of Appeal in that case warned that the

---

[103] David Ormerod (ed), *Smith and Hogan Criminal Law* (2008, 12th edn) p 1071.
[104] *Brutus v Cozens* [1973] AC 854, 862 per Lord Reid.
[105] Ibid.
[106] Ibid, p 862.
[107] [1960] 1 WLR 506.
[108] (1973) 58 Cr App R 539, CA.

section of the Act (then the old s 5 of the 1936 Act) should not be misused. In *Parkin v Norman*,[109] it was held that insulting behaviour was not to be construed as offensive or disgusting behaviour (two men masturbating in a public lavatory where they intended only each other to witness the conduct, but were caught by an undercover policeman). However, as already pointed out these cases are merely illustrative. As Lord Kilbrandon said in *Brutus v Cozens*:

> It would be unwise, in my opinion, to attempt to lay down any positive rules for the recognition of insulting behaviour as such, since the circumstances in which the application of the rules would be called for are almost infinitely variable; the most that can be done is to lay down limits, as was done in *Bryan v Robinson* (ante), in order to ensure that the statute is not interpreted more widely than its terms will bear.[110]

1.149 Unfortunately, it seems that Lord Kilbrandon's words have not been heeded and in the years since the 1986 Act was passed, the section has been interpreted very widely indeed. In *Masterson v Holden*[111] (a case from 1986 just before the Act came into force), two gay men were standing by a bus stop in Oxford Street at about 2 am kissing, cuddling, and one was fondling the other, both appearing to be unaware of other persons in the vicinity. Two other young men walked past, followed by two young women, who gasped. The young men then walked back to the defendants and one shouted: 'You filthy sods. How dare you in front of our girls?' The defendants were arrested and charged with using insulting behaviour.[112] The justices, being of opinion that the defendants' behaviour was insulting, particularly from the way in which the witnesses had *reacted*, and that a breach of the peace might have been occasioned, convicted the defendants. The Divisional Court upheld the conviction and stated *per curiam*: 'Overt homosexual conduct in a public street, indeed overt heterosexual conduct, may well be considered by many persons to be objectionable and may well be regarded by another person, particularly by a young woman, as conduct which insults her by suggesting that she is somebody who would find such conduct in public acceptable herself.' Surely, this case must now be consigned to the dustbin of history. It is very doubtful that such a case today would survive the Human Rights Act 1998. Moreover, given the essential element that the conduct must be directed 'towards another' it is doubtful whether the case would be made out under s 4 of the Public Order Act 1986.

Distribute or display

1.150 It is an alternative offence under s 4(1)(b) to distribute or display to another person any writing, sign, or other visible representation which is threatening, abusive, or insulting—with the requisite state of mind (see mental element below).

1.151 The term 'writing' includes typing, printing, lithography, photography, and other modes of representing or reproducing words in a visible form.[113]

---

[109] [1983] QB 92.
[110] [1973] AC 854, 866.
[111] [1986] 1 WLR 1017.
[112] At that time an offence contrary to the Metropolitan Police Act 1839, s 54(13)—'using insulting behaviour whereby a breach of the peace might have been occasioned'.
[113] Interpretation Act 1978, s 5 and Sch 1.

The term 'display' appears to connote an element of public showing—especially when read in the context of 'distribute or display' and in conjunction with s 4(2) which states, so far as is relevant, 'no offence is committed where . . . the writing or sign or other visible representation is distributed or displayed, by a person inside a dwelling and the other person is also inside that or another dwelling'. **1.152**

Thus, in *Chappell v DPP*,[114] the Divisional Court held that magistrates were correct to decide that the posting of an envelope, with writing containing abusive or insulting words concealed inside it, through the private letter box of another's home could not amount to a 'display'.[115] **1.153**

Mental element (mens rea)

The requisite mental element for an offence under s 4 is complex and divided into two parts. Firstly, there must be an element of intention or awareness for each in relation to the quality of the words or behaviour used. Section 6(3) of the Act provides: **1.154**

> A person is guilty of an offence under section 4 only if he intends his words or behaviour, or the writing, sign or other visible representation, to be threatening, abusive or insulting, or is aware that it may be threatening, abusive or insulting.

Secondly, and in addition, there must be an element of anticipated reaction by the other person. Section 4(1) provides that the acts in s 4(1)(a) or (b) must be committed **1.155**

> with intent to cause that person to believe that immediate unlawful violence will be used against him or another by any person, or to provoke the immediate use of unlawful violence by that person or another, or whereby that person is likely to believe that such violence will be used or it is likely that such violence will be provoked.

The second required mental element may be achieved in one of four alternative ways. The first two require intent (the 'intent' clauses), the other two do not (the 'whereby' clauses). Thus, the offence can be committed where, *in addition* to the intent under s 6(3) **1.156**

(a) the defendant *intended* to cause the other person to believe that immediate unlawful violence will be *used* against him or another; or

(b) the defendant *intended* to *provoke* the immediate use of unlawful violence by the other peson or another; or,

(c) *whereby* the other person was *likely* to believe that such (immediate unlawful) violence will be *used*; or,

(d) *whereby* it was *likely* that such (immediate unlawful) violence will be *provoked*.

As will be appreciated the first two of those options provide for subjective intent. The latter two 'whereby it was likely' options provide for an objective assessment. **1.157**

---

[114] (1988) 89 Cr App R 82.
[115] This case was decided before the coming into force of the Malicious Communications Act 1988. It is likely that such conduct would now be an offence under s 1 of that Act (amended by Criminal Justice and Police Act 2001, s 43, to include 'electronic communication' such as email).

1.158 It should also be noted that all of these variations are concerned with the anticipation of violence (*will be* used or *will be* provoked). The actual use of violence need not be proved, only the causing of anticipatory fear that it will be used.

1.159 Because of the variety of ways in which this offence can be committed, the prosecution should be careful to specify the way it puts its case so that the defence knows what it has to meet. If there is a substantial discrepancy between the particulars alleged and the facts found, it is likely to result in the conviction being quashed.[116]

1.160 As with other public order offences, the term 'violence' has a very broad meaning as provided by s 8. It includes violent conduct towards property as well as violent conduct towards persons, and it is not restricted to conduct causing or intended to cause injury or damage but includes any other violent conduct (for example, throwing at or towards a person a missile of a kind capable of causing injury which does not hit or falls short).

1.161 However, as with other public order offences, it must be *unlawful* violence. Accordingly, the defences of self-defence, reasonable defence of another, and prevention of crime are preserved.[117]

1.162 The term '*immediate* unlawful violence' has caused some difficulties. It does not mean 'instantaneous' but connotes proximity in time and in causation.[118] The Law Commission indicated that in their opinion, in replacing s 5 of the 1936 Act, the new offence should include an element of immediacy; in the case of behaviour provoking the use of violence, it must be the immediate use of such violence.[119] Indeed, the Divisional Court in *R v Horseferry Road Stipendiary, ex parte Siadatan*[120] said that it was most regrettable that the parliamentary draftsmen, when drafting s 4 did not achieve the same precision and clarity as the Law Commissioners had recommended. The Law Commission gave an example of the ambit of immediacy envisaged: A gang in one part of town uttering threats directed at persons, for example, of a particular ethnic or religious group resident in another part of town. The Law Commission report stated that this would be an offence even though the threat would not be capable of being performed until the gang arrived in the other part of town.

1.163 The case of *R v Horseferry Road Stipendiary, ex parte Siadatan*[121] concerned the publication of Salman Rushie's book *The Satanic Verses* in the late 1980s. Mr Siadatan sought to bring a private prosecution against Penguin Books Ltd for distributing the book which, he alleged, contained abusive and insulting writing whereby it was likely that unlawful violence would be provoked. The District Judge refused to issue a summons because Mr Siadatan had failed to demonstrate the likelihood of immediate unlawful violence as required by s 4(1). The Divisional Court upheld that ruling stating:

> It seems to us that the word 'immediate' does not mean 'instantaneous'; that a relatively short time interval may elapse between the act which is threatening, abusive or insulting and the

---

[116] *Winn v DPP* (1992) 156 JP 881.
[117] *R v Rothwell and Barton* [1993] Crim LR 626, CA; *R v Afzal* [1993] Crim LR 791.
[118] *R v Horseferry Road Stipendiary, ex parte Siadatan (DC)* [1991] 1 QB 260.
[119] Law Com 123, paras 5.43 and 5.44.
[120] *R v Horseferry Road Stipendiary*, 268 per Watkin LJ.
[121] Ibid, 260.

unlawful violence. 'Immediate' connotes proximity in time and proximity in causation; that it is likely that violence will result within a relatively short period of time and without any other intervening occurrence.[122]

However, the clarity of that decision was somewhat diluted in the case of *DPP v Ramos*.[123] **1.164** Mr Ramos sent two letters to an Asian community advice centre stating that a bombing hate campaign would ensue and that, if he was seen, the recipient would be killed. He was charged with distributing to another person letters containing writings which were threatening with the intent to cause that person to believe that immediate unlawful violence would be used against him contrary to s 4(1)(b). The District Judge ruled that as the letters were silent as to when the bomb would be detonated, it followed that it might be at some unspecified time in the future and as such lacked the element of immediacy required by the statute. The Divisional Court allowed the appeal by the DPP, holding:

> It was the state of mind of the victim which was crucial rather than the statistical risk of violence actually occurring within a short space of time. Provided, therefore, the victims believed and were likely to believe that something could happen at any time, there was a case to answer.

It is submitted that this judgment is wrong both in respect of its analysis of immediacy **1.165** ('at any time' cannot amount to 'immediate') and in relation to the mental element. In his Criminal Law Review commentary to the *Ramos* case, Professor Sir John Smith QC explained:

> In both assault and the offence under s.4 it is not enough that the victim is immediately put in fear. He must be put in fear of immediate violence, which is not the same thing. In the present case it is easy to understand that the recipients of the letters were 'immediately concerned for their own and others safety' as the magistrate found. It is less easy to see that it was open to him to infer that they feared immediate violence. . . . [This] is very far removed from the traditional examples of assault where the victim flinches from the upraised fist, the drawn sword or the charging horse . . .

> The court remarks that in both the 1986 and the 1861 (s.47 assault ABH) offences, 'it is the state of mind of the victims which is crucial rather than the statistical risk of violence actually occurring within a short space of time.' The state of mind of the victim is indeed an element in assault, *but not in either variety of the offence under s.4. The victim's actual apprehension can be no more than evidence of the defendant's intent or of the likelihood that the victim would believe that such violence would be used.*[124] (emphasis added)

Public or private place

As with other public order offences, the offence under s 4 can be committed in both public **1.166** and private places. However, s 4(2) provides an exception:

> no offence is committed where the words or behaviour are used, or the writing, sign or other visible representation is distributed or displayed, by a person inside a dwelling and the other person is also inside that or another dwelling.

---

[122] Ibid, p 269. See also *Valentine v DPP* [1997] COD 339, in which the Divisional Court held that the justices had been entitled to find the accused guilty where his threats caused a woman to fear 'immediate' violence the next time she went to work, but only because she might have gone to work the same night as the threats had been made.
[123] [2000] Crim LR 768.
[124] Ibid, 769.

1.167 An example of this in practice was the case of *Atkin v DPP*[125] (see above 1.138). Mr Atkin had invited the two customs officers over the threshold into his farmhouse, so there could be no offence since all three were inside the dwelling and the bailiff was unaware of the threats being made. To illustrate the point, had Mr Atkin issued the threat from his door-step (inside the dwelling) to the bailiff who was standing in the farmyard (outside the dwelling) and within earshot, then the offence would have been made out. Yet if Mr Atkin had issued the threat from inside his farmhouse towards the bailiff was within earshot but inside a neighbouring dwelling at the time, then no offence would be made out. The courts have held that communal parts of a block of flats, such as the landing and staircase, are not part of a dwelling.[126]

1.168 This 'dwelling' exception was clearly designed to remove from the ambit of 'public order' offences, those purely domestic disputes which could be dealt with as assaults.

1.169 For the purposes of public order offences, section 8 of the 1986 Act defines 'dwelling' as follows:

> 'dwelling' means any structure or part of a structure occupied as a person's home or as other living accommodation (whether the occupation is separate or shared with others) but does not include any part not so occupied, and for this purpose 'structure' includes a tent, caravan, vehicle, vessel or other temporary or movable structure.

1.170 In *R v CF*,[127] the Court of Appeal held that a police cell does not constitute a home or living accommodation and so the offence can be committed therein. That decision seemed to turn on the temporary nature of detention in a police cell. Professor Ormerod, in his *Criminal Law Review* commentary questioned whether, given the numbers currently housed, more than temporarily, in police cells there is really no reasonable argument on the point, as the Court suggested.[128] Moreover, surely one can argue that a prison cell is a dwelling or 'other living accommodation'.

F. Harassment, Alarm, or Distress: s 5

Historical development

1.171 The offence under s 5 was the most controversial of the statutory offences in the Public Order Act 1986 both before and during the passage of the Bill. Whereas the repealed s 5 of the Public Order Act 1936 (replaced by Public Order Act 1986, s 4) was considered the lowest-level public order offence prior to the 1986 Act, the offence under s 5 is more widely drawn and extends the criminal law into areas of annoyance, disturbance, and inconvenience. In particular it covers behaviour which falls short of violence or the threat or fear of violence.

---

[125] (1989) 89 Cr App R 199, DC.
[126] *Rukwira v DPP* [1993] Crim LR 882.
[127] [2007] 1 WLR 1021.
[128] [2007] Crim LR 574–5.

Indeed, it appears that the offence was something of an after-thought inserted into the Bill **1.172**
as a sweeping-up clause. It was not a recommendation of the Law Commission, nor did it
feature in the Green Paper.[129] The White Paper only put forward the proposal 'tentatively',
suggesting that:

> It is not easy to define the offence in a manner which conforms with the normally precise
> definitions of the criminal law, but which at the same time is sufficiently general to catch the
> variety of conduct aimed at. The Government recognises that there would be justifiable
> objections to a wide extension of the criminal law which might catch conduct not deserving
> of criminal sanctions.[130]

Today, s 5 is commonly used as a dragnet offence to catch all types of low-level anti-social **1.173**
behaviour.

Definition under the Public Order Act 1986, s 5

The offence is defined in s 5 as follows: **1.174**

   (1) A person is guilty of an offence if he—
      (a) uses threatening, abusive or insulting words or behaviour, or disorderly behaviour, or
      (b) displays any writing, sign or other visible representation which is threatening, abu-
         sive or insulting,
within the hearing or sight of a person likely to be caused harassment, alarm or distress
      thereby.
   (2) An offence under this section may be committed in a public or a private place, except
      that no offence is committed where the words or behaviour are used, or the writing, sign
      or other visible representation is displayed, by a person inside a dwelling and the other
      person is also inside that or another dwelling.
   (3) It is a defence for the accused to prove—
      (a) that he had no reason to believe that there was any person within hearing or sight
         who was likely to be caused harassment, alarm or distress, or
      (b) that he was inside a dwelling and had no reason to believe that the words or behav-
         iour used, or the writing, sign or other visible representation displayed, would be
         heard or seen by a person outside that or any other dwelling, or
      (c) that his conduct was reasonable.
   (4) . . . A constable may arrest a person without warrant if—
      (a) he engages in offensive conduct which the constable warns him to stop, and
      (b) he engages in further offensive conduct immediately or shortly after the warning.
   (5) In subsection (4) 'offensive conduct' means conduct the constable reasonably suspects
      to constitute an offence under this section, and the conduct mentioned in paragraph (a)
      and the further conduct need not be of the same nature.
   (6) A person guilty of an offence under this section is liable on summary conviction to a fine
      not exceeding level 3 on the standard scale.

The CPS Charging Standard describes the following types of conduct as examples which **1.175**
may at least be capable of amounting to disorderly behaviour:

- causing a disturbance in a residential area or common part of a block of flats;
- persistently shouting abuse or obscenities at passers-by;

---

[129] Green Paper, Cmnd 7891.
[130] White Paper, Cmnd 9510, para 3.26.

37

- pestering people waiting to catch public transport or otherwise waiting in a queue;
- rowdy behaviour in a street late at night which might alarm residents or passers-by, especially those who may be vulnerable, such as the elderly or members of an ethnic minority group;
- causing a disturbance in a shopping precinct or other area to which the public have access or might otherwise gather; and
- bullying.[131]

1.176 The Charging Standard comments that, 'Section 5 should be used in cases which amount to less serious incidents of anti-social behaviour. Where violence has been used, it is not normally appropriate to charge an offence under section 5 unless the physical behaviour amounts merely to pushing or undirected lashing out of a type likely to cause no more than a glancing blow, minor bruising or grazing. Such conduct may also be classified as disorderly and suitable for a charge under section 91 Criminal Justice Act 1967 in appropriate circumstances.'[132]

Jurisdiction

1.177 The offence under s 5 is, by virtue of s 5(6), triable summarily only—as is the racially or religiously aggravated form of the s 5 offence (see Crime and Disorder Act, s 31(1)(c) and (4)). This means that both forms of the offence may only be tried in the magistrates' court.

Essential elements of the offence

1.178 The offence under s 5(1) is wider than that under s 4 because it also includes conduct which is not threatening but merely 'disorderly'. No apprehension of fear or violence is required. Instead, the conduct must merely be likely to cause harassment, alarm, or distress.

1.179 There are a number of essential elements of the offence, some of which are in the alternative. We shall examine each below:

- uses threatening, abusive, or insulting words or behaviour;
- *or* disorderly behaviour;
- *or* displays any writing, sign, or other visible representation which is threatening, abusive, or insulting;
- *and* is within the hearing or sight of a person;
- *likely* to be caused harassment, alarm, or distress thereby;
- mental element (*mens rea*).

Threatening, abusive, or insulting words or behaviour

1.180 Those terms have already been analysed in relation to section 4 of the Public Order Act 1986 (see above at 1.143 et seq). They are to be given their ordinary meaning and are for

---

[131] See <http://www.cps.gov.uk/legal/p_to_r/public_order_offences/#_Section_5>.
[132] Ibid.

the tribunal of fact to determine.[133] For further discussion of the term 'abusive' in the context of section 5, see *R(DPP) v Humphrey*[134] and *Southard v DPP*.[135]

Disorderly behaviour

'Disorderly' is not defined in the Act. It is to be given its ordinary, everyday meaning without any resort to dictionaries or synonyms. The key authority on the point is *Chambers and Edwards v DPP*.[136] In that case, the appellants were demonstrators who persistently prevented a surveyor from using his theodolite by blocking its infra-red beam with their bodies or placards. The Crown Court concluded that their behaviour caused the surveyor harassment. Whilst there had been no threat or fear of violence, the surveyor had been inconvenienced and annoyed by their activities.   **1.181**

The Divisional Court held that no element of apprehension about one's personal safety was necessary for there to be harassment. The term 'disorderly' was to be given its ordinary meaning and it was a question for the tribunal of fact to determine.   **1.182**

The Divisional Court said that 'disorderly behaviour' was a separate, alternative constituent element from the use of threatening, abusive, or insulting words, or behaviour. It is intended to cover conduct which is not necessarily threatening, abusive, or insulting. Thus there need be no threatening, abusive, or insulting character to the behaviour for it to be disorderly. It was not necessary for the prosecution to prove any feeling of insecurity, in an apprehensive sense, on the part of any member of the public or any likelihood of that, to establish disorderly conduct in a harassment case.   **1.183**

Within the sight or hearing

This term requires careful analysis. The element is that the conduct must take place within the sight or hearing of a person *likely* to be caused harassment, alarm, or distress thereby. The prosecution do not have to prove that the words were *actually* heard or seen by a person. There must be a potential victim present rather than a hypothetical one, but it is no part of the offence that the conduct was directed at that other person. Thus it is sufficient that the words or conduct took place in the sight or hearing of a person who was likely to be caused harassment, alarm, or distress ie a person was present who was *able* have seen or heard the conduct.[137]   **1.184**

In *DPP v Orum*[138] the defendant was engaged in a drunken altercation with his girlfriend in the street in the early hours of the morning. Two police officers intervened and the defendant told one of the constables to 'fuck off'. The Divisonal Court held there was nothing to exclude a police constable from the category of people who could be caused harassment, alarm, or distress by the words or conduct to which s 5 applied, although it could not be assumed that every police officer was likely to be caused harassment, alarm, or distress   **1.185**

---

[133] *Brutus v Cozens* [1973] AC 854.
[134] [2005] EWHC 822 (Admin).
[135] [2006] EWHC 3449 (Admin).
[136] [1995] Crim LR 896.
[137] *Taylor v DPP* (2006) 170 JP 485.
[138] [1989] 1 WLR 88.

and that it was a question of fact in each individual case whether the words or conduct were capable of having that effect.

Harassment, alarm, or distress

1.186 Harassment, alarm, and distress are alternatives. However, as will be obvious, they do not mean the same thing. As we saw above in the case of *Chambers and Edwards v DPP*[139] 'harassment' does not demand any element of apprehension about one's personal safety. By contrast, in *Southard v DPP*[140] it was held that 'distress', by its very nature, involves an element of emotional disturbance or upset.

1.187 However, whilst these terms are alternatives, it may not be helpful to read them disjunctively. In *R(R) v DPP*[141] the Divisional Court, dealing in that case with an offence under section 4A said of 'distress':

> It is part of a trio of words: harassment, alarm or distress. They are expressed as alternatives, but in combination they give a sense of the mischief which the section is aimed at preventing. They are relatively strong words befitting an offence which may carry imprisonment [in the case of sections 4 and 4A] or a substantial fine. I would hold that the word 'distress' in this context requires emotional disturbance or upset. The statute does not attempt to define the degree required. It does not have to be grave but nor should the requirement be trivialised. There has to be something which amounts to real emotional disturbance or upset.

1.188 The case of *R(R) v DPP* is illustrative of the need for some real emotional disturbance, as well as for police officers to have a broad back. R was a 12-year-old boy, who was out with his sister well after midnight. Police officers stopped and arrested his sister on an allegation of criminal damage. R reacted badly and shouted abuse at the police officers and carried on after being told to be quiet. As the police left the scene in a police van, he made masturbatory gestures at the officers in the van and shouted, 'wankers'. At trial, the arresting officer said he had been offended by the remark but not annoyed. He said that he found it 'distressing' that a young boy was out at such a late hour and acting in that manner. In the Divisional Court, Toulson J said:

> It was a perfectly understandable use of English for the officer to say that he found it distressing that a small boy of 12 should be behaving as he was, out late at night and under no effective adult control. It was truly anti-social behaviour at a time when he ought to have been in bed. But the officer did not suggest that the behaviour caused him to suffer emotional disturbance and it would be most surprising if it had caused a mature police officer to suffer emotional disturbance. Although the case does not record the physical details of the parties involved, we are told that it is not in dispute that he was 4' 9' in height. The police officer was over 6' and weighed over 17 stone. He was, as the Magistrates recorded, an experienced police officer.

1.189 By contrast, the Divisional Court in *Southard v DPP*[142] said that the words 'fuck you' and 'fuck off' were potentially abusive, whether they were addressed to a police officer or an ordinary member of the public.

---

[139] [1995] Crim LR 896.
[140] [2006] EWHC 3449 (Admin).
[141] [2006] EWHC 1375 (Admin).
[142] [2006] EWHC 3449 (Admin).

Ultimately, whether a person was likely to be caused harassment, alarm, or distress is a ques- **1.190** tion of fact not law and as such can only be determined by the tribunal of fact in the circumstances of the particular case.

Mental element (mens rea)

As with other public order offences, the required mental element is either *intention* or **1.191** *awareness*. Section 6(4) of the Public Order Act 1986 explains:

> A person is guilty of an offence under section 5 only if he intends his words or behaviour, or the writing, sign or other visible representation, to be threatening, abusive or insulting, or is aware that it may be threatening, abusive or insulting or (as the case may be) he intends his behaviour to be or is aware that it may be disorderly.

Whether the accused had the intention or awareness for the purposes of an offence under **1.192** s 5 is an entirely subjective test, in the light of the whole of the evidence in the case.[143] In contrast to s 4 of the Public Order Act 1986, there is no 'whereby it is likely' clause; see 1.156.

Public or private place

Section 5(2) provides that: 'An offence under this section may be committed in public or **1.193** private, except that no offence is committed where the words or behaviour are used, or the writing, sign or other visible representation is displayed, by a person inside a dwelling and the other person is also inside that or another dwelling.'

Thus the 'dwelling' exception applies (see discussion above at 1.166 et seq in relation to **1.194** offences under s 4).

Specific defences

Section 5(3) provides three specific defences to an offence under s 5: **1.195**

> (3) It is a defence for the accused to prove—
>   (a) that he had no reason to believe that there was any person within hearing or sight who was likely to be caused harassment, alarm or distress, or
>   (b) that he was inside a dwelling and had no reason to believe that the words or behaviour used, or the writing, sign or other visible representation displayed, would be heard or seen by a person outside that or any other dwelling, or
>   (c) that his conduct was reasonable.

The first point of note is that these defences involve a 'reverse burden': the burden of proof **1.196** is on the defendant and the required standard of proof is to a balance of probabilities. Thus, once the prosecution has established a case to answer, it is for the defendant to show that it was more likely than not that, for example, his conduct was reasonable.

However, in *Sheldrake v DPP*,[144] the House of Lords considered whether such 'reverse **1.197** burdens' are incompatible with the presumption of innocence, as guaranteed by

---

[143] *DPP v Clarke* (1991) 94 Cr App R 359.
[144] [2004] UKHL 43.

Article 6(2) of the European Convention on Human Rights.[145] For further details of the decision in *Sheldrake* see 10.163 et seq.

1.198   Applying the principles identified in *Sheldrake* to s 5 of the Public Order Act 1986, it would seem that the 'reverse burden' of proof in s 5 is permissible. The defendant will, therefore, have to prove the defence on a balance of probabilities. No reverse burden is placed on any of the essential elements of the offence. For example, it is not an essential element for the prosecution to prove that the defendant must have *believed* that there was a person within hearing or sight who was likely to be caused harassment, alarm, or distress. The prosecution need only prove that there was such a person.[146] Moreover, the defences under s 5(3)(a) and (b) are subjective. They depend on the defendant's belief as to whether his conduct would be seen or heard. Thus, they are matters which it would be very difficult for the prosecution to disprove in the absence of the presumption.

1.199   The second point of note then, is that the first two defences under s 5(3)(a) and (b) are to be tested subjectively. However, the defence under s 5(3)(c)—whether the conduct was reasonable—is to be tested objectively in light of all the evidence.[147] That sits less easily within the series of tests set down by Lord Bingham in *Sheldrake*. If the reasonableness of a person's conduct is determinative of whether he is convicted, then why should it not be considered an essential element of the offence? Moreover, if reasonableness is to be assessed objectively, by definition it is not something which is within the defendant's knowledge making it difficult for the prosecution to disprove. Why should the burden not be on the prosecution to prove beyond reasonable doubt that the defendant's conduct was unreasonable in all the circumstances? This point has yet to be tested in the courts.

1.200   Thirdly, the question of whether the conduct was 'reasonable' has tended to engage the right to freedom of expression under Article 10(1) of the European Convention on Human Rights.[148] However, that fundamental right is not an unqualified right and according to Article 10(2) 'may be subject to such . . . restrictions or penalties as are prescribed by law and are necessary in a democratic society, in the interests of national security . . . for the prevention of disorder or crime . . . for the protection of the reputation or rights of others'. Thus, the need for the restriction must be convincingly established by a compelling

---

[145] European Convention for the Protection of Human Rights and Fundamental Freedoms (1953) (Cmd 8969) as scheduled by the Human Rights Act 1998, Sch 1.

[146] *Sheldrake* concerned a man convicted of being drunk in charge of a vehicle under the Road Traffic Act 1988, s 5(1)(b). Under s 5(2), 'It is a defence for a person charged with an offence under subsection (1)(b) to prove that at the time he is alleged to have committed the offence the circumstances were such that there was no likelihood of his driving the vehicle whilst the proportion of alcohol in his breath, blood or urine remained likely to exceed the prescribed limit.' The House of Lords held that this reverse burden did not infringe the presumption of innocence because 'the likelihood of driving' whilst under the influence was not an essential element of the offence of being drunk in charge of a vehicle. Accordingly, it was permissible to require the defendant to prove to the balance of probabilities that he was not likely to drive the car whilst under the influence in order to avail himself of the defence under the Road Traffic Act 1988, s 5(2).

[147] *DPP v Clarke* (1991) 94 Cr App R 359.

[148] European Convention for the Protection of Human Rights and Fundamental Freedoms (1953) (Cmd 8969) as scheduled by Human Rights Act 1998, Sch 1. See Ch 10.

countervailing consideration and the means employed must be proportionate to the end sought to be achieved.[149]

In *Percy v DPP*,[150] an experienced peace protestor who defiled the American flag in front of **1.201** US servicemen had her conviction quashed because the District Judge, who had convicted her of a s 5 offence, had failed to give sufficient weight to her Article 10 rights and whether, in the light of them, her conduct had been reasonable. For further details of this case see 10.44 et seq.

By contrast, in *Hammond v DPP*,[151] the appellant was an Evangelical Christian preacher **1.202** who carried a large placard bearing the words 'Stop Immorality! Stop Homosexuality! Stop Lesbianism!'—which insulted, distressed, and 'disgusted' the large crowd which gathered and indeed reacted angrily. A fracas broke out. The magistrates convicted Mr Hammond finding that the restriction on his free expression was aimed at a legitimate aim of preventing disorder. Prosecuting Mr Hammond was a proportionate response in view of the fact that his behaviour went beyond legitimate protest. The Divisional Court considered his actions in the light of both Articles 9[152] and 10 of the European Convention. The Court accepted that Article 10 was engaged but 'not without hesitation' upheld the magistrates' reasoning and finding that such conduct was not 'reasonable' within the meaning of s 5(3) of the Public Order Act 1986.[153] For further details of this case see 10.50 et seq.

Sentencing

The maximum penalty is a fine not exceeding level 3 on the standard scale[154] (Public Order **1.203** Act 1986, s 5(6)).

The offence under s 5 may alternatively be dealt with by way of a fixed penalty notice. **1.204** Under the Penalties for Disorderly Behaviour (Amount of Penalty) Order 2009 (SI 2009/83), the amount for this offence is currently £80.

The Sentencing Guidelines Council's *Magistrates' Court Sentencing Guidelines*[155] identifies **1.205** two starting points (based on a first time offender convicted after a contested trial).

---

[149] *Sunday Times v United Kingdom (No 2)* (1992) 14 EHRR 1233, the European Court of Human Rights said that: 'Freedom of expression constitutes one of the essential foundations of a democratic society subject to paragraph (2) of Article 10. It is applicable not only to information or ideas that are favourably received or regarded as inoffensive, or as a matter of indifference, but also to those that offend, shock or disturb. Freedom of expression as enshrined in Article 10 is subject to a number of exceptions which, however, must be narrowly interpreted and the necessity for any restrictions must be convincingly established.'

[150] [2001] EWHC 1125 (Admin); (2002) 166 JP 93.

[151] [2004] EWHC 69 (Admin); (2004) 168 JP 601. See also 10.50 and 10.39.

[152] Convention for the Protection of Human Rights and Fundamental Freedoms (1953)—Art 9 is the right to freedom of thought, conscience, and religion.

[153] Similarly, in *Norwood v DPP* [2003] Crim LR 888—where the defendant displayed a poster in his window bearing the words 'Islam out of Britain—Protect the British People' above a photograph of the World Trade Centre in flames on September 11th 2001—the Divisional Court held that the conduct was not reasonable.

[154] The 'standard scale' was set by the Criminal Justice Act 1982, s 37(2). Level 3 is currently £1,000.

[155] See Sentencing Guidelines Council website: <http://www.sentencing-guidelines.gov.uk>—effective from 9 December 2009 but updated regularly.

The lower level deals with offences involving 'shouting, causing a disturbance for some minutes'. The starting point is a band A fine (50 per cent of relevant weekly income). The higher level concerns offences involving 'substantial disturbance'. The suggested starting point is a band B fine (100 per cent of relevant weekly income). The guidelines identify high-level aggravating features such as group action and the length of the disturbance. Additional factors include the presence of a vulnerable person; the victim being a public servant; and the commission of the offence at a school, hospital, or other place where there may be vulnerable persons present. Mitigating factors include provocation; a brief or minor incident; or an incident which stopped as soon as the police arrived.

G. Intentional Harassment, Alarm, or Distress: Public Order Act 1986, s 4A

Historical development

1.206 The Criminal Justice and Public Order Act 1994[156] inserted s 4A into the 1986 Act to create the offence of *intentional* harassment, alarm, or distress. It requires threatening, abusive, or insulting words or behaviour, or disorderly behaviour, or displays etc as in s 5 above, but it also requires both an *intention* to cause a person harassment, alarm, or distress and the *actual* causing of harassment, alarm, or distress (as opposed to likely to cause it, which is required under s 5). Thus, although it is enumerated as s 4A it has little bearing on s 4 and is essentially a more serious version of s 5.

Definition under the Public Order Act 1986, s 4A

1.207 Section 4A of the Public Order Act 1986 (as inserted by Criminal Justice and Public Order Act 1994, s 154) provides as follows:

4A Intentional harassment, alarm or distress
(1) A person is guilty of an offence if, with intent to cause a person harassment, alarm or distress, he—
   (a) uses threatening, abusive or insulting words or behaviour, or disorderly behaviour, or
   (b) displays any writing, sign or other visible representation which is threatening, abusive or insulting,
thereby causing that or another person harassment, alarm or distress.
(2) An offence under this section may be committed in a public or a private place, except that no offence is committed where the words or behaviour are used, or the writing, sign or other visible representation is displayed, by a person inside a dwelling and the person who is harassed, alarmed or distressed is also inside that or another dwelling.
(3) It is a defence for the accused to prove—
   (a) that he was inside a dwelling and had no reason to believe that the words or behaviour used, or the writing, sign or other visible representation displayed, would be heard or seen by a person outside that or any other dwelling, or
   (b) that his conduct was reasonable.
(4) . . .

---

[156] Section 154.

(5) A person guilty of an offence under this section is liable on summary conviction to imprisonment for a term not exceeding 6 months or a fine not exceeding level 5 on the standard scale or both.

Jurisdiction

The offence under s 4A is, by virtue of s 4A(5) triable summarily only. The racially or reli- **1.208**
giously aggravated form under s 31(1)(b) of the Crime and Disorder Act 1998 is triable
either way (see Chapter 2 at 2.88 et seq).

Proportionality

As discussed above in relation to s 5, offences under s 4A often engage a person's right to **1.209**
freedom of expression under Article 10(1) of the European Convention of Human
Rights.[157] Accordingly, there must be a careful analysis as to the necessity and proportionality of bringing a prosecution at all: *Dehal v DPP*.[158] In that case, Mr Dehal was a Sikh who
sought to express his disagreement with the religious teachings at his temple by pinning a
notice to the temple's noticeboard denouncing its president as, among other things, 'a
hypocrite, a liar and . . . a proud, mad dog'. The justices and the Crown Court (on appeal
by way of rehearing) found that Mr Dehal intended to cause harassment, alarm, or distress
by displaying this insulting notice and indeed caused the president distress. What concerned Mr Justice Moses was that both the lower courts had failed to properly assess whether
bringing a criminal prosecution of this man, whose right to free expression was clearly
engaged, was a necessary and proportionate course of action in a democratic society.
Allowing the defendant's appeal Moses J said:

> What was needed was not merely a conclusion, namely that the prosecution was a propor-
> tionate response, but a careful analysis of the reasons why it was necessary to bring a criminal
> prosecution at all. In order to justify one of the essential foundations of a democratic society
> the prosecution must demonstrate that it is being brought in pursuit of a legitimate aim,
> namely the protection of society against violence and that a criminal prosecution is the only
> method necessary to achieve that aim. The court must carefully consider those consider-
> ations and set out their findings as to why they have reached their conclusion. So much is
> well-settled.[159]

Essential elements of the offence

The essential elements of the offence under s 4A are exactly the same as those for s 5 **1.210**
(see above 1.178 et seq). However, there are two additional elements which make the
offence more serious and thus punishable with up to six months' imprisonment:

- *actually causing* a person harassment, alarm, or distress; and
- *intention* to cause a person harassment, alarm, or distress.

---

[157] Convention for the Protection of Human Rights and Fundamental Freedoms (1953) as scheduled in
the Human Rights Act 1998, Sch 1.
[158] [2005] EWHC 2154 (Admin) Moses J. For further details see 10.41 et seq.
[159] see para 9.

Causation

1.211 In contrast with s 5, where the conduct need only be *'likely'* to cause a person harassment, alarm, or distress, for an offence under s 4A a person must *actually* have been caused harassment, alarm or distress 'thereby' (s 4A(1)).

1.212 There must be a causal connection between the activity of a particular defendant and the effect on the victim: *Rogers et al v DPP*.[160] In that case, a group of some 200 to 250 animal rights protesters gathered outside Mr Brown's farm to demonstrate against the cat breeding activity which he carried out there. The cats were lawfully bred for scientific research. The demonstrators became hostile and missiles were thrown at police officers. Ultimately, they pulled down a large security fence and attempted to breach police lines in order to enter the farm. Mr Brown was inside the farm. He heard the noise of demonstrators outside and watched their activities on closed circuit television. Rose LJ said that the fact that Mr Brown watched the incident on CCTV (and indeed chose to do so) did not break the causal connection between the activities of the defendants and the distress which he was thereby caused.

1.213 However, that causal connection might be inferred from the intention, even where there is a period of months between the act intended and the causal impact on its intended recipient. In *S v DPP*,[161] the appellant was an activist who sought to demonstrate against the activities of a laboratory. He took a photograph of a security guard at the laboratory and posted it on the internet, together with a speech bubble implying that the guard was a cannibal. Clearly, S intended to identify the security guard with the laboratory and cause him distress. However, the complainant did not access the website and see the photograph. Some five months later, however, he was shown a copy of the offending photograph printed off the website, which had since been removed from the internet. At that stage, as a result of the intervention of the police, the complainant was caused distress. However, the Divisional Court did not consider that this broke the required causal nexus:

> Once the appellant with the requisite intent had posted the image to the . . . website, he took the chance that the intended harassment, alarm or distress would be caused to the complainant. Whether it was ultimately triggered by a fellow activist, by a previously unknown and unconnected member of the public, or by a police officer who did not share the intention in the course of his duties, seems to me to be immaterial. Take the hypothetical example suggested by my Lord in the course of argument: a pervert posts a doctored photograph of an identifiable woman to a website, falsely representing her in circumstances of indecency. The image comes into the hands of the police in the course of a subsequent investigation. They show it to the woman who did not previously know of it and she suffers profound distress. It seems to me that if the man had the requisite intent and put the material into the public domain in that way but did nothing else, he could be convicted under section 4A.

---

[160] *Rogers, Blake, Wynn, Ross and Nicholls v DPP*, unreported, 22 July 1999, CO/4041/98.
[161] [2008] EWHC 438 (Admin).

Mental element (mens rea)

The offence under s 4A(1) requires specific intent to cause harassment, alarm, or distress. **1.214**
There is no question of awareness or recklessness here. However, intent may be inferred
from all the circumstances of the case.

In *Rogers v DPP*[162] (see facts above), the Divisional Court agreed with the magistrates' **1.215**
court that intent may be inferred where the accused's 'activities are committed in the context of a large crowd there to express disapproval of Mr Brown's activities and in the context
of the fence removal and penetration of the police line'—even where there was no evidence
that the defendants knew Mr Brown was inside the farm watching their activities on
CCTV.

Of course, each case is different. Intent may also be inferred from the very words used, **1.216**
though it does not automatically follow that the requisite intention is established, for
example, by the use of the words 'black bastard' (*DPP v Weeks*[163]). It is a matter for the tribunal of fact in each case.

Intoxication

Because the offence under s 4A requires specific intent, rather than mere awareness or **1.217**
recklessness, there is a potential defence that a person was so intoxicated that he was unable
to form the required intent. For a discussion as to the effect of voluntary, self-induced
intoxication see the section on riot above at 1.42 et seq.

Public or private

The offence under s 4A may be committed in a public or a private place, but the 'dwelling **1.218**
exception' applies (section 4A(2)). For a discussion of the 'dwelling exception' see above in
relation the offence under section 4 (at 1.166 et seq).

Note also the special defence under s 4A(3)(a) in relation to dwellings (see below **1.219**
at 1.220).

Special defences

For offences under s 4A, the Act provides special defences: **1.220**

> (3) It is a defence for the accused to prove—
> (a) that he was inside a dwelling and had no reason to believe that the words or behav-
> iour used, or the writing, sign or other visible representation displayed, would be
> heard or seen by a person outside that or any other dwelling, or
> (b) that his conduct was reasonable.

The legal burden of proof is on the defendant to prove these matters to the standard of a **1.221**
balance of probabilities. For a discussion of compatibility of these 'reverse burdens' with
the Human Rights Act 1998 and Article 6(2) of the European Convention on Human
Rights, and especially the requirement on the defendant to prove that his conduct was
reasonable see above in relation to the offence under s 5 (at 1.195 et seq).

---

[162] *Rogers, Blake, Wynn, Ross and Nicholls v DPP*, unreported, 22 July 1999, CO/4041/9.
[163] Unreported, 14 June 2000, CO/3957/99.

1.222 For a discussion as to the compatibility of the 'reasonableness' defence with the right to freedom of expression under Article 10(1) of the European Convention on Human Rights see above in relation to the offence under s 5 (at 1.200).

1.223 As to the requirement for proportionality under human rights legislation see *Dehal v DPP*[164] discussed above (at 1.209).

Police powers

1.224 The Criminal Justice and Police Act 2001, s 42(1), provides a constable with the power to make a direction stopping the harassment of a person in his home.

> 42 *Police directions stopping the harassment etc of a person in his home*
> (1) Subject to the following provisions of this section, a constable who is at the scene may give a direction under this section to any person if—
>   (a) that person is present outside or in the vicinity of any premises that are used by any individual ('the resident') as his dwelling;
>   (b) that constable believes, on reasonable grounds, that that person is present there for the purpose (by his presence or otherwise) of representing to the resident or another individual (whether or not one who uses the premises as his dwelling), or of persuading the resident or such another individual—
>   (i) that he should not do something that he is entitled or required to do; or
>   (ii) that he should do something that he is not under any obligation to do; and
>   (c) that constable also believes, on reasonable grounds, that the presence of that person (either alone or together with that of any other persons who are also present)—
>   (i) amounts to, or is likely to result in, the harassment of the resident; or
>   (ii) is likely to cause alarm or distress to the resident.
> (2) A direction under this section is a direction requiring the person to whom it is given to do all such things as the constable giving it may specify as the things he considers necessary to prevent one or both of the following—
>   (a) the harassment of the resident; or
>   (b) the causing of any alarm or distress to the resident.

1.225 By s 42(7) 'Any person who knowingly contravenes a direction given to him under this section shall be guilty of an offence and liable, on summary conviction, to imprisonment for a term not exceeding three months or to a fine not exceeding level 4 on the standard scale, or to both.'

1.226 For a full discussion of this see Chapter 3 at 3.143 et seq on police powers.

Sentencing

1.227 The maximum sentence for the basic offence under s 4A is a term of imprisonment not exceeding six months or a fine not exceeding level 5 on the standard scale or both: s 4A(5).

1.228 The Sentencing Guidelines Council's[165] *Magistrates' Court Sentencing Guidelines* identifies three starting points (based on a first time offender pleading not guilty and convicted

---

[164] [2005] EWHC 2154 (Admin).
[165] See <http://www.sentencing-guidelines.gov.uk>.

after trial). Depending on the nature of the offence, each starting point will be adjusted within a defined range according to the presence of aggravating and mitigating factors.

Threats, abuse, or insults made more than once but on the same occasion against the same person (eg while following them down the street) attract a starting point of a band C fine (150 per cent relevant weekly income). Group action or deliberately planned attack against a targeted victim attracts a starting point of a medium level community order. If a weapon is brandished or used or threats are made against a vulnerable person or if there is a course of conduct over a long period, the suggested starting point is twelve weeks' imprisonment. Again, these are starting points within a range of sentencing options. **1.229**

Aggravating features include: a high degree of planning; an offender deliberately isolating a victim; an offence committed within the vicinity of a victim's home; a large number of people present; actual or potential escalation into violence; serious impact on the victim. Mitigating factors, other than the defendant's personal mitigation, include: provocation; very short duration of the incident. **1.230**

2

OTHER PUBLIC ORDER OFFENCES

A. Overview	2.01	Sentence	2.84
B. Assault on or Obstruction of a		Forfeiture	2.87
Constable in the Execution of his Duty	2.02	Racially or religiously aggravated	
Assaulting a constable in the		offences	2.88
execution of his duty	2.03	The Test (s 28)	2.89
Resisting or wilfully obstructing		Racial or religious groups	2.90
a constable	2.12	Hostility	2.93
C. Prohibition of Political Uniforms	2.37	Sentencing	2.97
D. Prohibition of Quasi-Military		**G. Public Nuisance**	2.99
Organizations	2.42	Definition	2.101
Interpretation	2.44	Public nuisance vs private nuisance	2.106
Procedure	2.47	*Mens rea*	2.108
Defence	2.48	Vicarious liability	2.109
Powers of the High Court	2.49	Defences	2.110
E. Bomb Hoaxes	2.51	Sentence	2.111
Sentencing	2.52	**H. Criminal Damage**	2.112
F. Racial and Religious Hatred	2.56	Criminal damage	2.113
Stirring up racial and religious hatred		Aggravated criminal damage; arson;	
(or on grounds of sexual orientation)	2.57	threats to damage property,	
Racial hatred	2.60	possession with intent to destroy	
Religious hatred	2.62	or damage property	2.120
Actus reus	2.65	**I. Animal Research Facilities**	2.125
Mens rea	2.66	The legislative intent	2.126
Words, behaviour, written material		Interference in contractual relations	
stirring up racial and religious		so as to harm animal research	
hatred (s 18 racial hatred/		organization	2.131
s 29B religious hatred)	2.67	Intimidation of persons connected	
Publishing or distributing written		with animal research	
material stirring up racial or		organization	2.132
religious hatred	2.69	Criticism of the legislation	2.133
Public performance of a play stirring		Sentence	2.136
up racial or religious hatred	2.73	**J. Contamination or Interfering**	
Distributing, showing, or playing a		**with Goods**	2.146
recording stirring up racial or		Contamination of or interference	
religious hatred	2.75	with goods	2.147
Broadcasting a programme stirring up		Threatening to contaminate or interfere	
racial or religious hatred	2.78	with goods, or claiming to have	
Possession of written material or		done so	2.149
recording stirring up racial or		Possession of articles with a view	
religious hatred	2.80	to contaminating or interfering	
Defences	2.82	in goods	2.151
Liability of corporations	2.83	Sentence	2.152

K. Intimidation, including Watching		Drunk and disorderly person	
and Besetting	2.154	failing to leave	2.175
Origin of the offence	2.155	Alcohol consumption in a	
The offence	2.158	designated place	2.176
Elements of the offence	2.159	Drunk on an aircraft	2.177
Penalties	2.167	**M. Football Related**	
L. Drunk and Disorderly	2.168	**Disorder**	2.178
Drunk and disorderly	2.170	**N. Taking a Photograph of a**	
Drunk in a public place	2.173	**Police Officer**	2.183

A. Overview

2.01 The Public Order Act 1986 rewrote a number of common law offences, such as riot and affray, in statutory form and created others, such as violent disorder. These offences are discussed in Chapter 1. Many other offences are charged following public order incidents and these offences can be found both within the 1986 Act and in a range of other statutory provisions. This chapter, while not purporting to present an exhaustive list, examines a number of offences that arise within this context.

B. Assault on or Obstruction of a Constable in the Execution of his Duty

2.02 Section 89 of the Police Act 1996 creates two separate offences. It is an offence for any person

(a) to assault a constable in the execution of his duty; or
(b) to resist or wilfully obstruct a constable in the execution of his duty.

These summary only offences are perhaps those most regularly charged following any incident of public order or protest, and the offence of obstruction in particular is regularly employed against protestors who refuse to comply with police directions. In protest cases lay benches are often required to decide far from straightforward issues of law.

Assaulting a constable in the execution of his duty

2.03 Section 89 of the Police Act 1996 provides:

(1) Any person who assaults a constable in the execution of his duty, or a person assisting a constable in the execution of his duty, shall be guilty of an offence and liable on summary conviction to imprisonment for a term not exceeding six months or to a fine not exceeding level 5 on the standard scale, or to both.

The full range of assault charges is available to cover incidents of public disorder. They include, in ascending order of seriousness, common assault (Offences against the Person Act 1861, s 42, made summary only by the Criminal Justice Act 1988, s 39); assault occasioning actual bodily harm and wounding or causing grievous bodily harm without or with intent (contrary to the Offences Against the Person Act 1861, s 47; 20, and 18 respectively), as well as murder and manslaughter (contrary to common law). An examination of these offences is beyond the scope of this book but they are comprehensively addressed in most standard works on the criminal law.[1] However, the offence of assaulting a constable arises with such frequency, particularly within incidents of protest, that it merits individual consideration.

Elements of the offence

The offence under s 89 must involve an assault or battery. In short, an assault is any act **2.04** which intentionally or recklessly causes another person to apprehend immediate and unlawful personal violence. The act is not unlawful if, for example, it was done by accident, in lawful self-defence, or in defence of another. A battery is an act by which a person intentionally or recklessly applies unlawful force to the complainant. There is no need to prove any injury to the person assaulted.

Constable

It also must be proved that the victim of the assault or battery was a police officer of any **2.05** rank, or a person assisting such an officer. Every police officer in England and Wales holds the office of constable.[2] The constable does not have to be in uniform. The functions of police officers are increasingly being performed by people holding a variety of other offices, and there is a wealth of specific legislation in similar terms protecting them against assault in the execution of their duty.[3] It is well established that there is no need for the prosecution to prove that the accused knew, or even had reason to suspect, that the person he assaulted was a police officer.[4]

Execution of duty

This is discussed in full at 2.21 et seq, below. In the context of assaulting a constable in the **2.06** execution of his duty, it is no defence that a person believed, even on reasonable grounds, that the officer was acting outside his powers and therefore not in the execution of his duty. The offence will only not be proved if the officer was in fact acting outside the execution of his duty.

Self-defence

If, by way of example, an officer is acting outside the execution of his duty in carrying out **2.07** an unlawful arrest, the arrest itself is likely to be an assault. In these circumstances, the normal principles of self-defence apply and a person may act in reasonable self-defence. If the force used in self-defence is excessive or disproportionate, it will not be reasonable and the defence will fail.[5] The classic statement of the scope of this defence is that of the Privy Council in *R v Palmer*[6] approved and followed by the Court of Appeal in

---

[1] *Archbold Criminal Pleadings, Evidence and Practice* (2009), *Blackstone's Criminal Practice* (2009).
[2] *Lewis v Cattle* [1938] 2 KB 454.
[3] As to assaults on revenue and customs officers, see the Commissioners for Revenue and Customs Act 2005, s 32; on immigration officers, see the UK Borders Act 2007, ss 22 and 23; on those carrying out surveillance under the Regulation of Investigatory Powers Act 2000, s 76, see the Crime (International Co-operation) Act 2003, s 84; on traffic officers, see the Traffic Management Act 2004, s 10(1). For Police Community Support Officers, see 6.08 et seq.
[4] *R v Maxwell and Clanchy* (1909) 2 Cr App R 26.
[5] Criminal Justice and Immigration Act 2008, s 76.
[6] [1971] AC 814, 831–2 per Lord Morris.

R v McInnes[7]: in the context of a highly charged and rapidly evolving public order situation, the following well-known extract from the assessment of the level of force permitted to defend oneself is particularly pertinent:

> If there has been an attack so that defence is reasonably necessary, it will be recognised that a person defending himself cannot weight to a nicety the exact measure of his defensive action. If the jury thought that in a moment of unexpected anguish a person attacked had only done what he honestly and instinctively thought necessary, that would be the most potent evidence that only reasonable defensive action had been taken.

2.08   It follows that whilst an officer may be acting outside the execution of his duty, this does not mean that every act of violence against the officer will go unpunished, for the person can be charged on some other basis, for example, common assault or assault occasioning actual bodily harm. However, as courts of summary jurisdiction have no power to convict included offences, the prosecution would be wise to draft alternative counts in cases where the legality of the officer's conduct is in doubt (*Kerr v DPP*;[8] *Bentley v Brudzinski*[9]), or the issue is excessive self-defence.

2.09   On the face of it there should be no reason why a third person is not entitled to use force to assist another who is the subject of unlawful police conduct. Where the attacker is a civilian, then common law and statute allow a bystander to intervene to protect the victim. And if a police officer was, as a matter of law, acting outside the execution of his duty, there is no difficulty in that principle being transferred. However, in the scenario where the officer is acting within the execution of his duty but the bystander intervenes, genuinely believing on reasonable grounds that the officer is acting unlawfully, it must be assumed that mistake as to the lawfulness of the officer's actions is no defence.

Mistaken self-defence

2.10   A person's belief is relevant to self-defence. If a person is unaware his assailants are police officers who happen to be lawfully exercising their powers, and honestly believes that he is being assaulted or kidnapped, and uses force to resist, he will have a defence. His honest, albeit mistaken, belief in the necessity for self-defence will negative the *mens rea* for assault.[10] Equally, if a person goes to the aid of another he believes to be under attack by muggers, for example, but who is instead being arrested lawfully by plain clothes policemen, then he would be entitled to a defence.[11] However, this defence is not afforded to a person who uses force against someone he knows to be a constable, but mistakenly believes is acting outside the execution of his duty. It is a defence only if the constable is in fact acting outside the execution of his duty.

---

[7]   55 Cr App R 551.
[8]   [1995] Crim LR 394.
[9]   (1982) 75 Cr App R 217.
[10]   *Kenlin v Gardiner* [1967] 2 QB 510; *Ansell v Swift* [1987] Crim LR 194; *Blackburn v Bowering* [1994] 1 WLR 1324.
[11]   *Gladstone Williams* (1983) 78 Cr App R 276.

Sentencing

Sentencing guidelines can be found in the SGC Guidelines, *Assault and other offences against the person* (effective 3 March 2008, at pp 20–21) and the Magistrates' Courts Sentencing Guidelines.[12] **2.11**

Resisting or wilfully obstructing a constable[13]

Section 89 of the Police Act 1996 provides: **2.12**

> (2) Any person who resists or wilfully obstructs a constable in the execution of his duty, shall be guilty of an offence and liable on summary conviction for a term not exceeding one month or to a fine not exceeding level 3 on the standard scale, or to both.

Obstructs

While 'resists' implies some physical action by way of opposition, no physical act is necessary to constitute obstruction. It has been said that 'obstruction' takes place when a person makes it more difficult for him to carry out his duty.[14] But that will not always be sufficient. A constable has a duty to investigate a crime and, in pursuance of that, may ask questions of a person who he reasonably suspects has committed the crime, or has information about it. That person has a right to silence, but the exercise of that right may make it more difficult for the officer to carry out his duty. In *Rice v Connolly*,[15] mere silence was not an obstruction, nor was it an obstruction in *Green v DPP*[16] when a person advised another not to answer. However, this tension between the individual's rights and the officer's duty is not always resolved so clearly in favour of the individual. **2.13**

In *Sekfali & others v DPP*,[17] the Divisional Court considered the position of three defendants who were approached by police in order to ascertain whether they matched descriptions given to them by other witnesses. The officers identified themselves as police officers and showed their warrant cards. At this point the defendants ran off and were subsequently apprehended and arrested for obstruction. It was argued on their behalf that there was no duty which the law imposed upon the appellants to remain and answer questions when asked to do so by police officers, since the police had not arrested them, and therefore they were entitled to run away. The Court recognized that 'the position is that a citizen has no legal duty to assist the police' but, at paragraph 11, drew a distinction between saying nothing and running away: **2.14**

> The appellants would have been entitled to remain silent and not answer any questions put to them. They could have refused, if they had not been arrested, to accompany the police to any particular place to which they might have been requested by the police to go. They could have said that they had no intention of answering questions and they could, no doubt, have said that as a result they were intent on going on their way and have done so without giving rise to a case which would entitle the court to conclude that in departing they were intending

---

[12] *Blackstone's Criminal Practice 2009*, App 8.
[13] Obstruction and assault of Police Community Support Officers is addressed in the Police Reform Act 2002, s 46 and Sch 4, Part 1.
[14] Per Lord Goddard in *Hinchcliffe v Sheldon* [1955] 1 WLR 1207.
[15] [1966] 2 QB 414. See also 6.19 below.
[16] (1991) 155 JP 816.
[17] [2006] EWHC 894 (Admin).

to impede the police officers and obstruct the police officers in the exercise of their duty. Had they responded in that way, then it would have been for the police to have decided whether to arrest them; but they ran off, as the magistrates found, to avoid apprehension. That being a wilful act, taken so as to obstruct the police, was an act capable of constituted an offence contrary to section 89(2).

2.15 *Rice v Connolly* was distinguished on the basis that there is a difference between refusing to answer and giving a 'cock and bull story'. In *Rice v Connolly*, Lord Parker said:[18]

> In my judgment, there is all the difference in the world between deliberately telling a false story—something which on no view a citizen has a right to do—and preserving silence or refusing to answer—something which he has every right to do. Accordingly, in my judgment, it was not shown that the refusal of the defendant to answer the questions or to accompany the police officer in the first instance to the police box was an obstruction without lawful excuse.

2.16 This distinction between a refusal to act and a positive act of obstruction was also made by Bridge J in *Dibble v Ingleton*,[19] but the application of the rule can be uncertain. In *Ledger v DPP*,[20] officers attended Mr Ledger's house to investigate an alleged serious incident. Mr Ledger was drunk and refused to let the officers in the house or say whether there was anybody in the house. He was asked his name and address, which he gave as 'Freddie and the Dreamers'. In evidence, the officer said that he did not believe that this was his name but it was this answer that was held by the Court to justify his arrest for obstruction. This is perhaps a rather too narrow interpretation of the test, an opinion with which Professor Sir John Smith concurred in his Criminal Law Review Commentary:

> . . . it is plain that the appellant's reply was not intended to be believed. It was no more than a contemptuous way of telling the officers that he was not going to give his name and address. No doubt this behaviour was deplorable and very galling for the officers but, with respect, it does not appear to amount to an obstruction in law.

2.17 An individual may obstruct by omission in the limited circumstances where the individual is under an initial duty to act. The only positive obligation within the context of public order and protest is the common law offence of refusing to aid a constable who is attempting to prevent or quell a breach of the peace and who calls for assistance.[21] In *Lunt v DPP*,[22] the appellant refused to open his front door to officers who were attempting to exercise a lawful power under the Road Traffic Act 1988 to enter his premises. The officers did not give their reasons for wanting to enter the premises and forced an entry. The defendant was charged and convicted of obstruction. The Divisional Court upheld the conviction on the grounds that the officers had a right to enter and therefore the defendant was not entitled to keep the officers out. The Court held that the defendant had no right to be told of the 'precise legal authority under which the police authorities were acting'. However, it should surely be necessary to prove that a person accused of an offence by omission was aware of the facts giving rise to the duty to act. It is submitted there should

[18] [1966] 2 QB 414, 420.
[19] [1972] 1 QB 480, 488C–F.
[20] [1991] Crim LR 439.
[21] *Waugh*, The Times, 1 October 1986.
[22] [1993] Crim LR 535.

have been no duty to open the door unless the occupier was told that the officer had reasonable cause to suspect that a person had committed an offence under the Road Traffic Act 1988, that he wished to arrest that person and that he reasonably suspected that he was on the premises.[23]

Wilfully

'Wilfully' means that the act is done deliberately and intentionally, not by accident or inadvertence, but so that the mind of the person who does the act goes with it.[24] An obstruction must be wilful and a defendant does not commit wilful obstruction if he tries to help the police even if he actually makes their job more difficult,[25] or if he is not aware he is obstructing the police.[26] In contrast to the offence of assaulting a constable in the execution of his duty, a prosecutor must show that the defendant was aware that the person he obstructed was a police officer. However, the conduct need not be 'aimed at' a police officer, and the Divisional Court in *Lewis v Cox*[27] allowed a prosecutor's appeal in a case involving a defendant who had repeatedly opened the door of a police van to ask his friend where he was being taken. Here, because it could be inferred that the defendant knew that the police could not drive off while the van door was still open, he was aware that he was obstructing the police, and intended therefore to do so.[28]

2.18

Importantly in the public order and protest context, it is no defence for a defendant to argue that whilst he did obstruct, he was merely trying to prevent the arrest of a person he believed to be and was in fact innocent.[29]

2.19

Constable

This is discussed at 2.05 above.

2.20

Execution of his duty

Before any attempt is made to delineate the scope of a constable's duty, it worth asking what is a *duty*? Professor ATH Smith considered that:

2.21

> For the jurist, the word 'duty' has a number of possible meanings. When used in any rigorous sense, it bears connotations of obligation, and in its pristine Hohfeldian sense, it is the strict correlative of a right. So far as the scope of the duty in the offences of assault, resistance and obstruction is concerned, the law has developed in such a way that the law is not confined to duties *stricto sensu*, ie something that the officer is compelled by law to do. Rather, the courts have held that it is enough if the constable has a power to act as he does, and that he is not acting illegally in the exercise of that power at the time of the act complained of.

---

[23] Professor Spencer's commentary concurs with this view: [1993] Crim LR 535. For reasons to be given at the time of arrest see Ch 7 at 7.38 et seq.

[24] Per Lord Russell of Killowen CJ in *R v Senior* [1899] 1 QB 283, 290–1. See also *R v Walker* (1934) 24 Cr App R 117; *Eaton v Cobb* [1950] 1 All ER 1016; *Arrowsmith v Jenkins* [1963] 2 QB 561.

[25] *Wilmott v Atack* [1977] QB 498.

[26] *Ostler v Elliot* [1980] Crim LR 584.

[27] [1985] 1 QB 405.

[28] See also *Moore v Green* [1983] QB 667, 671.

[29] *Lewis v Cox* [1985] QB 509; *Hills v Ellis* [1983] QB 680.

2.22 The practical application of these principles gives rise to two questions in every case:

(a) Did the constable have a power to act as he did in those circumstances?

(b) If so, did he exercise that power excessively or disproportionately (taking into account, for example, a protestor's right to freedom of assembly)?

It is far more helpful to think in terms of the lawful and proportionate exercise of police powers, rather than to attempt to delineate duty. If an officer either does not have a power to act as he did, or exercised that power excessively or disproportionately, then he will be acting outside the execution of his duty.

2.23 However, many of the authorities adopt the language of duty. The duty of the police to keep the peace and the common law powers that flow from that (discussed in Chapter 6) are well established. Beyond that, any definition of the scope of an officer's duties has remained elusive. Parker LJ in *Rice v Connolly*[30] held:

> It is also in my judgment clear that it is part of the obligations and duties of a police constable to take all reasonable steps which appear to him necessary for keeping the peace, for preventing crime or for protecting property from criminal injury. There is no exhaustive definition of the powers and obligations of the police but they are at least those, and they would include the duty to detect crime and bring an offender to justice.

2.24 The powers of the police to keep the peace were also considered by the Divisional Court in *Coffin v Smith*,[31] a decision open to criticism. The police were called to a youth club to assist in removing trespassers. There was no evidence before the court that any breach of the peace was suspected. The appellants left as directed but remained outside the youth club, declining invitations to leave. The police were attempting to move the appellants away when one officer was assaulted. The Court concluded that the officers were acting within the execution of their duty both in assisting in the removal of the trespassers and also when attempting to move on the appellants as they stood in the street, on the grounds that

> a police officer's duty is to be a keeper of the peace and to take all necessary steps with that in view. These officers, just like ordinary officers on the beat, were attending a place where they thought that their presence would assist in keeping the peace . . . They were simply standing there on the beat in the execution of their duty when they were assaulted.

2.25 The judgment is problematic for two reasons. Firstly, there was in fact no evidence of any breach or potential breach of the peace or any concern held by an officer, and the evidence as far as it went pointed the other way. Secondly, the judgment equates the officer's duty with being 'on duty'.

2.26 The first criticism is limited to the facts of the judgment, and perhaps this case is best seen as the Divisional Court proceeding on the basis that a breach of the peace was indeed likely and affirming an officer's undisputed duty and corresponding powers to prevent a breach of the peace. On those grounds the judgment, albeit erroneous on the facts, does not give rise to problems of general application.

---

[30] [1966] 2 All ER 649, 651.
[31] (1980) 71 Cr App R 221.

The second criticism gives rise to wider difficulties. It must be too simplistic to suggest that **2.27** because an officer has 'clocked on', he is therefore acting, even *prima facie*, in the execution of his duty. The comment must be put in its context, namely an attempt by the Court to apply the proposition established by the Court of Appeal in *Waterfield and Lynn*[32] that it is not necessary for an officer's duty to be found in a specific rule of the common law or statute.[33] Ashworth J put forward a two-stage test:

> In the judgment of the court it would be difficult, and in the present case it is unnecessary, to reduce within specific limits the general terms in which the duties of police constables have been expressed. In most cases it is probably more convenient to consider what the police constable was actually doing and in particular whether such conduct was prima facie an unlawful interference with a person's liberty or property. If so, then it is relevant to consider whether (a) such conduct falls within the general scope of any duty imposed by statute or recognised at common law and (b) whether such conduct, albeit within the scope of such a duty, involved an unjustifiable use of powers associated with the duty.

This is a helpful, coherent, and practical test that is, in effect, another way of framing the two **2.28** questions set out at the beginning of this section. It asks first whether, in the act of touching, detaining, or searching, for example, there has been a potential interference in a person's rights. If there has been, then the second question is whether the police have powers in law to interfere in those rights and, furthermore, whether the officer has properly exercised those powers.

Returning to the criticism of *Coffin v Smith*, it is plain that the comment 'They were simply **2.29** standing there on the beat in the execution of their duty when they were assaulted', is, by lack of precision of language, a misapplication of the principle. The officers were not simply 'standing there', for their attempts to require the appellants to leave the area clearly amounted to an interference in the appellants' liberty to remain. Given there was such an interference, their actions required justification in law. Again, the judgment can be understood by applying the Court's erroneous factual assumption: the officers' actions were lawful if the officers perceived an immediate likelihood of a breach of the peace as they then have an undisputed power to remove persons from an area in order to keep the peace. On an application of *Waterfield*, there had been an interference, but the interference was justified in law.

On the assumption that the officers did fear a breach of the peace, the judgment of *Coffin* **2.30** *and Smith* should be seen as limited but not reaching the wrong conclusion. What cannot be good law is any suggestion that simply by being on duty, a constable is in the execution of his duty. These two cases are often quoted as examples of the principles to be applied in establishing the scope of a constable's duty. For the reasons set out above, the two-stage test in *Waterfield* should be seen as the correct statement of the law.

What takes an officer outside of his duty?

In the context of the questions discussed above, an officer who does not have a power to do **2.31** something, or exercises that power excessively or disproportionately will be acting outside the course of his duty.

---

[32] [1964] 1 QB 164.
[33] This in itself was an extension of the law as previously understood. In *Despard v Wilcox* (1910) 102 LT 103 the court were of the opinion that the duty must be specific and arise from statute or other legal source.

2.32 An officer who is trespassing will be acting outside his duty, but the practical application of this is often difficult. An officer who attends a property in response to a burglar alarm and finds the door open will have an implied permission to enter as well as a duty to investigate. An occupier has the right to ask them to leave and they would become trespassers if they stayed, but an offensive 'go away' may not be enough to withdraw this permission, and in any event the officers continue to be acting in the course of their duty during the reasonable time necessary for their departure.[34] Furthermore, even though told to go by the person who was in fact the owner, the constable, it seems, would be entitled to stay until he has taken reasonable steps to satisfy himself that it really was the owner who was instructing him to leave (and not the burglar)[35] as he has the duty to investigate the cause of the alarm.

2.33 It is clear law that a police officer is not acting in the execution of his duty if he seeks to restrain someone either when he has no grounds to arrest him, or when he is not purporting to arrest him, but merely to detain him or otherwise restrain him.[36] In the latter situation a police officer has no more right to lay hands on someone than any other member of the community. The person so restrained is entitled to use reasonable force to free himself.[37] In *Wood v DPP*[38] officers restrained the defendant who was leaving a restaurant who met the description of a person reported to have been offending within the premises. Others came out of the restaurant and referred to the defendant as the offender. The officer gave evidence that by this stage he believed he had reasonable grounds for arresting the defendant but he did not in fact arrest him. The defendant then assaulted the officers and was charged with assaulting a police officer in the execution of his duty. The argument that the distinction between detaining and arresting was mere semantics was rejected by the Divisional Court who quashed the convictions. The Court looked to the judgment of Winn LJ in *Kenlin & Another v Gardiner & Another*[39] who considered the case of two schoolchildren who were stopped by police officers who had their suspicions aroused. The officers showed their warrant cards and stated they were police. One of the children made to run away. The police officer caught hold of the arm of that boy and cautioned him, and the other then struggled with the other boy:

> So one comes back to the question in the end, in the ultimate analysis: was this officer entitled in law to take hold of the first boy by the arm—of course the same situation arises with the other officer in regard to the second boy a little later—justified in committing the technical assault by the exercise of any power which he as a police constable in the precise circumstances prevailing at that exact moment possessed?

---

[34] *R (Fullard) v Woking Magistrates' Court* [2005] EWHC 2922 (Admin); *Kay v Hibbert* [1977] Crim LR 226.

[35] See Criminal Law Review Commentary to *Kat v Hibbert* [1977] Crim LR 226.

[36] Though the use of 'kettling' in a group situation may be lawful. See 3.32, 4.67, 6.162 et seq, 10.164, and 10.167 et seq.

[37] See judgment of Lord Parker CJ in *Ludlow & others v Burgess* 75 Cr App R 227 and 2.07 et seq on self-defence. If the arrest is unlawful, other police officers who go to assist their colleague in the arrest are not acting in the execution of their duty, and if follows that an individual who reasonably resisted these officers would not be guilty of obstruction. *Cumberbatch v CPS; Ali v DPP* [2009] EWHC 3353 (Admin).

[38] [2008] EWHC 1056 (Admin); The Times, 23 May 2008. See also 7.02 et seq below.

[39] [1967] 2 QB 510.

I regret, really, that I feel myself compelled to say that the answer to that question must be in the negative. This officer might or might not in the particular circumstances have possessed a power to arrest these boys. I leave that question open, saying no more than I feel some doubt whether he would have had a power of arrest: but on the assumption that he had a power to arrest it is to my mind plain that neither of these officers purported to arrest either of these boys. What was done was not done as an integral step in the process of arresting, but was done in order to secure an opportunity, by detaining the boys from escape, to put them or either of them the question that was regarded as the test question to satisfy the officers whether or not it would be right in the circumstances, and having regard to the answer obtained from that question, if any, to arrest them.

I regret to say that I think there was a technical assault by the police officers . . .[40]

There is of course no such thing as a 'technical assault'. The language used demonstrates that even the most reluctant judge will be forced to accept the clear principle that where a police officer restrains a person, but does not at that time intend or purport to arrest him, then he is committing an assault, even if an arrest would have been justified.[41] And as such, the officer is outside the scope of his duty.

2.34 The limits to this principle that there is no power to detain short of arrest are found in the cases that address what is seen to be a *de minimis* interference with the person's liberty. In *Mepstead v DPP*[42] officers taking hold of a man's arm to explain a fixed penalty notice were held not to be acting outside of their duty, albeit the Court recognized that if they had held his arm for any length of time that then could have amounted to detention. Equally, in *Donnelly v Jackman*[43] the Court held, in relation to a tap on the arm by an officer, that 'it is not every trivial interference with a citizen's liberty that amounts to a course of conduct'. If, on the facts of the case, the physical touching by the officer did not amount to a 'detention' however transitory, then it is likely he remains within the exercise of his duty. Attracting somebody's attention by touching them is an obvious example.

2.35 A search must be carried out lawfully, otherwise the officer will be acting outside the execution of his duty. The courts when considering prosecutions for obstruction arising out of a refusal to cooperate with searches, notably in *R v Christopher Bristol*[44] and *O(A Juvenile) v DPP*,[45] have required officers to comply strictly with the provisions of the Police and Criminal Evidence Act 1984.

2.36 An 'off-duty' police officer is not necessarily acting outside the execution of his duty[46] if an incident occurs which justifies immediate action on his part as his obligations extend outside the hours of his shifts. However, it is essential in all cases that the officer is shown to have been acting lawfully, because even a minor, technical and inadvertent act of

---

[40] Ibid, at 519.

[41] Lord Justice Latham at para 7 of *Wood v DPP* and see also *Collins v Willcock* [1984] 1 WLR 1172 where a police officer was held to have committed a battery when, without purporting to exercise any lawful power of arrest, held a woman by the arm in order to question her.

[42] [1996] Crim LR 111.

[43] [1970] 1 WLR 562.

[44] [2007] EWCA Crim 3214.

[45] (1999) 163 JP 725 QB.

[46] *Albert v Lavin* [1982] AC 456.

unlawfulness on his part could mean that he cannot have been acting in the execution of his duty.[47]

C. Prohibition of Political Uniforms

2.37 Section 1(1) of the Public Order Act 1936 prohibits the public wearing of uniforms in a political context. The Act was enacted as a result of the Fascist marches of the 1930s where uniforms were commonly worn, for example, black shirts by the British Union of Fascists and the Imperial Fascist League, blue shirts by the Kensington Fascists, and grey by the United Empire Fascist Party.[48] Section 1(1) of that Act (which remains unaffected by the Public Order Act 1986) provides:

> Subject as hereinafter provided, any person who in any public place or any public meeting wears uniform signifying his association with any political organisation or with the promotion of any political object is guilty of an offence:

> Provided that, if the chief of police is satisfied that the wearing of any such uniform as aforesaid on any ceremonial, anniversary, or other special occasion will not be likely to involve risk of public disorder, he may, with the consent of a Secretary of State, by order permit the wearing of such uniform on that occasion either absolutely or subject to such conditions as may be specified in the order.

2.38 The offence is triable summarily only with a maximum penalty of three months' imprisonment or a fine not exceeding level 4 on the standard scale.[49] No further proceedings after charge shall be instituted without the consent of the Attorney General.[50]

2.39 While a number of prosecutions were brought under the Act shortly after it was enacted[51] and indeed some contemporary commentators regarded this section as the principal purpose of the Act,[52] it has seen little use. In *O'Moran v DPP*[53] the Divisional Court upheld the conviction of the appellants, members of the IRA, who had paraded at a funeral wearing black berets, dark glasses, black pullovers, and other dark clothing. It is a question of fact in each individual case as to what amounts to a uniform, and it does not require full and identical sets of clothing—a beret alone may amount to a uniform.

2.40 The definition of 'public place' in the 1936 Act applies (slightly narrower than that in the 1986 Act, s 16) and includes any highway and any other premises or place to which at the material time the public have or are permitted to have access, whether on payment or otherwise.[54]

---

[47] *Riley v DPP* (1989) 91 Cr App R 14; *Kerr v DPP* [1995] Crim LR 394.

[48] See I Brownlie, *Brownlie's Law of Public Order and National Security* (1981, 2nd edn) pp 181–2.

[49] Public Order Act 1936, s 7(2).

[50] Ibid, s 1(2).

[51] *R v Wood* (1937) 81 Sol Jo 108; *R v Charnley* (1937) 81 Sol Jo 108.

[52] J Baker, *The Law of Political Uniforms, Public Meetings and Private Armies* (1937) says 'the most important provision in the new Act is, probably, the one which prohibits the wearing of political uniforms in public': referenced in ATH Smith, *Public Order Offences* (1986) p 250.

[53] [1975] QB 864.

[54] *R v Edwards and Roberts* (1978) 67 Cr App R 228.

There is a related offence, triable summarily only, under s 13 of the Terrorism Act 2000, of **2.41** wearing an item of clothing or article in such a way as to arouse reasonable suspicion that he is a member or supporter of a proscribed organization. The test of 'reasonable suspicion' is a low one, and in the case of a defendant wearing a ring which bore the initials UVF, it mattered not that the defendant had received the ring as a gift and was not a member or supporter of the UVF—the objective reasonable basis for that suspicion existed.[55]

D. Prohibition of Quasi-Military Organizations

Section 2 of the 1936 Act prohibits quasi-military organizations. However, the archaic **2.42** linked offence of unlawful training and drilling in the use of arms prohibited by the Unlawful Drilling Act 1819 was repealed by the Statute Law Repeals Act 2008.

Section 2(1) provides: **2.43**

> If the members or adherents of any association of persons, whether incorporated or not, are—
> (a) organised or trained or equipped for the purpose of enabling them to be employed in usurping the functions of the police or of the armed forces or of the Crown; or
> (b) organised and trained or organised and equipped either for the purpose of enabling them to be employed for the use or display of physical force in promoting any political object, or in such manner as to arouse reasonable apprehension that they are organised and either trained or equipped for that purpose;
> then any person who takes part in the control or management of the association, or in so organising or training as aforesaid any members or adherents thereof, shall be guilty of an offence under this section.

Interpretation

The section gives rise to two questions that are without a clear answer: **2.44**

(a) What would amount to the 'usurpation' of 'the functions of the police or the armed forces' for the purposes of this section? (s 2(1)(a))
(b) What amounts to 'reasonable apprehension'? (s 2(1)(b))

Usurpation

Increasing use of private security firms to patrol housing estates or neighbourhoods as well **2.45** as individual properties in order to prevent and detect crime, certainly amounts to supplementing some of the police's functions, if not straightforward duplication. Modern warfare has seen increased use of private contractors (organized, trained, and equipped in the UK) employed to perform a wide variety of military activities that hitherto had been the function of the armed forces. ATH Smith in *Public Order Offences* (1986) considered this issue and concluded that 'The legal answer must be that none of these organisations seeks to "usurp" the functions of the police, in the sense of adversely performing or appropriating those functions.' Smith imports the element of 'adversely' into the definition of usurp, and certainly a number of the definitions given by the *Oxford English Dictionary*[56]

---

[55] Some assistance may be found in *Rankin v Murray* 2004 SLT 1164, Scottish High Court of Justiciary.
[56] The *New Shorter Oxford English Dictionary* (1993).

carry an element of 'wrongfulness', eg 'to appropriate (a right, prerogative, etc.) wrongfully; esp. seize or assume another's position or authority by force'. However, it is also defined as simply to 'encroach on another's rights, privilege, territory, etc.', something those private agencies are undoubtedly engaged in. Given this is a criminal statute it should be interpreted restrictively and must surely be read to include an element of unlawfulness in the appropriation.

Reasonable apprehension

2.46   What is a 'political object' will inevitably be case sensitive: successful prosecutions have been brought against those taking part in a Nazi organization called Spearhead[57] and against members of the Free Wales Army.[58] What amounts to the use or display of physical force is straightforward, but the 'reasonable apprehension' less so. In *Jordan and Tyndall*,[59] the Court of Appeal affirmed the trial judge's direction that a 'reasonable apprehension' meant 'an apprehension or fear which is based not upon undue timidity or excessive suspicion or still less prejudice, but one which is founded on grounds which to you appear to be reasonable. Moreover the apprehension or fear must be reasonably held by a person who is aware of all the facts . . . You must try to put yourselves in a position of a sensible man who knew the whole of the facts.'

Procedure

2.47   Offences under this section are triable either way.[60] Proceedings require the consent of the Attorney General.[61] The maximum penalty is two years' imprisonment or a fine or both on indictment; six months or a fine not exceeding the statutory maximum or both if tried summarily.[62] Specific provision is made (less essential since the introduction of the hearsay provisions in the Criminal Justice Act 2003) to allow for things done, or words spoken, or published by any person taking part in the organization, or training to be admissible as evidence of the purposes for which, or the manner in which, members or adherents of the association were organized, or trained, or equipped.[63]

Defence

2.48   It is a defence for a person to prove[64] that he neither consented to nor connived at the organization, training, or equipment of members or adherents of the association in contravention of the provisions of the section.[65] Section 2(6) also provides that s 2 does not prohibit the employment of a reasonable number of people as stewards to assist in the preservation of order at any public meeting held upon private premises, or the making of arrangements

---

[57] *R v Jordan and Tyndall* [1963] Crim LR 124, in which Jordan received nine months' imprisonment and Tyndall six months' imprisonment.

[58] *R v Evans and others*, The Times, 2 July 1969 in which two defendants received sentences of fifteen months' and a third was sentenced to nine months' imprisonment.

[59] See above.

[60] Public Order Act 1936, s 7(1).

[61] Ibid, s 2(2).

[62] Ibid, s 7(1).

[63] Ibid, s 2(4).

[64] Plainly this must be on the balance of probabilities.

[65] Public Order Act 1936, s 2.

for that purpose or the instruction of those people to be so employed in their lawful duties as stewards. These stewards are permitted to wear badges or other distinguishing signs.

Powers of the High Court

A High Court judge may grant a search warrant with a view to seizing evidence of the com- **2.49**
mission of an offence under s 2. The judge must be satisfied on information under oath that there is a reasonable ground for believing that an offence under s 2 has been committed and that evidence of it may be found at the place specified in the information.[66]

If an application is made by the Attorney General, and it appears to the High Court that an **2.50**
association is one to which s 2 applies, the Court may make any order as appears necessary to prevent any disposition without leave of the court of any property of the organization. It may also order an enquiry into the property and affairs of the organization in order to discharge its liabilities lawfully entered into, and to repay monies to good faith contributors and members and to meet the costs of winding up the organization. Any property which remains shall be forfeited to the Crown.[67]

E. Bomb Hoaxes[68]

Before the enactment of the Criminal Law Act 1977, bomb hoaxes were charged as a public **2.51**
nuisance.[69] The real thing is far more serious and still dealt with under the Explosive Substances Act 1883. Section 51 of the 1977 Act provides:

(1) A person who—
  (a) places any article in any place whatever; or
  (b) dispatches any article by post, rail or any other means whatever of sending things from one place to another,
  with the intention (in either case) of inducing in some other person a belief that it is likely to explode or ignite and thereby cause personal injury or damage to property is guilty of an offence.
In this subsection 'article' includes substance.
(2) A person who communicates any information which he knows or believes to be false to another person with the intention of inducing in him or any other person a false belief that a bomb or other thing liable to explode or ignite is present in any place or location whatever is guilty of an offence.

The offence is triable either way. The reference to 'any place whatever' in s 51(1)(a) does not require particularization of that place, a call stating 'there is a bomb' is sufficient, even if there is no reference to location.[70] Nor is it necessary to show that a defendant had any particular person in mind as the person in whom he intended to induce the belief that it is likely to explode or ignite.[71]

---

[66] Ibid, s 2(5).
[67] Ibid, s 2.
[68] See *R v Paul Michael Judge* [2009] 1 Cr App R (S) 439 for sentencing of defendant who made false distress call saying that a ship was aground, contrary to the Wireless Telegraphy Act 2006, s 47.
[69] See 2.99 et seq below.
[70] *R v Webb*, The Times, 19 June 1995.
[71] Criminal Law Act 1977, s 51(3).

Sentencing

2.52 The maximum penalty is seven years' imprisonment on indictment, or, if tried summarily, six months' imprisonment or a fine not exceeding the statutory maximum or both.[72]

2.53 Judges have been encouraged to pass deterrent sentences. In upholding a sentence of twelve months' imprisonment on two appellants who had telephoned the police to say that two incendiary devices had been placed at a number of shops, seemingly with the intention of causing financial loss:

> A bomb hoax of this kind, as this court has had occasion to say in the past, is a public nuisance, and it is important not to underestimate the anxiety and apprehension that this kind of behaviour engenders. The public rightly expect judges to pass severe sentences as a mark of public disapprobation of this kind of offence.[73]

2.54 Whilst that principle has not changed, it would appear that 'public disapprobation' of this kind of offending certainly has. Sentencing ranges referred to in earlier works on public order demonstrate that this offence has been viewed in a much more serious light in recent years. It is impossible to imagine a repetition in today's climate of the £50 fine imposed in 1986 for a hoax bomb alert at the South African Airways desk at Heathrow Airport.[74]

2.55 In *R v Harrison*,[75] the Court of Appeal upheld a sentence of four years' imprisonment on an appellant (with an antecedent history of like offences) who had made a series of phone calls to a theatre saying that a bomb had been planted. In *R v Harris*,[76] the Court of Appeal held that a total sentence (on a guilty plea) of three years' imprisonment was appropriate for an appellant who had manufactured two imitation bombs and taken one to a police station and one to a restaurant resulting in the premises and surrounding being evacuated. In *R v Philipson*,[77] a sentence imposed on a mentally disordered offender for communicating a bomb hoax was reduced to six months' imprisonment. The hoax was manifestly false and had caused no fear of disruption but the court found that a custodial sentence was warranted in the interests of protecting the public and the emergency services from such acts.[78]

F. Racial and Religious Hatred

2.56 The first offence of incitement to racial hatred was created by s 6 of the Race Relations Act 1965. Before then, such conduct was penalized, albeit rarely and without great success, under the common law offences of seditious libel, criminal libel, or public mischief. Even under the 1965 Act there were few prosecutions, and of those that were, a significant proportion of them were against black people, the most notable being the trial of Michael X for addressing a Black Power

---

[72] Ibid, s 51(4), as amended by the Criminal Justice Act 1991, s 24(4).
[73] *R v Dunbar* (1987) 9 Cr App R (S) 393.
[74] P Thornton, *Public Order Law* (1986) p 58.
[75] [1997] 2 Cr App R (S) 174.
[76] [2005] 2 Cr App R (S) 649.
[77] [2008] 2 Cr App R (S) 110.
[78] See also *R v Cook* [2006] 2 Cr App R 106.

meeting in Reading.[79] Many prosecutions failed because of the requirement to prove an intent to stir up racial hatred, and in the end, Lord Scarman concluded:

> Section 6 of the Race Relations Act is merely an embarrassment to the police. Hedged about with restrictions (proof of intent, requirement of the Attorney General's consent) it is useless to a policeman on the street.[80]

The Public Order Act 1986 was an attempt to cure these defects and this Act, along with subsequent legislation, now provides a broad range of provisions to deal with public order incidents involving both racial and religious hatred.

Stirring up racial and religious hatred (or on grounds of sexual orientation)

Part III of the Public Order Act 1986 introduced six specific offences addressing the stirring up of racial hatred. The Racial and Religious Hatred Act 2006[81] inserted like offences addressing religious hatred. The offences are triable either way and no proceedings may be instituted except by, or with the consent of, the Attorney General.[82] For the purpose of the rules against duplicity, each of ss 18–23 of the Act creates one offence. **2.57**

Hatred against a person on grounds of sexual orientation was added to the racial and religious hatred provisions, below, by the Criminal Justice and Immigration Act 2008, s 74, Schedule 16, but at the time of writing is not yet in force. **2.58**

There are two concepts that are common to many of the offences, and these will be examined first, before turning to the individual offences. **2.59**

Racial hatred

Section 17 of the Public Order Act 1986 provides: **2.60**

> In this part, 'racial hatred' means hatred against a group of persons . . . defined by reference to colour, race, nationality.

See 2.90, below, for a definition of 'racial group'. **2.61**

Religious hatred

Section 29A of the Public Order Act 1986 provides: **2.62**

> In this part 'religious hatred' means hatred against a group of persons defined by reference to religious belief or lack of religious belief.[83]

An attempt at a definition of 'religious' is notoriously elusive. A list of widely recognized religions was provided in the *Explanatory Memorandum*, along with those such as atheists and humanists who are without religion. **2.63**

---

[79] *R v Malik* [1968] 1 All ER 582.

[80] *Report on the Red Lion Square Disorders*, Cmnd 5919 (1975) para 125.

[81] SI 2007/2497 brought the 2006 Act into force on 1 October 2007 (except for the insertion of a s 29B(3)).

[82] Public Order Act 1986, s 27(3).

[83] When the Criminal Justice and Immigration Act 2008, s 74 and Sch 16 is in force a new s 29AB will be inserted to include hatred on grounds of sexual orientation.

2.64 There was widespread concern at these provisions as the Racial and Religious Hatred Bill passed through Parliament, both from religious groups who were concerned it would impede their proselytizing 'duties', as well as from comedians and commentators concerned it would restrict their right to mock and criticize. Therefore, in addition to the protections afforded by Articles 9, 10, and 11 of the European Convention on Human Rights, s 29J of the Act provides only in relation to the religious hatred offences:

> Nothing in this part shall be read or given effect in a way which prohibits or restricts discussion, criticism, or expressions of antipathy, dislike, ridicule, insult or abuse of particular religions or the beliefs or practices of their adherents, or of any other belief system or the beliefs or practices of its adherents, or proselytising or urging adherents of a different religion or belief system to cease practising their religion or belief system.

Actus reus

2.65 The *actus reus* of each offence of racial hatred, encompasses acts or material which is abusive, threatening, or insulting. The *actus reus* of each offence of religious hatred encompasses only acts or material which is threatening. This difference is deliberate, the result of extensive lobbying from both civil liberties and faith groups in response to the new provisions on religious hatred.[84]

Mens rea

2.66 The racial and religious offences are both made out if the prosecution are able to prove an intention to stir up racial hatred.[85] Historically, there had often been difficulties in proving this intention. In relation to the racial offence only, each section provides an alternative offence namely that, having regard to all the circumstances, racial hatred was likely to be stirred up. This alternative offence does not require intention, and for that reason it is likely to be a far more attractive option to prosecutors.

Words, behaviour, written material stirring up racial and religious hatred (s 18 racial hatred/s 29B religious hatred)

2.67 A person who uses threatening, abusive, or insulting words or behaviour, or displays any written material which is threatening, abusive, or insulting, commits an offence if he

(a) intends thereby to stir up racial hatred;[86] or,
(b) having regard to all the circumstances racial hatred is likely to be stirred up thereby.[87]

For the alternative racial hatred offence in (b), a person who is not shown to have intended to stir up racial hatred is not guilty of an offence under this section if he did not intend his words or behaviour, or the written material, to be, and was not aware that it might be, threatening, abusive, or insulting.[88]

---

[84] See, for example, *Racial and Religious Hatred Bill: Liberty's Briefing for Second Reading in the House of Commons* (June 2005).
[85] Public Order Act 1986, ss 18(1)(a) and 29B.
[86] Ibid, s 18(1)(a).
[87] Ibid, s 18(1)(b).
[88] Ibid, s 18(5).

A person who uses threatening words or behaviour, or displays any written material which **2.68**
is threatening, is guilty of an offence if he

(a) intends thereby to stir up religious hatred.[89]

Written material includes any sign or visible representation. The offence may be committed in a public or private place, but no offence is committed where the words or behaviour are used or the written material is displayed by a person inside a dwelling[90] and are not heard or seen except by other persons in that or another dwelling.[91] Furthermore, it is a defence for the accused to prove that he was inside a dwelling and had no reason to believe that the words or behaviour used, or the written material displayed, would be heard or seen by a person outside that or any other dwelling.[92]

Publishing or distributing written material stirring up racial or religious hatred

A person who publishes or distributes written material which is threatening, abusive or **2.69**
insulting commits an offence if

(a) he intends thereby to stir up racial hatred;[93] or
(b) having regard to all the circumstances racial hatred is likely to be stirred up thereby.[94]

A person who publishes or distributes written material which is threatening is guilty of an **2.70**
offence if

(a) he intends thereby to stir up religious hatred.[95]

It is a defence for an accused who is not shown to have intended to stir up racial hatred to **2.71**
prove that he was not aware of the content of the material and did not suspect, and had no reason to suspect, that it was threatening, abusive, or insulting.[96]

Publication or distribution means publication or distribution to the public or a section of **2.72**
the public.[97] While this new definition removes the previous exemption for material circulated to an association,[98] the decision in *R v Britton*[99] is not directly affected by the changes. The Court of Appeal held that the leaving by a 'wretched little youth' of a pamphlet entitled 'Blacks not wanted here' in the porch of the home of Sidney Bidwell, a Member of Parliament, was not a publication to the public at large. Lord Parker CJ in a narrow judgment held that an MP and his family were not a section of the public within the meaning of the Race Relations Act 1965 and the facts (late at night, at some distance from the street) militated against calling this a distribution. This judgment has been subject

---

[89] Ibid, ss 29B. When the Criminal Justice and Immigration Act 2008, s 74 and Sch 16 come into force this section will be amended to include the words 'or hatred on the grounds of sexual orientation'.
[90] Dwelling is defined in the Public Order Act 1986, ss 29 and 29N.
[91] Ibid, ss 18(2) and 29B(2).
[92] Ibid, ss 18(4) and 29B(4).
[93] Ibid, s 19(1)(a).
[94] Ibid, s 19(1)(b).
[95] Ibid, s 29C.
[96] Ibid, s 19(2).
[97] Ibid, ss 19(3) and 29C(2).
[98] Public Order Act 1936, s 5A(6).
[99] [1967] 2 QB 51.

to criticism,[100] and given the deliberate widening of the scope of the Act by the 1986 Act it is submitted that a similar case may well be decided differently today.

Public performance of a play stirring up racial or religious hatred

2.73   If a public performance of a play is given which involves the use of threatening, abusive, or insulting words or behaviour, any person who presents or directs the performance is guilty of an offence if

(a) he intends thereby to stir up religious hatred;[101] or

(b) having regard to all the circumstances (and, in particular, taking the performance as a whole) racial hatred is likely to be stirred up thereby;[102] or

(c) intends thereby to stir up religious hatred.[103]

The words play and public performance have the same meaning as in s 18 of the Theatres Act 1968.[104] The offence does not arise if the performance was given solely or primarily for the purposes of rehearsal, making a recording of the performance or enabling the performance to be included in a programme service.[105] Performers are protected unless they perform otherwise than in accordance with their direction.[106]

2.74   If a person presenting or directing the performance is not shown to have intended to stir up religious hatred, it is a defence for him to prove that he did not know and had no reason to suspect that the performance would use those offending words or behaviour, or that he had no reason to believe those words were threatening, abusive, or insulting, or that he did not know and had no reason to suspect that the circumstances in which the performance would be given would be such that racial hatred would be likely to be stirred up.[107]

Distributing, showing, or playing a recording stirring up racial or religious hatred

2.75   A person who distributes, shows, or plays a recording of visual images or sounds which are threatening, abusive, or insulting is guilty of an offence if

(a) he intends thereby to stir up racial hatred;[108] or

(b) having regard to all the circumstances racial hatred is likely to be stirred up thereby.[109]

2.76   A person who distributes, shows, or plays a recording of visual images or sounds which are threatening is guilty of an offence if

(a) he intends thereby to stir up religious hatred.[110]

---

[100] P Thornton, *Public Order Law* (1986) p 65; M Partington, 'Race Relations Act 1965: A Too Restricted View?' [1967] Crim LR 497.
[101] Public Order Act 1986, s 20(1)(a).
[102] Ibid, s 20(1)(b).
[103] Ibid, s 29D.
[104] Ibid, ss 20(5) and 29D(4).
[105] Ibid, ss 20(3) and 29D(2).
[106] Ibid, ss 20(4) and 29D(3).
[107] Ibid, s 20(2).
[108] Ibid, s 21(1)(a).
[109] Ibid, s 21(1)(b).
[110] Ibid, s 29E(1).

It is a defence for an accused who is not shown to have intended to stir up racial hatred to prove that he was not aware of the content of the recording and did not suspect, and had no reason to suspect, that it was threatening, abusive, or insulting.[111]   **2.77**

Broadcasting a programme stirring up racial or religious hatred

If a programme including any of the following and with the following intent, is included in a programme service, then the person providing the programme service, the person directing the programme, and the person by whom the offending words or behaviour are used are all guilty of an offence including   **2.78**

(a) threatening, abusive, or insulting visual images or sounds, if he intends to stir up racial hatred;[112]

(b) threatening, abusive, or insulting visual images or sounds, if having regard to all the circumstances racial hatred is likely to be stirred up thereby;[113]

(c) threatening visual images or sounds, if he intends thereby to stir up religious hatred.[114]

The defences for a person charged under (b) are set out in s 28(3)–(6). In summary, they are that the person either did not know the material would be in the programme; or that the programme would be included in a programme service; or that that they did not know and had no reason to suspect that racial hatred was likely to be stirred up; or that they did not know and had no reason to suspect that the material was threatening, abusive, or insulting.   **2.79**

Possession of written material or recording stirring up racial or religious hatred

A person who has the following material in his possession: **2.80**

(a) written material with a view to it being displayed, published, distributed, or included in a programme service (whether by that person or another); or

(b) recorded material (of visual images or sounds) with a view to it being distributed, shown, played, or included in a programme service (whether by that person or another),

is guilty of an offence if

(a) it is threatening, abusive, or insulting, and he intends racial hatred to be stirred up thereby, or, having regard to all the circumstances, racial hatred is likely to be stirred up thereby;[115] or

(b) it is threatening, abusive, or insulting, and he intends religious hatred to be stirred up thereby.[116]

It is a defence for an accused who is not shown to have intended to stir up racial hatred to prove that he was not aware of the content of the written material or recording

---

[111] Ibid, s 21(3).
[112] Ibid, s 22(1)–(2).
[113] Ibid, s 22(1)–(2).
[114] Ibid, s 29F.
[115] Ibid, s 23(1).
[116] Ibid, s 29G.

and did not suspect, and had no reason to suspect, that it was threatening, abusive, or insulting.[117]

2.81 A magistrate may issue a search warrant for premises if satisfied that there are reasonable grounds for suspecting that a person has possession of such written material or recording.[118]

Defences

2.82 In addition to the specific defences mentioned above, these provisions do not apply to fair and accurate reports of Parliamentary proceedings.[119] The truth of material, or belief in its truth, is not a defence.[120]

Liability of corporations

2.83 Where a body corporate is guilty of one of these offences, and it is shown that the offence was committed with the consent or connivance of a director, manager, secretary, or other similar body (or members if managed by its members), or a person purporting to act in any such capacity, such a person, as well as the body corporate is guilty of an offence and liable to be proceeded against and punished accordingly.[121]

Sentence

2.84 The maximum penalty on indictment is seven years' imprisonment, a fine, or both and six months' imprisonment or a fine not exceeding the statutory maximum or both if dealt with summarily. The maximum was increased from two years to seven years by s 40 of the Anti-terrorism, Crime and Security Act 2001.

2.85 A sentence of imprisonment was upheld in the case of *R v Saleem, Muhid & Javed*[122] which arose out of a demonstration in response to a Danish publication containing cartoons depicting the Prophet Mohammed. Placards declaring 'Be Prepared for the Real Holocaust' and 'Massacre Those Who Insult Islam' were held, and chants of 'Bomb, bomb the UK' were repeated. The Court took into account that the offending had occurred during a one-off demonstration, mounted at short notice without sophisticated planning and was thus not comparable to cases of solicitation to murder and stirring up racial hatred.[123] The sentence of four years' imprisonment imposed on Saleem for stirring up racial hatred contrary to s 18 (after trial) was reduced to thirty months' imprisonment after trial. Muhid and Javed were additionally charged with solicitation to murder and received total sentences of four years' imprisonment.

2.86 In *R v Gray*,[124] the Court of Appeal upheld a sentence of twelve months' imprisonment following a plea of guilty to the possession of magazines containing racist material,

---

[117] Ibid, s 23(3).
[118] Ibid, ss 25 and 29H.
[119] Ibid, ss 26 and 29K.
[120] *Birdwood*, unreported, 11 April 1995.
[121] Public Order Act 1986, ss 28 and 29M.
[122] [2008] 2 Cr App R (S) 12.
[123] *R v El-Faisal (Abdullah Ibrahim) (Reasons for Dismissal of Appeal)* [2004] EWCA Crim 456; *R v Abu Hamza* (2006) QB 659.
[124] [1999] 1 Cr App R (S) 50.

contrary to s 23. The defendant was also involved in their distribution. It is of note that the Court commented that reported decisions from the 1970s and 1980s were of limited value, since 'the grave social danger done by offences and remarks of a racist nature is now perhaps better known than it was then'.[125] This has now been recognized by Parliament with the significant increase to the maximum sentence.

Forfeiture

Following a conviction for an offence under s 18 (relating to display of written material), **2.87** 19, 20, 23, 29B (relating to a display of written material), 29C, 29E, or 29G, the court shall order to be forfeited any written material or recording produced to the court and shown to its satisfaction to be written material or a recording to which the offence relates. The order does not take effect until the time limits for appeal have expired or any appeal has been finally decided or abandoned.[126]

Racially or religiously aggravated offences

The Crime and Disorder Act 1998[127] (as extended by s 39 of the Anti-terrorism, Crime and **2.88** Security Act 2001) introduced an aggravated form of some existing offences. Section 29 covers offences of wounding or GBH contrary to s 20 Offences Against the Person Act 1865; assault occasioning actual bodily harm contrary to s 47 Offences Against the Person Act 1865; and common assault. Section 30 covers criminal damage. Section 31 covers the lesser public order offences in ss 4, 4A, and 5 of the Public Order Act 1986. Section 32 covers harassment contrary to ss 2 and 4 of the Protection from Harassment Act 1997. The justification for treating such conduct more severely than the basic versions of these crimes is helpfully summarized by Ivan Hare, *Legislating Against Hate—The Legal Response to Bias Crimes*:[128]

> The case for an explicit response to the phenomenon rests fundamentally on the realization that crimes motivated by hatred for the group to which the victim belongs are in some sense of a qualitatively distinct order of gravity. This perception arises from intuitive feelings of retribution and from awareness of the impact such offences have on the immediate victims and on society as a whole. In addition to being the target of an act of violence the victim is likely to feel a sense of injustice at having been discriminated against on the basis of his membership of, or association with, a particular group. The more general strain of the argument is that hate crimes entail a threat to the public welfare which makes it appropriate to punish them more severely.

[125] Therefore, the following are of limited value: *R v Relf* (1979) 1 Cr App R (S) 111: eleven months' imprisonment imposed for publishing leaflets containing derogatory references to the West Indian community which were displayed in various public places; *R v Edwards* (1983) 5 Cr App R (S) 145: twelve months' imprisonment imposed for a comic strip intended for publication in a magazine and designed to prejudice children against Jews.
[126] Public Order Act 1986, ss 25 and 29I.
[127] As extended by the Anti-terrorism, Crime and Security Act 2001, s 39, to add religiously aggravated offences.
[128] (1997) 17 OJLS 415.

If an offence is racially or religiously aggravated but falls outside those offences, then the sentencing judge is still entitled to increase the sentence taking into account those aggravating features by virtue of s 145 of the Criminal Justice Act 2003.[129]

The Test (s 28)

2.89 Any of the above offences become aggravated, either racially or religiously, if

(a) at the time of committing the offence, or immediately before or after doing so, the offender demonstrates towards the victim of the offence hostility based on the victim's membership (or presumed membership) of a racial or religious group; or

(b) the offence is motivated (wholly or partly) by hostility towards members of a racial or religious group.

Membership includes association with members of that group; presumed means presumed by the offender;[130] and the hostility can also be based on another factor at the same time.[131]

Racial or religious groups

2.90 A racial group means a group of persons defined by reference to race, colour, nationality (including citizenship), or ethnic or national origins.[132] This is a definition that follows closely the definition in both the Race Relations Act 1976[133] and the Public Order Act 1986.[134] In considering the use of words such as 'bloody foreigners' and 'get back to your own country', the House of Lords in *R v Rogers*[135] took a broad, non-technical approach to this definition, taking into account that the mischief of the section was aimed at racism and xenophobia. This broad approach followed the decision of the House of Lords in *Mandla v Dowell Lee*[136] where, in affirming that Sikhs were a racial group, Lord Fraser found that an ethnic group must have two essential characteristics: a long shared history, of which the group is conscious as distinguishing it from other groups; and a cultural tradition of its own including family and social customs and manners, often, but not necessarily associated with, religious observance. On these principles, 'foreigners' or 'Africans' may be a 'racial group' within the section.[137]

2.91 It would appear that Jews are protected under this definition,[138] as are gypsies (of Romany origin as opposed to 'travellers').[139] Rastafarians are not members of an ethnic group separate from the rest of the Afro-Caribbean community.

---

[129] Section 145 is identical to s 153 of the Power of Criminal Courts (Sentencing) Act 2000. Note that the Criminal Justice Act 2003, s 146, applies to aggravation on grounds of disability or sexual orientation.

[130] Crime and Disorder Act 1998, s 28(2).

[131] Ibid, s 28(3).

[132] Ibid, s 28(4).

[133] Ibid, s 3(1).

[134] Public Order Act 1986, s 16.

[135] [2007] 2 AC 62, HL; see also *DPP v M* [2004] 1 WLR 2758 ('bloody foreigners'); *AG's Ref (No 4 of 2004)* [2005] 2 Cr App R 26, CA ('immigrant doctor').

[136] In *Mandla v Dowell Lee* [1983] 2 AC 548, 562.

[137] *R v White (Anthony)* [2001] 1 WLR 1352.

[138] Lord Fraser approved the decision of the New Zealand Court of Appeal in *King-Ansell v Police* [1979] 2 NZLR 531.

[139] *Commission for Racial Equality v Dutton* [1989] QB 783.

A religious group means a group of persons defined by reference to religious belief or lack   **2.92**
of religious belief.[140]

Hostility

The hostility must be directed towards the victim at the time (or immediately before or   **2.93**
after) of the offence. That hostility is often evidenced by accompanying language, but a
judge would be entitled to conclude, on the basis of racial language used say, between five
and fifteen minutes earlier, that hostility shown at the later time was based upon the victim's
racial origin.[141] Whether the words or conduct actually demonstrated racial hostility is a
matter to be decided by the relevant tribunal of fact.[142]

A white offender chanting to a white police officer, 'I'd rather be a Paki, I'd rather be a   **2.94**
Paki, I'd rather be a Paki than a cop'[143] could not be guilty of an offence under s 28. It may
be that racial language of an offensive nature has been used, but unless the offender demonstrates hostility towards the victim based on *their* membership of a racial or religious
group, or that his racial hostility is a *motivation* for the offence, then the offending cannot
be brought within the section. In this case the offender's motivation was his dislike of
policemen.

The hostility need not be directed at a victim who is of a different racial, national, ethnic,   **2.95**
or religious group than the defendant;[144] and the section contemplates the possibility that
a defendant's hostility was based on a victim (of the same group) who has an association
with another group, or even that a defendant was mistaken that a victim belonged to
another group, even though in reality the victim was of the same group as the defendant.[145]
This reading of the section is not easily reconciled with the judgment in *DPP v Lal*,[146]
where the conviction of an Asian defendant who assaulted an Asian caretaker calling the
victim a 'white man's arse licker' and a 'brown Englishman' was overturned. However, that
decision was doubted by Baroness Hale in *Rogers*.[147]

In *Norwood v DPP*,[148] a BNP regional organizer displayed, in the first floor window of his   **2.96**
flat, a poster containing the words 'Islam out of Britain' and 'Protect the British people'.
Following a complaint, he was prosecuted for the racially aggravated form of s 5 of the
Public Order Act 1986. He contended that the poster was intended to refer to Muslim
extremism in the light of the events of 11 September 2001. He did not believe the poster
offensive or emotive, and that the poster was a BNP slogan against 'creeping Islamification'.
When considering the defence of whether the behaviour was reasonable, the Divisional
Court considered Article 10 of the European Convention on Human Rights within the
defence of reasonableness (an objective test) in s 5(3) of the Public Order Act 1986. Applying

---

[140] Crime and Disorder Act 1998, s 28(5).
[141] *R v Babbs* [2007] EWCA Crim 2737.
[142] *Johnson v DPP* [2008] EWHC 509 (Admin).
[143] *DPP v Howard* [2008] 4 Archbold News 3, DC.
[144] *R v White* [2001] 1 WLR 1352.
[145] See reference to 'presumed'.
[146] [2000] Crim LR 756.
[147] [2007] 2 AC 62, HL, para 15.
[148] [2002] EWHC 1546 (Admin).

the approach taken by Hallett J in *Percy v DPP*,[149] the questions to be asked were whether the defendant's conduct went beyond legitimate protest and whether the behaviour had not formed part of an open expression of opinion on a matter of public interest, but had become disproportionate and unreasonable. The Divisional Court upheld the conviction.

Sentencing

2.97 The racially or religiously aggravated form of each offence carries a higher maximum penalty and has attracted significantly higher sentences in practice.[150] The appropriate practice is for the sentencing tribunal to first identify the sentence that would have been passed in the absence of racial or religious aggravation, and then add an appropriate amount to reflect the aggravating element, indicating the extent of that extra amount.[151]

2.98 In sentencing those convicted of offences which do not have a specific aggravated form but which have nonetheless been racially or religiously[152] aggravated, s 145 of the Criminal Justice Act 2003 requires that the courts must[153] treat this element as an aggravating factor. The extent to which the sentence may be increased by reference to the aggravating effect of racial aggravation is not necessarily limited to two years and the appropriate amount will depend on the circumstances of the case.[154]

G. Public Nuisance

2.99 Historically, the conduct complained of was of a wondrous variety, including erecting a manufactory for hartshorn; keeping a ferocious dog unmuzzled; and keeping hogs near a public street and feeding them with offal. It also covers the emissions of smoke, noise, and smells from factories and mines. Today a vast swath of regulation exists to prohibit what had been prosecuted as public nuisance, from the Environmental Protection Act 1990 to the Dangerous Dogs Act 1991.[155] While the Courts have no power to abolish the offence,[156] the unanimous opinion of the House of Lords in *R v Rimmington and Goldstein* was that the most typical and obvious forms of public nuisance were now subject to statutory provision. It would almost always be preferable to prosecute the conduct under statutory law rather than common law, not only because of the primacy of Parliament, but also because statute defined the mode of trial, the maximum penalty, and might provide a statutory

---

[149] [2001] EWHC Admin 1125.
[150] *R v Kelly* [2001] 1 Cr App R (S) 341; *R v Bridger* [2006] EWCA Crim 3169.
[151] *R v Kelly and Donnelly* [2001] 2 Cr App R (S) 73; *R v Saunders* [2000] 1 Cr App R (S) 71, CA. In *R v Pells*; *AG's Ref (No 92 of 2003)*, The Times, 21 April 2004, CA, it was said that the observation in Saunders that, following a trial, a period of up to two years should be added to the term of imprisonment otherwise appropriate for the offence had it not been religiously aggravated, remained valid, but it needed to be read in the light of the Sentencing Advisory Panel's advice to the effect that the differential increase in the maximum penalties provided for by the Crime and Disorder Act 1998 carried no special significance and it would be wrong for courts to determine the sentencing range for the aggravated offences primarily by reference to the maximum sentences available: see *Archbold 2009*, para 5.89.
[152] Or aggravated on grounds of disability or sexual orientation: Criminal Justice Act 2003, s 146.
[153] Criminal Justice Act 2003, s 145(2)(a).
[154] *R v Morrison* [2001] 1 Cr App R (S) 5, CA.
[155] *R v Rimmington* [2006] 1 AC 459: a number of such offences are identified by Lord Bingham at para 29.
[156] Ibid, at para 31.

defence—all of which were absent from the common law crime. Furthermore, the common law offence should not be employed to avoid time limits or restrictions on penalty.[157]

In addition to these limitations on its use, an earlier Law Commission Report had expressed the hope that prosecutors would not feel the need to resort to the offence in public order situations.[158] Nonetheless, the door has been left open for occasions where a prosecutor can put forward the 'good reason' for prosecuting the common law offence of public nuisance. The common law principles contained within the offence of public nuisance are entirely consistent with Article 7(1) of the European Convention on Human Rights.[159] The crime is sufficiently defined[160] to meet the not particularly exacting[161] requirements of certainty set by the Convention. **2.100**

Definition

The House of Lords in *Rimmington and Goldstein* referred to numerous texts and cases on the definitions of the crime of public nuisance and only a selection find their way into the judgment.[162] The Court declined to define public nuisance except by example. The offence had developed into what Professor JR Spencer described as 'a rag bag of odds and ends which we should nowadays call "public welfare offences"',[163] and it would be beyond the scope of this work to embark upon a comprehensive examination of those sources. The common thread that can be found is, to use a phrase coined by Lord Bingham, 'the requirement of common injury'. In the first edition of his work in 1822, JF Archbold[164] published a precedent of an indictment for carrying on an offensive trade. The requirement of common injury was recognized in the particulars: **2.101**

> to the great damage and common nuisance of all the liege subjects of our said lord the King there inhabiting, being and residing, and going, returning, and passing through the said streets and highways.

Sir James Stephen in *A Digest to the Criminal Law* defined public nuisance as: **2.102**

> An act not warranted by law or an omission to discharge a legal duty, which act or omission obstructs or causes inconvenience or damage to the public in the exercise of rights common to all Her Majesty's subjects.[165]

This definition remained unchanged in the eighth and ninth editions of the Digest published in 1947 and 1950 and remains in similar terms in the current edition of *Archbold*,

---

[157] Ibid, at para 30.
[158] *Criminal Law: Offences Relating to Public Order*, Law Com 123 (1983).
[159] Per conclusions of Lord Bingham in *Rimmington and Goldstein* at paras 34–7.
[160] *Rimmington and Goldstein*, para 36.
[161] The standard as described by B Emmerson and A Ashworth, *Human Rights and Criminal Justice* (2001), para 10.23.
[162] *Rimmington*, paras 8–27.
[163] JR Spencer, 'Public Nuisance—A Critical Examination' [1989] CLJ 55, 59.
[164] JR Archbold, *A Summary of the Law Relating to Criminal Pleading and Evidence in Criminal Cases* (1822, 1st edn).
[165] Sir James Stephen, *A Digest to the Criminal Law* (1877) Ch XIX, p 108.

save in its reference to morals.[166] However, more helpful direction is discovered in an examination of what, on the facts, has amounted to public nuisance.

2.103   Returning to the first edition of Archbold, examples given of a public nuisance included using a shop in a public market as a slaughter house; erecting a privy near a highway; keeping hogs near a public street and feeding them with offal; keeping a fierce and unruly bull in a field through which there was a footway; and baiting a bull in the King's highway.

2.104   The examples arising from the case law are equally varied. Defendants responsible for impregnating the air with 'noisome and offensive stinks and smells' caused a nuisance to 'all the King's liege subjects' living in Twickenham and travelling and passing the King's highway.[167] A mother who took her young child through a public street well-knowing that the child suffered from the contagious, infectious, and dangerous disease of smallpox was convicted of the offence and sentenced to three months' imprisonment.[168] In 1991 an 'acid house party' which had lasted for about twelve hours overnight, with very loud music and which resulted in the nearby roads being blocked with traffic and surrounding woodland being littered with human excrement amounted to a public nuisance.[169] A plan to extinguish the floodlights at a Premier Division football match in order to make a fraudulent gain for a group of Far Eastern bookmakers would also have amounted to a public nuisance when those attending the match, presumably a crowd of thousands, would have been plunged into darkness.[170]

2.105   It is possible therefore to find some certainty. A legal adviser asked to give his opinion in advance should ascertain whether the act or omission contemplated was likely to inflict significant injury on a substantial section of the public exercising their ordinary rights as such. If so, an obvious risk of causing a public nuisance would be apparent; if not, not.[171]

Public nuisance vs private nuisance

2.106   Public nuisance differs from private nuisance only in the wider range of its impact.[172] In *AG v PYA Quarries Ltd*[173] (described as 'the leading modern authority on public nuisance' by Lord Bingham in *Rimmington and Goldstein*), the Court differentiated between public and private nuisance on what had become conventional grounds:

> The classic statement of the difference is that a public nuisance affects Her Majesty's subjects generally, whereas a private nuisance only affects particular individuals.
>
> . . .
>
> A public nuisance is a nuisance which is so widespread in its range or so indiscriminate in its effect that it would not be reasonable to expect one person to take proceedings on his own

---

[166] *Archbold's Criminal Pleading, Evidence and Practice 2009* (2009), 31–40.
[167] *R v White and Ward* (1757) 1 Bur 333.
[168] *R v Vantandillo* (1815) 4 M&S 73.
[169] *R v Ruffell* (1991) 13 Cr App R (S) 204, see also *R v Shorrock* [1994] QB 279.
[170] *R v Ong* [2001] 1 Cr App R (S) 404.
[171] The definition adopted by Lord Bingham when considering whether there was a definition that met the requirements of certainty in the European Convention on Human Rights: *Rimmington*, para 36.
[172] *R v Shorrock* [1994] QB 279.
[173] [1957] 2 QB 169.

responsibility to put a stop to it, but that it should be taken on the responsibility of the community at large.[174]

Any suggestion that public nuisance could be committed by isolated acts or a series of isolated acts[175] was rejected in *Rimmington and Goldstein*. The injury has to be suffered by the community—or a significant section of it—as a whole.[176] Therefore, despite previous authorities on the subject, it is now clear law that persistent and vexatious telephone calls to an individual victim lack the element of common injury to a section of the public and cannot amount to public nuisance[177] if targeted at the individual. If, however, the call was a hoax message of a public danger, such as a hoax telephone call that an explosive device had been placed in a railway station, that would be capable of constituting the offence even though made to one person alone.[178] **2.107**

Mens rea

A defendant is responsible for a nuisance which he knew, or ought to have known (because the means of knowledge were available to him), would be the consequence of what he did or omitted to do.[179] In *Rimmington and Goldstein*, Mr Goldstein, an orthodox Jew, was a supplier of kosher food. He owed a debt to his old friend Mr Ehrlich, who had pressed for repayment. Goldstein finally sent Ehrlich a cheque in the post and included in the envelope a small quantity of salt. This was a wry joke, in recognition of the age of the debt—salt being used as a preservative in kosher food. Unfortunately for Goldstein, when the envelope reached the sorting office, the salt leaked into the hands of a postal worker, who feared it was anthrax and called the police, who evacuated the building, thereby causing disruption to the postal system. He was convicted. However, on a correct application of the test, Lord Bingham held that his conviction must be quashed: **2.108**

> . . . the escape of the salt was not a result which Mr Goldstein intended. Nor, plainly was it a result which he knew would occur, since it would have rendered his intended joke entirely futile. It would seem far-fetched to conclude that he should reasonably have known that the salt would escape, at any rate without detailed consideration of the type of envelope used and the care taken in sealing it. He himself said that he had no idea the salt would leak out (see the Court of Appeal judgment, para 38). But neither at trial nor on appeal was this question squarely addressed. The emphasis was on a foreseeable consequence if there were an escape and not on the foreseeability of an unintended escape. In the event, I conclude that it was not proved against Mr Goldstein that he knew or reasonably should have known (because the means of knowledge were available to him) that the salt would escape in the sorting office or in the course of post.

Vicarious liability

In giving judgment in *R v Stephens*,[180] Mellor J held that all the prosecutor was required to prove was that 'the nuisance was caused in the carrying on of the works of the quarry', and **2.109**

---

[174] Ibid, per Romer J.
[175] An idea which originated in the judgment of Denning LJ in *PYA Quarries*.
[176] *Rimmington and Goldstein*, para 37.
[177] Ibid, para 38.
[178] Ibid, per Lord Nicholls, para 42.
[179] *R v Shorrock* [1994] QB 279, 289.
[180] (1866) LR 1 QB 702, 708–9.

it was irrelevant that the owner who was convicted was not present at the quarry due to age or infirmity and had in fact directed that refuse from the works should not fall into the river (the nuisance complained of). This strict approach was acknowledged by Wright J in *Sherras v De Rutzen*,[181] the rule being seen as an exception to the general rule that *mens rea* is an ingredient in every case, and the balance of authority weighs in favour of this interpretation applying to all forms of public nuisance.[182]

Defences

2.110 Statutory authorization for the conduct is a defence to public nuisance.[183]

Sentence

2.111 On indictment, the offence is punishable with imprisonment for life, and on summary conviction six months' imprisonment or a fine not exceeding the statutory maximum. The offence has been prosecuted infrequently in modern times and it is difficult to give a proper indication as to the sentencing range. There is some old authority that, in practice, the maximum should not exceed two years' imprisonment unless the case is a serious one.[184] More recently, the defendants who arranged to cause the abandoning of the Premiership match by switching off the floodlights (at 2.104 above) were sentenced to four years' imprisonment, taking into account the large sums of money that stood to be gained and the many thousands of people who would have been put at risk. The Court of Appeal upheld a twelve-month suspended prison sentence imposed on the organizer of the acid house party (at 2.104 above), but quashed the fine imposed, because of his lack of means.

H. Criminal Damage

2.112 The offences under the Criminal Damage Act 1971 include criminal damage; aggravated criminal damage; arson; threats to destroy or damage property; and possession of items with intent to destroy or damage criminal property.

Criminal damage

2.113 Section 1(1) of the Criminal Damage Act 1971 provides that a person who (a) without lawful excuse, (b) destroys or damages any property, (c) belonging to another, and (d) intending to destroy or damage any such property or being reckless as to whether any such property would be destroyed or damaged shall be guilty of an offence.[185]

---

[181] [1895] 1 QB 918.

[182] While the decision in *Stephens* was doubted in *Chisholm v Doulton* (1889) 22 QBD 736, it was *Stephens* and *Sherras* that were referred to without adverse comment in *Rimmington and Goldstein* and support can also be found for this position in the latest edition of David Ormerod, *Smith and Hogan Criminal Law* (2008, 12th edn) and also, by implication, in *R v Shorrock*.

[183] *Saunders v Holborn District Board of Works* [1895] 1 QB 64; *Managers of the Metropolitan Asylum District v Hill* (1881) LR 6 AC 193.

[184] *R v Morris* [1951] 1 KB 394; *R v Higgins* [1952] 1 KB 7.

[185] The Crime and Disorder Act 1998, s 30, creates the racially or religiously aggravated form of the offence: see 2.88.

Criminal damage is an offence triable either way[186] unless the value of the property alleged **2.114** to have been destroyed or the value of the alleged damage is less than £5,000, in which case the offence is treated as summary only.[187]

'Damage' is left undefined in the Act. What constitutes damage is a matter of fact and **2.115** degree, applying everyday common sense.[188] The Court of Appeal has upheld convictions where blankets soaked in water were said to be damaged[189] and water-soluble pavement paints were said to have damaged the pavement.[190]

'Property' is defined in the 1971 Act as meaning property of a tangible nature, whether real **2.116** or personal, and the Act makes specific provision that this includes wild creatures which have been tamed or are ordinarily kept in captivity but not does include mushrooms growing wild on any land; or flowers, fruit, or foliage, or a plant growing wild on any land.[191]

The requisite *mens rea* is either intention or recklessness. Following the House of Lords **2.117** decision in *R v G*,[192] the wider, subjective test of recklessness applies. A person acts recklessly with respect to

(a) a circumstance when he is aware of a risk that it exists or will exist;
(b) a result when he is aware of a risk that it will occur; and
(c) it is in the circumstances known to him, unreasonable to take the risk.

The meaning of 'lawful excuse' is explained in s 5 of the 1971 Act. What amounts to lawful **2.118** excuse is usually at the heart of protest related criminal damage cases, and this is discussed at length in 8.91 to 8.94.

The maximum sentence for criminal damage is ten years' imprisonment on indictment, or **2.119** six months or a fine not exceeding the statutory maximum if dealt with summarily. If, however, damage is quantified at less than £5,000 so that the offence must be treated as summary only, the maximum is reduced to three months' imprisonment or a fine not exceeding level 4 on the standard scale or both.[193]

Aggravated criminal damage; arson; threats to damage property, possession with intent to destroy or damage property

There are a number of aggravated forms of criminal damage set out in the Criminal Damage **2.120** Act 1971. Aggravated criminal damage, defined in s 1(2), is indictable only and includes the additional requirement that in committing the damage there was an intention or recklessness to endanger the life of another. Section 1(3) requires that an offence committed

---

[186] Magistrates' Court Act 1980, s 17 and Sch 1, para 29.
[187] Ibid, s 22 and Sch 2 (unless charged in the racially aggravated form).
[188] *Roe v Kingerlee* [1986] Crim LR 735.
[189] *Fiak* [2005] EWCA Crim 2381.
[190] *Hardman v Chief Constable of Avon and Somerset* [1986] Crim LR 330.
[191] Criminal Damage Act 1971, s 10(1).
[192] [2004] 1 AC 1034.
[193] Criminal Damage Act 1971, s 4(2).

under either s 1(1) or the aggravated form under s 1(2) by destroying or damaging property by fire shall be charged as arson.

2.121   The maximum sentence for criminal damage with intent to endanger life or recklessness as to whether life is endangered is life imprisonment.[194] The same applies for arson unless it is without intent or recklessness and is dealt with summarily, the maximum then being six months' imprisonment or a fine not exceeding the statutory maximum or both.

2.122   It is an offence for a person who, without lawful excuse, makes to another a threat to destroy or damage property belonging to that person or a third party, intending that the other would fear it would be carried out.[195] It is also an offence if a person threatens to damage his *own* property in a way which he knows is likely to endanger the life of that other or a third person.[196]

2.123   It is an offence if a person has anything in his custody or under his control intending without out lawful excuse to use it or cause or permit another to destroy or damage any property belonging to some other person[197] or to do the same to his own property in a way which he knows is likely to endanger the life of some other person.[198]

2.124   The maximum sentence for these two offences is ten years' imprisonment on indictment and six months' imprisonment or a fine or both if dealt with summarily.[199]

I. Animal Research Facilities

2.125   The Serious Organised Crime and Police Act 2005 introduced two offences designed to protect animal research facilities. It is an offence to interfere in contractual relations so as to harm an animal research organization and an offence to intimidate those connected with an animal research organization.

The legislative intent

2.126   In the 2004 White Paper, *Animal Welfare—Human Rights: Protecting People from Animal Rights Extremists*, the government maintained that 'the UK has in place one of the world's toughest regimes for licensing and controlling animal experiments' and lauded the 'extraordinary recent advances in genetics' arising from experiments involving animals. The paper pointed to the threat 'from a tiny minority of animal rights extremists' and promised to 'tighten the law' and ensure resources are available to increase protection to those working in this field.

2.127   'Animal rights extremist activity' was analysed in Section 3 of the Paper. It was accepted in the paper that the 'animal rights movement consists of a number of co-ordinated campaigns, some peaceful and some unlawful against a wide range of selected targets'.[200]

---

[194] Ibid, s 4(1).
[195] Ibid, s 2(a).
[196] Ibid, s 2(b).
[197] Ibid, s 3(a).
[198] Ibid, s 3(b).
[199] Ibid, s 4(2).
[200] *Animal Welfare—Human Rights: Protecting People from Animal Rights Extremists*, para 40.

The focus was very much on the approach taken by those campaigning to close down the animal research facility called Huntingdon Life Sciences (HLS).[201] The campaign focused activity on HLS's suppliers, customers, and shareholders. Supplier companies include those providing animals for the purpose of research at HLS, but also banks, fuel suppliers, and taxi companies. The 'criminal action ranges from threatening mail, aggravated trespass, e-mail, faxes and phone calls, to hoax explosive packages, serious assaults and, in the extreme, the use of explosive devices against property'.[202] The organization of this activity was described as 'a quasi-terrorist cellular structure'.[203]

The government's intended response was set out in Section 4 of the Paper and was described as a 'clear strategy to crack down on this sort of activity'. It was recognized that the conduct was already covered by a range of criminal offences[204] and the response was twofold: to systematically enforce the current law and to introduce new legislation to 'fill gaps in the law'. **2.128**

In response to increased animal rights activism, several changes had already been made to the law. Section 42 of the Criminal Justice and Police Act 2001 gave the police a new power to direct protestors away from homes, and in order to allow the police to control smaller groups the definition of 'public assembly' in s 16 of the Public Order Act 1986 was amended to reduce the definition of assembly from 20 or more persons to two or more persons.[205] Civil injunctions and preventative orders such as Anti-Social Behaviour Orders (ASBOs) were also being employed against animal rights activists.[206] **2.129**

At the time of the paper, the possibility of making it an offence to cause economic damage to the suppliers of firms or research groups had been considered. It was seen as 'a complex area which is difficult to define' but further consideration was promised. The subsequent Serious Organised Crime and Police Act 2005 contained two offences specifically directed at the protection of animal research organizations, though it should be noted that the Secretary of State may, by order, provide for these sections to apply to other persons or organizations in the same way they do to animal research organizations.[207] No proceedings for either offence may be instituted except by or with the consent of the Director of Public Prosecutions.[208] **2.130**

Interference in contractual relations so as to harm animal research organization

Section 145 of the Serious Organised Crime and Police Act makes it an offence if a person (A), with the intention of harming[209] an animal research organization[210] **2.131**

---

[201] Ibid, para 37.
[202] Ibid, para 42.
[203] Ibid, para 43.
[204] Set out in Annex A to the Paper.
[205] See 3.56 below.
[206] For injunctions, see 9.166 et seq. For ASBOs, see 9.178 et seq.
[207] Serious Organised Crime and Police Act 2005, s 149.
[208] Ibid, s 147.
[209] For the purposes of this section, to 'harm' an animal research organization means to cause the organization to suffer loss or damage of any description, or to prevent or hinder the carrying out by the organization of any of its activities.
[210] For definition of 'animal research organization' see s 148, in essence the holder of a licence (or a person specified) under the Animals (Scientific Procedures) Act 1986.

(a) does a relevant act, or threatens that he or somebody else will do a relevant act[211] (ie an act amounting to a criminal offence or a tortious act causing B to suffer loss or damage of any description, but the tortious act does not include an act which is actionable on the ground only that it induces another person to break a contract with B[212]);

(b) in circumstances in which that act or threat is intended or likely to cause a second person (B):

    (i) not to perform any contractual relationship obligation owed by B to a third person (C) (whether or not such non-performance amounts to breach of contract);

    (ii) to terminate any contract[213] B has with C; or

    (iii) not to enter into a contract with C.[214]

This section does not apply to any act done wholly or mainly in contemplation or furtherance of a trade dispute.[215]

Intimidation of persons connected with animal research organization

2.132 Section 146 of the Serious Organised Crime and Police Act 2005 makes it an offence if a person (A), with the intention of causing a second person (B) to abstain from doing something which B is entitled to do (or to do something which B is entitled to abstain from doing)

(a) threatens B that A or somebody else will do a relevant act (ie an act amounting to a criminal offence, or a tortious act causing B or another person to suffer loss or damage of any description); and

(b) A does so wholly or mainly because B is connected with an animal research organization[216] as set out, including an employee, student, or officer of an animal research organization, a lessor or licensor of premises occupied by such an organization or those having a financial interest in the organization, customers and suppliers, and family or friends of any of the above.[217]

Criticism of the legislation

2.133 The Joint Committee for Human Rights when reporting on the measures directed at animal research facilities set out in the Bill,[218] and recognizing that the new offences clearly engaged the right to freedom of expression in Article 10 of the European Convention on Human Rights, examined two distinct compatibility arguments. The first was the necessity

---

[211] Serious Organised Crime and Police Act 2005, s 145(1).

[212] Ibid, s 145(3).

[213] For the purposes of this section, 'contract' includes any other arrangement, and 'contractual' is to be read accordingly: s 145(4).

[214] Ibid, s 145(2).

[215] Ibid, s 145(6). Trade dispute has the same meaning as in Part 4 of the Trade Union and Labour Relations (Consolidation) Act 1992 with a slight amendment: see s 145(7).

[216] For definition of 'animal research organisation' see s 148, in essence the holder of a licence (or a person specified) under the Animals (Scientific Procedures) Act 1986.

[217] The persons protected are listed at s 146(2). This list may be changed by order of the Secretary of State.

[218] Joint Committee on Human Rights, Fifteenth Report, Section 2.

for the measures. The Committee felt they had no way of evaluating the government's claim for the necessity for the measures as set out in the 'Explanatory Notes', namely as a response to the 'systematic way in which animal rights extremists have used the conduct . . . with the calculated aim of disrupting organisations carrying out licensed animal research procedures'. In this context the Committee considered the extensive list of offences and police powers already available in relation to intimidatory forms of protest[219] and concluded that they were 'not so far persuaded that any of the specific examples of intimidation relied upon by the Government to justify the need for the new power is not already a criminal offence under existing provisions'.

2.134 The second concern was whether the provisions satisfied the requirements of legal certainty. The expansive reference to all criminal offences and torts (including the 'notoriously uncertain' economic torts of interfering with contractual relations and conspiracy) causing loss or damage was of concern to the Committee. In commenting on clauses 142–146 of the Bill the Committee concluded:

> In our view the legal uncertainty created by the definition of this offence is demonstrated by the chilling effect these provisions will have on activity such as seeking to persuade contractors not to contract with animal research organizations, and advocating boycotts of those contractors if they refuse. The Explanatory Notes state that there will be no interference with Article 10 rights, because of the requirement that the commission of a tort can only form the basis of the offence if the tort is one calling loss or damage to the person against whom it is directed. They state that the effect of this requirement is that 'the offence will not apply to any peaceful protest to the effect, for example, that a person should end a contractual relationship with an animal research organisation or to personal expression of opinion to that effect'. Such protests and expressions of opinion are not capable of causing loss or damage to the person at whom they are addressed.

> We are not persuaded that the offence does not have precisely the chilling effect which is disclaimed here. A campaign by a law-abiding organization such as the BUAV to attempt to persuade an airline not to transport animals to animal research organizations, widely assumed to be a perfectly legitimate form of protest activity in the past, may well be within the scope of the economic torts. A campaign advocating a boycott of such an airline if it refused to do so is even more likely to be within the scope of those torts. *In our view the offence fails to satisfy the requirement of legal certainty as it is currently defined, and is likely to be disproportionate in its effect because of the chilling effect it will have on these non-intimidatory forms of protest* [their emphasis].

2.135 Any human rights challenge based on justification would not appear to have any prospect of success, as a challenge to the level of the interference could not be based on the existence of other legislation fulfilling a similar function. Certainly, there does not appear to have been any such challenge in prosecutions brought to date. However, the legal certainty argument in relation to a prosecution based on a tortious relevant act may well be, on the facts of a particular case, one that is well-founded, both under the common law and on human rights grounds.

---

[219] At Annex A to the report *Animal Welfare—Human Rights: Protecting People from Animal Rights Extremists* published by the Home Office, Attorney General, and the DTI in July 2004.

Sentence

2.136   The maximum sentence under both these provisions is, on indictment, five years' imprisonment or a fine or both. On summary conviction to a maximum of twelve months' imprisonment or a fine not exceeding the statutory maximum or both.[220] Conduct that would otherwise be relatively low level offending unlikely to attract a custodial sentence— criminal damage, common assault, causing harassment alarm, or distress—if done with the intent in these sections becomes far more serious and a custodial sentence is usually imposed.

2.137   Before the enactment of the 2005 Act, animal rights activists engaged in the activity covered by these sections were charged under different legislative provisions, including blackmail, criminal damage, and harassment. This practice continues despite the new offences. The obvious reason for this is the significantly higher maximum penalties available— blackmail, for example, attracts a maximum sentence of fourteen years.

2.138   There is insufficient authority from the Court of Appeal to be able to elicit firm sentencing principles. Set out below is a summary of sentencing decisions, both from the Court of Appeal, but also first instance decisions of High Court judges, which have been used to inform subsequent sentencing tribunals and can properly be relied upon as informative indicators to the appropriate sentence. The cases considered are those where conduct encompasses activity targeted at animal research institutions however charged.

2.139   Prosecutors are increasingly seeking post-conviction ASBOs for those convicted of these offences. Care must be taken to ensure that the conditions imposed are not too broad and restrain a person from what would otherwise be legitimate protest as this may well amount to a breach of Articles 10 and 11 of the European Convention on Human Rights. For ASBOs, see 9.178 et seq.

R v Diane Jamieson[221]

2.140   Sentenced by Mr Justice Irwin at Preston Crown Court on 22 May 2008, she pleaded guilty to six counts of interfering with a contractual relationship so as to harm an animal research organization, contrary to s 145 of the Serious Organised Crime and Police Act 2005. She had written threatening and abusive letters to companies that had been identified on the Stop Huntingdon Animal Cruelty ('SHAC') website as companies associated with HLS. She was hitherto of good character. She was sentenced to fifty-one weeks' imprisonment on each count, to run concurrently, suspended for two years.

R v Joseph Harris[222]

2.141   The defendant pleaded guilty to three offences of interference with contractual relationships contrary to s 145 of the Serious Organised Crime and Police Act 2005. Each offence

---

[220] Serious Organised Crime and Police Act 2005, s 147. Under transitional provisions in s 175, twelve months should be read as six months in relation to offences committed before the commencement (not yet in force) of the Criminal Justice Act 2003, s 154(1) (limit on magistrates' court sentencing powers).

[221] Unreported, 22 May 2008.

[222] [2006] EWCA Crim 3303.

involved criminal damage to companies which traded directly or indirectly with HLS. The first involved forced entry, cutting tyre valves of heavy plant machines, and gluing locks causing £2,000 of damage. The second involved vandalizing another premises with slogans such as 'we found you, and 'this company kills puppies'. Locks had been glued, intercom systems had been damaged, air-conditioning wires cut, and the building flooded by a hose; and £11,400 of damage was caused. The third offence involved vehicles and windows being spray painted, tyres slashed, locks superglued, the intercom damaged, gas bottles opened, and oil spilled; all causing £15,200 of damage. The defendant was of good character and of high educational achievement. The Court of Appeal reduced three years' imprisonment at first instance to two years' imprisonment.

R v Suzanne Jaggers [223]

Sentenced by HHJ Kershaw at Leeds Crown Court on 5 February 2008, she pleaded guilty to one offence of sending a menacing message by telephone to HLS, contrary to s 127(1) of the Communications Act 2003. She had threatened that a director of HLS would be assaulted with a baseball bat. She was convicted after trial of one offence of blackmail by making a threat to Mr C of LC Kennels that his car would be bombed, with him in it, if he did not disassociate his business from HLS. She was treated as being of good character. She was sentenced to six months' imprisonment for the blackmail and three months consecutively for the Communications Act offence.

2.142

AG's Reference (No 113 of 2007) [224]

The defendant pleaded guilty to six counts of blackmail, one count of attempted blackmail, and five counts of interference with contractual relations so as to harm an animal research organization contrary to s 145 of the Serious Organised Crime and Police Act 2005. It was described by the court as 'a sustained campaign of intimidation over a period of almost five years'. Offences were committed between August 2001 and August 2006. Eleven victims were targeted, including sending letters such as 'Stop investing in HLS or you will die. Fuck you. We've got your address. Expect a visit or a car bomb' and 'Stop investing in animal killers at HLS. If no, we will visit you. And you will regret it. A.L.F.' One letter contained a white powder which resulted in the receiver being taken to a sterile area of hospital and was there for six to eight hours before being given the all clear. The office where this letter was received had to be sealed by chemical, biological, radiological, and nuclear trained officers and full decontamination procedures took place. In the event it was harmless but the complainant said the events had permanently affected her life. The defendant expressed regret and there was evidence she was suffering from significant anxiety and depression. She was sentenced by the trial judge to eight months' imprisonment. This was raised by the Court of Appeal to two years' imprisonment, albeit this reflected her substantial personal mitigation and the starting point was said to be six years after trial.

2.143

---

[223] Unreported, 5 February 2008.
[224] [2008] EWCA Crim 22.

R v Susanne Taylor; R v Theresa Portwine; R v Mark Taylor [225]

2.144   Sentenced by Mr Justice Goldring at the Central Criminal Court on 6 March 2007, Mark Taylor pleaded guilty to a conspiracy to interfere in contractual relations contrary to s 145 of the Serious Organised Crime and Police Act 2005 encompassing twenty occasions over three months in 2005. The majority of the offending was after he had been arrested for a first time, and two occasions after his second arrest. Susanne Taylor pleaded guilty to a similar conspiracy encompassing seventeen occasions, two of those occasions whilst on bail. Theresa Portwine pleaded guilty to a similar conspiracy encompassing ten occasions. She did not go to any protests after she was arrested. The protests were against companies believed to be trading with HLS. The behaviour at the protests was intended to frighten and intimidate. Large groups of protestors dressed in skeleton masks entered the grounds and offices of companies, and engaged in aggressive and abusive behaviour. Threats and abuse were directed at workers, including screams of 'killer' and 'murderer'. Physical pain and distress was also caused to those working at the targeted companies. Mark Taylor contested a Newton hearing that was resolved against him and he was sentenced as having a leading role. Goldring J indicated that given the numerous incidents, consecutive sentences would have been justified if indicted as substantives, and he therefore sentenced Mr Taylor to four years' imprisonment. Ms Taylor was sentenced to two and a half years and Ms Portwine to fifteen months' imprisonment.

R v Greg Avery; R v Natasha Avery; R v Heather Nicholson; R v Daniel Wadham; R v Gerrah Selby; and *R v Daniel Amos* [226]

2.145   Sentenced by Mr Justice Butterfield at Winchester Crown Court on 21 January 2009, the offences were described in sentencing remarks as a 'campaign of terror' conducted with 'military precision' against '40 companies over 6 years' causing an estimated '£12.6 million of financial loss'. This was a 'relentless, sustained, merciless and ruthless persecution'. The result was that 'certainly hundreds, probably thousands, of ordinary, decent men, women and children have had their lives made a living hell' by their activities. The criminal acts included making false allegations of paedophilia which left those accused having to barricade themselves in their homes out of fear of vigilante attacks and resign from their job. 'Extremely realistic' hoax bombs were sent to business and home addresses which required the bomb squad to evacuate premises and caused psychological damage to employees. The activity also included the sending of sanitary towels allegedly contaminated with the AIDS virus; demonstrations and damage at the homes of members of staff; threats or actual criminal damage to property including abusive words sprayed on the homes of employees; threats of physical assault and threats to kill; threatening and abusive telephone calls; emails and letters; repeated silent calls often in the middle of the night; delivery of unwanted material from mail order companies; and the coordinated sending of emails or telephone calls so as to block the company's systems. The defendants also took their campaign on an international level to Sweden, Germany, Switzerland, and France. All were sentenced for conspiracy to blackmail which carries a maximum sentence of fourteen years'

---

[225] Unreported, 6 March 2007.
[226] Unreported, 21 January 2009.

imprisonment and the Judge took the maximum as the starting point. Greg and Natasha Avery pleaded guilty. They were said to be the 'driving force' and were sentenced to nine years' imprisonment. Heather Nicholson, 'a trusted member of the inner circle' was sentenced to eleven years' imprisonment after trial. All three were said to be 'life-long, veteran, fanatical' activists as demonstrated by their previous convictions. Gavin Medd-Hall, who was said to be 'centrally involved' and had previous convictions, was sentenced to eight years' imprisonment after trial. Daniel Wadham, aged 21, played 'a full part in the conspiracy' and was involved in violent home visits in Sweden. He had one previous violent conviction relating to animals rights activity. He was sentenced to five years' imprisonment after trial. Gerrah Selby was said to be 'heavily involved in the campaign' and was involved in the serious activity on the continent and was heard shouting through a megaphone 'You are not going to be laughing when your children are screaming at night'. She was 20 years of age and not said to be the 'directing mind'. She was sentenced after trial to four years' detention in a young offender's institution. Daniel Amos was a 'very active trusted insider' who also took part in the activity on the continent. He was 22 and had no previous convictions. He was sentenced to six years after trial.

J. Contamination or Interfering with Goods

2.146 Section 38 of the Public Order Act 1986 created three new offences, triable either way,[227] of contamination of or interference with goods with the intention of causing public alarm or anxiety etc. This section was designed to address activities, including blackmail by extorting money from large companies, by contaminating or threatening to contaminate goods, usually foodstuffs, which are on sale in their stores throughout the country.

Contamination of or interference with goods

2.147 Section 38(1) provides:

It is an offence for a person, with the intention
(a) of causing public alarm or anxiety, or
(b) of causing injury to members of the public consuming or using the goods, or
(c) of causing economic loss to any person by reason of the goods being shunned by members of the public, or
(d) of causing economic loss to any person by reason of steps taken to avoid such alarm or anxiety, injury or loss,
to contaminate or interfere with goods, or make it appear that goods have been interfered with, or to place goods which have been contaminated or interfered with, or which appear to have been contaminated or interfered with, in a place where goods of that description are consumed, used, sold, or otherwise supplied.

2.148 The words 'contaminated or interfered with' are not defined in the Public Order Act 1986 and must therefore be given their ordinary meaning. It is not necessary to prove that the contamination should involve a poison or drugs, although if this has in fact happened and

---

[227] Public Order Act 1986, s 38(4).

shoppers are put at risk of injury the offence will be aggravated in terms of penalty. 'Goods' are defined as including substances whether natural or manufactured and whether or not incorporated in or mixed with other goods.[228]

Threatening to contaminate or interfere with goods, or claiming to have done so

2.149   Section 38(2) provides:

> It is also an offence for a person, with any such intention as is mentioned in paragraph (a), (c) or (d) of subsection (1), to threaten that he or another will do, or claim that he or another has done, any of the acts mentioned in that subsection.

2.150   A claim that another has done any such acts is not an offence where a person in good faith reports or warns that such acts have been, or appear to have been, committed.[229] The intention is the same as for having in fact carried out the contamination, although for obvious reasons the intention to cause injury does not apply.

Possession of articles with a view to contaminating or interfering in goods

2.151   Section 38(3) provides:

> It is an offence for a person to be in possession of any of the following articles with a view to the commission of an offence under subsection (1)—
> (a)   materials to be used for contaminating or interfering with goods or making it appear that goods have been contaminated or interfered with, or
> (b)   goods which have been contaminated or interfered with, or which appear to have been contaminated or interfered with.

Sentence

2.152   This is a serious offence. On indictment, the maximum penalty is ten years, a fine or both. On summary conviction, six months' imprisonment, a fine not exceeding the statutory maximum, or both.[230]

2.153   In *Cruickshank*,[231] the offender pleaded guilty to contaminating food in a supermarket by inserting pins, needles, or nails into various items. He persisted in this behaviour for three months, and some minor injuries were incurred by customers who bought the contaminated products. There was no logical explanation for the offender's behaviour, and no financial motive. Three years' imprisonment was upheld by the Court of Appeal.

K. Intimidation, including Watching and Besetting

2.154   Section 241 of the Trade Union and Labour Relations (Consolidation) Act 1992 re-enacts the nineteenth-century offence of intimidation, including watching and besetting. This offence has historically been employed in the context of trade union activity.

---

[228]   Ibid, s 38(5).
[229]   Ibid, s 38(6).
[230]   Ibid, s 38(4).
[231]   [2001] 2 Cr App R (S) 278.

Origin of the offence

The offence of intimidation, including watching and besetting, contrary to s 7 of the **2.155**
Conspiracy and Protection of Property Act 1875, arose out of the rise of trades union
activity in the nineteenth century but was more or less defunct until it enjoyed a modest
revival during the miners' strike of 1984–5 (out of 7,658 arrests made between 13 March
and 8 November 2004 during the strike 226 were for alleged offences under s 7). Some
benches of justices refused to entertain s 7 charges, taking the view that the conduct
complained of should have been charged under the s 5 of the Public Order Act 1936 or
not at all.

In a Criminal Law Review article in 1985,[232] F Bennion argued that although it was virtu- **2.156**
ally obsolete it should be preserved to punish 'illegal mass picketing'. The government
appeared to answer this appeal and specifically affirmed the offence in the Public Order Act
1986 by increasing the penalty.[233] The Trade Union and Labour Relations (Consolidation)
Act 1992 re-enacted the section without taking the opportunity to amend the archaic
wording of the provision.

Despite its history, the offence is not confined in its operation to industrial disputes[234], **2.157**
indeed the English criminal law contains no provision to deal specifically with picketing,
and has been used against animal rights and roads protestors[235] as well as those protesting
outside abortion clinics.[236] Historically, it was charged in respect of 'watching and besetting' private residences, but there is now separate legislation to protect homes.[237]

The offence

Section 241 of the Trade Union and Labour Relations (Consolidation) Act 1992 provides: **2.158**

(1) A person commits an offence who, with a view to compelling another person to abstain
from doing or to do any act which that person has a legal right to do or abstain from
doing, wrongfully and without legal authority—
  (a) uses violence to or intimidates that person or his wife or children, or injures his
    property,
  (b) persistently follows that person about from place to place,
  (c) hides any tools, clothes or other property owned or used by that person, or deprives
    him of or hinders him in the use thereof,
  (d) watches or besets the house or other place where that person resides, works, carries
    on business or happens to be, or the approach to any such house or place, or
  (e) follows that person with two or more other persons in a disorderly manner in or
    through any street or road.

---

[232] [1985] Crim LR 64.
[233] Public Order Act 1986, s 40 and Sch 2, para 1. This para was then repealed by the Trade Union and
Labour Relations (Consolidation) Act 1992, s 300(1), Sch 1.
[234] This has been long recognized; see, in relation to the offence under the 1875 Act, *Wilkins v Lyons*
[1899] 1 Ch 255 at 272.
[235] *Todd v DPP* [1996] Crim LR 344. It might even apply to stalking: Professor John Smith at [1996] Crim
LR 345.
[236] *DPP v Fidler & and another* [1992] 1 WLR 91.
[237] Criminal Justice and Police Act 2001, ss 42 and 42A. See 3.142 et seq.

Elements of the offence

With a view to compelling any other person

2.159 This element of *mens rea* governs all the offences created by the section. It imports not motive, but purpose—'with a view to'. Purpose is a more objective concept, not concerned with the different motives with which members of the group might have joined, say, a demonstration.[238] It requires more than the intention to persuade, as there must be an element of compulsion in the defendant's mind.[239] In *DPP v Fidler*,[240] the Divisional Court upheld the acquittal of protestors outside an abortion clinic who had used verbal abuse and approached persons attending the clinic but had not used or threatened physical force. In the absence of proof of compulsion, the charge was properly dismissed.

2.160 The 'other person' refers back to the person whom the defendant has a view to compel or 'any other person'; it is an offence to intimidate a worker with a view to compelling his employer.[241] It is immaterial that the compulsion is effective or not, as this *mens rea* element is concerned with intention.[242]

Wrongfully and without legal authority

2.161 Not all compulsion is wrongful. The authorities on the issue all arise out of picketing (which is not in itself unlawful) and this element will be discussed in that context below. As a matter of general principle, the conduct complained of must be independently unlawful—either a tort or a criminal offence.[243]

Intimidates

2.162 'Intimidate' is not a term of art and must be given a 'reasonable and sensible' interpretation.[244] Intimidation includes putting a person in fear by the exhibition of force or violence, or the threat of force or violence, and there is no limitation restricting the meaning to cases of violence or threats of violence to the person.[245] It certainly includes threats of breaches of contract.[246] It may even be that presence in very large numbers amounts in itself to intimidation.[247] Ultimately, it would appear that the question is one for the

---

[238] *DPP v Fidler* [1992] 1 WLR 91; *Lyons v Wilkins* (1899) 1 Ch 255, 270.
[239] *Bonsall* [1985] Crim LR 150; *McKenzie* [1892] 2 QB 519.
[240] [1992] 1 WLR 91.
[241] *Lyons v Wilkins* [1896] 1 Ch 811, though this decision has been subject to compelling criticism: see MA Hickling, *Citrine's Trade Union Law* (1967, 3rd edn) p 537 and F Bennion [1985] Crim LR at 67, both referred to by ATH Smith in *Public Order Offences* (1987) p 215.
[242] *Agnew v Munrow* (1891) 28 SLR 335.
[243] *Thomas and others v National Union of Mineworkers (South Wales Area) and others* [1986] 1 Ch 20.
[244] *Gibson v Lawson* [1891] 2 QB 545.
[245] *R v Jones* (1974) 59 Cr App R 120. Note that the court did not wish to define 'intimidation' exhaustively. See also *Connor v Kent* [1891] 2 QB 545 where the court again deliberately avoided any definition and held that intimidate is a word of everyday speech and must be interpreted on a case by case basis. See also *News Group Newspapers Ltd v SOGAT 82 (No 2)* [1987] ICR 181, 204–5 on the related tort of intimidation.
[246] *Rookes v Barnard* [1964] 1 AC 1129.
[247] The Court in *Bonsall* spoke of the 'terror that their very numbers convey'.

magistrates[248] but it must be shown that the victim of it was actually put in fear, even if the intimidation did not achieve its end.[249]

Persistently follows

There is only limited authority on what amounts to persistently following. The courts have **2.163** made no attempt to provide a definition.[250] Following a worker through the streets has been held to satisfy this test, as has following in a car.[251] Unlike the offence in subsec 1(e), the offence of 'persistently following' in 1(b) requires no element of disorderly conduct and can be committed by a sole person.

Hiding tools

In *Fowler v Kibble*,[252] a civil case, the Court of Appeal held that the hiding of the tools must **2.164** on its own be wrongful. Thus, on the grounds that the act of deprivation the Court was considering was effected without violence or threats, there was no offence when a workman did not let miners who were not members of a particular union have safety lamps, because the agreement with the employer did not extend to that union. The court went further when considering the application for the injunction, holding that the broad view of the statute was to prevent violence or the threat of it, which did not arise in that case.

Watching or besetting

This provision is the one that comes closest to criminalizing peaceful picketing and must **2.165** be read in accordance with the 'peaceful picketing' protection in s 220 of the same Act that makes it lawful for a person in contemplation or furtherance of a trade dispute to attend at or near his place of work (or that of a union member if a union representative) for the purpose of peacefully obtaining or communicating information, or peacefully persuading any person to work or abstain from working. Thus peaceful picketing is not 'unlawful' or 'wrongful' within the meaning of the Act.[253] However, if otherwise lawful picketing amounts to a nuisance, trespass, or some other tort, then it may become unlawful and be prosecuted as 'watching and besetting'. Any disparity between the early cases of *Lyons v Wilkins*[254] and *Ward Lock and Co Ltd v The Operative Printers' Society*[255] was resolved in the classic case on the limits of peace picketing, *Thomas and others v National Union of Mineworkers (South Wales Area) and others*.[256]

---

[248] It was held to be a matter for the jury in *R v Baker* (1911) 7 Cr App R 89. The offence is now triable summarily only.

[249] *Kennedy v Cowie* (1909) 47 SLR 209.

[250] *Smith v Thomasson* (1890) 62 LT 68.

[251] Ibid; *Wall* (1907) 21 Cox CC 401; *Elsey v Smith* [1983] IRLR 292 (a Scottish case).

[252] [1922] 1 Ch 140 (Sargant J) and [1922] 1 Ch 487 (Court of Appeal affirming decision of Sargant J).

[253] The immunity is limited to this s 421 of the 1990 Act, and does not afford a defence to, for example, offences of obstructing the highway, trespass, or obstruction of a constable: *M'Cusker v Smith* [1918] 2 IR 432; *Broome v DPP* [1974] AC 587; *Piddington v Bates* [1961] 1 WLR 162; *British Airports Authority v Ashton* [1983] 3 All ER 6.

[254] [1896] 1 Ch 811 and then [1899] 1 Ch 255.

[255] (1906) 22 TLR 327.

[256] The report at [1986] 1 Ch 20 (including the judgment of Scott J and a detailed summary of the submissions of both Louis Blom-Cooper QC and Anthony Scrivener QC) represents a detailed analysis of the law in this area.

2.166   The offence takes place where the person watched and beset, and those words are viewed as words of the ordinary English language and are a matter for the magistrates to decide.[257] Watching may involve little more than attending the place of the picket; 'beset' is defined in the *Oxford English Dictionary*[258] as 'surround with hostile intent, besiege, assail on all sides'.

Penalties

2.167   A person guilty of an offence under this section is liable on summary conviction to imprisonment for a term not exceeding six months or a fine not exceeding level 5 on the standard scale, or both.

L. Drunk and Disorderly

2.168   The experience of the courts is that a large proportion of non-protest related public order incidents are alcohol fuelled. The gravity of the offending is usually found, not in the intoxication itself, but in the acts that result, and is often most appropriately charged under the mainstream public order offences discussed in Chapter 1. However, there are a raft of offences found in disparate statutes that specifically relate to alcohol induced offending, some not requiring any offending above and beyond intoxication, others involving an element of 'disorderly' behaviour. Under the Penalties for Disorderly Behaviour (Amount of Penalty) Order 2002[259] as amended, many fall within the 'on the spot' penalty provisions attracting a fixed penalty notice.

2.169   A number of the offences are set out in brief form below.

Drunk and disorderly

2.170   It is an offence, contrary to s 91(1) of the Criminal Justice Act 1967 where any person is guilty, while drunk, of disorderly behaviour. In *Carroll v DPP*,[260] the offence is described as one of the most basic in the criminal calendar, and required proof of three elements: (a) that the defendant was drunk; (b) that he was in a public place; and (c) he was guilty of disorderly behaviour. Whether a defendant was drunk was a simple question of fact. On familiar principles it was the voluntary consumption of alcohol which was the requisite *mens rea*. There is no requirement of *mens rea* in relation to the third element, and 'disorderly conduct' is not furthered defined and is a matter for the court applying an everyday understanding of what those words mean.

2.171   The Court have to ask themselves, following the decision of the Divisional Court in *Lanham v Rickwood*,[261] 'no doubt as a matter of simple common sense, whether a person's loss of self-control is attributable to his having indulged in an excessive consumption of intoxicating liquor'. The offence relates only to intoxication by alcohol and cannot apply if

---

[257] *AG v O'Brien* [1936] ITLR 101 (a matter for juries at the time of the decision, the offence is now triable summarily only).

[258] The *Shorter Oxford English Dictionary* (1993).

[259] SI 2002/1873.

[260] [2009] EWHC 554 (Admin).

[261] (1984) 148 JP 573.

a person is under the influence of drugs.[262] Nonetheless, a person who has consumed both drink and drugs may well be drunk; the court would have to decide, 'as a matter of common sense', whether 'they are satisfied that, apart from the [consumption of drugs] he has consumed intoxicating liquor to an extent which affects his steady self-control'.[263] The 'steady self control test' was also used by Goff LJ in *Neale v RJME (a minor)*.[264]

This offence attracts a fixed penalty notice of £80. If the matter proceeds to court, on summary conviction the maximum penalty is a fine not exceeding level 3.   **2.172**

Drunk in a public place

Section 12 of the Licensing Act 1872 makes it an offence for a person to be 'found drunk   **2.173** on the highway or other public place, whether a building or not, or on any licensed premises'. The Licensing Act 1902 provides that such a person may be 'dealt with according to law', namely under the provisions in s 12 of the 1872 Act. The definition of 'public place' for this offence is to be found in s 8 of the 1902 Act, and includes 'any place to which the public have access, whether on payment or otherwise'. It has been held that the fact that a person's presence on the highway or in the public place need only be momentary and it is irrelevant that it may have been involuntary.[265]

This offence attracts fixed penalty of £50, or, on summary conviction a fine not exceeding   **2.174** level 1.

Drunk and disorderly person failing to leave

A person who is drunk or disorderly commits an offence contrary to s 143 of the Licensing   **2.175** Act 2003 if, without reasonable excuse, he fails to leave premises when requested to do so by the police or a 'relevant' person[266] at a licensed premises. A constable is obliged, if requested to do so by the relevant person at the premises, to help expel a drunk and disorderly person from the premises and help to prevent such a person from entering the premises. The maximum penalty, on summary conviction, is a fine not exceeding level 1. Those working at or in charge at the premises have, in effect, a duty to remove such persons from the premises as they commit an offence if they knowingly allow disorderly conduct.[267]

Alcohol consumption in a designated place

Section 12(2) of the Criminal Justice and Police Act 2001 as amended provides a constable   **2.176** with the power to require a person who he reasonably believes has been, is, or is about to consume alcohol in a designated public place [268] not to consume alcohol or to surrender the

---

[262] Ibid; and *Neale v RMJE (a minor)* (1984) 80 Cr App R 20.
[263] *Lanham v Rickwood.*
[264] (1984) 80 Cr App R 20.
[265] *Winzar v Chief Constable of Kent* (1983) The Times, 28 March 1983.
[266] Licensing Act 2003, s 143(2) defines a 'relevant person' and includes an employee or the licensee. For police entitlement to use force, see *Semple v DPP* [2001] EWHC 324 (Admin).
[267] Ibid, s 140(1).
[268] Designated by the local authority under s 13 of the 2001 Act. A licensed premises is not a designated public place: s 14 of the 2001 Act.

container of alcohol (other than a sealed container). If a person fails to comply with this requirement they commit and offence under s 12(4) of the 2001 Act.

Drunk on an aircraft

2.177 This is a far more serious offence than others in this category. A person who enters any aircraft when drunk, or is drunk on the aircraft, commits an offence under Article 65(1) of the Air Navigation Order 2000.[269] The offence is triable either way, and on indictment attracts a maximum penalty of five years' imprisonment, a fine or both. On summary conviction, a fine not exceeding the statutory maximum.[270] These offences are likely to cross the custody threshold, and a sentence of eight months was upheld in *R v Ayodeji*[271] at a time when the maximum sentence was two years.

M. Football Related Disorder

2.178 Public order incidents arising out of football related disorder are frequently charged under the mainstream public order offences.[272] There are, however, offences that relate to public order incidents arising specifically within the context of being a spectator at a designated[273] football match. This includes not only what takes place during the match, but also the period beginning two hours before the start (or if earlier, or if the match does not take place, then the advertised start of the match) and one hour after the end of the match (or one hour after the advertised end of the match if the match does not take place).[274]

2.179 As provided for by the Football (Offences) Act 1991, it is an offence, triable summarily only and with a maximum penalty of a fine not exceeding level 3, for a person at a designated football match to

(a) throw anything at or towards the playing area or area in which spectators or other persons are present;[275]

(b) engage or take part in chanting[276] of an indecent or racialist[277] nature;[278]

(c) go onto the playing area to which spectators are not generally admitted.[279]

---

[269] SI 2000/1562.

[270] Art 122(6) and Sch 12, Part B of the Air Navigation Order 2000.

[271] [2001] 1 Cr App R (S) 370, a case under the previous provisions in Art 57(1) of the Air Navigation Order 1995. At that time the maximum sentence was only two years.

[272] *R v Rees, McElroy, Carroll, Killick and Morris* [2006] 2 Cr App R (S) 20.

[273] A 'designated football match' is an association football match designated, or of a description designated, for the purpose of the Act by the Secretary of State: The Football (Offences) (Designation of Football Matches) Order 2004 (SI 2004/2410).

[274] Football (Offences) Act 1991, s 1(2).

[275] Ibid, s 2.

[276] 'Chanting' means the repeated uttering of any words or sounds (whether alone or in concert with one or more others): ibid, s 3(2)(a).

[277] 'Of racialist nature' means consisting of or including matter which is threatening, abusive, or insulting to a person by reason of his colour, race, nationality (including citizenship), or ethnic or national origins: ibid, s 3(2)(b).

[278] Ibid, s 3. 'You're just a town full of Pakis' was held to be a chant of a racialist nature, though each case had to be concerned taking into account the individual context: *DPP v Stoke on Trent Magistrates' Court* [2003] 3 All ER.

[279] Ibid, s 4.

The 'ticket touting' provisions in s 166 of the Criminal Justice and Public Order Act 1994 **2.180** makes it an offence, triable summarily only[280] and with a maximum penalty of a fine not exceeding level 5, for a person unauthorized to sell tickets by the organizers of the match to

(a) sell[281] a ticket for a designated[282] football match;
(b) otherwise to dispose of such a ticket to another person.

Within the limited provisions of the Football Spectators Act 1989 which are in force, it is **2.181** an offence

(a) to admit spectators to watch a designated football match unless it is played at licensed[283] premises;
(b) for any responsible person to contravene any term or condition of a licence granted to admit spectators to any premises for the purposes of watching any designated[284] match played there.

For the application of football banning orders to these offences, see 9.183 et seq. It **2.182** should also be noted that the Sporting Events (Control of Alcohol etc) Act 1985 provides a number of offences relating to the possession of alcohol and fireworks at sporting events.

N. Taking a Photograph of a Police Officer

Section 58A of the Terrorism Act 2000 was inserted by s 76 of the Counter Terrorism Act **2.183** 2008[285] and provides that:

(1) A person commits an offence who—
    (a) elicits or attempts to elicit information about an individual who is or has been—
        (i) a member of Her Majesty's forces,
        (ii) a member of any of the intelligence services, or
        (iii) a constable,
    which is of a kind likely to be useful to a person committing or preparing an act of terrorism, or
    (b) publishes or communicates any such information.
(2) It is a defence for a person charged with an offence under this section to prove that they had a reasonable excuse for their action.

---

[280] Section 166(3).

[281] 'Selling' includes offering to sell it, exposing it for sale, making it available for sale by another, advertising that it is available for purchase, and giving it to a person who pays or agrees to pay for some other goods or services or offers to do so: s 166(2).

[282] For meaning of 'designated' football match for these purposes, see Ticket Touting (Designation of Football Matches) Order 2007 (SI 2007/790).

[283] The licences are issued by the Football Licensing Authority under the Football Spectators (Seating) Order 2006 (SI 2006/1661).

[284] Designated for this purpose by the Football Spectators (Prescription) Order 2004 (SI 2004/2409 as amended).

[285] In force as of 19/1/09: The Counter-Terrorism Act 2008 (Commencement No. 2) Order 2009.

    (3) A person guilty of an offence under this section is liable—

        (a) on conviction on indictment, to imprisonment for a term not exceeding 10 years or to a fine, or to both;

        (b) on summary conviction—

        (i) in England and Wales or Scotland, to imprisonment for a term not exceeding 12 months or to a fine not exceeding the statutory maximum, or to both;

2.184 The obvious application of this legislation in the context of protest is the potential criminalization of the taking of photographs of police officers by the press and campaigning groups. The guidance issued on the exercise of these powers suggests that photographing police officers engaged on policing protests will not be limited by this legislation:

> It should ordinarily be considered inappropriate to use s 58A to arrest people photographing police officers in the course of normal policing activities, including protest, as without more, there is no link to terrorism.[286]

2.185 The Home Office guidance[287] supports this, and indicates that

> an officer making an arrest under s 58A *must reasonably suspect* that the information is of a kind likely *to be useful to a person committing or preparing an act of terrorism*. An example might be gathering information about the person's house, car, routes to work and other movements.

2.186 This Home Office guidance goes on to consider the statutory defence of reasonable excuse and, in bold letters, states:

> Important: Legitimate journalistic activity (such as covering a demonstration for a newspaper) is likely to constitute such an excuse. Similarly an innocent tourist or other sight-seer taking a photograph of a police officer is likely to have a reasonable excuse.

---

[286] www.metpolice.uk/about/photography.htm
[287] http://www.homeoffice.gov.uk/about-us/publications/home-office-circulars/circulars-2009/012-2009/index.html

3

PROCESSIONS, ASSEMBLIES, AND MEETINGS

A. Overview	3.01	**E. Parliament Square**	3.94
A right to assemble or process?	3.02	Background	3.95
B. Processions	3.07	The legislation	3.100
Procession	3.08	Designated area	3.101
Public place	3.10	Written notice	3.103
Advance notice of processions (s 11)	3.12	Authorization	3.107
Conditions imposed on public processions		Offences	3.112
(s 12)	3.28	Human rights compliance	3.117
Banning processions (s 13)	3.38	The Brian Haw litigation	3.122
Judicial review	3.47	The future	3.126
C. Assemblies	3.53	**F. Other Specific Areas**	3.130
Background	3.53	Trafalgar Square and Parliament	
Definition of 'public assembly'	3.56	Square Garden	3.130
No advance notice requirement	3.64	Royal Parks (including Hyde Park) and	
Police controls over public assemblies (s 14)	3.65	other Open Spaces	3.135
No power to prohibit assemblies	3.74	**G. Other Offences Specific to Location**	3.137
D. Meetings	3.76	Nucleas bases	3.137
Definition of public meeting	3.80	NHS facilities	3.138
Control of public meetings	3.84	At a person's home	3.142
Attempts to break up public meetings	3.87	**H. By-laws**	3.152
Police powers to attend meetings	3.88	Criminal proceedings	3.156
Election meetings	3.90		

A. Overview

Here we have to consider the right to demonstrate and the right to protest on matters of public concern. These are rights which it is in the public interest that individuals should possess; and, indeed, that they should exercise without impediment so long as no wrongful act is done. It is often the only means by which grievances can be brought to the knowledge of those in authority—at any rate with such impact as to gain a remedy. Our history is full of warnings against suppression of these rights.

Most notable was the demonstration at St Peter's Fields, Manchester, in 1819 in support of universal suffrage. The magistrates sought to stop it. At least 12 were killed and hundreds injured. Afterwards the Court of Common Council of London affirmed 'the undoubted right of Englishmen to assemble together for the purpose of deliberating upon public grievances'. Such is the right of assembly. So also is the right to meet together, to go in procession, to demonstrate and to protest on matters of public concern. As long as all is done peaceably and in good order, without threats or incitement to violence or obstruction to traffic, it is not prohibited.

3.01 This dissenting judgment of Lord Denning in *Hubbard v Pitt*[1] is a powerful vindication of the social value of protest, while at the same time confining it to little more than a privilege—the freedom to act in that way as long as no one else is affected adversely by the behaviour. Chapter 10 will examine how, through the enactment of the Human Rights Act 1998, this has developed into a 'right' to protest, while this chapter will focus on the restrictions that can be imposed by the police on processions, assemblies, and meetings, including the nationwide provisions in the Public Order Act 1986 as well as legislation directed at specific locations such as Parliament Square.

A right to assemble or process?

3.02 There is no statutory right to process or march recognized in the Public Order Act 1986 or in subsequent legislation directed at public order. Lord Bingham reflected in *R (on the application of Laporte) v Chief Constable of Gloucestershire Constabulary*,[2] that the 'approach of the English common law to freedom of expression and assembly was hesitant and negative, permitting that which was not prohibited'.

3.03 However, since the enactment of the Human Rights Act 1998, the right in Article 11 of the European Convention on Human Rights to freedom of peaceful assembly has been enshrined in domestic law, subject to the familiar provision for legislative restrictions on this right that 'are necessary in a democratic society in the interests of national security or public safety, for the prevention of disorder or crime, for the protection of health or morals or for the protection of the rights and freedoms of others'.

3.04 The arguments now focus on human rights jurisprudence, and the common law position is now of less relevance. The common law had, only to a limited extent, recognized such a right. In 1936, Lord Hewart CJ in *Duncan v Jones*[3] gave any such suggestion very short shrift:

> There have been moments during the argument in this case when it appeared to be suggested that the Court had to do with a grave case involving what is called the right of public meeting. I say 'called' because English law does not recognize any special right of public meeting for political or other purposes. The right of assembly, as Professor Dicey puts it, is nothing more than a view taken by the Court of the individual liberty of the subject.

3.05 In that case a police officer had stopped a person addressing a number of people in the street on the grounds that he reasonably apprehended that a breach of the peace would occur. That person resisted and was convicted of obstruction. In upholding the conviction, the Court were of the view that the law of unlawful assembly was irrelevant, and the only issue that fell to be decided was whether the officer had apprehended a breach of the peace. The Courts were less dismissive on other occasions and in that dissenting judgment in *Hubbard v Pitt*,[4] Lord Denning MR acknowledged a right to protest 'so long as no wrongful act

---

[1] [1976] QB 142.
[2] [2007] 2 AC 105. See also 4.61, 4.63 et seq; 6.147 et seq; 10.38, 10.80.
[3] [1936] 1 KB 218.
[4] [1976] QB 142.

is done'.[5] But if rights did exist under the pre-Human Rights Act common law, they did so, as Lord Bingham recognized, purely in the negative sense.[6] Processions, marches, and demonstrations were lawful only when they did not infringe any other law: 'They are, so long as they are peaceful and orderly, not actionable, even though they may cause some inconvenience to others.'[7] What value this 'right' provided was additionally undermined by the prominence which the law gives to the right to pass and repass along the highway, discussed in Chapter 4.

Nonetheless, although Part II of the Public Order Act 1986 makes no provision for positive **3.06** rights, it can be said that the imposition of controls and conditions on processions, assemblies, and meetings, does acknowledge by implication, that there is such a right if the specified conditions are fulfilled.[8]

B. Processions

The police can only impose controls on a march or demonstration under Part II of the **3.07** Public Order Act 1986 if it is a 'public procession'. The statutory definition in the Act is widely drawn in s 16: 'public procession' means a procession in a public place.

Procession

The word 'procession' is given no further definition and is rarely in issue. The Court of **3.08** Appeal considered the same definition under the previous Public Order Act 1936 to be 'very wide' and that since the dictionary definition included 'a proceeding of body of persons . . . in orderly succession' any procession was likely to be covered by the definition.[9]

The essence of a procession has been long established as simply a body of persons moving **3.09** along a route.[10] It is, however, not an immutable characteristic of a 'procession' for the purposes of the legislation that it should follow a pre-determined route or even that it should have a predetermined destination.[11]

Public place

'Public place' is further defined in s 16 as **3.10**

(a) any highway, or in Scotland any road within the meaning of the Roads (Scotland) Act 1984; and
(b) any place to which at the material time the public or any section of the public has access, on payment or otherwise, as of right or by virtue of express or implied permission.

---

[5] Ibid, 178; affirmed in *Kent v Metropolitan Police Commissioner*, The Times, 15 May 1981.
[6] See also *Duncan v Jones* [1936] 1 KB 218.
[7] Per Stuart Smith J in *News Group Newspapers Ltd v Society of Graphical and Allied Trades 1982 (No 2)* [1987] ICR 181.
[8] Other precedents for the right of assembly can be found in the Universal Declaration of Human Rights 1948; the American Declaration of the Rights and Duties of Man 1948; and the International Covenant on Civil and Political Rights 1966.
[9] *Kent v Metropolitan Police Commissioner*, The Times, 15 May 1981.
[10] *Flockhart v Robinson* [1950] 2 KB 498, affirmed in *Kay (FC) v Commissioner of Police for the Metropolis* [2008] 1 WLR 2723. See also 3.18 below.
[11] *Kay*, per Lord Rogers at paras 37–44 and Lord Carswell at para 61. See also 3.18 below.

This definition is wider than earlier definitions in that it includes all places of common resort and also private property to which the public has access otherwise than as a trespasser. This includes those places that everyone can access, most obviously the highway (including private roads), public transport, public houses and restaurants, parks and gardens, public footpaths, and public offices. It also includes places which can be attended on payment of a fee, such as a cinema or football ground, or places only open to a section of the public, a nightclub for example, open only to those who are over 18. Additionally, it includes places where the public can go to 'by virtue of . . . implied permission', such as some private land, for example; unfenced farm land or unfenced areas adjacent to the highway; or private land which is commonly walked on or played on without objection; or any land on which the public would in law be a visitor or licensee[12] as opposed to a trespasser.

3.11   The operation of this definition can be seen in the example of a garden surrounding a house that must be walked over to reach the front door. Whilst the garden is private property and easily demarcated, there is an implied permission for visitors to the house (a postman, for example) to walk across the garden to reach it. Whilst in 1978 the Court of Appeal in *R v Edwards and Roberts*[13] held that this did not make the garden a public place, the new definition would appear to overrule this, as at least a section of the public has implied permission to use the garden.

Advance notice of processions (s 11)

3.12   The Public Order Act 1986 provided for the first time a national requirement to give advance written notice of most public processions. This requirement extends to processions but not assemblies.

Background

3.13   Before the Public Order Act 1986, some hundred local Acts of Parliament, particularly in the larger cities, required advance notice to the police of processions, usually at least 24 or 36 hours before the event. And whilst the vast majority of local authorities had not seen the need for a legal requirement to give notice, it was estimated that the police were in fact informed in at least 80 per cent of cases where no requirement existed.[14]

3.14   Lord Scarman originally thought that there was no need for an advance notice requirement: 'It does present really insuperable difficulty for the urgently called demonstration.'[15] But in his later Brixton report he felt that subsequent events had shown that the need did exist.[16] The government in its White Paper[17] relied on the conclusions in favour of a requirement set out in the Report of the House of Commons Select Committee on Home Affairs in 1980, in particular that a notice requirement might 'serve as a formal trigger for discussion between police and organisers to agree the ground rules for a march . . . and

---

[12] See Occupiers Liability Act 1957.
[13] (1978) 67 Cr App R 228.
[14] *Report on the Red Lion Square Disorders*, Cmnd 5919 (1975) para 129.
[15] Ibid, para 128.
[16] *Report on the Brixton Disorders*, Cmnd 8427 (1981), para 7.45.
[17] *Review of Public Order Law*, Cmnd 9510 (1985), para 4.2.

would underline for organisers their responsibility for the safety and good behaviour of their supporters'.[18]

Advance notice provision (s 11(1))

Section 11(1) requires notice to be given for most, but not all, processions. The three **3.15** categories for which notice is required are processions

(a) intended to demonstrate support for or opposition to the views or actions of any person or body of persons;
(b) intended to publicize a cause or campaign; and
(c) intended to mark or commemorate an event.

It would appear that these categories will cover most types of procession. They clearly include all forms of political protest, whether against local, national, or international governments, whether criticizing action, inactions, or expressing a viewpoint. They cover (moving) rallies in support of political organizations and single issue groups (like Stop the War or CND) or in support of more obscure campaigns and causes. Ramblers' Association walks and cycle club Sunday rides are unlikely to be covered by this definition, but will be if intended to publicize the Rambler's Association's campaign to keep footpaths clear or if the Kenilworth Cycle Club is having a ride to commemorate a decade since it was founded.

Exception 1: 'commonly or customarily held' (s 11(2))

The advance notice provisions do not apply if 'the procession is one commonly or custom- **3.16** arily held in the police area (or areas) in which it is proposed to be held or is a funeral procession organised by a funeral director acting in the normal course of his business'.[19]

Processions commonly or customarily held include a wide range of public processions of a **3.17** national or local nature. The judges process annually to Westminster Abbey. There is the Notting Hill Carnival, the Lord Mayor's Show, and Chinese New Year celebrations in Soho and many local groups—religious and secular—have annual local parades, including Remembrance Day and Diwali parades.

Exactly what could amount to 'processions commonly or customarily held' was considered **3.18** by the House of Lords in *Kay (FC) v Commissioner of the Police for the Metropolis*.[20] The case arose from a notice handed out by police to participants in the Critical Mass cycle rides informing them that the ride was unlawful. The riders contended the rides were not unlawful and the matter was litigated as a 'friendly action' to seek a declaration from the courts. It was agreed between the parties that:

> Critical Mass is not an organization but the name given to a recurrent event. It takes place in central London on the evening of the last Friday of every month, as it has done so since April 1994. Similar events take place on the last Friday of the month in many other cities throughout the world. Critical Mass starts at the same location (the South Bank, near the National Theatre) at the same time (6pm). It is featured in Time Out Magazine. It is in the nature of

---

[18] HC (1979–80) 756, vol 1, para 35.
[19] Public Order Act 1986, s 11(2).
[20] [2008] UKHL 69.

Critical Mass that there is no fixed, settled, or predetermined route, end time, or destination; where Critical Mass goes, where and what time it ends, are all things which are chosen by the actions of the participants on the day.

3.19 Whilst the House of Lords was concerned that the issues were in fact broader, the question before them was whether the rides were commonly or customarily held. The answer is in an amalgam of two questions: 'Is it the same procession that takes place every month?' and 'Is that procession commonly or customarily held?' The Commissioner sought to argue that while each event constituted a procession, it was not the same procession each month because it didn't follow the same route. He relied upon the principle in *Flockhart v Robinson*[21] that 'A procession is not a mere body of persons: it is a body of persons moving along a route.' The House of Lords accepted that a procession must follow a route but rejected the suggestion that it must follow the same route (albeit that would be a material consideration) in order for it to be the same procession. The answer to the second question was found by giving 'the English language its natural meaning' and, per Lord Phillips, the 'common features' of the rides (the procession is made up of cyclists; starts at the same place at the same time; there is a common intention; it takes place within the same broad area; it is recognized by a single name) meant they were the same procession and that it was a procession commonly or customarily held.

Exception 2: 'not reasonably practicable' (s 11(1))

3.20 There is no requirement to give notice if 'it is not reasonably practicable' to do so.[22] The procedure for giving notice discussed at 3.22 and 3.23 below allows for the late delivery of notice in cases of demonstrations called at short notice. The exception discussed here exempts organizers from the requirement to give any notice at all. The circumstances to which it will apply are limited and will only apply to the procession which takes place almost instantly, as in the Union Movement procession in *Flockhart v Robinson*.[23] This would accord with a recent European Court of Human Rights decision considering the legality of a police decision to close down a necessarily spontaneous demonstration on the basis that no prior notification had been given. The Court found that: 'in special circumstances when an immediate response, in the form of a demonstration, to a political event might be justified, a decision to disband the ensuing, peaceful assembly solely because of the absence of the requisite prior notice, without any illegal conduct by the participants, amounts to a disproportionate restriction on freedom of peaceful assembly'.[24]

Processions without a determined route

3.21 The Critical Mass rides discussed above had no determined route. The Commissioner for the Police argued in the House of Lords that all processions falling within s 11(1) must have a predetermined route and, as such, those without predetermined routes are unlawful. This was questioned by all members of the court, and firmly rejected by some. Lord Phillips

---

[21] [1950] 2 KB 498.
[22] Public Order Act 1986, s 11(1).
[23] [1950] 2 KB 498.
[24] *Bukta and Others v Hungary* [2007] ECHR 25691/04 (17 July 2007).

provided three possible constructions for processions that do not have a determined route:

(a) the notification obligation does not apply to a procession that has no predetermined route (supported by Lord Roger at para 43, and Lord Brown at para 71);
(b) there is no obligation to give notice of a procession that has no predetermined route because it is not reasonably practicable to comply with s 11(1); and
(c) the notification obligation is satisfied if a notice is given that states that the route will be chosen spontaneously (supported by Baroness Hale at para 52).

As the issue was not required to be determined, no conclusion was reached as to the notice requirement of processions without a route. However, any of the options above were said to be preferable to the construction urged by the Commissioner.

Nature and delivery of notice to the police

The notice must be in writing and include the following:[25] **3.22**

(a) the fact that a procession is to be held (though it is not specified in the Act that the nature of the proposed procession is required to be set out);
(b) the date and starting time; and
(c) the proposed route, and the name and address of one of the organizers.

Delivery of the notice must be made[26] **3.23**

(a) to any police station in the police area in which it is proposed the procession will start, or, where it is proposed the procession will start in Scotland and cross into England, in the first police area in England on the proposed route;[27]
(b) either by hand or by recorded delivery post at least *six clear days* before the date of the procession. If sent by recorded delivery it must arrive at least six days before;[28] and
(c) if it is not reasonably practicable to deliver the notice at least six days before the procession, to deliver the notice by hand (not by post) as soon as is reasonably practicable.[29] This allows for demonstrations called at short notice in response to some event, for example where local parents call for a pedestrian crossing after a child has been killed on a road near a school.

Failure to comply: prosecution

It is a criminal offence to fail to comply with these advance notice requirements. It should **3.24** be noted at this stage that all offences in the Public Order Act 1986 for breaches of requirements, conditions, or bans relating to processions can only be brought in summary only proceedings in the magistrates' court. The organizer or organizers of the procession,

---

[25] Public Order Act 1986, s 11(3).
[26] Ibid, s 11(4)(b).
[27] Ibid, s 11(4).
[28] Ibid, 2 11(5)(b).
[29] Ibid, s 11(6).

but not the participants, may be prosecuted, and on conviction sentenced to a fine not exceeding level 3 on the standard scale,[30] if

(a) any of the notice requirements have not been satisfied; or

(b) the date, starting time, or route of the procession differs from the details on the written notice.

3.25 The word 'organizer' is not defined and must therefore be given its ordinary meaning. Clearly, there can be more than one organizer and responsibility does not rest solely with the organizer named on the written notice. On the facts in *Flockhart v Robinson*[31] it was held that the person who directed that procession along its route was the person who organized it. On this point, however, the judgment may well be limited to its particular facts, and the Court appeared to focus on the fact that the defendant's leading the procession was evidence that he was the organizer. In his dissenting judgment, Finnemore J held that because a person was the leader of the procession was not enough to constitute him its organizer.

3.26 It is a defence for the accused to prove on a balance of probabilities that

(a) he did not know of, and neither suspected nor had reason to suspect, that the notice requirements had not been satisfied or that the date etc differed from the notice;[32] or

(b) the differences of date, time, and route arose from circumstances either beyond his control or from something done with the agreement or by the direction of a police officer.[33]

3.27 It should be noted that the Public Order Act 1986 provides no immunities as a *quid pro quo* for the giving of notice on time. Other jurisdictions—for example, in the Public Assemblies Act 1979 in New South Wales, Australia—have protected those who give notice and process peacefully from prosecution for obstruction of the highway or other public nuisance. This means that the consent of the police to the proposed route of the procession would protect the organizer and marchers from being prosecuted for unexceptional behaviour. The domestic position is starkly different. In *Arrowsmith v Jenkins*[34] a conviction for obstructing the highway was upheld despite the fact that the police had notice of the meeting, that there was no intention to disrupt the highway, and meetings had been held there before without complaint. For obstruction of the highway see 4.19 et seq below.

Conditions imposed on public processions (s 12)

3.28 The Public Order Act 1986 not only introduced the written notice requirements, it also put in place a framework of controls the police were able to impose over public processions, involving either the imposition of conditions on the procession or, in more limited circumstances, prohibition.

---

[30] Ibid, s 11(10).
[31] [1950] 2 KB 498.
[32] Public Order Act 1986, s 11(8).
[33] Ibid, s 11(9).
[34] [1963] 2 QB 561.

Background

The current legislation was preceded by s 3 of the Public Order Act 1936, passed in the **3.29**
wake of fascist marches in the 1930s. It allowed the police to control public processions
where the police had reasonable grounds for apprehending that the procession might
occasion serious public disorder. This was the sole test for the imposition of such conditions
'as appear . . . necessary',[35] usually re-routing. The decision had to be taken by the chief
officer of police (the Chief Constable or, in London, the Metropolitan Police Commissioner
or the City of London Commissioner). If the chief officer was of the opinion that the
powers to impose conditions were insufficient to prevent serious public disorder, an order
could be applied for banning all or a class of processions for a period of up to three months.

On the whole the police used these powers sparingly. The White Paper[36] preceding the **3.30**
Public Order Act 1986 recognized that the excessive use of coercion in the management of
demonstrations was known to be counter-productive:

> The police prefer to discuss the plans for a march with the organizers and to negotiate an
> informal agreement about the route and other matters. In general these arrangements work
> well: the Metropolitan Police have given only two examples of cases where they have imposed
> formal conditions in order to prevent serious public disorder in the last five years. [Both were
> examples of straightforward re-routing.][37]

Imposing conditions

Section 12 of the Public Order Act 1986 allows for conditions to be imposed on a proces- **3.31**
sion if the senior police reasonably believes that

(a) it may result in serious public disorder;
(b) it may result in serious damage to property;
(c) it may result in serious disruption to the life of the community; or
(d) the purpose of the persons organizing is the intimidation of others with a view to com-
    pelling them not to do an act they have a right to do, or to do an act they have a right
    not to do.

The first test re-enacts the test from the 1936 Act. The addition of the second condition is **3.32**
relatively clear. However, the third test has been far more controversial[38] as 'disruption to
the community' is widely drawn. This provision was intended, as evidenced by the White
Paper *Review of Public Order Law*[39] that preceded the 1986 Act, to prevent marches from
causing unreasonable disruption, such as to local residents, other users of the highway, and
adjoining shops and premises; to limit traffic congestion; to prevent a bridge from being
blocked; to reduce the severe disruption sometimes suffered by pedestrians, business,
and commerce; or to keep Oxford Street[40], or shopping centres, or city centres, free from

---

[35] Public Order Act 1936, s 1(1).
[36] Cmnd 9510.
[37] Ibid, para 4.19.
[38] It remains controversial: See *Liberty's Response to the JCHR on 'Policing and Protest'* (June 2008).
[39] Cmnd 9510, para 4.23.
[40] It was exactly this situation that became the actual facts of the procession in *Austin and Saxby v
Commissioner of Police for the Metropolis* [2005] EWHC 480 and Tugenhat J in the High Court referred

demonstrators during business hours. This test more than any other extends the basis for imposing conditions beyond the concept of public disorder, as 'serious disruption' is open to be interpreted as 'serious inconvenience'. The balance has always been between the freedom of assembly and the rights of pedestrians and motorists to use the highway unhindered by protestors; in including this provision the 1986 Act has, as it clearly intended, titled the balance in favour of the latter.

3.33 The last test, intimidation of others, is directed at those who organize processions with more malicious intent; those whose overt or covert purpose is to intimidate or coerce. The example given in the White Paper to illustrate this test was of a National Front counter-demonstration to a march by the Troops Out Movement in Manchester in 1984 with literature describing their purpose as being to 'stop this vermin . . . don't let them march'. In a present day context, a Unite Against Fascism counter-demonstration to an authorized English Defence League march past a mosque (using similar literature) may fall within the test as being the intimidation of the English Defence League march with a view to compelling them not to do an act they have a right to do, namely to march through the streets of London. It is worth noting that the word 'compelling' is derived from the offence of intimidation contrary to the Conspiracy and Protection of Property Act 1875, and this suggests that the provision was also directed at the control of picketing.

3.34 The tests only have effect when the senior police officer, having regard to the time or place at which, and the circumstances in which, any public procession is being, or is intended to be held and to its route, reasonably believes that any one or more of the tests is applicable to a particular procession.[41] In relation to a procession that is being held or where persons are assembling with a view to taking part in a procession, the senior police officer means the most senior in rank of the police officers present at the scene, and the direction need not be given in writing.[42] In other circumstances, it is defined as 'the chief officer of police' (either the Chief Constable or Commissioner of Police[43]) and the direction must be given in writing.

3.35 The chief officer may give directions imposing on the persons organizing or taking part in the procession such conditions as appear to him necessary to prevent such disorder, damage, disruption, or intimidation, including conditions as to the route of the procession or prohibiting it from entering any public place specified in the directions.[44] It is clear that the powers are greater than simple re-routing, and the section is drafted widely enough to allow the imposition of conditions such as perhaps restricting the number of people on the procession and its duration.[45]

---

back to the White Paper. This was a case brought for false imprisonment arising out of the police 'kettling' or detainment tactics. The case reached the House of Lords on the Art 5 issue: [2009] 1 AC 564.

[41] Public Order Act 1986, s 12(1).
[42] Ibid, s 12(2)–(3).
[43] Section 15 provides that the chief officer of police may delegate his functions under ss 12–14A to an assistant chief constable or, in the City of London and the Metropolitan Police District, an assistant commissioner of police as applicable.
[44] Ibid, s 12(1).
[45] Compare with test for assembles at 3.65 et seq.

Section 12 does not permit the police to ban the procession, nor to disband a procession **3.36** already underway, although the police have other common law powers and can also act to control a procession if it is necessary to avoid an imminent breach of the peace, whether by the individuals who form part of the procession or anyone else.[46]

Failure to comply with conditions: prosecution

There are three summary offences of failing to comply with police conditions imposed on **3.37** a public procession:

(a) it is an offence if an organizer organizes a procession and knowingly fails to comply with a condition.[47] The maximum penalty on summary conviction is three months' imprisonment or a fine not exceeding level 4 on the standard scale or both.[48] It is a defence to prove that the failure to comply with the condition arose from circumstances beyond the defendant's control;[49]

(b) it is an offence if a participant takes part in a procession and knowingly fails to comply with conditions.[50] The maximum penalty on summary conviction is a fine not exceeding level 3.[51] It is a defence to prove that the failure to comply with the condition arose from circumstances beyond the defendant's control;[52] and

(c) it is an offence to incite somebody else knowingly to participate in a procession in breach of a condition.[53] The maximum penalty on summary conviction is three months' imprisonment, a fine not exceeding level 4,[54] or both.

Banning processions (s 13)

If at any time the chief officer of police reasonably believes that, because of particular **3.38** circumstances existing, the powers under s 12 will not be sufficient to prevent the holding of public processions in that district or area from resulting in serious public disorder, he is required (there is no discretion) under s 13 to put in motion the procedure for applying for a banning order. The question is not whether the applicants or those on the march

---

[46] See High Court decision in *Austin and Saxby v Commissioner of Police for the Metropolis* [2005] EWHC 480, para 72. This was a case brought for false imprisonment arising out of the police 'kettling' or detainment tactics. The case was appealed to the Court of Appeal and House of Lords on the issue of Art 5 of the European Convention on Human Rights and the lawfulness of the detention. The overlap between Public Order Act 1986 powers and those under the common law to avoid a breach of the peace are discussed at length in the High Court judgment.

[47] Public Order Act 1986, s 12(4) and see *DPP v Baillie* [1995] Crim LR 426: Mr Baillie had distributed information about free festivals to travellers. He was served with a notice under s 14 requiring him to comply with certain conditions about a proposed festival which the police believed was to take place. He was prosecuted for breaching those conditions even though the event had not yet taken place. He was acquitted on appeal by the Crown Court, and the Divisional Court upheld that acquittal. The Court concluded that there was no evidence that brought the police within s 14(1) but left open the question of whether an offence under s 14 had been committed before the public assembly had occurred.

[48] See discussion above as to whether the Crown can prove a person is the organizer.

[49] Public Order Act 1986, s 12(4).

[50] Ibid, s 12(5).

[51] Ibid, s 12(9).

[52] Ibid, s 12(5).

[53] Ibid, s 12(6).

[54] Ibid, s 12(10).

themselves are likely to cause serious public disorder, simply whether serious public order would result.[55]

3.39   The chief officer is the Chief Constable outside London, and the Metropolitan Police Commissioner, or the City of London Police Commissioner in London. The chief officer may delegate his function to an assistant chief constable outside London, or an assistant commissioner of police in London.[56]

Procedure outside London

3.40   Outside of London, the Chief Constable is concerned with circumstances in any district or part of a district. The Chief Constable applies to the council of the district in which the procession is to be held, specifying in the application the length of the ban required (up to three months) and whether the ban should extend to all processions or a class of procession. Despite the initial intention of the government to allow a single march to be banned—recognizing that blanket bans meant 'the innocent suffer with the guilty'[57]—the 1986 Act did in the end provide no power to request or make a ban of one particular procession. On receiving such an application, a council may, with the consent of the Secretary of State, make an order either in the terms of the application or with such modifications as may be approved by the Secretary of State.[58]

3.41   Local authorities have no power of their own to seek a ban with or without the consent of the Home Secretary. The initiative must come from the police.

Procedure in London

3.42   In London, the Commissioner is concerned with circumstances in his police area or part of it. The Commissioner himself makes the Order after obtaining the consent of the Home Secretary.[59] Therefore local authorities in London have no part in the formal process of making banning orders, although they may seek to persuade the Commissioner in a particular case.

3.43   Whether made in London or elsewhere, an existing order may be varied or revoked during its currency by using the same procedure as for making the order.[60] It is unclear whether the order can be relaxed for one particular procession if the full procedure is complied with. It appears possible that the order could read, for example, 'all public processions, except traditional May processions, processions of a religious character, and the Stop the War march on 17th May'. Blanket bans have been used to cover a single march.[61] Therefore, while there is no provision for the banning of a single march, this can be cured by either a blanket ban or by allowing a number of specified marches within the order, and then allowing further marches if and when applications were made to vary the order. Class bans are rare.

---

[55]   *Kent v Metropolitan Police Commissioner*, The Times, 15 May 1981.
[56]   Public Order Act 1986, s 15.
[57]   Cmnd 9510, para 4.14,
[58]   Public Order Act 1986, s 13(2).
[59]   Ibid, s 13(4).
[60]   Ibid, s 13(5).
[61]   For example, a seventeen-day ban in July 1981 of all public processions in Grimsby, Hull, Cleethorpes, and Scunthorpe was imposed in order to stop a proposed National Front march in Grimsby.

One example was the one month ban in parts of the Midlands in 1974 of any procession in connection with the death of James McDade, a member of the IRA.

The Act makes no reference to the renewal of orders, but there is nothing to prevent the making of a fresh order in the same or modified terms on the expiry of the existing order. Banning orders are rare and there is a dearth of authority on the procedure under the 1986 Act; the case of *Kent v Metropolitan Police Commissioner*[62] relates to a ban in 1981 and addressed the similar test under the 1936 Act. **3.44**

The Convention jurisprudence is discussed in Chapter 10 but in this specific context, orders banning processions can be justified only in extreme circumstances. In *Christians against Racism and Fascism v UK*,[63] the appellant association had planned to hold a procession to promote its aims—unity in the love of God and opposition to fascism and racism—at a time when a blanket ban was in place. While, on the facts existing at the time, the European Court held that a ban was justified, the Court stressed the strict test of necessity: **3.45**

> A general ban on demonstrations can only be justified if there is a real danger of their resulting in disorder which cannot be prevented by less stringent measures. In this connection, the authority must also take into account the effect of a ban on processions which do not by themselves constitute a danger for public order. Only if the disadvantage of such processions being caught by the ban is clearly outweighed by the security considerations justifying the issue of the ban, and if there is no possibility of avoiding such undesirable side effects of the ban by a narrow circumspection of its scope in terms of its territorial application and duration, can the ban be regarded as necessary within the meaning of Article 11(2) of the Convention.[64]

Failure to comply with a ban: prosecution

The 1986 Act creates three summary offences of failing to comply with an order prohibiting public processions. It is an offence to **3.46**

(a) knowingly organize a banned procession.[65] The maximum penalty on summary conviction is three months' imprisonment and/or a fine not exceeding level 3 on the standard scale;[66]

(b) take part in a banned procession knowing it is banned.[67] The maximum conviction on summary conviction is a fine not exceeding level 3;[68] and

(c) to incite somebody else knowingly to take part in a banned procession.[69] The maximum penalty on summary conviction is three months' imprisonment and/or a fine not exceeding level 4.[70]

---

[62] The Times, 15 May 1981: see discussion at 3.50 below.
[63] (1980) 21 DR 138. See also 10.143–10.144.
[64] Ibid, at para 5.
[65] Public Order Act 1986, s 13(7).
[66] Ibid, s 13(11).
[67] Ibid, s 13(8).
[68] Ibid, s 13(12).
[69] Ibid, s 13(9).
[70] Ibid, s 13(13).

Judicial review

3.47 There is no statutory or other right of appeal against the imposition of conditions or a ban made under the Public Order Act 1986.

3.48 In limited circumstances the order of the chief officer of police or local council may be amenable to judicial review with the quashing of the order being one remedy available to the Divisional Court. Judicial review is available because of the words 'reasonably believes' as a prerequisite to the operation of the procedure to impose conditions or a ban; the chief officer or senior officer (or anyone who has been lawfully delegated powers) must act reasonably in exercising these powers. The test of reasonableness of his decision, although a question of fact, is always treated as a question of law and therefore may be challenged by way of judicial review.

3.49 The scope of judicial review is limited in that the judge does not consider the merits of the original decision, only whether that decision was lawful. An examination of judicial review and public law principles is beyond the scope of this book[71] but broadly speaking, the decision may be unlawful if it was improperly reached (for example, the procedure was not complied with or improper considerations were taken into account) or because the decision was so unreasonable, irrational, or arbitrary that no reasonable chief officer could have come to that conclusion.[72]

3.50 In *Kent v Metropolitan Police Commissioner*[73] (a case considering the similar test under the Public Order Act 1936), a blanket ban had been put in force across London in the face of serious disorders in Brixton, Wanstead, Finsbury Park, and Ealing. CND wanted to march during the course of the ban, and there was no suggestion that the CND march itself would result in disorder. CND sought a declaration that the order was null and void and that CND were lawfully entitled to march during the prohibited period. The Court of Appeal upheld the ban despite expressing concern that the Commissioner's reasons for his order seemed meagre, although 'The Court could not say that the Commissioner was at fault or that the order made was ultra vires, especially when the Home Secretary had agreed with it.'

3.51 A similar reluctance was shown when the London Borough of Lewisham tried to obtain an order of mandamus against the Commissioner to ban a National Front march.[74] Slynn J said:

> No doubt I have power to grant mandamus.[75] Circumstances could arise in which I could make an order. For example, if the Commissioner failed to take into account all relevant matters or if the Commissioner was of the opinion that his powers to prevent serious public disorder under subsection (1) [of the Public Order Act 1936, s.3 imposition of conditions], . . . and other powers, were not sufficient to prevent public disorder, but nevertheless failed

---

[71] For an authoritative and comprehensive guide see Michael Fordam, *Judicial Review Handbook* (2008, 5th edn).
[72] *Associated Provincial Picture House Limited v Wednesbury Corporation* [1948] 1 KB 223.
[73] The Times, 15 May 1981.
[74] The Times, 12 August 1977.
[75] Now called a 'mandatory order'.

to take action. Or if the Commissioner took a view of the circumstances which was wholly untenable, I consider that the court could intervene.

Nevertheless, the Court in that case did not intervene.

These cases are from the late 1970s and early 1980s. The enactment of the Human Rights **3.52** Act 1998 has required a far more intensive level of review by the administrative court when considering decisions involving fundamental freedoms,[76] a review that goes far beyond the '*Wednesbury* unreasonable' test applied at the time. The test of proportionality would now require the Commissioner's response to be appropriate and necessary to achieve a legitimate aim, and this requires a substantive review. Similar cases may well be decided very differently if they arose today.

C. Assemblies

Background

Prior to the 1986 Act there had been no statutory restrictions on the holding of assemblies **3.53** in public as the previous legislation only controlled processions. The 1986 Act provided police with a new power to impose conditions on those organizing or taking part in an assembly, and it was picketing that many felt to be the target of the new legislation. The White Paper refers to picketing at Warrington and 'of course the mass pickets during the miners' dispute'.[77] Whilst the police's common law powers allowed the imposition of control during the course of the picket, for example, to prevent a breach of the peace or to control numbers, the 1986 Act powers can operate both before and during the picket. The government stated that the right of peaceful picketing will not in any way be infringed and that it is not intended that the power should be used to undermine the right of pickets in reasonable numbers to stand by the entrance to a workplace.[78]

The government also considered[79] whether, following the shooting of a policewoman **3.54** outside the Libyan People's Bureau in April 1984, demonstrations outside embassies, particularly by foreign nations, should be subject to special controls. But it concluded it would be neither practicable nor desirable to make any changes to public order law in this respect; the police's existing statutory and common law powers, coupled with the new 1986 Act powers, were quite adequate.

These new controls include a police power to impose conditions as to the place and **3.55** duration of the assembly and the number of persons at the assembly, with penalties for non-compliance. In contrast with processions here is no power or procedure to ban an assembly falling within these provisions.

---

[76] See, inter alia, *R v Secretary of State for the Home Department, ex parte Daly* [2001] 2 AC 532 and Michael Fordham, *Judicial Review Handbook* (2008, 5th edn), Parts 58–59.
[77] Cmnd 9510, para 5.1. See also Peter Thornton, *We Protest: The Public Order Debate* (NCCL 1985), pp 59–60.
[78] Ibid, para 5.14.
[79] Ibid, para 5.12.

Definition of 'public assembly'

3.56   The Public Order Act, s 16, as amended, defines 'public assembly' as meaning an assembly of two or more persons in a public place which is 'wholly or partly open to the air'. As originally drafted, the Act referred to 'twenty or more persons': the number was reduced to two by s 57 of the Anti-social Behaviour Act 2003. The definition of public place is discussed at 3.10 above.

3.57   This part of the Public Order Act 1986 therefore only governs an assembly

(a)   which is held in public. Private assemblies, whether held indoors or outdoors, cannot be controlled by these provisions; and

(b)   which is held out of doors or one which is at least partly open to the air.[80]

This probably includes a marquee with its sides up (but not down), but presumably does not include a hall with its doors left open on a warm summer's day.

3.58   The common law offence of unlawful assembly was abolished by s 9(1) of the 1986 Act. 'Assembly' in the 1986 Act is not further defined, and leaves open the question of when two people are simply standing having a conversation and when they become an 'assembly', and also the distinction to be drawn between 'assembly' and 'procession'.

3.59   Despite the comments made in *DPP v Roffey*[81]—in the context of the criminal offence of flying too near an assembly—that an assembly means no more than a gathering of persons, whether stationary or in motion, it would seem that in the public order context an assembly must at least be static, but little clear guidance has emerged as to the distinction between a procession and an assembly. In *DPP v Jones*,[82] the notice that was purported to be served on an assembly under s 14 sought to regulate the movement to the demonstration as well as the demonstration itself. The Crown sought to argue that an assembly can move:

> [Counsel for the Crown] submits that an assembly is not a static activity and that section 14 clearly envisages that it may move. That, he says, is implicit in the words of the section 'a place at which the assembly may be 'or continue to be'. He emphasizes the words 'or continue to be'. So here, he submits, the conditions provide for an entrance point for those taking part in the assembly and an exit point for those who wish to leave it. It is his submission that the assembly is permitted in the whole area between points 1 and 2 on the map. Therefore, he submits, this whole area is 'the place at which the assembly may be or continue to be.' The effect is, he says, that people may come and go from the permitted area defined in conditions 3 and 4 to the entrance and exit point at point 1. The fact that the permitted area is designated as an area where the demonstration is permitted, does not prevent the whole area between points 1 and 2 being the place where the assembly may occur.

3.60   This argument was rejected. The Court concluded that the conditions directed at an embarkation and disembarkation point at a point geographically distinct from the area defined for the assembly, could not relate to the assembly and were *ultra vires* the Deputy Chief Constable's powers under s 14 of the 1986 Act. This, by inference, supports the

---

[80]   For discussion of problems of definition arising from 'partly open to the air' see D Bonner and R Stone, '*The Public Order Act 1986: Steps in the Wrong Direction*' [1987] PL 202, 223.

[81]   [1959] Crim LR 283.

[82]   [2002] EWHC 110.

submission that an assembly relates to a static demonstration. This definition would at least dovetail with the definition of 'procession' which has at its heart 'a body of persons moving along a route'.

Whilst an assembly has to consist of at least two persons, the geographical delineation can be broad. In *Broadwith v Chief Constable of Thames Valley Police Authority*,[83] counsel for the appellant, who had been convicted of breaching a condition imposed on an assembly when he had in fact been on his own, a short distance from the main assembly (albeit demonstrating at the same time and against the same target as the assembly on which the condition was imposed), sought to argue: **3.61**

> ... that section 14 of the 1986 Act is not directed to individuals but to groups of 20 [*the law at the time*] or more and, at the time of his arrest, the appellant was not only on his own but was walking away from the larger group and, therefore, he was not part of any assembly.

Lord Justice Rose rejected this argument: **3.62**

> So far as that submission is concerned, it seems to me that there are a number of difficulties. First of all, groups, whether they be of 20 or more or less than that size, can only consist of individuals. It may be necessary according to the particular circumstances, in order to ensure that an assembly proceeds on permitted lines, to take steps in relation to controlling the movements of particular individuals.

> 29. Furthermore, it is not, to my mind, an accurate description of the appellant as being not part of an assembly because he was walking away from the other larger group. The fact is that, although he was so walking, he had come with others intending to demonstrate and was deliberately seeking to enter the part of Burford Road which was closed by the police presence, in accordance with the notice which had been served, and was doing so prior to the time of 1.30, when an assembly in Burford Road was, in accordance with the notice, to be permitted.

An attempt at certainty in a definition based on the current authorities appears elusive; a fact conceded by Tugendhat J in *Austin and Saxby v The Commissioner of Police and the Metropolis*:[84] **3.63**

> There is room for uncertainty as to whether a group is at any given time a procession or an assembly, or perhaps both at once.

No advance notice requirement

Unlike the law relating to processions, there is no legal requirement to give advance notice, either to the police or to the local authority, of the holding of a public assembly. **3.64**

Police controls over public assemblies (s 14)

Section 14 of the Public Order Act provides the framework for imposing conditions on public assemblies. **3.65**

---

[83] [2000] All ER (D) 225.
[84] See High Court decision in *Austin and Saxby v Commissioner of Police for the Metropolis* [2005] EWHC 480. See also 3.74, 3.75, 4.67, 4.73 et seq; 6.162 et seq; 10.164, 10.167 et seq.

Imposing conditions

3.66 The senior police officer may impose conditions on an assembly if, having regard to all the circumstances, he reasonably believes that it may result in

(a) serious public disorder: s 14(1)(a);

(b) serious damage to property: s 14(1)(a);

(c) serious disruption to the life of the community: s 14(1)(a); or

(d) the purpose of the organizer(s) is the intimidation of others with a view to compelling them 'not to do an act they have a right to do, or to do an act they have a right not to do': s 14(1)(b).

These tests are the same as the tests for imposing conditions on processions: see discussion at 3.28.

3.67 For an assembly being held, the senior police officer is the most senior in rank of the police officers present at the scene. In relation to an assembly intended to be held it is the chief officer of police (the Metropolitan or City of London Police Commissioner, or outside London the Chief Constable). These functions may be delegated to an assistant commissioner of police or an assistant chief constable.[85]

3.68 When the Public Order Act 1986 first came into force, commentators[86] were of the opinion that the 'intimidation of others' test was directed primarily at picketing and demonstrations in support of picketing. The White Paper[87] gave picketing as 'the obvious example' and suggested that this test should apply either to picketing which obstructs the free passage of the highway or to other forms of picketing which are not obstructive but can nevertheless be intimidatory. In a present day context, this is more relevant in the context of assemblies that seek to target and intimidate those who have dealings—business or personal—with, for example, animal experimentation facilities (though this has now been separately legislated for in s 145 of the Serious Organised Crime and Police Act 2005), or nuclear, or military bases.

3.69 The use of the words 'right to do' and 'right not to do' are adapted from the offence of intimidation contrary to s 7 of the Conspiracy and Protection of Property Act 1875. The 'rights' in question were presumably intended to refer to the right to go to work and the right to refuse to come out on strike. However, the legal basis of these 'rights' is unclear; whether they are statutory or common law rights, or even fundamental freedoms is at best dubious.

3.70 Intimidation for the purposes of the Conspiracy and Protection of Property Act 1875 includes putting a person in fear by the exhibition of force or violence, and there is no limitation restricting the meaning of 'intimidation' to cases of violence or threats of violence to the person[88] as it can also include threats of breaches of contract.[89] However, intimidate

---

[85] Public Order Act 1986, s 15.

[86] P Thornton, *Public Order Law* (1987) p 153.

[87] Cmnd 9510, para 5.10.

[88] *R v Jones* (1974) 59 C App R 120.

[89] *Rookes v Barnard* [1964] AC 1129.

must be given a 'reasonable and sensible interpretation';[90] 'abuse, swearing, and shouting' in one particular set of circumstances has been held not to amount to a threat of violence for the purposes of intimidation.[91]

Conditions

Once the tests are satisfied, directions may be given imposing on the organizers or **3.71** participants such conditions as are required to prevent disorder, damage, disruption, or intimidation. Unlike the provisions imposing conditions on processions which allow for any conditions necessary to be imposed, in relation to assemblies the police are limited to conditions restricting the place, maximum duration, or maximum numbers of the assembly as appear necessary.

When imposing conditions, the chief officer of police must identify which limb was relied **3.72** upon (and if it is s 14(1)(a) then to specify which of the three grounds contained in that limb). The reasons given do not have to be in great detail, but have to be sufficient to enable demonstrators to understand why the decision was made and sufficient for, if required, a court to understand whether the decision was reasonable.[92] The conditions must be reasonable and proportionate to the legitimate aim of maintaining public order.[93]

Failure to comply with conditions: prosecution

Section 14 of the Public Order Act 1986 creates three summary only offences of failing to **3.73** comply with police conditions on assemblies:

(a) it is an offence if an organizer organizes an assembly and knowingly fails to comply with a condition.[94] The maximum penalty on summary conviction is three months' imprisonment and/or a fine not exceeding level 4;[95]

---

[90] *Gibson v Lawson* [1891] 2 QB 545.
[91] *News Group Newspapers Ltd v Society of Graphical and Allied Trades* 1982 [1987] ICR 181. See also *Police v Reid* [1987] Crim LR 702 (anti-apartheid demonstration shouting at guests arriving at South Africa House reception held to be causing discomfort, not intimidation); and *Thomas v National Union of Mineworkers (South Wales Area)* [1985] 2 WLR 1081.
[92] *R(on the application of Louis Brehony) v Chief Constable of Greater Manchester* [2005] EWHC 640 (Admin) challenged by way of an application for judicial review a decision of the Chief Constable of Greater Manchester imposing a condition prohibiting him and fellow members of a group known as 'Victory to the Intifada' from demonstrating outside the Marks & Spencer store in Manchester City Centre on Saturdays from 29 November 2004 until 3 January 2005 and requiring them to relocate their protest to the Peace Gardens. This group had been demonstrating every Saturday outside the store for about four years. The store is in the pedestrianized shopping area in the centre of the city. The purpose of the demonstration, as it is put in the grounds in support of the claim, was to highlight the support given by Marks & Spencer to the government of Israel and to urge the public to boycott goods on sale at the store. In the summer of 2004 a counter-demonstration was formed outside the store, whose purpose was to express support for the government of Israel and opposition to the Victory to the Intifada group. The police imposed the conditions because of the increased number of people in the area during the Christmas period. The Court declined to interfere with the Chief Constable's decision having considered both reasonableness and the proportionality.
[93] Ibid, at para 18, applying the test set out by Dyson LJ in *R(Samaroo) v Secretary of State for the Home Department* [2001] EWCA Civ 1139.
[94] Public Order Act 1986, s 14(4).
[95] Ibid, s 14(8).

(b) it is an offence if a participant takes part in an assembly and knowingly fails to comply with a condition.[96] The maximum penalty on summary conviction is a fine not exceeding level 3;[97] and

(c) it is an offence to incite somebody else knowingly to participate in an assembly in breach of a condition.[98] The maximum penalty on summary conviction is three months' imprisonment and/or a fine not exceeding level 4.[99]

It is a defence to charges (a) and (b) to prove that the failure to comply with the condition arose from circumstances beyond the defendant's control.[100]

No power to prohibit assemblies

3.74   There is no power to ban assemblies. However, it may be perceived by organizers and participants that the conditions imposed are so onerous that they amount to a *de facto* ban. This was recognized by Tugendhat J in the High Court proceedings in *Austin and Saxby v Commissioner of Police for the Metropolis*:[101]

> In Smith para 8-07 and in D Feldman *Civil Liberties and Human Rights in England and Wales* 2nd ed Oxford 2002, a point is made, which I accept. As Professor Feldman states it, at p1063, 'Conditions which are so demanding that they amount in effect to a ban are an improper use of the power and so are unlawful on ordinary public law principles'. But this procession was not banned. It had already taken place to the extent of reaching Oxford Circus. And if the conditions do no more than is necessary and proportionate in the circumstances of the case to achieve the statutory public order objectives, then bringing the procession to an end will not be unlawful.[102]

The law remains uncertain as to whether directions under s 14 may be used to bring an existing assembly to an end.

3.75   In the High Court in *Austin and Saxby*, Tugendhat J concluded that a direction under s 14 as to the maximum duration of an assembly can include a direction that its members disperse by a specified route, or even stay in a specified place for as long as is necessary for the dispersal to be effected consistently with the objective of preventing disorder, damage, disruption, or intimidation.[103] In this context, Tugendhat J also noted that the direction must be in accordance with Articles 10 and 11 of the European Convention on Human Rights and other public law requirements. The Court of Appeal, however, expressed reservations about the judge's conclusions[104] but, in the event, the Court of Appeal did not embark on a detailed examination of these provisions as that was not required given their

---

[96]   Ibid, s 14(5).

[97]   Ibid, s 14(9).

[98]   Ibid, s 14(6).

[99]   Ibid, s 14(10).

[100]   Ibid, s 14(4)(5).

[101]   See High Court decision in *Austin and Saxby v Commissioner of Police for the Metropolis* [2005] HRLR 20; [2005] UKHRR 1039. See also fn 88, 3.74.

[102]   Ibid, para 92.

[103]   Ibid, para 95. The police could also use their common law powers to prevent a breach of the peace.

[104]   [2007] EWCA Civ 989, paras 79–80.

decision on other aspects of the case, and the House of Lords' decision[105] was confined to the Article 5 of the European Convention on Human Rights issue.[106]

D. Meetings

The law has long recognized the right of public meeting, 'a right which has long passed out **3.76** of the region of discussion or doubt'.[107]

Open air meetings, or those at least 'partly open to the air', at which two or more persons **3.77** are present in a public place are 'assemblies' for the purposes of the Public Order Act 1986 and are subject to the controls discussed above.[108] But the Act provides no controls over public meetings held indoors or in closed premises, for example council meetings which are open to the public. It was felt that it was neither necessary nor desirable to have these controls because serious public disorder was less frequently associated with indoor meetings and because the existing law provided adequate coverage.[109]

Private meetings are governed by the law of contract and the terms of the letting and hiring **3.78** of halls. The public have no right to attend private meetings unless specifically invited, whether on payment or otherwise. The organizers have the right to refuse entry and those who attend without permission or who breach the conditions of their attendance are trespassers and can be ejected from the meeting, if necessary by force.[110] In a recent, well publicized example, an 82-year-old was forcibly ejected from the Labour party conference after shouting 'nonsense' as the then Foreign Secretary defended government policy on Iraq. Otherwise, the attendance of persons at a meeting is governed by the terms of the contract. In clear cases an interlocutory injunction will be granted to prevent the wrongful exclusion of members from meetings of an association.[111]

The police have no right to attend private meetings unless they are invited by the **3.79** organizers.[112] They do, however, have a right to enter to prevent crime or deal with a breach of the peace or to pursue a criminal. It should also be noted that the public order offences examined in Chapter 1 can be committed in private as well as in public so that the police will be entitled to enter private premises for the purposes of arrest. However, if there is no legal justification for their entry they will not be in the execution of their duty for the purposes of the offences of assault and obstruction contrary to s 51 of the Police Act 1964.[113] A policeman who has entered private premises without permission becomes a trespasser at

---

[105] [2009] UKHL 5.
[106] See Ch 10 on human rights.
[107] *Ex parte Lewis* (1888) 21 QBD 191, 196.
[108] See 3.65 et seq.
[109] Cmnd 9510, para 5.17.
[110] *Marshall v Tinnelly* (1937) 81 SJ 902.
[111] *Woodford v Smith* [1970] 1 All ER 1091, relating to a local ratepayers and residents' association.
[112] *Davis v Lisle* [1936] 2 KB 434, following *Great Central Railway Co v Bates* [1921] 3 KB 578; *R v Prebble* (1858) 1 F&F 325.
[113] *Davis v Lisle* [1936] 2 KB 434; *R v Prebble* (1858) 1 F&F 325 and *R v Richards and Leeming* (1985) 81 Cr App R 125. See also Ch 2.

the very latest on being told to leave and refusing to do so.[114] As an example, the police were not entitled to remove drinkers at a late hour from a barn attached to a public house where there was no nuisance, no breach of the peace, and no danger of one.[115]

Definition of public meeting

3.80   There is no definition of 'public meeting' in the Public Order Act 1986. Similarly, there is no definition in the Public Meeting Act 1908 or the Representation of the People Act 1983.

3.81   The definition found in s 9 of the Public Order Act 1936 is retained in that Act for the offence prohibiting the wearing of uniforms in connection with political objects 'in any public place or at any public meeting',[116] an offence under that Act which remains in force. For those purposes, a 'meeting' is defined as 'a meeting held for the purpose of the discussion of matters of public interest or for the purpose of the expression of views on such matters' and a 'public meeting' as 'any meeting in a public place and any meeting which the public or any section thereof are permitted to attend, whether on payment or otherwise'.

3.82   There is a dearth of authorities on the subject of what is a public meeting. Using the earlier definition in s 9 of the 1936 Act as a guide, it must be a 'meeting', but this could apply to any small (two or more) or larger group of persons meeting for a particular purpose. What that purpose is gives rise to difficulties; the definition in s 9 of the 1936 Act required it to be for the purpose of discussion of matters of *public* interest and this will of course remain the definition for the purposes of those sections of the 1936 Act that remain in force. However, there seems no reason why in other contexts, matters of a *private* interest could not be discussed at a public meeting. There is some case law on what is a lawful public meeting, and this indicates that a lawful meeting may be held on a highway even if it might amount to an obstruction,[117] and a public meeting does not cease to be lawful because there is disorderly opposition from other persons.[118]

3.83   The meeting must also be held in a public place. The definition of public place is discussed more fully at 3.10 et seq above. The essence of that definition is that the meeting must be held at 'any place to which at the material time the public or any section of the public has access, on payment or otherwise, as of right or by virtue of express or implied permission'. This excludes private meetings held on private premises, such as private members' clubs and meetings by invitation or limited ticket sale. A public meeting should be one which is genuinely open to the public. However, since the amendment to s 16 of the Public Order Act 1986 reducing the numbers to qualify for an assembly to two, any outdoor public meeting will be controlled as an assembly. Only if the venue for the meeting is not wholly or partially open to the air will the Public Order Act 1986 provisions governing assemblies not apply.

---

[114] See *Davis v Lisle.*
[115] *R v Prebble* (1858) 1 F&F 325.
[116] Public Order Act 1936, s 1(1) and see 2.37 et seq.
[117] *Burden v Rigler* [1911] 1 KB 337.
[118] *Beatty v Gillbanks* (1882) 9QBD 308; *Duncan v Jones* [1936] 1 KB 218.

Control of public meetings

It is the responsibility of those holding public meetings to see that the premises are fit **3.84**
for the purpose of the meeting and the intended size of the meeting, to comply with the
contractual conditions imposed by the lettors or hirers of the hall or meeting-place, including health and safety arrangements, and to ensure that the meeting is conducted in an
orderly manner.

Section 2(6) of the 1936 Act specifically provides that the prohibition in s 2 of that Act on **3.85**
members of organizations being trained for the purpose of usurping the functions of the
police shall not be construed as prohibiting the employment of a reasonable number of
persons as stewards to assist in the preservation of order at a public meeting held upon
private premises, or the making of arrangements for that purpose or the instruction of the
persons to be so employed in their lawful duties as stewards or their being furnished with
badges or other distinguishing signs.

While stewards may wear 'badges or other distinguishing signs', they are not permitted **3.86**
to wear a uniform to promote a political object or signify association with a political
organization[119] or usurp the functions of the police or the armed forces or use or display
force to promote a political object.[120] In the course of their duties as stewards they may
use reasonable force where necessary to control disorder, to prevent crime[121] and to eject
members of the public who have strayed beyond the bounds of reasonable participation.

Attempts to break up public meetings

The limited provisions of s 1 of the Public Meeting Act 1908 create three criminal **3.87**
offences summarized in the marginal note as 'Penalty on endeavour to break up a public
meeting':

(a) any person who at a lawful public meeting acts in a disorderly manner for the purpose
of preventing the transaction of the business for which the meeting was called together
is guilty of an offence: s 1(1);[122]

(b) any person who incites others to commit such an offence is guilty of an offence:
s (2);[123] and

(c) if any constable reasonably suspects any person of committing an such an offence, he
may if requested so to do by the chairman of the meeting require that person to declare
to him immediately his name and address. If that person refuses or fails so to declare
his name and address or gives a false name and address he is guilty of an offence.[124]

This section does not apply to election meetings which are governed by s 97 of the
Representation of the People Act 1983.

---

[119] Public Order Act 1936, s 1 (see 2.37 et seq).
[120] Ibid, s 2 (see 2.37 et seq).
[121] Criminal Law Act 1967, s 3.
[122] And shall on summary conviction be liable to imprisonment for a term not exceeding six months or to
a fine not exceeding level 5 on the standard scale or to both.
[123] With the same punishment scale.
[124] And shall on summary conviction be liable to a fine not exceeding level 1 on the standard scale.

Police powers to attend meetings

3.88 When a public meeting is held on private premises such as a room in a town hall (which is private despite being owned by a public body) or at the South Place Ethical Society at Conway Hall in London, the right of the police to be present is a murky area of the law, particularly when those present or those holding the meeting have decided that police officers should be excluded. Generally, the police will not attend such meetings unless invited to do so. But in what is now an old case, in an area of the law that has not been considered by the appellate courts in recent decades, the Divisional Court in *Thomas v Sawkins*[125] appeared to decide that police have the right, although uninvited, to attend public meetings held on private premises if they reasonably apprehend a breach of the peace. The extent of the court's ruling is uncertain. The meeting, which was open to the public without payment, was convened in order to protest against the Incitement to Disaffection Bill and to demand the dismissal of the Chief Constable of Glamorgan. The case was unusual in that Sawkins, a police sergeant, was ejected from the meeting by Thomas who subsequently brought a private prosecution against Sawkins for assault while resisting his ejection. In fact no breach of the peace took place. The magistrates found that the police were entitled to enter and remain during the meeting because they had reasonable grounds to believe that if they were not present there would be seditious speeches and other incitements to violence and a breach of the peace. They therefore concluded that there had been no assault. The findings were upheld on appeal when much emphasis was laid upon the fact that the meeting was in public.

3.89 The application of this case is not easy, and each case will turn on its own facts. The police might argue, for example, that a meeting convened to protest against the passage of a Race Relations Bill might permit their attendance if held in Bradford, but not if held in Devon. But, it would appear that the police will not be entitled to attend public meetings on private premises unless there are clear grounds for believing that a breach of the peace will take place. Annoyance and disturbance at a meeting by cries of 'Hear, Hear' (or something a little less archaic), putting questions to the speaker and making observations on his statements would not be a breach of the peace.[126] Once lawfully in attendance at a public meeting, a police officer can also arrest anyone committing a wide range of public order offences.[127]

Election meetings

3.90 Election meetings are governed by the provisions of the Representation of the People Act 1983 which permits a candidate in an election to use certain schools and halls for public election meetings free of charge, provided that the candidate bears the expense of any damage caused.[128] The aim of the legislation is to ensure that candidates of all parties, however impecunious, have a public platform for their views. Two conditions must be

[125] [1935] 2 KB 249.
[126] *Wooding v Oxley* (1839) 9 C & P 1. For breach of the peace, see Ch 6.
[127] See Ch 1.
[128] Representation of the People Act 1983, ss 95 and 96, and Sch 5.

complied with; the purpose of the meeting must be to further the candidature of the person holding the meeting, and the meeting must be public.

Local authorities are under no general statutory duty to make facilities available for **3.91** ordinary public meetings. But they have no discretion to refuse election meetings unless the meeting will not fulfil the two conditions set out above. All candidates in a local or general election are entitled to inspect the list of meeting halls and school premises available in that and neighbouring constituencies.

The Court of Appeal Civil Division has examined the right of a candidate of the British **3.92** National Party to have a suitable schoolroom made available for a public meeting in a local government election[129] in a narrow judgment that focused on the procedural issue. The Inner London Education Authority had refused permission to the candidate on the grounds that violence would inevitably ensue and damage would be caused to the school in Bethnal Green. The candidate sought declaratory and mandatory relief from the Queen's Bench Division that a room must be made available. The Education Authority resisted and successfully argued that the proceedings were an abuse of process as the correct route of challenge should have been on judicial review. The Court of Appeal overturned that decision and held that while the duty of the local authority or the local education authority is a duty imposed by the statute, nevertheless the entitlement of the candidate under the statute is a private right which is capable of being enforced by action in the Queen's Bench Division for a declaration and for injunctive relief. The matter was remitted and the court then did permit the meeting to take place.

It is an offence, contrary to s 97(1) of the Representation of the People Act 1983 and pun- **3.93** ishable summarily by a fine not exceeding level 5, for a person at a lawful public meeting to act, or incite others to act, in a disorderly manner for the purpose of preventing the transaction of the meeting's business. A 'lawful public meeting' for the purposes of this section means a political meeting held in any constituency between the date of the issue of the writ for the return of a Member of Parliament for the constituency and the date at which a return to the writ is made, or a meeting held with reference to a local government election in the electoral area for that election in the period beginning with the last date on which notice of the election may be published in accordance with the local government election rules and ending with the day of the election.[130]

E. Parliament Square

Sections 132–138 of the Serious Organised Crime and Police Act 2005 imposes on those **3.94** wishing to protest within the vicinity of Parliament obligations and potential restrictions that go far beyond the rules governing peaceful assembly elsewhere in the country. The legislative provisions are examined below, but a brief consideration of the background to the new legislation may be helpful.

---

[129] *Ettridge v Morrell*, unreported, 1 January 1987 (Court of Appeal).
[130] Representation of the People Act 1983, s 97(2).

Background

3.95 There are a number of authorities involved in managing Parliament Square. Parliament Square Garden is managed by the Greater London Authority under the GLA Act 1999. The perimeter pavements to the east and south of the Square are managed by Westminster City Council. The Trafalgar Square and Parliament Square Garden Byelaws 2000 set out what is prohibited or permitted in both squares.

3.96 Sessional Orders are passed at the beginning of the Parliamentary Session. The Sessional Order instructs the Commissioner of the Metropolitan Police to make sure that passages through the streets leading to parliament are kept free and open during the sitting of Parliament. The Commissioner in turn has the power, under s 52 of the Metropolitan Police Act 1839, to make regulations as occasion requires for preventing obstruction in the street during public processions and to give directions to constables for preventing any obstruction of the thoroughfares in the immediate neighbourhood of Parliament.[131] Section 54 of the 1839 Act prohibits 'nuisances by persons in the thoroughfares' and makes it an offence to disregard the directions of the commissioners of police, and also, inter alia, to 'blow any horn or use any other noisy instrument, for the purpose of calling persons together'.

3.97 The House of Commons Procedure Committee conducted a short inquiry into a number of existing Sessional Orders, including that relating to the Metropolitan Police, and published a Report in November 2003. The Committee recommended that the government should introduce appropriate legislation to prohibit long-term demonstrations and to ensure that the laws about access were adequate and enforceable, concluding that 'legislation on demonstrations is the only way to ensure that the police have adequate powers to achieve the result intended by the Sessional Order'. This has been used by the government as an *ex post facto* justification for the introduction of new legislation.[132] However, it seems to have been overlooked that the Public Order Act 1986 already contained the power for a senior police officer to impose conditions when he or she considers that an assembly may cause 'serious disruption to the life of the community'.[133] Given that the White Paper before the 1986 Act considered disruption to shoppers in Oxford Street as potentially fulfilling such a test, this power could no doubt have been called upon if any serious or prolonged disruption to parliamentarians was reasonably envisaged.

3.98 The proposals that eventually resulted in Serious Organised Crime and Police Act 2005 were first put before the Commons on 3 November 2004 by Peter Hain MP, Leader of the House,[134] and were a joint venture between the government and the Commons Procedure Committee. The specific concerns that were raised as requiring new legislation were, inter alia: that terrorists might secrete themselves or their bombs behind cardboard posters; that

---

[131] The directions of the Commissioner should be understood to relate to those assemblies which are capable of being obstructive in accordance with the Metropolitan Police Act 1839, s 52 (irrespective of the wording of the sessional order) or else risk being *ultra vires: Papworth v Coventry* [1967] 1 WLR 66.

[132] Home Office Consultation Document, *Managing Protest Around Parliament* (2007) para 2.3.

[133] Public Order Act 1986, s 14.

[134] Hansard, HC col 373 et seq (3 November 2004).

demonstrators would physically prevent MPs from entering or leaving the House; that Parliament Square was being aesthetically 'defaced' by Brian Haw, the anti-war protestor (when the Bill was originally introduced it allowed a senior police officer to remove someone from the vicinity of Parliament if they are 'spoiling the visual aspect, or otherwise spoiling the enjoyment by members of the public' of the area, though that clause disappeared by the Second Reading); that MPs or parliamentary workers would variously be deafened or distracted from their work by demonstrators' cacophonous use of loudhailers; and that long-term demonstrators such as Brian Haw deterred other, perhaps more persuasive demonstrators, from using Parliament Square to address their concerns to MPs and the media.[135]

The last explanation is at best deliberately misleading, for it was indeed Mr Haw himself **3.99** who was the primary focus of this legislation, and no doubt because of the media coverage and negative publicity for government policies his protest had attracted. In 2002, Westminster City Council had unsuccessfully applied for an injunction to stop his protest on the basis he was obstructing the highway (in the terms of the criminal offence), but the application was dismissed by the High Court on the basis that although there was an obstruction in fact, it was not unreasonable, as he was using the highway in a reasonable manner to exercise his right to freedom of expression under Article 10 of the European Convention on Human Rights.[136] The existing civil and criminal legislation appeared powerless in the face of his continuing protest and Caroline Flint, Minster of State at the Home Office, made it fairly clear at the Report Stage that the government intended that Mr Haw should fall within the new regime.[137]

The legislation

The Secretary of State is empowered by s 138 of the Serious Organised Crime and Police **3.100** Act 2005 to designate an area, no more than one kilometre in a straight line from the point nearest to it in Parliament Square.[138] Any demonstration within the designated area is subject to a new authorization regime and criminal sanctions are introduced for breaches of those requirements. These provisions are found within ss 132–137 of the 2005 Act.

Designated area

The area itself is defined by a Statutory Instrument[139] rather than the Act. It specifically **3.101** excludes Trafalgar Square, a traditional site of protest on the northern boundary of the area. Apart from Parliament itself the designated area includes Whitehall, Downing Street, Westminster Abbey, the Middlesex Guildhall (now the Supreme Court), New Scotland Yard, and the Home Office. It also covers a small section of land on the other bank of the

---

[135] This is taken from an examination of the background to the legislation in Ian Loveland 'Public Protest in Parliament Square' [2007] EHRLR, Issue 3.
[136] *Westminster City Council v Haw* [2002] EWHC 2073 (QB). For more on the Brian Haw case, see 3.122 et seq below.
[137] Hansard, HC, cols 1220–1230 (3 November 2004).
[138] Serious Organised Crime and Police Act 2005, s 133.
[139] The Serious Organised Crime and Police Act 2005 (Designated Area) Order 2005 (SI 2005/1537).

River Thames, including County Hall, the Jubilee Gardens, St Thomas' Hospital, and the London Eye.

3.102 As it currently stands the area is bounded by an imaginary line starting at the point where Hungerford Bridge crosses Victoria Embankment; continuing along Hungerford Bridge to the point where it crosses Belvedere Road; rightwards along Belvedere Road as far as Chicheley Street; leftwards along Chicheley Street as far as York Road; rightwards along York Road, crossing Westminster Bridge Road into Lambeth Palace Road; along Lambeth Palace Road as far as Lambeth Bridge; over Lambeth Bridge; leftwards along Millbank as far as Thorney Street; along Thorney Street as far as Horseferry Road; leftwards along Horseferry Road as far as Strutton Ground; along Strutton Ground crossing over Victoria Street into Broadway; along Broadway as far as Queen Anne's Gate; along Queen Anne's Gate as far as Birdcage Walk; rightwards along Birdcage Walk as far as Horse Guards Road; along Horse Guards Road as far as the Mall; rightwards along the Mall; across the north end of Whitehall as far as Northumberland Avenue; along Northumberland Avenue as far as Victoria Embankment; leftwards along Victoria Embankment returning to the starting point.

Written notice

3.103 A person seeking authorization for a demonstration in the designated area must give written notice to the Commissioner of Police for the Metropolis.[140] That notice must be given, if reasonably practicable, not less than six clear days before the day on which the demonstration is to start, or, if that is not reasonably practicable, then as soon as it is, and in any event not less than twenty-four hours before the time the demonstration is to start.[141] The provision for the 'spontaneous protest' in earlier Acts is therefore explicitly abandoned, given that in no circumstances is it permissible to demonstrate without having given at least twenty-four hours notice, even if that which is demonstrated against (a military coup or a particular vote in Parliament, for example) only took place that day. Whilst, as discussed below, the domestic courts have said that the restrictions imposed by s 132 do not infringe the right to freedom of peaceful assembly,[142] this inflexible procedural requirement would appear to be contrary to the jurisprudence of the European Court of Human Rights in the subsequent case of *Bukta & others v Hungary*,[143] where the Court found:

> in special circumstances when an immediate response, in the form of a demonstration, to a political event might be justified, a decision to disband the ensuing, peaceful assembly solely because of the absence of the requisite prior notice, without any illegal conduct by the participants, amounts to a disproportionate restriction on freedom of peaceful assembly.

3.104 If there are grounds for justifying the very late or complete lack of notice, there may then still be grounds for arguing that a prosecution for breach of the notice requirement would be contrary to a person's rights under the Convention.

---

[140] Serious Organised Crime and Police Act 2005, s 133(1).
[141] Ibid, s 133(2).
[142] *See Blum v DPP* [2006] EWHC 3209 (Admin) and other cases discussed below at 3.117–3.120 and at 10.111–10.116.
[143] [2007] ECHR 25691/04 (17 July 2007).

The notice must be given by the organizer of the demonstration or, if it is a lone demonstra- **3.105** tion, by that person.[144] It must state the date and time when the demonstration is to start, the place where it is to be carried on, how long it is to last, whether it is to be carried on by a person by himself or not, and the name and address of the person giving notice.[145]

The notice must be given by delivering it to a police station in the metropolitan police **3.106** district or sending it by recorded delivery to such a police station.[146] Oral notice by telephone or in person is therefore not sufficient. It should be noted that s 7 of the Interpretation Act 1978 under which service of a document is deemed to have been effected at the time it would be delivered in the ordinary course of post does not apply.[147]

Authorization

If a notice is received at the appropriate place, in the appropriate time and in the appropri- **3.107** ate form, the Commissioner *must* give authorization for the demonstration. There is no power for the Commissioner to ban the demonstration, but in giving authorization the Commissioner is entitled to impose such conditions on the demonstrations as in the Commissioner's reasonable opinion are necessary for the purpose of preventing any of the following:[148]

(a) hindrance to any person wishing to enter or leave the Palace of Westminster;
(b) hindrance to the proper operation of Parliament;
(c) serious public disorder;
(d) serious damage to property;
(e) disruption to the life of the community;
(f) a security risk in any part of the designated area; and
(g) risk to the safety of members of the public (including any taking part in the demonstration).

This amounts to a far broader test than in the legislation applicable nationwide. **3.108** Notwithstanding there are no advance notice requirements on assemblies outside the designated area, to impose conditions on such an assembly already underway, the senior police officer has to reasonably believe that it may result in serious public disorder, serious damage to property, or serious disruption to the life of the community or that the purpose of assembly is to coerce by intimidation.[149] That the balance between the right to protest and the ability of pedestrians and road users not to be inconvenienced (discussed at the time of the enactment of the Public Order Act 1986) has swung ever more in favour of the latter group, is clear in the additional tests.

Within the designated area 'serious disruption' has been reduced to 'disruption', which is **3.109** notable as it is difficult to imagine an assembly of any size causing no disruption whatsoever.

---

[144] Serious Organised Crime and Police Act 2005, s 133(3).
[145] Ibid, s 133(4).
[146] Ibid, s 133(5).
[147] Ibid, s 133(6).
[148] Ibid, s 134(3).
[149] As discussed at 3.66 et seq above.

At the time of 1986 Act, concerns were addressed as to the breadth of the 'serious disruption' test, as it could easily be interpreted as meaning 'serious inconvenience'.[150] Within the new test this concern is ever more apparent, particularly in the light of the additional tests: it is also now permissible to impose conditions simply to avoid a 'hindrance' to users of Parliament. Finally, the use of the words 'security risk' inevitably means that the test is now so widely drawn as to permit conditions to be imposed on almost all medium sized demonstrations.[151] It will be interesting to note however, the extent to which the Commissioner is willing to disclose to any Court investigating a challenge to the imposition of conditions imposed on the basis of 'security risk' the nature and source of the material relied upon.

3.110 The conditions that may be imposed, are also widely drawn, and extend the existing power of the police to control an assembly. The conditions may (in particular) impose requirements as to

(a) the place where the demonstration may, or may not, be carried on;
(b) the times at which it may be carried on;
(c) the period during which it may be carried on;
(d) the number of persons who may take part in it;
(e) the number and size of banners or placards used; and
(f) maximum permissible noise levels.[152]

3.111 The police may now set down the time at which an assembly may take place, not simply control its duration as under the Public Order Act 1986. The significance of this is obvious; heads of state or other visiting dignitaries against whom individuals or groups wish to protest can be brought to and from Parliament at times when demonstrations are prohibited, effectively nullifying the power and intention of the protest. Nationally, the police are able to control the number of persons on the demonstration (but only to prevent the far more serious disorder as discussed above), but the 2005 Act also permits control of the number and size of the banners and the maximum noise levels.

Offences

3.112 All the offences created are summary only. Section 132 creates offences of demonstrating without authorization in the designated area. It is an offence to organize, or to take part, or to carry on alone, a demonstration for which authorization has not been given under s 134(2). It is a defence to any of these charges for a defendant to show that he reasonably believed that authorization had been given. A person guilty of organizing such a demonstration is liable on conviction to a maximum term of imprisonment of six months or

[150] P Thornton, *Public Order Law* (1987) p 133.
[151] Liberty's *Response to the Home Office Consultation: Managing Protest Around Parliament* (2008).
[152] Independent of this provision, s 137 bans the use of loudspeakers within the designated area at any time and for any purpose (subject to a number of exceptions, including where consent of the local authority has been granted). The use of loudspeakers is also governed by of the Control of Pollution Act 1974, s 62(1) and of the Noise and Statutory Nuisance Act 1993, s 8. In addition, the use of amplification equipment on Parliament Square Garden requires the prior permission of the Mayor of London under the Trafalgar Square and Parliament Square Byelaws.

a fine not exceeding level 4 on the standard scale[153] or both.[154] Those convicted of taking part in a demonstration or demonstrating alone are liable to a fine not exceeding level 3.[155]

The offences in s 132(1) do not apply if the demonstration is a public procession—whether **3.113** or not notice is required to be given under s 11 of the Public Order Act 1986.[156] Processions in the designated area are still governed by the controls under the 1986 Act and are not further regulated by the 2005 Act.[157] This means, for example, that a spontaneous protest by way of procession around Parliament Square may be lawful despite being an obstruction to traffic and pedestrians, whereas a static demonstration on Parliament Green which is not obstructive may be unlawful. Similarly, the offences do not apply to peaceful picketing which is lawful under s 220 of the Trade Union and Labour Relations (Consolidation) Act 1992.[158]

It is an offence for a person to take part or organize a demonstration which has been **3.114** authorized but to then knowingly fail to comply with a condition imposed which is applicable to that individual.[159] More widely, it is also an offence to take part or organize a demonstration which has been authorized, but which has changed its nature beyond that particularized in the notice (ie time, place, number of persons). In those circumstances a person is guilty if they knew or should have known that the demonstration was carried on otherwise than in accordance with those particulars.[160] It is a defence to both charges to show that the failure to comply or the divergence from the particulars arose from circumstances beyond the defendant's control or from something done with the agreement, or by the direction, of a police officer.[161] If convicted of either charge, an organizer is liable to imprisonment not exceeding six months, to a fine not exceeding level 4, or both. A participant guilty of either charge is liable to a fine not exceeding level 3.[162]

The senior police officer may give directions to the organizers or participants in a demon- **3.115** stration to comply with additional or varied conditions if he reasonably believes it is necessary to prevent any of the disruptions and hindrances mentioned in s 134(3)(a)–(g).[163] A person taking part or organizing the demonstration who knowingly fails to comply with such a varied or additional condition is guilty of an offence[164] and if convicted, an organizer is liable to imprisonment not exceeding six months, to a fine not exceeding level 4, or both and a participant to a fine not exceeding level 3.[165]

---

[153] Currently £2,500.
[154] Public Order Act 1986, s 136(1).
[155] Ibid, s 136(2). Currently £1,000.
[156] Ibid, s 132(3).
[157] However, the 2005 Act specifically excludes from the scope of the Public Order Act 1986, any control over assemblies in the designated area: s 132(6).
[158] Ibid, s 132(4).
[159] Ibid, s 134(7)(a).
[160] Ibid, s 132(7)(b).
[161] Ibid, s 134(8).
[162] Ibid, s 136(3).
[163] Ibid, s 135(1).
[164] Ibid, s 135(3).
[165] Ibid, s 136(3).

3.116 It is also an offence under s 136(4) to incite any person to do, or fail to do, anything that would result in an offence under Part 4. A person convicted under this section is liable to imprisonment not exceeding six months, to a fine not exceeding level 4, or both. Buried deep within a schedule to the Serious Crime Act 2007 is an amendment to subsec 4 that is not yet in force. The offence is changed to 'encouraging or assisting' the other offences, thus widening the ambit even further.[166]

Human rights compliance

3.117 In *Stephen Blum, Aqil Shaer, Maya Evans and Milan Rai v DPP, CPS and SSHD*,[167] the Divisional Court reviewed the convictions of four defendants charged with protesting in the designated area without obtaining authorization. Before the District Judges all appellants had contended first that s 132(1)(a) and (b) were not compatible with Articles 10 and 11 of the European Convention on Human Rights. That led them to argue either that the subsections should be subject to a proviso and read down, pursuant to s 3 of the Human Rights Act 1998, or, alternatively, simply that it was unlawful to convict the appellants under s 6(1) of the Human Rights Act 1998. In the case of Milan Rai, it was further argued that it was an abuse of process to prosecute, having regard to the infringement of Mr Rai's rights under Articles 10 and 11.

3.118 Before the Divisional Court the appellants no longer contended that s 132(1)(a) and (b) were incompatible with Articles 10 and 11. The appellants no longer argued that any part of the sections should be read down, pursuant to the court's obligation under s 3 of the Human Rights Act 1998. Instead it was argued that the decision of the police to arrest, of the CPS to prosecute and the decision of the court to convict had interfered with important convention rights and thus had to be justified under convention law. The submission in simple terms was that the State, in its various public authority guises (police, CPS, courts) must be able to justify the necessity to act on the individual facts of each case. Thus, the questions that arose in each case were said to be: were the arrest, detention, prosecution, and conviction of the appellant in each individual case strictly necessary, particularly where each had acted peacefully and in one case silently and without any form of obstruction? Was each necessary and proportionate for the achievement of legitimate aims, or was it heavy-handed and unnecessary? It was further submitted that no consideration was given to that question of justification by the District Judges in the individual cases, and that the convictions should be quashed for that reason also.

3.119 The Court conducted a wide review of the European case law on the subject, and is a helpful resource for that alone. The Court concluded that one case in particular was particularly problematic for the appellants. In *Ziliberberg v Moldova*[168] at para 11 that judgment reads:

> The present case resembles the *Ezelin* case in that there were no reprehensible acts committed
> by the applicant. At the same time it is distinguishable in that the demonstration in the

---

[166] See s 63(2) and Sch 6, Part 2, para 64(1), (2) of the Serious Crime Act 2007, with reference to the new offences of assisting and encouraging in ss 44–46 of the Serious Crime Act 2007.

[167] [2006] EWHC 3209 (Admin). This decision has been endorsed by the ECtHR. See also 3.103 above and 10.111–116 below.

[168] Application No 61821/00 of 4 May 2004. See also 10.111.

present case was not authorised in accordance with the law, as it was in the *Ezelin* case. The applicant does not dispute that the organisers of the demonstration did not apply for an authorisation. As such the right to freedom of assembly covers both private meetings and meetings in public thoroughfares. Where the latter are concerned, their subjection to an authorisation procedure does not normally encroach upon the essence of the right. Such a procedure is in keeping with the requirements of Article 11(1), if only in order that the authorities may be in a position to ensure the peaceful nature of a meeting, and accordingly does not as such constitute interference with the exercise of the right.[169]

3.120 While the authorities offered support for the proposition that Articles 10 and 11 had to be considered where public order offences included the defence of reasonableness, Lord Justice Waller concluded:

It seems to me that nothing said in the above authorities relied on by Mr Thornton can cut across the reasoning in *Ziliberberg*. Once it is accepted that the sections requiring authorization are compatible with Article 10 and Article 11, it simply cannot be a legitimate line of argument to say—'that may be so, but you must look at the activity taking place without authorisation, when considering whether there has been an infringement of Article 11 itself'. Once an authorization procedure is Article 11 compliant, Parliament must be entitled to impose sanctions where authorization has not been obtained, otherwise the finding that the sections are compatible is illusory.

3.121 The concession that s 132(1)(a) and (b) were not incompatible with Articles 10 and 11 was said to have been rightly made by the Divisional Court, in both *Tucker v Director of Public Prosecutions*[170] and *Moase v City of Westminster Magistrates' Court*.[171] Human rights arguments will of course remain relevant to individual considerations of the reasonableness and proportionality of conditions imposed. In addition, there is the prospect, as discussed above, of challenging the notice requirements in a case where there is a pressing and immediate need to protest.

The Brian Haw litigation

3.122 A number of cases have focused on the protest by Brian Haw.[172] Of little general application is the litigation that focused on whether the new legislation applied to a continuing protest. The judgment at first instance, *R (on the application of Haw) v Secretary of State for the Home Department*,[173] effectively disapplied s 132 in relation to Mr Haw, and Mr Haw alone. Mr Haw's argument was based on pure statutory construction; the phrase 'when the demonstration starts' in s 132(1)(c) removed pre-existing demonstrations from the authorization requirement since it would have been impossible for Mr Haw to have obtained authorization when his demonstration started in 2001. However, the commencement

---

[169] *Rassemblement Jurassien v Switzerland*, No 8191/78, Commission decision of 10 October 1978, DR 17, p 119.
[170] [2007] EWHC 3019 (Admin). See 10.14.
[171] [2008] EWHC 2309 (Admin) 27 June 2008.
[172] For a more detailed examination, see I Loveland, 'Public Protest in Parliament Square' [2007] EHRLR Issue 3 and Leslie Blake, '"Hybrid Bills" and Human Rights: The Parliament Square Litigation 2002–2007" (2008) 19 King's Law Journal 183.
[173] [2006] QB 359.

order made under s 178 in respect of ss 132–138[174] sought to provide that references to a demonstration 'starting' were taken as embracing demonstrations which either started or continued after 1 August 2005. Mr Haw's submission was that the 'continuing' element of the Order was *ultra vires* in so far that it extended the scope of the statutory scheme and that there was, in s 178 at least, no such amending power. The submission was an orthodox one; penal statutes should be strictly construed, and a literal construction should be adopted unless the meaning was ambiguous or obscure or led to an absurd result. The majority decided in favour of Mr Haw and applied a literal construction, holding there was no obscurity and as such no reference should be made under *Pepper v Hart*[175] to ministerial statements. The Court of Appeal[176] took a different view, reasoning that s 132 should not be construed in isolation. The Court held that as s 132(6) disapplied s 14 of the Public Order Act 1986 to assemblies that were also a demonstration in the designated area and made no time limitation on the application of this provision then:

> . . . it is inconceivable that Parliament would have repealed[177] section 14 with respect to demonstrations which had already started, if it did not intent to apply the provisions of 132 to 138 of the Act to such demonstrations.
>
> The only sensible conclusion to reach in these circumstances is that Parliament intended that those sections of the Act should apply to a demonstration in the designated area, whether it started before or after they came into force. Any other conclusion would be wholly irrational and could fairly be described as manifestly absurd.[178]

3.123 Consequently Mr Haw's demonstration was held to fall under the provisions and during the night of 23 May 2006, two weeks after the Court of Appeal decision, seventy-eight police officers[179] removed the banners and posters that formed part of the demonstration and imposed conditions that Mr Haw's demonstration could occupy only an area 3 metres square. Mr Haw remained.

3.124 A subsequent prosecution of him in the magistrates' court in 2007 for breaching the conditions imposed was dismissed following a ruling of no case to answer by the District Judge on the grounds that firstly, the authorization came only from a superintendant and the Act requires it to be given by the Commissioner, and that secondly, the conditions were not sufficiently clear to allow Mr Haw to comply properly. The Divisional Court in *DPP v Brian Haw*[180] upheld the acquittal and in doing so made two points of general application.

3.125 The court disagreed with the District Judge and ruled that the Commissioner was able to delegate functions to police officers appropriately, even though there was no specific provision for this in legislation. However, the acquittal was upheld because the conditions were unworkable, were plainly not reasonable, and did not satisfy the test of certainty

---

[174] Serious Organised Crime and Police Act 2005 (Commencement No 1, Transitional and Transitory Provisions) Order 2005 (SI 2005/1521).

[175] [1993] AC 593.

[176] [2006] EWCA Civ 532.

[177] Clearly s 14 has not been repealed, merely disapplied within the designated area.

[178] [2006] EWCA Civ 532, at paras 22–23.

[179] The Daily Telegraph, 26 May 2006.

[180] [2007] EWHC 1931 (Admin); (2008) 1 WLR 379.

required when considering whether the restrictions on Convention rights were 'according to law'.

The future

In July 2007, the Prime Minister Gordon Brown stated that the law governing protest in Parliament Square should be reconsidered: **3.126**

> Whilst balancing the need for public order with the right to public dissent, I think it right—in consultation with the Metropolitan Police, Parliament, the Mayor of London, Westminster City Council and liberties groups—to change the laws that now restrict the right to demonstrate in Parliament Square.[181]

The legislative process towards that avowed intent began in the Home Office Consultation Document, *The Governance of Britain: Managing Protest around Parliament* of October 2007. In the foreword to that document, the natural correlation between protest and place has been expressly acknowledged by the Home Secretary: **3.127**

> We are clear that there should be no unnecessary restrictions on people's right to protest. This is particularly important in the vicinity of Parliament given that it is the forum of our democracy—the seat of our elected representatives. Therefore it is right that we review provisions that have generated such concern. If left unchecked, such concerns can in turn contribute to a wider cynicism towards the political process.[182]

The White Paper, *The Governance of Britain—Constitutional Renewal*[183] was published in March 2008 and explained the government's response to the consultation process: **3.128**

> The Way Forward
>
> 25. The Government has considered the arguments on how best to balance competing rights in the context of a dynamic security situation and proposes to repeal sections 132–138 of the Serious Organised Crime and Police Act 2005.
>
> 26. Given the strength of feeling in responses to the consultation document on potential restrictions on legitimate protest, and in the absence of greater evidence of a policing problem, the Government will not pursue harmonization of the sorts of conditions that can be placed on marches and assemblies in the Public Order Act 1986.
>
> 7. In moving to repeal sections 132–138 of the Serious Organised Crime and Police Act, the Government nonetheless takes seriously the need to ensure that the operation of Parliament is safeguarded. For many years this principle has been given expression in sessional orders which provided the Metropolitan Police with clarity on the House's expectations on the Commissioner.
>
> 28. The Government believes that Parliament itself is well placed to contribute to proper consideration of what needs to be secured in order to ensure that Members are able freely and without hindrance to discharge their roles and responsibilities.

Clause 1 of the Draft Constitutional Renewal Bill repeals ss 132–138 of the 2005 Act. If the Bill goes through in its current form, public order and protest in the vicinity of **3.129**

---

[181] The Prime Minster, the Rt Hon Gordon Brown, 3 July 2007, quoted in the Home Office Consultation, *Managing Protest Around Parliament* (October 2007) p 8.
[182] Home Office Consultation, *Managing Protest Around Parliament* (2007) p 4, per the Rt Hon Jacqui Smith MP.
[183] Cm 7342-1.

Parliament will revert to being controlled by the Public Order Act 1986, sessional orders, and by-laws. At the time of writing however, the Constitutional Renewal Bill has not been introduced to Parliament and the Queen's Speech of 2008 was ambiguous as to whether there is any prospect of that happening in the near future.

F. Other Specific Areas

Trafalgar Square and Parliament Square Garden

3.130 Trafalgar Square was a private possession of the Crown but was constituted as part of the metropolis by the Trafalgar Square Act 1844. By s 383 of the Greater London Authority Act 1999, the functions of the Secretary of State in s 2 of the 1844 Act relating to care, control, management, and regulation of the Square were transferred to the Mayor and the Greater London Authority.

3.131 Whilst Trafalgar Square has long been associated with public protest, under the common law there was said to be no *right* of public meeting in the square.[184] In *Rai and others v UK*,[185] the European Commission considered government policy that did not permit meetings in Trafalgar Square on issues related to Northern Ireland. The Commission considered the origin and scope of the policy and concluded:

> Having regard to the fact that the refusal of permission did not amount to a blanket prohibition on the holding of the applicant's rally but only prevented the use of a high profile location (other venues being available in Central London) the Commission concludes that the restriction in the present case may be regarded as proportionate and justified as necessary in a democratic society . . .

3.132 The land compromising Parliament Square Gardens means the site in Parliament Square on which the Minister of Works was authorized by the Parliament Square (Improvement) Act 1949 to lay out the garden referred to in that Act as 'the new central garden'. It was vested in the Secretary of State for Culture, Media, and Sport, but by s 384 of the Greater London Authority Act 1999 it was transferred to and vested in the Crown as part of the hereditary possessions and revenues of the Crown. The care, control, management, and regulation of the central garden of Parliament Square have become functions of the Mayor and the Greater London Authority.

3.133 Both squares are now regulated by the Trafalgar Square and Parliament Square Garden Byelaws 2000.[186] Written permission[187] of the Mayor of London (or anyone authorized by the Mayor under s 380 of the Greater London Authority Act 1999 to give such permission) is required by reg 4 to, amongst other things:

> (5) use any apparatus for the transmission, reception, reproduction or amplification of sound, speech or images, except apparatus designed and used as an aid to defective

---

[184] *Ex parte Lewis* (1888) 21 QBD 191.

[185] (1995) 82-A DR 134; See also *Pendragon v UK* [1999] EHRLR 223.

[186] As amended by the Trafalgar Square and Parliament Square Garden (Amendment No 1 Byelaws 2002).

[187] Addressed to: Squares Management team, Post Point 23, GLA, City Hall, The Queen's Walk, More London, London, SE1 2AA.

hearing, or apparatus used in a vehicle so as not to produce sound audible to a person outside that vehicle, or apparatus where the sound is received through headphones;

(9) make or give a public speech or address; and

(10) organize or take part in any assembly, display, performance, representation, parade, procession, review or theatrical event.

3.134 Where an authorized person has reasonable ground for belief that a person has contravened any one or more of these by-laws, that person shall give on demand his name and address to that authorized person.[188]

Royal Parks (including Hyde Park) and other Open Spaces

3.135 The Royal Parks and Other Open Spaces Regulations 1997[189] sought to harmonize the regulation of open spaces in London and revoked the Trafalgar Square Regulations 1952[190] and the Royal and other Parks and Gardens Regulations 1977.[191] The Regulations originally also applied to Trafalgar Square but this area was removed from their scope by The Royal Parks and other Open Spaces (Amendment) Regulations 2004, SI 2004/1308.

3.136 The Regulations set out comprehensively what is not permitted unless the written permission of the Secretary of State has been obtained,[192] the most relevant to the scope of this book being the following subsections of regulation 4:

(10) use any apparatus for the transmission, reception, reproduction or amplification of sound, speech or images, except apparatus designed and used as an aid to defective hearing, or apparatus used in a vehicle so as not to produce sound audible to a person outside that vehicle, or apparatus used where the sound is received through headphones;

(15) make or give a public speech or address except in the public speaking area in Hyde Park;[193] and

(17) organize or take part in any assembly, display, performance, representation, parade, procession, review or theatrical event.

There is no right to hold meetings in the Royal Parks,[194] but it is Royal Parks policy that demonstrations should be held in Hyde Park as opposed to the other Royal Parks. Exceptions are considered where there is a specific relationship between the Park and the purpose of the demonstration.

---

[188] 'Authorized person' means a constable, or any person acting to enforce these by-laws in accordance with an authorization given by the Mayor under s 380 of the Act.

[189] SI 1997/1639 as amended by The Royal Parks and other Open Spaces (Amendment) Regulations 2004, SI 2004/1308.

[190] SI 1952/776.

[191] SI 1977/217.

[192] Applications to demonstrate in Hyde Park should be addressed to the Park Manager, Hyde Park, The Park Office, Ranger's Lodge, Hyde Park, London, W2 2UH.

[193] Speakers' Corner.

[194] *Bailey v Williamson* (1873) LR 8 QB 118.

G. Other Offences Specific to Location

Nuclear bases

3.137 New offences introduced in the Criminal Justice and Immigration Act 2008 (s 75, Sch 17) extend the offences in Nuclear Material (Offences) Act 1983 relating to nuclear facilities. These provisions are not yet in force. The most significant offences in the context of public order and protest are those that make it an offence punishable by imprisonment for life if convicted of any one of a number of criminal offences (including offences against the person and criminal damage) if the act was directed at a nuclear facility or interfered with such a facility and caused death, injury, or damage from the emission of ionizing radiation or the release of radioactive material.[195]

NHS facilities

3.138 The Criminal Justice Act 2008 introduces offences specific to causing nuisance or disturbance on NHS premises. By virtue of s 119,[196] a person commits an offence if

(a) the person causes, without reasonable excuse and while on NHS premises, a nuisance or disturbance to an NHS staff member who is working there or is otherwise there in connection with work;

(b) the person refuses, without reasonable excuse, to leave the NHS premises when asked to do so by a constable or an NHS staff member; and

(c) the person is not on the NHS premises for the purpose of obtaining medical advice, treatment, or care for himself or herself.

A person who commits an offence under this section is liable on summary conviction to a fine not exceeding level 3 on the standard scale.[197]

3.139 For the purposes of this section a person ceases to be on NHS premises for the purpose of obtaining medical advice, treatment, or care for himself or herself once the person has received the advice, treatment, or care, and a person is not on NHS premises for the purpose of obtaining medical advice, treatment, or care for himself or herself if the person has been refused the advice, treatment, or care during the last eight hours.[198]

3.140 A power to remove a person causing nuisance or disturbance is also provided.[199] If a constable reasonably suspects that a person is committing or has committed an offence under s 119, the constable may remove the person from the NHS premises concerned. If an authorized officer[200] reasonably suspects that a person is committing or has committed an offence under s 119, the authorized officer may remove the person from the NHS premises

---

[195] Criminal Justice and Immigration Act 2008, s 75, Sch 17, para 3, adding s 1A to the Nuclear Material (Offences) Act 1983.

[196] Currently, SI 2008/3260 has only brought into force the definitions subsec (s 119(4)).

[197] Criminal Justice Act 2008, s 119(2).

[198] Ibid, s 119(3).

[199] Currently, SI 2008/3260 has only brought into force the definitions in s 120(5)–(6).

[200] An 'authorized officer' is a duly authorized NHS staff member: s 120(5).

concerned, or authorize an appropriate NHS staff member to do so.[201] It has been specifically provided that any person removing another person from NHS premises under this section may use reasonable force if necessary.[202]

An authorized officer cannot remove a person under this section or authorize another person to do so if the authorized officer has reason to believe that the person to be removed requires medical advice, treatment, or care for himself or herself, or the removal of the person would endanger the person's physical or mental health. Appropriate national authorities are given the power to prepare and publish guidance about these removal powers.[203]   **3.141**

At a person's home

The Serious Organised Crime and Police Act 2005 included new provisions to give further protection to people in their homes. As part of a broader move to strengthen police powers against protestors, particularly animal rights activists, the Criminal Justice and Police Act 2001 was amended and protests or demonstrations outside a person's home are almost certain to be covered by these provisions.   **3.142**

Police directions to stop the harassment of a person in his home (Criminal Justice and Police Act 2001, s 42)

If a person is present outside or in the vicinity of someone's home, the police are empowered to give any direction including a direction to leave the property and not return within a period not exceeding three months.[204] That direction may be given if   **3.143**

(a) the police have reasonable ground for believing that the person is present for the purpose of representing to or persuading, the resident or another individual at the dwelling (it does not have to be that individual's dwelling[205]):
(i) that he should not do something he is entitled or required to do or
(ii) that he should do something that he is not under any obligation to do;[206] and
(b) that the constable has reasonable grounds for believing that the presence of the person (either alone or together with other persons present):
(i) mounts to, or is likely to result in, the harassment of the resident or
(ii) is likely to cause alarm or distress to the resident.[207]

The direction is for the purpose of preventing harassment, alarm or distress of the resident and may be given orally, to an individual or a group,[208] and can include conditions as the   **3.144**

---

[201] Ibid, s 120(2).
[202] Ibid, s 120(3).
[203] Most of s 121 is in force (except s 121(4) which refers back to a part of s 120 that is not in force): SI 2008/3260.
[204] Criminal Justice and Police Act 2001, s 42(4), substituted by s 127(1), (2) of the Serious Organised Crime and Police Act 2005 as of 1 July 2007 (SI 2005/1521, Art 3(1)(m)).
[205] 'Dwelling' has the same meaning as in Part I of the Public Order Act 1986.
[206] Criminal Justice and Police Act 2001, s 42(1)(b).
[207] Ibid, s 41(1)(c).
[208] Ibid, s 42(3).

police see fit, including those as to the distance from the premises at which persons must remain, or the number of persons allowed to remain at the premises.

3.145 An officer has no power to give a direction if there is a more senior ranking officer at the scene, nor does he have a power to direct a person to refrain from peaceful picketing which is lawful under s 220 of the Trade Union and Labour Relations (Consolidation) Act 1992.

3.146 Any person who knowingly fails to comply with a requirement in a direction given to him (other than a requirement under subsec 4(b) not to return within a certain period) shall be guilty of an offence and liable, on summary conviction, to imprisonment for a term not exceeding *three months* or to a fine not exceeding level 4 on the standard scale, or to both.[209]

3.147 Any person to whom a constable has given a direction (including a requirement under subsec 4(b) not to return within a certain period) commits an offence if he returns to the vicinity of the premises within the period specified in the direction beginning with the date on which the direction is given, and does so for the required purpose of representing to or persuading. A person guilty of this offence shall be liable, on summary conviction, to imprisonment for a term not exceeding six months or to a fine not exceeding level 4 on the standard scale, or to both.[210]

Offence of harassment of a person in his home (Criminal Justice and Police Act 2001, s 42A)

3.148 Section 126 of the Serious Organised Crime and Police Act 2005 added a new s 42A to the 2001 Act. The purpose of the new offence was described by the Home Office as:

> . . . to give the police the ability to deal with harassing or intimidatory behaviour by individuals towards a person in his home even after an incident has taken place. Currently the police's ability to give directions to protestors under section 42 of the 2001 Act and to arrest them if they knowingly contravene a direction is only effective if the police are in attendance at the scene of a protest. Section 42 does not cover a situation where, for example, a resident makes a complaint about the presence of protestors outside his home, but the protestors disappear before the police arrive, or the police are not able to give a direction as they do not have the resources to enforce it at the scene.
>
> . . .
>
> This means that the police can deal with the protestors *after* the event. This will be useful if, for example, there is evidence of a protest on CCTV but the police were not present, or the police were present and could identify the protestors but there was some difficulty in enforcing a direction at the scene of the protest.[211]

The government conceded that 'the new offence in section 42 has broad application' and that 'the police will therefore need to consider the use of these powers proportionately'.[212]

---

[209] Ibid, s 42(7).
[210] Ibid, s 42(7A).
[211] Home Office Circular 34/2005, paras 39 and 41.
[212] Ibid, para 45.

It is an offence under s 42A if **3.149**

(a) a person is present outside or in the vicinity of any premises that are used by any individual as his dwelling;[213] and

(b) the person is present there for the purpose (by his presence or otherwise) of representing to, or persuading, the resident or another individual (whether or not that individual uses the premises as his dwelling) that he should not do something he is entitled or required to do, or that he should do something that he is not under any obligation to do;[214] and

(c) that person intends his presence to amount to, or ought to know that his presence is likely to result in, the harassment of, or to cause alarm or distress to, the resident;[215] and

(d) the presence of that person amounts to, or is likely to result in, the harassment of, or causes alarm or distress to, the resident or other individual at the dwelling or a person in another dwelling in the vicinity of the resident's dwelling.[216]

The reference to presence includes presence alone or together with other persons present. The 'ought to have known' test is fulfilled on an objective standard, namely whether a reasonable person in possession of the same information would think that the person's presence would have that effect.[217] A person guilty of this offence shall be liable on summary conviction to a maximum of six months' imprisonment or a fine up to level 4 or to both.[218]

This provision is capable of limiting extensively the right to protest if given too broad an **3.150** interpretation. Harassment is loosely defined and police have said that very mild behaviour (six women standing by the road with a banner) was causing harassment.[219] There is no definition at all of 'vicinity' and the police have been recorded as using an expansive interpretation, in one case the police concluding that an assembly outside the gates of a factory was 'in the vicinity of the dwelling' because some of the employees of that factory lived 'near the factory'.[220] This lack of clarity, coupled with an absence of a 'reasonableness' provision as is found in offences under the Protection from Harassment Act 1997 (thereby allowing a defendant to invoke their Convention rights that it was reasonable for them to invoke their rights of assembly as they did), means there is real potential for a breach of Article 11 of the European Convention on Human Rights. In order to avoid this, the Court must, as required by the Human Rights Act 1998, interpret the language of the provision narrowly so as to make it compatible with Convention rights by interfering with the rights to free expression and assembly only as is strictly necessary.

---

[213] Criminal Justice and Police Act 2001, s 42A(1)(a).
[214] Ibid, s 42(1)(b).
[215] Ibid, s 42(1)(c).
[216] Ibid, s 42A(1)(d).
[217] Ibid, s 42A(4).
[218] Ibid, s 42A(5)–(6).
[219] Liberty website, *Harassment and Interference with Contracts* at <http://www.yourrights.org.uk/yourrights/the-right-of-peaceful-protest/harassment-and-interference-with-contracts.html>.
[220] Ibid.

3.151 The section has one, rather anomalous, result. Taking, as an example, a CND protest that takes place at the home of a celebrity who hosts a birthday party for hundreds of people and invites the CEO of a nuclear installation. The protestors direct their protest only at the CEO, calling for him to give up his job, and are aware their presence will cause the CEO distress. The CEO is covered under three of the four elements of the offence—he is at a premises used as a dwelling (s 42A(1)(a)); the protestors are seeking to persuade him to give up a job he is entitled to do (s 42A(1)(b)); and their presence has caused him distress (s 42A(1)(d)). However, perhaps a legislative oversight, the requirement of intention or knowledge in s 42A(1)(c) is directed only at the resident. The protestors are not guilty of the offence unless they also intended their presence would amount to, or knew or ought to have known that their presence was likely to result in, the harassment of, or to cause alarm or distress to, the celebrity who was not a target of the protest.

H. By-laws

3.152 By-laws[221] cover nearly every activity in public places including processions and assemblies. In addition to the legislation discussed in this chapter, in an individual case it may be that there are further requirements imposed by local by-laws. The wording of each by-law may differ from one locality to another, but many by-laws are repeated in different parts of the country. A copy of the by-laws is usually available on the internet[222] and should be on sale in the local town hall and also available for inspection.

3.153 By-laws are the laws and regulations of local authorities. They are authorized by various enabling statutes and must be confirmed by the relevant Secretary of State. The Local Government Act 1972, s 235, for example, enables district councils and London boroughs to make by-laws for good rule and government, and for the suppression of nuisances. This general power covers topics such as music near houses, churches, and hospitals; noisy hawking; indecent language; indecent shows and nuisances contrary to public decency; wilful jostling; flags; defacing pavements; advertising bills and advertising vehicles; dangerous games, and spitting.

3.154 Other statutes authorize the making of by-laws on specific topics: preservation of order and prevention of damage in national parks and country parks (National Parks and Access to the Countryside Act 1949, s 90 and Countryside Act 1968, s 41); prevention of nuisance and preservation of order on commons (Commons Act 1899, s 1 and 10); access to and preservation and protection of ancient monuments (Ancient Monuments and Archaeological Areas Act 1979, s 19); and regulation of pleasure fairs and roller skating rinks (Public Health Act 1961, s 75). Prosecutions on the railways are governed by by-laws made under the Transport Act 2000 and Railways Act 2005.[223]

---

[221] Also spelt 'Bylaw' or 'Bye-law'. For further discussion see 4.94–4.102 and 5.149–5.151.

[222] For example: <http://www.warwickdc.gov.uk/WDC/Council_x2c_+government+and+democracy/Councils/Bylaws/default.htm>.

[223] See *DPP v Inegbu* [2008] EWHC 3242 (Admin) [2008] All ER(D) 269 (Nov) for resolution of apparent lacuna in law given absence of savings provisions for method of proving by-laws in criminal proceedings.

Typical by-laws governing the use of parks, gardens, and open spaces vested in or **3.155** maintained by a local authority will, among other things

(a) prohibit holding or taking part in public discussion or any public meeting, and giving or reading any public speech, lecture, sermon, or address;
(b) prohibit bill-posting or the erection of placards or notices;
(c) prohibit wilful obstruction or annoyance of any other person or officer of the council;
(d) prohibit the erection of a stall or booth or other structure;
(e) prohibit the playing of a radio, loudspeaker, or musical instrument so as to cause a nuisance or annoyance;
(f) prohibit the sale or distribution of books, pamphlets, leaflets, or advertisements; and
(g) provide for a person's removal by an officer of the council or a constable for infringement of any by-law.[224]

Criminal proceedings

The penalty for infringing a by-law is a fine at the level set out in the by-law or, where not **3.156** expressed, a fine not exceeding level 2.[225] Any person may institute the criminal proceedings for breach of a by-law unless the statute under which the by-law is made restricts the right to prosecute.[226]

Where a charge is brought, the defendant may challenge the validity of the by-law (even **3.157** though confirmed by the Secretary of State) on the grounds that it is *ultra vires* the enabling statute or obviously unreasonable or inconsistent with or repugnant to the general law. The magistrates are bound to decide on any objection to the validity of a by-law and an appeal against their decision lies to the Divisional Court by way of case stated.[227]. In *Boddington v British Transport Police*,[228] the House of Lords held that *Anisimic Ltd v Foreign Compensation Commission*[229] made obsolete the distinction between procedural errors and other errors of law, by extending the doctrine of *ultra vires* so that any misdirections in law could render the relevant decision *ultra vires* and a nullity.

The burden is on the defence to show that, on a balance of probabilities, the by-law was **3.158** *ultra vires* and so the prosecution is not required to prove its validity to the criminal standard. But, if the presumption of legality in its favour is overcome by a defendant, then the by-law is of no legal effect whatsoever. It is necessary in every case to examine the particular statutory context to determine whether a court has jurisdiction to rule on a defence based on arguments of invalidity of subordinate legislation or an administrative act under it.

---

[224] See also Transport for London by-laws.
[225] Local Government Act 1972, s 237.
[226] *R v Stewart* [1896] 1 QB 300.
[227] Magistrates' Court Act 1980, s 145. An appeal by way of case stated is on a matter of law and can only be made once the proceedings are complete.
[228] (1998) 2 WLR 639.
[229] (1979) AC 147.

3.159   *Bugg v Director of Public Prosecution*,[230] despite being now overruled to the extent that the distinction it makes between procedural and substantive errors of law was said to be incorrect, does remain helpful as an example of the grounds on which a by-law has been successfully challenged. The RAF Alconbury By-laws 1985 and the HM Forest Moor and Menwith Hill Station By-laws 1986[231] (made by the Secretary of State for Defence under Part II Military Lands Act 1892), which purported to exclude members of the public from service bases, were substantially invalid for failure to state with sufficient clarity the area they covered.

3.160   More recently and since the enactment of the Human Rights Act 1998, in *Kay Tabernacle v Secretary of State for Defence*,[232] the challenge to the Atomics Weapon Establishment (AWE) Aldermaston Byelaws 2007 was in part successful on the basis of the same common law principle that by-laws must not be vague or imprecise. The Administrative Court, in considering the human rights and common law arguments set out clearly the applicable legal principles to a challenge to by-laws:

(a)   the Secretary of State is a public authority within the meaning of s 6 of the Human Rights Act 1998 and by-laws, as secondary legislation, are susceptible to judicial review if they unjustifiably interfere with the human rights of those affected by them or are otherwise unlawful;

(b)   one of the consequences of the requirement that an interference is 'prescribed by law' is that the law must not be so vague as to have unforeseeable application.[233] A person must know with reasonable certainty when he or she is breaking the law;[234]

(c)   when it comes to justification under Articles 10(2) or 11(2), the authorities acknowledge that exercise of the right to freedom of assembly and exercise of the right to free expression are often closely associated;[235]

(d)   it is possible to distinguish between interferences which 'encroach on the essence of the right' and interferences which impact on the manner and form in which rights are exercised. It is axiomatic that particularly convincing justification is required in relation to the former, but that the discretionary area of judgment will be wider in the latter;

(e)   in domestic law, by-laws are susceptible to judicial review on grounds of, among other things, irrationality.

Private law

3.161   Under the civil law, arguments relying on a breach of a by-law may also in some cases be sufficient to sustain an action in damages.[236] However, a finding of invalidity in the course of criminal proceedings will not necessarily sustain an action in damages in the civil courts.

---

[230] (1993) QB 473.
[231] 1986/481.
[232] [2008] EWHC 416 Admin.
[233] *Gaweda v Poland* (2002) 12 EHRC 486.
[234] *Staden v Tarjani* (1980) 78 LGR 614.
[235] *R (Laporte) v Chief Constable of Gloucestershire Constabulary* [2007] 2 AC 105.
[236] *Newman v Francis* (1953) 51 LGR 168). The slightly differently formulated test of Simon Brown LJ in *Percy v Hall* [1997] QB 924 was said to have the same effect.

In *Percy v Hall*,[237] the protestors at RAF Alconbury brought claims for wrongful arrest and false imprisonment arising out of actions taken by the police to enforce the by-laws referred to above. The protestors were arrested 150 times and brought their action against 66 constables of the Ministry of Defence Police who carried out the arrests. The Court held that the proper approach to determining the validity of by-laws was that laid down in *Fawcett Properties Ltd v Buckinghamshire County Court*,[238] per Lord Denning:

> By-laws and planning conditions will only be held void for uncertainty if they can be given no meaning or no sensible or ascertainable meaning. Even if the by-laws were invalid, at the time of the events complained of, they appeared to be perfectly valid to the police and they were in law to be presumed valid and in the public interest they needed to be enforced. The court were of the opinion that it is one thing to accept that a subsequent declaration as to their invalidity operates retrospectively to entitle a person convicted of their breach to have that conviction set aside; quite another to hold that it transforms what judged at the time was to be regarded as the lawful discharge of the constables' duty, into what must later be found actionably tortious conduct. If there was a right of redress on the part of those arrested under what ultimately are found to be defective by-laws it could only be against the Secretary of State as the maker of an invalid instrument. Police officers are not to be deprived of the defence of lawful justification wherever they can show they were acting in the reasonable belief that the plaintiffs were committing a by-law offence.

The threatened breach of a by-law may be restrained by an injunction[239] and the finding of invalidity in respect of a by-law by a criminal court does not provide a private law defence to other members of the public if there is a breach of that injunction. The Divisional Court has held that a protestor who acted in breach of an injunction not to go on certain land was in breach of the injunction, notwithstanding the fact that the Court accepted she was on the land only to remove notices declaring the lawfulness of what were in fact invalid by-laws.[240] The Court stated that what members of the public should do is either ignore the notices or seek a court order requiring removal of the notices.

---

[237] (1997) QB 994.
[238] (1964) AC 636.
[239] *Burnley BC v England* (1977) 76 LGR 393.
[240] *Secretary of State for Defence & Ministry of Defence v Percy* [1999] 1 All ER 732.

4

USE OF THE HIGHWAY

A. Introduction	4.01	Terrorism Act 2000	4.80
B. Definition of the Highway	4.03	Criminal Justice and Public	
C. Use of the Highway	4.05	Order Act 1994	4.92
D. Obstruction of the Highway	4.19	G. By-laws	4.94
Essential elements of the offence	4.20	H. Street-based Prostitution	4.103
E. Picketing	4.51	Loitering or soliciting	4.108
Picketing in the employment law context	4.53	Jurisdiction and penalty	4.109
Consumer picketing	4.68	Essential elements	4.110
F. Police Road Blocks	4.72	Kerb crawling	4.125
At common law	4.73	Essential elements	4.128
Police and Criminal Evidence Act 1984	4.77	Persistent soliciting	4.142

A. Introduction

Many forms of protest take place on the 'highway', the legal term for streets, pavements, **4.01** squares, and other public spaces over which the general public has the right of passage 'to pass and repass without let or hindrance'. Thus the 'highway' is the ultimate public place and is often the focal point at which the individual and the state come into contact. If the highway is obstructed or used unreasonably then criminal offences may be committed. Even the most peaceful conduct may sometimes amount to criminal conduct.

It is therefore necessary to examine the scope of the term 'highway' and the use which may **4.02** lawfully be made of it in the context of public order law. This chapter is not concerned with traffic offences. The law on processions and assemblies is dealt with in Chapter 3 and the law of trespass in Chapter 5. Instead, here we are concerned with the offence of obstruction of the highway;[1] the right of passage; picketing; police powers such as road-blocks and 'kettling'; highway by-laws; and the street-based prostitution offences of soliciting and kerb crawling.

---

[1] Highways Act 1980, s 137.

B. Definition of the Highway

4.03 There is no statutory definition of the term 'highway'. The Highways Act 1980, s 328(1) defines 'highway' only as 'the whole or a part of a highway other than a ferry or waterway'. Section 328(2) states 'where a highway passes over a bridge or through a tunnel, that bridge or tunnel is to be taken for the purposes of this Act to be a part of the highway'. The Highways Act 1835,[2] s 5 states 'the word "highways" shall be understood to mean all roads, bridges, carriageways, cartways, horseways, bridleways, footways, causeways, churchways, and pavements'. In the Road Traffic Act 1991 the term 'road' means 'any length of highway or of any other road to which the public has access, and includes bridges over which a road passes'.[3] Thus, we must turn to the common law for a definition.

4.04 At common law a 'highway' is a way over which there exists a public right of passage, that is to say a right for all Her Majesty's subjects at all seasons of the year freely and at their will *to pass and repass* without let or hindrance: *Ex parte Lewis*.[4] A highway may be dedicated subject to certain restrictions and obstructions[5] and it may be limited to a recognized class of traffic, that is it need not be a way for vehicles because, if they are open to the public, footpaths and bridleways are also highways. It is, however, an essential characteristic of a highway that every member of the public should have the right to use it and it cannot be dedicated to a limited section of the public.[6]

C. Use of the Highway

> On a highway I may stand still for a reasonably short time, but I must not put my bed upon the highway and permanently occupy a portion of it. I may stoop to tie up my shoelace, but I may not occupy a pitch and invite people to come upon it and have their hair cut. I may let my van stand still long enough to deliver and load goods, but I must not turn my van into a permanent stall.[7]

4.05 The highway is, by definition, a place of public access—but what use may the public rightfully make of it? The starting point is the right of passage—or as it is known 'the right to pass and repass'. The purpose of the highway is to allow the public to travel from A to B and back again, if they so wish. So the right of the public on the highway is to pass along it. But that does not mean that one must keep moving—one has the right to stop and look around, change a tyre, consult a map. Yet, once one is allowed to stop, for how long may one stop

---

[2] The Highways Act 1835 has been largely repealed and replaced with modern legislation. However, the interpretation clause of s 5 remains in force.

[3] The Road Traffic Act 1991, s 82 states 'road' has the same meaning as in the Road Traffic Regulation Act 1984. Section 142 of the 1984 Act has had the above definition substituted (1 November 1991) by New Roads and Street Works Act 1991.

[4] (1888) 21 QBD 191, 197 per Wills J. See generally *Halsbury's Laws of England* (4th edn, 2004 reissue) vol 21, para 1 et seq.

[5] Ibid, paras 131–6.

[6] Ibid, para 1.

[7] *Iveagh v Martin* [1961] 1 QB 232, 273 per Paull LJ.

and for what purpose may one stop without interfering with the right of others to pass and repass? That has been the question for the courts through the ages.

In *Harrison v Duke of Rutland*[8] Mr Harrison had used the public highway, which crossed   **4.06**
the Duke of Rutland's land, in order to disrupt grouse shooting. He was forcibly restrained by the Duke's servants and sued for assault. The Duke pleaded justification on the basis that Mr Harrison had been trespassing. The majority (Kay LJ and Lopes LJ) held that the public right of access to the highway extended only to the right of passing and repassing and that if a person uses the highway for any other purpose (as here, to disrupt the lawful activity of grouse shooting) then he was a trespasser. But Lord Esher MR contemplated that there may be 'reasonable and usual' uses of the highway beyond passing and repassing. He said:

> Highways are, no doubt, dedicated prima facie for the purpose of passage: but things are done upon them by everybody which are recognised as being rightly done, and as constituting a reasonable and usual mode of using a highway as such. If a person on a highway does not transgress such reasonable and usual mode of using it, I do not think he will be a trespasser.[9]

In *Hickman v Maisey*[10] the defendant was a racing tout who used the public highway cross-   **4.07**
ing the plaintiff's property for the purpose of observing the horses training in order to obtain tips. The Court of Appeal in that case followed the approach of Lord Esher MR in *Harrison v Duke of Rutland*, stating that a man who stopped by the side of the road to rest or take a sketch would not be a trespasser, but the defendant's activities fell outside 'an ordinary and reasonable user of the highway' and so amounted to trespass. Collins LJ said:

> in modern times a reasonable extension has been given to the use of the highway as such . . . The right of the public to pass and repass on a highway is subject to all those reasonable extensions which may be recognised as necessary to its exercise in accordance with the enlarged notions of people in a country becoming more populous and highly civilised, but they must be such as are not inconsistent with the maintenance of the paramount idea that the right of the public is that of passage.[11]

So does the public simply have the right *to pass and repass* and no more, or does there exist   **4.08**
a right to assemble there? This was the debate which divided the House of Lords three to two in *DPP v Jones (Margaret) & Another*.[12] This landmark case decided that, provided the activity did not cause a public or private nuisance, obstruct the highway, or unreasonably impede the right of passage, there is a right of public assembly on the highway.

The issue in *DPP v Jones* was one of fundamental constitutional importance: what are   **4.09**
the limits of the public's right of access to the public highway? Dr Margaret Jones was amongst a group of peaceful demonstrators who gathered on the verge of the A344, adjacent to the perimeter fence of Stonehenge. The police inspector in charge of policing the

---

[8] [1893] 1 QB 142.
[9] Ibid, pp 146–7.
[10] [1900] 1 QB 752.
[11] Ibid, pp 757–8.
[12] [1999] 2 AC 250.

demonstration concluded that the demonstrators constituted a 'trespassory assembly'[13] and so asked them to move on. Some did, but Dr Jones did not and determined to test her rights under the law. She was duly arrested and charged with 'trespassory assembly' under s 14B(2) of the Public Order Act 1986[14]—that is, taking part in an assembly which she knew was prohibited by an order under s 14A.

4.10 Where certain conditions are met under s 14A of the Public Order Act 1986 the chief officer of police may apply to the local council for an order prohibiting for a specified period 'trespassory assemblies' within a specified area. An assembly[15] will be 'trespassory' where it takes place 'without the permission of the occupier of the land or so as to exceed the limits of any permission . . . or the limits of the public's right of access'.[16] So the question was what are the limits of the public's right of access?

4.11 Dr Jones was convicted in the magistrates' court but appealed to the Crown Court which overturned the conviction on the basis that none of the demonstrators had been 'destructive, violent, threatening a breach of the peace or doing anything other than reasonably using the highway'. The Divisional Court reinstated the convictions, holding that the fact that the defendants were entirely peaceful was irrelevant—the right of access to the public highway is limited to the right to pass and repass and to do anything which is incidental to that right. Peaceful assembly is not incidental to the right to pass and repass. Thus, assembly on the highway, however peaceable, exceeds the limits of the right of public access and is therefore conduct which amounts to trespassory assembly.

4.12 On appeal to the House of Lords, Lord Irvine of Lairg LC, analysed the older authorities and giving the leading opinion for the majority in *DPP v Jones*, held that a person's right to use the highway was not restricted to the right to pass and repass and any acts incidental or ancillary to that right:

> In truth, very little activity could accurately be described as 'ancillary' to passing along the highway: perhaps stopping to tie one's shoe-lace, consulting a street-map, or pausing to catch one's breath. But I do not think that such ordinary and usual activities as making a sketch, taking a photograph, handing out leaflets, collecting money for charity, singing carols, playing in a Salvation Army band, children playing a game on the pavement, having a picnic, or reading a book, would qualify. These examples illustrate that to limit lawful use of the highway to that which is literally 'incidental or ancillary' to the right of passage would be to place an unrealistic and unwarranted restriction on commonplace day-to-day activities.[17]

4.13 Lord Irvine favoured a broader 'reasonable user' approach. However, he did not accept that this approach would materially realign the interests of the general public and landowners. It would not permit the unreasonable or obstructive uses of the highway. It would not 'afford carte blanche to squatters or other uninvited visitors' because their activities would

---

[13] See Ch 5 for full discussion of the law of trespass, in particular 5.127 and 5.136–38.

[14] As inserted by the Criminal Justice and Public Order Act 1994, s 70.

[15] An assembly for the purposes of this offence means an assembly of twenty or more persons: Public Order Act 1986, s 14A(9).

[16] Ibid, s 14A(5).

[17] [1999] 2 AC 240, 255–6.

almost certainly be unreasonable or obstructive or both. His Lordship concluded, therefore:

> the public highway is a public place which the public may enjoy for any reasonable purpose, provided the activity in question does not amount to a public or private nuisance and does not obstruct the highway by unreasonably impeding the primary right of the public to pass and repass: *within these qualifications there is a public right of peaceful assembly on the highway.*

Lord Slynn of Hadley and Lord Hope of Craighead strongly dissented, taking a much more **4.14** restrictive view. Lord Slynn focused on Lord Esher MR's use of words in *Harrison v Duke of Rutland*: 'It does not seem to me that his words "any reasonable or usual mode of using the highway as a highway" or "a reasonable and usual mode of using the highway *as such*" (emphasis added) were intended to include acts done by people which were not in the ordinary sense of the term "passing and repasssing"'.[18]

Lord Hope noted that, for the tort of trespass, the purpose of the trespasser need not be **4.15** unlawful, it being enough that the user of the soil was there for a purpose other than that which is the proper use of the highway, namely that of passing and repassing along it. Thus, Lord Hope said it was irrelevant whether the assembly was or was not peaceful or causing an obstruction. His Lordship looked at some of the older authorities which indicated an unwillingness on the part of judges to favour resort to the courts for a remedy where the trespass was so trivial or technical that no reasonable person would object (for example, a clergyman holding a service on the beach[19] or a man setting up appliances on the highway to catch moths[20]). He said that 'the fact that some activities on the highway are or ought to be tolerated does not mean that they are being done there in the exercise of the public's right to access it. It is the extent of the right of access, not the question whether the activity ought to be tolerated, which is the issue in the present case.'[21]

Lord Hope was concerned for the rights of landowners—who were not even represented at **4.16** the appeal. He said that the right of assembly, which the appellant was seeking to establish, had less to do with the right of passage than with what would be described in terms of property law as the right to remain.[22] He said that, 'it is not difficult to see that to admit a right in the public in whatever numbers to remain indefinitely in one place on a highway for the purpose of exercising the freedom of the right to assemble could give rise to substantial problems for landowners in their attempts to deal with the activities of demonstrators, squatters and other uninvited visitors'.[23]

There must be a consideration of time, however. Lord Clyde, in the majority with Lords **4.17** Hutton and Irvine LC, said it was all a question of nature and degree. Responding to Lord Hope's concerns that the right to assembly would entail a right to remain, he stated that there was no right to remain on the highway, so that any stopping and standing *must be*

---

[18] Ibid, p 262.
[19] *Llandudno Urban District Council v Woods* [1899] 2 Ch 705.
[20] *Fielden v Cox* (1906) 22 TLR 411.
[21] [1999] 2 AC 240, 273.
[22] Ibid, p 275.
[23] Ibid, p 276.

reasonably limited in time. While the right may extend to a picnic on the verge, it would not extend to camping there.[24] Likewise, he said that, 'if a group of people stand in the street to sing hymns or Christmas carols they are in my view using the street within the legitimate scope of the public right to access it, provided of course that they do so *for a reasonable period* and without any unreasonable obstruction to traffic'.[25] Applying that to the right of assembly, Lord Clyde said:

> The test then is not one which can be defined in general terms but has to depend on the circumstances as a matter of degree. It requires a careful assessment of the nature and extent of the activity in question. If the purpose of the activity becomes the predominant purpose of the occupation of the highway, or if it becomes more than reasonably transitional in terms of either time or space, then it may come to exceed the right to use the highway.[26]

4.18 Lord Clyde's observations have a particular resonance when examining the offence of obstruction of the highway[27]—where factors such as the nature and extent of the activity, its duration of time and use of space are all considerations to be weighed in the balance when determining whether the conduct was reasonable.[28]

D. Obstruction of the Highway

4.19 It is a summary only offence under s 137 of the Highways Act 1980 to wilfully obstruct the highway. Under s 137(1):

> If a person, without lawful authority or excuse, in any way wilfully obstructs the free passage along a highway he is guilty of an offence and liable to a fine not exceeding level 3[29] on the standard scale.

Essential elements of the offence

4.20 There are three essential elements of the offence:

- obstruction;
- wilfulness; and
- without lawful authority or excuse (reasonableness).

4.21 At the outset, it is important to understand that the key issue will usually be whether the activity is *reasonable*. It will be very easy for a technical obstruction to take place and for that obstruction to be deliberate, but the question is whether, in all the circumstances, it was reasonable.

4.22 The key authority is *Hirst and Agu v Chief Constable of West Yorkshire*.[30] The case concerned animal rights supporters, who had been demonstrating against the use of animal fur both

---

[24] Ibid, p 280.
[25] Ibid, p 281.
[26] Ibid, p 281.
[27] s 137 Highways Act 1980.
[28] See *Hirst & Agu v Chief Constable of West Yorkshire* (1987) 85 Cr App R 143.
[29] At the time of writing, level 3 on the standard scale is £1,000.
[30] (1987) 85 Cr App R 143.

outside and in the doorway of a furrier's shop in Bradford. They handed out leaflets, held banners, and attracted groups of passers-by who blocked the street. In the Divisional Court Glidewell LJ said that the issue of whether they were guilty of the statutory offence turned on three questions:

(a) was there an obstruction (unless *de minimis*, 'any stopping on the highway', is *prima facie* an obstruction)?
(b) Was the obstruction deliberate?
(c) And was the obstruction without lawful authority or excuse?[31]

Let us examine those questions in turn.

Obstruction

The public's primary right of access to the highway is for passage—'the right to pass and repass'. Accordingly, unless the obstruction is so small and trifling that one can consider it comes within the rubric *de minimis*, any stopping on the highway, whether it be on the carriageway or on the footway, will *prima facie* amount to an obstruction.[32] To quote Lord Parker CJ in *Nagy v Weston*,[33] 'Any occupation of part of a road thus interfering with people having use of the whole road is an obstruction.' **4.23**

So the threshold for causing an obstruction is very low, but again the question will be was it reasonable? Glidewell LJ gave a 'mundane example': **4.24**

> suppose two friends meet in the street, not having seen each other for some time, and stop to discuss their holidays and are more or less stationary for a quarter of an hour or 20 minutes. Obviously, they may well cause an obstruction to others passing by. What they are discussing has nothing to do with passing or re-passing in the street. They could just as well have the conversation at the home of one or other of them or in a coffee shop nearby. Is it to be said that they are guilty of an offence and the reasonableness of what they are doing is not in issue? In my judgment it cannot be said.[34]

The act of obstruction is made out by the act of stopping on the highway, as a result of which the free passage of other users of the highway is impeded. It is the stopping, not the impeding of others, which amounts to the physical element of the offence. **4.25**

In *Waite v Taylor*[35] a busker was convicted of the offence for juggling with fire sticks in Union Street, Bath. May LJ found that the underlying principle of obstruction lay in the fact that the stopping was outside the primary purpose of passage: **4.26**

> In so far as a highway is concerned members of the public have the right to pass and repass along it. That does not, however, mean that one must keep moving all the time. However, if one does stop on a highway then *prima facie* obstruction occurs, because by stopping you are on a piece of the very highway that somebody else may wish to pass and repass along. Where, however, your stopping is really part and parcel of passing and repassing along the highway and is ancillary to it (such as a milkman stopping to leave a milk bottle on a doorstep) then it

---

[31] Ibid, pp 150–1.
[32] *Hirst and Agu v Chief Constable of West Yorkshire* (1987) 85 Cr App R 143, 151 Glidewell LJ.
[33] [1965] 1 WLR 280, 284.
[34] *Hirst and Agu*, p 150.
[35] (1985) 149 JP 551.

is not an obstruction within the meaning of the subsection with which we are concerned . . . On the other hand, where stopping on the highway cannot properly be said to be ancillary to or part and parcel of the exercise of the right to pass and repass along that highway, then the obstruction becomes unreasonable and there is an obstruction contrary to the provisions of the subsection.

4.27 The stopping must be *unreasonable*. So Glidewell LJ in *Hirst and Agu*[36] said that *Waite v Taylor* applied too rigid a test. The stopping of the animal rights protestors outside the furrier's shop was not part and parcel or even ancillary to the right of passage. Nevertheless, the question was whether their actions were reasonable. In the light of the House of Lords decision in *DPP v Jones*[37] stressing the reasonable user test—that must be correct.

4.28 Moreover, it will be a good defence if there was, in fact, little or no *actual* obstruction of others. It is not essential for the prosecution to prove actual obstruction of another but if no other is actually obstructed, then it is would be difficult to show that the use of the highway was unreasonable. *Hubbard v Pitt*[38] was a case concerning a demonstration by local residents against the activities of an Islington estate agent. Lord Denning MR held that the presence of half a dozen people on the pavement outside the estate agent's premises, for three hours on a Saturday morning, without interfering with the passage of other people was not an obstruction.

Wilfulness

4.29 The second essential element of the offence is that it must be 'wilful' or deliberate. This connotes a measure of intention but it is not to be confused with malice. The act of obstruction is simply stopping on the highway and thereby interfering with the right of others to pass and repass. So 'wilful' obstruction merely amounts to intentional or deliberate stopping. As Glidwell LJ explained in *Hirst and Agu*,[39] 'Clearly, in many cases a pedestrian or a motorist has to stop because the traffic lights are against the motorist or there are other people in the way, not because he wishes to do so. Such stopping is not wilful. But if the stopping is deliberate, then there is wilful obstruction.'

4.30 Wilful then means intentional, as opposed to accidental, that is, by an exercise of free will.[40] Thus it would be a defence to say that 'my car broke down, I had no choice in the matter'. Moreover, it seems that the intention must be to obstruct the free passage of the highway. In *Eaton v Cobb*[41] the driver of a motor car pulled over to the side of the road and opened his off-side door, striking a cyclist who was passing. The magistrates found that the driver had looked in his rear-view mirror but did not see the cyclist approach, whereas the cyclist had his head down and was unable to react in time to avoid the opening door. Lord Goddard CJ in the Divisional Court concluded that although the driver

---

[36] Op cit.
[37] [1999] AC 240. See 4.08–4.18 above.
[38] [1976] QB 142, 174–5, per Lord Denning.
[39] *Hirst and Agu*, p 151.
[40] *Arrowsmith v Jenkins* [1963] 2 QB 561.
[41] [1950] 1 All ER 1016. This was a case of wilfully obstructing the free passage of the highway, under the Highways Act 1835, s 72—the precursor to the offence under the Highways Act 1980, s 137.

had wilfully opened his door, he had not done so intending to obstruct the highway. The motorist had deliberately opened the door, but the consequences were accidental and not 'wilful'.

However, the decision in *Eaton v Cobb* appears to be at odds with Glidewell LJ's formula- **4.31** tion in *Hirst and Agu* above, where he said that if the stopping is deliberate, then there is wilful obstruction. Perhaps the better answer in *Eaton v Cobb* was that the driver did wilfully obstruct the highway—because he wilfully opened the door and the door obstructed the free passage of the cyclist—but his conduct was reasonable in all the circumstances, because he looked in his mirror and opening a car door to alight from a vehicle is patently ancillary to the proper use of the highway for passage. Thus again, once a person has deliberately stopped on the highway, the real issue will be whether that conduct was reasonable.

Whether an activity is reasonable is always a question of fact not law and will depend on all **4.32** the circumstances of the case—the duration of the obstruction, the manner of it, the space occupied, and the extent to which others were inconvenienced.

Without lawful authority or excuse (reasonableness)

The prosecution must prove the absence of lawful authority or excuse. In fact, authority **4.33** and excuse are two different things. As Glidewell LJ explained in *Hirst and Agu*,[42] 'Lawful authority includes permits and licences granted under statutory provision . . . such as for market and street traders and, no doubt, for those collecting for charitable causes on Saturday mornings. Lawful excuse embraces activities otherwise lawful in themselves which may or may not be reasonable in all the circumstances.'

'Lawful authority' is aimed at those who have been granted some form of statutory power **4.34** or permission from the market trader in Glidewell LJ's example (under a permit from the local authority) to the police officer setting up a road block[43] or directing traffic (under statutory powers[44]). For the statutory protection for picketing in contemplation or furtherance of a trade dispute see the section on picketing below.[45] Most defendants will be unable to avail themselves of this defence.

'Lawful excuse', however, appears to be much wider and amount to an assessment of **4.35** reasonableness. In *Nagy v Weston*[46] Lord Parker CJ said '[after obstruction and wilfulness] two further elements must be proved, first that the defendant has no lawful authority or reasonable excuse, and, secondly, that the user to which he was putting the highway was an unreasonable user. *For my part, I think that excuse and reasonableness are really the same ground.*'

---

[42] *Hirst and Agu*, p 151.
[43] See, for example, *Johnson v Phillips* [1975] 3 All ER 682: a police officer would have lawful authority to create road blocks or barriers in certain limited circumstances or to control traffic where life or property were at risk.
[44] For example, the Police and Criminal Evidence Act 1984, s 4—see below at 4.77.
[45] Trade Union and Labour Relations (Consolidation) Act 1992, s 220—see below at 4.53.
[46] [1965] 1 All ER 78, 80.

4.36   However, the courts have been clear to emphasize, as did Glidewell LJ in *Hirst and Agu*,[47] that 'for there to be a lawful excuse for what would otherwise be an obstruction of the highway, *the activity in which the person causing the obstruction is engaged must itself be inherently lawful*. If it is not, the question whether it is reasonable does not arise.'[48]

4.37   If, however, the activity is inherently lawful (for example, distributing leaflets demonstrating against the fur trade), then whether there is a lawful excuse turns on whether the conduct was reasonable. Again, therefore, one must look at the nature of the activity, its duration in time, the space occupied, and the extent of the interference caused to others— its reasonableness.

Reasonableness and human rights

4.38   The final question, whether the prosecution have proved that the defendant obstructed the highway 'without lawful excuse', is 'to be answered by deciding whether the activity in which the defendant was engaged was or was not *a reasonable user* of the highway': *Hirst and Agu*.[49] In that case Glidewell LJ explained:

> For instance, what is now relatively commonplace, at least in London and large cities, distributing advertising material or free periodicals outside stations, when people are arriving in the morning. Clearly, that is an obstruction; clearly, it is not incidental to passage up and down the street because the distributors are virtually stationary. The question must be: *is it a reasonable use of the highway or not?* . . . It may be decided that if the activity grows to an extent that it is unreasonable by reason of the space occupied or the duration of time for which it goes on that an offence would be committed, but it is a matter on the facts for the magistrates.[50]

4.39   In so holding Glidewell LJ applied the reasoning of the Divisional Court in *Nagy v Weston*,[51] where the activity in question, the sale of hot dogs in the street, 'could not . . . be said to be incidental to the right to pass and repass along the street.' The question was one of fact: 'whether the activity was or was not *reasonable*'. Thus, in *DPP v Jones*[52] when the House of Lords held that the public's right of access to the highway was not restricted to the right of passage but to any reasonable use—including peaceful non-obstructive assembly—Lord Irvine of Lairg LC said that, 'I find it satisfactory that there is a symmetry in the law between the activities on the public highway which may be trespassory and those which may amount to unlawful obstruction.'[53]

4.40   Into the assessment of reasonableness, one must now factor fundamental human rights.[54] It will be apparent from the cases discussed above that cases of wilful obstruction of the highway often arise out of otherwise lawful demonstrations. As a result, the rights to

---

[47] Ibid, p 150 but see also *Nagy v Weston* [1965] 1 All ER 78.

[48] See also *Birch v DPP* (1999) unreported CO 2381/99, 10 December 1999.

[49] *Hirst and Agu*, per Glidewell LJ at p 150.

[50] Ibid, p 150.

[51] [1965] 1 WLR 280 at 4.08–4.18 above.

[52] [1999] 2 AC 240.

[53] Ibid, pp 258–9. Though it should be noted that the opinions of Lord Slynn and Lord Hope in *DPP v Jones* made it quite clear they thought that there was little to be gained by comparing obstruction and trespass cases.

[54] See generally Ch 10 on human rights issues.

freedom of expression and freedom of assembly under Articles 10 and 11 of the European Convention on Human Rights will be engaged. Although those rights are not unqualified, and thus may be restricted where there is a pressing social need, the courts have recognized the fundamental importance of those rights to the lifeblood of a democracy: see for example *R v Secretary of State for Home Department ex p Simms*[55] and *Handyside v United Kingdom*.[56]

Indeed, the state has a positive obligation to facilitate peaceful protest. In *Stankov v Bulgaria*,[57] the European Court of Human Rights held: **4.41**

> Freedom of assembly and the right to express one's views through it are among the paramount values of a democratic society. The essence of democracy is its capacity to resolve problems through open debate. Sweeping measures of a preventive nature to suppress freedom of assembly and expression other than in cases of incitement to violence or rejection of democratic principles—however shocking and unacceptable certain views or words used may appear to the authorities, and however illegitimate the demands made may be—do a disservice to democracy and often even endanger it.
>
> In a democratic society based on the rule of law, political ideas which challenge the existing order and whose realisation is advocated by peaceful means must be afforded a proper opportunity of expression through the exercise of the right of assembly as well as by other lawful means.

Accordingly, any interference with those rights must be narrowly interpreted and the necessity for any restrictions must be convincingly established: *Sunday Times v United Kingdom (No 2)*.[58] **4.42**

Moreover, the decision to bring a prosecution at all in such cases must be proportionate. In *Dehal v DPP*[59] Moses J said: 'In order to justify one of the essential foundations of democratic society the prosecution must demonstrate that it is being brought in pursuit of a legitimate aim, namely the protection of society against violence and that a criminal prosecution is the only method necessary to achieve that aim'.[60] **4.43**

In *Ezelin v France*[61] the European Court of Human Rights emphasized the importance of peaceful, non-violent, non-obstructive protest and held that punitive measures, however minimal, imposed on a demonstrator after the event are to be considered as much an interference with freedom of assembly as the arrest and physical removal of the demonstrator at the time. The Court went so far as to say: 'The freedom to take part in a peaceful **4.44**

---

[55] [2000] 2 AC 115, 126 per Lord Steyn.
[56] (1976) 1 EHRR 737, para 49.
[57] [2001] ECHR 29225/95.
[58] [1992] 14 EHRR 123.
[59] [2005] EWHC 2154 (Admin) Moses J at para 9—in the context of a case of the Public Order Act 1986, s 4.
[60] See 1.209 and 10.41 et seq. Where there is a question of ' reasonableness' in the context of the Public Order Act 1986, s 4 and s 5,the European Convention on Human Rights, Art 10 requires a strict assessment of necessity and proportionality of any interference with that right. See *Percy v DPP* [2001] EWHC 1125 (Admin), (2002) 166 JP 93; *Hammond v DPP* [2004] EWHC 69 (Admin), (2004) 168 JP 601; *Norwood v DPP* [2003] Crim LR 888.
[61] (1991) 14 EHRR 362, paras 51–3.

assembly . . . is of such importance that it cannot be restricted in any way . . . so long as the person concerned does not himself commit any reprehensible act[62] on such an occasion.'

4.45 A useful illustration of the Strasbourg approach in the context of a peace demonstration on the highway, is *G v Germany*.[63] In that case the Commission concluded that 'the right to freedom of peaceful assembly is one of the foundations of a democratic society and should not be interpreted restrictively'. On the facts of the case, which involved requirements to give advance notice of a demonstration, the Commission found that the defendant's conviction was justified and 'necessary in a democratic society for the prevention of disorder and crime', but only because of the deliberate blocking of a public road leading to army barracks, 'thereby causing more obstruction than would normally arise from the exercise of the right of peaceful assembly'. The repeated sit-ins blocking the approach road tipped the balance between the public interest and the applicant's interest in favour of the public, so that the applicant's conviction was held to be not disproportionate.

4.46 For a clear exposition of a High Court judge putting all this together and working through the thought process in a topical obstruction of the highway case see *Westminster City Council v Brian Haw*.[64] Since 2001, Brian Haw has mounted a 24-hour-a-day vigil in Parliament Square in opposition to the British government's policy on Iraq. He lives, eats, and sleeps on the square opposite the Houses of Parliament, from where he displays placards and photographs in support of his views. Westminster City Council applied for an injunction to stop Mr Haw's demonstration, alleging it amounted to obstruction of the highway. Gray J rejected that application on the basis that, taking into account the duration, place, purpose, and effect of the obstruction, as well as the exercise of the Convention right to free speech, Mr Haw's use of the highway was not unreasonable.

4.47 The Court found that by virtue of his bed overhanging the pavement by about 2 feet it amounted to an obstruction and that this obstruction was wilful in the sense that it was deliberate. But the location of the protest was crucial to the question of reasonableness. Mr Haw was expressing his views on government policy and sought peacefully to influence Parliament. Where better to express those views than outside Parliament? Gray J was mindful of the fundamental importance of the right to freedom of expression. He said:

> I certainly do not accept that Article 10 is a trump card entitling any political protestor to circumvent regulations relating to planning and the use of the highways and the like, but in my judgment the existence of the right to freedom of expression conferred by Article 10 is a significant consideration when assessing the reasonableness of any obstruction to which the protest gives rise.[65]

---

[62] 'Reprehensible conduct' would include, for example, conduct likely to cause a breach of the peace or unreasonable obstruction of the highway.
[63] (1989) 60 DR 256, 263.
[64] [2002] EWHC 2073, QB.
[65] Ibid, para 24.

This case is also interesting because of the long duration of the protest. In *DPP v Jones*[66]   **4.48**
Lord Clyde explained, 'if the purpose of the activity becomes the predominant purpose of
the occupation of the highway, or if it becomes more than reasonably transitional in terms
of either time or space, then it may come to exceed the right to use the highway'. So one
factor militating against the conduct being reasonable is its long duration. Yet in *Haw*, the
protest had been ongoing for some fifteen months (and is still ongoing at the time of
publication in 2010). In that case, Gray J said this:

> It is an important feature of this case that the obstruction has been continuing for some 15
> months, albeit in circumstances where the subject matter of the placards has remained topi-
> cal throughout that period. The duration of the obstruction is an indication of unreasonable-
> ness. Against that, the point is fairly made for the defendant that, given that his objective is
> to influence Parliament in relation to policy towards Iraq, the location opposite the Houses
> of Parliament is a suitable one. The defendant asserts an entitlement to continue to protest
> for so long as it is necessary for him to achieve, if he can, the change in policy which he is
> advocating. As to the extent of the interference with the right of passage and re-passage,
> according to the unchallenged evidence, the pavement which surrounds the grassed area in
> Parliament Square is not easily reached by pedestrians. There are no designated pedestrian
> crossings, and access to pedestrians is, according to the evidence, if anything, discouraged. In
> stark contrast to the pavement on the other side of the roads around Parliament Square, rela-
> tively few pedestrians use the inner pavements. The evidence of observations carried out by
> the street enforcement officers of the Council is that less than 30 pedestrians per hour use
> those inner pavements. There is no evidence of any actual obstruction of any pedestrian seek-
> ing to walk along the pavement. In all the time that the defendant has been present, the police
> have not once considered it necessary to take action against Mr Haw or even to warn him of
> any possible future action. There is no suggestion of any violence or disorder or breach of the
> peace arising out of the presence of Mr Haw in Parliament Square. The unchallenged evi-
> dence is that the defendant goes to great pains to ensure that the area is kept clean and tidy.
> . . . Apart from these considerations, which all bear on the question of reasonableness, here is
> another, to my mind, significant, consideration which I should also take into account. It is
> the fact that the defendant is exercising his right to freedom of expression, and doing so on a
> political issue.

Power to order offender to remove obstruction

Once a person has been convicted of the offence of obstructing the highway, the courts   **4.49**
have power to order the offender to remove any continuing obstruction, provided that it is
in his power to do so. Failure to do so can lead to a new offence, punishable by ever larger
fines and costs.

Section 137ZA of the Highways Act provides as follows: **4.50**

(1) Where a person is convicted of an offence under section 137 above in respect of the
obstruction of a highway and it appears to the court that—
(a) the obstruction is continuing, and
(b) it is in that person's power to remove the cause of the obstruction,

---

[66] [1999] 2 AC 240, 281. For an obstruction of long duration see *Schmidberger v Republik Österreich*
at 10.65.

the court may, in addition to or instead of imposing any punishment, order him to take, within such reasonable period as may be fixed by the order, such steps as may be specified in the order for removing the cause of the obstruction.

(2) The time fixed by an order under subsection (1) above may be extended or further extended by order of the court on an application made before the end of the time as originally fixed or as extended under this subsection, as the case may be.

(3) If a person fails without reasonable excuse to comply with an order under subsection (1) above, he is guilty of an offence and liable to a fine not exceeding level 5 on the standard scale; and if the offence is continued after conviction he is guilty of a further offence and liable to a fine not exceeding one-twentieth of that level for each day on which the offence is so continued.

(4) Where, after a person is convicted of an offence under subsection (3) above, the highway authority for the highway concerned exercise any power to remove the cause of the obstruction, they may recover from that person the amount of any expenses reasonably incurred by them in, or in connection with, doing so.

E. Picketing

The picket line can . . . quickly become a source of conflict as tensions rise and incomes (of the pickets) fall, aggravated in some cases still further by the presence of replacement workers doing the jobs once done by the strikers . . . The picket line can also quickly become a source of great tension between competing liberal values: the liberty of the employer to conduct business without restraint on the one hand, and the liberty of the pickets to freedom of assembly on the other. The way in which the courts hold the balance between these conflicting liberties has changed over time. In recent years there has been more open acknowledgement on the part of the courts of the rights of the picket and the civil liberties dimension to cases in which employers have sought injunctions to restrain peaceful protest.[67]

4.51 A comprehensive review of the law of picketing is beyond the scope of this chapter and this book—but there are aspects of picketing which affect both the use of the highway and public order law generally.[68] The highway, by definition, is a way over which there exists a public right of passage for all of Her Majesty's subjects.[69] Accordingly, pickets, whether acting against job losses or the sale of fur coats, have the right to use the highway just like anyone else. Moreover, the House of Lords in *DPP v Jones*[70] has recognized the right of assembly on the highway. However, like anyone else, the pickets' use of the highway must be strictly limited to that which is *reasonable*.

4.52 There is no comprehensive right to picket enshrined in statute. However, the courts have come to recognize the civil liberties aspects of picketing, on both sides of the divide. In *Hubbard v Pitt*,[71] Lord Denning MR said:

Picketing is lawful so long as it is done merely to obtain or communicate information, or peacefully to persuade; and is not such as to submit any other person to any kind of

---

[67] Hugh Collins, KD Ewing, and Aileen McColgan, *Labour Law: Text & Materials* (2005) pp 915–16.
[68] See in particular Ch 2 for offences of obstructing a police officer in the execution of his duty; assaulting a police officer in the execution of his duty; and watching and besetting.
[69] *Ex parte Lewis* (1888) 21 QBD 191, 197.
[70] [1976] QB 142.
[71] Ibid, 177.

constraint or restriction of his personal freedom: see *Hunt v Broome* [1974] AC 587, 597 per Lord Reid.

Picketing in the employment law context

The statutory protection for peaceful picketing in the context of employment disputes is to be found in s 220 of the Trade Union and Labour Relations (Consolidation) Act 1992 which provides as follows: **4.53**

> *Peaceful Picketing*
> 220 (1) It is lawful for a person in contemplation or furtherance of a trade dispute to attend—
> (a) at or near his own place of work, or
> (b) if he is an official of a trade union, at or near the place of work of a member of a union whom he is accompanying and whom he represents,
> for the purpose only of peacefully obtaining or communicating information, or peacefully persuading any person to work or abstain from working.

The first point of note is that s 220(1) potentially provides the defence of 'lawful authority'[72] for what would otherwise be obstruction of the highway 'at *or near* his own place of work'.[73] Nevertheless, whether the picket is actually near the place of work will be a matter of fact and degree for the magistrates. **4.54**

Secondly, the 'lawful authority' is strictly limited to activity which is 'for the purpose *only* of peacefully obtaining or communicating information, or peacefully persuading any person to work or abstain from working'.[74] Thus, any activity which exceeds the ambit of that definition section will not be protected by the statute. **4.55**

In *Broome v DPP*,[75] the appellant was a trade union official who had been convicted of obstruction of the highway. He had been picketing outside a building site in Stockport during a national strike. A lorry driver called Dickinson called at the site and was accosted by the appellant, who tried to dissuade him from entering and delivering supplies. However, it transpired that the driver was at the wrong site. He departed for the correct site in Short Street and he told the appellant of his destination. The appellant took a short cut to Short Street and again asked Dickinson to draw to the side of the road and endeavoured to persuade him not to enter the site. After a few minutes of conversation, Dickinson was not persuaded and manoeuvred his vehicle to enter the site. At that point, the appellant stood in front of the lorry holding a poster, shouting in a renewed effort to persuade the driver from delivering his supplies. The driver asked him to move, but he refused. A police inspector intervened and told the appellant that the driver wished to enter the site. The appellant said he would not allow him to do so. The police inspector warned him that if he did not move aside he would be arrested. The appellant refused to move and so was arrested. The appellant's argument was that this was an entirely peaceful picket **4.56**

---

[72] Highways Act 1980, s 137, and see discussion of lawful authority above.
[73] Trade Union and Labour Relations (Consolidation) Act 1992, s 220(1)(a).
[74] Ibid, s 220(1).
[75] [1974] 2 WLR 58. The case is also known as *Hunt v Broome*.

which lasted no more than a few minutes and that the picket was protected by statutory authority.[76]

4.57   The House of Lords accepted that the statute potentially provided 'lawful authority' for what would otherwise have been an offence of obstructing the highway. However, in Broome's case, by detaining the driver and refusing to allow him to enter after his powers of persuasion had failed, his conduct exceeded the ambit of the statutory protection and therefore it provided no defence. In the leading speech, Lord Reid said:

> His attendance there is only made lawful by [the] subsection . . . if he attended only for the purpose of obtaining or communicating information or 'peacefully persuading' the lorry driver. Attendance for that purpose must I think include the right to try to persuade anyone who chooses to stop and listen, at least so far as this is done in a reasonable way with due consideration for the rights of others. A right to attend for the purpose of peaceful persuasion would be meaningless unless this were implied . . .

> But I see no ground for implying any right to require the person who it is sought to persuade to submit to any kind of constraint or restriction of his personal freedom. One is familiar with persons at the side of the road signalling to a driver requesting him to stop. It is then for the driver to decide whether he will stop or not. That, in my view, a picket is entitled to do. If the driver stops, the picket can talk to him but only for so long as the driver is willing to listen. That must be so because if the picket had the statutory right to stop or to detain the driver that must necessarily imply that the Act has imposed on those passing along the road a statutory duty to remain for longer that they chose to stay.[77]

4.58   Ominously, Lord Reid went on to say that an alternative purpose, in excess of that permitted by statute, could be inferred by sheer weight of numbers:

> [I]f a picket has a purpose beyond those set out in the section, then his presence becomes unlawful and in many cases such as I have supposed it would not be difficult to infer as a matter of fact that pickets in unreasonably large numbers do have the purpose of preventing free passage. If that were the proper inference then their presence on the highway would become unlawful.[78]

4.59   Thus, in *Tynan v Balmer*[79] it was held that some forty pickets on the move circling around the main entrance to a factory was an unreasonable use of the highway and therefore an obstruction of the highway.

4.60   The third, rather obvious, point is that the picketing must be 'peaceful'. The only lawful purpose of picketing permitted by s 220 is '*peacefully* obtaining or communicating information, or *peacefully* persuading any person to work or abstain from working'. Clearly, any violent or threatening conduct may be dealt with under the various offences of the Public Order Act 1986 discussed in Chapter 1 or the other offences discussed in Chapter 2, such as obstruction of a police officer[80] or obstruction of the highway,[81] disscussed in this Chapter.

---

[76] At that time, the statutory authority was the Industrial Relations Act 1971, s 134—which was framed in almost identical terms to the present Trade Union and Labour Relations (Consolidation) Act 1992, s 220.

[77] [1974] 2 WLR 58, 63–4.

[78] Ibid, p 64.

[79] [1967] 1 QB 91.

[80] See Ch 2.

[81] See above at 4.19 et seq.

Picketing and breach of the peace

The power of arrest for an anticipated breach of the peace is often used in the context of **4.61** picketing. A police officer (indeed any citizen) has the common law power to take preventative action short of arrest where he reasonably believes a breach of the peace is 'imminent'.[82] The preventive action taken must be reasonable and proportionate; and there is no power to take action short of an arrest when a breach of the peace is not so imminent as would be necessary to justify arrest: *R (Laporte) v Chief Constable of Gloucestershire Constabulary*.[83]

In the context of picketing, the police have often sought to use this power to take preventa- **4.62** tive action. The case of *Piddington v Bates*[84] concerned the policing of a picket at a printers' works. The premises had a front and a back entrance. Some eighteen men arrived wearing picket badges. A police constable informed them that, in his view, two pickets were suffi-cient at each of the front and rear entrances. The appellant said that he was going to the back entrance and that, if the constable wished to prevent him, he had better arrest him. He then gently pushed past the constable and was gently arrested on the grounds that, in the officer's view, picketing by more than two persons at each entrance might lead to intimida-tion and a breach of the peace—unless steps were taken to prevent it. In the Divisional Court, upholding the conviction, Lord Parker CJ said that for preventative action to be taken the constable must reasonably anticipate a real, not a remote, possibility of a breach of the peace.[85]

However, in *R (Laporte) v Chief Constable of Gloucestershire Constabulary*[86] Lord Bingham **4.63** of Cornhill said that he respectfully regarded *Piddington v Bates* as 'an aberrant decision'. He said 'it is not enough to justify action that a breach of the peace is anticipated to be a real possibility'. The test is whether there exists a reasonable apprehension that a breach of the peace is 'imminent'. The term 'imminent' is to be applied narrowly[87] and connotes a sense of immediacy[88]—that is the breach of the peace is about to happen[89] unless preventative action is taken.

The case of *Moss v McLachlan*[90] arose in the context of the 1984–5 miners' strike, where **4.64** there was violent conflict in the Nottinghamshire coalfields between striking members of the National Union of Mine Workers, and working miners, many of whom belonged to the Union of Democratic Mine Workers. The latter were determined to continue working, the former equally determined to stop them. The police struggled to keep the peace and there were ugly clashes. The appellants were four of approximately sixty striking miners intent on

---

[82] *Albert v Lavin* [1982] AC 546. See also breach of the peace powers at 6.125 et seq below.
[83] [2007] 2 AC 105, [2007] 2 WLR 46. See also 3.02, 4.63 et seq; 10.38, and 10.80.
[84] [1961] 1 WLR 162.
[85] Ibid, p 169.
[86] *Laporte*, para 47.
[87] Ibid, see especially Lord Mance at para 141.
[88] *R v Howell* [1982] QB 416: 'the arrestor reasonably believes that such a breach will be committed in the immediate future'.
[89] *Redmond-Bate v Director of Public Prosecutions* (1999) 163 JP 789, 791 per Sedley LJ. In that case, the agreed issue was whether it was reasonable for a constable, in the light of what he perceived, to believe that the appellant, a female lay preacher, was 'about to cause' a breach of the peace—a test equated with imminence.
[90] [1985] IRLR 76.

a mass demonstration at one of several nearby collieries. They were stopped in their car by the police less than five minutes' drive from the nearest pit, where the police feared a violent episode. The men tried to push on and were arrested. In the judgment of the Divisional Court, Skinner J said that the fact the men were in 'close proximity both in place and time' meant that a breach of the peace was 'imminent and immediate'.[91]

4.65 That case was cited with approval by the House of Lords in *R (Laporte) v Chief Constable of Gloucestershire Constabulary*.[92] However, Lord Mance went further and was clear to reject the idea that imminence could be understood in a flexible sense:

> [I reject] the suggestion [in *Moss v McLachlan*] that imminence is a flexible concept, different degrees of which may justify different forms of preventative action. I regard the reasonable apprehension of an imminent breach of the peace to be an important threshold requirement, which must exist before any form of preventative action is permissible at common law. Where reasonable apprehension of an imminent breach of the peace exists, then the preventative action must be reasonable and proportionate. But the threshold for preventative action is neither a broad test of reasonableness nor flexible.[93]

4.66 Fourthly, then, where there is a reasonable apprehension of an imminent breach of the peace, the police may take such steps as are reasonable and proportionate to prevent it. Those steps may include imposing restrictions on the numbers participating in a picket (*Piddington v Bates*[94]) or setting up road blocks to prevent people attending pickets (*Moss v McLachlan*[95]) —but only where those steps are reasonable and proportionate to the nature of the imminent breach of the peace in the circumstances of each case. Blanket restrictions as a matter of policy laid down in advance of any picket are unlikely to meet that test.

4.67 Fifthly, in extreme and exceptional circumstances, where there are simply no other means whatsoever whereby an imminent breach of the peace can be obviated, reasonable and proportionate preventative action may be taken by the police, even against innocent third parties: *Austin and Saxby v Commissioner of Police of the Metropolis*.[96] So for example, the presence of innocent third parties holding a perfectly lawful meeting (or picket) might incite an imminent breach of the peace by an opposing group. Where all possible practical steps have been taken (including making advance preparations and imposing conditions) to deal with the anticipated breach of the peace by the opposing group and there is a reasonable belief that there are no other means to prevent an imminent breach of

---

[91] In *Foy v Chief Constable of Kent*, unreported, 20 March 1984, the same 'intercept policy' was applied to stop a group of Kent miners at the Dartford Tunnel, some 200 miles from their destination of the Nottingham coalfields. The miners ultimately abandoned their application for an interim injunction to restrain the Chief Constable. Some 25 years on, in the light of *Laporte*, it is submitted that this case would have to be decided differently today.

[92] *Laporte*. See Lord Bingham of Cornhill at para 51 and Lord Rodger of Earlsferry at paras 70–1.

[93] Ibid, para 140–1.

[94] Op cit.

[95] Op cit.

[96] [2007] EWCA Civ 989, [2008] 2 WLR 415, CA, following the *obiter* speeches of Lords Rodger and Mance in *R (Laporte) v Chief Constable of Gloucestershire Constabulary* [2007] 2 WLR 46.

the peace, the police may be entitled (where it is strictly necessary) to disperse the meeting or picket.[97]

Consumer picketing

Thus far, we have only discussed the law of the highway as it pertains to picketing in the **4.68** area of labour disputes. However, a significant feature of protesting in the modern setting is consumer picketing, for example anti-apartheid activists seeking to boycott Barclay's bank in the 1970s and 1980s. In *Hubbard v Pitt*[98] Lord Denning MR said:

> I see no valid reason for distinguishing between picketing in furtherance of a trade dispute and picketing in furtherance of other causes. Why should workers be allowed to picket and other people not? I do not think there is any difference drawn by the law save that, in the case of a trade dispute, picketing is covered by statutory provisions:[99] and, in the case of other causes, it is left to the common law. But, broadly speaking, they are in line one with the other.

The case of *Hubbard v Pitt* concerned a group of local residents in the London Borough of **4.69** Islington who regularly picketed outside a local estate agent's office complaining that his commercial activities were forcing out working class tenants in favour of well-to-do families and changing the character of the area. The estate agent sought an injunction which was granted. The Court of Appeal upheld the injunction, but Lord Denning MR (dissenting) said he would have dismissed the injunction. He said that the trial judge's ruling that the right to picket was confined to the context of industrial disputes should not be allowed to stand. In an enduring judgment, Lord Denning concluded that the consumer pickets were not unlawful: they behaved in an orderly and peaceful manner throughout; they were arranged with the full knowledge and agreement of the police; the presence of half a dozen people on a Saturday morning for three hours was not an unreasonable use of the highway and did not interfere with the free passage of other people to and fro; there was nothing in the nature of a public nuisance, no crowds gathered, no queues were formed, no obstruction caused, no breaches of the peace; nor was it a nuisance for people to attend at or near the plaintiff's premises in order to communicate information or in order peacefully to persuade, unless associated with obstruction, violence, intimidation, molestation, or threats.

The case of *Hirst and Agu v Chief Constable of West Yorkshire*[100] also concerned a consumer **4.70** boycott of a furrier's shop in Bradford by a group of animal rights activists. In that case, both Glidewell LJ and Otton J (Divisional Court) cited with approval the dissenting remarks of Lord Denning MR in *Hubbard v Pitt*. They held that the convictions for

---

[97] Ibid, see in particular the Court of Appeal's judgment at para 35, in which Sir Anthony Clarke MR, advances a series of propositions distilled from the authorities. The Court of Appeal placed great reliance on the Irish nineteenth-century case of *O'Kelly v Harvey* (1883) 14 LR Ir 105.

[98] [1976] QB 142, 177.

[99] Thus, a consumer picket could not claim 'lawful authority' for obstructing the highway by virtue of the Trade Union and Labour Relations (Consolidation) Act 1992, s 220.

[100] (1987) 85 Cr App R 143. See full discussion of this case above in relation to the offence of obstruction of the highway.

obstructing the highway should be quashed because the lower court had failed to consider the reasonableness of the pickets' use of the highway.

4.71 However, *Hubbard v Pitt* was prescient. The way in which consumer pickets are often now dealt with is not through the criminal law but by civil law injunctions.[101]

F. Police Road Blocks

4.72 There are a range of police powers[102] which concern the use of the highway as it relates to public order law.

At common law

4.73 The police have the power, 'in very exceptional circumstances', to erect and maintain a full cordon upon the highway around a group of protestors in order to prevent an imminent breach of the peace. So long as it continues to be necessary to prevent disorder, reasonable and proportionate, such a cordon will not amount to a deprivation of liberty under Article 5 of the European Convention, even when it continues for several hours: *Austin and Another v Commissioner of Police of the Metropolis*.[103]

4.74 In *Austin* the House of Lords considered the controversial police technique of 'kettling'. That case arose from the May Day demonstrations of 2001. The demonstration was planned and the police were aware of it, but the organizers had deliberately given no notice to the police and had refused to cooperate with them. Thus the police were taken by surprise when some 3,000 protestors entered Oxford Circus in London at 2pm. Police intelligence suggested there was a hard core of 500–1,000 people intent on violent confrontation amongst the demonstrators (though there were also non-demonstrators caught up in the crowd). Accordingly, the police set up cordons at each of the exits to Oxford Circus. The plan was to control the release and dispersal of the crowd. However, the trial judge found, a large proportion of the crowd were openly hostile to the police and thus delayed the controlled release. In the result, many of the 3,000 were detained within the cordon for up to seven hours, without food, shelter, or toilet facilities. Ms Austin had an 11-month-old baby whom she needed to collect from a child minder. The Court of Appeal said that although this situation was 'a serious interference with human dignity',[104] it did not amount to a deprivation of liberty under Article 5 of the European Convention. The House of Lords upheld that ruling, approving the distinction made between a restriction of the liberty of movement and a deprivation of liberty under Article 5.

4.75 A police constable has the power to stop and turn back motor vehicles if he has reasonable grounds for apprehension that a breach of the peace is imminent: *Moss v McLachlan*.[105] However, the test of imminence is to be applied strictly and the preventative measure of

---

[101] For a full discussion of injunctions see Ch 9.
[102] For a full discussion of police powers, please see Chs 6 and 7.
[103] [2009] UKHL 5. For *Austin* and 'kettling' see also 3.32, 4.67, 6.162 et seq; 10.164, and 10.167 et seq.
[104] [2007] EWCA Civ 989, [2008] 2 WLR 415, para 8.
[105] [1985] IRLR 76 DC.

turning back a vehicle must be reasonable and proportionate to the anticipated breach of the peace: *Laporte*.[106]

A constable has the power at common law to control traffic on public roads: *Gelberg v Miller*[107] and also *Daniel v Morrison*.[108] A constable may also cause others to disobey traffic regulations, but only when life and/or property are at risk: *Johnson v Phillips*.[109] **4.76**

Police and Criminal Evidence Act 1984

Section 4(1) of the Police and Criminal Evidence Act 1984 permits a police officer, on **4.77** written authorization by an officer not below the rank of superintendent,[110] to conduct 'road checks' for the purpose of ascertaining whether a vehicle is carrying

(a) a person who has committed an offence other than a road traffic offence or a [vehicle] excise offence;
(b) a person who is a witness to such an offence;
(c) a person intending to commit such an offence; or
(d) a person who is unlawfully at large.

Road checks are limited to a particular 'locality' for up to seven days[111] (although this is **4.78** renewable) and must be based on a reasonable suspicion that the person is in the locality.

Section 1 of the Police and Criminal Evidence Act 1984 also provides that a constable, **4.79** whether in uniform or not, may stop and search any person or vehicle, and may detain the person or vehicle for the purpose of searching, provided he has reasonable grounds to suspect that he will find stolen or prohibited articles eg offensive weapons.

Terrorism Act 2000

Section 44 of the Terrorism Act 2000 provides a power of stop and search, the exercise of **4.80** which is governed by s 45. When an authorization is given under s 44, any constable in uniform is authorized

(a) to stop a vehicle in an area or at a specified place and to search (i) the vehicle, (ii) the driver of the vehicle, (iii) a passenger in the vehicle, and (iv) anything in or on the vehicle or carried by the driver or a passenger; and
(b) to stop a pedestrian in an area or at a specified place and to search (i) the pedestrian, and (ii) anything carried by him.

For the authorization to be given, the person giving it must consider it 'expedient' for the **4.81** prevention of acts of terrorism (s 44(3)).

---

[106] [2006] UKHL 55, [2007] 2 AC 105, [2007] 2 WLR 46.
[107] [1961] 1 All ER 291.
[108] (1980) 70 Cr App R 142.
[109] [1975] 3 All ER 682.
[110] Unless it is 'a matter of urgency' in which case an officer below the rank of superintendent may authorize such a road check: see Police and Criminal Evidence Act 1984, s 4(5) and (6).
[111] Ibid, s 4(12). See 6.119.

4.82   Once 'authorization' has been given, however, a constable does not require reasonable grounds for suspicion (s 45(1)), as he would under s 1 or s 4 of the Police and Criminal Evidence Act 1984. However, s 44 powers may be exercised only for the purpose of searching for articles of a kind which could be used in connection with terrorism. A constable may seize and retain an article which he discovers in the course of a s 44 search and which he reasonably suspects is intended to be used in connection with terrorism (s 45(2)). A constable exercising this power may not require a person to remove any clothing in public except for headgear, footwear, an outer coat, a jacket, or gloves (s 45(3)).[112]

4.83   If a constable proposes to search a person or vehicle under s 44, he may detain the person or vehicle for such time as is reasonably required to permit the search to be carried out at or near the place where the person or vehicle is stopped. If a person or vehicle is stopped under s 44, a written statement is to be provided. Moreover, the vehicle driver or the pedestrian may request a written statement that it or they were stopped by virtue of s 44. Such an application must be made within twelve months of the stop (s 45(4)–(6)). Under s 47, any person who fails to stop a vehicle when required to do so by a constable acting under a s 44 authorization, or who wilfully obstructs a constable exercising such a power, commits a summary offence. It is punishable by up to six months' imprisonment or a fine up to level 5, or both.

4.84   The House of Lords examined the legality of the use of s 44 powers in *R (Gillan) v Metropolitan Police Commissioner*.[113] In August 2003, the Assistant Commissioner of the Metropolitan Police authorized the use of s 44 across the whole Metropolitan Police District for a period of twenty-eight days, the maximum possible period.[114] Mr Gillan was a PhD student on his way to protest peacefully at an arms fair being held at the ExCel Centre in the Docklands area of east London. He was stopped at random by two police officers. They searched his rucksack for 'articles concerned with terrorism' under s 44. They found nothing incriminating. The incident lasted no more than twenty minutes. Likewise, Ms Quinton was a freelance journalist on her way to film the same protest. She was wearing a photographer's jacket and carrying a camera. Upon being stopped by a police officer, she produced her press pass. Nevertheless, she was searched for articles connected with terrorism. The police search form records the encounter as lasting no more than five minutes. Ms Quinton estimated it lasted more like thirty minutes. The Divisional Court dismissed the claimants challenge to the legality of the use of s 44, as did the Court of Appeal.

---

[112] Where the stop and search under the Police and Criminal Evidence Act 1984, s 1 is conducted in public view, it is similarly limited to outer clothing. Any search which requires the removal of more than outer clothing cannot be conducted in public see s 2(9)(a) of the 1984 Act and Code A para 3.5. However, the Terrorism Act 2000, s 44 goes further by empowering a constable to require the removal of footwear and headgear in public.

[113] [2006] 2 AC 307. For a discussion of these powers see Clive Walker, '"Know Thine Enemy as Thyself": Discerning Friend from Foe under Anti-terrorism Laws' (2008) 32 University of Melbourne Law Review 275. See also 6.87 et seq and 10.87 below.

[114] In fact, there had been a succession of authorizations since the Act came into force in February 2001, of which the authorization in August 2003 was only the latest.

The House of Lords also dismissed the appeal. Lord Bingham gave the leading speech in which he began by recognizing that: **4.85**

> it is an old and cherished tradition of our country that everyone should be free to go about their business in the streets of the land, confident that they will not be stopped and searched by the police unless reasonably suspected of having committed a criminal offence. So jealously has this tradition been guarded that it has almost become a constitutional principle. But it is not an absolute rule. There are, and have for some years been, statutory exceptions to it.[115]

He held that as a matter of construction, the word 'expedient' under s 44(3) has a meaning quite distinct from 'necessary'. Thus, in order for an authorization to be given under s 44, the decision-making officer did not require reasonable grounds for considering that the powers were necessary and suitable for the prevention of terrorism—only that it was 'expedient' to do so. Moreover, the Act put in place a series of safeguards and restraints on the use of the power—including time limits, geographical areas, the rank of the authorizing officer, and confirmation by the Home Secretary. **4.86**

The House of Lords also held that the powers did not conflict with the European Convention on Human Rights. A stop and search did not involve 'a deprivation of liberty' within the meaning of Article 5 because the stop would ordinarily be for a very brief period of time and did not involve the stopped person being arrested, handcuffed, confined, or removed to a different place. Thus, the action was more properly to be described as being detained in the sense of being kept from proceeding or being kept waiting. If it did amount to a detention, it could be justified as being 'in order to secure the fulfilment of any obligation prescribed by law' as set out in Article 5(1)(b). In relation to the right to privacy, the intrusion would normally be insufficiently serious to engage Article 8. If it did, a proper exercise of the power could be justified as being in pursuit of a legitimate aim and proportionate under Article 8(2). If the power was properly exercised it was difficult to see how it could infringe Articles 10 (right to freedom of expression) and 11 (right to freedom of assembly), but if it was misused then they could be infringed. If either were engaged then, provided that the exercise of the power was lawful, it would be expected that the justifications of those articles would also apply. In each case the provision had to be 'lawful' for the purposes of the European Convention in that the exercise of the power to stop and search had to be governed by rules of law which were not arbitrary but were clear and accessible. The law was held to be sufficiently clear and free from arbitrariness. **4.87**

In January 2010, in *Gillan and Quinton v United Kingdom* (Application no. 4158/05), the European Court of Human Rights (fourth section) took a very different view from the House of Lords in relation to Article 5. The Court went on to hold that there had been a violation of Article 8 (right to privacy) because the interference was not in accordance with the rule of law. For a more detailed discussion of the Strasbourg judgment see 6.87 et seq. **4.87A**

Under s 48 of the Terrorism Act 2000 'authorization' may be given to prohibit or restrict the parking of vehicles on a specified road if the person giving it considers it 'expedient for **4.88**

---

[115] Ibid, para 1, p 332.

the prevention of acts of terrorism' (s 48(1) and (2)). The power may then be exercised by a constable placing a traffic sign on the road concerned (s 49(1)). A constable exercising the power may suspend a parking place (s 49(2)).

4.89 The period of authorization must not exceed twenty-eight days (s 50(1) and (2)). An authorization may be renewed in writing by the authorizer or by a person who could have authorized it and s 50 applies as if it were a new authorization (s 50(3)).

4.90 Section 51 of the Terrorism Act 2000 makes it an offence for any person who contravenes any relevant restriction or prohibition on parking. It is a defence for a person charged under s 51 to show to the balance of probabilities that he had a 'reasonable excuse' for the act or omission in question (s 51(3)). Under s 51(4), possession of a current disabled person's badge does not of itself constitute a reasonable excuse.

4.91 The offences under s 51 are triable summarily only. For an offence contrary to s 51(1), a person is liable to a fine not exceeding level 4 (s 51(5)). For the offence contrary to s 51(2), a person is liable to imprisonment for a term not exceeding three months, a fine not exceeding level 4 on the standard scale, or both (s 51(6)).

Criminal Justice and Public Order Act 1994

4.92 Where incidents of serious violence are reasonably believed to be imminent, the authorization of the use of s 60 of the Criminal Justice and Public Order Act 1994 enables police officers in uniform to stop any pedestrian or vehicle in order to search for offensive weapons or dangerous implements. Like s 44 of the Terrorism Act 2000, the officer does not require reasonable grounds for suspecting that the stopped person is carrying such articles. All that is required is that the conditions for authorization and the duration of the authorization set out in s 60 are met.

4.93 Any person who fails to stop, or to stop a vehicle, when required to do so by a police officer acting in the exercise of his powers conferred by s 60, shall be guilty of an offence and upon summary conviction liable to imprisonment for a term not exceeding one month or a fine not exceeding level 3 on the standard scale, or both.

G. By-laws

4.94 Many activities on the highway and in other public places such as parks and gardens are restricted by virtue of by-laws. A by-law is a local law made by a local government authority, who are authorized to make such laws by various enabling statutes. Once drafted by the local authority, the by-laws must be confirmed by the relevant Secretary of State, designated in the enabling statute, before they have the force of law. Sections 236–238 of the Local Government Act 1972 provide the correct procedure by which by-laws are enacted and confirmed. A copy of the by-laws in force in the local area must be available for inspection at the local town hall and on sale for a small payment.

4.95 For example, s 235 of the Local Government Act 1972 enables district councils in England; councils for principal areas in Wales; and London Boroughs to make by-laws for 'good rule and government' and for the 'prevention and suppression of nuisance therein'. This general power has been used to address a wondrous variety of minor nuisances from 'wilful jostling' and 'indecent bathing' to 'noisy hawking' and 'flags'.

By-laws have sometimes been used as a way to counter demonstrations. In the 'climate camp' demonstrations against Kingsnorth power station in Kent in August 2008, the police learned that protestors aimed to take to the River Medway in home-made rafts or coracles, dressed as pirates, as part of the Great Rebel Raft Regatta. The police sought a method of preventing this and so, in coordination with the local harbour master, invoked the Medway Ports Authority Bylaws 1991 which stated that any regattas or other processions on the river required the permission of the harbour master. Since no notice had been given and no permission sought, the harbour master issued a 'special direction' under s 21 of the Medway Ports Authority Act 1973 directing the pirate coracles off the water, in order to ensure 'the safety of navigation'. When the pirates refused to comply with that direction issued by a police officer acting on the authority of the harbour master, they were charged (and ultimately convicted) of obstructing a police officer in the execution of his duty.[116]   **4.96**

The penalty for infringing a by-law is a fine at the level set out in the by-law or, where not expressed, a fine not exceeding level 2.[117]   **4.97**

Responsibility for instituting criminal proceedings under a by-law is usually designated in the enabling legislation.   **4.98**

When a charge is brought, a defendant may challenge the validity of a by-law (notwithstanding the fact that it has been confirmed by the Secretary of State) on the grounds that it is *ultra vires* (outside the power) of the enabling statute and/or obviously unreasonable or inconsistent with or repugnant to the general law. The magistrates are bound to decide on any objection to the validity of the by-law, as part of the trial at the first instance. Thereafter, an appeal against their decision lies to the Divisional Court by way of case stated.   **4.99**

For an example of a successful *ultra vires* challenge to by-laws in the context of political protest see *Tabernacle v Secretary of State for Defence*.[118] That case involved a challenge by way of judicial review (rather than in the course of criminal proceedings) by members of the Aldermaston Women's Peace Camp to the validity of the Atomic Weapons Establishment (AWE) Aldermaston Byelaws 2007 regulation 7(2)(f), which prohibited camping in 'Controlled Areas' near the nuclear weapons base. The Court of Appeal held that the by-laws violated the rights of Aldermaston Women's Peace Camp (which had been assembling peacefully at the site for over twenty-three years) to freedom of expression and association under Articles 10 and 11 of the European Convention on Human Rights and as a result were *ultra vires*.   **4.100**

An important aspect of that judgment concerned the 'manner and form' argument. Often, the State will seek to argue that the restrictions imposed on a demonstration—whether by conditions under s 14 of the Public Order Act 1986 or by-laws or some other legal   **4.101**

---

[116] For an analysis of this offence see Ch 2 at 2.12 et seq.
[117] Local Government Act 1972, s 237.
[118] [2009] EWCA Civ 23.

mechanism—do not extinguish the essence of the right to free expression but merely the 'manner and form' of its exercise.[119] Thus, in the case of the Aldermaston Women's Peace Camp, the Secretary of State's argument was that the women were free to protest all they wanted about nuclear weapons, but were simply prohibited from camping in a Controlled Area. Giving the judgment of the Court of Appeal, Laws LJ said that such arguments should be 'treated with considerable care'[120] and in this case carried 'little weight'.[121] Laws LJ explained:

> [The] 'manner and form' may constitute the actual nature and quality of the protest; it may have acquired a symbolic force inseparable from the protestors' message; it may be the very witness of their beliefs. It takes little imagination to perceive, as I would hold, that that is the case here. As I have said, the AWPC has been established for something like 23 years. Some of those involved may have been steadfast participants the whole time. Others will have come and gone. But the camp has borne consistent, long-standing, and peaceful witness to the convictions of the women who have belonged to it. To them, and (it may fairly be assumed) to many who support them, and indeed to others who disapprove and oppose them, the 'manner and form' *is* the protest itself.[122]

4.102 For a more detailed discussion of by-laws see 3.152–61 (see also 5.149–51).

H. Street-based Prostitution

4.103 There are a number of street-based prostitution offences which concern the highway and public order. It is not an offence to engage in prostitution *per se*. Instead, the law seeks to curtail the *public* activities of prostitutes, their pimps, and clientele. The gravamen of these offences is not the sexual exploitation of women (or men) but the nuisance factor and annoyance caused to local residents and passers-by as a result of prostitutes soliciting on the street or of prospective clients kerb crawling in search of prostitutes. Accordingly, in construction and purpose, these are not so much sexual offences as public order offences.

4.104 Prior to the Street Offences Act 1959, street-based prostitution was prosecuted in various ways—most commonly under s 3 of the Vagrancy Act 1824[123] which made it an offence for a 'common prostitute' to engage in 'riotous or indecent behaviour' whilst wandering in a public street or place of public resort. Alternatively, it was prosecuted under various local Acts or by-laws aimed at suppressing 'annoyance' or 'nuisance' by the activities of prostitutes.

4.105 The law was reformed as a result of the Wolfenden Committee,[124] which reported in 1957[125] and led to the Street Offences Act 1959. That the principal aim of these

---

[119] The distinction between a right's essence and the manner and form of its exercise has long been recognized in the jurisprudence of the European Court of Human Rights see: *Ziliberberg v Moldova* (Application 61821/00) (and see 10.111 below); *Ashingdan v United Kingdom* (1985) 7 EHRR 528, para 57; *F v Switzerland* (1987) 10 EHRR 411; and *Rai, Allmond & 'Negotiate Now' v United Kingdom* (1995) 19 EHRR CD 93.

[120] Ibid, para 35.

[121] Ibid, para 38.

[122] Ibid, para 37.

[123] 5 Geo 4 c 83.

[124] Chaired by Sir John Wolfenden.

[125] Report of the Wolfenden Committee, Cmnd 247 (1957).

street-based offences was to address public order issues was plain from the Wolfenden Committee's report. It took the view that prostitution itself should not be outlawed because, 'no amount of legislation directed towards its abolition will abolish it'.[126] Instead,

> What the law can and should do is to ensure that the streets of London and our big provincial cities should be freed from what is offensive and injurious and made tolerable for the ordinary citizen who lives in them and passes through them.

That thread runs throughout the Street Offences Act 1959 and the street-based prostitution offences which appeared in the subsequent Sexual Offences Act 1985 and Sexual Offences Act 2003. **4.106**

The three offences of 'street-prostitution' we examine here are **4.107**

(a) loitering or soliciting;
(b) kerb crawling; and
(c) persistent soliciting.

Loitering or soliciting

Section 1 of the Street Offences Act 1959 provides as follows: **4.108**

> (1) It shall be an offence for a common prostitute (whether male or female[127]) to loiter or solicit in a street or public place for the purpose of prostitution.

Jurisdiction and penalty

The offence under s 1 is triable only on summary jurisdiction before the magistrates' court (s 1(2)). The maximum penalty is a fine not exceeding level 2 on the standard scale or for an offence committed after 'a previous conviction',[128] to a fine not exceeding level 3 on that scale.[129] Moreover, this offence is likely to attract an anti-social behaviour order (ASBO) under the Crime and Disorder Act 1998.[130] **4.109**

Essential elements

There are four essential elements to this offence, though it may be committed in alternative ways, for example by loitering *or* soliciting in a street *or* a public place. Let us briefly examine those essential elements: **4.110**

- common prostitute;
- loiter or solicit;
- street or public place; and
- for the purpose of prostitution.

---

[126] Ibid, para 225.
[127] The addition of the clause '(whether male or female)' was inserted by the Sexual Offences Act 2003, s 56 and Sch 1—in force as of 1 May 2004.
[128] See 9.178 et seq.
[129] That this offence is met with a financial penalty is ironical—for there is often only one obvious way of paying off the fine. Often, prostitutes have been imprisoned for non-payment of fines.
[130] See Chapter 9.

Common prostitute

4.111   'Prostitute' has never been defined in statute. At common law, the case of *de Munck*[131] established that sexual intercourse is not a vital element. Darling J famously stated that 'prostitution is proved if it is shown that a woman offers her body commonly for lewdness for payment in return'.[132] That definition should not be taken to mean offers her body in a passive or submissive role as opposed to an active role.[133] However, there must be an offer of some direct physical contact of a sexual nature: *Armhouse Lee Ltd v Chappell*.[134]

4.112   It is immaterial whether the sexual services are actually carried out or intended to be carried out. The essence of prostitution is the making of an *offer* of sexual services in return for a reward. The mischief that the Act intended to address was the harassment and nuisance to members of the public on the streets by prostitutes offering sex for reward: *McFarlane*.[135]

4.113   The term 'common prostitute' now refers to both male and female prostitutes. Section 1(1) of the 1959 Act had to be amended by the Sexual Offences Act 2003[136] to insert the words 'whether male or female'. Prior to that amendment, it was clear from the Wolfenden Report and the history of the Bill's passage through Parliament the term 'common prostitute' had meant only female and not male prostitutes: *DPP v Bull*.[137]

4.114   The word 'common' is not mere surplusage. It denotes a prostitute who offers him or herself commonly ie 'who is prepared for reward to engage in acts of lewdness with all and sundry, or with anyone who may hire her [or him] for that purpose', as opposed to a single act of lewdness for reward: *R v Morris-Lowe*.[138]

Loiter or solicit

4.115   'Loiter or solicit' should be read as alternatives, so that s 1(1) of the 1959 Act in fact creates two offences—though there is a degree of overlap.

4.116   'Loiter' appears to cover a wider range of behaviour than 'solicit'. Loitering is simply lingering with no intent to move on either by foot or in a vehicle.[139] According to the editors of

---

[131]   [1918] 1 KB 635.

[132]   Ibid, p 637.

[133]   *Webb* [1964] 1 QB 357.

[134]   The Times, 7 August 1996, DC. That case concerned a woman who engaged in telephone sex conversations for reward.

[135]   (1994) 99 Cr App R 8. In that case Lord Taylor CJ, giving the judgment of the Court of Appeal, declined to distinguish between a 'clipper' (a woman who offered sexual services in return for payment in advance, never intending to provide them) and a 'hooker' (a woman who did intend to provide the sexual services she offered for reward).

[136]   Sexual Offences Act 2003, s 56 and Sch 1—in force from 1 May 2004.

[137]   [1995] 1 Cr App R 413.

[138]   [1985] 1 All ER 400. That case concerned a man who was charged with trying to procure women to become common prostitutes. He advertised in the local paper for young women to train as masseuses. His defence was that he had no intention of setting up a massage business but had simply wished to entice the women to engage in a single act of lewdness with him. The Court of Appeal said a single act would not have been sufficient to make the women 'common prostitutes'.

[139]   *Bridge v Campbell* (1947) 177 JP 444.

Rook and Ward on Sexual Offences[140] 'loitering' for the purpose of prostitution is an offence even though the prostitute does not actively solicit clients; simply lingering in the hope that clients will approach is sufficient.

'Solicit' then connotes some active display of invitation to the prospective client. However, that does not require the use of spoken words. A physical gesture or some other signal will suffice. In *Horton v Mead*,[141] a man was seen to enter some seven public lavatories in the Piccadilly Circus and Leicester Square area of London over the space of two hours, remaining in each for a prolonged period. In each he was seen to 'smile in the face of gentlemen, purse his lips and wriggle his body'. Moreover, in upholding the conviction the Court of Appeal said it is immaterial whether the signal reaches the mind of the intended recipient or is understood by him. It is the act of inviting, not the receiving of the invitation, that is essential. **4.117**

In *Behrendt v Burridge*[142] a woman advertised her services to passers-by by seating herself on a stool in a downstairs bay window of a house, illuminated by a red light. She sat 'silent and motionless'[143] dressed in a low-cut top and mini-skirt. However, two men were seen to enter the house and one was proved to have paid for sexual services. The Divisional Court held that although she had not actively approached any client by word or gesture, her presence at the window, in the circumstances described above, amounted to 'soliciting' in the sense of tempting or alluring prospective clients. According to Boreham J, 'This young woman . . . might just as well have had at her feet an advertisement saying, "I am a prostitute. I am ready and willing to give the services of a prostitute."'[144] Again, we can see the public order agenda of these offences. It is the public display to innocent passers-by that the offence seeks to prohibit. **4.118**

Street or public place

This element emphasizes the public order aspect of the offence. The terms 'street' and 'public place' are alternatives. The term 'street' is defined in s 1(4) of the 1959 Act: **4.119**

> For the purposes of this section 'street' includes any bridge, road, lane, footway, subway, square, court, alley or passage, whether a thoroughfare or not, which is for the time being open to the public; and the doorways and entrances of premises abutting on a street (as hereinbefore defined), and any ground adjoining and open to a street, shall be treated as forming part of the street.

As one can see, the term 'street' is drafted sufficiently widely to catch every area of public access and indeed some private places adjacent to the street. The fact that the definition begins with the word 'includes' suggests that the list is not exhaustive. **4.120**

---

[140] *Rook and Ward on Sexual Offences: Law & Practice* (2004) para 12.22, p 360.
[141] [1913] 1 KB 154—a case decided under the precursor to s 32 Sexual Offences Act 1956 (now repealed).
[142] (1976) 63 Cr App R 202.
[143] Ibid, p 206 per Boreham J.
[144] Ibid, p 206.

4.121   In *Smith v Hughes*,[145] the Divisional Court gave short shrift to the argument that a prostitute who solicited men from a balcony some ten feet above the pavement was not caught by the definition. Lord Parker CJ said:

> . . . it can matter little whether the prostitute is soliciting while in the street or standing in a doorway or on a balcony, or at a window, or whether the window is shut or open or half-open; in each case her solicitation is *projected to and addressed to somebody walking in the street*. For my part, I am content to base my decision on that ground and that ground alone.[146] (emphasis added)

4.122   Both *Smith v Hughes*[147] and *Behrendt v Burridge*[148] tend to confirm the public policy aim of the Act to enable people to walk along the street without being accosted by prostitutes. In both cases it was the potential 'victim' of the solicitation (or prospective client) who was 'in the street' rather than the prostitute herself.

4.123   'Public place' is not defined in the Act. It is difficult to see what other area might be a 'public place' that is not within the definition of 'street' under s 1(4). Whether a place is a street or a public place will be a question of fact and degree for the magistrates to determine.[149]

For the purpose of prostitution

4.124   The loitering or soliciting in the street or public place must be 'for the purpose of prostitution', which may be inferred from the circumstances.[150] As explained above in relation to the definition of 'common prostitute', the purpose of prostitution is not restricted to sexual intercourse but must involve an offer of some direct physical contact of a sexual nature for reward.[151]

Kerb crawling

4.125   Section 1 of the Sexual Offences Act 1985 defines the offence of 'kerb crawling' as follows:

> (1) A person commits an offence if he solicits another person (or different persons) for the purposes of prostitution—
> > (a) from a motor vehicle whilst it is in the street or public place; or
> > (b) in a street or public place while in the immediate vicinity of a motor vehicle that he has just got out of or off,
>
> persistently or in such a manner or in such circumstances as to be likely to cause annoyance to the person (or any of the persons) solicited, or nuisance to other persons in the neighbourhood.

---

[145] [1960] 1 WLR 830.
[146] Ibid, p 832.
[147] Ibid.
[148] (1976) 63 Cr App R 202.
[149] *Glynn v Simmonds* [1952] 2 All ER 57; *Elkins v Cartlidge* [1947] 1 All ER 829.
[150] *Knight v Fryer* [1976] Crim LR 322.
[151] *Armhouse Lee Ltd v Chappell*, The Times, 7 August 1996, DC.

Jurisdiction and penalty

The offence of kerb crawling is triable summarily only. The maximum penalty is a fine not **4.126** exceeding level 3 on the standard scale.[152] Moreover, this offence is likely to attract an ASBO under the Crime and Disorder Act 1998.[153]

Who can commit the offence?

Kerb crawling is, in effect, the corollary of soliciting. Whereas soliciting is the offence com- **4.127** mitted by the prostitute, kerb crawling is the offence committed by the prospective client. As originally framed in 1985, the offence could only be committed by a man soliciting a woman. However, as a result of amendment by the Sexual Offences Act 2003,[154] the offence is now gender-neutral and thus may be committed by either a man or a woman soliciting another person of either sex.

Essential elements

The offence of kerb crawling shares many of the same essential elements as soliciting, with **4.128** public order aspects of the offence to the forefront. The conduct must be either 'persistent' or such as is 'likely to cause annoyance' to the person solicited or likely to cause 'nuisance' to the neighbourhood. The essential elements are:

• solicits;
• persistently or 'likely to cause annoyance' or 'nuisance';
• street or public place;
• from/in the vicinity of a motor vehicle; and
• for the purpose of prostitution.

Solicits

For a definition and discussion of the meaning of 'solicits' see above at 4.119 et seq in **4.129** relation to the offence of 'soliciting' by a common prostitute.

In *Darroch v DPP*,[155] the Divisional Court held that 'soliciting involved some positive **4.130** indication, by act or word, to a prostitute that her services were required'. The act of persistently driving a motor vehicle around an area frequented by prostitutes did not of itself constitute an act of soliciting women for the purposes of prostitution.

Persistently

The solicitation requires either a measure of 'persistence' or, in the alternative, some likeli- **4.131** hood of annoyance or nuisance. Again, we see the public order aspect of the offence. It is not an offence to protect the prostitute from being exploited. It is designed to keep the streets free of pests. Thus, 'persistence' 'connotes a degree of repetition of either more than

---

[152] Sexual Offences Act 1985, s 1(2).
[153] See 9.178 et seq below.
[154] See s 56 and Sch 1, para 4, which came into effect from 1 May 2004.
[155] (1990) 91 Cr App R 378.

one invitation to one person or a series of invitations to different people': per Lord Parker CJ in *Dale v Smith*.[156]

Likely to cause annoyance or nuisance

4.132   The parallels with other forms of public order offences are clearly apparent here. The offence can be committed either 'persistently' (see above) or alternatively, 'in such a manner or in such circumstances as to be likely to cause annoyance to the person (or any of the persons) solicited, or nuisance to other persons in the neighbourhood'.

4.133   On the face of it there are two potential 'victims' of the offence: either the person(s) who are solicited or persons in the neighbourhood generally. However, the key word is 'likely'. In *Paul v DPP*[157] the Divisional Court held that Parliament had used the word 'likely' so that it should not be necessary for the prosecution to call evidence to prove that a specific member of the public had in fact been caused annoyance or nuisance.[158] In that case, the appellant had solicited a prostitute in a street where there were no other vehicles or pedestrians in the area at that time. The prostitute pleaded guilty to 'loitering' and so did not give evidence of her 'annoyance.' The Divisional Court said he was rightly convicted of conduct which was likely to cause nuisance to persons in the neighbourhood on the basis that it was sufficient that the area was heavily populated and that residents were likely to be affected.

4.134   In *Paul v DPP*, Woolf LJ also held that in determining whether the conduct was likely to cause annoyance or nuisance the magistrates were entitled to apply their local knowledge of the area where the offence occurred. In that case, the justices knew that the Studley Road area of Luton was a frequent haunt of prostitutes with a constant procession of cars there at night—which somewhat undermined the defendant's contention that he and the lady were well-known to each other because of work he had done for her previously and she had flagged him down to ask for a lift home.

4.135   The words 'annoyance' and 'nuisance' are not defined in the Act. It is submitted that they bear their ordinary meaning. They are questions of fact and degree for the magistrates. Since no evidence is required to show that a member of the public in fact experienced annoyance or nuisance, this can be inferred from the circumstances.

Street or public place

4.136   Section 4(4) of the Sexual Offences Act 1985 defines 'street' as follows:

> For the purposes of this Act 'street' includes any bridge, road, lane, footway, subway, square, court, alley or passage, whether a thoroughfare or not, which is for the time being open to the public; and the doorways and entrances of premises abutting on a street (as hereinbefore

---

[156] [1967] 1 WLR 700. That was a case of 'persistent importuning' under the Sexual Offences Act 1956, s 32 (now repealed) in which the defendant had on two successive days approached young boys, at Forster Square railway station in Bradford, and said 'hello' followed by an invitation to look at indecent photographs.
[157] (1990) 90 Cr App R 173.
[158] In *Paul v DPP*, ibid, the Divisional Court found instructive the conjoined cases of *Parkin v Norman* and *Valentine v Lilley* [1983] QB 92, [1982] 2 All ER 583 which were concerned with the use of the word 'likely' in the Public Order Act 1936, s 32.

defined), and any ground adjoining and open to a street, shall be treated as forming part of the street.

This definition is the same as that in relation to 'soliciting' under s 1(4) of the Street Offences Act 1959. For a discussion of the meaning of 'street' and 'public place' see above at 4.103 et seq in relation to soliciting. **4.137**

From or in the immediate vicinity of a motor vehicle

As the name of the offence suggests, it is aimed at preventing the influx into a neighbour-hood of people in or on motor vehicles soliciting other people for the purposes of prostitution and causing annoyance or nuisance. However, that should not be taken to mean that the vehicle need either be moving or stationary or that the presence of the vehicle itself causes annoyance or nuisance.[159] **4.138**

The alternative element in s 1(1)(b), that the soliciting may be committed by a person 'in a street or public place while in the immediate vicinity of a motor vehicle that he has just got out of or off', are meant to cover a person who stops his vehicle and steps out of it and solicits another. Clearly the words 'immediate vicinity' and 'just got out of' is designed to connote a measure of proximity in time and place to the vehicle. Ultimately, these are questions of fact for the magistrates. **4.139**

'Motor vehicle' has the same meaning as in the Road Traffic Act 1988,[160] which is 'a mechanically propelled vehicle intended or adapted for use on roads'.[161] Accordingly, one cannot commit the offence of kerb crawling from or in the immediate vicinity of a bicycle[162] (though if it is persistent a charge may be brought under s 2—see below). **4.140**

For the purpose of prostitution

For a definition and discussion of the meaning of 'for the purpose of prostitution' see above at 4.124 in relation to the offence of 'soliciting'. **4.141**

Persistent soliciting

Section 2(1) of the Sexual Offences Act 1985 provides as follows: **4.142**

A person commits an offence if in a street or public place he persistently solicits another person (or different persons) for the purpose of prostitution.

Jurisdiction and penalty

The offence is triable summarily only. The maximum penalty is a fine not exceeding level 3 on the standard scale.[163] However, a person convicted of this offence may also attract an ASBO under the Crime and Disorder Act 1998. **4.143**

---

[159] See *Rook and Ward on Sexual Offences* (2004) para 12.51, p 372.
[160] Sexual Offences Act 1985, s 1(3), as amended by the Road Traffic (Consequential Provisions) Act 1988 (c 54, SIF 107:1), s 4, Sch 4, para 29.
[161] Road Traffic Act 1988, s 185(1)(c).
[162] See the report in The Times, 1 March 2007, for an example of this practice in Bournemouth.
[163] Sexual Offences Act 1985, s 2(2).

Who can commit the offence?

4.144 As with the offence under s 1 of the Sexual Offences Act 1985, the offence under s 2 (as originally drafted) could only be committed by a man soliciting a woman. However, as a result of amendment by the Sexual Offences Act 2003,[164] the offence is gender-neutral and thus may be committed by either a man or a woman persistently soliciting another person of either sex.

Essential elements

4.145 There are four essential elements to the offence of persistent soliciting, which significantly overlap with the offence of soliciting under s 1 of the Sexual Offences Act 1985:

- solicit;
- persistently;
- street or public place; and
- for the purpose of prostitution.

For a discussion of the meanings of these terms see above in relation to s 1 of the Sexual Offences Act 1985 (kerb crawling).

4.146 In *Darroch v DPP*,[165] the Divisional Court held that soliciting involved some positive indication, by act or word, to a prostitute that her services were required. The act of persistently driving a motor vehicle around an area frequented by prostitutes did not of itself constitute an act of soliciting women for the purposes of prostitution under s 2 of the Sexual Offences Act 1985. Moreover, the Divisional Court in that case went on to say that only one act of soliciting could not amount to persistent soliciting.

4.147 Like the offence under s 1 ('kerb crawling'), the offence of 'persistent soliciting' under s 2 is the corollary offence to 'loitering or soliciting by a common prostitute': it is the offence committed by the prospective client rather than by the prostitute. The differences between the offences under s 1 (kerb crawling) and s 2 (persistent soliciting) are twofold. Firstly, under s 2 there is no requirement to show a connection with a motor vehicle. Secondly, under s 2 there is no requirement to show a likelihood of causing annoyance or nuisance—persistence alone is sufficient. Accordingly, the latter offence covers a wider range of conduct. Since the maximum penalty is the same for both offences, one wonders why Parliament bothered with the narrower offence of kerb crawling, other than that it has a headline grabbing description.

---

[164] See s 56 and Sch 1, para 4, which came into effect from 1 May 2004.
[165] (1990) 91 Cr App R 378.

5

TRESPASS TO LAND

A. Introduction	5.01	Trespass on a protected site	5.140
B. Civil Law of Trespass to Land	5.06	Other offences involving trespass	5.149
The scope of the tort of trespass to land	5.06	By-laws	5.149
Defences to tort of trespass	5.11	Being in a prohibited place for a	
Who can sue for trespass?	5.16	purpose prejudicial to the safety	
Remedies against trespassers	5.18	or interests of the State	5.152
C. Criminal Law	5.41	Offences under the Vagrancy Act 1824	5.155
Development of the criminal		Failure to leave an exclusion zone	5.158
law of trespass	5.41	Violence for securing entry	5.159
Criminal Justice and Public Order Act		Trespass during currency of interim	
1994, Part V	5.47	possession order	5.160
Aggravated trespass	5.47	Adverse occupation of residential	
Powers to remove persons committing		premises	5.161
or participating in aggravated trespass	5.66	Trespassing with a weapon of offence	5.165
Powers to remove trespassers present on		Trespassing on premises of foreign	
land for purpose of residing there	5.74	missions, etc	5.167
Powers to remove trespassers		Obstruction of enforcement officers or	
with caravans	5.91	court officers executing High Court	
Powers to remove those preparing		or county court process	5.170
for or attending raves	5.98	Trespassing on licensed aerodromes	5.176
Unauthorized campers:		Trespassing on a railway	5.177
powers of removal	5.113	Poaching	5.178
Public Order Act 1986, ss 14A–C	5.126	Burglary	5.179
Trespassory assemblies	5.126	Trespass with intent to commit a	
Serious and Organised Crime and		sexual offence	5.181
Police Act 2005, s 128	5.140		

A. Introduction

Trespass to land is generally defined as an unlawful entry upon land in the possession of another.[1] It is traditionally a 'tort' or 'civil wrong' and thus litigated in the civil courts as an action for possession of land, or for damages, rather than being prosecuted in the criminal courts. Therefore, a sign proclaiming 'trespassers will be prosecuted' is usually more of a threat than a reality. However, there are a number of circumstances in which trespass

5.01

---

[1] See *Blackstone's Commentaries* (1876) vol 3, p 184; D Elvin and J Karas, *Unlawful Interference with Land* (2002, 2nd edn) p 5; *Halsbury's Laws of England* (1999, 4th edn) paras 505 et seq; *Clerk & Lindsell On Torts* (2009, 19th edn) Ch 19.

to land may form part of a criminal charge. Generally, trespass to land is only criminalized when accompanied by some aggravating feature or ulterior motive. However, recent legislation has significantly increased the number and type of locations at which trespass to land *per se* constitutes a criminal offence.[2]

5.02 Trespass to land is to be distinguished from trespass to the person (assault, battery, and false imprisonment), and trespass to goods (unlawful interference with another's possessions). As *torts*, trespass to the person and trespass to goods are generally beyond the scope of this work and throughout this chapter 'trespass' will be used as shorthand for 'trespass to land'. For the meaning of the *offences* of assault and battery see 2.04. For police powers in relation to stop, search, and arrest which would otherwise raise issues of false imprisonment, see Chapters 6 and 7.

5.03 The background to the increased criminalization of trespass over the past two decades began with political concern in the early 1990s about new age travellers, rave culture, and the activities of hunt saboteurs and animal rights activists. This gave rise to the Criminal Justice and Public Order Act 1994. Part V of the 1994 Act still provides for the bulk of criminal trespass offences, which have been progressively amended and expanded by subsequent legislation, particularly that aimed at tackling 'anti-social behaviour'. In addition, post-11 September 2001, a raft of measures have been introduced under the banner of 'prevention of terrorism'. In practice, these powers are frequently used in 'ordinary' public order situations and in the policing of protest. They are discussed in detail below.

5.04 An additional factor in the increased use of trespass law, whether civil or criminal, in the context of public order and protest activity is the growing privatization of public space. Thus, while shopping precincts, town centres, recreational areas, etc were once public land, they are now frequently owned by private companies. In such a situation, a protestor will require the permission of the landowner or face being a trespasser. The implications of this development on the Convention rights to freedom of expression (Article 10) and association (Article 11) are considered in Chapter 10.

5.05 Although this work is primarily focused on the criminal law, the first part of this chapter looks at the civil law relating to trespass. Civil law remedies, and in particular injunctions, are increasingly being used in the public order context, especially in relation to protest activity and travellers. The key principles underpinning the law of trespass are therefore considered below. Civil remedies, including injunctions, are discussed in further detail in Chapter 9.

B. Civil Law of Trespass to Land

The scope of the tort of trespass to land

5.06 Trespass to land can be committed in a number of ways: by a person unlawfully entering onto another's land in person, or by causing animals[3] or objects to do so (eg by throwing stones,

---

[2] The Serious and Organised Crime and Police Act 2005, s 128, as amended by the Terrorism Act 2006, creates a new offence of entering or being on any protected site in England and Wales or Northern Ireland as a trespasser. Protected sites include nuclear bases and other sites of political or royal significance. This provision is discussed at 5.140 et seq below.

[3] *League Against Cruel Sports Ltd v Scott* [1986] QB 240.

pouring water, tipping rubbish[4]). It is also a trespass to remove unlawfully any part of land in the possession of another (including buildings or other fixtures attached to the land);[5] or to leave anything on the land.[6] Trespass can also be committed where a person has entered the land of another lawfully, but then exceeds the scope of the permission allowing him to remain.[7] In this situation, the person entering the land is treated as a trespasser *ab initio*.[8]

Entry onto another's land must be intentional before it amounts to trespass, but this means **5.07** only that the entry must not have been involuntary—eg tripping and falling over a neighbour's boundary would not amount to trespass. However, a mistake of fact or law does not amount to a defence: entering a neighbour's property mistakenly believing it to be one's own is a trespass.[9]

It is not necessary for the person in possession of the land to show that the trespasser has **5.08** caused any damage, the tort is actionable *per se*.[10]

A person does not trespass on land if his entry onto it was in accordance with permission **5.09** granted by the possessor of the land; or was justified by operation of law;[11] was made under a right of easement, licence,[12] customary right, or other right of way, user or *profit à prendre*.[13] However, if a person uses land in ways not authorized by the right under which he is permitted to use the land, then he becomes a trespasser.

In *DPP v Jones*,[14] the House of Lords considered whether using the highway for the pur- **5.10** poses of a peaceful assembly is consistent with the public's right of access. The majority of their Lordships held that reasonable use of the highway will not amount to trespass pro- vided it is consistent with the primary right to pass and repass. Therefore, a peaceful assem- bly that does not cause obstruction will not amount to trespass on the highway.[15]

Defences to tort of trespass

Necessity

A person may lawfully deviate onto private land in order to overcome an obstruction to a **5.11** right of way created by the person in possession of the land.[16] Similarly in 'clear and simple

---

[4] *Whalley v Lancashire and Yorkshire Railway Co* (1884) 13 QBD 131; *Kynoch Ltd v Rowlands* [1912] 1 Ch 527.
[5] *Lavender v Betts* [1942] 2 All ER 72.
[6] *Mace v Philcox* (1864) 15 CBNS 600; *Westripp v Baldock* [1939] 1 All ER 279.
[7] *Hillen v ICI (Alkali) Ltd* [1936] AC 65, HL.
[8] *Six Carpenters' Case* (1610) 8 Co Rep 146a.
[9] *Baseley v Clarkson* (1682) 3 Lev 37; *Turner v Thorne and Thorne* (1959) 21 DLR (2d) 29.
[10] *Stoke-on-Trent Council v W&J Wass Ltd* [1988] 1 WLR 1406.
[11] See, for example, National Parks and Access to the Countryside Act 1949, s 60, which provides for lawful access for recreational purposes to land subject to an access agreement or order; see also the Countryside and Rights of Way Act 2000, s 2(1).
[12] *Whelan v Leonard* [1917] 2 IR 323.
[13] *Mannall v Fisher* (1859) 5 CBNS 856; *Pannell v Mill* (1846) 3 CB 625. A *profit à prendre* is a right to take natural resources from the land—for example, a right to fish or hunt on land may constitute a *profit à prendre*, as may a right to collect firewood, or to take minerals from the soil.
[14] [1999] 2 AC 240. See 5.127 and 5.136 et seq below.
[15] See Ch 4 for further discussion of rights in respect of public highways.
[16] *Stacey v Sherrin* (1913) 29 TLR 555.

cases or in an emergency',[17] it may be lawful to enter onto another's land without permission in order to abate a nuisance or trespass by encroachment. However, the instances in which this is appropriate will be rare. The common law remedy of 'self-redress' or 'abatement' and what constitutes a 'clear and simple case' is discussed at 5.34 et seq below.

5.12   In *Monsanto plc v Tilly*[18] the Court of Appeal emphasized that the availability of 'necessity' as a defence to trespass is strictly circumscribed.[19] In that case, the defendants to an injunction prohibiting them from entering onto land and there destroying genetically modified crops had sought to establish a defence of necessity. They argued that destruction of the crops was necessary in order to protect public health and the environment. The Court of Appeal rejected this argument, finding, as a matter of fact, that the defendants' real aim was to gain publicity for their cause rather than to abate an immediate and obvious danger. The issue of 'necessity' as a defence generally is considered in Chapter 8.

Human rights

5.13   To date, arguments based on the State's positive obligations under Articles 10 and 11 to facilitate peaceful protest have not succeeded in carving out a 'human rights' defence to allegations of civil trespass. In *Appleby v United Kingdom*,[20] environmental campaigners sought to demonstrate against plans to build on the only public playing field in their town. They wished to campaign and hand out leaflets in the town centre. However, the town centre was located within a privately owned shopping precinct and the owners of the precinct refused permission to campaign there. The would-be campaigners argued that the failure of the local authority (which had sold the land to the private developers) to secure a right of access to the town centre for members of the public to express their views peacefully on matters of public interest was a dereliction of their positive obligations under Articles 10 and 11 and that spaces, such as town centres, which traditionally fulfilled public functions should be classed as 'quasi public' spaces with attendant public rights of access, even where they were privately owned.

5.14   The European Court of Human Rights rejected this argument, holding that 'While it is true that demographic, social, economic and technological developments are changing the ways in which people move around and come into contact with each other, the Court is not persuaded that this requires the automatic creation of rights of entry to private property, or even, necessarily, to all publicly owned property (government offices and ministries, for instance).'[21] However, it was an important factor in the Court's decision that there were other fora in which the campaigners could carry out their activities. The Court expressly left open the possibility that in different factual circumstances, for example in the context of a corporate town where the entire municipality was controlled by a private body, positive

---

[17] *Burton v Winters* [1993] 1 WLR 1077 at p 1082.
[18] [2000] Env LR 313, CA.
[19] Ibid, paras 27–34; and *Southwark Borough Council v Williams* [1971] 1 Ch 734.
[20] (2003) 37 EHRR 38.
[21] Ibid, para 47.

obligations might arise to facilitate public access to private land for the purposes of expression and assembly.[22]

Defences to possession proceedings based on Article 8 rights are considered in 5.21 below. **5.15**

Who can sue for trespass?

The general rule is that a person suing for trespass must be in exclusive possession of the land upon which the trespass has occurred. Thus, the owner of land cannot sue if he has leased the land to someone else and is no longer in occupation of it.[23] In such a situation the tenant could sue.[24] If land is vacant, then the owner has sufficient possession to sue in trespass unless he has no intention of returning.[25] In recent years, the general rule has been relaxed to allow those with other types of right over land to sue for trespass if those rights are interfered with. For example, a company that has leased the right to grow genetically modified crops on a particular piece of land is 'in possession' of the soil in which the crops grow and therefore has sufficient right to maintain an action in trespass if the crops are interfered with.[26] Likewise, a developer with a licence to occupy land for the purposes of development has sufficient interest to sue for ejectment of trespassers.[27] **5.16**

Perhaps surprisingly, a person suing for trespass does not need to show that their possession of the land is lawful: actual possession is sufficient except where the defendant to the claim can show a better right to possession of the land than the claimant.[28] **5.17**

Remedies against trespassers

Orders for possession

A person entitled to the immediate possession of land (usually the owner or tenant) can sue a trespasser for the return of the possession of the land, provided the claim is brought within the time limit for such proceedings. In the case of unregistered land this remains twelve years. However, Part 9 of the Land Registration Act 2002 disapplies this time limit in respect of registered land and creates a new regime for claims of adverse possession (claims to possession of land by trespassers who have been in occupation without permission for the specified period). **5.18**

The procedure for bringing possession proceedings is set out in Part 55 of the Civil Procedure Rules ('CPR'). In addition, ss 75 and 76 of the Criminal Justice and Public **5.19**

---

[22] For further discussion of protest rights and private land see Jacob Rowbottom, 'Property and Participation: A Right of Access for Expressive Activities' [2005] 2 EHRLR 186–202; Kevin Gray and Susan Gray, 'Civil Rights, Civil Wrongs and Quasi-Public Space' [1999] EHRLR 45; B Fitzpatrick and N Taylor, 'Trespassers Might be Prosecuted: The European Convention and Restrictions on the Right to Assemble' [1998] EHRLR 292.

[23] *Wallis v Hands* [1893] 2 Ch 75.

[24] *National Provincial Bank v Ainsworth* [1965] 2 All ER 472, HL.

[25] *R v St Pancras Assessment Committee* (1877) 2 QBD 581; *Trustees, Executors and Agency Co Ltd v Short* (1888) 13 App Cas 793, PC.

[26] *Monsanto v Tilly* [2000] Env LR 313.

[27] *Manchester Airport v Dutton* [1999] 3 WLR 524, CA.

[28] *Doe d Hughes v Dyeball* (1829) Mood & M 346; *Asher v Whitlock* (1865) LR 1 QB 1; *Perry v Clissold* [1907] AC 73.

Order Act 1994 provide for interim possession proceedings, backed by criminal penalties. These are discussed below. In regular possession proceedings, the claimant must show

(a) that he has superior title to the land as compared to the defendant; and
(b) that he was entitled to immediate possession of the land as at the date of the commencement of the proceedings.

Where possession proceedings are brought against trespassers, the claimant must also show that

(c) the land is in the sole occupation of the trespasser(s);[28a] and
(d) the 'trespasser' is not a former tenant or sub-tenant.[29]

5.20 In cases where the claimant is a private landlord and the defendant was a trespasser *ab initio*, the court has no discretion, it must grant the claimant an order for possession forthwith.[30] The only considerations for the court are

(a) the claimant's status in respect of the land; and
(b) the trespasser's lack of any tenancy, licence or other legal right to remain.

Once these are established, an order for possession forthwith follows as of right; the court has no discretion to suspend possession unless the claimant agrees.[31]

5.21 In *Kay v Lambeth LBC*,[32] the House of Lords considered whether the position is any different in respect of possession proceedings brought by public authorities. The case concerned two sets of possession proceedings brought by local authorities against (a) former homeless people who had been accommodated by a housing trust, which had been granted a head lease by the local authority, but which had been terminated; and (b) gypsies who had moved their caravans onto local authority land without consent. Both sets of defendants sought to defend the claims on the basis that summary eviction would violate their right to respect for their homes under Article 8 of the European Convention on Human Rights. These defences were rejected. The majority of their Lordships held that in possession proceedings against trespassers, even those brought by public landlords, no case-by-case assessment based on a defendant's individual circumstances is required. A court deciding an application for possession need not consider anything other than the parties' respective entitlements to possession of the land under existing domestic law unless, exceptionally, the defendant can show a seriously arguable case that the relevant domestic law of property under which he falls to be evicted is incompatible with the European Convention, or that the decision to seek eviction is *Wednesbury* unreasonable. In respect of trespassers' rights,

---

[28a] In *Secretary of State for the Environment, Food and Rural Affairs v Meier* [2009] IWLR2780, the House of Lords confirmed that a possession order is not available unless the trespassers is in actual occupation of the lord, i.e a stated intention to move into the land is not sufficient, although an injunction may be available in such circumstances.
[29] CPR 55.1(b).
[30] *McPhail v Persons Unknown* [1973] Ch 447.
[31] Ibid.
[32] [2006] 2 AC 465.

the majority of their Lordships in *Kay* expressly endorsed the position laid down in *McPhail v Names Unknown*,[33] ie that an order for possession against a trespasser follows as of right.

This approach has subsequently been confirmed by the House of Lords in *Doherty v Birmingham City Council*,[34] notwithstanding the decision of the European Court of Human Rights in *McCann v UK*.[35] In addition, in *Boyland & Son v Persons Unknown*,[36] the Court of Appeal held that s 89 of the Housing Act 1980 does not grant the court power to suspend possession orders so as to allow trespassers time to vacate land. **5.22**

Interim possession orders

Interim possession orders, introduced in Part V of the Criminal Justice and Public Order Act 1994, were intended to provide a new 'quick and effective' remedy against squatters of residential and business premises, backed by criminal sanctions for non-compliance, and enforceable by the police, instead of county court bailiffs (who would enforce regular possession proceedings).[37] **5.23**

The procedures for interim possession proceedings are now contained in section III of rule 55 of the CPR. The conditions for obtaining such an order are that **5.24**

(a) the only claim made is a possession claim against trespassers for the recovery of premises. 'Premises' has the same meaning as in s 12 of the Criminal Law Act 1977, ie 'any building, any part of a building under separate occupation, and land ancillary to a building, the site comprising any building or buildings together with any land ancillary thereto';

(b) the claimant has an immediate right to possession of the premises;

(c) the claimant has had such a right throughout the period of alleged unlawful occupation;

(d) the claim is made within twenty-eight days of the date on which the claimant first knew, or ought reasonably to have known, that the defendant (or any of the defendants), was in occupation;

(e) the defendant(s) did not enter or remain on the premises with the consent of a person who, at the time consent was given, had an immediate right to possession of the premises;

(f) the claimant has complied with the rules for service; and

(g) the claimant has given the undertakings set out in CPR 55.25.[38]

An application for an interim possession order will be heard as soon as practicable but not less than three days after the date on which the claim form was issued.[39] Once an interim possession order has been made, it must be served within forty-eight hours after it is sealed and the defendant must vacate the premises within twenty-four hours of the service of the order.[40] A date will be set for the full possession hearing not less than seven days after the **5.25**

---

[33] Op cit.

[34] [2008] 3 WLR 636.

[35] [2008] 2 FLR 899, ECHR.

[36] (2007) HLR 24.

[37] Comments of the then Home Secretary introducing the Bill: Hansard, HC cols 29–30(11 January 1994).

[38] CPR Parts 55.21 and 55.25.

[39] CPR Part 55.22(6).

[40] CPR Parts 55.25(3) and 55.26.

date on which the interim order was made.[41] If the defendant has left the premises, he may apply on grounds of urgency for the interim order to be set aside before the date of the full possession hearing.[42]

5.26   Where an interim possession order has been made in respect of any premises and served in accordance with the rules of court, it is an offence, contrary to s 76(2) of the Criminal Justice and Public Order Act 1994, if a person is present on the premises as a trespasser at any time during the currency of the order. Save that, no offence is committed if the person leaves the premises within twenty-four hours of the time of service of the order and does not return, or, if a copy of the order was not fixed to the premises in accordance with the rules of court.[43] A person who is in occupation of the premises at the time the order is served is treated as a trespasser for the purposes of s 76.[44]

5.27   It is also an offence under s 76(4) if a person who was in occupation of the premises at the time of service of the order leaves but then re-enters the premises as a trespasser or attempts to do so after the expiry of the order but within one year of the date on which the order was served.[45]

5.28   The offences under s 76 are triable summarily only and are punishable with a term of imprisonment of up to six months and/or a fine not exceeding level 5 on the standard scale.

5.29   Further offences are committed, contrary to s 75(1) and (2) of the 1994 Act, if, for the purposes of obtaining or resisting an interim possession order, a person makes a statement which he knows to be false or misleading in a material particular; or is reckless as to the same. The offence is triable either way and is punishable, on indictment, with imprisonment of up to two years and/or a fine. If tried summarily, the maximum penalty is a term of imprisonment of up to six months and/or a fine not exceeding the statutory maximum.

Injunctions

5.30   An order in the form of an injunction is available to restrain an act of trespass and, in certain circumstances, a pre-emptory injunction may be available to restrain an *anticipated* trespass. The circumstances in which an injunction may be granted are discussed in Chapter 9.

5.31   The test to be applied in granting such an order to restrain an anticipated trespassory protest has yet to be clarified. However, it is clear that any prior restraint on activity which engages Article 10 rights will be subjected to the most careful scrutiny.[46] In *Heathrow Airport v Garman & Others*[47] representatives of Heathrow Airport sought an injunction

---

[41]   CPR Part 55.25(4).
[42]   CPR Part 55.28.
[43]   Criminal Justice and Public Order Act 1994, s 76(1).
[44]   Ibid, s 76(6).
[45]   Ibid, s 76(4).
[46]   *R (Laporte) v Chief Constable of Gloucestershirec Constabulary* [2007] 2 AC 105, para 37; *Sunday Times v United Kingdom (No 2)* (1991) 14 EHRR 229, para 51.
[47]   [2007] EWHC 1957, QB, unreported 6 August 2007.

prohibiting a planned protest by environmental activists that threatened to disrupt the operation of the airport. There was a dispute between the protestors and the airport author-ities as to precisely the form that the disruption was likely to take: the former referred in their literature publicizing the planned protest to 'eight days of education, sustainable liv-ing and direct action against the root causes of climate change'. However, the claimants referred to the defendants' previous direct action at Drax power station and Nottingham East Midlands Airport, which had resulted in the suspension of normal activities at both locations for a number of hours.

In seeking the injunction, the airport authorities sought to rely on the law of trespass, as well as nuisance, breach of by-laws, and the Protection from Harassment Act 1997. The protesters argued that since the injunction would interfere with their rights under Articles 10 and 11 of the European Convention on Human Rights, the applicable test was whether an injunction was necessary and proportionate in a democratic society to protect one of the legitimate aims contained in Articles 10(2) and 11(2). The airport argued that the test was that ordinarily applicable to the grant of an interim injunction, namely, the balance of convenience.[48] In the event, the point was not decided because Swift J found that even on the more rigorous test of necessity an injunction was justified in this case.   **5.32**

In *Hampshire Waste Services Ltd v Intending Trespassers upon Chineham Incinerator*[49] an injunction was granted prohibiting an anticipated trespassory incursion in the course of a 'day of global action against incinerators' at specified sites even though the persons against whom the injunction was sought were not identified individuals. Sir Andrew Morritt VC held that it was sufficient that those constrained by the injunction could be identified by an adequately precise definition: for example, 'Persons entering or remaining without the consent of the claimants . . . in connection with the 'Global Day of Action Against Incinerators' . . . on or around 14 July 2003.'[50]   **5.33**

Self-help or abatement

A person against whom trespass is committed may use reasonable force to eject a trespasser,[51] or, in 'clear and simple' or urgent cases, to abate a trespass by encroachment, for example by removing an overhanging branch or encroaching tree root,[52] but, except in cases of emer-gency, force is unlikely to be reasonable where it is possible to seek a court order for eviction or abatement.[53]   **5.34**

In *Burton v Winters*,[54] the Court of Appeal considered the limits of self-redress in the con-text of a boundary dispute between neighbours. The defendants garage encroached on the claimant's land by 4½ inches. This was a trespass by encroachment, but the judge at first instance found the trespass to be so slight as to warrant only a remedy in damages.   **5.35**

---

[48] *American Cyanamid v Ethicon* [1975] AC 367.
[49] [2004] Env LR.
[50] Ibid, para 10. Civil injunctions are considered further in Ch 9.
[51] *Hemmings v Stoke Poges Golf Club* [1920] 1 KB 720.
[52] *Burton v Winters* [1993] 1 WLR 1077 at p 1082.
[53] Ibid; *Sedleigh-Denfield v O'Callaghan* [1940] AC 880, 911.
[54] Ibid.

He refused to exercise his discretion to issue an injunction requiring the defendants to remove the garage altogether. Dissatisfied with this result, the claimant took matters into her own hands and built a wall on the defendants land, blocking access to the garage. The defendants duly obtained an injunction against the claimant to restrain her from further trespass on their land and, when the claimant refused to comply, committal proceedings were commenced for contempt of court.

5.36   Ultimately, the case came before the Court of Appeal, which had to decide, amongst other things, the extent to which the claimant was entitled, at common law, to take direct action to abate the trespass to her land. Perhaps unsurprisingly, the Court of Appeal held that the claimant's counter trespass was not a proportionate response. The Court emphasized that 'self-redress' or 'abatement' to rectify a trespass to land was only available in 'clear and simple' cases, such as the removal of an overhanging branch or an encroaching root, or in an emergency where it was not possible to wait for 'the slow progress of the ordinary forms of justice'. Since Mrs Burton's case was neither simple nor urgent (she had in fact waited for court proceedings to take their course, she had just not liked the result), self-redress was not a remedy available to her. She was duly committed to prison to serve a two-year sentence for contempt of court.

5.37   Those seeking to enforce their rights directly against trespassers in person should also be aware of s 6(1) of the Criminal Law Act 1977. This makes it a summary offence for any person (including the owner of the property), without lawful authority, to use or threaten violence for the purpose of securing entry into any premises where

(a)   there is someone present on those premises at the time who is opposed to the entry which the violence is intended to secure; and

(b)   the person using or threatening the violence knows that that is the case.

Section 6(1A) exempts displaced residential occupiers,[55] protected intending occupiers,[56] and those acting on their behalf from prosecution under s 6(1). However, other interests or rights in the premises do not constitute 'lawful authority' for the purposes of s 6(1).[57]

The role of the police in ejecting trespassers

5.38   It is well established that a private individual or body seeking to exercise his right to self-redress to evict a trespasser may call upon others to assist with the eviction.[58] This includes calling for the assistance of the police.[59] Those who assist, including the police, will act within the law provided that the person seeking the eviction is within his rights to do so and any force used is the minimum reasonably necessary.[60] If, however, the person or body seeking the eviction is not lawfully entitled to do so, even if he, in good faith, believes that he is,

---

[55]   See the Criminal Law Act 1977, s 12, for definition.

[56]   See ibid, s 12A, for definition.

[57]   Ibid, s 6(2).

[58]   *Wheeler v Whiting* (1840) 9 C & P 262.

[59]   *R v Chief Constable of Devon and Cornwall, ex p Central Electrical Generating Board* [1982] QB 458.

[60]   *Hall v Davis* (1825) 2 C & P 33; *Thomas v Marsh and Nest* (1833) 5 C & P 596; *Hemmings v Stoke Poges Golf Club Ltd* [1920] 1 KB 720, CA.

then those who assist, including the police, will also be acting unlawfully.[61] For this reason, Sedley LJ in *Porter*[62] suggests that, in certain situations, it may be prudent for the police simply to be on hand in case of a breach of the peace, but to leave the actual eviction to the landowner or his agents. Equally, however, there is judicial endorsement of the involvement of police officers in actually effecting evictions.[63] As a matter of practice, it is clear that the police frequently do assist in the eviction of trespassers, particularly in the context of protest activity.[64]

Whilst it is clear that the police have the *power* to assist with the eviction of trespassers, even where only a tort and no crime has been committed, the question of whether they will be acting in the exercise of their *duty* when doing so has yet to be resolved.[65] In most cases this distinction is irrelevant: what matters is whether the police were acting lawfully or not. However, the distinction becomes significant if an officer is assaulted in the course of evicting a trespasser. If the officer was *voluntarily* (lawfully) assisting in the eviction, then the trespasser would be guilty of common assault. If the officer was acting in the exercise of his *duty*, then the trespasser would be guilty of the offence of assaulting an officer in the course of his duty. Resistance to removal falling short of assault might also amount to obstruction of an officer in the execution of his duty.[66] In *Porter v Commissioner of Police for the Metropolis*,[67] the Court of Appeal (Civil Division) considered this issue obiter, but each of the three members of the Court expressed a different view. **5.39**

Damages

Damages for wrongful occupancy of land are available against a trespasser in the event of his having funds to pay them. **5.40**

C. Criminal Law

Development of the criminal law of trespass

Although there are some longstanding criminal offences containing an element of trespass—for example, burglary (contrary to s 9 of the Theft Act 1968—see 5.179 et seq below), or 'being in . . . a prohibited place for a purpose prejudicial to the safety or interests of the state' (contrary to s 1 of the Official Secrets Act 1911—see 5.152 et seq), there has recently been an explosion of offences criminalizing unlawful presence on private or Crown land. **5.41**

---

[61] *Foulkes v Chief Constable of Merseyside* [1998] 3 All ER 705.
[62] *Porter v Metropolitan Police Commissioner*, 20 October 1999, unreported, p 30.
[63] See comments of Judge LJ in *Porter*, pp 8–9; and those of May LJ at p 23.
[64] See, for example, the evidence to the Parliamentary Joint Committee on Human Rights of Phil McLeish, an environmental activist and member of Climate Camp: Seventh Report of Session 2008–09, Vol 2, Ev 29, Q134–148.
[65] See *R v Prebble & others* [1858] 1 F&F 325; *R v Roxburgh* (1871) 12 Cox CC 8; cf *Coffin v Smith* (1980) 72 CAR 221; *R v Commissioner of the Metropolitan Police, ex p Porter*, above.
[66] Per Lawton LJ in *R v Chief Constable of Devon and Cornwall, ex p CEGB* [1982] QB 458, 473E–F.
[67] Unreported, 20 October 1999.

5.42 The Criminal Law Act 1977 introduced criminal offences relating to the trespassory occupation of residential premises and entry onto diplomatic missions.[68] Then in 1986, with the passage of the Public Order Act 1986, the Thatcher government introduced for the first time a two-stage law of criminal trespass, which empowered police officers in specified circumstances to direct trespassers to leave land, with criminal sanctions for failure to comply. This followed the previous summer's 'Battle of the Beanfield' in which police had clashed with members of the peace convoy and other travellers seeking to hold a festival at Stonehenge to celebrate the summer solstice. Prior to this it had, for a brief time, been a criminal offence to conspire to trespass on land (even though a trespass by one person in similar circumstances was not an offence).[69] But this had been abolished by s 1 of the Criminal Law Act 1977, which limited indictable conspiracies to agreements to pursue a course of conduct which, if carried out would necessarily amount to or involve the commission of a criminal offence (and not a tort).[70]

5.43 In 1991, the Home Office published a consultation paper on 'squatting' with a view to considering the ways in which the law might be strengthened to safeguard the rights of property owners. This expressly included the possibility of introducing new criminal legislation. This was followed in 1994 by the introduction, in Part V of the Criminal Justice and Public Order Act 1994, of interim possession orders with criminal sanctions attached.[71]

5.44 Part V of the 1994 Act also expanded the two-stage criminal trespass law introduced in the Public Order Act 1986. Section 34 of the 1986 Act had provided for criminal sanctions for failure to comply with a direction to leave land, but only where such a direction had been given by police to two or more trespassers who had the common purpose of residing on the land (and other criteria were met). This offence was re-enacted, with minor amendments, in s 61 of the 1994 Act.[72] But, in addition, the 1994 Act introduced a raft of new criminal trespass measures: a new offence of aggravated trespass;[73] new offences relating to raves;[74] new powers for the prohibition of trespassory assemblies;[75] and new powers, backed by criminal sanctions, for local authorities to deal with unauthorized campers.[76]

5.45 These powers were further enhanced over the following decade by the introduction of the Protection from Harassment Act 1997, which provides for a statutory power to grant an injunction restraining a course of conduct which amounts to harassment,[77] and the

---

[68] See 5.37 and 5.161 et seq for discussion of offences contrary to ss 6–10 of the 1977 Act, which remain in force.

[69] *Kamara v DPP* [1974] AC 104.

[70] Note, however, that since *aggravated* trespass is a criminal offence, conspiracy to commit aggravated trespass is also an offence—see reports of arrest in April 2009 of 114 people on suspicion of conspiracy to commit aggravated trespass in what was billed as 'the biggest pre-emptive raid on environmental protestors in UK history' at <http://www.guardian.co.uk/environment/2009/apr/13/nottingham-police-raid-environmental-campaigners>.

[71] See 5.26 above.

[72] See 5.74 et seq below.

[73] See 5.47 et seq below.

[74] See 5.98 et seq below.

[75] See 5.126 et seq below.

[76] See 5.113 et seq below.

[77] See Ch 9.

Anti-social Behaviour Act 2003, which provides for the making of anti-social behaviour orders, effectively banning the recipient of the order from specified geographical locations and from engaging in specified activity.[78] Although these latter legislative provisions do not expressly involve trespass, or create new trespassory offences, the powers they convey are often used to restrain protest on private property.[79]

Most recently, the Serious Organised Crime and Police Act 2005, as amended by the **5.46** Terrorism Act 2006, creates a new offence of entering or being on a 'protected site' as a trespasser. 'Protected sites' include nuclear facilities and various military bases; Royal residences and political sites; including, amongst other places, Parliament, 10 Downing Street, Chequers, and GCHQ.[80] When originally introduced, this provision was said to be in response to the intrusion by 'comedy terrorist' Aaron Barschak dressed as Osama Bin Laden at Prince William's 21st birthday party at Windsor Castle and was even described by the then Home Secretary at the Bill's second reading in the House of Commons as 'a sledge hammer to crack a nut'.[81] However, by the time of the first statutory instrument made under s128 of the 2005 Act, designating various military bases as 'protected sites', the Ministry of Defence was openly acknowledging that the purpose of the order was to deter protestors from entering military sites where 'by actively trespassing, [they] place themselves at risk of being mistaken for terrorists'.[82] On the day this provision came into force, 1 April 2006, two grandmothers from Yorkshire, aged 70 and 64, were arrested for (and subsequently convicted of) trespassing at Menwith Hill military base.[83] Although the government has indicated an intention to repeal the requirement to obtain prior authorization for demonstrations in the designated area around Parliament Square and the attendant criminal sanctions contained in ss 132–7 of the 2005 Act (see Chapter 3, 3.94 et seq), no such intention has been expressed in relation to s 128.

Criminal Justice and Public Order Act 1994, Part V

Aggravated trespass

Section 68(1) of the 1994 Act provides as follows: **5.47**

(1) A person commits the offence of aggravated trespass if he trespasses on land . . . and, in relation to any lawful activity which persons are engaging in or are about to engage in on that or adjoining land . . . , does there anything which is intended by him to have the effect—

(a) of intimidating those persons or any of them so as to deter them or any of them from engaging in that activity,
(b) of obstructing that activity, or
(c) of disrupting that activity.

---

[78] See Ch 9.
[79] See, for example, *Heathrow Airport v Garman and others* [2007] EWHC 1957, QB; and the cases considered at paras 25–8 of Liberty's written evidence to the JCHR, Seventh Report of Session 2008–09, Vol II, Ev 158.
[80] See 5.140 et seq below.
[81] Hansard, HC, col 1059 (7 December 2004).
[82] Explanatory Memorandum to the Serious Organised Crime and Police Act 2005 (Designated sites) Order 2005, SI 2005/3447 available at <http://www.opsi.gov.uk/si/em2005/uksiem_20053447_en.pdf>.
[83] See report in the Independent, 6 April 2006 at <http://www.independent.co.uk/news/uk/crime/helen-and-sylvia-the-new-face-of-terrorism-472993.html>.

5.48 Charges under this section are frequently brought against protestors who would not otherwise be subject to the criminal law—ie because their behaviour was unthreatening and caused no damage to person or property.

5.49 The section as originally enacted was limited to trespass on land 'in the open air', but these words were repealed by s 59 of the Anti-social Behaviour Act 2003. Section 68 of the 1994 Act does not contain any positive definition of 'land', although subsec 68(5) specifies that

> [i]n this section 'land' does not include—
>
> (a) the highways and roads excluded from the application of s 61[84] by paragraph (b) of the definition of 'land' in subsection (9) of that section; or
> (b) a road within the meaning of the Roads (Northern Ireland) Order 1993.

It has been successfully argued, at first instance before a District Judge, that, in the absence of a positive definition of 'land' in s 68, charges alleging that aggravated trespass had been committed in a building fell to be dismissed, because s 68, as amended by the Anti-social Behaviour Act 2003, was ambiguous as to whether buildings are included within the meaning of 'land' for the purposes of that section. The District Judge rejected the prosecution submission that, in the absence of a positive definition of 'land' within s 68, reference should be made to s 128 of the Explanatory Notes to the Anti-social Behaviour Act 2003, which specifies that the effect of s 59 of the 2003 Act is that the offence of aggravated trespass may now be committed in a building or in the open air. The District Judge also found it inappropriate to have recourse to the definition of 'land' contained in the Interpretation Act 1978. This decision is currently subject to appeal by way of case stated.[85]

5.50 It is, however, clear that 'land' for the purposes of s 68 of the 1994 Act does not include land forming part of a highway unless it is 'a footpath, bridleway or byway open to all traffic within the meaning of Part III of the Wildlife and Countryside Act 1981, . . . a restricted byway within the meaning of Part II of the Countryside and Rights of Way Act 2000 or . . . a cycle track under the Highways Act 1980 or the Cycle Tracks Act 1984'.[86] In other words, there is no offence of aggravated trespass on the highway unless the highway in question falls into one of the specified categories. The terms defined by reference to Part III of the Wildlife and Countryside Act 1981 are as follows:

> 'footpath' means a highway over which the public have a right of way on foot only, other than such a highway at the side of a public road
>
> 'bridleway' means a highway over which the public have the following, but no other, rights of way, that is to say, a right of way on foot and a right of way on horseback or leading a horse, with or without a right to drive animals of any description along the highway
>
> 'byway open to all traffic' means a highway over which the public have a right of way for vehicular and all other kinds of traffic, but which is used by the public mainly for the purpose for which footpaths and bridleways are so used.[87]

---

[84] For discussion of Criminal Justice and Public Order Act 1994, s 61 see 5.74 et seq below.
[85] *CPS v North West Surrey Magistrates Court* [2009].
[86] See the Criminal Justice and Public Order Act 1994, ss 68(5) and 61(9)(b).
[87] All definitions are from the Wildlife and Countryside Act 1981, Part III, s 66.

Part II of the Countryside and Rights of Way Act 2000 defines 'restricted byway' as follows:

'restricted byway' means a highway over which the public have restricted byway rights, with or without a right to drive animals of any description along the highway, but no other rights of way.

'restricted byway rights' means—

(a) a right of way on foot,
(b) a right of way on horseback or leading a horse, and
(c) a right of way for vehicles other than mechanically propelled vehicles.[88]

The Highways Act 1980, as amended by the Cycle Tracks Act 1984, defines 'cycle track' as follows: **5.51**

'cycle track' means a way constituting or comprised in a highway, being a way over which the public have the following, but no other, rights of way, that is to say, a right of way on pedal cycles (other than pedal cycles which are motor vehicles within the meaning of [the Road Traffic Act 1988]) with or without a right of way on foot.[89]

The offence of aggravated trespass is triable summarily only and carries a maximum penalty **5.52** of three months' imprisonment, or a fine of up to level 4 on the standard scale, or both.

As set out above, s 68(1) specifies three ways in which the offence of aggravated trespass **5.53** may be committed. Namely, by doing an act that is intended to have the effect of

(a) intimidating persons so as to deter them from engaging in lawful activity;
(b) obstructing that activity; or
(c) disrupting that activity.

However, in *Nelder v DPP*,[90] a case concerning hunt saboteurs who had run towards a hunt blowing horns and shouting, the Divisional Court held that these three ways overlap and that a charge will not be void for duplicity if it specifies all three ways of committing the offence in a single charge. The information laid against the defendants in *Nelder* was expressed in the following terms: that they 'did trespass on land in the open air in relation to a lawful activity which persons were engaged in on that or adjoining land in the open air did together with others blow horns, whistle, holler and shout which was intended to have the effect of intimidating those persons present or any of them as to deter, disrupt or obstruct that activity'. The Divisional Court held that even though, on the facts, there was no evidence of intimidation, the defendants had been properly convicted under the charge as it stood. The Court observed that although it would have been preferable for the charge to have specified the way in which the prosecution in fact put its case—namely that the actions of the defendants had been intended to disrupt and/or obstruct the hunt, rather than to cause intimidation—there was no requirement that these ways of committing the offence be laid as separate charges.

---

[88] Both definitions are from the Countryside and Rights of Way Act 2000, Part II, s 48(4).
[89] Highways Act 1980, s 329(1), as amended by the Cycle Tracks Act 1984.
[90] The Times, 11 June 1998.

5.54   In *DPP v Barnard*,[91] the Divisional Court held that there are three distinct elements that must all be proved under s 68(1) of the Criminal Justice and Public Order Act 1994: (a) trespass on land; (b) the doing of some act, that must be some distinct and overt act beyond the trespass itself; and (c) the intention by the second act to intimidate, obstruct or disrupt.[92] It is apparent from the wording of s 68(1) itself that there is in fact a fourth essential element of the offence, namely, that the activity the accused intended to disrupt or obstruct was itself lawful within the meaning of s 68(2). This fourth element has been the focus of judicial consideration in *Nelder v DPP*[93] and *R v Jones; Ayliffe v DPP*.[94] The four elements are considered separately below.

Trespass on land

5.55   There is no statutory definition of what constitutes 'trespass' for the purposes of s 68 of the Criminal Justice and Public Order Act 1994. It is submitted that the meaning is as in tort,[95] save that under the criminal law there can be no 'innocent' or 'mistaken' trespass. Under the civil law, a person may commit a trespass by mistake, for example, by entering the wrong house by accident. However, under the criminal law a person does not 'enter as a trespasser' without knowing that fact, or at very least being reckless as to that fact.[96] It is submitted, therefore, that a person is not guilty of an offence under s 68 unless it is proved that he knew (or was reckless to the fact) that he was trespassing.

5.56   Aside from the issue of the defendant's knowledge in relation to trespass, it is surprising how difficult it can be in many cases for the prosecution to prove the fact of trespass if this aspect of the case is challenged. In practice this element of the offence is often assumed and is not disputed by defendants. However, it may be a fruitful line of defence. It is often difficult to prove the precise boundaries of private property and the location of public highways. Public highways and roads are expressly excluded from the definition of 'land' in s 68(1) by operation of s 68(5). However, it is still possible to trespass on land for the purposes of s 68(1) by making unlawful use of a public footpath or bridleway, because lawful use of these rights of way generally extends only to rights to pass and repass and, unlike highways and roads, they are not exempt under s 68(5). It may be arguable that the principle enunciated in *DPP v Jones*,[97] discussed at 5.127 and 5.136 et seq below, that reasonable use of the highway, not inconsistent with the primary right to pass and repass, is not unlawful, should be extended to other public rights of way. However, activity which causes obstruction of a public footpath or bridleway would certainly fall outside the principle in *DPP v Jones*.

---

[91] [2000] Crim LR 371.
[92] Laws LJ at p 4 of the transcript of judgment 15 October 1999.
[93] Op cit.
[94] [2007] 1 AC 136.
[95] See 5.01 et seq above.
[96] See, in relation to burglary contrary to the Theft Act 1968, s 9, *R v Collins* [1972] 2 All ER 1105; *R v Jones; R v Smith* [1976] 1 WLR 672.
[97] [1999] 2 AC 240.

Act additional to mere act of trespass

The words of s 68(1) specify that a 'person commits the offence of aggravated trespass if he **5.57** trespasses on land . . . *and*, in relation to any lawful activity which persons are engaging in or are about to engage in on that or adjoining land . . ., *does there anything* which is intended by him to have the effect' of achieving any of the ends set out in s 68(1)(a) to (c). The effect of the words 'and . . . does there anything', as explained in *DPP v Barnard*,[98] is that there must be a distinct second act additional to the act of trespass before the offence is made out. Thus in *Barnard* itself, there was no offence disclosed in law where the act pleaded in the information as being intended to have the effect of intimidating, obstructing or disrupting lawful activity was 'unlawfully enter[ing] onto the land'. It was held that this amounted to no more than a restatement of the act of trespass and not a distinct and overt second act as required by the section. The Divisional Court observed that an allegation that the defendant 'occupied the land with others' with the requisite intention might suffice, as a strict matter of law, but Laws LJ stated that he would expect something more than mere occupation with others to be pleaded in any satisfactory information.

Intention to intimidate, obstruct, or disrupt

As for the requisite intention, in *Winder v DPP*[99] the Divisional Court held that it was suf- **5.58** ficient for the offence to be made out if, at the time of the second act, the defendant had a general intent to intimidate, obstruct, or disrupt lawful activity on the land, even if he did not intend that the second act itself should intimidate, obstruct, or disrupt. In *Winder*, the defendants, who were anti-hunt protestors, ran towards a fox hunt. They intended to disrupt the hunt when they reached it, but did not intend their approach itself to disrupt, obstruct, or intimidate. Nonetheless, the Divisional Court found that the act of running towards the hunt was more than merely preparatory to the intended disruption and, given that the defendants were trespassing at the time, the offence was made out.

Lawful activity

An offence under s 68(1) of the Criminal Justice and Public Order Act 1994 is only made **5.59** out if the activity the trespasser intended to obstruct/disrupt, etc was itself lawful. Section 68(2) provides that:

> Activity on any occasion on the part of a person or persons on land is 'lawful' for the purposes of this section if he or they may engage in the activity on the land on that occasion without committing an offence or trespassing on the land.

In *R v Jones; Ayliffe v DPP*,[100] anti-war protestors argued that the activity they sought **5.60** to obstruct at various naval and other military bases around the UK was not itself lawful activity within the meaning of ss 68(1) and 68(2) because it amounted to the international law crime of aggression. The House of Lords held that the reference to 'offence' in s 68(2) is to an offence under the domestic criminal law, and does not include offences under

---

[98] [2000] Crim LR 371.
[99] [1996] 160 JP 713.
[100] [2007] 1 AC 1994.

customary international law, such as the crime of aggression, that have not been incorporated into domestic law.

5.61 Even where the disrupted activity was partially unlawful within the meaning of s 68(2), an offence under s 68(1) may still be committed. In *Nelder*,[101] the Divisional Court held that where hunt saboteurs had disrupted a hunt that had itself trespassed on railway property, the protestors had nonetheless been rightly convicted because their disruption of the hunt had continued for an 'appreciable time over an appreciable distance'[102] after the hunt had returned to land on which it had permission to be. The Court observed that its decision would have been different had it been the hunt's central objective to hunt on land over which it had no permission to go, or if the protestors had limited their activity to the period where the hunt was trespassing on railway property.

5.62 The 'persons' referred to in s 68(1) who are engaging in or about to engage in the relevant lawful activity must be physically present on the land at the time of offence. Thus in *DPP v Tilly*[103] no offence under s 68(1) was committed when anti-genetically modified crop protestors trespassed on land and destroyed crops, because no one engaged in, or about to engage in, activity relating to the crops was present at the time. The section was found to criminalize 'a situation in which people are meant to be intimidated, or cannot get on with what they are entitled to do. Thus, to suffer inconvenience or anxiety they must be present.'[104] This approach clearly derives from the words in s 68(1): 'in relation to any lawful activity which persons *are engaging in or are about to engage in on that or adjoining land*'.

Defences

5.63 Unlike the other offences created under Part V of the Criminal Justice and Public Order Act 1994, s 68 does not specify any statutory defences, such as, for example, those specified in s 69(4), that the defendant may show that he was not trespassing or that he had a reasonable excuse for failing to leave the land as soon as practicable. In practice, persons charged under s 68(1) usually dispute one or more of the essential elements of the offence discussed above. Since it is for the prosecution to prove each of these elements to the criminal standard, they are not strictly speaking defences, but rather the defendant putting the prosecution to proof of every necessary element.

5.64 In practice, it will be necessary for the defendant to make clear that every element of the offence is in dispute, if this is indeed the case. With the issue of trespass, for example, it is often taken to be proved on the basis of a statement from one of those whose activity was disrupted that the land was private and that the accused had no permission to be there. If the accused believes there may be reason to doubt this assertion, for example, because there was a public right of way, or the boundaries of the land and land to which he—or the public generally—had access were uncertain, then this should be challenged during the relevant part of the prosecution case. A defence request for pre-trial disclosure may also

---

[101] The Times, 11 June 1998.
[102] Simon Brown LJ at p 6 of judgment 3 June 1998.
[103] [2002] Crim LR 128.
[104] Ibid, para 26.

clarify the issue. This might include, for example, a request for land registry documents, or licences demonstrating the authority for the activity the accused is alleged to have disrupted.

A frequent form of defence raised against charges of aggravated trespass, particularly in protest cases, is justification, either under s 3 of the Criminal Law Act 1967 (use of reasonable force in the prevention of crime or in effecting lawful arrest); the common law doctrine of self-defence, or, more frequently, defence of others or property;[105] and/or necessity or duress of circumstances. These defences are considered in detail in Chapter 2 and 8 of this work. **5.65**

Powers to remove persons committing or participating in aggravated trespass

Section 69(1) of the Criminal Justice and Public Order Act 1994 confers power on the senior police officer present to direct a person or persons to leave land if the officer reasonably believes **5.66**

(a) that person or persons to be committing, to have committed, or to intend to commit the offence of aggravated trespass; or

(b) that two or more persons are trespassing on land[106] and are present there with the common purpose of intimidating persons so as to deter them from engaging in a lawful activity or of obstructing or disrupting a lawful activity.

A direction under s 69(1) may be communicated to the persons to whom it applies by any constable at the scene.[107] **5.67**

Section 69(3) makes it a criminal offence for a person knowing that a direction under s 69(1) has been given which applies to him to fail to leave the land as soon as practicable, or, having left, to re-enter the land as a trespasser within three months of the direction having been given. **5.68**

The authors suggest that s 69(3) must be read as creating an offence of failing to comply with a *lawful* direction and that if a reasonable doubt is raised about the legality of the direction given, then an essential element of the offence is missing. It may, in appropriate circumstances, be open to a defendant to challenge the lawfulness of a direction if the wording used is ambiguous or overly broad.[108] For example, it is common practice for police dealing with an alleged incident of aggravated trespass to hand out printed pro forma sheets to those to whom the direction applies, setting out the terms of the direction. The pro forma usually contains a list of all of the possible reasons for which a direction might validly be given. It is for the police attending the scene to delete the reasons which do not apply in a particular case before the form is handed out. If this is not done, it may be arguable that an unamended pro forma, which specifies reasons for the direction which clearly do not apply, **5.69**

---

[105] Now to be read in conjunction with the Criminal Justice and Immigration Act 2008, s 76.
[106] The discussion at 5.49 above in respect of the meaning of 'land' for the purposes of s 68 of the 1994 Act applies equally to s 69.
[107] Criminal Justice and Public Order Act 1994, s 69(2).
[108] See Ch 10 (10.82 et seq) below for a discussion of the concept of legal certainty.

undermines the legality of the direction and/or the accused's knowledge that a direction had been given which applied to him.

5.70 The offence is triable summarily only and is punishable with a term of imprisonment of up to three months or a fine not exceeding level 4 on the standard scale, or both.

5.71 It is not necessary for the purposes of the offence under s 69(3) for the accused to have committed aggravated trespass under s 68(1). In *Capon v DPP*,[109] the Divisional Court considered an appeal by way of case stated brought by a group of campaigners against fox hunting who had been convicted of the offence under s 69(3). The group had been trespassing on land in order to observe and record the digging out of a fox. The court below had found as a matter of fact that the appellants had not committed an offence of aggravated trespass contrary to s 68(1), because they had no intention to disrupt, obstruct, or intimidate, but merely to be present and observe. Nonetheless, the Divisional Court upheld the appellants' convictions under s 69(3), because it was sufficient that the police officer who had given the direction under s 69(1) had reasonably believed them to be committing aggravated trespass, had given a direction to that effect and the appellants had been aware that a direction had been given.

5.72 Section 69(4) provides that it is a defence to proceedings for an offence under s 69(3) for the accused to show

(a) that he was not trespassing on land, or
(b) that he had a reasonable excuse for failing to leave the land as soon as practicable or as the case may be, for re-entering the land as a trespasser.

5.73 There is at present no direct authority as to whether s 69(4) places an evidential or a legal burden on the accused to show either of the matters set out in (a) and (b) above. Following the reasoning in *Sheldrake v DPP*,[110] it is strongly arguable, at least in relation to the issue of whether or not the accused was trespassing, that the accused should bear only an evidential burden: ie that it should be for the accused only to raise some evidence to challenge the allegation that he was trespassing and that it should then fall to the prosecution to prove the trespass beyond reasonable doubt. This is particularly the case where there is an issue as to the boundaries of the land in question: this issue is far more likely to be within the particular knowledge of the occupier of the land than of the accused; and thus it is arguably in breach of the presumption of innocence within Article 6(2) of the European Convention on Human Rights to place more than an evidential burden on the accused in this respect. Obiter comments to this effect were made by the court in relation to a similar defence under s 61(6) of the 1994 Act in *R (Fuller) v Chief Constable of Dorset Police*.[111] Such arguments have particular force in respect of s 69(4)(a) given that the substantive offence under s 68(1) requires the prosecutor to prove the fact of trespass to the criminal standard. In this context it would be surprising if Parliament intended to impose more than

---

[109] Independent, 23 March 1998.
[110] [2005] 1 AC 264.
[111] [2003] 1 QB 480, para 55.

an evidential burden on a defendant to show that he was not trespassing for the purposes of s 69.

Powers to remove trespassers present on land for purpose of residing there

Directions to leave the land

Section 61 of the Criminal Justice and Public Order Act 1994 replaces ss 34–39 of the Public Order Act 1986. Section 61(1) provides that: **5.74**

> If the senior police officer present at the scene reasonably believes that two or more persons are trespassing on land and are present there with the common purpose of residing there for any period, that reasonable steps have been taken by or on behalf of the occupier to ask them to leave and—
>
> (a) that any of those persons has caused damage to the land or to property on the land or used threatening, abusive or insulting words or behaviour towards the occupier, a member of his family or an employee or agent of his, or
> (b) that those persons have between them six or more vehicles on the land,
>
> he may direct those persons, or any of them, to leave the land and to remove any vehicles or other property they have with them on the land.[112]

Section 61(2) makes clear that a direction under s 61(1) may be given both in respect of persons who are reasonably believed by the senior police officer present to have entered land as trespassers and those who were not originally trespassing, but who have subsequently become trespassers. **5.75**

The direction may be communicated by any constable at the scene, it does not have to be communicated by the senior officer who gave the direction.[113] **5.76**

In *R (Fuller) v Chief Constable of Dorset Police*,[114] Stanley Burnton J held that it is implicit in s 61(1) that the power to give a direction can only lawfully be exercised where trespassers have failed to comply with the steps taken by the occupier to ask them to leave. In other words, a direction cannot lawfully be given until the trespassers have had an opportunity to comply with the occupier's requests. Further, an order given under s 61(1) must be an order to leave immediately: an order to leave at some future time, even where the time is specified, will be invalid. **5.77**

Definitions

Section 61(9) provides definitions of key terms within the section: **5.78**

'Trespass' is defined as:

(a) in England and Wales, subject to the extensions effected by s 61(7), trespass as against the occupier of the land;
(b) in Scotland, entering, or as the case may be remaining on, land without lawful authority and without the occupier's consent.

---

[112] This section replaces the Public Order Act 1986, ss 34–39.
[113] Public Order Act 1994, s 61(3).
[114] [2003] 1 QB 480.

Section 61(7) extends the definition of trespass, for the purposes of s 61, to include, in respect of common land, 'infringement of the commoner's rights'. 'Common land' and commoner's rights are defined in s 22 of the Commons Registration Act 1965. In summary, 'common land' is land, other than a town or village green or highways, over which there are rights of 'sole or several vesture or herbage or of sole or several pasture'[115] and also that for which, for a period of not less than twenty years, a significant number of the inhabitants of the locality have indulged in lawful sports and pastimes as of right.[116] 'Rights of common' are defined as including 'cattlegates or beastgates (by whatever name known) and rights of sole or several vesture or herbage or of sole or several pasture, but . . . not . . . rights held for a term of years or from year to year'.[117]

5.79 References in s 61 to 'the occupier' include the commoners (ie those with rights of common) or any of them or, in the case of common land to which the public has access, the local authority as well as any commoner.[118]

5.80 'Occupier' is defined as

   (a) in England and Wales, the person entitled to possession of the land by virtue of an estate or interest held by him; and
   (b) in Scotland, the person lawfully entitled to natural possession of the land.[119]

5.81 'Land' does not include buildings, other than agricultural buildings[120] and scheduled monuments.[121] Nor does it include land forming part of a highway unless it is a footpath, bridleway, or byway open to all traffic within the meaning of Part III of the Wildlife and Countryside Act 1981; is a restricted byway within the meaning of Part II of the Countryside and Rights of Way Act 2000, or is a cycle track under the Highways Act 1980, or the Cycle Tracks Act 1984;[122] or, with certain specified exceptions, a road within the meaning of the Roads (Scotland) Act 1984.

5.82 'Vehicle', within the meaning of the section, is given a very wide definition and includes 'any chassis or body, with or without wheels'; it does not have to be in a fit state for use on the roads.

5.83 A person may be regarded for the purposes of s 61 as having a purpose of residing in a place notwithstanding that he has a home elsewhere.[123]

Offence of failing to leave or re-entering after direction

5.84 Section 61(4) of the Criminal Justice and Public Order Act 1994 makes it a criminal offence where a person, who knowing that a police direction under s 61(1) has been given which applies to him, fails to leave the land as soon as reasonably practicable, or,

---

[115] Commons Registration Act 1965, s 22(1).
[116] Ibid, s 22(1A).
[117] Ibid, s 22(1).
[118] Criminal Justice and Public Order Act 1994, s 61(7)(b).
[119] Ibid, s 61(9).
[120] Within the meaning of, in England and Wales, the Local Government Finance Act 1988, Sch 5, paras 3–8, or, in Scotland, the Valuation and Rating (Scotland) Act 1956, s 7(2).
[121] Within the meaning of the Ancient Monuments and Archaeological Areas Act 1979.
[122] See 5.50 above for further explanation of these terms.
[123] Criminal Justice and Public Order Act 1994, s 61(9).

having left, re-enters the land as a trespasser within three months of the day on which the direction was given.

The offence is summary only. The maximum penalty is three months' imprisonment and/ or a fine of upto level 4 on the standard scale. **5.85**

Defences

Section 61(6) specifies that it is a defence to proceedings for this offence for the accused to show **5.86**

(a) that he was not trespassing on the land; or
(b) that he had a reasonable excuse for failing to leave the land as soon as reasonably practicable or, as the case may be, for again entering the land as a trespasser.[124]

Human rights considerations

The comments made in 5.69 above in respect of the legal certainty of directions made under s 69(1) of the 1994 Act are also applicable to directions made under this section. **5.87**

The fact that the procedure under s 61 is effective without trespassers having had a previous opportunity to be heard before a court does not mean that s 61 is incompatible with Article 6 of the European Convention on Human Rights. The opportunity of a person prosecuted under s 61(4) to challenge his arrest and prosecution in court proceedings is sufficient.[125] **5.88**

A prosecution under s 61(4) may amount to a violation of a person's Article 8 rights, but not necessarily. Prosecution will be justified under Article 8(2) if it pursues a legitimate aim and is necessary and proportionate.[126] **5.89**

Power to seize and remove vehicles

Section 62 provides that a constable may seize and remove a vehicle where a direction has been given under s 61 and the constable reasonably suspects that a person to whom the direction applies has, without reasonable excuse, failed to remove the vehicle from the land, or has re-entered the land as a trespasser with the vehicle within three months of the direction being given. Section 67 of the 1994 Act provides for regulations specifying charges in respect of the removal, retention, disposal, and destruction of vehicles seized under s 62.[127] Sections 62 and 67 have been held to be compatible with Article 1 of the First Protocol of the European Convention (the right to peaceful enjoyment of possessions).[128] **5.90**

Powers to remove trespassers with caravans

The Anti-social Behaviour Act 2003, ss 60–4 insert new ss 62A–E into the Criminal Justice and Public Order Act 1994. These provisions confer powers on the police to direct **5.91**

---

[124] For the burden of proof in respect of these defences see 5.73 and 10.172.
[125] *R (Fuller) v Chief Constable of Dorset Police*, para 57.
[126] Ibid, paras 59 and 60.
[127] See Police (Retention and Disposal of Vehicles) Regulations 1995, SI 1995/723.
[128] *R (Fuller) v Chief Constable of Dorset Police*, paras 61–3.

trespassers to leave land and to remove any vehicles they have with them where the senior officer present at the scene reasonably believes:

> s 62A(2) ...
>
> (a) that the person and one or more others ('the trespassers') are trespassing on the land;
> (b) that the trespassers have between them at least one vehicle on the land;
> (c) that the trespassers are present on the land with the common purpose of residing there for any period;
> (d) if it appears to the officer that the person has one or more caravans in his possession or under his control on the land, that there is a suitable pitch on a relevant caravan site for that caravan or each of those caravans;
> (e) that the occupier of the land or a person acting on his behalf has asked the police to remove the trespassers from the land.

5.92 Section 62A(1) specifies that the power to issue a direction under this section arises where the senior officer present at the scene reasonably believes that the conditions (plural) in subsec 2 are satisfied ie all of the conditions must be satisfied before a direction can lawfully be given. As with directions under s 61 of the 1994 Act, a direction under s 62A may be communicated by any constable present at the scene.[129]

Definitions

5.93 Section 62D defines the terms 'trespass' and 'occupier' for the purposes of ss 62A–C in respect of common land. Section 62E provides definitions of other key terms for the purposes of ss 62A–D. Of note is the fact that although the definition of 'land' for the purposes of these provisions is similar to that for the purposes of s 61, in that it does not include buildings other than agricultural buildings and scheduled monuments, highways are not exempt for the purposes of ss 62A–D.

5.94 'Relevant caravan site' for the purposes of this section means a caravan site situated within the area of the local authority concerned, and which is managed by such a local authority or a registered social landlord.[130] Section 62A(5) places an officer proposing to give a direction under this section under an obligation to consult every local authority within whose area the land is situated as to whether there is a suitable pitch for any caravan affected by the direction.

Offence of failing to leave or re-entering after a direction

5.95 Section 62B makes it an offence where a person, knowing that a direction has been given under s 62A which applies to him, to fail to leave the land as soon as reasonably practicable or to re-enter the land in the area of the relevant local authority as a trespasser with the intention of residing there within three months of the date of the direction. The 'relevant local authority' is defined in s 62E. The offence is triable summarily and is punishable with a prison sentence of up to three months and/or a fine not exceeding level 4 on the standard scale.

---

[129] Criminal Justice and Public Order Act 1994, s 62A(3); See 5.69 above for discussion of the requirement of legal certainty.

[130] Ibid, s 62A(6).

Defence

Section 62B(5) provides that it is a defence for the accused to show that he was not trespass-   **5.96**
ing on the land, or that he had a reasonable excuse for failing to leave the land as soon as
reasonably practicable, or for entering, within three months of the direction, land in the
area of the relevant local authority as a trespasser with the requisite intent. It is also a
defence under this subsection if, at the time the direction was given, the accused was under
18 years of age and residing with his parent or guardian.[131]

Powers to seize and remove vehicles

Section 62C provides for police powers to seize and remove vehicles where a constable   **5.97**
reasonably suspects that a person to whom a direction under s 62A(1) has been given has
failed to remove a vehicle or has re-entered land in the area of the relevant local authority as
a trespasser with a vehicle within three months of the direction. Section 67 provides for the
making of regulations prescribing charges in respect of the removal, retention, disposal,
and destruction of vehicles seized under s 62C.[132]

Powers to remove those preparing for or attending raves[133]

Directions to leave the land

Section 63 of the Criminal Justice and Public Order Act 1994 confers powers on a police   **5.98**
officer of at least the rank of superintendent in specified circumstances, discussed below, to
direct persons to leave land and to remove any vehicles or other property where he reasonably believes that:

s 63(2) . . .

  (a) two or more persons are making preparations for the holding there of a gathering to
      which [s 63] applies;[134]
  (b) ten or more persons are waiting for such a gathering to begin there, or
  (c) ten or more persons are attending such a gathering which is progress.

Definitions

Gatherings to which s 63 applies are defined in s 63(1) as gatherings: **5.99**

  on land in the open air of 20 or more persons (whether or not trespassers) at which amplified
  music is played during the night (with or without intermissions) and is such as, by reason of
  its loudness and duration and the time at which it is played, is likely to cause serious distress
  to the inhabitants of the locality; and for this purpose

  (a) such a gathering continues during intermissions in the music and, where the gathering
      extends over several days, throughout the period during which amplified music is played
      at night (with or without intermissions); and
  (b) 'music' includes sounds wholly or predominantly characterized by the emission of a
      succession of repetitive beats.

---

[131] For the burden of proof in relation to these defences see discussion at 5.73 and 10.172 above.
[132] See fn 125 above.
[133] These powers are in addition to the powers to deal with public nuisance, see Ch 2.
[134] See 5.99 below.

5.100 A direction under s 63, if not communicated to those to whom it applies by the officer giving the direction, may be communicated by any constable at the scene.[135] Persons shall be treated as having had a direction communicated to them if reasonable steps have been taken to bring it to their attention.[136]

5.101 Section 64 confers a power on the police to enter land without a warrant where an officer of at least the rank of superintendent reasonably believes that circumstances exist which would justify the giving of a direction under s 63. The purposes for which such an entry may lawfully be effected are

(a) to ascertain whether such circumstances exist;
(b) to exercise any power conferred on a constable by s 63 or s 64(4).

Definitions

5.102 Section 63(10) defines 'land in the open air' as including a place that is partly open to the air and specifies that the terms 'occupier', 'trespasser', and 'vehicle' for the purposes of s 63 have the same meaning as in s 61.[137]

5.103 Section 58 of the Anti-social Behaviour Act 2003 inserted a new subsec 1A into s 63 of the 1994 Act, extending the definition of gatherings for the purposes of s 63 to include trespassory gatherings on land of twenty or more persons which would meet the definition within s 63(1) were they to have taken place in the open air. In short, the new s 1A provides that *indoor* gatherings may also be caught by the provisions of ss 63–6, provided that twenty or more persons there present are trespassing.

First rave offence: failing to leave or re-entering after direction (s 63(6))

5.104 Under s 63(6), a person knowing that a direction under s 63(2) has been given which applies to him, commits a criminal offence if he

(a) fails to leave the land as soon as reasonably practicable; or
(b) having left again enters the land within the period of seven days from the giving of the direction.

Statutory defences

5.105 It is a defence under s 63(7) to a charge under s 63(6) for a person to show that he had a reasonable excuse for failing to leave the land as soon as reasonably practicable or, as the case may be, for again entering the land. Unlike the statutory defences contained in s 69(4)(a) and s 61(6)(a), considered above, it is no defence to a charge under s 63(6) to show that the accused was not trespassing. This is because an offence under s 63(6) may be committed even if the accused was not trespassing at the time. In contrast to the issue of trespass, the defence of 'reasonable excuse' contained in s 63(7) is more likely to be within the particular knowledge of the accused and therefore arguments that s 63(7) imposes an evidential as

---

[135] Criminal Justice and Public Order Act 1994, s 63(3).
[136] Ibid, s 63(4).
[137] See 5.82.

opposed to a legal burden on the accused are likely to carry less weight than in respect of the defences under s 69(4)(a) and s 61(6)(a).[138]

Section 63 specifies that certain activity and persons are exempt from prosecution under s 63(6) and 63(7A).[139] These are **5.106**

(a) licensable activity within the meaning of s 1(1)(c) of the Licensing Act 2003 provided that it is carried out in accordance with an authorization within the meaning of s 136 of that Act;[140]
(b) the occupier of the land in question, any member of his family and any employee or agent of his and any person whose home is situated on the land.[141]

Second rave offence: preparing for/attending a rave within twenty-four hours of direction (s 63(7A))

Section 63(7A), inserted into Criminal Justice and Public Order Act 1994 by s 58 of the Anti-social Behaviour Act 2003, creates a further criminal offence where a person, knowing that a direction under s 63(2) has been given which applies to him, makes preparations for, or attends, a gathering as defined in s 63(1) or (1A) within twenty-four hours from the time the direction was given. This offence is triable summarily only and is punishable with a prison sentence of up to three months and/or a fine not exceeding level 4 on the standard scale.[142] **5.107**

Third rave offence: proceeding to a rave contrary to direction (s 65)

A third criminal offence in respect of raves is created by s 65. This provides that where a direction under s 63(2) has been given, a constable in uniform within a five-mile radius of the boundary of the site of the rave may stop any person he reasonably believes to be on his way to the rave and direct him not to proceed. Knowing failure to comply with such a direction is a summary offence punishable with a fine not exceeding level 3 on the standard scale.[143] **5.108**

Powers to seize and remove vehicles and sound equipment

Section 64(4) provides for a power of seizure and removal in respect of vehicles and sound equipment. The power is exercisable where a direction has been given under s 63 and a constable reasonably suspects that any person to whom the direction applies has, without reasonable excuse **5.109**

(a) failed to remove the vehicle or sound equipment from the land; or
(b) entered the land as a trespasser with the vehicle or sound equipment within seven days from the order being given.

---

138 See *Sheldrake v DPP* [2005] 1 AC 264.
139 See 5.107 below.
140 Criminal Justice and Public Order Act 1994, s 63(9).
141 Ibid, s 63(5) read with s 63(10).
142 Ibid, s 63(7B).
143 Ibid, s 65(4).

Although the subsection does not expressly refer to any requirement that the person to whom the direction applies must know that such a direction has been given, this can be inferred from the reference to 'reasonable excuse': presumably lack of knowledge of an applicable direction would always amount to a reasonable excuse for failing to comply. Vehicles and sound equipment belonging to an exempt person, as defined in s 63(10) (ie the occupier of the land, his family, employees, agents, or any person whose home is situated on the land) may not be seized under this section.

Forfeiture of sound equipment

5.110   Section 66 provides for a court to order forfeiture of sound equipment where a person has been convicted of an offence under s 63. Section 66(3) specifies that in considering whether to order forfeiture, the court shall have regard to the value of the property and the likely financial and other effects on the offender of the making of the order (taken together with any other order that the court contemplates making).

5.111   Where forfeiture has been ordered, a third party who can satisfy the court that he is the owner of the property, may make an application for return of the property to him, but only if he satisfies the court either that he had not consented to the offender having possession of the property or that he did not know, and had no reason to suspect, that the property was likely to be used at a gathering to which s 63 applies.[144] Any such application must be made within six months from the date of the forfeiture order.[145]

5.112   The provisions of s 67 and the regulations[146] made thereunder governing the removal, retention, disposal, and destruction of vehicles apply to vehicles seized under s 64(4).

Unauthorized campers: powers of removal

5.113   Section 77 of Criminal Justice and Public Order Act 1994 confers powers on local authorities to direct unauthorized campers to leave the land on which they have set up camp and to remove any vehicle or other property they have with them on the land. Section 77(3) makes it a summary offence for a person, knowing that an applicable direction has been given, to fail to leave the land or to remove the vehicle or other property as soon as practicable, or, having removed the vehicle or property, to re-enter the land with a vehicle within three months of the date on which the direction was given. This offence is punishable with a fine not exceeding level 3 on the standard scale.

Directions to leave: residing in a vehicle

5.114   The circumstances in which a direction may be made are that it must appear to the local authority that persons are residing in a vehicle or vehicles within its area:

(a) on any land forming part of a highway;

(b) on any other unoccupied land; or

(c) on any occupied land without the consent of the occupier.

---

[144] Ibid, s 66(5) and (8).
[145] Ibid, s 66(7).
[146] See Police (Retention and Disposal of Vehicles) Regulations 1995, SI 1995/723.

Section 77(6) defines 'land' as meaning land in the open air. 'Vehicle' is given a broad **5.115** definition, which is materially the same, although not identically worded, to that applicable to s 61.

Notice of a direction given under s 77(1) must be served on the persons to whom the direc- **5.116** tion applies, but it is sufficient for the direction to specify the land and (except where the direction applies to only one person) to be addressed to all occupants of the vehicles on the land, without naming them.[147] Where it is impracticable to serve notice of a direction under s 77(1) on a person to whom it applies, the notice will be treated as having been properly served if a copy of it is fixed in a prominent place to the vehicle or vehicles concerned.[148]

The local authority is also required to take such steps as may be reasonably practicable to **5.117** secure that a copy of a notice of direction under s 77(1) is displayed on the land in question (otherwise than being fixed to a vehicle) in a manner designed to ensure that it is likely to be seen by any person camping on the land.[149] In addition, the local authority is required to give notice of any direction under s 77(1) to the owner of the land and to any occupier of the land, unless after reasonable inquiries it is unable to ascertain their name and address. By virtue of s 79(4), the owner and occupier of the land are entitled to appear and to be heard in any prosecution brought under s 77(3) against unauthorized campers on their land.

Section 77(4) clarifies that a direction made under s 77(1) continues to operate so as to **5.118** require persons who re-enter the land within three months of the date of the order to leave and remove their vehicles and property, just as they were required to do when the direction was first given.

Statutory defence

Section 77(5) provides that it is a defence to an offence under s 77(3) for an accused to show **5.119** that his failure to leave or to remove the vehicle or other property as soon as practicable or his re-entry with a vehicle was due to illness, mechanical breakdown, or other immediate emergency.[150]

*Application to the magistrates' court: Criminal Justice and
Public Order Act 1994, s 78*

Section 78(1) provides that: **5.120**

A magistrates' court may, on a complaint made by a local authority, if satisfied that persons and vehicles in which they are residing are present on land within that authority's area in contravention of a direction given under section 77, make an order requiring the removal of any vehicle or other property which is so present on the land and any person residing in it.

---

[147] Criminal Justice and Public Order Act 1994, s 77(2).
[148] Ibid, s 79.
[149] Ibid, s 79(3).
[150] Since these matters are predominantly within the knowledge of the accused it is likely that this subsection would be construed as imposing a legal burden on the accused. See 5.73 and 10.172 for further discussion of the burden of proof.

Such an order may authorize the local authority to take such steps as are reasonably necessary to ensure that the order is complied with.[151] In particular, the magistrates may authorize the local authority to enter the land and take specified steps to secure entry to the vehicles or property subject to the order and to make them suitable for removal.[152] The local authority must give the owner and occupier of occupied land at least twenty-four hours notice of their intention to enter onto the land, unless it is not possible, after reasonable enquiries, to ascertain their names and addresses.[153]

5.121 Section 78(5) provides that a summons issued by a magistrates' court in response to a complaint made by a local authority under s 78(1) may be directed to the occupant of a particular vehicle on the land in question, or to all occupants of vehicles on the land in question, without naming him or them. However, if the person or persons to whom the summons is directed fails to attend court, the magistrates do not have power to issue a warrant for their arrest. This is because s 78(6) expressly disapplies s 55(2) of the Magistrates' Courts Act 1980, under which the court would ordinarily have power to issue a warrant for arrest in such circumstances. The court may, however, proceed to hear the complaint in the person's absence, if satisfied that the summons was served on them within a reasonable time before the hearing, or if they have attended court in relation to the matter on a previous occasion.[154]

5.122 A summons issued under s 78(5) is deemed to have been properly served if, where it is impracticable to serve it directly on the person or persons to whom it applies, it is fixed in a prominent place on the vehicle or vehicles concerned.[155]

5.123 The local authority is required to display a copy of the summons on the land (otherwise than by being fixed to a vehicle) and to give notice to the owner and occupier of the land. The owner and occupier are also entitled to be heard in any proceedings under s 78.[156]

5.124 It is a summary criminal offence, punishable by a fine not exceeding level 3 on the standard scale to wilfully obstruct any person in the exercise of any power conferred on him by an order made under s 78(1).[157]

Guidance on use of powers under ss 77 and 78

5.125 The Department of the Environment and the Welsh Office issued Circular 18/94 (Welsh Office (76/94) Gypsy Sites Policy and Unauthorised Camping) to provide guidance on the exercise of the powers under s 77. More recently, the Office of the Deputy Prime Minister also produced 'Guidance on Managing Unauthorised Camping' (February 2004) and a 'Guide to effective use of enforcement powers—Part 1: Unauthorised Encampments' (February 2006). The 2004 and 2006 Guidance both apply to England. The National Assembly for Wales/Home Office have produced 'Guidance on Managing Unauthorised

---

[151] Criminal Justice and Public Order Act 1994, s 78(2).
[152] Ibid.
[153] Ibid, s 78(3).
[154] Magistrates' Courts Act 1980, s 55(1) and (3).
[155] Criminal Justice and Public Order Act 1994, s 79(2).
[156] Ibid, s 79(4).
[157] Ibid, s 78(4).

Camping' (January 2005). All of the guidance emphasizes the importance of local authorities taking humanitarian considerations into account and of making adequate enquiries prior to taking eviction action to ensure that the individuals concerned do not have pressing needs which would make it inhumane to proceed. A number of cases have confirmed that, whatever the legal status of the various guidance documents, the extent of a local authority's compliance with it, or deviation from it will, at very least, be relevant to any question of whether the authority's action was *Wednesbury* unreasonable.[158]

Public Order Act 1986, ss 14A–C

Trespassory assemblies

Sections 70 and 71 of the Criminal Justice and Public Order Act 1994 insert new ss 14–C **5.126** into the Public Order Act 1986, and in so doing introduce a new concept into the law of public order: the 'trespassory assembly'. This is an assembly of twenty or more persons[159] which is 'held on land [in the open air][160] to which the public has no right of access or only a limited right of access, and . . . takes place . . . without the permission of the occupier of the land or so as to exceed the limits of any permission of his or the limits of the public's right of access'.[161]

At first blush this provision appears to be targeted largely at assemblies on private property. **5.127** However, the extension of the provision to land to which the public has limited rights of access, where such limits are exceeded, in fact means that the provision covers virtually all public space. There can be very few public places to which the public has wholly unfettered rights of access. The leading case on trespassory assembly, *DPP v Jones*[162] concerned a peaceful assembly on the grass verge beside a public road near to Stonehenge and involved a finely balanced analysis by the House of Lords of the limits of the public right of access to public highways. This case is considered in more detail below.

Sections 14A–C of the Public Order Act 1986 are significant because they provide, for the **5.128** first time, powers to ban certain types of public assembly. When the 1986 Act was originally passed, consideration was given to making public assemblies akin to processions and extending the power to ban processions to assemblies also. However, the White Paper[163] concluded that:

> Meetings and assemblies are a more important means of exercising freedom of speech than are marches: a power to ban them, even as a last resort, would be potentially a major infringement of freedom of speech (especially at election time). It might also be difficult to enforce: and there was no strong request from the police for a power to ban.

---

[158] *R v Hillingdon LBC, ex p McDonagh* [1998] 31 HLR 531; *R v Lincolnshire CC and Wealden DC, ex p Atkinson, Wales and Stratford* (1995) 8 Admin LR 529; *R v Leeds CC, ex p Maloney* (1998) 31 HLR 552, QBD.
[159] Public Order Act 1986, s 14A(9).
[160] See definition of land, ibid, in s 14A(9).
[161] Ibid, s 14A(5).
[162] [1999] 2 AC 240.
[163] Cmnd 9510, para 5.3.

In the event, the powers relating to assemblies were therefore limited to imposing conditions.[164] This, however, changed with the passage of ss 70 and 71 of the Criminal Justice and Public Order Act 1994. Some commentators have speculated that this was prompted by governmental frustration at the failure to secure convictions following the 'Battle of the Beanfield', at which there had been violent clashes between police and those seeking to celebrate the summer solstice at Stonehenge.[165]

The circumstances in which a ban may be imposed

5.129 Within the City of London or the metropolitan police area, the Commissioner of Police may, with the consent of the Secretary of State, make an order prohibiting trespassory assemblies within an area within his district not exceeding a 5-mile radius from a specified centre and for a period not exceeding four days, provided that he reasonably believes that a trespassory assembly is intended to be held and 'may result in (i) serious disruption to the life of the community, or (ii) where the land, or building or monument on it, is of historical, architectural, archaeological or scientific importance, in significant damage to the land, building or monument'.[166] Outside of the City of London and the metropolitan police area, the chief police officer (Chief Constable), where he reasonably believes the same set of conditions apply, may apply to the appropriate district council for an order under s 14A prohibiting for a specified period the holding of trespassory assemblies in the district or a specified part of it.[167] And on receipt of such an application, the council, with the consent of the Secretary of State, may make an order either in the terms of the application or with such modifications as may be approved by the Secretary of State.[168]

5.130 Section 14A(9) specifies that:

> 'limited', in relation to a right of access by the public to land, means that their use of it is restricted to use for a particular purpose (as in the case of a highway or road) or is subject to other restrictions.

5.131 For the purposes of ss 14A–C, 'assembly' means an assembly of twenty or more persons[169] and 'land' means land in the open air.[170] It is of note that s 57 of the Anti-social Behaviour Act 2003, which amends the definition of 'public assembly' for the purposes of s 14 of the Public Order Act 1986 from being an assembly of *twenty* or more persons to an assembly of *two* or more persons, does *not* apply to trespassory assemblies for the purposes of ss 14A–C. Trespassory assemblies still require the presence of twenty or more persons.

---

[164] Public Order Act 1986, s 14. See Ch 3 for discussion of assemblies generally.

[165] Andy Worthington, 1 June 2009 at <http://www.guardian.co.uk/commentisfree/libertycentral/2009/jun/01/remembering-the-battle-of-the-beanfield>.

[166] Public Order Act 1986, s 14A(4).

[167] Ibid, s 14A(1).

[168] Ibid, s 14A(2).

[169] In contrast to public assemblies, held in a public place as defined in s 16 of the 1986 Act, the number of participants required for a trespassory assembly for the purposes of ss 14A–C remains twenty or more—ie the reduction to two or more persons effected by the Anti-social Behaviour Act 2003, s 57 applies only to public assemblies and not to trespassory assemblies.

[170] Public Order Act 1986, s 14A(9).

The geographical reach of an order under s 4A may be substantial, it may extend to an area   **5.132**
with a radius of up to 5 miles from a specified centre and may be for a period of up to four
days.[171]

Once an order under s 14A is in place, it is a criminal offence contrary to s 14B, to organize,   **5.133**
take part in, or incite another to take part in a trespassory assembly within the specified
area. Section 14C confers power on a constable in uniform, within the area specified in an
order under s 14A, to stop those whom he reasonably believes to be on their way to an
assembly prohibited by the order and to direct them not to proceed in the direction of the
assembly. Knowing failure to comply with such a direction is a criminal offence contrary to
s 14C(3).

An order made under s 14A may be revoked or varied by a subsequent order made in the   **5.134**
same way.[172] And any order made under s 14A shall, if not made in writing, be recorded in
writing as soon as practicable after being made.[173]

The offences of organizing[174] or inciting[175] another to participate in a trespassory assembly   **5.135**
are both punishable with imprisonment of up to three months[176] and/or a fine not exceeding level 4 on the standard scale.[177] The offence of taking part[178] in a trespassory assembly
is punishable with a fine not exceeding level 3 on the standard scale.[179]

In *DPP v Jones*,[180] the House of Lords considered the extent to which static assemblies   **5.136**
on the highway are automatically trespassory in that they exceed the primary right to
pass and repass along the highway. The case concerned a peaceful assembly of more than
twenty people on the grass verge of the A344 road adjacent to the perimeter fence
of Stonehenge to mark the tenth anniversary of the 'Battle of Beanfield'. The key issue
before their Lordships was the extent of the public right of access to the highway and,
in particular, whether the right was strictly limited to the right to pass and repass, or whether
the right of access extended to other reasonable uses not inconsistent with the primary
right to pass and repass. If the public right was limited to passing and repassing, then
any static assembly on the highway would be in excess of that right and therefore
trespassory.

The majority of their Lordships rejected a strict interpretation. Lord Irvine of Lairg LC found   **5.137**
the public's right of access extends to all reasonable activity that does not amount to a public
or private nuisance, or an obstruction of the highway unreasonably impeding the primary
right of the general public to pass and repass.[181] Lord Clyde emphasized the primacy of the

---

[171] Ibid, s 14A(6).
[172] Ibid, s 14A(7).
[173] Ibid, s 14A(8).
[174] Contrary to s 14B(1).
[175] Contrary to s 14B(3).
[176] This will be increased to 51 weeks if/when s 280(2), (3) and related provisions are brought into force.
[177] Public Order Act 1986, ss 14B(5) and (7).
[178] Contrary to s 14B(2).
[179] Ibid, s 14B(6).
[180] [1999] 2 AC 240. See also 4.08–18 above.
[181] Ibid, pp 254H–255A.

right to pass and repass, but concluded that other usual and reasonable uses of the highway that are consistent with that right are within the scope of the public's right of access.[182] And Lord Hutton held that the common law fell to be extended to include reasonable use of the highway beyond passing and repassing, provided always that the use is not inconsistent with the paramount purpose of a highway, which is for the public to pass and repass.[183]

5.138   On the facts as found in *Jones*, the majority held that the entirely peaceful, non-obstructive assembly had been within the (extended) right of public access to the highway and was not therefore trespassory for the purposes of ss 14A–C. However, *Jones* is *not* authority for the proposition that all peaceful, non-obstructive assemblies on the highway will be non-trespassory. Both Lord Clyde and Lord Hutton stressed that it will be a question of fact whether any given assembly amounts to a reasonable use of the highway, to be determined by reference to its duration, purpose, the space it occupies, and its effects.[184]

5.139   In the case of *Gypsy Council v United Kingdom*[185] the European Court of Human Rights considered the compatibility of ss 14A–C with European Convention rights. The Gypsy Council complained that an order under s 14A banning Horsmondon fair, a traditional gathering of cultural and social importance to the gypsy community, was contrary to the participants' rights under Articles 8, 11, and 14. The European Court of Human Rights rejected the claim as manifestly ill-founded, finding that although the ban did constitute an interference with Convention rights, it was in accordance with the law (the statutory provisions were sufficiently clear and precise to meet the requirements of legal certainty), pursued a legitimate aim (preventing public disorder) and was necessary in a democratic society.

Serious and Organised Crime and Police Act 2005, s 128

Trespass on a protected site

5.140   Section 128 of the Serious Organised Crime and Police Act 2005, as amended by the Terrorism Act 2006, introduces a new offence of trespassing on a protected site. This represents a further significant extension of the criminal law of trespass. When originally proposed, this measure was said to be in response to the intrusion at Windsor Castle during Prince William's 21st birthday celebrations and was described by the then Home Secretary as 'a sledge hammer to crack a nut'.[186] However, the Explanatory Memorandum that accompanied the first order specifying designated sites makes clear that, in practice, use of the measures against protestors was at the forefront of government thinking.[187] The Memorandum acknowledges that during the passage of the Serious Organised Crime and Police Bill through Parliament, a commitment was made that designations under s 128 would be made sparingly. However, it goes on to commend the deterrent effect of an

---

[182]   Ibid, p 279F.
[183]   Ibid, p 292G.
[184]   Ibid, pp 281D–F; 293B–D.
[185]   Application No 00066336/01, 14 May 2002.
[186]   Hansard, HC, col 1059 (7 December 2004).
[187]   The Memorandum is available online at <http://www.opsi.gov.uk/si/em2005/uksiem_20053447_en.pdf>.

offence of criminal trespass on Ministry of Defence sites where protest activity there has the potential to impede the operation of the site.

A 'site' for the purposes of s 128 is 'the whole or part of any building or buildings, or any **5.141** land, or both'.[188] The 'protected sites' to which s 128 applies are 'nuclear site[s] or . . . designated site[s]'.[189] 'Nuclear site' is defined as follows:

(1B) (a) so much of any premises in respect of which a nuclear site licence (within the meaning of the Nuclear Installations Act 1965) is for the time being in force as lies within the outer perimeter of the protection provided for those premises; and
(b) so much of any other premises of which premises falling within paragraph (a) form a part as lies within that outer perimeter.
(1C) For this purpose—
(a) the outer perimeter of the protection provided for any premises is the line of the outermost fences, walls or other obstacles provided or relied on for protecting those premises from intruders; and
(b) that line shall be determined on the assumption that every gate, door or other barrier across a way through a fence, wall or other obstacle is closed.

'Designated site' means a site specified or described (in any way) in an order made by the **5.142** Secretary of State, and designated for the purposes of s 128 by the order. A 'designated site' for the purposes of s 128 is *not* the same as the 'designated area' defined in s 138 of the Serious and Organised Crime and Police Act 2005 for the purposes of ss 132–7 of that Act.[190] A site may only be designated by the Secretary of State for the purposes of s 128 if it is Crown land; or it is land belonging to Her Majesty in her private capacity or to the immediate heir to the Throne in his private capacity; or it appears to the Secretary of State that it is appropriate to designate the site in the interests of national security.[191] The meaning of 'Crown land' is further defined in s 128(8)(b) and (9).

Two orders have been made designating various military bases, Royal residences, and politi- **5.143** cal sites, including the Palace of Westminster and Portcullis House, 10 Downing Street, Chequers, GCHQ premises, and other places, as designated sites for the purposes of s 128.[192] A further order has been made amending the previous order in so far as it related to Chequers.[193]

Section 128(7) of the 2005 Act specifies that, for the purposes of s 128, a person who is on **5.144** any protected site as a trespasser does not cease to be a trespasser by virtue of being allowed time to leave the site.

Further, a person accused of an offence under s 128 cannot rely on any right of the public **5.145** to 'access land' under s 2(1) of the Countryside and Rights of Way Act 2000, because

---

[188] Serious Organised Crime and Police Act 2005, s 128(8)(a).
[189] Ibid, s 128(1A).
[190] See Ch 3 (3.94 et seq) and Chapter 4 (4.100) for discussion of ss 132–8 of the 2005 Act.
[191] Ibid, ss 128(2) and (3).
[192] Serious Organised Crime and Police Act 2005 (Designated Sites) Order 2005, SI 2005/3447; Serious Organised Crime and Police Act 2005 (Designated Sites under Section 128) Order 2007, SI 2007/930.
[193] Serious Organised Crime and Police Act 2005 (Designated Sites under Section 128) (Amendment) Order 2007, SI 2007/1387.

s 131(1) of the Serious and Organised Crime Act 2005 disapplies that provision to land in respect of which a designation order is in force. 'Access land' is defined in s 1 of the Countryside and Rights of Way Act 2000. Broadly speaking it is open land, common land, and private land that has been dedicated as 'access land' in accordance with s 16 of the Countryside and Rights of Way Act 2000. Section 2 of the Countryside and Rights of Way Act 2000 gives the public, subject to specified restrictions, the right to enter and remain on any access land for the purposes of open-air recreation. The effect of s 131(1) of the 2005 Act is to disapply this right in respect of designated sites. Thus, in so far as any designated site for the purposes of s 128 extends over open, common, or designated land, it is no defence to a charge under that section to argue that one was exercising a right to open-air recreation under the Countryside and Rights of Way Act 2000.

5.146 Section 131(2) provides that 'the Secretary of State may take such steps as he considers appropriate to inform the public of the effect of any designation order, including, in particular, displaying notices on or near the site to which the order relates.' However, he may only do so if a person with sufficient interest in the land consents.[194] It is a defence for a person charged with an offence under s 128 to prove that he did not know, and had no reasonable cause to suspect, that the site in relation to which the offence is alleged to have been committed was a protected site.[195]

5.147 The offence is triable summarily only and carries a maximum penalty of six months' imprisonment and/or a fine not exceeding level 5 on the standard scale.[196] Proceedings for this offence may not be commenced without the consent of the Attorney General.[197]

5.148 A list of designated sites and the background to the enactment of the provisions can be found on the Home Office website.[198, 199]

Other offences involving trespass

By-laws

5.149 There are many by-laws which create criminal trespass offences, see, for example, those discussed in the cases of *Secretary of State for Defence v Percy*,[200] *DPP v Hutchinson*,[201] and *Tabernacle v Secretary of State for Defence*.[202] The by-law under challenge in the case of *Tabernacle* was paragraph 7(2)(f) of the Atomic Weapons Establishment (AWE) Aldermaston Byelaws 2007. This prohibited camping in 'tents, trees, caravans or otherwise' within 'controlled areas' owned by the Ministry of Defence within the vicinity of AWE

---

[194] Serious Organised Crime and Police Act 2005, s 131(3) and (4).
[195] Ibid, s 128(4).
[196] Ibid, s 128(5), read in conjunction with s 175.
[197] Ibid, s 128(6).
[198] See <http://security.homeoffice.gov.uk/legislation/current-legislation/terrorism-act-2006/criminal-trespass-sites>.
[199] Further information about the provisions, cases in which they have been applied, and the campaign to change them can be found on the website: <http://www.repeal-socpa.info>.
[200] [1999] 1 All ER 732.
[201] [1990] 3 WLR 196.
[202] [2009] EWCA Civ 23.

Aldermaston. Contravention of paragraph 7(2)(f) was made a criminal offence by virtue of paragraph 9 of the same provisions. In the circumstances of this case, this by-law was found to be unlawful because it amounted to a disproportionate interference with the rights to freedom of expression and freedom of assembly.

In general, by-laws are rules made by government departments, local authorities, corpora-   **5.150**
tions, and associations under statutory authority for the regulation, administration, or management of a certain district, property, or undertaking.[203] They are binding on all persons within the area or organization to which they relate. They require confirmation by a Secretary of State before they can be brought into force. Guidance directed to local authorities on the making of by-laws, including model by-laws, can be found on the website of the Department for Communities and Local Government.[204]

It is a valid defence to a criminal charge under a by-law to show that the provision is *ultra*   **5.151**
vires the powers under which it was made.[205]

Being in a prohibited place for a purpose prejudicial to the safety or interests of the State

It is an offence contrary to s 1 of the Official Secrets Act 1911 to approach, inspect, pass   **5.152**
over, be in the neighbourhood of, or enter any prohibited place, as defined in s 3 of the 1911 Act, for any purpose prejudicial to the safety or interests of the State. Section 3 defines 'prohibited place' as follows:

(a) any work of defence, arsenal, naval or air force establishment or station, factory, dock-yard, mine, minefield, camp, ship, or aircraft belonging to or occupied by or on behalf of His Majesty, or any telegraph, telephone, wireless or signal station, or office so belonging or occupied, and any place belonging to or occupied by or on behalf of His Majesty and used for the purpose of building, repairing, making, or storing any munitions of war, or any sketches, plans, models, or documents relating thereto, or for the purpose of getting any metals, oil, or minerals of use in time of war;

(b) any place not belonging to His Majesty where any [munitions of war], or any [sketches, models, plans] or documents relating thereto, are being made, repaired, [gotten] or stored under contract with, or with any person on behalf of, His Majesty, or otherwise on behalf of His Majesty; and

(c) any place belonging to [or used for the purposes of] His Majesty which is for the time being declared [by order of a Secretary of State] to be a prohibited place for the purposes of this section on the ground that information with respect thereto, or damage thereto, would be useful to an enemy; and

(d) any railway, road, way, or channel, or other means of communication by land or water (including any works or structures being part thereof or connected therewith), or any place used for gas, water, or electricity works or other works for purposes of a public character, or any place where any [munitions of war], or any [sketches, models, plans] or documents relating thereto, are being made, repaired, or stored otherwise than on

---

[203] For further discussion of by-laws generally see Ch 3 (3.152–61) and Ch 4 (4.94–102).
[204] See<http://www.communities.gov.uk/localgovernment/360902/byelaws/localgovernmentlegislation/guidancenotesarrangements/>.
[205] *Boddington v British Transport Police* [1999] 2 AC 143.

behalf of His Majesty, which is for the time being declared [by order of a Secretary of State] to be a prohibited place for the purposes of this section, on the ground that information with respect thereto, or the destruction or obstruction thereof, or interference therewith, would be useful to an enemy.

5.153 There are in addition two statutory instruments specifying further prohibited places for the purposes of the 1911 Act: the Official Secrets (Prohibited Place) Order 1955[206] and the Official Secrets (Prohibited Places) Order 1994;[207] these orders specify various nuclear sites, including those at Sellafield, Capenhurst, Harwell, and Windscale. Further, paragraph 2 of Schedule 17 to the Communications Act 2003 provides that 'for the purposes of the Official Secrets Act 1911, any electronic communications station or office belonging to, or occupied by, the provider of a public electronic communications service shall be a prohibited place'.

5.154 An offence contrary to s 1 of the 1911 Act is indictable only, with a maximum penalty of fourteen years' imprisonment.

Offences under the Vagrancy Act 1824

5.155 Section 4 of the Vagrancy Act 1824 provides that 'every person wandering abroad and lodging in any barn or outhouse, or in any deserted or unoccupied building, or in the open air, or under a tent, or in any cart or wagon, . . . and not giving a good account of himself or herself' commits an offence; as does any person 'being found in or upon any dwelling house, warehouse, coach-house, stable, or outhouse, or in any enclosed yard, garden, or area, for any unlawful purpose'.

5.156 The unlawful purpose must be the commission of some offence which would subject the party to criminal proceedings.[208] In *L v CPS*,[209] the Divisional Court held that the scope of s 4 is to be restrictively interpreted and that the words 'unlawful purpose' should be read as 'then and there about to commit an offence'. The court concluded that hiding from the police after an offence has allegedly been committed did not fall within the section. Further, the list of buildings to which the section expressly refers is exhaustive, therefore, being found within an enclosed office has been held not to fall within the scope of s 4.[210] Likewise, a university campus is not an 'enclosed area' for the purposes of this section.[211] In *L v CPS*, Auld LJ expressed the view that a prosecution under s 4 of the 1824 Act 'is and should be a choice of last resort for a prosecutor when seeking to mark suspicious conduct'.[212] Nonetheless, the charge is still used, for example, where there is insufficient evidence to charge burglary.

---

[206] SI 1955/1497.
[207] SI 1994/968.
[208] *Hayes v Stevenson* (1860) 25 JP 39.
[209] [2008] 1 Cr App R 8.
[210] *Talbot v DPP* [2000] 1 WLR 1102.
[211] *Akhurst v DPP* [2009] EWHC 806 (Admin).
[212] *L v CPS*, para 36.

The offence is triable summarily only and punishable with a maximum of three months' **5.157** imprisonment and/or a fine not exceeding level 3 on the standard scale.[213]

Failure to leave an exclusion zone

Where a person, following conviction for an offence or as a condition of release from **5.158** prison, has been prohibited from entering a specified place or from doing so during a specified period,[214] s 112 of the Serious and Organised Crime and Police Act 2005 confers a power on the police to direct that person to leave if the officer believes, on reasonable grounds, that the person is in the place at a time when he would be prohibited from entering it. The direction may be given orally and it is an offence knowingly to contravene such a direction. The offence is triable summarily only and carries a maximum penalty of four months' imprisonment and/or a fine not exceeding level 5 on the standard scale.[215]

Violence for securing entry

This is discussed at 5.37 above.

5.159

Trespass during currency of interim possession order

This is discussed at 5.26 et seq above.

5.160

Adverse occupation of residential premises

It is an offence, contrary to s 7 of the Criminal Law Act 1977, as amended,[216] if **5.161**

(a) any person is on residential premises ('premises' means a building or land ancillary to a building, which includes the garden of a private house and, for the purposes of this section, any access to premises[217]) as a trespasser, and

(b) a displaced residential occupier or 'a protected intending occupier' (defined as a person with a freehold or leasehold interest, or a tenancy or other defined authority to occupy the premises, who requires the premises for his own occupation as a residence but who has been excluded from occupation by a trespasser, and who carriers and produces a signed and witnessed notice to that effect[218]), or person acting on behalf of a displaced residential occupier or a protected intending occupier, requires the trespasser to leave, and

(c) the trespasser fails to leave.

It is a defence for the accused to prove (i) that he believed that the person requiring him **5.162** to leave was not a person within (b),[219] or (ii) that the premises were used mainly for

---

[213] If/when the Criminal Justice Act 2003, Sch 32, Part 2, para 146, is brought into force, the maximum penalty for an offence contrary to the first part of the Vagrancy Act 1824, s 4, will be a fine not exceeding level 1 on the standard scale and the maximum penalty in respect of an offence contrary to the second part of s 4 will be a fine not exceeding level 3 on the standard scale. Neither offence will carry any term of imprisonment.

[214] For example by the imposition, under the Crime and Disorder Act 1998, s 1C(2) (as amended), of an anti-social behaviour order following conviction, or as a licence condition under the Criminal Justice Act 2003, s 250.

[215] Serious Organised Crime and Police Act 2005, s 112(5) read in conjunction with s 175.

[216] By the Criminal Justice and Public Order Act 1994, s 73.

[217] Criminal Law Act 1977, ss 12(1)(a) and 7(4).

[218] Ibid, s 12A

[219] Ibid, s 7(2).

non-residential purposes,[220] or (iii) that the notice under (b) was either defective or not produced.[221] As to whether these statutory defences impose a legal or merely an evidential burden on the accused, see the observations at 5.73 and 10.172.

5.163 This offence is triable summarily only and carries a maximum penalty of imprisonment of up to six months and/or a fine not exceeding level 5 on the standard scale.[222]

5.164 Section 12(8) of the Criminal Law Act 1977 confirms that 'no rule of law ousting the jurisdiction of magistrates' courts to try offences where a dispute of title to property is involved shall preclude magistrates' courts from trying offences under this part of this Act.' This applies to the offences created by ss 6–10 of the Act.

Trespassing with a weapon of offence

5.165 It is an offence, contrary to s 8 of the Criminal Law Act 1977, for any person on premises (meaning a building or land ancillary to a building[223]) as a trespasser to have with him without lawful excuse a weapon of offence, namely any article made or adapted for use for causing injury to or incapacitating a person, or intended by the person having it with him for such use. This offence is triable summarily only and carries a maximum penalty of three months' imprisonment and/or a fine not exceeding level 5 on the standard scale.

5.166 There are also two further offences, under s 20(1) and (2) of the Firearms Act 1968, of trespassing with a firearm or imitation firearm, without reasonable excuse in a building (s 20(1)), or on land (s 20(2)). 'Land' for the purposes of s 20(2) includes land covered with water. The offence of trespassing with a firearm in a building is an either way offence, unless the weapon is an airgun or an imitation firearm, in which case it is triable summarily only. If tried summarily, the offence is punishable with imprisonment of up to six months and/or a fine not exceeding level 5 on the standard scale. If tried on indictment, the offence under s 20(1) is punishable with a term of imprisonment not exceeding five years and/or a fine. The offence under s 20(2) is triable summarily only and is punishable with imprisonment of up to three months and/or a fine not exceeding level 4 on the standard scale.

Trespassing on premises of foreign missions, etc

5.167 In the case of *Kamara v DPP*,[224] students from Sierra Leone were convicted of conspiracy to trespass at common law, having occupied their High Commission in London with the aid of an imitation firearm (they were also convicted of unlawful assembly). However, s 1 of the Criminal Law Act 1977 (following the Law Commission's proposals: Working Paper No 54) abolished the offence of conspiracy to trespass.

5.168 It is, however, an offence, contrary to s 9 of the Criminal Law Act 1977, to enter or be on the premises of a diplomatic mission, or consular premises, or any other premises entitled to similar inviolability, including closed diplomatic missions or consular premises, or the

---

[220] Ibid, s 7(3).
[221] Ibid, s 12A(9).
[222] Ibid, s 7(5).
[223] Ibid, s 12(1)(a).
[224] [1974] AC 104.

residence of diplomats or other similarly accredited persons, as a trespasser. Proceedings under this section may not be instituted except with the consent of the Attorney General.[225] A certificate issued by or under the authority of the Secretary of State shall be conclusive evidence of a premise's status as a diplomatic mission or other premises protected under this section.[226]

It is a defence for an accused to prove that he believed that the premises in question were not premises to which s 9 applies.[227] The section does not specify whether the belief must be reasonably or honestly held. The authors would submit that in the absence of an express requirement of reasonableness, the subsection should be read as requiring a subjective belief only. The offence is triable summarily only and is punishable with imprisonment of up to six months and/or a fine not exceeding level 5 on the standard scale.   **5.169**

Obstruction of enforcement officers or court officers executing High Court or county court process

It is an offence contrary to s 10 of the Criminal Law Act 1977, as amended,[228] for a person to resist or intentionally obstruct a court officer (including bailiffs), or an enforcement officer, or person acting under the authority of an enforcement officer, engaged in executing any process or writ issued by the High Court or by any county court for the purpose of enforcing any judgment or order for the recovery of any premises or for the delivery of possession of any premises.   **5.170**

The offence of resisting or intentionally obstructing a court officer only applies where the judgment or order that the court officer is seeking to enforce was made in possession proceedings against a trespasser.[229]   **5.171**

'Enforcement officer' means an individual who is authorized to act as an enforcement officer under the Courts Act 2003. 'Officer of a court' means any sheriff, under sheriff, deputy sheriff, bailiff, or officer of a sheriff; and any bailiff or other person who is an officer of a county court within the meaning of the County Courts Act 1984.[230]   **5.172**

It is a defence for the accused to prove that he believed that the person he was resisting or obstructing was not a court officer, or an enforcement officer, or a person acting under the authority of the same.[231]   **5.173**

Section 10(5) provides that an enforcement officer or any officer of a court may arrest without warrant anyone who is, or whom he, with reasonable cause, suspects to be, guilty of an offence under this section.   **5.174**

---

[225] Criminal Law Act 1977, s 9(6).
[226] Ibid, s 9(4).
[227] Ibid, s 9(3). See 5.73 and 10.172 above in relation to burden of proof.
[228] By the Courts Act 2003.
[229] Ibid, s 10(2).
[230] Ibid, s 10(6).
[231] Ibid, s 10(3).

5.175 An offence under s 10 is triable summarily only and is punishable with a term of imprisonment of up to six months and/or a fine not exceeding level 5 on the standard scale.[232]

Trespassing on licensed aerodromes

5.176 In addition to any applicable by-laws, s 39 of the Civil Aviation Act 1982 makes it an offence to trespass on any land forming part of an aerodrome licensed in pursuance of an Air Navigation Order. However, no offence is committed unless it is proved that, at the material time, notices warning trespassers of their liability under this section were posted so as to be readily seen and read by members of the public, in such positions on or near the boundary of the aerodrome as appear to the court to be proper. The offence is triable summarily only and the maximum penalty is a fine not exceeding level 3 on the standard scale.

Trespassing on a railway

5.177 In addition to any applicable by-laws, trespassing on any railway lines, sidings, embankments, tunnels, cuttings, or similar railway works is an offence contrary to s 55 of the British Transport Commission Act 1949. Section 1 of the Criminal Justice and Police Act 2001 makes this a 'penalty offence' for which an on-the-spot penalty of £50 is payable in the case of those over the age of 16 and £30 for those under the age of 16.[233]

Poaching

5.178 Section 30 of the Game Act 1831; s 1 of the Night Poaching Act 1828; s 1 of the Deer Act 1991; and Schedule 1, paragraph 2(1) of the Theft Act 1968 all create various poaching offences involving trespass to land.

Burglary

5.179 It is an offence under s 9 of the Theft Act 1968 if a person

    (a) enters any building or part of a building as a trespasser and with intent to steal, commit unlawful damage or inflict grievous bodily harm,[234] or

    (b) having entered as a trespasser steals, or attempts to steal, or inflicts or attempts to inflict grievous bodily harm.[235]

5.180 'Building' for the purposes of this provision includes an inhabited vehicle or vessel.[236] The offence is triable either way and carries a maximum penalty on indictment of fourteen years' imprisonment in respect of offences committed in a dwelling and a maximum of ten years in respect of all other offences.[237] If tried summarily, the maximum penalty is six months' imprisonment and/or a fine not exceeding the statutory maximum.

---

[232] Ibid, s 10(4).
[233] Penalties for Disorderly Behaviour (Amount of Penalty) Order 2002 (SI 2002/1837), as amended by SI 2009/83, Art 2, Sch, Part 2.
[234] Theft Act 1968, s 9(1)(a).
[235] Ibid, s 9(1)(b). The Sexual Offence Act 2003, s 63, replaces the previous offence of burglary with intent to rape (see below).
[236] Theft Act 1968, s 9(4).
[237] Ibid, s 9(3).

Trespass with intent to commit a sexual offence

It is an offence, contrary to s 63 of the Sexual Offences Act 2003 knowingly or recklessly to **5.181** trespass on any premises intending to commit a relevant sexual offence. 'Relevant sexual offence' means any offence under Part 1 of the Sexual Offences Act 2003, this includes in the region of seventy different offences ranging from rape,[238] to sexual assault,[239] to exposure,[240] and voyeurism.[241] The offence contrary to s 63 is triable either way and carries a maximum sentence of imprisonment of ten years when tried on indictment and a maximum sentence of six months' imprisonment and/or a fine not exceeding the statutory maximum when tried summarily.

---

[238] Sexual Offences Act 2003, s 1.
[239] Ibid, s 3.
[240] Ibid, s 66.
[241] Ibid, s 67.

6

POLICE POWERS BEFORE ARREST

A. The Nature of Policing	6.01		An inspector's 'authorization'	6.82
Information gathering	6.01		A constable's powers	6.85
Responding to protest	6.06		Terrorism Act 2000, s 44	6.87
Police community support officers			The commander or assistant chief	
and accredited persons	6.08		constable's 'authorization'	6.90
Private security companies	6.16		The constable's power	6.97
B. Contact with the Police Short of Arrest	6.18		Code A and the conduct of the search	6.102
C. Establishing Identity	6.26		Searches and the European	
Name, address, date of birth,			Convention on Human Rights	6.112
and personal details	6.27		Road traffic stops	6.118
Disguises	6.33		Stop and seizure of vehicles	6.118
An inspector's 'authorization'	6.34		Road checks	6.119
A constable's power	6.40		Road stops	6.122
The power and the European			**F. Breach of the Peace**	6.125
Convention on Human Rights	6.42		What is a breach of the peace?	6.129
Fingerprints	6.43		Definition	6.129
Photographs and filming	6.44		Breach of the peace and the	
Photographs: following exercise of			criminal law	6.139
other police powers	6.44		Who may take action?	6.141
Photographs: overt surveillance	6.45		When may action be taken?	6.142
D. Control of Movement	6.55		What action may be taken?	6.153
Directions to leave and alcohol-related			Arrest	6.156
disorder	6.57		Limits on pickets	6.160
Dispersal of groups and anti-social			Police powers and private property	6.161
behaviour	6.60		The application of human rights	
A superintendent's 'authorization'	6.60		principles	6.162
A constable's 'direction'	6.64		Against whom may action be taken?	6.168
'Removal' of children to their home	6.67		**G. The Use of Force by the Police**	6.174
Police cordons	6.69		Sources of power to use force	6.175
E. Stop and Search: Before Arrest	6.72		What is 'reasonable' force?	6.181
Police and Criminal Evidence			The European Convention	6.184
Act 1984, s 1	6.73		Equipment	6.195
Criminal Justice and Public Order			Policing protests	6.201
Act 1994, s 60	6.82		**H. Conclusion**	6.205

A. The Nature of Policing

Information gathering

6.01 The policing of public order is, as with all other areas of policing, now intelligence-led, on a national scale. Within the framework of the National Intelligence Model, information is collected, recorded, disseminated, and retained in order to identify material which can be assessed for intelligence value and inform decision-making about priorities and tactical options.[1] Special Branch (and counter-terrorism units) have specific responsibility for dealing with material relating to 'national security, domestic extremism, terrorism and other unlawful subversive activity'.[2] Under the umbrella of the National Domestic Extremism Co-ordinator (NDEC) of the Association of Chief Police Officers (ACPO), three units—the National Public Order Intelligence Unit (NPOIU); the National Extremism and Tactical Co-ordination Unit (NECTU); and the National Domestic Extremism Team (NDET)—have, respectively, intelligence, prevention, and enforcement functions. [3]

6.02 However, within each police force an officer of ACPO rank is responsible for the 'force level intelligence capability'. He is responsible for a force intelligence unit or bureau which processes intelligence and disseminates it to local basic command units within the police force.[4] The police recognize that it is important to establish strong links between special branch and the force intelligence capability[5] and that 'Information gathered within special branch units can be relevant to identified priority policing issues such as criminal damage, violence, and public disorder'.[6]

6.03 Specialist police teams exist to obtain information about protestors. Evidence Gathering Teams (EGT) attend demonstrations to obtain 'intelligence by taking photographs and making notes of significant events which may be thought to be of potential evidential value' and Forward Intelligence Teams (FIT) 'monitor people's movements at events . . . to assist in the efficient deployment of resources'.[7] The Metropolitan Police Service has a Public

---

[1] See 'Practice Advice: Introduction to Intelligence-Led Policing' August 2007 produced on behalf of the Association of Chief Police Officers (ACPO) by the National Centre for Policing Excellence and to be found on the ACPO website: <http://www.acpo.police.uk> policies directory, <http://www.acpo.police.uk/asp/policies/Data/Intelligence_led_policing_17x08x2007.pdf> (last accessed 6 November 2009).

[2] Para 1.10 of 'Practice Advice: Resources and the People Assets of the National Intelligence Model' August 2007, produced on behalf of ACPO by the National Policing Improvement Agency, and to be found on the ACPO website <http://www.acpo.police.uk>, policies directory, <http://www.acpo.police.uk/asp/policies/Data/resources_people_assets_nim_17x08x07.pdf> (last accessed 6 November 2009).

[3] See Her Majesty's Inspectorate of Constabulary report 'Adapting to Protest', Part 2, 25 November 2009, pp 147–8.

[4] 'Practice Advice' above, paras 1.1–1.3.

[5] Ibid, para 1.1.

[6] Ibid, para 1.10.

[7] See para 2 of judgment of Laws LJ in *Wood v Commissioner of Police of the Metropolis* [2009] HRLR 25. For a fuller account of FITs' and EGTs' roles, concerns expressed about them, and HMIC's recommendations see Her Majesty's Inspectorate of Constabulary report 'Adapting to Protest', Part 2, 25 November 2009, pp 6 and 126 onwards and recommendation 10 at p 166.

Order Intelligence Unit (CO11) deployed at protests 'to recognise those known to be extreme protestors'[8] and are also responsible for training and policy.

It is little wonder that stories are emerging of a police strategy, through 'overt surveillance' **6.04** and other methods, whereby different units of the police force build intelligence databases, some of application to all the public, and some specific to protestors; and even pass on information to the targets of the protestors. These include the databases of 'Crimint' (Criminal Intelligence), CO11, NPOIU, NECTU, NDET, the Police National Information and Coordination Centre (PNICC), as well as the automatic number plate recognition (ANPR) computer of the Police National Computer (PNC).[9]

The courts, both European and domestic, in *S and Marper v UK*[10] and *Wood v Commissioner* **6.05** *of Police of the Metropolis*[11] have considered the compatibility or otherwise of parts of this strategy—the taking, retention and use of photos, fingerprints and DNA—with Article 8 of the European Convention on Human Rights. By their own admission, the courts have only just begun the process of testing its legality.[12] These cases are considered below and in Chapters 7 and 10.

Responding to protest

In March 2004 NECTU was created by ACPO. It 'promotes a co-ordinated response to **6.06** domestic extremism by providing tactical advice to the police service, and information and guidance to industry and government' and NDET (above) is responsible for its enforcement.[13]

---

[8] Lord Bingham in *R (on the application of Laporte) v Chief Constable of Gloucestershire* [2007] 2 AC 105, HL, para 8. For *Laporte* see 4.61 et seq, 6.146 et seq, 10.38, and 10.80.

[9] Guardian, 15 September 2008 'Fears over privacy as police expand surveillance project' at <http://www.guardian.co.uk/uk/2008/sep/15/civilliberties.police> (last accessed 25 November 2009); Guardian, 6 March 2009 'Caught on film and stored on database: how police keep tabs on activists' at <http://www.guardian.co.uk/uk/2009/mar/06/police-surveillance-database-activists-intelligence> (last accessed 25 November 2009); Guardian, 6 March 2009 'Revealed: police databank on thousands of protestors' at <http://www.guardian.co.uk/uk/2009/mar/06/police-surveillance-protestors-journalists-climate-kingsnorth> (last accessed 25 November 2009); Guardian, 20 April 2009 'Secret police intelligence was given to E.ON before planned demo' at <http://www.guardian.co.uk/uk/2009/apr/20/police-intelligence-e-on-berr> (last accessed 25 November 2009); Guardian, 26 October 2009, 'Police in £9m scheme to log "domestic extremists" ', <http://www.guardian.co.uk/uk/2009/oct/25/police-domestic-extremists-database> (last accessed 25 November 2009); Daily Mail, 26 October 2009 'Police compiling database of "domestic extremist" protestors', <http://www.dailymail.co.uk/news/article-1223026/Police-compiling-database-protestors-committed-crimes.html?ITO=1490> (last accessed 25 November 2009). See also paras 2–13 of judgment of Laws LJ in *Wood* for the police's own account of what they do with photographic material, and the lawfulness of this strategy generally below and 10.148.

[10] (2009) 48 EHRR 50 and see 7.77 and 10.155.

[11] [2009] HRLR 25 and see 6.45 and 10.157.

[12] Lord Collins in *Wood v Commissioner of Police of the Metropolis* [2009] HRLR 25, para 100. See generally on data collection and surveillance *MS v Sweden* (1997) EHRR 313 and Dr Victoria Williams, *Surveillance and Intelligence Law Handbook* (2006).

[13] From the home page of NECTU at <http://www.netcu.org.uk> (last accessed 19 September 2009).

6.07   Police forces have specialist police support units (PSU) or public order units trained and deployed to deal with public disorder.[14] For example, the Territorial Support Group (TSG) is primarily responsible for controlling public disorder within London. Established in January 1987 to replace the Special Patrol Group following the death of Blair Peach, a schoolteacher, who died from a blow to the head as police tried to disperse a crowd during an anti-racism demonstration in West London, the TSG describes itself as 'London's first response to any planned or spontaneous events, which may involve public disorder. They have policed every major public order incident in the capital'.[15] The TSG, however, receives a high level of complaints for among other things 'oppressive behaviour', a large proportion of which are not upheld.[16]. Reviews of the policing of the G20 protests in London in April 2009, have shown that the police also rely on untrained officers in policing large scale protests, a practice which has been criticized and is likely to be reviewed and changed.[17]

Police community support officers and accredited persons

6.08   At the other extreme—the policing of low level crime and anti-social behaviour—the police are losing their monopoly.[18]

6.09   Police 'community support officers' (PCSOs) play a deliberately visible role in dealing with low level public disorder. They are the creature of Police Reform Act 2002, Part 4, Chapter 1 (as amended). They are under the direction and control of and employed and 'designated' by chief constables (s 38(1) and (2)). The police must be satisfied that they are suitable, capable, and trained to carry out their functions (s 38(4)). They must wear an approved uniform and, if requested, must produce evidence of their designation, when exercising any of their powers (s 42).

6.10   The Act gives PCSOs various powers, beyond those of ordinary citizens, which may be tailored by the chief constable to suit their force area (s 38(5), (5A), (6), (7) and s 38A[19] and Schedule 4, Part 1 of the Act.[20]).

6.11   Some of the PCSOs' powers relate to specified offences, set out in Schedule 4, Part 1, Paragraphs 2(6), 3, and 3A of the Act, which include

- those susceptible to a fixed penalty notice (under Criminal Justice and Police Act 2001, Part 1, Chapter 1[21]);

---

[14] See Her Majesty's Inspectorate of Constabulary report 'Adapting to Protest', Part 2, 25 November 2009, Ch 5.

[15] See <http://www.met.police.uk/co/territorial_support.htm> (last accessed 19 September 2009).

[16] See the Guardian, 7 November 2009, 'Scotland Yard riot squad faces calls to end "culture of impunity"' at <http://www.guardian.co.uk/politics/2009/nov/06/police-scotland-yard-riot-squad> (last accessed 7 November 2009).

[17] See para 6.202.

[18] For a historical examination of 'the pluralization of policing' see Tim Newburn and Robert Reiner, 'From PC Dixon to Dixon PLC: Policing and Police Powers Since 1954' [2004] Crim LR 101.

[19] Inserted by the Police and Justice Act 2006, s 7(2).

[20] See also the Police Reform Act 2002 (Standard Powers and Duties of Community Support Officers) Order 2007, SI 2007/3202. Annex A has an explanatory note with a table of the powers.

[21] See Sch 4, Part 1, para 1. See also 9.73.

- failure to disperse for anti-social behaviour (Anti-social Behaviour Act 2003, s 32(2)[22]);
- offences under some by-laws;
- offences which appear to the PCSOs to have caused injury, alarm, or distress to any other person;
- offences which appear to the PCSOs to have caused damage to any other person's property;
- anti-social behaviour under s 1 of the Crime and Disorder Act 1998;[23] and
- some road traffic offences.

PCSOs' powers to deal with these offences are also in Schedule 4, Part 1 of the Act and include broadly the following: **6.12**

- the power to issue fixed penalty notices (paragraph 1);
- the power to require a person's name and address where the PCSO has reason to believe that a person has committed one of the relevant offences (paragraph 1A[24]), or is acting in an anti-social manner (paragraph 3[25]) or in relation to a road traffic offence (paragraph 3A[26])
- the power to 'detain' for up to thirty minutes a person who has not given his name and address, while waiting for a police officer to arrive to deal with the person (paragraph 2(3)) or to accompany him to a police station (paragraph 2(4));[27] and
- the power to search, seize, and retain items from someone who has been detained (paragraph 2A[28]).

PCSOs have other powers which are not contingent on particular offences such as the power **6.13**

- to disperse groups and remove young people to their place of residence (paragraph 4A,[29] equivalent to police powers under s 30 of the Anti-social Behaviour Act 2003[30]);
- to enter property to save life and limb or prevent serious damage to property (paragraph 8, equivalent to police power under s 17 of PACE[31]);

---

[22] See 6.64 and Ch 9.
[23] For ASBOs, see Ch 9.
[24] Inserted by the Serious Organised Crime and Police Act 2005, Sch 8(1), para 2. It is a summary offence punishable by a fine not exceeding level 3 to fail to do so (para 1A(5)).
[25] Equivalent to powers of a police officer under the Police Reform Act 2002, s 50, see 6.30.
[26] Inserted by the Serious Organised Crime and Police Act 2005, Sch 8, Part 1, para 6. See 6.29 for similar police powers.
[27] It is a summary offence punishable by a fine not exceeding level 3 to abscond (para 2(5)). It has been pointed out that the Act does not specifically prohibit immediate detention for a further thirty minutes though this is unlikely to be looked upon favourably by the courts. Nor does the Act spell out what the police should do once they arrive, though presumably the officer will consider exercising a power of arrest. See M Zander, *The Police and Criminal Evidence Act 1984* (2005, 5th edn) para 12.10, p 414.
[28] Inserted by the Serious Organised Crime and Police Act 2005, Sch 8, Part 1, para 4, equivalent to powers of a police officer under the Police and Criminal Evidence Act 1984 (PACE), s 32, on which see 7.45.
[29] Inserted by the Anti-social Behaviour Act 2003, s 33(3).
[30] See 6.64 and 6.67.
[31] See 6.178 and 7.51.

- to stop vehicles used to cause alarm (paragraph 9, equivalent to police powers under s 59 of the Police Reform Act 2002[32]);
- to carry out road checks (paragraph 13, equivalent to police powers under s 4 of PACE and s 163 of the Road Traffic Act 1988[33]);
- to cordon off areas (paragraph 14, equivalent to police powers under s 36 of the Terrorism Act 2000[34]);
- to stop and search vehicles and people in authorized areas under the Terrorism Act 2000, but only under the supervision of an officer (paragraph 15, equivalent to police powers under s 44 of the Terrorism Act 2000[35]);
- to take photos of those arrested, detained or given a fixed penalty notice (paragraph 15ZA[36]equivalent to police powers under s 64A(1A) of PACE[37]);
- to exercise general stop, search, and seizure powers;[38] and
- to use reasonable force in the exercise of their powers.[39]

6.14 PCSOs (and other accredited persons, below) must 'have regard' to any relevant provisions of the Codes of Practice which accompany the Police and Criminal Evidence Act 1984 (s 67(9) and (9A)[40]) These Codes are made pursuant to PACE, ss 66 and 67. The burden on police officers is more rigorous. The language in the codes ('must', 'shall') indicates that the codes should be followed by police officers, although PACE does not expressly say so. PACE does, however, (s 67(10)) say that failure to comply with the Code is not a criminal offence or give rise to civil proceedings and the Notes for Guidance which accompany the Codes are explicitly not part of the Codes (Code C paragraph 1.3 and Code D paragraph 2.2). Nevertheless, evidence obtained in breach of the Codes may sometimes be excluded in criminal proceedings.[41]

6.15 'Accredited persons' (who may for example be traffic wardens, store detectives, or door supervisors) play a similar, increasing, and controversial role. They have been described by the Magistrates' Association of England and Wales as a 'third-tier' police force.[42] They, too, are the creation of the Police Reform Act 2002. Under s 40 a chief constable has the power to establish a 'community safety accreditation scheme', through which organizations, not directly run by the police, cooperate with the police, among other things, to combat 'crime and disorder, public nuisance and other forms of anti-social behaviour'. Under s 41, subject to checks about the suitability of the organization and

---

[32] See 6.118.
[33] See 6.119 and 6.122.
[34] See 6.71.
[35] See 6.93 et seq.
[36] Inserted by the Serious Organised Crime and Police Act 2005, Sch 8, Part 1, para 12.
[37] See 6.44.
[38] See Code A Annex C to PACE for search powers of PCSOs generally. See 6.72 et seq for equivalent police powers.
[39] See 6.178.
[40] See also Code B, para 2.13; Code C, para 1.16; Code D, para 2.22. S 67(9A) inserted by the Police Reform Act 2002, s 107(1), Sch 7, para 9(7).
[41] See also 7.60 et seq for the implications of failing to make a lawful arrest.
[42] The Times, 25 July 2009 'Magistrates protests as 'bouncers' get powers to give on-the-spot fines' at <http://www.timesonline.co.uk>, report at <http://www.timesonline.co.uk/tol/news/uk/crime/article6727070.ece> (last accessed 19 September 2009).

employees, the police may grant accreditation to employees. Schedule 5 sets out the powers which follow with accreditation. These include the power to issue a fixed penalty notice to anyone whom the accredited person has reason to believe has committed or is committing a relevant offence (similar to those enforced by PCSOs, above), the power to require him to give his name and address and the power to photograph him, but not the power to detain.

Private security companies

Private security companies and neighbourhood and police wardens play an increasing role in patrolling the streets and places to which the public have access. Unless they are accredited persons, they have no special powers beyond those of any other citizen to deal with a breach of the peace, arrests, or use force.[43] **6.16**

Where protestors come into direct contact with the target of their campaign, they will often be confronted by security guards protecting people and private property. Security guards may, as the agents of property owners, use self-help to eject trespassers.[44] Their activities are regulated by the Private Security Industry Act 2001. The Act sets up a regulator, the Security Industry Authority (s 1). The Authority maintains a register of approved contractors providing security industry services (ss 14–18). The Authority also issues licences to and keeps a public register of individuals working within the security industry and carrying out 'licensable conduct' or 'designated activities' (s 1(2)(a), s 3(3), s 12 and Schedule 2). These cover the activities of 'security operatives' whose role is 'guarding premises against unauthorized access or occupation, against outbreaks of disorder or against damage; guarding property against damage or theft . . .; guarding . . . individuals against . . . . injuries that might be suffered in consequence of the unlawful conduct of others' (paragraph 2(1) of Part 1 of Schedule 2). It is an offence not to have a licence where one is required or to employ someone who is not licensed (s 3(1)[45] and s 5(1)[46]). The Authority also has the power to prosecute those who commit offences under the Act.[47] **6.17**

B. Contact with the Police Short of Arrest

Contact between citizens and the police short of arrest, when the police are not otherwise exercising any of their coercive powers, is a vexed area. There is a fine line between conduct **6.18**

---

[43] See 6.125 et seq on breach of the peace; 7.33 on citizen's arrest; and 6.177 and 6.179 on use of force. For the Police Federation's mixed reaction to these developments see the Police Federation comments on 'Auxillary Police' released on 14 November 2009, at <http://www.polfed.org/federationpolicy/DBB5F2A29D8E42499B5DB0063E7BD5A3.asp> (last accessed 14 November 2009).

[44] See Ch 5.

[45] Summary only, maximum penalty six months' imprisonment and/or a level 5 fine.

[46] Either way. When tried summarily maximum is six months' imprisonment and/or a level 5 fine. When tried on indictment maximum is five years.

[47] *R (on the application of Securiplan Plc, Ullmann Sabrewatch Ltd and Lucas) v Security Industry Authority and Hutchins (interested party)* [2009] 2 All ER 211, DC.

which amounts to obstruction of a police officer in the execution of his duty and conduct which is not.[48]

6.19 The comments by Lord Parker in *Rice v Connolly*[49] are probably the best starting point. Commenting on the position of citizens he said:

> It seems to me quite clear that though every citizen has a moral duty or, if you like, a social duty to assist the police, there is no legal duty to that effect, and indeed the whole basis of the common law is the right of the individual to refuse to answer questions put to him by persons in authority, and to refuse to accompany those in authority to any particular place; short, of course, of arrest. (page 419)

6.20 As to the police:

> It is . . . in my judgment clear that it is part of the obligations and duties of a police constable to take all steps which appear to him necessary for keeping the peace, for preventing crime or for protecting property from criminal injury. There is no exhaustive definition of the powers and obligations of the police, but they are at least those, and they would further include the duty to detect crime and to bring an offender to justice. (page 419)

6.21 The police may therefore speak to a person in the ordinary course of the officer's duty without detaining him or exercising any element of compulsion.[50] Where a citizen is abusive, uncooperative, and positively hostile to the officers, uses obscene language calculated to provoke and antagonize the officers and then tries to walk away, the citizen is guilty of obstruction.[51] Indeed the citizen commits an obstruction if, when asked to stop for questioning, he runs away, without at least taking his leave.[52] However, a citizen is entitled to give unhelpful but truthful answers and then walk away. While this is 'unfortunate' it does not amount to an obstruction or increase the reasonableness of an officer's suspicion so as to justify the exercise of a formal power, such as search or arrest.[53]

6.22 Where the police have grounds to suspect[54] someone of an offence, but do not exercise their powers of arrest (see Chapter 7), the police should caution him before questioning him (PACE Code C 10.1/Code G 3.1). At the same time, the person must be told that he is not under arrest and is free to leave if he wants to (Code G, paragraph 3.2). Where, for example, the police are called to a disturbance in the street, they may not, at first, know who has committed an offence and who is a bystander or witness. Anyone they suspect may have committed an offence should be cautioned and also told that they are not under arrest and may leave.

---

[48] See also Ch 2, Part B on assault on or obstruction of a constable in the execution of his duty.
[49] [1966] 2 QB 414, DC and see 2.13.
[50] Code A, notes for guidance, note 1.
[51] *Ricketts v Cox* (1982) 74 Cr App R 298, DC (a decision criticized by the commentator in the report at [1982] Crim LR 184).
[52] *Sekfali v DPP* (2006) 170 JP 393, DC, per Newman J at p 396.
[53] *Samuels v Commissioner of Police for the Metropolis*, 3 March 1999, CA.
[54] Code C, note 10A 'There must be some reasonable, objective grounds for the suspicion, based on known facts or information which are relevant to the likelihood the offence has been committed and the person to be questioned committed it.'

In some circumstances, the police must also make records of voluntary encounters and **6.23** provide receipts to the person stopped (Code A, paragraphs 4.11–20, see also notes for guidance). These requirements emerged from the Macpherson enquiry into the murder of Stephen Lawrence.[55] Evidence given to the enquiry highlighted the universal complaint by minority ethnic communities that they were disproportionately the subject of supposedly voluntary stops.[56] In an attempt to monitor patterns in the encounters and ease community relations, an officer who requests a person in a public place to 'account for themselves' (their actions, behaviour, presence in an area, or possession of anything) must make a record of the encounter and provide a receipt to the person.[57] The record must identify the name of the officer who has made the stop and the 'self-defined ethnic background' (paragraph 4.17) of the person stopped. Additional requirements to state a reason for the stop and to give a record to the person stopped have been dispensed with as too bureaucratic and time-consuming.[58]

These formalities do not apply to 'general conversations such as when giving directions to **6.24** a place, or when seeking witnesses', nor where 'an officer is seeking general information or questioning people to establish background to incidents which have required officers to intervene to keep the peace or resolve a dispute' (Code A, paragraph 4.13). They may not apply where there is public disorder (Code A, note for guidance 20).

The police may do things—such as ask questions, carry out a search, enter property—with **6.25** the consent of the citizen. Consent cannot be inferred from silence or from the fact that a person has remained with the police.[59] The police may not search a person (as opposed to a property or vehicle), even with consent, where they would have no power to carry out the search in the absence of consent (Code A, paragraph 1.5).

C. Establishing Identity

Often the police's objective will not be to arrest or to control public disorder; it will simply **6.26** be to identify the participants. This section deals with some of their powers to do so.

Name, address, date of birth, and personal details

As a general rule, there is no requirement to give the police one's name, address or other **6.27** personal details.

As Lord Bingham observed in *R (on the application of Laporte) v Chief Constable of* **6.28** *Gloucestershire Constabulary*, a citizen's refusal to give his name 'however irritating to the police was entirely lawful'.[60] There is no obligation to provide a name and address even

---

[55] The Stephen Lawrence Inquiry, Report of an Inquiry by Sir William Macpherson, February 1999, Cm 4262-I.

[56] See para 45.8 of the Macpherson report, for stops and searches, see below.

[57] Code A, para 4.12.

[58] The Police and Criminal Evidence Act 1984 (Codes of Practice) (Revisions to Code A) (No 2) Order 2008, SI 2008/3146.

[59] See for example *Osman v DPP* (1999) 163 JP 725, QB.

[60] [2007] 2 AC 105, HL, para 55.

during a formal search and the police have no power of detention in order to obtain it (paragraph 4.2 of Code A[61]). The aim of a search is to search, not to question (although it may be legitimate to ask questions where the police need to identify if there is for example a bomb or dangerous weapon to hand—so called 'safety interviews' before arrest [62]).

6.29 There are exceptions where it is an offence not to answer questions or provide information. The most common ones stem from police powers under Part VII of the Road Traffic Act 1988 to police the roads and these encounters also often result in the police issuing 'HORT/1' forms ('producers') requiring drivers to produce driving documents.[63] For example, under s 164 the police may require a driver to produce his licence and give his date of birth. Section 165 contains similar powers to require names, addresses, and insurance certificates. Section 168 imposes a duty to give the police one's name and address where the police suspect reckless or careless driving. Where an accident has taken place and someone is injured or damage is caused, s 170 imposes upon a driver the obligation to stop and give his name and address to anyone who may have a good reason for requiring it and also to report the accident and provide insurance certificates. Under s 172 the keeper of a vehicle must identify the driver of a vehicle which may have committed a road traffic offence.[64]

6.30 If a police officer has reason to believe that a person has been acting, or is acting in an anti-social manner, he may require that person to give his (correct) name and address and it is an offence to fail to do so (Police Reform Act 2002, s 50[65]). A person's anti-social manner is defined rather broadly—'a manner that caused or was likely to cause harassment, alarm or distress to one or more persons not of the same household as himself'.[66] However, where this precondition is not met—for example where someone is required to give his name and address as a condition for release from a cordon, or during a search or simply because he is attending a demonstration, as has been reported—exercise of this power may be unlawful.[67]

6.31 A Police Community Support Officer can ask for a name and address where he has reason to believe that a person has committed a relevant offence.[68] Separately, the police are using against campaigners their power, exercisable at ports and borders, to interview in order to establish whether a person is involved in terrorism (under the Terrorism Act 2000, Schedule 7).

---

[61] See paras 6.30 and 6.72.
[62] See *R v Ibrahim* [2009] 1 WLR 578, CA.
[63] See also 6.122 et seq.
[64] The section was considered compatible with the European Convention on Human Rights, Art 6, in *O'Halloran and Francis v United Kingdom* (2008) 46 EHRR 21.
[65] Summary only, maximum sentence a level 3 fine.
[66] Crime and Disorder Act 1998, s 1, see Chapter 9.
[67] See for example HMIC report 'Adapting to Protest', Part 2, 25 November 2009, p 126 and recommendation 8(a) at p 165.
[68] See 6.12.

After arrest, a detainee need not provide his name and address, though the failure to do so **6.32** may have other implications. It may trigger the police's power to search in order to verify identity, take fingerprints and refuse bail if charged.[69]

Disguises

The police have the power to require a person to remove his face coverings at any time in **6.33** any place within a given locality (Criminal Justice and Public Order Act 1994, s 60AA,[70] see also Code A, paragraphs 2.15–18).[71]

An inspector's 'authorization'

The power may only be exercised by officers where there has been an 'authorization' to carry **6.34** out searches in a given area (without suspicion about the person searched). An authorization may be given by an inspector on one of two grounds.

First, the power may be used where an authorization has already been given under s 60(1) **6.35** of the Criminal Justice and Public Order Act 1994, for the purposes of stopping and searching on the grounds that there may be violence, particularly involving weapons (s 60AA(1)(a)[72]).

Second, an authorization can be given (s 60AA(1)(b) and s 60AA(3)) where an inspector **6.36** reasonably believes

- that activities may take place in a locality that are likely to involve the commission of offences;[73] and
- that it is expedient[74] in order to prevent or control the activities, to give an authorization.

Authorizations under s 60AA must be in writing and spell out the grounds, locality, and **6.37** period of the authorization (s 60AA(6)).

Authorizations under both s 60(1) and s 60AA(3) can be for up to twenty-four hours and **6.38** may be extended by a further twenty-four hours by a superintendent if it appears that it is expedient to do so having regard to offences which have been committed (s 60(3) and s 60AA(4)). According to paragaph 2.17 of Code A 'the period authorized shall be no longer than appears reasonably necessary to prevent, or seek to prevent the commission of offences'.

Code A (note 13) also gives some guidance about the scope of the locality to which the two **6.39** authorizations may apply:

It is for the authorising officer to determine the geographical area in which the use of the powers is to be authorised. In doing so the officer may wish to take into account factors such

---

[69] See Ch 7.

[70] Inserted by the Anti-terrorism Crime and Security Act 2001, s 94(1).

[71] See also 6.109.

[72] See 6.82.

[73] The Act does not define the term 'offences' but note for guidance 10 of Code A says that the purpose of s 60AA is to deal with 'intimidatory or violent protests'.

[74] See 6.93.

as the nature and venue of the anticipated incident, the number of people who may be in the immediate area of any possible incident, their access to surrounding areas and the anticipated level of violence. The officer should not set a geographical area which is wider than that he or she believes necessary for the purpose of preventing anticipated violence, the carrying of knives or offensive weapons . . . or, in the case of s 60AA, the prevention of commission of offences.

A constable's power

6.40 The authorization gives any uniformed officer the power to require any person to remove any item which the officer reasonably believes a person is wearing wholly or mainly in order to conceal his identity (s 60AA(2))(a)). However, as note for guidance 4 to Code A warns:

> Many people customarily cover their heads or faces for religious reasons—for example, Muslim women, Sikh men, Sikh or Hindu women, or Rastarfarian men or women. A police officer cannot order the removal of a head or face covering except where there is reason to believe that the item is being worn by the individual wholly or mainly for the purpose of disguising identity, not simply because it disguises identity. Where there may be religious sensitivities about ordering the removal of such an item, the officer should permit the item to be removed out of public view. Where practicable, the item should be removed in the presence of an officer of the same sex as the person and out of sight of anyone of the opposite sex.

6.41 It is an offence to fail to remove an item when required to do so (s 60AA(7)[75]). An authorization also gives the officer the power to seize any item which the officer reasonably believes a person intends to wear to conceal his identity (s 60AA(2)(b)). The police may also retain and dispose of items seized under this power (Criminal Justice and Public Order Act 1994, s 60A[76]). The authorization does not give the police the power to stop and search for disguises. An officer need not, therefore, comply with the requirements imposed by PACE for the conduct of searches[77] when exercising powers under s 60AA. However, where a police officer is exercising a search power[78] and an authorization is in force, the officer may seize any item which the officer reasonably believes is intended to be used for concealing identity (Code A, paragraph 2.15).

The power and the European Convention on Human Rights

6.42 In *DPP v Avery*[79] Newman J (paragraph 17 onwards) also commented, in passing, on the rationale behind the power to require the removal of masks and the compatibility with the Human Rights Act of the predecessor to the power under s 60AA(1)(a) to require the removal of masks where violence with weapons is feared. Heather Avery was an animal rights campaigner who had refused a request by an officer to remove her mask during a protest. Newman J accepted that the wearing of a mask can be a potent means of demonstrating in a lawful manner and, indeed, that the wearing of apparel to the head

---

[75] Summary only, maximum penalty is one month imprisonment and/or a level 3 fine.
[76] Inserted by the Crime and Disorder Act 1998, s 26. See also the Police (Retention and Disposal of Items Seized) Regulations 2002, SI 2002/1372, and, generally, Police (Property) Regulations 1997.
[77] *DPP v Avery* [2002] 1 Cr App R 31, DC; PACE, s 2(2)(3) and s 3. See para 6.102 et seq.
[78] See 6.72 et seq.
[79] [2002] 1 Cr App R 31, DC.

and face can be required by custom or religion. However, he also noted that masks are used to conceal identity and this hinders the police's ability to arrest those responsible for offences at that time or control future demonstrations by identifying potential trouble-makers. Concluding[80] that he was 'satisfied as to the legality of the provision' (he did not spell out which Convention principles or Articles he was applying), Newman J recognized that the power was available 'only in anticipation of violence'.[81] Since that judgment, s 60AA (in particular s 60AA(1)(b) and s 60AA(3), above[82]) has been passed and this does not place any limit on the offences which may lead to an authorization being made.

Fingerprints

When it comes into force, a police officer will have the power (PACE, s 61(6A)[83]) to take a person's fingerprints without consent, without an arrest and away from a police station if **6.43**

- he reasonably suspects that a person is committing or attempting to commit an offence or has committed or attempted to commit an offence;[84] and
- either his name is unknown and cannot readily be ascertained, or the officer has reasonable grounds for doubting whether a name furnished by the police is his real name.

Photographs and filming

Photographs: following exercise of other police powers

The police (and PCSOs[85]) have the power (under PACE, s 64A[86] and Code D, s 5) to photograph or film a person, without his consent (and to remove anything on his head) somewhere other than at the police station where, among other things **6.44**

- he has been arrested;[87]
- he has been given a direction to leave a locality (Violent Crime Reduction Act 2006, s 27[88]);
- he has been detained by a PCSO (Police Reform Act 2002, Schedule 4, Part 1, paragraph 2(3)[89]);

---

[80] Ibid, para 18.
[81] See also the judgment of Brooke LJ at paras 24 and 26.
[82] See above at 6.36.
[83] Inserted by the Serious Organised Crime and Police Act 2005, s 117, not yet in force. For the taking of fingerprints after arrest see Ch 7.
[84] Unlike other subsecs to s 61, s 61(6A) does not limit the term 'offence' to a 'recordable offence'.
[85] See 6.08 et seq.
[86] Inserted by the Anti-terrorism Crime and Security Act 2001, s 92. See also 7.74.
[87] Ibid.
[88] See 6.57.
[89] See 6.11 et seq.

- he has been given a penalty notice for disorderly behaviour (under Criminal Justice and Police Act 2001, Part 1, Chapter 1[90]);
- he has been given a fixed penalty notice by a PCSO (under Police Reform Act 2002, Schedule 4, Part 1, paragraph 1[91]).

Photographs: overt surveillance

6.45 In *Wood v The Commissioner of Police of the Metropolis*[92] the Court of Appeal considered the growing police practice of overtly filming protestors or those connected with campaigns and retaining and using that information. The judgment gave a flavour of the issues future courts will need to tackle when considering the lawfulness of the wider strategy of overt surveillance.

6.46 Andrew Wood was the media coordinator of the Campaign Against the Arms Trade (CAAT) and had no criminal convictions. He attended the AGM of a company involved in organizing trade fairs for the arms industry. The company had been subject to demonstrations in the past, where criminal offences had taken place and there was police intelligence that there might be disorder at this one. Andrew Wood did nothing wrong at the meeting, but two other campaigners, including one who had convictions arising from protests, were ejected for chanting slogans and there was evidence that Andrew Wood made contact with them after the meeting. The police photographed Andrew Wood outside the meeting, followed him to the underground, asked him who he was and sought to obtain his identity by asking railway staff to identify him from his travel document.

6.47 The photographs were retained by CO11, the public order unit of the Metropolitan Police, in case a criminal offence taking place at the time of the AGM came to light, or if they were needed in civil proceedings, or for use at another event involving the company due to take place several months later. They were kept under strict controls. Copies were taken out of the unit only at later public order events in order to identify people involved in unlawful activity. They were reviewed after about a year and only retained if they had 'ongoing significant intelligence value'.

6.48 More generally, the case also revealed that there was a database of images held by CO11. It emerged that 'the criteria for inclusion on the database [were]: observed or suspected participation in unlawful activity at the event when the pictures were taken, or participation of such activity at an earlier time. Mere presence at a demonstration or other event is not enough' (paragraph 11 of the judgment). The Metropolitan Police have created a policy on 'the Use of Overt Filming/Photography' which they describe as 'a particularly useful tactic to combat crime and gather intelligence and evidence relating to street crime, anti-social behaviour and public order' (paragraph 13 of the judgment).[93]

---

[90] See Ch 9.
[91] See 6.11 et seq.
[92] [2009] HRLR 25. See 6.05 and 10.148 et seq.
[93] See also 6.03.

As to the law, the Court of Appeal found that Andrew Wood's rights of privacy under **6.49** Article 8 had been infringed by the retention of his photos for more than a few days after the meeting.[94]

The Court unanimously found that Article 8(1) was engaged. Laws LJ, giving the first and **6.50** principal judgment reasoned as follows. The central value protected by the Article 8 right is 'the personal autonomy of every individual' (paragraph 20) and 'an individual's personal autonomy makes him—should make him—master of all those facts about his own identity, such as his name, health, sexuality, ethnicity, his own image . . . and also of the "zone of interaction" . . . between himself and others. He is the presumed owner of these aspects of his own self; his control of them can only be loosened, abrogated, if the State shows an objective justification for doing so' (paragraph 21).

There are, however, three qualifications to this. 'First, the alleged threat or assault to the **6.51** individual's personal autonomy must . . . attain "a certain level of seriousness". Secondly, the touchstone for Article 8(1)'s engagement is whether the claimant enjoys on the facts a "reasonable expectation of privacy" . . . Thirdly, the breadth of Article 8(1) may in many instances be greatly curtailed by the scope of the justifications available to the State pursuant to Article 8(2)' (paragraph 22).

The mere taking of someone's photograph in a public street is not an interference with **6.52** privacy (paragraph 35). There must be 'aggravating circumstances' (paragraph 36). In Andrew Wood's case the circumstances which engaged Article 8 were that the photos were taken by the police, an emanation of the State (paragraph 28) and while Andrew Wood did not know why they were being taken it was implicit that they would be kept and used (paragraphs 43 and 46).

The court then considered whether Article 8(2), containing the exceptions to the right to **6.53** privacy, applied. It was readily accepted by the court that the photographs were taken for a legitimate aim—for the prevention of disorder or crime and perhaps also in the interests of public safety or the protection of the rights and freedoms of others. Only Laws LJ commented on whether they were taken in accordance with the law, concluding that they were, pursuant to the police's common law powers to detect and prevent crime (applying *Rice v Connolly*[95] and *Murray v UK*[96]). The final and critical point was whether the police's actions had been proportionate. This is a fact-sensitive question (Dyson LJ at paragraph 85). Laws LJ (paragraph 58 onwards) and Dyson LJ (paragraph 83 onwards) found *S and Marper*[97] (the case in which the European Court ruled that the retention by the police of DNA samples of innocent people was unlawful) distinguishable. Laws LJ expressed the view that there is a 'qualitative difference between photographic images on the one hand and fingerprints and DNA on the other, not least as regards the reach of the use to which they might be put' (paragraph 59). Dyson LJ and Lord Collins took the view that, given Andrew Wood's connections with the suspect who had been ejected and had criminal

---

[94] Arts 10 and 11 were not engaged on the facts of this case—Laws LJ at para 61.
[95] [1966] 2 QB 414, 419, per Lord Parker CJ.
[96] (1994) 19 EHRR 193.
[97] For *Marper*, see also 7.77 and 10.155.

convictions for protests, the police were justified in taking and retaining photos for a few days (while the police operation at the AGM was concluded), but retention beyond that point, certainly for several months for use at another event, was disproportionate (Dyson LJ at paragraph 88, Lord Collins at paragraph 97, Laws LJ dissenting at paragraphs 56 to 60).

6.54 Andrew Wood's judicial review of the police's decision to take his photographs and obtain details of his identity, refused by the Administrative Court, was therefore allowed by the Court of Appeal. The Home Office is working with ACPO to develop new guidance in the light of the *Wood* judgment.[98]

D. Control of Movement

6.55 Three such powers are dealt with elsewhere in this chapter and book. A failure to comply constitutes a separate offence, beyond simple obstruction of the police (Police Act 1996, s 89(2)[99]). Often, a decision (an authorization) by a senior officer will trigger a power for any officer to take action and/or make it an offence for a person not to comply with the police's requirements.

6.56 Three such powers are dealt with here and elsewhere in this book. First, the police's powers to prevent or abate a breach of the peace includes the power to contain or cordon people (an example being the case of *Austin*) and to prevent them from going to their destination (an example being *Laporte*).[100] Second, any officer may direct a person who is harassing someone else at their home to leave the vicinity and it is an offence to fail to comply (Criminal Justice and Police Act 2001, s 42[101]). Third, a senior officer may direct someone who is participating in an aggravated trespass to leave the land and it is an offence not to leave or to return (Criminal Justice and Public Order Act 1994, s 69 [102]).

Directions to leave and alcohol-related disorder

6.57 Any police officer has the power to give a 'direction' to someone to leave a locality where there has been alcohol-related disorder and not to return for up to forty-eight hours (Violent Crime Reduction Act 2006, s 27(1)[103]). The power has increasingly been used against groups of football supporters congregating at pubs on match day.

---

[98] See Joint Committee on Human Rights 'Follow-up' report published 28 July 2009, p 25, para 56 and see also HMIC report 'Adapting to Protest', Part 2, 25 November 2009, p 8, Ch 7, p 129 onwards and recommendation 8(b) at p 165.

[99] See Ch 2.

[100] See generally on breach of the peace, 6.125 et seq below. For *Austin* see 4.73 et seq, 6.162 et seq, and 10.167. For *Laporte*, see 4.61 et seq, 6.146 et seq, 10.38, and 10.80.

[101] See Ch 3 at G.

[102] See Ch 5.

[103] See also Home Office guidance 'Giving directions to individuals to leave a locality (s 27 of the Violent Crime Reduction Act 2006) Practical Advice'—produced by COI on behalf of the Home Office, August 2007, Ref: 282381.

A direction may be given (s 27(2)) where **6.58**

- the presence of the person is likely, in all the circumstances, to cause or contribute to the occurrence of alcohol-related crime or disorder in that locality; and
- the direction is necessary for the purposes of removing or reducing the likelihood of there being such crime or disorder during the period of time the direction is in effect.

The direction cannot have the effect of preventing a person from going home, to work, to **6.59** be educated, to obtain medical treatment, or somewhere the person is required to attend (s 27(4)). The police must give the person the direction in writing (s 27(3)) and they have the power to photograph the person who has been given a direction (s 27((7) amending PACE, s 64A). The police must make a record of the direction (s 27(5)). It is an offence to fail to comply with a direction (s 27(6)[104]).

Dispersal of groups and anti-social behaviour

A superintendent's 'authorization'

A superintendent has the power to give an 'authorization', lasting for up to six months, **6.60** for other officers to disperse groups of people in an area (the 'dispersal area') where there has been a history of anti-social behaviour (Anti-social Behaviour Act 2003, ss 30–6[105]).

The criteria (s 30(1)) for giving the authorization are that the superintendent has reason- **6.61** able grounds for believing that

- members of the public have been intimidated, harassed, alarmed, or distressed as a result of the presence or behaviour of groups of two or more people 'in public places' in the locality; and
- 'anti-social behaviour' is a significant and persistent problem in the locality.

'Anti-social behaviour' is behaviour by a person which causes or is likely to cause harass- **6.62** ment, alarm, or distress to one or more other persons not of the same household as the person (s 36). This is the same wording as s 1 of the Crime and Disorder Act 1998 (and Police Reform Act 2002, s 50).[106] 'Public place' means any highway or place where the public or any section of the public has access on payment or otherwise, as of right or by permission, express or implied (s 36[107]). This includes therefore cinemas, restaurants, coffee bars, and pubs.[108]

---

[104] Summary only, maximum sentence a level 4 fine.
[105] The Secretary of State may issue a code of practice and an officer must have regard to it (s 34). The Home Office has issued a circular on the use of this power Home Office Circular 004/2004. ACPO has issued a policy 'Practice Advice on Part 4 of the Anti-social Behaviour Act 2003' 2005 produced with the National Centre for Policing Excellence. See also *Carter v Crown Prosecution Service* [2009] EWHC 2197 (Admin).
[106] See Ch 9 and 6.30.
[107] The same definition is used in the Public Order Act 1986, s 16, see 3.10.
[108] *R (W) v Commissioner of Police of the Metropolis* [2007] QB 399, CA, per May LJ at para 4.

6.63 The authorization must be in writing and spell out not only the locality and period of the authorization but also its grounds (s 31(1)), this last requirement being important given the 'considerable encroachment upon the rights of individuals inherent in the granting of such authorizations' (Hallett LJ at paragraph 16 in *Sierny v Director of Public Prosecutions*[109]). An authorization may not be made in respect of those involved in lawful picketing or approved processions, but others, such as those involved in static demonstrations can be affected (s 30(5)). An authorization cannot be made without the consent of the local authority and without publication of its existence in a local newspaper or by posting a notice of it in conspicuous places within the locality or both (s 31(2) and (3)).

A constable's 'direction'

6.64 The authorization gives any police officer the power to give a 'direction' to people to disperse (immediately or within a given time or in a specified way), to leave the locality and/or not to return for up to twenty-four hours (s 30(4)). The direction may be given orally (s 32). It is an offence to fail to comply with a direction (s 32(2)[110]).

6.65 An officer may make the direction if he has reasonable grounds for believing that the presence or behaviour of a group of two or more people in any public place has resulted or is likely to result in any members of the public being intimidated, harassed, alarmed, or distressed (s 30(3)). Unless there are exceptional circumstances a reasonable belief must depend, in part at least, on some behaviour of the group which indicates in some way or other intimidation, harassment, alarm, or distress. Otherwise, use of the direction would constitute an illegitimate intrusion into the rights of the group and would not be proportionate.[111]

6.66 In *R (on the application of Singh) v Chief Constable of the West Midlands Police*[112] the Court of Appeal considered the lawfulness of a direction to a group of religious protestors, following authorizations which had been based on widespread anti-social behaviour by seasonal revellers and skate boarders. Hallett LJ said that an authorization and subsequent direction can apply to anti-social behaviour of a kind which was not envisaged when the authorization was given (paragraphs 101 and 103). Furthermore, Parliament did intend the dispersal regime to apply to protests (paragraph 79). However, whether or not a group's behaviour on any particular occasion warrants a dispersal direction will depend on the circumstances. Police officers must act proportionately and sensibly and on an objective basis. 'Articles 10 and 11 are there to protect peaceful and lawful protest' (paragraph 90) but, taking into account the rights of other members of the public in the vicinity, the Court concluded that the police's exercise of their powers was proportionate and lawful.

'Removal' of children to their home

6.67 If, following a superintendent's authorization, a police officer finds someone whom he has reasonable grounds for believing is under 16 and not under the effective control of an adult

---

[109] (2006) 170 JP 697, DC.
[110] Summary only, maximum penalty is three months' imprisonment and/or a level 4 fine.
[111] *MB v DPP* (2007) 171 JP 10, DC.
[112] [2006] 1 WLR 3374, CA.

he may 'remove' that person to his place of residence (Anti-social Behaviour Act 2003, s 30(6)). However the power may not be exercised if the officer has reasonable grounds for believing that the child would if taken to their home be likely to suffer significant harm and if the power is exercised the local authority must be notified (s 32(6)).

The power applies between 9 pm and 6 am. The exercise of the power, challenged by **6.68** Liberty for having a curfew effect, was considered in *R (W) v Commissioner of Police of the Metropolis*.[113] Giving the judgment of the court, May LJ (paragraph 18 onwards) said that the power to remove carries with it a power to use reasonable force if necessary. Children are free to enter the dispersal area without fear of being removed, provided they do not participate in anti-social behaviour and provided they avoid others who are behaving anti-socially. The 'discretionary power can only be used if, in the light of its purpose, it is reasonable to do so; . . . constables must have regard to circumstances such as how young the child is; how late at night it is; whether the child is vulnerable or in distress; the child's explanation for his or her conduct and presence in the area; and the nature of the actual or imminently anticipated anti-social behaviour' (paragraph 35).

Police cordons

The principal police power to set up cordons in order to control protestors and public **6.69** disorder derives from their power to deal with breaches of the peace, where the power has been exercised to encircle or contain protestors. This somewhat controversial area of the law involving the decision in *Austin v Commissioner of Police of the Metropolis*[114] is considered further below.[115]

Perhaps surprisingly, their power to set up scene of crime cordons, to keep people outside a **6.70** given area, rests on relatively recent and heavily criticized authority. In *DPP v Morrison*[116] the Divisional Court considered the lawfulness of a cordon preventing the public from using a public right of way over private premises (a shopping mall). Hooper J (paragraph 23), having considered *Ghani v Jones*[117] and Code B of PACE, decided that there was a power to cordon off the area on the basis that the police were entitled to assume that the owner of the land had given them consent. Indeed the court said that 'consent could not lawfully be withheld' and doubted 'whether the owner of land over which a public right of way passes can either consent or not consent to an obstruction of the right of way'. The fiction of implied consent has been criticized on practical grounds and in principle, not least because the exercise of the power may conflict with the owner's right to withdraw consent and his rights under Article 8. Yet, at the moment, there is no obvious alternative basis on which it can comfortably be justified.[118]

---

[113] [2007] QB 399, CA.
[114] [2009] 1 AC 564, HL.
[115] For *Austin*, see 4.73 et seq; 6.162 et seq; and 10.167. See generally on breach of the peace, 6.125 et seq below.
[116] (2003) 167 JP 577, DC.
[117] [1970] 1 QB 693, CA.
[118] See commentary to *Morrison* at [2003] Crim LR 727, 728, and M Zander, *The Police and Criminal Evidence Act 1984* (2005, 5 edn) pp 24–5.

6.71 In contrast, there are explicit and far-reaching powers under terrorism legislation to create 'cordoned areas'. A superintendent can designate an area as a cordoned area if, and only if, he considers it expedient for the purposes of a terrorist investigation (Terrorism Act 2000, s 33(2)). A terrorist investigation includes investigations into the commission, preparation, or instigation of acts of terrorism.[119] A cordoned area must, so far as is reasonably practicable, be demarcated by a police tape with the word 'police' on it, or any other way considered appropriate (s 33(4)(b)). The designation can last for up to fourteen days from the date it is made but may be extended until up to twenty-eight days after the date it was first made (s 35). Once an area has been designated, any officer has the power to order a person or driver of a vehicle to leave it and restrict further access to it (s 36(1)). It is an offence, without reasonable excuse, to fail to comply with a police officer's order (s 36(2)(3).[120]

E. Stop and Search: Before Arrest

6.72 There is no common law police power to search before arrest: *Ghani v Jones*[121] but there are a multiplicity of statutory powers. Annex A to Code A of PACE sets out a list of police powers (Annex C sets out PCSOs' principal search and seizure powers[122]). Code A itself applies to all of them (see below). Most powers require the person conducting the search to have a reasonable suspicion about the person he is searching. Two, controversial powers, do not.[123]

Police and Criminal Evidence Act 1984, s 1

6.73 Section 1(1) of PACE authorizes a police officer to 'search any person or vehicle or anything which is in or on a vehicle' and to 'detain a person or vehicle for the purpose of such a search'. The power may be exercised anywhere the public have ready access. It cannot be exercised in a 'dwelling'. In some circumstances it may be exercised in a garden or yard or other land used as a dwelling (s 1(4)) and (s 1(5)).

6.74 The police may search for (s 1(2))

- stolen articles;
- offensive weapons (s 1(7)(a), s 1(9), Code A notes for guidance paragraph 23);
- articles made or adapted or intended by the suspect to be used to commit offences such as burglary, theft, taking motor vehicles, fraud, criminal damage (s 1(7)(b) and s 1(8));
- bladed or sharply pointed articles (other than a folding pocket knife) carried in public (s 1(8A)[124] and Criminal Justice Act 1988, s 139); and
- fireworks (s 1(8B)[125]).

---

[119] Terrorism Act 2000, s 92. See 6.92 for the definition of terrorism, Terrorism Act 2000, s 1.
[120] Summary only, maximum penalty is three months' imprisonment and/or level 4 fine.
[121] [1970] 1 QB 693, CA at p706.
[122] See 6.13.
[123] For concerns about the inappropriate use of all these powers during protests, see HMIC report 'Adapting to Protest', Part 2, 25 November 2009, p 7, p 122 onwards, recommendation 9 at p 165.
[124] Inserted by the Criminal Justice Act 1988, s 33.
[125] Inserted by the Serious Organised Crime and Police Act 2005, s 115.

A police officer may seize any of the articles for which he is looking if in the course of the   **6.75**
search he discovers them (s 1(6)).

The power may only be exercised where the officer has 'reasonable grounds for suspect-   **6.76**
ing' that he will find these articles (s 1(3)). The term 'reasonable grounds for suspecting' is
considered in Chapter 7 in relation to the power of arrest.[126] Code A to PACE,[127]
paragraphs 2.2–2.11 provides further clarification of its meaning in the context of
searches.

Paragraph 2.2 for example states: **6.77**

> Reasonable grounds for suspicion depend on the circumstances in each case. There must be
> an objective basis for that suspicion based on facts, information, and/or intelligence which
> are relevant to the likelihood of finding an article of a certain kind. Reasonable suspicion can
> never be supported on the basis of personal factors. It must rely on intelligence or informa-
> tion about, or some specific behaviour by, the person concerned. For example, other than in
> a witness description of a suspect, a person's race, age, appearance, or the fact that the person
> is known to have a previous conviction, cannot be used alone or in combination with each
> other, or in combination with any other factor, as the reason for searching that person.
> Reasonable suspicion cannot be based on generalisations or stereotypical images of certain
> groups or categories of people as more likely to be involved in criminal activity. A person's
> religion cannot be considered as reasonable grounds for suspicion and should never be
> considered as a reason to stop or stop and search an individual.

Paragraph 2.6 clarifies how to apply the term to gangs: **6.78**

> Where there is reliable information or intelligence that members of a group or gang habitu-
> ally carry knives unlawfully or weapons or controlled drugs, and wear a distinctive item of
> clothing or other means of identification to indicate their membership of the group or gang,
> that distinctive item of clothing or other means of identification may provide reasonable
> grounds to stop and search a person. [See Note 9]

Note 9 to paragraph 2.6 states: 'Other means of identification might include jewellery,   **6.79**
insignias, tattoos or other features which are known to identify members of the particular
gang or group.'

Reasonable grounds may be confirmed or dispelled by questioning. Reasonable grounds   **6.80**
cannot be provided by a refusal to answer questions.[128] There is no power to stop or detain
in order to find grounds for a search (Code A, paragraphs 2.9–2.11).

Kent police's use of this power at a 'climate camp' at Kingsnorth Power Station in Summer   **6.81**
2008 is subject to a judicial review, *R (on the application of E, T and Morris) v Chief Constable
of Kent Police*.[129] Rather than being selected for a search according to whether there was a
reasonable suspicion about them, almost everyone wishing to attend the climate camp was
subject to a s 1 stop and search. This policy was criticized in a report, commissioned by

---

[126] See 7.05 et seq.
[127] The Code of Practice for the exercise by police officers of statutory powers of stop and search; and police
officers and police staff of requirements to record public encounters.
[128] See 6.18.
[129] Claim No CO/10579/2008. Permission was granted on 6 May 2009. Interim hearing on 12 January
2010, case ongoing at the time of writing.

Kent police,[130] as being 'inappropriate' (page 26, paragraph 5.2.6) and 'disproportionate and counter-productive' (page 7, paragraph 2.4 and page 24 and page 29 paragraph 6.3). The Applicants in the judicial review argue that the police policy was indiscriminate and therefore unlawful. The police initially sought to justify it on the basis of a 'group suspicion', relying on *Laporte*, *Austin*, and *Cumming*.[131] However, at an interim hearing they accepted that the police did not have the requisite individual suspicion and that this was an interference with Articles 10 and 11 rights.

Criminal Justice and Public Order Act 1994, s 60[132]

An inspector's 'authorization'

6.82 An inspector has the power to give an 'authorization' for stop and search, without reasonable or any suspicion of possession of a prohibited article, to take place in a locality within the local police area[133] for up to twenty-four hours[134] (Criminal Justice and Public Order Act 1994, s 60).[135] The power is directed at those carrying weapons—dangerous instruments (with a blade or pointed) or offensive weapons (s 60(11)).

6.83 An authorization may be made where the inspector reasonably believes that in the local police area (s 60(1))

- incidents involving serious violence may take place and it is expedient[136] to authorize searches to prevent them; or
- an incident involving serious violence has already taken place, weapons which were used are being carried in the area and it is expedient to authorize searches in order find them; or
- people are carrying weapons without good reason.

6.84 Authorization under s 60 must be in writing and spell out the grounds, locality, and period of the authorization (s 60(9)(9ZA)).

A constable's powers

6.85 The authorization confers on any police officer the power within the locality defined by the authorization to stop and search for weapons (s 60(4))

- any pedestrian or anything carried by him;
- a vehicle, its driver, and any passenger.

6.86 It is an offence for a person to fail to stop when required to do so (s 60(8)[137]). No reasonable suspicion is required. Once the authorization has been given the officer may make any

---

[130] Strategic Review of Operation Oasis (Camp for Climate Change), report by ACC Andy Holt and Superintendent David Hartley, South Yorkshire Police published on 23 July 2009. See also 6.30.
[131] For *Laporte*, see 4.61 et seq, 6.146 et seq, 10.38, and 10.80. For *Austin*, see 4.73 et seq, 6.162 et seq, and 10.167. For *Cumming*, see 7.15 and 7.16.
[132] As amended by the Knives Act 1997, s 8; the Crime and Disorder Act 1998, s 25; the Anti-terrorism, Crime and Security Act 2001, Schs 7 and 8; SI 2004/1573; the Serious Crime Act 2007, s 87.
[133] See 6.39.
[134] See 6.38.
[135] See also PACE, Code A paras 2.12 to 2.14.
[136] See 6.93.
[137] Summary only, maximum penalty is one month imprisonment and/or a level 3 fine.

search he thinks fit whether or not he has any grounds for suspecting the person or vehicle is carrying weapons (s 60(5)).[138] The officer has the power to seize, retain, keep safe, dispose of, or destroy any weapon found during the search (s 60(6), s 60A).[139] Separately, the authorization also triggers the power of a constable to require the removal of disguises.[140]

Terrorism Act 2000, s 44

Section 44 of the Terrorism Act 2000 contains perhaps the most controversial stop and search power: the power, in order to prevent acts of terrorism, of a senior police officer to give an authorisation for individual officers to stop and search without suspicion. **6.87**

The future of the power is in issue as a result of the case of Kevin Gillan (a peaceful anti-weapons protestor) and Pennie Quinton (a journalist) who in 2003 were stopped and searched for about twenty minutes near an arms fair in East London by officers purportedly exercising this power. They challenged the exercise of the power by both judicial review and a County Court claim for damages. When the House of Lords examined their case, in *R (Gillan) v Commissioner of Police of the Metropolis*,[141] it considered a number of ingredients of these powers and concluded that the searches were 'prescribed by law' under Article 5(1), 'in accordance with the law' under Article 8(1) and lawful.[142] When their case came before the European Court of Human Rights, in *Gillan and Quinton v UK*,[143] the European Court disagreed with many of the House of Lords' findings and concluded that Kevin Gillan and Pennie Quinton's rights under Article 8 had been violated. Examining whether the provision afforded legal protection for those exercising Convention rights against arbitrary interference by public authorities, as part of its analysis of whether the search powers were 'in accordance with the law' under Article 8, the European Court found that neither the power of the senior officer to give an authorisation nor the power of individual officers to stop and search pursuant to such an authorisation were sufficiently circumscribed or subject to adequate legal safeguards against abuse (paras 79 and 87). **6.88**

We shall now consider the detail of the provisions and the two courts' observations on them. **6.89**

The commander or assistant chief constable's 'authorization'

A senior officer has the power to give an 'authorization' for stop and search, without reasonable or any suspicion of possession of a prohibited article, if he 'considers it expedient for the prevention of acts of terrorism' (section 44).[144] **6.90**

---

[138] See 6.99.

[139] The Police (Retention and Disposal of Items Seized) Regulations 2002, SI 2002/1372, see also, generally, Police (Property) Regulations 1997.

[140] See 6.35.

[141] [2006] 2 AC 307, HL and commentary at [2006] Crim LR 752. See also para 4.84 et seq, 6.87 et seq, 113 et seq and 10.87.

[142] See Lord Bingham, para 31 et seq.

[143] Application no. 4158/05, 12 January 2010, see in particular paras 76 et seq.

[144] See also PACE, Code A, paras 2.19 to 2.26 and Home Office Circular 027/2008 at <http://www.homeoffice.gov.uk/about-us/publications/home-office-circulars/circulars-2008/027-2008>.

6.91 Authorization is given by an officer of the rank of commander or assistant chief constable level (section 44(4)). The Home Secretary must be notified and confirm the authorization (section 46).

6.92 'Terrorism' is defined in s 1 of the Terrorism Act 2000[145] to include:

- serious violence, damage to property, risk to the health and safety of the public;
- used or threatened to influence the government or an international governmental organization or the public; and
- for the purpose of advancing a political, religious, racial, or ideological cause.

6.93 The term 'expedient' was considered in *Gillan* by Lord Bingham in the House of Lords (paragraphs 13 to 15, see also Lord Scott at para 59 onwards). He concluded that an authorization may be given if, and only if, the stop and searches will be of significant practical value in preventing terrorism. Both Lord Bingham and the European Court expressed the view that the term 'expedient' has a meaning quite distinct from 'necessary' – the European Court observed that it means no more than 'advantageous' or 'helpful' – but the European Court concluded from this that the criteria for exercise of the power do not satisfy the Convention requirement that the power should be exercised with proportionality (para 80).

6.94 The authorization may cover any area within the authorizing officer's force area. In *Gillan* the House of Lords examined an authorization which covered the whole of the Metropolitan Police District (paragraph 17). It was challenged on the basis that the threat of terrorism was to Central London, not 'the dormitory suburbs of outer London' which did not offer spectacular terrorist targets. For Lord Bingham this was 'not . . . an unattractive submission' but, in dismissing it, he relied on secret security intelligence from the police and Home Office that any part of London was threatened and also that the power gave the police the facility to disrupt terrorist activities at an early stage, and not just near their culmination. The court did not have any grounds to interfere with these judgments.[146]

6.95 The authorization may have effect for up to twenty-eight days, but may be extended (s 46). In *Gillan* Lord Bingham considered another 'not . . . unattractive submission'—that a succession of authorizations, between February 2001 and September 2004, amounted to a continuous ban and was unlawful (paragraph 18 onwards). But, having examined the facts, he concluded that it was lawful. Its renewal had not been a 'routine bureaucratic exercise', the process had complied with the letter of the statute and the decisions reflected the level of the terrorist threat in London at that time.

6.96 The European Court, however, drew different conclusions from these two features of the power. Noting that authorisations are renewable and had become a 'rolling programme', and that police force areas cover extensive regions with concentrated populations, the Court remarked on 'The failure of the temporal and geographical restrictions provided by Parliament to act as any real check on the issuing of authorisations by the executive' (para 81).

---

[145] Amended by the Terrorism Act 2006, s34 and the Counter-Terrorism Act 2008, s75.
[146] Reliance was placed on *A v Secretary of State for the Home Department* [2004] UKHL 56, [2005] 2 AC 68, paragraph 29.

The European Court also took into account the limits of the Home Secretary's powers to interfere with authorisations, of the High Court to interfere with these decisions on a judicial review and of the role of the Independent Reviewer who, by virtue of section 126 of the Act, prepares annual reports on their use (paras 80 and 82).

The constable's power

The effect of the authorization is to confer on any uniformed police officer the power **6.97** within the area specified by the authorization to stop and search:

- a pedestrian or anything carried by him (section 44(2)); and
- a vehicle, its driver, a passenger, and anything in the vehicle or carried by the driver or passenger (section 44(1)).

It is an offence for a person to fail to stop when required to do so or wilfully to obstruct a **6.98** police officer exercising these powers (section 47(1)).[147] The power may be exercised only for the purposes of searching for articles of a kind which could be used in connection with terrorism (section 45(1)(a)), though, as the European Court observed, this is a very wide category which could cover many articles commonly carried by people in the street (para 83). A police officer may seize and retain an article which is discovered during the search and which he reasonably suspects is intended to be used in connection with terrorism (section 45(2)).

The heart of the power under section 44 (and indeed under section 60)[148] is that the officer **6.99** need have no suspicion, reasonable or subjective, about the person selected to be searched. The power is exercisable whether or not the officer has any grounds for suspecting the presence of articles which could be used for terrorism (section 45(1)(b)). According to Lord Bingham, the powers under section 44 'cannot, realistically, be interpreted as a warrant to stop and search people who are obviously not terrorist suspects, which would be futile and time-wasting. It is to ensure that a constable is not deterred from stopping and searching a person whom he does suspect as a potential terrorist by the fear that he could not show reasonable grounds for his suspicion.' (paragraph 35, see also Lord Brown at para 92). The purpose of the power is to deter potential terrorists and by occasionally finding terrorists and their equipment (Lord Brown, paragraph 77). The way it is exercised must be effective in order to achieve this end. It would not be effective if those searched were selected entirely randomly (Lord Hope, paragraph 41; Lord Scott, paragraph 66), nor on the simple basis that one in every ten people is stopped (Lord Scott, paragraph 66). Nor would it be practical or effective to stop everyone (Lord Brown, paragraph 77). The selection can be on 'hunch' (Lord Hope, paragraph 46) or intuition based on training (Lord Brown, paragraph 78). Although neither appellant in *Gillan* was of Asian origin some of the Lords addressed the concern that the powers may be exercised in a racially discriminatory way and there may be no way to spot or challenge this.[149]

---

[147] Summary only, maximum penalty is six months' imprisonment and/or level 5 fine.
[148] See para 6.82 et seq.
[149] See the judgments of Lord Hope, para 38 et seq and Lord Brown, para 83 et seq; *R (European Roma Rights Centre) v Immigration Officer at Prague Airport (United Nations High Commissioner for Refugees intervening)* [2005] 2 AC 1, HL; Code A para 2.25.

6.100 For the European Court this feature of the power reinforced its view that the exercise of the power by individual police officers carried with it a 'clear risk of arbitrariness' (para 85). The Court was concerned about the breadth of the discretion of the officer carrying out the search (para 83) and that judicial review and an action in damages were of limited value to those seeking to challenge those exercising it, as the case of Kevin Gillan and Pennie Quinton itself demonstrated (para 86). The Court cited official statistics which showed that the number of searches under s 44 was increasing, that exercise of the power to search had never led to an arrest for a terrorism offence and that those searched included those 'so far from any known terrorism profile that, realistically, there was not the slightest possibility of him / her being a terrorist, and no other feature to justify the stop' (para 84). The statistics also showed that the risk of discriminatory use of the powers against those of black and Asian origin was a very real consideration (para 85). The European Court was also concerned that such a widely framed power could be misused against demonstrators in breach of Articles 10 and 11 (para 85).

6.101 Even before the European judgment, wider concerns had been expressed that section 44 was being used, but should not have been used, against peaceful protestors and as a public order tactic.[150] On 7 May 2009 the Metropolitan Police Service, with the approval of the Metropolitan Police Authority, announced it would refine its use of the power[151] and it appears that, so far as London is concerned, authorisations for the use of the power now only apply to iconic and strategically important sites identified by the police in consultation with boroughs, in the light of the police's assessments, based on intelligence, of the level and nature of the terrorism threat.[152] In the light of the judgment of the European Court in *Gillan and Quinton*, it is likely that the legislation itself, and not just the policies and guidelines for those applying it, will be reviewed and may be amended. But until then, section 44 remains good (but tainted) law.

Code A and the conduct of the search

6.102 Sections 2 and 3 of PACE and Code A govern the exercise by police officers of all statutory powers to search a person or a vehicle without first making an arrest. Section 45 of the Terrorism Act 2000 contains additional requirements applicable to Terrorism Act 2000, section 44 searches.

---

[150] At p17 of the National Policing Improvement Agency 'Practice Advice on Stop and Search in Relation to Terrorism' 2008 on the NPIA website, <http://www.npia.police.uk>, at <http://www.npia.police.uk/en/docs/Stop_and_Search_in_Relation_to_Terrorism_-_2008.pdf> (last accessed 19th September 2009). House of Lords and House of Commons, Joint Committee on Human Rights, 'Demonstrating Respect for Human Rights? A Human Rights Approach to Policing Protest' March 2009 HL Paper 47-1, HC 320-1, recommendation 6 and para 93 and their 'Follow-up' report published 28 July 2009 at p22, para 46 onwards.

[151] Report 10 of the 7 May 2009 meeting of the Strategic and Operational Policing Committee of the Metropolitan Police Service.

[152] Evidence of Assistant Commissioner Yates to the Home Affairs Committee enquiring into the Home Office's response to terror attacks, 10th November 2009, viewable at http://www.parliamentlive.tv/Main/Player.aspx?meetingId=5133 (last accessed 21st November 2009).

Paragraph 1 to Code A sets out some fundamental principles: **6.103**

    1.1 Powers to stop and search must be used fairly, responsibly, with respect for people being searched and without unlawful discrimination. [It is] unlawful for police officers to discriminate on the grounds of race, colour, ethnic origin, nationality or national origins when using their powers.

    1.2 The intrusion on the liberty of the person stopped or searched must be brief . . .

    1.4 The primary purpose of stop and search powers is to enable officers to allay or confirm suspicions about individuals without exercising their power of arrest.

Paragraph 3.2 says 'The co-operation of the person to be searched must be sought in every   **6.104**
case, even if the person initially objects to the search . . .'

Before police officers carry out a search they should (PACE, section 2(2) and (3)) take   **6.105**
reasonable steps[153] to:

* identify themselves as police officers if they are not in uniform;[154]
* give their name and the police station to which they are attached;
* give the object of the proposed search;
* give the grounds for making the search.

A search will be unlawful unless the police comply with these statutory requirements   **6.106**
because 'any search of a person, even upon reasonable suspicion, is on the face of it a trespass requiring proper justification in law. A search conducted under statutory powers which does not even require reasonable suspicion in relation to the individual is doubly appropriate for that qualification.'[155]

The formality and excessive use of time in complying with these requirements could be   **6.107**
reduced if the police had in their pockets pre-prepared slips of paper with the relevant information (Sedley LJ in *Osman v DPP*).[156] Before a search the police must normally also tell the person to be searched of their right to a record of the search (see below and PACE, section 2(2) to (5)).

The police may detain a person or vehicle for 'such time as is reasonably required to permit   **6.108**
a search to be carried out either at the place where the person or vehicle was first detained or nearby' (PACE, section 2(8)).[157]

There is no power to require a person to remove any of his clothing in public other than   **6.109**
an outer coat, jacket, or gloves (PACE, section 2((9)(a)). In addition, headgear and footwear

---

[153] The test is not whether it is 'reasonable in all the circumstances': *R v Christopher Bristol* (2008) 172 JP 161, CA.

[154] For plain-clothed officers *see B v DPP* (2008) 172 JP 449, DC.

[155] Sedley LJ in Divisional Court in *Osman v DPP* (1999) 163 JP 725, QB, 729. See also *Bonner v DPP* [2005] ACD 56, DC; *R v Fennelly* [1989] Crim LR 142, CC; *B v DPP* (2008) 172 JP 449, DC.

[156] (1999) 163 JP 725, 729.

[157] Also the Terrorism Act 2000, section 45(4)); Code A, paragraphs 3.3, 3.4, and note 6 in Notes for Guidance.

may also be removed during searches under section 44 of the Terrorism Act 2000.[158] However, by virtue of paragraph 3.6 of Code A:

> Where on reasonable grounds it is considered necessary to conduct a more thorough search (e.g. by requiring a person to take off a T-shirt), this must be done out of public view, for example, in a police van . . . or police station if there is one nearby. . . . Any search involving the removal of more than an outer coat, jacket, gloves, headgear or footwear . . . may only be made by an officer of the same sex as the person searched and may not be made in the presence of anyone of the opposite sex unless the person being searched specifically requests it.[159]

6.110 The police must make a record of the search (PACE, section 3(1)), stating among other things the object of the search, the grounds for making it, the date and time when it was made, the place where it was made, what if anything was found, whether any injury or damage resulted from the search and the identity of the officer involved (PACE, section 3(3)).

6.111 The person searched (or who was in charge of the vehicle searched) is entitled to a copy of the 'record' or 'written statement' of the search at the time of the search or, on request, within twelve months of it.[160] In some circumstances (for example when the officer has to respond to an incident with a higher priority) the police are only required to give a 'receipt' and explain how a full record can be obtained (PACE, Code A, paragraphs 4.2A, 4.10A, and 4.10B).

Searches and the European Convention on Human Rights

6.112 The House of Lords' and European Court's analysis of the lawfulness of the searches, under section 44 of the Terrorism Act 2000, of Kevin Gillan and Pennie Quinton, included observations which may be relevant to the exercise of all search powers. Again, however, the European Court and House of Lords came to different conclusions.[161]

6.113 The European Court determined that Article 5 was engaged (see paras 56 and 57). The court re-iterated that the Article, containing the protection against the deprivation of liberty, is concerned with more than mere restrictions on the liberty of movement (these are governed by Article 2 of the Fourth Protocol, which the United Kingdom has not ratified). The difference between a deprivation of and a restriction on liberty is nonetheless merely one of degree or intensity, not one of nature or substance so 'the starting point must be [a person's] concrete situation and account must be taken of a whole range of criteria such as the type, duration, effects and manner of implementation of the measure in question' (applying *Guzzardi v Italy*).[162] Turning to the facts of the case, the Court observed that although the length of time during which each applicant was stopped and searched did not

---

[158] Terrorism Act 2000, s 45(3), see also Code A, note for guidance 8. See also para 6.33.

[159] See also paras 7.45 and para 7.70.

[160] PACE, s 3(7); Criminal Justice and Public Order Act 1994, s 60(10A)(10), inserted by Knives Act 1997, s 8(8). See also Terrorism Act 2000, s 45(5), (6).

[161] See on Convention rights generally Chapter 10, paras. 10.87, 10.97, 10.148 and 10.157 on the case of *Gillan* and *Gillan and Quinton* in particular.

[162] (1980) 3 EHRR 333. Also *Ashingdane v UK* (1985) 7 EHRR 528 and *HL v United Kingdom* (2005) 40 EHRR 32.

exceed 30 minutes, during this period they were entirely deprived of any freedom of movement. They were obliged to remain where they were and submit to the search and if they
had refused they would have been liable to arrest, detention at a police station and criminal
charges. Applying *Foka v Turkey*,[163] the Court concluded that this element of coercion is
indicative of a deprivation of liberty within the meaning of Article 5(1).

The European Court's judgment may therefore end a trend in domestic cases, particularly   **6.114**
those where police powers to address public disorder have been examined, to deny the
application of Article 5 to detentions which occur during police operations where detention is not the primary aim.[164] The House of Lords judgment in *Gillan* was part of this
trend. Giving the lead judgment in that case Lord Bingham (paragraph 21 onwards) also
noted the relationship between Article 5 and Article 2 of the Fourth Protocol and also
applied *Guzzardi v Italy*, but concluded that Article 5 did not apply to section 44 searches.
For Lord Bingham it was significant that a search 'will ordinarily be relatively brief. The
person stopped will not be arrested, handcuffed, confined or removed to any different
place. I do not think, in the absence of special circumstances, such a person should be
regarded as being detained in the sense of confined or kept in custody, but more properly
of being detained in the sense of kept from proceeding or kept waiting' (paragraph 25).
According to Lord Bingham (paragraph 26) had Article 5 been engaged, the exception to
that right under Article 5(1)(b) (the fulfilment by the citizen of some other prescribed legal
obligation) would have applied.[165]

The European Court did not consider the application of Article 5 further because its pri-   **6.115**
mary conclusion was that Article 8 – the right to private life - was engaged and had been
violated (see paragraphs 6–65). The Court re-iterated that the concept of 'private life' is a
broad term, not susceptible to an exhaustive definition. In an echo of the Court of Appeal's
reasoning in *Wood v The Commissioner of Police of the Metropolis*[166] the European Court in
Gillan and Quinton confirmed that 'There is . . . a zone of interaction of a person with others, even in a public context, which may fall within the scope of "private life"' (para 61).
Applying this to a search, the Court said 'the use of the coercive powers . . . to require an
individual to submit to a detailed search of his person, his clothing and his personal belongings amounts to a clear interference with the right to respect for private life. Although the
search is undertaken in a public place, this does not mean that Article 8 is inapplicable.
Indeed . . . the public nature of the search may, in certain cases, compound the seriousness
of the interference because of an element of humiliation and embarrassment' (para 63).

For Lord Bingham in the House of Lords in *Gillan* the circumstances in which Article 8   **6.116**
might apply to a search were much more limited. He said there might be an interference

---

[163] (2008), Application No.: 00028940/95, 24/6/2008.
[164] See the commentary on *Gillan* in [2006] Crim LR 752, 755; *Austin v Commissioner of Police of the
Metropolis* [2009] 1 AC 564, HL considered at 4.73 et seq, 6.162 et seq and 10.167 et seq ; and *R (on the application of Laporte) v Chief Constable of Gloucester* in the Divisional Court [2004] 2 All ER 874, DC considered
at 4.61 et seq, 6.146, 10.38, 10.80.
[165] For a criticism of this element of his reasoning see R Clayton and H Tomlinson, *The Law of Human
Rights* (2009, 2nd edn) p 584, para 10.32 applying *Engel v Netherlands* (No 1) (1979–80) 1 EHRR 647,
para 69. See generally Ch 10.
[166] See para 6.45 et seq.

with the right where (for instance) an officer in the course of a search perused an address book, or diary, or correspondence but he doubted whether an ordinary superficial search of a person or bags reaches a sufficient level of seriousness to engage the Convention (paragraph 29, see also Lord Brown at paragraph 74). In any event, one of the exceptions in Article 8(2)—such as the interests of national security, public safety, the prevention of disorder or crime, or for the protection of the rights and freedoms of others- would apply to a properly authorized and conducted search.

6.117 As to Articles 10 and 11 of the Convention, the European Court, having found that Article 8 had been violated, did not consider it necessary to examine the arguments that section 44 of the Terrorism Act 2000 might have a chilling effect on protests and might delay contemporaneous reporting of protests and therefore violated these rights (paragraphs 88–90).[167] In the House of Lords, Lord Bingham (at paragraph 30) had found it 'hard to conceive of circumstances in which the power, properly exercised in accordance with the statute and Code A, could be held to restrict' Article 10 and 11 rights and in any event he would expect the justifications in paragraphs (2) of Articles 10 and 11 to apply. He did however refer to one such circumstance where Articles 10 and 11 might apply: 'if the power were used to silence a heckler at a political meeting', a barely concealed reference to the removal of Walter Wolfgang from the 2005 Labour Party Conference for heckling Jack Straw about the Iraq war. It remains to be seen whether, particularly in the light of the European Court judgment, there will be circumstances where the courts will prefer to rely on Articles 10 or 11, rather than Article 8, when considering the lawfulness of the police's use of stop and search powers. One such circumstance may be the increasing use of the power against journalists and photographers.[168]

Road traffic stops

Stop and seizure of vehicles

6.118 A police officer may stop a vehicle where he has reasonable grounds for believing that it is being driven in a careless or inconsiderate way or off road[169] and it is causing alarm, distress, or annoyance to members of the public (Police Reform Act 2002, s 59(1)). It is an offence to fail to stop when required to do so (s 59(6)).[170] An officer may seize the vehicle if it appears to the police officer that the person responsible has used the vehicle in the same way after the officer has warned the person not to (s 59(4)). A warning need not be given if, among other things, it is impracticable to give one (s 59(5)). The police may enter property other than a home and may use reasonable force to stop and seize the vehicle (s 59(3)).

---

[167] See also para 85 of the judgment and para 6.20.
[168] See, for example, the Independent, 4 December 2009, 'Photographers snap over use of Section 44 by police officers' at http://www.independent.co.uk/news/uk/home-news/photographers-snap-over-use-of-section-44-by-police-officers-1833839.html (last accessed 14 January 2010).
[169] Road Traffic Act 1988, s 3 and s 34.
[170] Summary only, maximum penalty is level 3 fine.

Road checks

By virtue of PACE, s 4 the police can set up systematic road checks or road blocks.　**6.119**

A superintendent's 'authorization'

A police superintendent[171] has the power to give an 'authorization', lasting up to seven　**6.120**
days[172] for a road check or road block to be conducted in a specified locality. The purpose
of the road check is to ascertain whether a vehicle is carrying someone who has committed
an offence; a witness to an offence; a person intending to commit an offence; or a person
who is unlawfully at large. A road check may only be authorized if the offence in question
is indictable and the superintendent has reasonable grounds for suspecting that the person
sought is, or is about to be, in the locality of the search. The authorization must specify
whether the road checks will be continuous or take place at specified times and their
purpose.

The constable's power

The authorization gives a constable the power to stop any vehicle selected by any criterion　**6.121**
(s 4(2)). It is an offence for a driver not to stop at a road check when required to do so (Road
Traffic Act 1988, s 163, see below). The power is to ascertain whether a vehicle is carrying
the person sought. There is no power to carry out a search. An officer would have to rely on
his general powers under PACE to justify a search of a motor vehicle.[173] Anyone stopped at
a road check is entitled to obtain a 'written statement' of the purpose of the road check
within twelve months of the stop (s 4(15)).

Road stops

Section 163(1) and (2) of the Road Traffic Act 1988 states that a driver of a car on a road　**6.122**
'must stop the vehicle on being required to do so' by a uniformed officer. Section 163(3)
says that 'If a person fails to comply with this section he is guilty of an offence'.[174] Section
163(2) contains a similar provision applicable to cyclists. There are two views on what this
section means.

On one, narrow, view—for which the authority is *Steel v Goacher*[175]—the section simply　**6.123**
creates an obligation, backed up by a tailor-made criminal offence, on a driver to stop when
asked to do so by an officer. According to this interpretation, the section does not create a
distinct police power to stop a vehicle. The section simply assists the police, once the driver
has stopped, to exercise some other power—such as the power to question, check, search,
or arrest—which would be thwarted if the driver were not obliged to stop. On this interpretation, it is submitted, the driver is only obliged to stop if the officer is entitled to exercise that other power. It has been argued by those who prefer this view that a police officer

---

[171] PACE, s 4(3) or an officer of a lower rank in the case of urgency s 4(5). See also 4.77.
[172] Extendable for a further seven days (ibid, s 4(11)(a), s 4(12)).
[173] See 6.73 on these powers.
[174] Summary only, maximum penalty level 5 fine. See also reference to this power in PACE, s 4(2), the
power to carry out road checks, considered above.
[175] (1983) 147 JP 83, DC. See also *Winter v Barlow* [1980] RTR 209, DC.

must, once he stops a vehicle, also give his reasons for doing so, otherwise the stop will be unlawful.[176]

6.124 Another interpretation—for which the authority is *Beard v Wood*[177]—is that s 163 creates not only an obligation on the driver to stop, and indeed stand still while the police carry out their enquiries,[178] but also a distinct police power, which is not dependent on the lawful exercise of another police power, to stop the driver. But when may the power be exercised? Observations by Watkins LJ in *Lodwick v Sanders*[179] suggest that at its narrowest the power to stop can be exercised in order for an officer to police Part VII of the Road Traffic Act 1988 (by virtue of which the police may among other things establish drivers' identities and see relevant driving documents[180]) although it has been suggested that the power may be used to police all road traffic offences.[181]

F. Breach of the Peace

> Every constable, and also every citizen, enjoys the power and is subject to a duty to seek to prevent, by arrest or other action short of arrest, any breach of the peace occurring in his presence, or any breach of the peace which (having occurred) is likely to be renewed, or any breach of the peace which is about to occur.[182]

6.125 With this concise sentence, Lord Bingham answered three of the five key questions relating to questions relating to breach of the peace, which we shall deal with here:

- what is a breach of the peace?
- who may take action?
- in what circumstances may action be taken?
- what action may be taken?
- against whom may action be taken?

6.126 The concept of a breach of the peace and the powers that go with it are as old as the common law itself. Once a breach of the peace has occurred or is imminent, the police (indeed any citizen) may take steps to prevent it—by moving people on; diverting them away; stopping them from moving forward; detaining them so long as is necessary; and even using force. These powers are commonly used in the context of public protest, where the threat of violence by protestors or others becomes apparent, and in other incidents of relatively minor public disorder.

---

[176] R Clayton and H Tomlinson, *Civil Actions Against the Police* (2005, 3rd edn) p 341, para 7–159 and p 345, para 7–173.

[177] [1980] RTR 454, QB.

[178] Watkins LJ in *Lodwick v Sanders* [1985] 1 WLR 382, 389, DC.

[179] [1985] 1 WLR 382, DC at p389. But see different views of Webster J in the same case on the scope of s163. See also Lord Widgery in *Beard v Wood* 1980] RTR 454, 459, QB.

[180] See 6.29.

[181] *Wilkinson's Road Traffic Offences* (2007, 23rd edn) p 1/464, (para 6.14).

[182] Lord Bingham in *R (on the application of Laporte) v Chief Constable of Gloucestershire Constabulary* [2007] 2 AC 105, HL at para 29; endorsed by Lord Brown at para 110.

Furthermore, the police (or any citizen) may arrest and detain a person for a breach of the **6.127** peace or to prevent a threatened renewal of a breach of the peace, or to prevent a serious or imminent breach of the peace. Once arrested the person must be taken to a police station and then produced before a magistrates' court to show cause under the Justice of the Peace Act 1361 why he should not be bound over. There is also a complaint procedure whereby a person may be required to attend a magistrates' court with a view to being bound over.[183]

If bound over to be of good behaviour or keep the peace for a specified period and for a **6.128** specified sum in case of a breach, the person is not subject to a conviction or a penalty because this is not a charge and a breach of the peace is not a criminal offence. He merely gives an undertaking as to his future conduct, with or without (often without) any admission about his past behaviour.[184]

What is a breach of the peace?

Definition

The classic definition of breach of the peace was given by the Court of Appeal by Watkins **6.129** LJ in *R v Howell*:[185] 'We are emboldened to say that there is a breach of the peace whenever harm is actually done or is likely to be done to a person or in his presence to his property or a person is in fear of being so harmed through an assault, an affray, a riot, unlawful assembly or other disturbance.' This imposes a higher threshold than the hitherto conflicting authority set by the Court of Appeal in *R v Chief Constable of Devon & Cornwall, ex parte Central Electricity Generating Board*[186] in which Lord Denning said that 'There is a breach of the peace whenever a person who is lawfully carrying out his work is unlawfully and physically prevented by another from doing it.'[187] The *Howell* definition has since been approved both by the European Court of Human Rights (in *Steel v UK*[188]) and by the House of Lords in *R (on the application of Laporte) v Chief Constable of Gloucestershire Constabulary*,[189] Lord Bingham[190] emphasizing that in *Howell* 'The court concluded that the essence of the concept was to be found in violence or threatened violence.'

A person also commits a breach of the peace if his actions provoke violence in others, **6.130** provided violence is the natural consequence of the person's behaviour.[191] Failing to acknowledge that others cannot, in some circumstances, reasonably be expected to put up with disruptive activities would be to ignore 'the infirmity of human temper'.[192]

---

[183] See the Magistrates Courts Act 1980, s 115 and Ch 9.
[184] See Ch 9.
[185] [1982] QB 416, 427, CA.
[186] [1982] QB 458.
[187] Ibid, p 471.
[188] (1999) 28 EHRR 603, paras 25–9 and 55.
[189] [2007] 2 AC 105, HL.
[190] Ibid, para 27, with the agreement of Lord Brown at para 113. See also *Percy v DPP* [1995] 1 WLR 1382, DC.
[191] See *Steel v UK* (1999) 28 EHRR 603, paras 27 and 55 approving Collins J in *Percy v DPP* [1995] 1 WLR 1382, 1392, DC.
[192] As Channell J put it in *Wise v Dunning* [1902] 1 KB 167, 179.

6.131 Thus, in *Laporte*, Lord Carswell[193] reviewing the case law, particularly authorities involving demonstrations, identified three classes of cases into which most if not all instances of breach of the peace fitted.

6.132 'In the first class, which one might regard as the most direct . . . the person . . . is himself committing or about to commit a breach of the peace' and Lord Carswell cited *Moss v McLachlan*[194] (striking miners being stopped from travelling to confront working miners at a pit) as an example.

6.133 'The second category . . . concerns people whose acts are lawful and peaceful in themselves but are likely to provoke others into committing a breach of the peace' and Lord Carswell cited *Humphries v Connor*,[195] and *Wise v Dunning*,[196] cases where the natural consequence of sectarian actions, words, and emblems in the sight of opponents would have been to cause a violent response.

6.134 'In the third class of case the actions are not necessarily provocative per se, but a counter-demonstration is arranged, of such a nature that the confluence of demonstrations is likely to lead to a breach of the peace. This situation not infrequently arises in the context of parades in Northern Ireland' and Lord Carswell, former Chief Justice of Northern Ireland, cited *O'Kelly v Harvey*,[197] a case not without modern echoes, where the Orange Party and Land League Party planned opposing demonstrations.

6.135 In this context, cases involving freedom of expression require special care because the legitimate exercise of this right may offend, shock, or disturb others.[198] Thus, in *Redmond-Bate v DPP*,[199] where three Christian fundamentalist women were preaching on the steps of Wakefield Cathedral, Sedley LJ in the Divisional Court said that 'Free speech includes not only the inoffensive but the irritating, the contentious, the eccentric, the heretical, the unwelcome and the provocative provided it does not tend to provoke violence.' It had therefore been 'both illiberal and illogical' for the police officers dealing with them and the lower courts to conclude that there was a reasonable apprehension that violence might be provoked.

6.136 When deciding who is responsible for the breach of the peace, the courts also examine the reasonableness of the actions of both sides and the rights, particularly any European Convention rights, they may be exercising. According to Simon Brown LJ in the Divisional Court in *Nicol and Selvanayagam v DPP*:[200]

---

[193] *Laporte*, paras 94–9.

[194] (1985) 149 JP 167, DC.

[195] (1864) 17 ICLR 1.

[196] [1902] 1 KB 167.

[197] (1883) 10 LR Ir 287 at first instance in the Exchequer Division and (1884–85) 14 LR Ir 105 on appeal.

[198] See *Handyside v UK* (1979–80) 1 EHRR 737, para 49.

[199] [2000] HRLR 249, DC, paras 20 and 21. See also 10.149.

[200] (1996) 160 JP 155, 163, DC. Comments approved and quoted by the European Court of Human Rights in *Steel v UK* (1999) 28 EHRR 603, paras 27–8 and 55 and reinforced by Lord Brown, as he had then become, *in R (on the application of Laporte) v Chief Constable of Gloucestershire Constabulary* [2007] 2 AC 105, HL, para 121. See also *Bibby v Chief Constable of Essex Police* (2000) 164 JP 297, CA and *Foulkes v Chief Constable of Merseyside Police* [1998] 3 All ER 705, CA.

the court would surely not find a [breach of the peace by a defendant] proved if any violence likely to have been provoked on the part of others would be not merely unlawful but wholly unreasonable—as, of course, it would be if the defendant's conduct was not merely lawful but such as in no material way interfered with the other's rights. A fortiori, if the defendant was properly exercising his own basic rights, whether of assembly, demonstration or free speech.

In that case, the court took the view that the actions of animal rights campaigners **6.137** who sought to disrupt a fishing competition by throwing sticks at the competitors' fishing lines, were unreasonable and they had therefore committed a breach of the peace.

The definition is sufficiently clear to be prescribed by law within the meaning of **6.138** Article 10(2) of the European Convention according to the European Court of Human Rights.[201]

Breach of the peace and the criminal law

A breach of the peace is not a criminal offence, except in Scotland at common law,[202] but it **6.139** is a concept which may lead to police action (see below). It is an 'offence', in a different context; under Article 5(1)(c) in cases where the courts have examined the procedural rights of a person who has been arrested and detained by the police, and then appears in court at risk of being committed to prison.[203]

Powers to deal with a breach of the peace, which were expressly preserved by the Public **6.140** Order Act 1986 (see s 40(4)), are independent of procedures for dealing with criminal offences. PACE, its Codes, and the Bail Act 1976 do not apply.[204] However, the courts do carefully examine the content and scope of the criminal law when interpreting equivalent breach of the peace powers in order to ensure that police powers and citizens' rights under the two regimes are broadly compatible.[205] They have not, however, yet determined whether the ingredients of an actual (as opposed to an apprehended), breach of the peace must also amount to the commission of an identifiable criminal offence.[206]

---

[201] *Steel v United Kingdom* (1999) 28 EHRR 603, paras 25–9 and 55.
[202] Conduct is criminal in Scotland if it is genuinely alarming and distressing to any reasonable person (*Smith v Donnelly* 2002 JC 65). See also *Jones v Carnegie* 2004 JC 136 endorsing the test in *Ferguson v Carnochon* (1889) 16 R (J) 93 that it is an offence if conduct by one or more persons 'will reasonably produce alarm in the minds of the lieges'; see also *Lucas v United Kingdom* Application No 39013/0 at 10.59 below.
[203] See 6.156 et seq and Ch 9. See, in *R (on the application of Laporte) v Chief Constable of Gloucestershire Constabulary* [2007] 2 AC 105, HL, Lord Bingham at para 28; Lord Brown at para 111; Lord Mance at para 137. See also *Steel v UK* (1999) 28 EHRR 603, paras 46–50; Dyson LJ in the Court of Appeal in *Williamson v Chief Constable of West Midlands* [2004] 1 WLR 14, CA at para 9; *R v County of London Quarter Sessions Appeals Committee, ex parte Metropolitan Police Commissioner* [1948] 1 KB 670, 673, 676, DC; Lord Bingham in *Customs & Excise Commissioners v City of London Magistrates' Court* [2000] 1 WLR 2020, 2025.
[204] See 6.159.
[205] *Williamson v Chief Constable of West Midlands* [2004] 1 WLR 14, CA and PACE; *Austin v Commissioner of Police of the Metropolis* (2008) 2 WLR 415, CA and Public Order Act 1984, s 12 and s 14. *McLeod v Metropolitan Police Commissioner* [1994] 4 All ER 553, CA and powers of entry under PACE, s 17. *R (on the application of Laporte) v Chief Constable of Gloucestershire Constabulary* [2007] 2 AC 105, HL and power of arrest under PACE, s 24 and power to control demonstrations under the Public Order Act 1986.
[206] See Lord Mance in *R (on the application of Laporte) v Chief Constable of Gloucestershire Constabulary* [2007] 2 AC 105, HL, para 137.

Who may take action?

6.141 All citizens, police officers or otherwise, have the same power to deal with a breach of the peace. In the words of Lord Diplock in *Albert v Lavin*:[207] 'At common law this is not only the right of every citizen, it is also his duty, although, except in the case of a citizen who is a constable, it is a duty of imperfect obligation.' Indeed for the police, 'A constable's ultimate duty is to preserve the Queen's peace.'[208] If called upon by a police officer, it is an offence at common law for a citizen to fail to come to the assistance of a police officer in order to preserve the public peace.[209]

When may action be taken?

6.142 Action may be taken where a breach of the peace[210]

- is occurring;
- has occurred and is likely to be renewed; and
- is about to occur.

6.143 There will be little room for confusion over whether a breach of the peace is occurring. In any event, any ambiguities are likely to be caught by one of the two other circumstances in which action may be taken or by the inclusion, within the *Howell* definition of a breach of the peace (above) of the fear or the threat of violence.

6.144 In *Chief Constable of Cleveland Police v McGrogan*[211] the Court of Appeal considered the circumstances in which breach of the peace powers could be exercised where a breach of the peace had occurred and was likely to be renewed. The powers being exercised were arrest and detention and the circumstances were an assault by a man on a woman at their home. The police had arrested and justified the continued detention of the man because they feared that, if he were released without having been bound over by a court, he would return home and there would be more violence.

6.145 Wall J (paragraphs 35–6) adopted the trial judge's formulation of the law: 'the power to detain to prevent a further breach of the peace is limited to circumstances where there is a real (rather than fanciful) apprehension based on all the circumstances that if released the prisoner will commit or renew his breach of the peace within a short time . . .' and added two further conditions: '(1) that the officer making the decision for continued detention must have an honest belief that further detention is necessary in order to prevent a breach of the peace, and (2) that there must be, objectively, reasonable grounds for that belief.'

---

[207] [1982] AC 546, 565, HL.

[208] Lord Brown in *R (on the application of Laporte) v Chief Constable of Gloucestershire Constabulary* [2007] 2 AC 105, HL, para 123, see also Lord Rodger at para 61. See Ch 2 for consideration of a police officer's duty.

[209] *R v Brown* 174 ER 522 cited by Lord Rodger in *R (on the application of Laporte) v Chief Constable of Gloucestershire Constabulary* [2007] 2 AC 105, HL, para 83 and endorsed by Lord Brown at para 123.

[210] See Lord Bingham in *Laporte* quoted at 6.125 and Lord Diplock in *Albert v Lavin* at 6.153. See aslo para 6.156.

[211] [2002] 1 FLR 707, CA.

Unsurprisingly, the exercise of preventative powers, to deal with a breach of the peace **6.146**
which has not taken place, but is about to occur, has proved to be the most contentious. In
the words of Lord Rodger [212] 'For the most part, the common law is concerned to punish
those who have committed an offence and to deter them and others from doing so in the
future. It does not step in beforehand to prevent people from committing offences. The
duty to prevent a breach of the peace is therefore exceptional. And, if not kept within
proper bounds, it could be a recipe for officious and unjustified intervention in other
people's affairs.' All the more so where freedoms of expression and assembly are engaged
because, as Lord Bingham observed [213] 'Any prior restraint on freedom of expression calls
for the most careful scrutiny.'

The powers were considered in the House of Lords in *R (on the application of Laporte) v* **6.147**
Chief Constable of Gloucestershire Constabulary. [214] Anti-war protestors planned a large and
public demonstration outside RAF Fairford. The police were concerned that violence and
criminal offences would take place and devised a detailed plan to deal with the protests.
Jane Laporte, whose conduct and intentions, it was accepted, were entirely peaceful,
travelled to the demonstration on one of three coaches carrying 'a diverse group of varying
ages and affiliations' from London to Fairford to attend the protests. About 5 km from
Fairford, the coaches were stopped and searched and various items (including material
which might be used to conceal identities or be used for criminal offences) were found and
seized. Out of the 120 people travelling on the coaches, eight were of concern to the police,
identified by the police as 'members of an anarchist organisation known as the Wombles'.
Jane Laporte challenged by judicial review the police's decision to order the coaches and all
but three of their occupants to return to London, thereby preventing protestors from
attending the demonstration at Fairford. She argued that her rights under Articles 10 and
11 had been breached.

The House of Lords, allowing her appeal, confirmed that before any preventative action **6.148**
can be taken, the threat of a breach of the peace must be 'imminent' and this is an objective
test. Lord Mance's comments [215] encapsulate the view of the House of Lords. 'I regard the
reasonable apprehension of an imminent breach of the peace as an important threshold
requirement, which must exist before any form of preventive action is permissible at common law. Where a reasonable apprehension of an imminent breach of the peace exists, then
the preventive action taken must be reasonable or proportionate. But the threshold for
preventive action is neither a broad test of reasonableness nor flexible.' In the words of
Lord Bingham 'The test is the same whether the intervention is by arrest or . . . by action

---

[212] *R (on the application of Laporte) v Chief Constable of Gloucestershire Constabulary* [2007] 2 AC 105, HL,
para 62.
[213] *R (on the application of Laporte) v Chief Constable of Gloucestershire Constabulary* [2007] 2 AC 105, HL,
para 37 citing *The Sunday Times v United Kingdom (No 2)* (1992) 14 EHRR 229, para 51 and *Hashman and
Harrup v United Kingdom* (2000) 30 EHRR 241, para 32.
[214] [2007] 2 AC 105, HL. For *Laporte*, see also 4.61 et seq, 6.167 et seq, 10.38, and 10.80.
[215] Ibid, para 141.

short of arrest'.[216] In doing so, the House of Lords rejected the police's argument[217] based on *Moss v McLachlan*[218] that the police's actions need simply be reasonable and imminence goes only to the reasonableness of the actions.

6.149 But what does 'imminent' mean? Lord Rodger acknowledged that 'There is no need for the police officer to wait until the opposing group hoves in sight before taking action. That would be to turn every intervention into an exercise in crisis management'.[219] Similarly, Lord Carswell said this of the imminence test: 'I do consider, however, that it can properly be applied with a degree of flexibility which recognizes the relevance of the circumstances of the case. In particular it seems to me rational and principled to accept that where events are building up inexorably to a breach of the peace it may be possible to regard it as imminent at an earlier stage temporally than in the case of other more spontaneous breaches'.[220] Lord Rodger recognized the realities of modern policing: 'a senior officer at the centre of a police operation, receiving reports from his officers on the ground, plus intelligence and advice on how to interpret the data, may have good reason to appreciate that a breach of the peace is 'imminent' or 'about to happen', even though that would not be apparent to officers lacking these advantages'.[221]

6.150 In the circumstances of *Laporte*, the breach of the peace was not imminent. The police had identified and disarmed those people on the coach who intended violence. They had made plans to deal with breaches of the peace at RAF Fairford itself. The test is objective but, tellingly perhaps, the officer who made the decision did not consider the threat of the breach of the peace to be imminent, prompting Lord Rodger to comment that if the officer 'had concluded that a breach of the peace at Fairford was imminent, I might have been disposed to accept that'.[222] As one commentator observed, it is unclear what the courts could or would have decided if the police had not been so honest about the adequacy of their powers under the Public Order Act 1986 and in assessing the imminence of any breaches of the peace.[223]

6.151 Having declared that the test applied by the court in *Moss v McLachlan* was wrong, the House of Lords in *Laporte* considered how they would have applied the *Laporte* test—of imminence—to the facts of *Moss v McLachlan*. In *Moss v McLachlan* the court examined the lawfulness of the police's tactic, during the 1980s miners' strike, of setting up road blocks at a motorway exit to prevent striking miners from travelling on to picket working miners' collieries between 1 ½ and 5 miles from the road block. The police sought to justify the road blocks because they prevented violent clashes between the striking and working miners. Lords Bingham, Rodger, and Carswell[224] broadly took the view that the breach of

---

[216] Ibid, paras 39 and 45. See para 50 too where Bingham sets out his conclusions from a review of the authorities. Also Lord Rodger, para 66; Lord Carswell, para 101; Lord Brown, para 114.
[217] Summarized by Lord Bingham from para 40.
[218] (1985) 149 JP 167. See also *Minto v Police* [1987] 1 NZLR 374.
[219] *Laporte*, para 69.
[220] Ibid, para 102, see also Lord Mance, para 141.
[221] Ibid, para 67.
[222] Ibid, para 71. See also Lord Carswell, para 104.
[223] See [2007] Crim LR 576, 579.
[224] *Laporte*, paras 51, 71, and 102.

the peace was imminent. For Lord Bingham it was significant that 'four members of one belligerent faction [were] within less than five minutes of confronting another belligerent faction, and no designated, police-controlled, assembly point separated [them] from the scene of apprehended disorder'. Lord Brown regarded the decision 'as going to the further-most limits of any acceptable view of imminence, and then only on the basis that those prevented from attending the demonstration were indeed manifestly intent on violence'.[225] Lord Mance took the view that the court's decision in that case—that the police's actions were lawful—was probably wrong and certainly unclear. The court's incorrect formulation of the test, he said, had led the court to the wrong conclusion.[226]

Lord Bingham[227] observed that any extension of police preventative powers to control **6.152** protestors, generally, should be made by Parliament, not judges. While Lord Bingham expressed no opinion on whether they should be extended, the Court of Appeal did in *Austin v Commissioner of Police of the Metropolis*.[228] It endorsed 'the desirability of a thorough consideration of this area of the law in order to see whether it would be possible to make clear provisions appropriate to cover a case of this kind in the future'.[229]

What action may be taken?

In the words of Lord Diplock in the House of Lords in the leading case of *Albert v Lavin*[230] **6.153** 'every citizen in whose presence a breach of the peace is being, or reasonably appears to be about to be, committed has the right to take reasonable steps to make the person who is breaking or threatening to break the peace refrain from doing so; and those reasonable steps in appropriate cases will include detaining him against his will'. Reasonable force may be used.[231] However, the power to take steps to deal with a breach of the peace only lasts so long as the threat of a breach of the peace exists.[232] Thus, in *Albert v Lavin*, it was lawful for a police officer to detain a queue jumper whose actions might otherwise have provoked a violent response from others waiting for a bus, but probably only until the bus had gone, it is submitted.

Action short of detention by force (or arrest, see below) may be taken. It may be something **6.154** minor such as gently putting one's hand on a person's elbow to escort him away from a breach of the peace[233] or removing an orange lily from a lapel.[234] Words may be all that is needed. It may be enough simply to issue a warning, backed up, in the event that the

---

[225] Ibid, para 118.
[226] Ibid, para 150.
[227] Ibid, para 52, see also Lord Brown, para 132.
[228] [2008] QB 660, CA.
[229] *Austin* in the Court of Appeal, para 84.
[230] [1982] AC 546, 565, DC.
[231] Hodgson J in the Divisional Court in *Albert v Lavin* [1982] AC 546, 553 cited with approval by Lord Bingham in *R (on the application of Laporte) v Chief Constable of Gloucestershire Constabulary* [2007] 2 AC 105, HL, para 30. See 6.174 et seq.
[232] Hodgson J in the Divisional Court in *Albert v Lavin* [1982] AC 546, 553, DC. Compare with *McGrogan*, above at 6.144.
[233] *King v Hodges* [1974] Crim LR 424, DC.
[234] *Humphries v Connor* (1864) 17 ICLR 1.

warning is ignored, with the power to arrest for breach of the peace[235] or for obstruction of the police.[236] It may be justifiable to ban a public meeting.[237] The police may do nothing. They may decide that they have to ration the resources they allocate to policing protests even where those protests might lead to a breach of the peace.[238]

6.155 Three circumstances merit particular discussion.

Arrest

6.156 Any citizen, including the police, has a power of arrest where:[239]

(1) a breach of the peace is committed in the presence of the person making the arrest[240] or

(2) the arrestor reasonably believes that such a breach will be committed in the immediate future by the person arrested although he has not yet committed any breach, or

(3) where a breach of the peace has been committed and it is reasonably believed that a renewal of it is threatened.

6.157 Exceptionally the police have the power to arrest in order to prevent a breach of the peace, but there must be a sufficiently serious or imminent threat to the peace to justify the 'extreme step of depriving of his liberty a citizen who is not at the time acting unlawfully'.[241] By analogy, it is submitted that the police may only arrest in other circumstances where there is no other alternative way of abating the breach of the peace.

6.158 The person carrying out the arrest simply need say 'I am arresting you for a breach of the peace' in order to effect the arrest.[242] The arrested person must be taken to a police station and then brought before a justice of the peace as soon as reasonably practicable to determine if a breach of the peace has occurred and a bind over to keep the peace should be made.[243] In the meantime detention is justified if it is in order to prevent a breach of the peace.[244] There is also authority that detention is justified, after arrest, to take a person to

---

[235] *R v Howell* [1982] QB 416, CA.

[236] Under Police Act 1996, s 89(2), see Ch 2. See comments by Lord Rodger in *R (on the application of Laporte) v Chief Constable of Gloucestershire Constabulary* [2007] 2 AC 105, HL, para 74.

[237] *Duncan v Jones* [1936] 1 KB 218, though in the light of the 'constitutional shift' given to freedom of expression and assembly by the Human Rights Act 1998, as Sedley J characterized it in *Redmond-Bate v DPP* (1999) 163 JP 789, 795, this case may be decided differently now, see 6.135. See also comments of Lord Bingham at para 34 of *Laporte*.

[238] *R v Chief Constable of Sussex ex p International Traders Ferry Ltd* [1999] 2 AC 418, HL. See Lord Brown's comments on this case, in *Laporte*, from para 124, especially his comments on Lord Cooke's justification (at p 454 of the *International Traders case*), for acknowledging that it is 'the lawless elements acting on the side of protestors who have won the day'.

[239] Watkins LJ in the Court of Appeal in *R v Howell* [1982] QB 416, CA.

[240] It has been argued that the absence of the term 'reasonably believes' from this limb of the arrest power, but not from the two others, limits the power of arrest when a breach of the peace is actually taking place—Richard Card, *Public Order Law* (2000) p 25.

[241] Beldam LJ in *Foulkes v Chief Constable of the Merseyside Police* [1998] 3 All ER 705, 711, CA. See also *Bibby v Chief Constable of Essex Police* (2000) 164 JP 297, CA. For compatibility of arrest for breach of the peace with the ECHR see also *Steel v United Kingdom* (1999) 28 EHRR 603.

[242] *R v Howell* [1982] QB 416, CA.

[243] Dyson LJ in *Williamson v Chief Constable of West Midlands* [2004] 1 WLR 14, CA, paras 19–21. See Ch 9 on the court and breach of the peace and 6.139 on the application of Art 5(1)(c).

[244] *Chief Constable of Cleveland Police v McGrogan* [2002] 1 FLR 707, CA, above.

court to be bound over even when the threat of a breach of the peace has passed.[245] However, it has been argued that the common law power to detain in these circumstances has been abolished by s 115(1) of the Magistrates' Courts Act 1980 which requires all bind over proceedings to be initiated by a complaint.[246]

In *Williamson v Chief Constable of West Midlands*[247] Dyson LJ in the Court of Appeal con- **6.159** firmed that breach of the peace is not an offence within the meaning of the Police and Criminal Evidence Act 1984 (or, therefore, its codes). He also considered the implications. Section 39 and Code C (the Code of Practice for the detention, treatment, and questioning of persons by police officers[248]) do not apply, though it is good practice for them to be observed.[249] There is no power to grant bail, for example under s 34(5) of PACE or s 1 of the Bail Act 1976.[250]

Limits on pickets

Pickets during trade disputes are treated no differently from any other non-industrial **6.160** picket. Although s 220 of the Trade Union and Labour Relations (Consolidation) Act 1992 provides a statutory right to picket 'Even that limited right is subject to the overriding right and duty of the police to take steps to prevent an apprehended breach of the peace.'[251] Thus, in the celebrated case of *Piddington v Bates*[252] the court approved a police decision to limit the number of pickets[253] and in *Kavanagh v Hiscock*[254] the court approved a police cordon preventing pickets getting close enough to a coach of working electricians to talk to them. The Department for Business Innovation and Skills ('BIS' formerly 'BERR') has issued a Code of Practice on Picketing.[255] Section C covers the criminal law and section D deals with police powers.

Police powers and private property

'The Queen's peace' is a wider concept than public order.[256] Thus, a breach of the peace **6.161** may take place on private land[257] and there does not need to be a disturbance to a member

---

[245] For example, Dyson LJ in *Williamson v Chief Constable of West Midlands* [2004] 1 WLR 14, CA, para 21.

[246] R Clayton and H Tomlinson, *Civil Actions Against the Police* (2005, 3rd edn) pp 235–7.

[247] [2004] 1 WLR 14.

[248] See Ch 7.

[249] Confirming *Constable of Cleveland Police v McGrogan* [2002] 1 FLR 707, CA. Note, however, that according to Code C 1.10 of PACE, the Code applies to all people in custody 'whether or not they have been arrested'.

[250] Dyson LJ at para 15 in *Williamson*.

[251] *Harvey on Industrial Relations and Employment Law* NII3205, at p NII/458, issue 197.

[252] [1961] 1 WLR 162, QB.

[253] Note that in *Laporte* Lord Bingham described the case as 'aberrant' (para 47). See also comments of Lord Rodger at para 67 and Lord Mance at paras 140–1.

[254] [1974] QB 600, DC.

[255] Code of Practice, Picketing PL928 (1st Revision) <http://www.berr.gov.uk/whatwedo/employ-ment/employment-legislation/employment-guidance/trade-unions/page22266.html> (last accessed 19th September 2009, section on employment, policy and legislation), to be transferred to website <http://www.bis.gov.uk>.

[256] *McQuade v Chief Constable of Humberside* [2002] 1 WLR 1347, CA per Laws LJ at para 19.

[257] Contrast the offence contrary to Public Order Act 1986, s 5. See Glidewell LJ in the Court of Appeal in *McConnell v Chief Constable of Greater Manchester* [1990] 1 WLR 364, CA.

of the public outside the premises for a breach of the peace to have occurred.[258] Police powers reflect this. The police have a common law power to enter premises to deal with or prevent a breach of the peace, even where they would otherwise be trespassers.[259] There is no limit to the type of premises the police may enter though the police should act with 'great care and discretion' particularly when entering contrary to the wishes of the owners or occupiers[260] and must observe Article 8 and Article 1 Protocol 1 of the European Convention.[261] The police may eject trespassers where there is an actual or threatened breach of the peace.[262]

The application of human rights principles

6.162 The exercise by the police of breach of the peace powers are measured against human rights standards (and general public law principles[263]). These are dealt with more fully in Chapter 10.

6.163 The potential application of Article 5 (the right to liberty and security) was considered by the House of Lords in *Austin v The Commissioner of Police of the Metropolis*.[264] Louis Austin, a peaceful protestor, had been held within a preventative police cordon (a form of containment now known as a 'kettle' designed to quell disorder) during May Day demonstrations in Oxford Street, Central London with about 3,000 others for about seven hours until their controlled release. Lord Hope, giving the lead judgment, with which the other Law Lords agreed, concluded that Article 5 was not engaged at all.[265]

6.164 Lord Hope's reasoning was as follows. He recognized that the right not to be deprived of one's liberty is an absolute right, but is narrowly defined. Whether there has been a deprivation of liberty as opposed to something less is a matter of degree and intensity. He recognized that those who drafted Article 5 had not expressly included the maintenance of public order and the protection of public safety as lawful grounds for the deprivation of liberty. However, he concluded that it was permissible to do so, take what he called a 'pragmatic approach' and put into the balance 'the lives of persons affected by mob violence' and, more widely, 'the interests of the community' by relying on Article 2 (the right to life).

---

[258] Laws LJ at para 27 in *McQuade*, applying *McConnell*.
[259] The power was preserved of PACE, s 17(6). See *McLeod v Metropolitan Police Commissioner* [1994] 4 All ER 553.
[260] Neill LJ in the Court of Appeal in *McLeod v Metropolitan Police Commissioner* [1994] 4 All ER 553.
[261] *McLeod v United Kingdom* (1999) 27 EHRR 493.
[262] See judgment of Judge LJ in the Court of Appeal in *Porter v Commissioner of Police of the Metropolis*, unreported, 20 October 1999, CA, where the court also considered whether, in the absence of a breach of the peace, the police have the power to eject trespassers, see para 5.38. See also *Semple v DPP* [2009] EWHC 3241 (Admin).
[263] *Boddington v British Transport Police* [1999] 2 AC 143, HL.
[264] [2009] 1 AC 564, HL. Also considered at 4.73 et seq and10.167. See also David Mead, 'Of Kettles, Cordons and Crowd Control—Austin v Commissioner of Police for the Metropolis and the meaning of "deprivation of liberty"' in (2009) 3 EHRLR 376–94. See also *Gillan and Quinton v UK*, considered at para 6.112 et seq.
[265] Ibid, para 11 onwards.

Applying these principles to the kettle, Lord Hope concluded[266] that measures of this kind **6.165** do not fall within Article 5(1) so long as they are not arbitrary—that is, that they are resorted to in good faith, are proportionate and are enforced for no longer than is reasonably necessary. Discomfort was kept to a minimum. The cordon was maintained only so long as was reasonably thought necessary to protect the demonstrators and neighbourhood properties from violence.

The Lords' decision in *Austin* is now before the European Court of Human Rights[267] **6.166** and the use of the kettle has been closely examined and may be reviewed following its use at the G20 protests in London in April 2009.[268] The Joint Committee on Human Rights[269] recommended that containment should only be used where 'it is necessary and proportionate to do so generally and in relation to each individual contained'. Where it is used it should among other things: only be imposed for the minimum period of time necessary; there should be clear communication between the police and those contained; those contained should be given access to facilities such as toilets, medical assistance, and water; the police should establish a means of considering individual circumstances and identifying who can be let out (with a presumption that people should be allowed to leave where possible).

Articles 10 and 11, qualified rights, were engaged in *Laporte*.[270] It was common ground **6.167** that the police had acted in the interests of national security, for the prevention of disorder or crime, or for the protection of the rights of others, legitimate purposes under Articles 10(2) and 11(2). However, on the facts, the House of Lords concluded that the police's actions were unlawful because they were not necessary in a democratic society. They were premature and indiscriminate and were accordingly disproportionate. In coming to this conclusion the House of Lords took into account the following, among other, factors: the police had removed from the coach the equipment troublemakers might have used; the police could or should have identified and removed the troublemakers only and allowed the others to continue to RAF Fairford; any violence which might have occurred would have taken place at RAF Fairford where the police had plans in place.[271]

---

[266] Ibid, para 37, and see also Lord Scott at para 39, and Lord Neuberger at para 60 on the principle and its application to the facts in *Austin*. See Lord Neuberger at para 61 floating the possibility that the situation was also lawful because those affected had implicitly consented to it.

[267] *Austin v UK*, Application No 39692/09. See also, from the same incident, *Lowenthal and O'Shea v UK*, Application No 41008/09 and *Black v UK*, Application No 40713/09.

[268] See for example reports of Joint Committee on Human Rights Follow-Up report published July 2009 p 9 onwards, para 17 onwards; HMIC report, Part 1, published July 2009 at p8, and recommendations 5–9 at pp 10–11, and p 54, and Annex I at p 102; Home Affairs Committee Report, published 2009 at Ch 4, p 14 onwards, para 38 onwards and recommendations 16–22 at pp 28–9. See comments on 'crowd dynamics' and containment in HMIC report 'Adapting to Protest', Part 2, 25 November 2009, Ch 4. The use of this power at the G20 protests in London in April 2009 is also subject to a judicial review, *Abbott v Commissioner of the Police for the Metropolis*, Claim No: CO/6790/2009. Permission was granted on 23 November 2009.

[269] Follow-Up report, p14, para 29.

[270] See also 4.61 et seq, 6.146 et seq, 10.38, and 10.80.

[271] See, for example, Lord Bingham at para 55, Lord Rodger at para 85 onwards, Lord Brown at para 118.

Against whom may action be taken?

6.168 The words of Lord Diplock in *Albert v Lavin*[272] are the best starting point: 'every citizen in whose presence a breach of the peace is being, or reasonably appears to be about to be, committed has the right to take reasonable steps' to deal with it. For Lord Bingham in *Laporte*[273] this is a 'simple and workable test . . . There is very unlikely to be doubt about who to take action against, since this will be apparent to the senses of the intervener'. Similarly for Sedley LJ in *Redmond-Bate v DPP*,[274] 'the critical question . . . is where the threat is coming from, because it is there that preventive action must be directed'. Having said this, in *Joyce v Hertfordshire Constabulary*[275] the Divisional Court considered a case where a police officer encountered a struggle between football supporters and police officers, without knowing how it started. Kerr LJ said 'the rights and wrongs do not matter', the officer was entitled to intervene against a football supporter.

6.169 The wider problem which has confronted the judges is whether there is 'a principle whereby if it is the only way to prevent a third party (A) causing a breach of the peace, a police officer . . . may request another person (B) to desist from entirely lawful and innocent conduct, and, if B refuses to desist, may physically restrain B or charge B with wilfully obstructing the police officer . . . in the execution of her or his duty'.[276] This was the situation in *Laporte* and *Austin*. They were innocent people detained in order to allow the police to deal with a potentially violent situation.

6.170 The House of Lords in *Laporte* did not express a unified view but the themes which could be extracted were summarized by Sir Anthony Clarke MR giving the judgment of the whole Court of Appeal in *Austin v Commisioner of Police of the Metropolis* when he said:[277]

> As we read the speeches of Lord Rodger and Lord Brown they give some support for the following propositions:
> i)   where a breach of the peace is taking place, or is reasonably thought to be imminent, before the police can take any steps which interfere with or curtail in any way the lawful exercise of rights by innocent third parties they must ensure that they have taken all other possible steps to ensure that the breach, or imminent breach, is obviated and that the rights of innocent third parties are protected;
> ii) the taking of all other possible steps includes (where practicable), but is not limited to, ensuring that proper and advance preparations have been made to deal with such a breach, since failure to take such steps will render interference with the rights of innocent third parties unjustified or unjustifiable; but
> iii) where (and only where) there is a reasonable belief that there are no other means whatsoever whereby a breach or imminent breach of the peace can be obviated, the lawful exercise by third parties of their rights may be curtailed by the police;

---

[272] [1982] AC 546, 565, HL.
[273] *Laporte*, para 49.
[274] (1999) 163 JP 789, para 6.
[275] (1985) 80 Cr App R 298, DC. But see also *Cumberbatch v CPS* [2009] EWHC 3353 (Admin).
[276] Lord Mance in *Laporte*, para 147. For obstructing a police officer in the execution of duty see 2.12.
[277] [2008] QB 660, paras 35 and 36.

iv) this is a test of necessity which it is to be expected can only be justified in truly extreme and exceptional circumstances; and

v) the action taken must be both reasonably necessary and proportionate.
While it cannot we think be said that Lord Mance expressly supports those propositions, they seem to us to be consistent with his views.[278] They are not inconsistent with the speech of Lord Carswell and Lord Bingham did not address these questions at all.[279]

Some of the members of the House of Lords in *Laporte* considered the compatibility of their views with the European Convention authorities.[280] Typical was the reasoning of Lord Mance. He recognized[281] that in *Ezelin v France*[282] the Court said that 'the freedom to take part in a peaceful assembly—in this instance a demonstration that had not been prohibited—is of such importance that it cannot be restricted in any way . . . so long as the person concerned does not himself commit any reprehensible act on such an occasion'. However, he went on to observe[283] that the Commission and Court 'have accepted the legitimacy of general statutory restrictions on demonstrations in the form of a public procession, where necessary to avoid a breach of the peace . . . So the general statements in *Ezelin* . . . may by parity of reasoning be subject to a similar qualification which would permit preventive action against an innocent person where it was reasonably apprehended that there was no other possible means of avoiding an imminent breach of the peace . . .' **6.171**

Sir Anthony Clarke MR in the Court of Appeal in *Austin v Commissioner of Police of the Metropolis*[284] had also analysed the views of the Lords in these authorities[285] and concluded: **6.172**

> In these circumstances we read Lord Rodger, Lord Brown and Lord Mance as being of the view that the approach identified in the five propositions set out above is not inconsistent with the Strasbourg jurisprudence. They are in our opinion consistent with it. Moreover, provided that it is recognized, as their Lordships each did, that the primary focus should be on the wrongdoers and not innocent demonstrators or those who are not demonstrators but are present by chance, and that, save in a case of absolute necessity, the right of freedom of expression under Article 10 and the freedom of assembly and association under Article 11 must be protected, the propositions seem to us to represent a fair and reasonable balance between the interests of all those involved.

The Court of Appeal in *Austin* concluded by adopting the five propositions they had extracted from *Laporte*.[286] **6.173**

---

[278] See para 148 of his judgment.

[279] See paras 43, 45, and 55 of his judgment.

[280] See for example the comments of Lord Bingham at paras 35–7; Lord Rodger at paras 81–85; Lord Brown at paras 121, 127, and 130; Lord Mance from para 135 and from para 144. Authorities considered included *Ziliberberg v Moldova* Application No 61821/00; *Ezelin v France* (1992) 14 EHRR 362 (followed by the Divisional Court in *Blum v DPP* [2007] UKHRR 233, DC); *Christians against Racism and Fascism v United Kingdom* (1980) 21 DR 138. See Ch 10.

[281] *Laporte*, para 144.

[282] (1992) 14 EHRR 362.

[283] *Laporte*, para 149, citing *Christians against Racism and Fascism v United Kingdom* (1980) 21 DR 138 and *Ziliberberg v Moldova* Application No 61821/00.

[284] [2008] QB 660.

[285] Ibid, para 38 onwards.

[286] Ibid, para 119(ii).

G. The Use of Force by the Police

6.174 Widespread concerns about the high profile policing of the G20 protests in London on 1 and 2 April 2009—not least the death of Ian Tomlinson who was not a protestor—have led to a spate of independent reviews of the strategies, training, and equipment the police deploy to deal with protests. At the time of writing, a number of reports have been published[287] and the police are revising their approach but have not finalized or made public their reforms.[288] It should not be forgotten, however, that the use of force is also a day-to-day means by which the police address public disorder, most of which does not stem from protests. This part of this chapter seeks to identify and put in context the justifications for the use of force by the police generally and particular considerations which apply to the policing of protests.[289]

Sources of power to use force

6.175 The police may make physical contact with others if it does not go beyond what are generally acceptable standards of conduct in ordinary life: *Collins v Wilcock*.[290]. Thus, for example, the police were acting lawfully in *Mepstead v DPP*[291] when an officer took hold of a man's arm, not intending to detain or arrest him, but in order to draw his attention to what was being said to him. There is a hint, in the reference made by Goff LJ in *Collins v Wilcock*[292] to 'a person who is acting reasonably in the exercise of a duty', that there may be some further latitude to a police officer in the amount of force he may use.

6.176 By virtue of s 117 of PACE the police may use reasonable force, if necessary, in the exercise of any of their powers under PACE. This may apply, therefore, to the exercise of powers to search (ss 1, 2, and 32[293]), to enter property to arrest (s 17[294]), to arrest (s 24), as well as powers exercised once the person is in detention at the police station (eg ss 36, 37, and 54). Accordingly, when in *Kenlin v Gardiner*[295] the police restrained suspects in order to question them, having no power to do so, they committed an assault (and the person restrained was not committing an assault when, in turn, he used force, to resist the restraint).

---

[287] See the House of Lords and House of Commons Joint Committee on Human Rights Report, 'Demonstrating Respect for Rights? Follow-Up', 22nd Report of Session 2008–09, HL Paper 141, HC 522, published 28 July 2009; House of Commons Home Affairs Committee report 'Policing of the G20 Protests', 8th Report of Session 2008–09, HC 418, published 29 June 2009; HMIC report 'Adapting to Protest', Part 1 published 7 July 2009 and Part 2 published 25 November 2009.
[288] See HMIC report 'Adapting to Protest', Part 2, 25 November 2009, p 34 and Ch 5, pp 104–5, which cites the ACPO Public Order and Public Safety Update Reports to HMIC, dated 13 October 2009, and 29 October 2009, and The Metropolitan Police Service's letter to HMCIC dated 7 September 2009.
[289] See also Ch 8; paras. 4.73 et seq, 6.162 et seq, and 10.167 et seq (on kettling); para 6.72 et seq (on stop and search).
[290] [1984] 1 WLR 1172, 1177–8, DC per Goff LJ. See also Ch 2, especially 2.33 to 2.34.
[291] [1996] COD 13, QB. See also *McMillan v Crown Prosecution Service* (2008) 172 JP 485, DC.
[292] *Collins v Wilcock*, p 1178. See also *Semple v DPP* [2009] EWHC 3241 (Admin) for the police power to use force to assist publicans under s 143(4) Licensing Act 2003.
[293] Terrorism Act 2000, s 114 provides similar powers to the police when exercising stop and search powers under s 44 of that Act.
[294] *O'Loughlin v Chief Constable of Essex* [1998] 1 WLR 374, CA.
[295] [1967] 2 QB 510, DC.

Similarly, in *Wood v DPP*[296] the police were acting unlawfully when they restrained a suspect in order to identify him, as they did not intend to or purport to carry out an arrest, even though they had the power to do so.

By virtue of s 3 of the Criminal Law Act 1967 'A person may use such force as is reasonable **6.177** in the circumstances in the prevention of crime, or in effecting or assisting in the lawful arrest of offenders or suspected offenders or of persons unlawfully at large.' This applies to anyone, not just police, but also civilians.[297]

PCSOs may use reasonable force in the exercise of their powers provided the police **6.178** themselves may use force when exercising similar powers.[298] When entering premises, they may only use force in the company of a police officer, or for the purpose of saving life or limb, or preventing serious damage to property.[299] PCSOs may also use reasonable force[300] when exercising their power to detain someone who has not given his name and address.[301]

All citizens have the right, in common law, to use reasonable force in self-defence when **6.179** attacked. Force may be used in response to an apprehended attack, provided it is imminent.[302] Force may be used in the defence of others.[303]

Anyone may use reasonable force to stop or prevent a breach of the peace,[304] when acting **6.180** through necessity to prevent death or serious injury[305] and in order to protect property (under the Criminal Damage Act 1971, s 5(2)[306]).

What is 'reasonable' force?

Force may be used where it is reasonable and proportionate and reasonably necessary.[307] **6.181**

The question whether force is 'reasonable in the circumstances' has been re-stated so far as **6.182** s 3 of the Criminal Law Act 1967 and self-defence are concerned, by s 76 of the Criminal Justice and Immigration Act 2008. There are two questions when anyone uses force. Firstly, a subjective test—what are the circumstances as the person using force believed them to be?

---

[296] The Times, 23 May 2008. But see *Semple v DPP* [2009] EWHC 3241 (Admin).
[297] See generally the discussion in Ch 8, Part C the prevention of crime.
[298] Police Reform Act 2002, s 38(8), see also PACE, Code C, para 1.14. See 6.08 et seq for PCSOs' powers.
[299] Police Reform Act 2002, s 38(9).
[300] Ibid, Sch 4, Part 1, paras 4, 4ZA, 4ZB as amended by Serious Organised Crime and Police Act 2005, Sch 9, para 4.
[301] Police Reform Act 2002, Sch 1, Part 1, para 2.
[302] *AGs Reference (No 2 of 1983)* [1984] QB 456, CA; *R v Colin Chisam* (1963) 47 Cr App R 130, CA; *R v Bird* [1985] 1 WLR 816, CA; *Palmer v The Queen* [1971] AC 814, PC.
[303] *R v Colin Chisam* (1963) 47 Cr App R 130, CA; *R v Duffy* [1967] 1 QB 63, CA; and see Criminal Justice and Immigration Act 2008, s 76(10).
[304] See 6.153 et seq.
[305] See Ch 8, Part E.
[306] See Ch 8, Part D.
[307] *Palmer v The Queen* [1971] AC 814, PC, see p 831 cited with approval in *Tomlinson v Commissioner of Police of the Metropolis* [2006] EWHC 2810, QB, para 12. See also Criminal Justice and Immigration Act 2008, s 76(7)(b)—see Ch 8.

Secondly, an objective test—was the degree of force used, reasonable in these circumstances?[308]

6.183 The courts apply the reasonable force test in the same way regardless of the source of the police power to use force.[309] The courts allow police officers the same margin for judgment, discretion, and error they allow any citizen. 'One does not use jewellers' scales to measure reasonable force' when assessing what force is reasonable in order to effect an arrest under s 3 of the Criminal Law Act 1967.[310]

The European Convention

6.184 Where the police use force, the State is responsible and the European Convention is, potentially, applicable.[311]

6.185 Article 2(1) guarantees the right to life. By virtue of Article 2(2), the right is not violated where death results from the use of force which is no more than absolutely necessary (a) in defence of any person from unlawful violence; (b) in order to effect a lawful arrest or to prevent the escape of a person lawfully detained; and (c) in action lawfully taken for the purpose of quelling a riot or insurrection. Article 2 applies to situations where the State is permitted to use force and that force may result, as an unintended outcome, in the deprivation of life.[312]

6.186 Police officers policing public disorder or protests should therefore refrain, unless absolutely necessary, from using force which might cause death.[313] Further, in their planning and preparations for the policing of protests the police should seek to avoid the risks of loss of life and, it is submitted, minimize the use of force generally. For example, in *Gulec v Turkey*[314] the police's recourse to firing live rounds into a crowd to disperse protestors breached Article 2 not only because a protestor was killed but also because the police's failure to plan so that they could rely on less extreme measures—such as truncheons, riot shields, water cannon, rubber bullets or tear gas—was 'incomprehensible and unacceptable'.[315]

---

[308] These questions are addressed in Ch 8, 8.64 et seq.

[309] See, for example, *Tomlinson v Commissioner of Police of the Metropolis* [2006] EWHC 2810, QB, para 11 where force used to prevent a breach of the peace, under Criminal Law Act 1967, s 3, under PACE, s 117 and in self-defence was considered. In *Tomlinson*, the court cited *R v Clegg* [1995] 1 AC 482, HL where, according to Lord Lloyd at p 496 force used to prevent crime, arrest offender, and self-defence was considered.

[310] Lane J, *Reed v Wastie* [1972] Crim LR 221, DC. See also Criminal Justice and Immigration Act 2008, s 76(7)(a). For the use of dogs to assist in an arrest see *Pollard v the Chief Constable of West Yorkshire Police* [1999] PIQR P219; *Roberts v Chief Constable of Kent* [2008] EWCA Civ 1588; *Coles v Chief Constable of South Yorkshire Police* 12 October 1998, CA.

[311] See Ch 10.

[312] *Giuliani and Gaggio v Italy*, App No 23458/02, 25 August 2009 at para 204.

[313] See *Andreou v Turkey* (2009) Application No 00045653/99, 27 October 2009, para 47 onwards; *Giuliani and Gaggio v Italy*, Application No 23458/02, 25 August 2009, paras 204–213; *McCann v UK* (1995) 21 EHRR 97. On the State's positive obligation to take steps to preserve life, see *Osman v UK* (2000) 29 EHRR 245.

[314] (1999) 28 EHRR 121.

[315] Ibid, para 71. See also *Ergi v Turkey* (2001) 32 EHRR 18 and *Huohvanainen v Finland* (2008) 47 EHRR 44.

Article 3 prohibits in absolute terms torture and inhuman or degrading treatment or **6.187** punishment. However, Article 3 does not prohibit the use of force in well-defined circumstances, such as to effect an arrest, provided the use of force is indispensable and not excessive.[316] And 'In order to fall within the scope of Article 3, the ill-treatment must attain a minimum level of severity, the assessment of which depends on all the circumstances of the case, such as the duration of the treatment, its physical or mental effects and, in some cases, the sex, age and state of health of the victim, etc.'[317] The Court recognizes that the minimum severity requirement is in the nature of things relative.[318]

The European Court, in cases where it has determined that assaults by the police have **6.188** engaged Article 3, has decided what level of injury is required to meet the minimum severity threshold. In *Karabulut v Turkey*[319] the applicant was arrested during a peaceful but unlawful demonstration and suffered a blow to the front of the head which caused a swelling of 2 cm. In non-protest cases, such as *RL and M-J D v France*[320] the applicants suffered numerous bruises which led to them being unfit for work for between six and ten days. In *Allaham v Greece*[321] the applicant alleged that he was brutally beaten on the head by one officer while another held him still. He suffered headaches, dizziness, and a perforated eardrum, resulting in a significant long-term loss of hearing. Handcuffing may, depending on the circumstances, engage Article 3.[322]

Although Article 3 is an absolute right, the European Court recognizes that whether it is **6.189** engaged in any particular case may depend on the conduct of the person subjected to force (if he threatens violence or may abscond) and also on the police's rights to act in self–defence.[323] Even in these circumstances, however, following *RL and M-J D v France*,[324] the police may only use force which is reasonable, proportionate, and necessary, taking into account alternative ways of dealing with the situation. In *Karabulut v Turkey*, above,[325] it was relevant not only that the applicant had not been violent or put up resistance, but also that the police had had the opportunity to prepare for the demonstration as they had prior notice of it.

Article 3 may also be engaged in altogether different circumstances—by imposing an obli- **6.190** gation on the police to prevent protestors from causing other citizens to suffer inhuman

---

[316] *Karabulut v Turkey*, Application No 16999/04, 27 January 2009, para 42, citing *Kurnaz and Others v Turkey*, Application No 36672/97, § 52, 24 July 2007.

[317] *Raninen v Finland* (1998) 26 EHRR 563, para 55, reiterating principles set out in *Ireland v the United Kingdom* (1979–80) 2 EHRR 25.

[318] *Selmouni v France* (2000) 29 EHRR 403, para 100.

[319] Application No 16999/04, 27 January 2009, paras 10 and 41. Also *Balçik v Turkey*, Application No 25/02, 29 November 2007, para 20 et seq, in particular paras 27–34.

[320] [2005] Crim LR 307, Application No 44568/98, paras 64–5, but see dissenting judgment at paras 1–11. See also *RIVAS v France* [2005] Crim LR 305, Application No 59584/00, para 39.

[321] (2009) 49 EHRR 10, p 223.

[322] Contrast *Raninen v Finland* (1998) 26 EHRR 563 with *Tarariyeva v Russia* (2009) 48 EHRR 26.

[323] *Raninen v Finland* (1998) 26 EHRR 563, para 56: *RIVAS v France*; and *RL and M-J D v France*.

[324] *RL and M-J D v France*, paras 68–73. See also *RIVAS v France*, paras 40–1.

[325] Application No 16999/04, 27 January 2009, para 43. See also *Balçik v Turkey*, Application No 25/02, 29 November 2007.

and degrading treatment. In *(E) (a child) v Chief Constable of the Royal Ulster Constabulary*[326] the House of Lords examined a challenge to the policing of protests in Belfast on the grounds that not enough had been done to restrain loyalist protestors who sought, through increasing violence, to stop Roman Catholic parents and children from taking their normal route on foot through a loyalist area to a Catholic girls' primary school.

6.191 The House of Lords (Lord Carswell in particular from paragraph 41 onwards) confirmed that the State has a positive obligation to take steps to prevent the infliction by third parties of inhuman or degrading treatment.[327] As with Article 2(above), the authorities' obligation under Article 3 is to do all that can reasonably be expected to avoid a real and immediate risk of inhuman or degrading treatment being inflicted, once they have or ought to have knowledge of the existence of the risk.[328] The test is therefore one of reasonableness and proportionality. The police are uniquely placed through their experience and intelligence to make a judgement on the wisest course to take in all the circumstances.[329]

6.192 Confronted with concern that police resources could and should be directed away from the demonstrations and towards serious harm and even death orchestrated elsewhere in Belfast by the same group, Baroness Hale in *(E) (a child)* said that 'As a general principle, a police officer is not entitled to stand by and let one person kill or seriously ill-treat another, when he has the means of preventing it, just because he fears the wider consequences of doing so.'[330]

6.193 Article 8 (the right to respect for private and family life) may also be engaged when the police strike a person, as the right may, depending on the circumstances, include a person's 'physical integrity', in other words, his body.[331] Indeed, there may be circumstances where the level of force used is not sufficient for Article 3 to be engaged, but is enough for Article 8 to apply.[332] However, Article 8 is, unlike Article 3, a qualified right and so one of the exceptions to that right, set out in paragraph 2 (eg the prevention of disorder or crime) may apply.

6.194 Similarly, the use of force may be relevant to Article 11. In *Balçik v Turkey*[333] the police's 'forceful intervention' to disperse an unlawful but peaceful, demonstration, was found to

---

[326] [2009] 1 AC 536, HLNI, considered by Gordon Anthony in 'Positive Obligations and Policing in the House of Lords' in (2009) 4 EHRLR 538–51.

[327] Ibid, Lord Carswell, paras 44–5. There was a slight difference of opinion over whether the positive obligation was absolute or not, or whether, if absolute, it was only its content which distinguished it from the negative obligation on the state not to inflict inhuman and degrading treatment on its citizens—see Lord Carswell at para 45 and Baroness Hale at para 10.

[328] Lord Carswell at para 48.

[329] Lord Carswell at para 58.

[330] *(E) (a child)*, para 14. Contrast this with the decision of the House of Lords in *R v Chief Constable of Sussex ex p International Traders Ferry* [1999] 2 AC 418, HL where a challenge to the police's decision to ration its policing of protests at Shoreham against the export of livestock, so that adequate policing levels across Sussex generally could be maintained, was dismissed.

[331] *Connors v UK* (2005) 40 EHRR 9, para 82; *Storck v Germany* (2006) 43 EHRR 6, para 143.

[332] *Raninen v Finland* (1998) 26 EHRR 563, para 63.

[333] Application No 25/02, 29 November 2007, see para 35 et seq, especially para 53. See also *Karabulut v Turkey*, Application No 16999/04, 27 January 2009, at para 30 et seq. Contrast the 'reasonable and calm'

breach not only Article 3, but also Article 11. The backdrop to the Court's reasoning was that 'it is important for the public authorities to show a certain degree of tolerance towards peaceful gatherings if the freedom of assembly guaranteed by Article 11 of the Convention is not to be deprived of all substance' (paragraph 52).

Equipment

ACPO have issued a number of guidances on the use of equipment used to manage public order and protest.[334] They are supplemented by Safety Manuals and Notices on their use (which, like many police documents, are not in the public domain).[335]   **6.195**

The guidance on the use of handcuffs for example begins by saying:[336] 'Any intentional application of force to the person of another is an assault. The use of handcuffs amounts to such an assault and is unlawful unless it can be justified. Justification is achieved through establishing not only a legal right to use handcuffs, but also good objective grounds for doing so in order to show that what the officer . . . did was a reasonable, necessary and proportionate use of force.'   **6.196**

Interestingly enough, the guidance on the use of CS gas which predated the G20 protests[337] says: 'Chief officers may wish to consider policies relating to possession of incapacitant spray at pre-planned public order events. It should be noted that there are no group tactical options for its use at such events and therefore use will be at the discretion of individual officers in accordance with the overriding principle of reasonableness and necessity.'   **6.197**

The policy on the use of tasers[338] should be read now in the light of the recommendation of the Joint Committee on Human Rights that tasers 'should not be used against peaceful protestors'[339] and the Home Affairs Committee's comments that 'it would not endorse any move to authorise its wider use beyond dealing with a violent threat' and that tasers should not be used in large public protests.[340]   **6.198**

The police have contemplated, instead, the use of 'distance weapons' such as water canons for policing protests. The Home Affairs Committee, however, rejected their use apparently on similar grounds to their rejection of the use of tasers: 'British policing is based on   **6.199**

---

police action in *Rai v UK*, application number 26258/07, decision 17th November 2009, where no breach of Art 11 was found.

[334] See the ACPO website, <http://www.acpo.police.uk>, policies directory, <http://www.acpo.police.uk/policies.asp> (last accessed 19 September 2009).

[335] These, and training, do not however guarantee consistent or satisfactory use of equipment, shields for example—see for example HMIC report 'Adapting to Protest', Part 2, 25 November 2009, pp 5–6, Ch 5 and p 101, and see 6.202 below.

[336] 'Guidance on the Use of Handcuffs' 19 September 2006 at para 2.1.2. See also 'Guidance on the Use of Limb Restraints' issued 19 September 2006.

[337] 'Guidance on the Use of Incapacitant Spray' dated 19 September 2006 at para 2.5.12.

[338] 'Operational Use of Taser by Authorised Firearms Officers' dated December 2008.

[339] Demonstrating Respect for Human Rights? A Human Rights Approach to Policing Protest, March 2009 HL Paper 47-1, HC 32, see also recommendation 34 and para 193.

[340] Home Affairs Committee Report, published June 2009, p 22, para 66 onwards and p 30, para 27 onwards.

consent and face-to-face engagement, the use of Taser has the potential to erode that relationship and create a rift between the police and the policed'.[341]

6.200 At the time of the G20 protests, the police appear formally to have endorsed 'distraction' tactics against protestors, such as a slap in the face or a baton strike to the leg, justified in order to prevent an escalation of violence and to give an officer a window of opportunity in which to apply better control.[342] However, given that 'the images of "distraction" tactics in action have the potential to undermine the public's trust in the police' it is likely that the police will comply with the Home Affairs Committee's recommendation that the police clarify how and when these tactics should legitimately be used.[343]

Policing protests

6.201 The policing of large scale protests is likely to be overhauled as a result of lessons from the G20 protests.[344] Her Majesty's Inspectorate of Constabulary (HMIC) proposes that it should be based on 'the original British policing model'. This model, which HMIC attributes to Sir Robert Peel, the founder of the modern police force, 'places a high value on tolerance and winning the consent of the public' through 'an approachable, impartial, accountable style of policing based on minimal force'.[345] Quoting from his Nine Principles of Good Policing, HMIC noted that 'Sir Robert Peel recognised that "the degree of cooperation of the public that can be secured diminishes proportionately to the necessity of the use of physical force"'.[346] Accordingly HMIC propose that the police service should adopt 'an overarching set of fundamental principles' on the use of force, based on necessity and minimum use of force, which should run 'as a golden thread' though all aspects of police business.[347] Three particular proposals relevant to the policing of public order and protest emerge from HMIC's and others' reviews.

6.202 Firstly, it emerged that many officers untrained, inexperienced, and ill-equipped to deal with public disorder were on the front line in dealing with the G20 protestors. Common standards for public order training are contained in the ACPO Manual of Guidance for Public Order Standards, Tactics and Training (2004).[348] However, the Manual is out of date and training is limited and inconsistent.[349] Accordingly HMIC recommends that the police revise their public order training so that it provides national consistency and affords explicit training on the legal framework for policing public order, particularly on the

---

[341] Home Affairs Committee Report, published June 2009, p 22, para 71 and p 30, para 29.

[342] See evidence to Home Affairs Committee report, June 2009, p 19, para 55 onwards; see also HMIC Part 1 Report, p 58.

[343] Home Affairs Committee Report, published June 2009, p 19, para 58.

[344] On the policing of small events, see the comments at paras 91–2 of Lord Collins in the *Wood* case, above at 6.45 and HMIC report 'Adapting to Protest', Part 2, 25 November 2009, p 12.

[345] See HMIC report 'Adapting to Protest', Part 2, 25 November 2009, p 5, p 11, p 13, recommendation 6 at p 165.

[346] HMIC report 'Adapting to Protest', Part 2, 25 November 2009, p 32.

[347] See HMIC report 'Adapting to Protest', Part 2, 25 November 2009, p 7, p 29 onwards, pp 116–18 and recommendation 1 at p 161.

[348] See also ACPO's Personal Safety Manual (2007), considered in HMIC Part 1 Report, p 58.

[349] See HMIC report 'Adapting to Protest', Part 2, 25 November 2009, p 7, Ch 5, p 100 onwards and also Ch 6, p 111 onwards.

circumstances where force may be used. The objective is to ensure that officers apply their powers appropriately and proportionately to public order scenarios ranging from mass peaceful protest to serious violent disorder.[350] HMIC (and the Home Affairs Committee) recommend that those responsible for planning the policing of the protests should ensure that properly trained officers principally should be on the front line.[351]

Secondly, for individual police officers to be accountable for their actions they must be identifiable. The Joint Committee on Human Rights, among others, was concerned that at the G20 there was a widespread failure to comply with existing ACPO guidance[352] that individual police officers should display their identifying badges or identify themselves when asked and the Committee were surprised that their supervising officers did not deal with this at the time.[353] This is not a new issue: it had been highlighted in reports on at least three other demonstrations in the twenty-five years before the G20 protests.[354] Accordingly, the Committee recommend that there should be a legal requirement for police officers to wear identification numbers when on duty or to identify themselves when asked.[355] **6.203**

Thirdly, HMIC looked at police forces' policies for policing protests and concluded that they are out of date, incomplete, inconsistent, and deficient.[356] The principal national manuals providing guidance to those in charge of public order policing (as well as frontline officers and their trainers, above) are the ACPO Manual of Guidance on Keeping the Peace (2007) and the ACPO Manual of Guidance on Public Order Standards, Tactics and Training (2004). These are being reviewed by the police.[357] HMIC recommends that the policing of public order should be codified in order to ensure consistency of standards, guidance, and training.[358] As to the content of the policies, those planning the policing of protests should so far as possible ensure that their plans minimize recourse to the use of force, particularly potentially lethal force.[359] Furthermore, 'In planning future public order operations for protest the police should . . . [d]emonstrate explicit consideration of **6.204**

---

[350] See HMIC report 'Adapting to Protest', Part 2, 25 November 2009, Ch 5 at p 98 onwards; Ch 6 especially at p 111 onwards; recommendations 1 and 4 at p 161 onwards.

[351] HMIC Part 1 Report, p 11, recommendation 10 and p 62; and Home Affairs Committee report, June 2009, p 20 para 60, see also p 24 para 75.

[352] See reference in HMIC Part 1 Report at p 57 to the 'Dress Code Standard Operating Procedures (2008)' issued on 18 June 2009, para 13.6.27.

[353] Joint Committee Report, July 2009, p 17, para 37 onwards.

[354] See HMIC report 'Adapting to Protest', Part 2, 25 November 2009, p 174.

[355] See Joint Committee Report, July 2009, p 3 and p17, para 39. See also the Home Affairs Committee Report, June 2009, Summary and p 9, para 23 and recommendation p 27; and HMIC Part 1 Report, p 11 recommendation 12 and p 62.

[356] See HMIC report 'Adapting to Protest', Part 2, 25 November 2009, p 14, p 64 onwards, Ch 7.

[357] See 6.174.

[358] Using the powers to codify under the Police Act 1996, s 39A, introduced by the Police Reform Act 2002. See HMIC report 'Adapting to Protest', Part 2, 25 November 2009, p 7, Ch 2, p 66 onwards and recommendation 2 at p 162.

[359] See HMIC report 'Adapting to Protest', Part 2, 25 November 2009, Ch 6, especially p 118 and recommendation 1 at p 161.

the facilitation of peaceful protest throughout the planning process and the execution of the operation'.[360]

H. Conclusion

6.205 Any examination of police powers in the context of demonstrations risks misleading. Police powers are invariably exercised at the expense of freedom. However, as the European Court observed: 'although the essential object of Article 11 is to protect the individual against arbitrary interference by public authorities with the exercise of the rights protected, there may in addition be positive obligations to secure the effective enjoyment of these rights'.[361] These views have been echoed by, among others, the Home Affairs Committee. The concluding remarks of its report into the policing of the G20 protest[362] bear repeating:

> the police must constantly remember that those who protest on Britain's streets are not crimi-
> nals but citizens motivated by moral principles, exercising their democratic rights. The
> police's doctrine must remain focused on allowing this protest to happen peacefully. Any
> action which may be viewed by the general public as the police criminalizing protest on the
> streets must be avoided at all costs.

---

[360] See HMIC Part 1 Report p 7; p 11 recommendation 11; p 10 recommendation 1 (see also reference at p 37) and HMIC report 'Adapting to Protest', Part 2, 25 November 2009, p 16, Ch 7.
[361] *Djavit An v Turkey* (2005) 40 EHRR 45, para 57.
[362] Report June 2009, p 25, para 78 and p 31, para 32.

7

ARREST, DETENTION, AND BAIL

A. Arrest	7.01	Granting bail (with or without		
What is an arrest	7.01	conditions)		7.122
The police's power of arrest	7.02	Bail conditions from the police station		
The arresting officer's own suspicion:		(Bail Act 1976, s 3A)		7.122
Castorina 1	7.07	Bail conditions from the court		
Reasonable grounds for the		(Bail Act 1976, s 3)		7.126
officer's suspicion: *Castorina 2*	7.08	Implications of breaching bail		7.131
The discretion to arrest: *Castorina 3*	7.18	Breach of street bail		7.131
The citizen's power of arrest	7.33	Breach of bail from the police station		
Information to be given on arrest	7.38	to return to the police station		7.132
Search of a person after arrest	7.45	Breach of bail to attend court		
Entry and search of property on arrest	7.49	(Bail Act, s 7)		7.134
After arrest: street bail or police station	7.54	Impact on sentencing of commission		
The implications of failing to make		of offence while on bail		7.139
a lawful arrest	7.60	Refusing bail		7.140
B. Detention at the Police Station	7.65	The police's power to refuse bail		7.141
The role of the custody officer	7.66	The courts' power to refuse bail		7.144
Collecting personal information	7.72	Reviews and challenges to bail decisions		7.155
A detainee's rights	7.78	Records of decisions		7.155
Consultation of the Codes	7.78	Varying bail conditions		
Legal advice	7.79	following street bail		7.157
The right to have someone		Defence applications to vary bail		
informed when arrested	7.83	conditions from the police station		7.159
Special groups	7.85	Prosecution applications for		
Conditions during detention	7.89	reconsideration of bail decision		
Police detention and charge	7.94	by the police or magistrates		7.160
The decision to detain	7.95	Applications to vary bail conditions		
Further investigations	7.99	after first court hearing		7.161
Is there sufficient evidence to		Appeals against bail conditions,		
charge?	7.103	from a magistrates' court to		
The decision to charge	7.105	the Crown Court		7.162
C. Bail Conditions and Remands		Renewed applications for bail to the		
in Custody After Charge	7.109	same court		7.163
Introduction	7.109	Appeals against refusals of bail by		
The European Convention	7.112	a magistrates' court to the		
PACE and the Bail Act	7.121	Crown Court		7.164
		Appeals to the High Court		7.165

A. Arrest

What is an arrest?

7.01   There is no statutory definition of what constitutes, as a matter of fact, an arrest. Leading judges and academics have defined it. The term 'arrest' is an ordinary English word according to Viscount Dilhorne.[1] 'An arrest occurs when a police officer states in terms that he is arresting or when he uses force to restrain the individual concerned. It occurs also when by words or conduct he makes it clear that he will, if necessary, use force to prevent the individual from going where he may want to go' according to Lord Devlin.[2] There is no magic formula, only the obligation to make it plain to the suspect by word and deed that he is no longer a free man.[3] The person carrying out the arrest must also intend to bring the person arrested 'within the machinery of the criminal law' according to Professor Glanville Williams.[4] Otherwise the restraint is an assault even if an arrest would have been justified.[5]

The police's power of arrest

7.02   Arrest by police officers for a public order offence is nearly always effected by arrest without warrant under Part III of the Police and Criminal Act 1984. These arrests may take place in any part of the United Kingdom by virtue of Part X of the Criminal Justice and Public Order Act 1994. The other power often used where there is or may be public disorder is the power to arrest for breach of the peace, discussed in Chapter 6. The discrete power to arrest for breach of bail is discussed below.[6] The police may also arrest with a warrant, such as one issued by a justice of the peace under s 1 of the Magistrates' Courts Act 1980 or following a request for extradition, including a European Arrest Warrant, under the Extradition Act 2003.

7.03   This section will consider the critical question: When will an arrest without warrant be lawful? The answer lies in Part III, s 24 in particular, of the Police and Criminal Evidence Act 1984 (PACE),[7] Article 5 of the European Convention on Human Rights[8] and Code of Practice G to PACE, on the statutory power of arrest by police officers[9]. Section 24 has been closely examined in the case of *Castorina v Chief Constable of Surrey*[10] and other cases, particularly on issues such as reasonable grounds to arrest, necessity for arrest, and *Wednesbury*

---

[1]   *Spicer v Holt* [1977] AC 987, 1000, HL.

[2]   *Shabaan Bin Hussien v Chong Fook Kam* [1970] AC 942, 947, PC. See also Lord Parker CJ in *Alderson v Booth* [1969] 2 QB 216, 220–1.

[3]   *R v Inwood* [1973] 1 WLR 647, 652–3. See also *R v Fiak* [2005] EWCA Crim 2381, CA (Crim Div), paras 13–14.

[4]   'Requisites of a Valid Arrest' [1954] Crim LR 6, 15.

[5]   *Wood v DPP*, The Times, 23 May 2008, following *Kenlin v Gardner* [1967] 2 QB 510 DC.

[6]   See 7.131 et seq.

[7]   See Terrorism Act 2000, s 40 onwards for power to arrest for terrorism offences.

[8]   See Ch 10.

[9]   See for example paras 1.2–1.3. See 6.14.

[10]   (1988) 138 NLJ Rep 180, CA.

reasonableness for arrest, as viewed in the light of Article 5 of the European Convention. Each of these subjects will be considered in turn.

Under section 24 of PACE[11] a police officer may arrest without a warrant **7.04**

- anyone who is about to commit an offence or whom he has reasonable grounds for suspecting to be about to commit an offence;
- anyone who is in the act of committing an offence or whom he has reasonable grounds for suspecting to be committing an offence;
- where an offence has been committed or where a police officer has reasonable grounds for suspecting that an offence has been committed, anyone who is guilty of the offence, or anyone whom the officer has reasonable grounds for suspecting to be guilty.

For an arrest to be lawful, it must pass the three hurdles set by Woolf LJ in *Castorina v Chief* **7.05** *Constable of Surrey*:[12]

(1) Did the arresting officer suspect that the person who was arrested was guilty of the offence? The answer to this question depends entirely on the findings of fact as to the officer's state of mind.

(2) Assuming the officer had the necessary suspicion, was there reasonable cause for suspicion? This is a purely objective requirement to be determined by the judge if necessary on [the] facts found by a jury.

(3) If the answer to the two previous questions is in the affirmative, then the officer has a discretion which entitles him to make an arrest and in relation to that discretion has been exercised in accordance with the principles laid down by Lord Greene MR in *Associated Provincial Picture Houses Ltd v Wednesbury Corporation*.[13]

Since the decision in *Castorina*, its third limb in particular, one must be mindful of three **7.06** developments. First the Human Rights Act 1998 has been passed and Article 5 in particular is engaged. Second, conventional administrative law principles have of course developed in the sixty plus years since *Wednesbury* was decided.[14] And third, since an amendment to PACE in 2005, an arrest may now only be made if it is necessary, for one of a number of explicit and exclusive reasons (examined below).[15]

The arresting officer's own suspicion: *Castorina 1*

The arresting officer must actually suspect that the person arrested committed the offence. **7.07** 'Suspicion in its ordinary meaning is a state of conjecture or surmise, where proof is lacking: "I suspect but I cannot prove."'[16] The suspicion must be genuine.[17] The Crown

---

[11] Subsections (1), (2), and (3), substituted by the Serious Organised Crime and Police Act 2005, s 110.
[12] *Castorina* was confirmed by Sir Anthony Clarke MR in *Raissi v Commissioner of Police of the Metropolis* [2009] 2 WLR 1243, CA quoting from pp 20–1 of the transcript of *Castorina*.
[13] [1948] 1 KB 223, CA, considered at 7.27 et seq.
[14] See for example M Fordham, *The Judicial Review Handbook* (2008, 5th edn).
[15] Subsections (4) and (5), substituted by the Serious Organised Crime and Police Act 2005, s 110 and examined at paras 7.18 et seq.
[16] Lord Devlin in *Shaaban Bin Hussien v Chong Fook Kam* [1970] AC 942, 948, PC. Reaffirmed, for example, by Hallett LJ in *Chief Constable of West Yorkshire v Armstrong* [2008] EWCA Civ 1582, CA, para 10.
[17] Lord Hope in *O'Hara v Chief Constable of the Royal Ulster Constabulary* [1997] AC 286, 298, HL.

must prove this subjective suspicion at any trial. If they fail to do so, the arrest is unlawful.[18]

Reasonable grounds for the officer's suspicion: *Castorina 2*

7.08   The requirement that there be reasonable suspicion is part of the compromise English law has evolved to accommodate the potential of conflict between two rival public interests—the preservation of an individual's liberty and the detection of crime.[19] It is the route by which the arresting officer is held accountable[20] and the European Convention's protection against arbitrary arrest and detention.[21]

7.09   'All that the objective test requires is that [the arresting officer's] grounds be examined objectively and that they be judged at the time that the power was exercised'.[22] Reasonable suspicion 'presupposes the existence of facts or information which would satisfy an objective observer that the person concerned may have committed the offence. What may be regarded as "reasonable" will however depend upon all the circumstances.'[23] A number of factors may, cumulatively, amount to reasonable suspicion.[24] The threshold for the existence of reasonable grounds is low.[25]

7.10   Admissible evidence is not required. As Auld LJ said 'it is important not to lose sight of the distinction between availability of evidence and information amounting to *prima facie* proof and information, maybe falling short of admissible evidence, capable of amounting to reasonable grounds for suspicion'.[26] An officer is entitled to act on anonymously received information.[27] The arresting officer's belief may derive from hearsay information, including what he has been told by others, not least another officer.[28] The information may also come from the police national computer.[29]

7.11   However, it is the reasonableness of the arresting officer's suspicions, rather than the knowledge and views of other officers, which must be examined. Thus, an officer may not arrest simply because instructed to do so by an officer, even a senior officer. '"Following orders" is

---

[18]   See for example *Siddiqui v Swain* [1979] RTR 454, 457, DC; *Chapman v DPP* (1989) 89 Cr App R 190, DC; *R v Olden* [2007] EWCA Crim 726, CA.

[19]   See Lord Diplock in *Holgate-Mohammed v Duke* [1984] AC 437, 445.

[20]   *O'Hara v Chief Constable of RUC*, 299 per Lord Steyn.

[21]   *Fox, Campbell and Hartley v UK* (1991) 13 EHRR 157, para 32.

[22]   *O'Hara v Chief Constable of the RUC*, 298 per Lord Hope.

[23]   *Fox, Campbell and Hartley v UK*, para 32. See also *Dallison v Caffrey* [1965] 1 QB 348, 370–1, CA; Lord Hope in *O'Hara v Chief Constable of the RUC*, p 298; and PACE, Code G, Note for Guidance 2.

[24]   See for example Hallett LJ in *Chief Constable of West Yorkshire v Armstrong*, para 19. Also see Hughes LJ in the Court of Appeal in *Buckley v Chief Constable of Thames Valley Police* [2009] EWCA Civ 356, para 16.

[25]   See Sir Anthony Clarke MR in *Raissi v Commissioner of Police of the Metropolis* [2009] 2 WLR 1243, CA, para 20.

[26]   *Al Fayed v Commissioner of Police of the Metropolis* (2004) 148 SJLB 1405, CA [2004] EWCA Civ 1579 at para 50.

[27]   *DPP v Wilson* [1991] RTR 284, DC.

[28]   Lord Steyn in *O'Hara v Chief Constable of the RUC*, p 293. For the position of officers coming to the assistance of other officers, see *Joyce v Hertfordshire Constabulary* (1985) 80 Cr App R 298, DC, *Cumberbatch v CPS* [2009] EWHC (Admin) and 6.168.

[29]   *Hough v Chief Constable Staffordshire Police* [2001] All ER (D) 63 (Jan), [2001] PoLR 6, and see comments on this judgment in R Clayton and H Tomlinson, *Civil Actions Against the Police* (2005, 3rd edn) p 200, para 5.078.

not a defence.'[30] It is not necessary, when establishing the arresting officer's reasonable belief, to establish that the information supplied by a third party was in fact true[31] (a suspect's remedy against the person who supplied incorrect information to the arresting officer may be to sue that person for negligence [32]). If the arresting officer does not have reasonable grounds for suspicion, the arrest is not lawful if, unknown to him, another officer does have reasonable grounds.[33] In this respect, the requirements of domestic law are more exacting than Article 5(1)(c) of the European Convention, but this does not mean that domestic law is wrong.[34]

The source and quality of the information is, however, relevant when assessing whether the arresting officer's suspicion was reasonable. So where a junior officer relies on a briefing from a senior officer he need not have a detailed account of the evidence, provided there is an outline, because it comes from a source which it is reasonable to rely on.[35] Conversely, an officer may rely solely on information from an informant, but he should treat it with very considerable reserve and hesitate before regarding it, without more, as a basis for reasonable suspicion.[36]   **7.12**

The courts have not however come to a settled view on whether an officer should investigate further before his suspicion can be considered reasonable. In urgent cases, involving serious offences, there appears to be no such requirement.[37] The same may apply to minor cases.[38] This was the view of Purchas LJ in *Castorina* itself, a case of burglary where the police arrested an employee suspected of being involved in an inside job. This view was reiterated forcefully by Hughes LJ in *Buckley v Chief Constable of Thames Valley Police*.[39] However, it has been said that 'Castorina is an oversimplification of the position' and that a reasonable person would and should not only carry out obvious and straightforward enquiries but also ask questions of the suspect before his suspicion could be considered reasonable.[40] Indeed, in *Chief Constable of West Yorkshire v Armstrong* Hallett LJ accepted 'the proposition that the thoroughness of an investigation may well be relevant as part of the whole surrounding circumstances'.[41] There may be circumstances, provided there is no   **7.13**

---

[30] See Sir Anthony Clarke in *Raissi v Commissioner of Police of the Metropolis*, para 14 following *O'Hara v Chief Constable of the RUC*. See also Simon Brown LJ in *Hough v Chief Constable of Stafforshire*, para 16.

[31] Lord Hope in *O'Hara v Chief Constable of the RUC*, p 298.

[32] *Hough v Chief Constable of the Staffordshire Constabulary*. See also *Ahmed v Shafique Arora* [2009] EWHC 618, QB.

[33] Lord Steyn in *O'Hara v Chief Constable of the Royal Ulster Constabulary*, p 291–2.

[34] Ibid, followed by Simon Brown LJ in *Hough v Chief Constable of Staffordshire*, para 20.

[35] *R v Olden* [2007] EWCA Crim 726, para 22; Sedley LJ in *Clarke v Chief Constable of North Wales* [2000] PoLR 83, [2000] All ER (D) 477, para 23; *Raissi v Commisioner of Police for the Metropolis*.

[36] Lord Donaldson in *James v Chief Constable of South Wales*, 16 April 1991, CA, the Independent, 28 April 1991.

[37] *Hough v Chief Constable of the Staffordshire Constabulary*, per Simon Brown LJ at para 17 (a road stop, based on information from the police national computer of someone suspected of firearms offences); *Chief Constable of West Yorkshire v Armstrong* [2008] EWCA Civ 1582 (where a vicious rapist who might have struck at any time was on the loose).

[38] *McCarrick v Oxford* [1983] RTR 117, CA (suspected driving while disqualified).

[39] [2009] EWCA Civ 356, para 10.

[40] R Clayton and H Tomlinson, *Civil Actions Against the Police* (2005, 3rd edn) p 199, para 5.074; and R Clayton and H Tomlinson 'Arrest and Reasonable Grounds for Suspicion' (1988) 7 September, LSG 22.

[41] [2008] EWCA Civ 1582, para 14.

urgency, which makes it incumbent upon an officer to make further enquiries before 'suspicion could properly crystallise'. It is also arguable that now, by virtue of s 24(4) and (5) of PACE and under the third limb of *Castorina*, an arrest is only necessary when appropriate further enquiries have been made.[42]

7.14 An arresting officer should have an accurate understanding of the offence for which he is arresting a suspect. If the officer is wrong to apply the offence at all to the suspect's circumstances, then there can be no reasonable suspicion.[43] As to the depth of the officer's knowledge of the applicable law, in *Mossop v DPP* Scott Baker LJ said that the officer had to have reasonable grounds for suspicion that all the elements of the offence had been committed.[44] In that case the arrest was unlawful because the arresting officer did not know that the offence of possession of an offensive weapon could only be committed in a public place. Where more complicated offences are being investigated, however, it may be enough for the arresting officer to take a broad brush approach.[45]

7.15 What if the police come across a number of people, only one of whom may have committed the offence? In *Cumming v Chief Constable of Northumbria*[46] the Court of Appeal considered the lawfulness of the arrests of six people, narrowed down by the police from a wider group of potential suspects, one or more of whom may have committed the offence being investigated. Latham LJ, holding that the arrests were lawful, said 'Where a small number of people can be clearly identified as the only ones capable of having committed the offence, I see no reason why that cannot afford reasonable grounds for suspecting each of them of having committed that offence, in the absence of any information which could or should enable the police to reduce the number further' (at paragraph 41).

7.16 *Cumming* is also authority for the proposition that reasonable suspicion may be based solely on the fact that a person had the opportunity to commit an offence.[47] But in *Samuels v Commissioner of Police for the Metropolis*,[48] a case which might readily be transposed to the situation of protestors near the site of their protest, the Court of Appeal concluded that an officer who stopped a person who was in a high risk area for burglary and who answered back when challenged, did not have reasonable suspicion to conduct a search.

7.17 What, then, in a suspect's personal background, is relevant to establishing reasonable suspicion? Previous convictions for similar offences may not be sufficient.[49] Nor, in the absence of other factors, will connections to someone whom the police suspect has committed an offence.[50] However, in *Clements v DPP*[51] it was held that the fact that the suspect was a

[42] See 7.22 et seq.
[43] *DPP v Todd* [1996] Crim LR 344, DC. But see *Percy v Hall* [1997] QB 924, CA.
[44] [2003] EWHC 1261 (Admin), para 11.
[45] *Coudrat v Commissioners for Customs and Excise* [2005] STC 1006 per Smith LJ at para 32.
[46] [2003] All ER (D) 305 (Dec), [2004] PoLR 61, CA.
[47] Ibid, para 41 per Latham LJ.
[48] 3 March 1999, CA.
[49] *Fox, Campbell and Hartley v UK* (1991) 13 EHRR 157 at paras 34–6.
[50] *Buckley v Chief Constable of Thames Valley Police* [2009] EWCA Civ 356, para 8; *Raissi v Commissioner of Police of the Metropolis* [2009] 2 WLR 1243, CA, and [2009] 2 WLR 1243 in the Court of Appeal.
[51] [2005] EWHC 1279 (Admin).

young man on an anti-war demonstration was a factor an officer could take into account when considering whether he was likely to commit criminal damage near the perimeter fence of a military base.

The discretion to arrest: *Castorina 3*

Where an officer has reasonable grounds to suspect a person, the officer then has a discretion to arrest. There are three elements to any examination of the lawfulness of the decision to arrest.[52] First, s 24(5) of PACE sets out reasons for which an arrest may take place. Second, s 24(4) sets out the test—based on necessity—the officer must apply when considering whether the reasons are made out in a particular case. Third, by virtue of the third limb of *Castorina*, *Wednesbury* principles apply to that decision. **7.18**

The reasons for arrest: s 24(5)

A police officer may arrest for any offence for one of a number of stated reasons: **7.19**

- to enable the name or address of the person in question to be ascertained (where the name or address is not known and/or where there are reasonable grounds to doubt one of them) (s 24(5)(a) and (b)[53]);
- to prevent the person suffering physical injury or causing physical injury to someone else (s 24(5)(c)(i) and (ii), and note that the Home Office propose to expand and clarify this reason so that it applies more clearly to continuing offences, anti-social behaviour, and low-level disorder[54]);
- to prevent the person causing loss of or damage to property (s 24(5)(c)(iii)), to which the Home Office proposals, above, also apply);
- to prevent the person causing an unlawful obstruction of the highway (s 24(5)(c)(v)[55]);
- to prevent any prosecution from being hindered by the disappearance of the suspect (s 24(5)(f)[56]); or
- to allow the prompt and effective investigation of the offence or suspect (s 24(5)(e)).

This last reason is the least precise and most open-ended.[57] According to Code G (paragraph 2.9) it covers cases where there are reasonable grounds to believe that the person may make contact with co-suspects, may make contact with witnesses or where it is necessary to obtain evidence by questioning (this last ground being most commonly used). In relation **7.20**

---

[52] See, further, 'The New Powers of Arrest: Plus Ça Change: More of the Same or Major Change?' [2007] Crim LR 459 by RC Austin, to whom we are indebted for some of the observations in this section.

[53] See also Code G, para 2.9 and also observations by Ed Cape, *Defending Suspects at Police Stations* (2006, 5th edn) p 40 para 2.14. This power should be considered in the light of the police's powers to take fingerprints (s 61(6A), see 6.43) and photographs (s 64A(1B), see 6.44).

[54] Home Office, 'PACE Review—Government proposals in response to the Review of the Police and Criminal Evidence Act 1984', August 2008, Ch 3, p 4 and Ch 7, pp 12–13, paras 7.13–7.15.

[55] See Chapter 4.

[56] See also Code G, para 2.9(f).

[57] It was considered in passing by Underhill J in the High Court in *R (on the application of C) v Chief Constable of A* [2006] EWHC 2352 (Admin).

to indictable offences, it may include instances where there is a need to conduct a search[58] or take samples, photos, etc.[59]

7.21 For the sake of completeness it should be noted that there is also the power to arrest to prevent an offence against public decency (s 24(5)(c)(iv)) and to protect a child or vulnerable person (s 24(5)(d)). All these considerations should be read in the light of the police's power to grant 'street bail' discussed below. Code G spells out that 'The criteria are exhaustive. However, the circumstances that may satisfy those criteria remain a matter for the operational discretion of individual officers'.[60] As the power of arrest applies to any offence, it is submitted that, in the light of the police's obligation to act proportionately, the less serious the offence, the less an arrest is justified.[61]

The 'necessity' test: s 24(4)

7.22 The power of arrest 'is exercisable only if the constable has reasonable grounds for believing that for any of the reasons mentioned in subsec (5) [above] it is *necessary* to arrest the person in question' (s 24(4) emphasis added).

7.23 In *Bull, Farrelly and Fox*[62] a Northern Ireland case, Kerr LCJ said that, when determining whether an arrest is necessary, all obviously relevant circumstances should be taken into account. There should be some evaluation of the feasibility of achieving the object of the arrest by some alternative means. However, arrest need not be in every instance a matter of last resort. It may be enough for it to be the practical and sensible option. Code G also clarifies how an arresting officer should interpret the term 'necessary'. Paragraph 1.3 says: 'The use of the power must be fully justified and officers exercising the power should consider if the necessary objectives can be met by other, less intrusive means. Arrest must never be used simply because it can be used. . . . When the power of arrest is exercised it is essential that it is exercised in a non-discriminatory and proportionate manner'. It has been argued that the term 'necessary' may require the officer to carry out the further enquiries before arresting.[63]

7.24 The officer must have reasonable grounds for the belief that an arrest is necessary. These grounds are distinct from the grounds founding the officer's suspicion that the suspect may have committed an offence (above, *Castorina*). However, it is submitted that these grounds will be subject to a similar analysis: did the officer actually believe that an arrest was necessary and would these grounds also satisfy an objective observer.[64]

---

[58] PACE, ss 18 and 32 considered at 7.45 et seq, 7.52 and 7.53.
[59] See 7.72 et seq. See also Home Office Review of PACE, above, at paras 7.14 and 7.15.
[60] Code G, para 2.7, see also para 2.8.
[61] See 7.27 et seq.
[62] [2009] NIQB 2, QBD, paras 16–8.
[63] See RC Austin, 'The New Powers of Arrest: Plus Ça Change: More of the Same or Major Change?' [2007] Crim LR 459, 465, where it is also argued that the term 'believing', considered below, may have the same effect. See *Bull, Farrelly and Fox* [2009] NIQB 2, QBD and also 7.13.
[64] See 7.07 and 7.08 et seq.

It remains to be seen whether and to what extent the term 'believing' in s 24(4) is more **7.25** exacting than the term 'suspecting'.[65] Authorities such as *Baker v Oxford*[66] and *Johnson v Whitehouse*[67] suggest that there is a difference between the two words. The word 'believe' has a 'greater force'[68], though the distinction may be 'a fine one'.[69]. The latest observations on this point come from Kerr LCJ in *Bull, Farrelly and Fox* who said that 'Belief involves a judgment that a state of affairs *actually exists*; suspicion that a state of affairs *might well* exist.'[70]

There is still scope for the police to continue their practice of de-arresting suspects, that is **7.26** releasing suspects from arrest,[71] often after the detainee's removal from the scene of the incident but before his arrival at the police station.

Wednesbury and Wednesbury Plus

Conventional administrative law principles apply to the officer's decision to arrest, follow- **7.27** ing the third limb of *Castorina*. The application of the *Wednesbury* test (the well-known administrative law test[72]) in this context means this. The arrest is unlawful if the police officer's decision was so unreasonable, or capricious, or arbitrary that no reasonable police officer could have come to the conclusion that in all the circumstances he had the power to make an arrest at that particular moment. This requirement of *Wednesbury* reasonableness in the decision-making process may be modified by virtue of the application of Article 5 of the European Convention, imposing a more restrictive discretion upon the arresting officer. This is the so-called '*Wednesbury* plus' test.[73]

The test was developed in two cases examining the version of s 24 of PACE which preceded **7.28** the current version, in which the courts considered the lawfulness of the arrests of other- wise willing volunteers and their detention for interview for short periods of time so that the investigating officers could put pressure on them to speak and exert some control over the situation.

In *Cumming v Chief Constable of Northumbria* Latham LJ,[74] having found that the right to **7.29** liberty under Article 5 was engaged and that any decision to arrest had to take into account the importance of that right, said: 'The court must consider with care whether or not the decision to arrest was one which no police officer, applying his mind to the matter could reasonably take bearing in mind the effect on the appellants' right to liberty . . .'

---

[65] Ed Cape suggests that it is 'a more difficult test to satisfy' in *Defending Suspects at Police Stations* (2006, 5th edn) p 40 at 2.14. So too does RC Austin in 'The New Powers of Arrest: Plus Ça Change: More of the Same or More Change?' [2007] Crim LR 459, 464.
[66] [1980] RTR 315, DC, comments by Park J at p 320.
[67] [1984] RTR 38, 47, DC.
[68] Ibid, p 47 per Nolan J.
[69] *Wills v Bowley* [1983] 1 AC 57, 103, HL per Lord Bridge.
[70] [2009] NIQB 2, QBD at para 14.
[71] PACE, s 30(7) and (7A), amended by the Criminal Justice Act 2003, s 4(4). See also street bail, below.
[72] *Associated Provincial Picture Houses Ltd v Wednesbury Corporation* [1948] 1 KB 223, CA.
[73] Auld LJ in *Al Fayed v Commissioner of the Police of the Metropolis* (2004) 148 SJLB 1405, [2004] EWCA Civ 1579, para 97.
[74] [2003] All ER (D) 305 (Dec), [2004] PoLR 61, para 43.

7.30 In *Al Fayed v Commissioner of Police of the Metropolis*[75] Auld LJ stated: 'The requirement of *Wednesbury* reasonableness . . . may, depending on the circumstances of each case, be modified where appropriate by the human rights jurisprudence . . . so as to narrow, where appropriate, the traditionally generous ambit of *Wednesbury* discretion.' He added that, Article 5 being one of the most fundamental human rights, 'The more substantial the interference [with that right], the narrower the otherwise generous *Wednesbury* ambit of reasonableness becomes . . .'

7.31 Both cases were discussed, followed, and applied to the current version of s 24 by Underhill J in *R (on the application of C) v Chief Constable of A*.[76] He concluded[77] that consideration of whether the exercise of the discretion to arrest was lawful under s 24(5) 'involves a detailed and fact-sensitive enquiry into the decision-making process of the constable making the arrest'.

7.32 The discretion to arrest must also be exercised in good faith.[78] However, 'a collateral motive for an arrest on otherwise good and stated grounds does not necessarily make it unlawful. It depends on the motive'.[79]

The citizen's power of arrest

7.33 Everyone has a power of arrest by virtue of s 24A of PACE.[80] This includes, for example, private security guards, store detectives, and police community support officers (and others accredited under the Police Reform Act[81]). This power is distinct from PCSOs' separate power to detain someone who has not given a satisfactory name or address[82] which the courts may not have treated as an arrest following the reasoning in *Laporte* and *Austin* but may now do so in the light of the European Court's judgment in *Gillan and Quinton*.[83]

7.34 The power to arrest only relates to indictable offences, including offences triable either way.[84] In the context of public order these include violent disorder, affray,[85] theft and serious criminal damage. The citizen's power is to arrest:

- anyone who is in the act of committing an offence or whom he has reasonable grounds for suspecting to be committing an offence;

---

[75] (2004) 148 SJLB 1405, CA, [2004] EWCA Civ 1579, para 83. See also *Paul v Chief Constable of Humberside Police* [2004] PoLR 179,[2004] All ER (D) 333 (Mar), para 30.

[76] [2006] EWHC 2352 (Admin). See also *Bull, Farrelly and Fox* [2009] NIQB 2, QBD.

[77] Ibid, para 27.

[78] See authorities, before the current version of s 24, such as *Holgate-Mohammed v Duke* [1984] AC 437, 443, HL; *Paul v Chief Constable of Humberside Police* [2004] All ER (D) 333 (Mar), [2004] PoLR 179, CA, from para 35.

[79] *R v Chalkley* [1998] QB 848, CA: a case in which the police conducted an arrest in order to plant a listening device in a suspect's home.

[80] Substituted by the Serious Organised Crime and Police Act 2005, s 110. See also 7.01.

[81] See Ch 6.

[82] See Ch 6.

[83] For *Laporte*, see 4.61 et seq, 6.146 et seq, 10.38, and 10.80. For *Austin*, see 4.73 et seq, 6.162 et seq, and10.167. For *Gillan and Quiton* see 6.55 et seq. See also Ed Cape, *Defending Suspects at Police Stations* (2006, 5th edn) p 49, 2.33.

[84] Interpretation Act 1978, Sch 1; see also the Magistrates' Courts Act 1980, s 17, s 22, and Sch 1. But see PACE, s 24A(5) for offences to which s 24A does not apply.

[85] See Ch 1.

- where an offence has been committed, anyone who is guilty of the offence, or anyone whom the person carrying out the arrest has reasonable grounds for suspecting to be guilty.

Interestingly enough, the circumstances in which the police may arrest are slightly wider. Under s 24(2) they may arrest not only where an offence has been committed, but also when they have reasonable grounds for suspecting that an offence has been committed.[86] **7.35**

The citizen's power of arrest is only exercisable if **7.36**

- it appears to the person making the arrest that it is not reasonably practicable for an officer to make the arrest instead; and
- the person carrying out the arrest has reasonable grounds for believing that it is necessary to arrest to prevent the suspect suffering physical injury, causing physical injury to someone else, causing loss of or damage to property or making off before a police officer can assume responsibility for him.

The person carrying out the arrest must then deliver the person arrested to a police officer or a justice of the peace as soon as is reasonably practicable.[87] **7.37**

Information to be given on arrest

By virtue of s 28 of PACE no arrest by a police officer or citizen is lawful unless the person arrested, at the time of or as soon as is practicable after the arrest, is **7.38**

- told that he is under arrest (s 28(1), he must also be told why an arrest is considered necessary[88]); and
- informed of the ground for the arrest (s 28(3) although this information need not be imparted by the arresting officer[89]).

However, these steps are not required if it was not reasonably practicable because the person arrested escaped before there was time to inform him[90] or as a result of that person's violent conduct.[91] **7.39**

The fundamental obligation to inform someone arrested of the reason for his arrest is deep seated in common law[92] and Article 5. In *Fox, Campbell and Hartley v United Kingdom*,[93] the European Court said: **7.40**

> Paragraph (2) of Article 5 contains the elementary safeguard that any person arrested should know why he is being deprived of his liberty. This protection is an integral part of the scheme

---

[86] See 7.04 and, for the practical significance of this distinction *R v Self* [1992] 1 WLR 657, CA (and *Stanley v Benning*, 14 July 1998, CA).

[87] *John Lewis & Co v Tims* [1952] AC 676, HL; *Dallison v Caffrey* [1965] 1 QB 348, CA.

[88] Code G, Note for Guidance 3.

[89] *Dhesi v Chief Constable of the West Midlands Police* [2000] PoLR 120, CA.

[90] PACE, s 28(5).

[91] *DPP v Hawkins* [1988] 1 WLR 1166, QB.

[92] *Christie v Leachinsky* [1947] AC 573, 587, HL, per Viscount Simon. Reiterated, since PACE, in for example *Clarke v Chief Constable of North Wales* [2000] PoLR 83, [2000] All ER(D) 477, para 25.

[93] (1991) 13 EHRR 157, para 40.

of protection afforded by Article 5: by virtue of paragraph (2) any person arrested must be told in simple, non-technical language that he can understand, the essential legal and factual grounds for his arrest . . . Whilst this information must be conveyed 'promptly' . . . it need not be related in its entirety by the arresting officer at the very moment of the arrest. Whether the content and promptness of the information conveyed were sufficient is to be assessed in each case according to its special features.

7.41 Domestic courts have accepted this formulation. While recognizing that each case turns on its own facts, in *Taylor v Chief Constable of Thames Valley Police* Clarke LJ observed that the question (above) posed in *Fox, Campbell and Hartley* will suffice.[94]

7.42 In *Fox, Campbell and Hartley* the European Court also said that it is not enough for the arrested person just to be told for what offence he has been arrested.[95] Code G advises 'when a person is arrested on suspicion of committing an offence they must be informed of the suspected offence's nature, when and where it was committed. . . .'[96] This requirement was considered in *Taylor v Chief Constable of Thames Valley*,[97] a protest case. The Court of Appeal said that it was sufficient for the 10-year-old suspect to be told, when arrested at a demonstration several weeks after the alleged offence, just the offence for which he had been arrested (violent disorder), the place (Hillgrove Farm) and the date of the alleged offence. It was not necessary to specify the exact way he had committed the offence (throwing stones). In *R v Kirk*[98] the court said that if a person has been arrested for two offences, he must be told of the more serious one. These authorities may have superseded the decision in *R v Hamilton*[99] that no reason need be given where it is obvious.

7.43 Vague or technical language should be avoided. 'Although no constable ever admits to saying "You're nicked for handling this gear" or "I'm having you for twoc-ing this motor", either will do and, I have no doubt, frequently does', according to Sedley LJ.[100] However, the words 'That's enough, you're locked up' were held to be insufficient where there were several possible offences.[101] Arrest is a continuing act so if an arrest is at first unlawful—as a result for example of a delay in informing the person of his arrest or the ground for the arrest—it can become lawful from the time the error is corrected.[102]

7.44 A person must also be cautioned on arrest, unless it is impracticable to do so.[103] The arresting officer must make a record in his pocket book of the nature and circumstances of

---

[94] [2004] 1 WLR 3155, CA, paras 25–6 and 35.
[95] *Fox, Campbell and Hartley*, para 41.
[96] Note for Guidance 3. See also Code C, Note for Guidance 10B.
[97] [2004] 1 WLR 3155, CA.
[98] [2000] 1 WLR 567, CA.
[99] [1986] Crim LR 187.
[100] *Clarke v Chief Constable of North Wales Police* [2000] PoLR 83, [2000] All ER (D) 477. See also Code G, Note for Guidance 3.
[101] *R v Lowe* [1986] Crim LR 49.
[102] *Lewis v Chief Constable of the South Wales Constabulary* [1991] 1 All ER 206, CA.
[103] Code G, para 3.4; Code C, para 10.4 onwards. See *DPP v Lawrence* [2008] 1 Cr App R 10, DC for the treatment of comments made by a suspect which form the offence itself and Code C, Section 11.

the offence leading to the arrest, the reason(s) arrest was necessary, the giving of the caution, and anything said by the person at the time of arrest.[104]

Search of a person after arrest

A police officer may search a person arrested for any offence under s 32 of PACE **7.45** (a common law power exists too[105]):

- if the constable has reasonable grounds for believing that the arrested person may present a danger to himself or others (s 32(1)); or
- for anything which he might use to escape but only if he has reasonable grounds for believing that the person to be searched may have such a thing concealed on him and only to the extent reasonably required to discover any such thing (ss 32(2)(a)(i), 32(3), 32(5)); or
- for anything which might be evidence relating to the offence but only if he has reasonable grounds for believing that the person to be searched may have such a thing concealed on him and to the extent reasonably required to discover such evidence (ss 32(2)(a)(ii), 32(3), 32(5)[106]).

There is only limited guidance about the conduct of PACE searches post-arrest in **7.46** s 32 and Code B of PACE itself (see paragraph 1.1 and s 7). The police should give reasons for the search before it takes place unless it is unnecessary or impracticable to do so and searches should not be carried out as a matter of routine.[107] The power does not authorize the police to require a person to remove any of his clothing in public other than an outer coat, jacket, or gloves, but it does authorize a search of a person's mouth (s 32(4)[108]). Presumably, by analogy with searches under s 1 of PACE,[109] more extensive searches are permissible, for example in a police vehicle or at a nearby police station, if there are reasonable grounds for a more extensive search, or if the person detained consents.

Where the police are searching someone on arrest, they have the power to seize anything **7.47** relevant to one of the three aims of the search, above (s 32(8) and (9)[110]). They may use reasonable force (s 117[111]). There is no express obligation in s 32 on the police to make a record of the search.

Separately, the police have the power under s 54(6A)[112] to search anyone 'in police deten- **7.48** tion otherwise than at a police station' to ascertain if he has anything on him which he may

---

[104] Code G, Section 4.
[105] See *R (Rottman) v Commissioner of Police of the Metropolis* [2002] 2 AC 692, HL.
[106] See also *R v Churchill* [1989] Crim LR 226, CA.
[107] *Brazil v Chief Constable of Surrey* [1983] 1 WLR 1155, QB see in particular Goff LJ at p1162 and *Lindley v Rutter* [1981] QB 128, DC.
[108] Amended by Criminal Justice and Public Order Act 1994, s 59.
[109] See 6.73 et seq and 6.103 et seq.
[110] See also para 7.1(b) of Code B, *R v Naylor* [1979] Crim LR 532.
[111] See 6.176.
[112] Inserted by the Criminal Justice Act 1988, s 147. See also 7.70 and 7.73.

use to cause injury to himself or someone else, to damage property, to interfere with evidence or to assist him to escape.

Entry and search of property on arrest

7.49 The police have many powers to enter and search property of which at least four are particularly relevant to arrest (a detailed examination of these powers, and linked powers to seize and retain material and the rights of the owners of property seized to secure its return are beyond the scope of this book[113]). Code B[114] applies to the exercise of these powers (see paragraph 2.3).

7.50 Firstly, the police have the power to enter property with the consent of the owner, who may, of course, not necessarily be the suspect (see Code B, s 5).

7.51 Secondly, the police have the power to enter property without a warrant to carry out an arrest[115] and also to save life or limb or to prevent serious damage to property[116] (PACE, s 17).

7.52 Thirdly, following an arrest for an indictable offence, the police have the power to enter and search, for evidence relating to the offence, any property 'in which [the person arrested] was when arrested or immediately before' (s 32(2)(b)).[117] Section 32(7) sheds some light on an issue which frequently arises. Where the person was arrested in a property which consists of two or more 'separate dwellings' the power of search only applies to the dwelling in which the person was and to any parts of the property which are used in common with others. This will apply where the property searched is a flat within a block and may also apply where it is a bedroom in a shared flat or house.

7.53 Fourthly, the police also have the power to search premises 'occupied or controlled by' a person arrested for an indictable offence on the authority of an inspector (s 18). This may be his home and may not necessarily be the place where he was arrested. The police's power applies if the police have reasonable ground for suspecting that there is evidence that relates to the offence for which the person has been arrested and to any other indictable offence connected to or similar to that offence.

After arrest: street bail or police station

7.54 After arrest by the police, the suspect must normally be taken to the police station as soon as practicable (s 30(1) and (1A)[118]). The police may delay taking the detainee to the police station (or granting street bail, considered below) where it is necessary in order to carry out

---

[113] For which, see for example, R Stone, *The Law of Entry, Search and Seizure* (2005, 4th edn).

[114] Code of Practice for searches of premises by police officer and the seizure of property found by police officers on persons or premises.

[115] *O'Loughlin v Chief Constable of Essex* [1998] 1 WLR 374, CA.

[116] *Baker v CPS* (2009) 173 JP 215, DC.

[117] See *R v Badham* [1987] Crim LR 202, CC and *R v Beckford (Junior)* (1992) 94 Cr App R 43, CA for authorities on when s 18 (below) and s 32 powers are applicable.

[118] Substituted by the Criminal Justice Act 2003, s 4(2).

investigations (such as a search of property under s 18, above) which it is reasonable to carry out immediately.[119] There are proposals by the Home Office to establish 'Short Term Holding Facilities' in shopping and town centres to relieve police stations of the burden of dealing with suspects who need not be held for a long time and for whom the only measures necessary may be to establish their name and address (by the taking of fingerprints, photographs, and DNA samples) and then release them with a view to a disposal which does not involve charging them.[120]

The police may after arrest grant 'street bail'.[121] Instead of taking a detainee to the police station, a police officer may, at any time before a detainee arrives at the police station, release the person on condition that he attend a police station at a later date (s 30A[122]). There is no statutory limit to the period for which a person may be bailed although a Home Office circular advises a maximum of six weeks.[123] Having said this, the police may re-arrest a suspect released on police bail before his return to the police station if new evidence justifying a further arrest has come to light since his release.[124]   **7.55**

The Home Office circular sets out some of the factors to take into account when considering whether the use of street bail is appropriate in any given case: **7.56**

- 'the nature of the offence'. The circular confirms that 'there is no definitive list of offences to which street bail can be granted. It is a matter for the officer's discretion'. However, it is 'unlikely' that street bail would be granted in relation to a serious offence;
- 'the ability to progress the investigation at the station';
- 'confidence in the suspect answering bail'. The power may be used where the police are satisfied that the suspect has given his correct name and address;
- 'the level of awareness and understanding of the procedure by the suspect'; and
- 'The arresting officer must / should not grant street bail if there are reasonable grounds to believe that the arrested person might continue to commit that or another offence if released.'

Officers are also reminded to ensure 'that street bail is used fairly, objectively and without any bias against ethnic or other groups within the community'. However, the principles and details of the Bail Act 1976 do not apply to police 'street bail'[125] and it has been pointed out that the arrested person has no statutory right to make representations and there is no duty on the officer to listen to them, take them into account or record them.[126]   **7.57**

---

[119] PACE, s 30(10) and (10A), inserted by the Criminal Justice Act 2003, s 41.

[120] See the PACE Review, 'Government proposals in response to the Review of the Police and Criminal Evidence Act 1984' August 2008 Ch 3, p 5 and Ch 10, p 21, paras 10.18–10.20. See generally on street disposal and street justice, Ed Cape, 'Modernising Police Powers—Again?' [2007] Crim LR 934, 941.

[121] See also for bail generally, 7.109 et seq.

[122] Inserted by the Criminal Justice Act 2003, s 4(7). Section 30A(3A) and (3B) were inserted by the Police and Justice Act 2006, Sch 6(2), para 2.

[123] Home Office circular 061/2003 found in <http://www.homeoffice.gov.uk/circulars>, accessed through the Home Office home page: <http://www.homeoffice.gov.uk>, then 'about us', then 'publications', then 'home office circulars'.

[124] PACE, s 30C(4) inserted by the Criminal Justice Act 2003, s 4. See also 7.131.

[125] PACE, s 30C(3), inserted by the Criminal Justice Act 2003, s 4.

[126] Ed Cape 'Modernising Police Powers—Again?' [2007] Crim LR 934, p 943.

7.58 When granting street bail, the police have the power to impose such bail conditions (other than recognizances, securities, sureties, and residence at a bail hostel (s 30A(3A)) as appear to them to be necessary, among other things, to secure that the person (s 30A(3B))

- surrenders to custody;
- does not commit offences on bail; or
- does not interfere with witnesses or otherwise obstruct the course of justice.

7.59 The officer must give the bailed person a notice in writing stating (s 30B[127])

- the offence for which he has been arrested;
- the ground on which he was arrested;
- that he is required to attend the police station, which one, and at what time; and
- the bail conditions, if any and the opportunities to apply to vary them.[128]

The implications of failing to make a lawful arrest

7.60 If the police carry out an unlawful arrest, measures taken thereafter are also unlawful.[129] The consequences can in principle be significant and some, immediate.

7.61 The arrested person may use force to resist arrest. In the words of Lord Simonds in the seminal House of Lords case, *Christie v Leachinsky*[130] '. . . it is the corollary of the right of every citizen to be thus free from arrest that he should be entitled to resist arrest unless that arrest is lawful . . . Blind, unquestioning obedience is the law of tyrants and of slaves: it does not yet flourish on English soil.' These words have been tempered, first by Lord Goddard who remarked that a citizen 'must not use more force than necessary'[131] and then by Sedley LJ advising that a citizen risks committing further serious offences (such as assault with intent to resist arrest) 'unless his knowledge of the law is very sound'.[132]

7.62 There is authority which supports the argument that a person who has been unlawfully arrested cannot, after being charged, be refused bail,[133] but note that an unlawful arrest can be cured by a subsequent lawful arrest.[134]

7.63 The mere fact that an arrest was unlawful cannot prevent an accused being convicted of a criminal offence. However, in extreme cases criminal proceedings may be stayed as an abuse of process.[135] At trial, the credibility of officers giving evidence—for example, eyewitness accounts of an incident—may be undermined by errors they may have made at

---

[127] Inserted by the Criminal Justice Act 2003, s 4.
[128] See 7.155 et seq and 7.157 et seq.
[129] But see *Lewis v Chief Constable of the South Wales Constabulary* [1991] 1 All ER 206, CA, considered at 7.43.
[130] [1947] AC 573, 591, HL.
[131] *R v Wilson* [1955] 1 WLR 493, 494, CA.
[132] In *Clarke v Chief Constable of North Wales Police* [2000] PoLR 83, CA, [2000] All ER (D) 477, para 36.
[133] *Hutt v Commissioner of the Police of the Metropolis* [2004] PoLR 13, CA.
[134] See 7.43.
[135] For example, *R v Horseferry Road Magistrates' Court ex p Bennett* [1994] 1 AC 42, HL and *R v Mullen* [2000] QB 520, CA.

the arrest stage. Evidence, such as comments made after caution, may be excluded at trial under ss 76 or 78 of PACE.

The victim of an unlawful arrest may make a complaint to the Independent Police **7.64** Complaints Commission.[136] Civil and/or criminal legal proceedings may be brought for, among other things, false imprisonment and trespass to the person (assault).[137]

B. Detention at the Police Station

This part of this chapter will deal with what detainees can expect of their time at a **7.65** police station: standard police procedures and powers during their detention; the detainees' basic rights; the conditions in which they should be kept; and how long they can be kept in custody. The key sources are Parts IV and V of PACE and Code C to PACE.[138] The PACE Codes are under review and proposals for change have been made.[139]

The role of the custody officer

Custody officers play a pivotal role in the detention of suspects at the police station. They **7.66** must be an officer of at least the rank of sergeant (s 36(3)) unconnected with the investigation (s 36(5)).[140] Custody officers must treat the detainee in accordance with PACE and its Codes of Practice (s 39(1)(a)[141]). They must perform their functions as soon as practicable. A custody officer will not, however, be in breach of the Code if delay is justifiable and reasonable steps are taken to prevent unnecessary delay (para 1.1.A). This may be the case, for example, where a large number of suspects are brought into the station simultaneously (Note for Guidance 1H). Custody officers must keep a custody record, now normally a computer log, evidencing compliance with the Codes (s 39(1)(b) and Code C, s 2 generally). A detainee is entitled to a copy of the custody record (paragraph 2.4A).

When a detainee first arrives under arrest at a police station he should be brought before the **7.67** custody officer (Code C, paragraph 2.1A). The custody officer is responsible for informing the detainee of his rights (see below) and for his welfare generally including his mental and physical well-being (see Code C, s 9). If necessary a doctor or mental health worker will be called and advise whether the suspect is fit to be detained and fit to be interviewed. Drunken prisoners are a problem frequently met by custody officers.

---

[136] Set up under the Police Reform Act 2002, Part II.

[137] For more detail on these remedies see for example J Harrison, S Cragg, and H Williams, *Police Misconduct: Legal Remedies* (2005, 4th edn); R Clayton and H Tomlinson, *Civil Actions Against the Police* (2005, 3rd edn).

[138] The Code of Practice for the detention, treatment and questioning of persons by police officers. For detention for terrorism see also Code H, the Code of Practice in connection with the detention, treatment, and questioning by police officers of persons under s 41 of, and Schedule 8 to, the Terrorism Act 2000.

[139] See the Home Office's PACE Review, 'Government proposals in response to the Review of the Police and Criminal Evidence Act 1984' August 2008.

[140] Proposals to extend this role to 'staff custody officers' appear to have been reversed—see the Serious Organised Crime and Police Act 2005, s 120 and 121, and the Policing and Crime 2009, Schedule 7, Part 13.

[141] See para 6.14.

7.68 The custody officer must record on the custody record the offence for which the detainee has been arrested and the reasons for arrest as relayed by the arresting officer (Code C, paragraphs 2.1, 3.4, 10.3, and Code G, paragraphs 2.2 and 4.3). The custody officer is entitled to assume that the arrest was lawful and is not expected to test the arresting officer's assessment.[142] The custody officer must record any comments the detainee may make in relation to the arresting officer's account, though the detainee should not be invited to comment (Code C, paragraph 3.4). The custody officer should not put any specific questions to the detainee about the offence (Code C, paragraph 3.4). There are separate provisions governing the interviewing of suspects.[143]

7.69 If a suspect is detained, his detention must be properly authorized by the custody officer.[144] There is no statutory obligation to invite or take into account a detainee's observations on whether detention should be authorized. If the custody officer authorizes a person's detention, the detainee must be informed of the grounds as soon as practicable and before he is questioned about any offence (Code C, paragraph 3.4).

7.70 The custody officer has the power to search a detainee to ascertain what he has with him and to seize and retain anything (PACE, s 54[145]) although not everyone need be searched (Code C Note for Guidance 4A). More thorough searches may take place.[146]

7.71 Detainees (and their lawyers) who have concerns about any aspect of the detainee's detention and treatment at the police station may ask the custody officer to note those concerns in the custody record. The custody officer, however, has control and discretion over what is entered in the custody record. Code C does however require the police to report any complaint about a detainee's treatment since his arrest to an inspector (Code C, paragraph 9.2). A detainee, or more likely his lawyer, may of course seek to put any complaints direct to the inspector on duty.

Collecting personal information

7.72 A detainee does not have to identify himself. However, a failure to provide a name and address may influence the police's decision on bail after charge.[147] Furthermore, a detainee may be forced to submit to searches and provide samples which may lead to identification — these are considered, below.

7.73 Section 54A[148] and Code D para 5.1 onwards, give the police, on the authority of an inspector, the power to search or examine a detainee in order to establish his identity, where

---

[142] *Al Fayed v Commissioner of Police of the Metropolis* (2004) 148 SJLB 1405, [2004] EWCA Civ 1579, para 101.

[143] See Code C, s 11 onwards; Code of Practice E on audio recording interviews with suspects; and Code of Practice F on visual recording with sound of interviews with suspects.

[144] See 7.94.

[145] See Code C, para 4.1. See also power to search after arrest but before arrival at the police station at 7.45 et seq and 7.48.

[146] See s 55 and Code C, Annex A for strip searches (defined in para 9 of Annex A to Code C) and intimate searches (defined in s 65(1)).

[147] See Code C, para 10.9 and Code G, para 3.7; and see bail generally from 7.109.

[148] Inserted by the Anti-terrorism, Crime and Security Act 2001, s 90.

the detainee refuses to identify himself or the police have reasonable grounds for suspecting that the person is not who he claims to be. The police may also search for and photograph identifying marks (s 54A(5)). As a matter of practice, the police will often ask about and make a written record of the appearance, personal details, and circumstances (antecedents) of someone who has been charged.

The police's power to photograph[149] a detainee in custody stems from s 64A.[150] A detainee's **7.74** photograph may be taken with or without consent (s 64A(1)), including from a camera system in the police station, (Code D, paragraph 5.15). Clothing covering the face may be removed (Code D, paragraph 5.13). Force may be used (Code D, paragraph 5.14). Any photograph, including photographs taken away from the police station,[151] may be retained and used or disclosed to any person for the investigation of any crime—for example to distinguish that person from others arrested at the same time, or where the person's identity is in doubt, or for identification procedures, or to ascertain whether the detainee may be connected with other offences or even to circulate to some of the public[152] (s 64A(4), Code D Note for Guidance 5B).

The police may also take a variety of samples from a detainee, normally either with the **7.75** suspect's consent, or without consent where the suspect has been arrested for a recordable offence.[153] By virtue of s 61[154] and Code D, paragraph 4.1 onwards[155] the police may take fingerprints. This power may also be exercised when a person has been warned, repri-manded, cautioned, charged, or convicted (s 61(4), (6)). The police's powers to take impressions of a detainee's footwear is derived from s 61A[156] and Code D, paragraph 4.16 onwards. The police also have the power to take body samples, some of which include a person's DNA profile. There are two types, defined in s 65 and both covered by Code D, s 6. Non-intimate samples—including hair, saliva, and skin—are governed by s 63.[157] Intimate samples—including bodily fluids such as blood and urine—are governed by s 62 (these may only be taken with consent, but inferences may be drawn from a refusal, with-out a good reason, to consent[158]). Force may be used, where consent is refused, to take fingerprints and non-intimate samples.[159]

---

[149] Including filming by virtue of the Police and Criminal Evidence Act 1984, s 64A(6).
[150] Inserted by the Anti-terrorism, Crime and Security Act 2001, s 92.
[151] See 6.44 et seq.
[152] *Hellewell v Chief Constable of Derbyshire* [1995] 1 WLR 804, QB and *R (on the application of Ellis) v Chief Constable of Essex Police* [2003] EWHC 1321 (Admin).
[153] Recordable offences include all imprisonable offences and some non-imprisonable ones. See Code D Note for Guidance 4A and PACE, s 27(4).
[154] Amended by the Criminal Justice Act 2003, s 9 and the Criminal Justice and Police Act 2001, s 78. See also 6.43.
[155] The Code of Practice for the identification of persons by police officers.
[156] Inserted by Serious Organised Crime and Police Act 2005, s 118.
[157] As amended by the Criminal Justice Act 2003, s 10(1)(2): the Criminal Justice and Public Order Act 1994, s 55(2), s 55(3), s 168(2), Sch 10, para 58(a).
[158] See the Police and Criminal Evidence Act 1984, s 62(10).
[159] Code D, paras 4.6 and 6.7; and see PACE, s 117 and the Police Reform Act 2002, s 38(8) and Sch 4, para 29.

7.76 The police may carry out speculative searches of detainees' fingerprints, foot impressions, and DNA samples against other records held by the police or law enforcement agencies in the UK or abroad in order to ascertain, for example, whether the detainee may be connected with other offences (s 63A[160]). They may then be retained, even where the detainee has not been convicted of an offence, and used in order, among other things, to prevent or detect crime or investigate an offence (s 64(1A)[161]).

7.77 In *S and Marper v United Kingdom*[162] the European Court found that the indiscriminate and indefinite retention of personal information, DNA profiles in particular, of persons suspected but not convicted of offences infringed their rights under Article 8. Behind the headlines, it is worth recalling that the European Court was considering the lawfulness of the retention of three types of personal data: cellular material, DNA profiles, and fingerprints. The Court attached particular significance to the 'highly personal nature of cellular samples' (paragraph 72) and acknowledged that 'the level of interference with the . . . right to private life may be different for the three different categories of personal data' (paragraph 120). In November 2009 the government issued its proposals, in response to *Marper* and after consultation, on the retention and use of DNA profiles, and other personal information.[163] The Home Office proposes to retain for six years the profiles of adults arrested but not convicted of a recordable offence[164] and to retain indefinitely the profiles of adults who have been convicted of a recordable offence. Similar provisions will apply to fingerprints. The proposals are different for juveniles.

A detainee's rights

Consultation of the Codes

7.78 Detainees have the right to consult the Codes of Practice at the police station (see for example Code C paragraphs 1.2 and 3.1 (iii) and Code D paragraph 2.1).

Legal advice

7.79 A detainee has the right to consult a solicitor privately at any time and as soon as practicable (s 58 and Article 6[165]). The detainee can choose which solicitor he wants (Code C, Note for Guidance 6B). If the detainee does not have a chosen solicitor ('own solicitor'), or if that solicitor is not available, the custody officer will put the detainee in contact with a police station 'duty solicitor', who will normally be from a local independent high street

---

[160] Inserted by the Criminal Justice and Public Order Act 1994, s 56 and amended subsequently. See also Code D Notes for Guidance 4B, 6E, and Annex F.

[161] Inserted by the Criminal Justice and Police Act 2001, s 82. See Code D, Annex F too.

[162] (2009) 48 EHRR 50. See also the wider issue of the collation, retention, and use of databases of personal information, considered in *Marper* and also *Wood v Commissioner of Police of the Metropolis* [2009] HRLR 25 considered in Ch 6.

[163] See Home Office consultation, launched May 2009 'Keeping the Right People on the DNA database, Science and Public Protection' and its response, dated 11 November 2009, 'Keeping the Right People on the DNA Database: Summary of Responses'.

[164] See 7.75 above, for definition.

[165] See for example *Averill v UK* (2001) 31 EHRR 36; *Salduz v Turkey* (2009) 49 EHRR 19, p 421; and *Panovits v Cyprus*, Application No 4268/04, 11 December 2008.

solicitors' firm. Often a trained solicitor's representative will attend (see Code C, paragraph 6.12). The police should not do or say anything to dissuade a detainee from obtaining legal advice (Code C, paragraph 6.4). A detainee must be asked if he would like to see a solicitor, even if he has already declined legal advice, if a solicitor arrives at a police station to see him (at for example the request of a third party, Code C, paragraph 6.15).

Code C states that a detainee must be told that 'free independent legal advice is available' and that he may communicate privately with a solicitor 'whether in person, in writing or by telephone' (paragraphs 3.1(ii) and 6). However, where a detainee is relying on publicly funded advice—which is free to him regardless of means—these rights must be read in the light of the procedures and funding arrangements put in place by the Legal Services Commission (LSC) in its contract with solicitors.[166]

7.80

Exercise of the right may be delayed where the suspect has been arrested for an indictable offence[167] for up to thirty-six hours if the police have reasonable grounds for believing that the exercise of the right will, among other things, lead to 'interference with or harm to evidence connected with' the offence or 'alerting of other persons suspected of having committed' the offence who have not yet been arrested.[168] A detainee who wants legal advice may not normally be interviewed until he has received advice, unless among other things awaiting the arrival of the solicitor would cause unreasonable delay in the investigation (Code C, paragraph 6.6, see also 11.2).

7.81

'The right to consult or communicate in private is fundamental' (Code C Note for Guidance 6J) and part of a detainee's rights under Article 6(3)(c) of the European Convention.[169] The European Court has therefore determined that it is not permissible for the police to sit in on an interview between a detainee and his solicitor.[170] Domestic case law, which suggests that it is permissible for an interview with a solicitor to take place in a cell or that it may take place on the phone in the custody area where a custody officer is in earshot of the detainee's side of the conversation, has been criticized academically on the grounds that it is inconsistent with Convention authority.[171] Deliberate eavesdropping and recording of privileged conversations are 'categorically unlawful',[172] subject to limited statutory powers (covert surveillance under the Regulation of Investigatory Powers Act 2000, Part II has been approved by the House of Lords[173]).

7.82

---

[166] See Final Unified Contract Crime Specification (July 2008) for Invitation to Tender (080407), reflected in Code C, particularly Note for Guidance 6B2. See also the LSC review of funding: 'Best Value Tendering for CDS Contracts 2010', consultation paper March 2009 and LSC response dated July 2009. LSC materials can be found in the Criminal Defence Service section of their website: <http://www.legalservices.gov.uk>.

[167] See 7.34.

[168] See s 58(6) onwards; see also Annex B to Code C. See *R v Samuel* [1988] QB 615, CA; *R v James* [2008] EWCA Crim 1869; *R v Alladice* (1988) 87 Cr App R 380, CA; and comments by Keene LJ in *R (Faisaltex Ltd) v Preston Crown Court* [2009] 1 Cr App R 37, para 47.

[169] See for example *S v Switzerland* (1992) 14 EHRR 670, para 48.

[170] *Brennan v United Kingdom* (2002) 34 EHRR 18.

[171] *R (on the application of M) v Commissioner of Police of the Metropolis* [2001] PoLR 264, DC and see commentary at [2002] Crim LR 215.

[172] *R v Grant* [2006] QB 60, para 52 per Laws LJ.

[173] *McE v Prison Service of Northern Ireland* [2009] 2 WLR 782, HL.

The right to have someone informed when arrested

7.83   A detainee has the right to have 'one friend or relative or other person who is known to him or who is likely to take an interest in his welfare' informed as soon as is practicable that he is being detained (PACE, s 56 and paragraph 3.1(i), and ss 5 of Code C). If the person cannot be contacted, the detainee may chose up to two alternatives and the custody officer has a discretion to allow further attempts until the information has been relayed (Code C, paragraph 5.1, Notes for Guidance 5C and 5D). The police have the power to delay the exercise of this right, similar to their power to delay access to legal advice (above, but see Code C, Annex B, paragraph 5). If a friend enquires about a detainee's whereabouts, this information shall be given out if the detainee agrees (Code C, paragraph 5.5).

7.84   In addition a detainee should be given writing materials in order to write letters to people outside and allowed to telephone one person for a reasonable time, though neither the telephone call nor the letter will be confidential (Code C, paragraphs 5.6 and 5.7). A detainee may receive visits at the custody officer's discretion (Code C, paragraph 5.4 and note 5B). These rights too may be delayed or denied.

Special groups

7.85   The police must make additional provision for special groups such as the deaf, the mentally vulnerable,[174] and the blind. We shall touch upon the position only of the young, foreigners, and those who do not understand English.[175]

7.86   Where a juvenile, a person under seventeen,[176] has been arrested the custody officer must ascertain the person responsible for his welfare and inform that person of the juvenile's arrest as soon as practicable (Code C, paragraph 3.13[177]). Even if a juvenile is not living with his parents, the police should give consideration to informing them (Code C Note for Guidance 3C). The police must arrange for juveniles to be assisted at the police station by an 'appropriate adult' (Code C, paragraph 3.15). This is in addition to a solicitor. An appropriate adult may be among other things, a parent or guardian or some other responsible adult aged eighteen or over (Code C, paragraph 1.7). A detainee should always be given an opportunity to consult with a solicitor in the absence of the appropriate adult. Discussions between the detainee and solicitor, even when the appropriate adult is present, are subject to legal privilege.[178]

7.87   Nationals of a foreign country have the right to contact their embassy (Code C, paragraph 3.3 and Section 7). Indeed, the UK has bilateral agreements with a number of countries requiring the UK police to notify the embassy of the arrest of a citizen from one of those

---

[174] See for example Code C Annex E.
[175] See Ed Cape, *Defending Suspects at Police Stations* (2006, 5th edn), in particular Ch 11 for a comprehensive account for all groups.
[176] Code C, para 1.5, Code D, para 2.4, and PACE, s 37(15). The age of criminal responsibility is ten years: Children and Young Persons Act 1933, s 50 as amended.
[177] See para 3.14 too for juveniles subject to a court order, Children and Young Persons Act 1933, s 34 as amended by PACE, s 57.
[178] See Code C Note for Guidance 1E and *A Local Authority v B* [2009] 1 FLR 289.

countries (Code C, paragraph 7.2 and Annex F). Consular officers may visit one of their nationals in police detention in private (Code E, paragraph 7.3). However, notwithstanding these agreements, if a detainee is a political refugee (whether for reason of race, nationality, political opinion, or religion) the embassy shall not be given any information about him except at the detainee's express request (Code C, paragraph 7.4).

The police must make provision for suitably qualified interpreters to be available for detainees who do not understand English (Code C, paragraph 3.12 and s 13). **7.88**

Conditions during detention

Code C (s 8) sets out what physical conditions the police should provide for detainees. **7.89**

For example, so far as is practicable, not more than one detainee should be in a cell. Cells should be adequately heated, cleaned, ventilated, and lit. Clean bedding should be supplied 'of a reasonable standard'. Access to toilet and washing facilities must be provided. **7.90**

At least two light meals and one main meal should be offered in any twenty-four hour period. Drinks should be provided at meal times and regularly between meals. As far as practicable meals shall offer a varied diet, and meet any specific dietary needs, or religious beliefs the detainee may have. The detainee may, at the custody officer's discretion, have meals supplied by his family or friends (Code C, paragraph 8.6). **7.91**

Detainees must be allowed periods of rest. In any period of twenty-four hours a detainee must be allowed a continuous period of at least eight hours for rest, normally at night, free from questioning, travel, or any interruption in connection with the investigation (Code C, paragraph 12.2, see also Annex G on fitness to be interviewed). **7.92**

The custody officer must ensure that a detainee receives appropriate medical attention as soon as reasonably practicable if, among other things, the person is injured (Code C, paragraph 9.5). If a detainee has a particular prescribed medicine, the custody officer must, after consultation with a doctor, ensure that he receives it (Code C, paragraph 9.9). **7.93**

Police detention and charge

Part IV of PACE ('Detention') regulates the police's powers to detain a suspect at a police station (s 34(1)). The decision to detain is the custody officer's. **7.94**

The decision to detain

The Act is founded on two presumptions. The first is that a detainee should be released from custody unless his detention can be justified (s 34(2)). The second is that 'All persons in custody must be dealt with expeditiously, and released as soon as the need for detention no longer apples' (Code C, paragraph 1.1). In the words of counsel for the police in *Mercer v Chief Constable of the Lancashire Constabulary*:[179] the police have 'to prove that the detention was lawful minute by minute and hour by hour, because what may originally have **7.95**

---

[179] [1991] 1 WLR 367, 373, CA.

been a lawful detention may become unlawful because of its duration or of a failure to comply with the complex provisions' of PACE. In addition, there are time limits beyond which detention may not be extended.

7.96 So far as the first presumption is concerned, the justification for detention is dealt with in s 37(1) and (2) ('Duties of custody officer before charge'). Commenting on these provisions, the Court of Appeal said:[180] 'The statutory framework seems clear enough. The person under arrest may be detained at the police station for as long as necessary for the custody officer to "determine" whether there is sufficient evidence to charge him,[181] or to secure or preserve evidence relating to the offence for which he was arrested, or to obtain such evidence in the course of an interview or interviews . . . [O]nce the custody officer has sufficient evidence to charge, he is not entitled to continue the detention without charge.' This framework is consistent with the detainee's rights under Article 5(1)(c) of the European Convention (the right to liberty).[182]

7.97 So far as the second presumption is concerned, the justification for detention must be regularly reviewed.[183] A custody officer should review whether it is appropriate to detain a suspect 'as soon as practicable after the person arrested arrives at the police station'.[184] Thereafter detention should be kept under review by an inspector unconnected with the investigation (the 'review officer'). That officer's first review should take place not later than six hours after detention was first authorized and further reviews should take place at intervals of no more than nine hours, although there is scope for reviews to be postponed where it is not practicable to carry one out within the required timescale.[185] The review officer must give the detainee or his solicitor the opportunity to make representations about detention (section 40(12)).

7.98 The time limits beyond which a detainee may not be detained without charge are set out at ss 41–4 (also Code C, Section 15). Normally a person should not be kept in detention without being charged for more than twenty-four hours. However, an officer of at least the rank of superintendent may authorize detention up to thirty-six hours. The test at this stage is threefold: the superintendent must have reasonable grounds for believing that (a) detention is necessary to obtain evidence (b) the offence investigated is indictable and (c) the investigation is being conducted 'diligently and expeditiously'. Beyond that, a magistrates' court may issue a 'warrant of further detention' and an 'extension' to a warrant with the result that the maximum period during which a person is detained can be up to, but not more than, ninety-six hours. Different provisions apply to terrorist cases. Suspects may be

[180] *R (on the application of G) v Chief Constable of West Yorkshire* [2008] 1 WLR 550, CA, para 12.
[181] See 7.103 et seq and 7.105 et seq. For further discussion see Ed Cape, *Defending Suspects at Police Stations* (2006, 5th edn) p 59, para 2.50 onwards and p 365, para 10.6 onwards; and also Ed Cape 'Detention Without Charge: What Does "Sufficient Evidence to Charge" Mean?' [1999] Crim LR 874.
[182] See Auld LJ in *Al Fayed v Commissioner of Police of the Metropolis* [2004] EWCA Civ 1579, (2004) 148 SJLB 1405, at para 88 (and paras 85–104 for his further analysis of the section).
[183] See Ed Cape, *Defending Suspects at Police Stations* (2006, 5th edn) p 62 onwards, para 2.58 onwards for the detail on periods of detention and reviews.
[184] PACE, s 37(10). See also Code C, Section 15.
[185] PACE, s 40 and Code C, para 15 and s 40(4).

detained, pre-charge, for up to twenty-eight days.[186] Proposals to extend to forty-two days the time limits for pre-charge detention of terrorist suspects were shelved by the Home Secretary.[187]

Further investigations

The steps investigating officers may take, and the powers they may exercise, in order to **7.99** secure sufficient evidence to satisfy a custody officer that there is enough evidence to charge, are beyond the scope of this book. However, it is worth noting that the Crown Prosecution Service may have input into these decisions[188] and that investigating officers have an obligation to pursue all reasonable lines of enquiry including those which point away from the suspect.[189] Here, we consider the likely impact of these enquiries on the suspect's detention.

The principal and most frequent investigatory tool of the police, and the one which most **7.100** directly affects a suspect's continued detention, is a formal tape recorded interview.[190] The police will seek to obtain answers from questions and ensure that a court may draw adverse inferences from silence.[191] The suspect has a choice: he can answer questions or remain silent. Sometimes solicitors advise clients to say nothing or to say 'No comment.' Sometimes they advise them to set out their defence in a 'prepared statement'. This is a set piece document with the suspect's words prepared with the help of the solicitor and handed to the police at any time while the suspect is questioned at the police station. If the suspect exercises his right to remain silent the court may, in some circumstances, draw adverse inferences against him.

Where there have been multiple arrests, the police may interview all detainees before **7.101** making a decision on detention or charge for any of them.[192] The police may detain a suspect for interview even if the interviewee indicates that he does not propose to answer any questions.[193] However, interviewing must cease when the investigating officer is satisfied that all relevant questions have been put, the suspect has been given an opportunity to put forward an innocent explanation, and the officer reasonably believes there is sufficient evidence to provide a realistic prospect of conviction in which case he must (without delay) inform the custody officer.[194] A person may not normally be questioned (or, therefore, detained for questioning) further about the alleged offence after charge or after he has been told that he may be prosecuted (Code C, paragraphs 16.4, 16.5, and 16.9).

---

[186] See Code H which applies to those arrested and detained on suspicion of terrorism under Terrorism Act 2000, s 41 and Sch 8. See also Ed Cape, *Defending Suspects at Police Stations* (2006, 5th edn) Ch 9.

[187] See clause 22 of the Counter-Terrorism (Temporary Provisions) Bill 2007–2008 and statement by the Home Secretary, Jacqui Smith, to the House of Commons on 13 August 2008.

[188] See for example paras 5.2, 5.6, and 5.8 of DPP's Guidance on Charging, see 7.105.

[189] See para 3.5 of Code of Practice to the Criminal Procedure and Investigations Act 1996.

[190] See Code C, ss 11, 12, 14, and, generally, Ed Cape, *Defending Suspects at Police Stations* (2006, 5th edn) Ch 7.

[191] Criminal Justice and Public Order Act 1994, ss 34–48; see also Code C, Annex C on inferences from silence.

[192] Sedley LJ in *Clarke v Chief Constable of North Wales* [2000] PoLR 83, CA, [2000] All ER(D) 477.

[193] Code C Note for Guidance 1K.

[194] Code C, para 11.6, Note for Guidance 11B, and para 16.1.

7.102 Interviews apart, some enquiries are lengthy or cannot be conducted at the time a person is first held at a police station (for example identification procedures). In these circumstances the suspect may be released from the police station and bailed to return at a later date (s 34(2) and (5) known as 'section 47(3) bail' or 'deferred bail'[195]). There is no statutory time limit within which the police must require the suspect to return or conclude their investigation (although it should be borne in mind that there is a six-month time limit for initiating prosecutions for most summary only offences[196]). Furthermore, the courts will only close down ongoing investigations on the basis that there is no prospect of a prosecution in the most exceptional cases.[197]

Is there sufficient evidence to charge?

7.103 Throughout this process, the custody officer must consider whether or not there is sufficient evidence to charge the suspect (s 37(7)[198]). When making this decision he must apply 'the Threshold Test'.[199] According to that test the custody officer must conduct:

> an overall assessment of whether in all the circumstances of the case there is at least a reasonable suspicion against the person of having committed an offence . . . and that at that stage it is in the public interest to proceed. The evidential decision in each case will require consideration of a number of factors including: the evidence available at the time and the likelihood and nature of further evidence being obtained; the reasonableness for believing that evidence will become available; the time that will take and the steps being taken to gather it; the impact of the expected evidence on the case, and the charges the totality of the evidence will support.

7.104 Although the Crown Prosecution Service are heavily involved throughout the decision-making process,[200] according to s 37(7) and (7A)[201] of PACE it is for the custody officer, where the test is satisfied, to

- consult the Crown Prosecution Service (CPS) on how the case should be resolved (PACE, s 37B[202]), and the custody officer may release the suspect on bail or authorize his continues detention while the consultation takes place (s 37(7)(a)[203]);

---

[195] See *R (Torres) v Commissioner of Police of the Metropolis* [2007] EWHC 3212 (Admin) on s 34(5) and the imposition of bail conditions under s 37, see 7.122.

[196] The Magistrates Court Act 1980, s 127. See also the DPP's Guidance on Charging, para 8.6, for guidance on period of time for releases on bail under s 37, and 7.105.

[197] Underhill J in the High Court in *R (on the application of C) v Chief Constable of A* [2006] EWHC 2352 (Admin), para 32.

[198] Amended by the Criminal Justice Act 2003, s 28, Sch 2, para 2 and then by the Police and Justice Act 2006, s 11.

[199] This test is set out at para 3.10 and applicable by virtue of para 8.4 of the DPP's Guidance on Charging (below at 7.105). The test was considered in *R (on the application of G) v Chief Constable of West Yorkshire* [2008] 1 WLR 550, CA. See comment on this decision by Ed Cape 'Police Station Law and Practice Update' in the Journal of the Legal Action Group issues April 2007, April 2008, and October 2009. See Home Office Review of PACE, August 2008 at Ch 15, esp paras 15.3–15.6 for rationale for this test at this stage of the investigation and proposals for reform.

[200] See para 8 of DPP's Guidance on Charging below at 7.105.

[201] Inserted by the Criminal Justice Act 2003, s 28, Sch 2, paras 1 and 2.

[202] Inserted by Criminal Justice Act 2003, s 28, Sch 2, paras 1 and 3.

[203] Also Code C, para 16.1B and Note for Guidance 16AB.

- release the suspect without charge and on bail to return to the police station pending other decisions or enquiries (s 37(7)(b));[204]
- release the suspect without charge and with no obligation to return to the police station (s 37(7)(c)); or
- charge the suspect (s 37(7)(d)) and caution him (Code C, paragraph 16.2), note any comments made (Code C, paragraph 16.8) and bail him to attend court (see below).

The decision to charge

The decision to charge is now, in most cases, made by the CPS. This follows the recommendation by Auld LJ that 'The Crown Prosecution Service should determine the charge in all but minor, routine offences.'[205] Accordingly, the DPP issued a Guidance on Charging[206] which custody officers must observe.[207] The Guidance confirms that Crown Prosecutors are 'responsible for the decision to charge and the specifying or drafting of the charges in all indictable only, either way or summary offences'. The exceptions are summary offences punishable by less than three months' prison, most road traffic offences, absconding from bail, and offences under s 5 of the Public Order Act 1986, where the decision to charge remains with the custody officer.[208]   **7.105**

When determining whether and what offence to charge the Crown Prosecutor and (where they retain the power to make the decision) custody officers apply the criteria in the Code for Crown Prosecutors.[209] This requires two tests to be passed: (a) the 'evidential test'—Is there enough evidence to provide a 'realistic prospect of conviction'? (paragraph 5.2)[210] and (b) a 'public interest test'—Is it in the public interest to prosecute? (paragraph 5.6).   **7.106**

A charge is not the only procedure by which criminal proceedings may begin. Public prosecutors have the power to lay an information in order to obtain a summons to bring a suspect before a magistrates' court, under s 1 of the Magistrates' Courts Act 1980. In pilot areas they have the power to issue a 'written charge' and 'requisition' under s 29 of the Criminal Justice Act 2003.[211] When this scheme is effective across the country public prosecutors will no longer have the power to obtain a summons (s 29(4)).   **7.107**

However, a charge (or equivalent) is not the only possible outcome. The CPS or police may conclude that a simple caution, conditional caution, reprimand, warning, or youth   **7.108**

---

[204] See 7.102.

[205] 'Review of the Criminal Courts of England and Wales', recommendation 154, at <http://www. criminal-courts-review.org.uk/auldcomts.htm>, (last accessed 19 September 2009).

[206] Issued in accordance with PACE, s 37A, inserted by Criminal Justice Act 2003, s 28, Sch 2, para 3 Third edition, published in February 2007. To be found in the Legal Resources/the Director's Guidance section of the CPS website, <http://www.cps.gov.uk>.

[207] See s 37A(3), and Code C 16.1A, and the DPP Guidance at para 2.

[208] DPP Guidance, paras 3.1 and 3.3.

[209] Ibid, paras 3.6 and 3.8. See Code for Crown Prosecutors to be found in the Legal Resources section of the CPS website, <http://www.cps.gov.uk>. In limited circumstances, the police may apply the 'threshold test': see paras 3.9–3.11 of the Guidance.

[210] Note that this is a higher test than the threshold test, set out at 7.103, which requires there only to be 'a reasonable suspicion against the person of having committed an offence'.

[211] In force in certain pilot areas by virtue of the Criminal Justice Act 2003 (Commencement No 16) Order 2007, SI 2007/1999 and Criminal Justice Act 2003 (Commencement No 21) Order 2008, SI 2008/1424.

conditional caution is appropriate.[212] Indeed, the CPS or police may take no further action and the suspect's detention or obligations to answer bail end.[213]

C. Bail Conditions and Remands in Custody After Charge

Introduction

7.109 The police's and courts' powers to impose bail conditions, and to refuse bail altogether, are designed, among other things, to prevent the commission of offences. They can be seen as part of a panoply of powers—which also include injunctions, anti-social behaviour orders (ASBOs), and conditional discharges[214]—available to maintain public order. Bail, however, is different because the rules of evidence are less strict, the test the court has to apply when deciding whether to restrict bail is less demanding, and there has been no finding against the defendant.[215]

7.110 Doubts have been raised, particularly when it comes to political protest, about the imposition of unnecessarily wide bail conditions which inevitably restrict the rights to protest enshrined in Articles 10 and 11. The concerns have been broadened by the introduction of police powers to impose bail conditions pre-charge, including street bail. These powers, combined with potentially lengthy periods of investigation by the police (which the courts are reluctant to curtail[216]) accentuate questions about scrutiny. They also raise questions of proportionality, not least because the implications of breaching bail include the possibility of being remanded in custody and there are proposals to make breach of bail conditions a criminal offence.

7.111 The rest of this chapter will identify the law which those making bail decisions should apply when balancing the real needs for bail conditions, particularly those aimed at preventing further offences, with important human rights, particularly where the defendant wishes to continue to protest. It will also touch upon some of the procedures for challenging bail decisions.[217] As with so many other areas of law, the European Convention on Human Rights provides the framework and the parameters, and domestic law provides the detail. We shall therefore begin with the Convention.[218]

The European Convention

7.112 All citizens have a right to bail. The right stems from the right to liberty (Article 5) and the presumption of innocence (Article 6).

---

[212] See DPP's Guidance on Charging, para 9 and Note for Guidance 16A to Code C. These methods of 'diversion' from prosecution are discussed in Ch 9.

[213] See DPP Guidance on Charging, para 6 and PACE, s 34(2) and (5), and s 37(7)(c).

[214] See Ch 9.

[215] See below, for example 7.113, 7.120, and 7.129.

[216] See 7.102.

[217] The detail of the procedures in the courts is beyond the scope of this book. But see the Criminal Procedures Rules 2005, Part 19 and *Blackstones Criminal Practice 2010* (2010) p 1353, para D7.46 for practice in magistrates' courts; and p 1360, para D7.60 for practice in the Crown Court. Indeed, see Section D7, on Bail, pp 1333 onwards of *Blackstones* for bail from courts, generally.

[218] See Ch 10 for a detailed examination of relevant human rights.

The European Court has identified five risks which may justify the refusal of bail, in addition to the continuing requirement that there be reasonable suspicion of the defendant:[219] **7.113**

- the suspect would fail to appear for trial;[220]
- the suspect would prejudice the administration of justice;[221]
- the suspect's release would cause public disorder;[222]
- bail should be refused for the suspect's own protection;[223]
- the suspect would commit a further offence.

When assessing the risk that a suspect would commit a further offence, courts should consider the nature and gravity of a suspect's past convictions, of the current allegation, and of the feared further offence. When considering the relevance of past convictions, the court may take into account their nature and the sentence imposed.[224] The domestic court may take into account the seriousness of the allegations the defendant faces, but must also establish, in the light of the circumstances of the case and the suspect himself, that the danger of repetition is plausible and the decision to refuse bail is appropriate.[225] The court may, in special circumstances take into account the danger that a person may repeat, if not detained, serious offences similar to those of which he is suspected.[226] **7.114**

Further, the European Court has said that, when assessing any risk as a ground for refusing bail, objections raised in a general and abstract fashion do not justify the continuation of detention.[227] Grounds given for refusing bail in particular cases should not be stereotyped.[228] **7.115**

In practice bail conditions can be and are imposed in order to avert any of these risks too.[229] However, the only express reference in the European Convention to the justification for imposing bail conditions is in the final sentence of Article 5(3): 'Release [from detention] may be conditioned by guarantees to appear for trial.' This has justified, for example, conditions such as a surety,[230] the surrender of travel documents[231] and the imposition of a **7.116**

---

[219] See *Brogan v UK* (1989) 11 EHRR 117; *Nikolova v Bulgaria* (2001) 31 EHRR 3, para 58; and *Letellier v France* (1992) 14 EHRR 83, para 35.

[220] See *Stögmüller v Austria* (1979–80) 1 EHRR 155, para 15; *Neumeister v Austria* (1979–80) 1 EHRR 91, para 10; *Letellier v France*, para 43; *Goral v Poland* Application No 38654/97.

[221] See *Wemhoff v Germany* (1979–80) 1 EHRR 55, para 14; *Clooth v Belgium* (1992) 14 EHRR 717, paras 43 and 44.

[222] See *Letellier v France*, para 51.

[223] See *Letellier v France*, para 51; *I A v France* 1998-VII RJD 2951, para 108.

[224] *Toth v Austria* (1992) 14 EHRR 551, para 70.

[225] *Clooth v Belgium*, para 40.

[226] *Matznetter v Austria* (1979–80) 1 EHRR 198, para 9.

[227] *Clooth v Belgium*, para 44.

[228] *Yagci and Sargan v Turkey* (1995) 20 EHRR 505, para 52.

[229] See paras 2.35–2.36 of Law Commission report 'Bail and the Human Rights Act 1998' and the 'Guidance for bail decision-takers and their advisers' which accompanied it (Law Com No 269) at <http://www.lawcom.gov.uk/docs/lc269.pdf> (last accessed 19 September 2009).

[230] *Neumeister v Austria*, para 14.

[231] *Stögmüller v Austria*, para 15.

residence requirement.[232] There is some authority that Article 5 will not normally be engaged by the imposition of bail conditions.[233]

7.117 However, where the courts have considered the consequences of failing to comply with bail conditions, they have been more ready to apply Convention rights. Thus, in *Iwanczuk v Poland*, the European Court applied Article 5 to the setting of the level of a security as liberty was at stake.[234] In *R (CPS) v Chorley Justices*[235] Latham LJ considered the lawfulness of a doorstep condition imposed by a magistrates' court. He took the view that Article 5 was engaged because any breach of a lawfully imposed bail condition might lead to an arrest under s 7 of the Bail Act 1976.

7.118 Indeed, Latham LJ also reasoned that Article 8 was engaged because it was a condition which was capable of interfering with the defendant's private and family life and indeed his home. It is submitted, on similar grounds, that proposed bail conditions which may interfere with a citizen's rights to protest should be measured against the requirements of Articles 10 and 11.[236] The question then is whether the bail conditions are 'a proportionate and appropriate response to the problem presented by the particular defendant in the particular case'.[237]

7.119 As to the general approach decision makers should take to the grant of bail, the Law Commission in its Guidance to those making decisions on bail, 'Bail and the Human Rights Act 1998',[238] advise that bail conditions (as an alternative to unconditional bail) should only be imposed where they are necessary to address the risks and the proposed conditions should not violate the defendant's other Convention rights under Articles 8–11 of the European Convention.[239] In turn, bail should only be refused where it is necessary to avert these risks, the risks are real, and the risks cannot be sufficiently reduced by the imposition of bail conditions.[240]

7.120 Finally, in *R v Havering Magistrates' Court, ex parte DPP*, Latham LJ, reviewing domestic authorities, concluded that the existing procedures for court bail hearings were compatible with Article 5 and that Article 6(3) did not apply.[241] Accordingly, evidence relevant to the decision on bail does not have to achieve the criminal standard of proof. Inadmissible evidence, including hearsay, can be considered, though the courts must take into account

---

[232] *Schmid v Austria*, Application 10670/83, (1985) 44 DR 195.
[233] From the Scottish High Court of Justiciary, *McDonald v Procurator Fiscal* (2003) SLT 467. See generally *Guzzardi v Italy* (1981) 3 EHRR 333. But see also, on control orders under the Prevention of Terrorism Act 2005, cases such as *Secretary of State for the Home Department v JJ* [2008] 1 AC 385, HL.
[234] (2004) 38 EHRR 8, para 66.
[235] [2002] 166 JP 764, HC.
[236] See Law Commission 'Guidance for bail decision-takers and their advisers', para 24.
[237] Latham J in *R (CPS) v Chorley Justices* [2002] 166 JP 764, HC at p769 onwards.
[238] 'Guidance for bail decision-takers and their advisers'.
[239] Ibid, paras 21 and 24.
[240] Ibid, paras 1–3 and 20.
[241] [2001] 1 WLR 805, DC, in particular paras 10, 35, and 39–42. See *In re Moles* [1981] Crim LR 170, QB; *R v Mansfield Justices ex parte Sharkey* [1985] QB 613, QB (considered below at 7.129); *R v Liverpool City Justices ex p DPP* [1993] QB 233, QB. See later cases such as *R (on the application of Thomas) v Greenwich Magistrates Court* [2009] Crim LR 800, DC and *R (on the application of Ajaib v Birmingham Magistrates' Court* [2009] EWHC 2127 (Admin).

the quality of the material and a defendant must have an opportunity to challenge and answer it.

PACE and the Bail Act

The source of the relevant domestic legislation on bail is fragmented. Provisions governing **7.121** the police's decisions[242] to grant bail are in Parts III and IV of PACE[243] and also in the Bail Act 1976[244] and, perhaps unsurprisingly, the Home Office proposes a new, single statutory approach to police bail, to include other reforms of bail [245]. Where a defendant appears in court having been charged at the police station, the court must remand the defendant[246] and the remand must either be on bail or in custody, applying the Bail Act 1976 (in particular s 4).[247] The criteria to be taken into account vary. They depend for example on whether the decision is to grant bail (with or without conditions) or to refuse bail. They also depend on whether the decision is the police's or the courts'.

Granting bail (with or without conditions)

Bail conditions from the police station (Bail Act 1976, s 3A)

A custody officer releasing a suspect from a police station, whether on condition to return **7.122** to the police station or after charge, has the power to impose bail conditions (ss 37, 38, 40(10), 47(1), and (1A)[248] in PACE, Part IV[249]). When making any decision on bail under Part IV of PACE, custody officers must observe ss 3A and 3 of the Bail Act 1976[250] (see PACE, s 47(1)).

Accordingly (Bail Act 1976, s 3A(5)) no conditions shall be imposed unless it appears to **7.123** the officer that it is necessary [251]

- to prevent the suspect from failing to surrender to custody; or
- to prevent him from committing an offence while on bail; or
- to prevent him from interfering with witnesses or otherwise obstructing the course of justice; or

---

[242] See 7.94 et seq. See also DPP Guidance on Charging, para 4.1, for input by the CPS into the police's decisions.

[243] In particular ss 30, 30A (street bail, see above 7.55 et seq), 34, 37, 38, 46, and 47.

[244] In particular ss 3, 3A, 5, 5A, 5B, 6, and 7. The Bail Act 1976 applies to 'bail in criminal proceedings' which includes 'bail grantable in connection with an offence to a person who is under arrest' s 1(1)(b).

[245] See Home Office PACE Review—Government Proposals in response to the Review of the Police and Criminal Evidence Act 1984, Home Office publication August 2008 (Ch 3, Summary of Proposals, Bail and Ch 11, Bail, para (11.2)).

[246] Magistrates' Courts Act 1980, ss 5, 10, 15, 18, and 55 and Football Spectators Act 1989, s 21C.

[247] See also Bail Act 1976, s 1(6) and Magistrates' Courts Act 1980, s 128.

[248] Added by the Criminal Justice and Public Order Act 1994, s 27(1)(b) and amended by the Police and Justice Act 2006, s 10, Sch 6, Part 1, para 1, Part 3 para 6.

[249] See *R (Torres) v Commissioner of Police of the Metropolis* [2007] EWHC 3212 (Admin): custody officers releasing detainees on bail under s 34(5) may only impose conditions under s 37.

[250] Section 3A added by the Criminal Justice and Public Order Act 1994, s 27(3). See below, 7.126 for s 3. Neither s 4 nor, therefore Sch 1, apply.

[251] See Latham LJ in *R (CPS) v Chorley Justices* (2002) 166 JP 764, HC for consideration of the term 'necessary' and the application of Art 5.

- for his own protection or, if he is a child or young person, for his own welfare or in his own interests.

7.124 The police may impose on a person any bail condition available to the court.[252]

7.125 There are no statutory time limits within which the person should be required to attend the police station if bailed to attend a police station following street bail[253] or from the police station.[254] However, if the person has been charged, the court date given will normally be no later than the first sitting of the magistrates' court after charge (PACE, s 47(3A)[255]).

Bail conditions from the court (Bail Act 1976, s 3)

7.126 The courts' power to grant bail stems from s 3 of the Bail Act 1976. The court may grant unconditional bail or by virtue of s 3(6)[256] may impose such bail conditions as appear to be necessary[257] among other things

- to secure the suspect's surrender to custody;
- to ensure that he does not commit an offence on bail;
- to ensure that he does not interfere with witnesses or otherwise obstruct the course of justice whether in relation to himself or any other person; or
- for his own protection or, if he is a child or young person, for his own welfare or in his own interests.[258]

7.127 There is no exhaustive list of conditions which may be imposed. Conditions of most relevance in public order cases include

- residence;[259]
- not to approach a given place;[260]
- not to contact specified people or organizations (which may be either the victims/complainants or the defendant's co-accused);
- not to attend demonstrations.

7.128 A court may not remand a defendant in custody because he refuses to consent to bail conditions as this is not one of the grounds for refusing bail.[261]

---

[252] See 7.127. But the police may not impose a condition to reside at a bail hostel, to be available for reports or to see a lawyer, Bail Act 1976, s 3A(2).

[253] See 7.55.

[254] See 7.102.

[255] Inserted by the Crime and Disorder Act 1998, s 46.

[256] See also Bail Act 1976, Sch 1, Part I, para 2(1), considered at 7.152, applicable by virtue of Bail Act 1976, s 4(5) and Sch 1, Part I, para 8, commented on by Lord Lane in *R v Mansfield Justices ex parte Sharkey* [1985] QB 613, QB. These considerations apply to bail decisions for both imprisonable and non-imprisonable offences, *R v Bournemouth Magistrates Court, ex p Cross, Griffin and Pamment* (1989) 89 Cr App R 90, DC.

[257] See Latham LJ in *R (CPS) v Chorley Justices* (2002) 166 JP 764, DC.

[258] These are described in s 3(6) as 'the normal powers to impose conditions of bail', a term used in this and other Acts (eg PACE, s 47(1A)).

[259] See the Criminal Procedure Rules 2005, rule 19.25, which requires a defendant to notify the prosecutor of the proposed address as soon as practicable.

[260] *R v Bournemouth Magistrates Court, ex p Cross, Griffin and Pamment* (1989) 89 Cr App R 90, DC; *R v Mansfield Justices, ex parte Sharkey* [1985] 1 QB 613, QB.

[261] *R v Bournemouth Magistrates Court, ex p Cross, Griffin and Pamment* (1989) 89 Cr App R 90, DC.

In *R v Mansfield Justices, ex parte Sharkey and others*,[262] cases arising from the 1980s' miners' **7.129** strike and therefore pre-dating the Human Rights Act 1998, the High Court upheld the lawfulness of magistrates' practice of imposing a condition, applicable to all defendants, regardless of their personal circumstances. The common condition prevented striking miners from attending the target of their strike, except peacefully to picket their own workplace.[263] Lord Lane laid out the following principles:

- 'the question the magistrates should ask themselves is a simple one: is this condition necessary for the prevention of the commission of an offence by the defendant when on bail? They are not obliged to have substantial grounds. It is enough if they perceive a real and not a fanciful risk of an offence being committed. [The Bail Act's provisions] give the court a wide discretion to inquire whether the condition is necessary';[264]
- the magistrates' discretion must be exercised reasonably, following *Wednesbury* principles;[265]
- the magistrates were 'certainly entitled to use their knowledge of events . . . because it was only on the basis of that knowledge . . . they could properly reach a conclusion as to the necessity of imposing a bail condition';[266]
- against this background, the personal circumstances of each defendant did not affect the likelihood that the defendants would rejoin the picket and commit further offences.[267]

The court did however express concerns about the appearance of summary or group **7.130** justice—such as putting all defendants in the dock together even where their cases arose from different circumstances and the clerk's practice of attaching the standard conditions to bail forms even before the magistrates had made a decision on applications for unconditional bail.[268]

Implications of breaching bail

Breach of street bail

Where a suspect has been granted street bail[269] the police have the power to arrest him if he **7.131** fails to attend the police station or where they have reasonable grounds for suspecting that the suspect has broken any bail conditions (PACE, s 30D[270]). The police must then take the suspect to a police station as soon as practicable for the investigation to continue or for new bail conditions to be imposed by a custody officer. The Home Office propose to create new offences of failing to attend a police station in response to street bail and failing to observe police bail conditions.[271]

---

[262] [1985] QB 613, QB.
[263] See Ch 4 for peaceful picketing.
[264] [1985] QB 613, 625. This 'essentially simple question' was approved in *R (CPS) v Chorley Justices* (2002) 166 JP 764, eg by McCombe J at p 771.
[265] [1985] QB 613, p 625.
[266] Ibid, p 626.
[267] Ibid, p 628.
[268] Ibid, p 628. See also 7.120.
[269] See 7.55.
[270] Inserted by the Criminal Justice Act 2003, s 4.
[271] Home Office Review, August 2008, Ch 3, p 5 and Ch 11, p 23, paras 11.3–11.4.

Breach of bail from the police station to return to the police station

7.132 Where a suspect has been granted bail from the police station to return to the police station the police also have the power to arrest him if he fails to attend the police station or where they have reasonable grounds for suspecting that the suspect has broken any bail conditions (s 46A[272]). The suspect must then be taken to the police station as soon as practicable. If the suspect is simply re-bailed, the custody officer may only release him on unconditional bail or the same bail conditions as before arrest (ss 37C and 37CA[273]). Alternatively, the investigation may continue and the suspect may be charged, after consultation with the CPS,[274] and then a fresh decision on bail is made under s 38 of PACE whereby bail may be refused.[275]

7.133 It is an offence to fail to return to the police station when bailed from the police station.[276] It is not an offence to fail to observe bail conditions imposed on release from the police station, but there are proposals to create such an offence.[277]

Breach of bail to attend court (Bail Act, s 7)

7.134 The police's and courts' powers in relation to a defendant who has been bailed, whether by the police or the court itself, to attend court depend on whether

- the defendant is not likely to attend court or may break or has broken bail conditions; or
- the defendant has actually failed to attend court.

7.135 Where the police have reasonable grounds to believe that a defendant is not likely to attend court, or is likely to break or has broken any bail conditions, the police have the power to arrest him without a warrant and the defendant will be brought to court (Bail Act 1976, s 7(3) and (4)[278]). The court will conduct a summary hearing.[279] If the court determines that the defendant is not likely to attend court or has broken or is likely to break any bail condition, it may remand the defendant in custody or grant bail, on the same conditions as before or different ones (Bail Act 1976, s 7(5)[280]). It is not an offence simply to breach bail conditions. Nor does it normally amount to a contempt of court. In some circumstances breach of bail may amount to a separate criminal offence (such as witness intimidation).

---

[272] Inserted by the Criminal Justice and Public Order Act 1994, s 29.

[273] Inserted by the Criminal Justice Act 2003, Sch 2, para 3 and Police and Justice Act 2006, Sch 6(3), para 8, respectively.

[274] See DPP Guidance on Charging, (para 10.1).

[275] See 7.141.

[276] Bail Act 1976, s 6, punishable if sentenced in the magistrates' court with up to three months' imprisonment and/or a fine not exceeding level 5, but, if committed to the Crown Court for sentence, with up to twelve months' imprisonment and/or an unlimited fine.

[277] Home Office Review, August 2008, Ch 3, p 5 and Ch 11, p 23, paras 11.3–11.4.

[278] The power of arrest is preserved by PACE, s 26 and Sch 2. See *R (Ellison) v Teesside Magistrates' Court* (2001) 165 JP 355, DC.

[279] For the procedure to be followed see *R v Liverpool City Justices, ex p DPP* [1993] QB 233, QB; *R v Havering Magistrates Court, ex parte DPP* [2001] 1 WLR 805, DC; and *R (on the application of Thomas) v Greenwich Magistrates' Court* [2009] Crim LR 800, DC.

[280] See *R v Havering Magistrates' Court, ex parte DPP*; *R (Hussain) v Derby Magistrates' Court* [2001] 1 WLR 2454, DC; *R (Vickers) v West London Magistrates' Court* (2003) 167 JP 473, QB.

The Bail Act 1976 does not empower a court to punish a person for breach of a bail condition.[281]

Where the defendant has actually failed to attend court the position is as follows.[282] It is an offence to fail to attend court without reasonable cause when required to do so (Bail Act 1976, s 6(1)).[283] If the defendant had reasonable cause not to attend, he still commits an offence if he fails to attend 'as soon after the appointed time as is reasonably practicable' (Bail Act 1976, s 6(2)). **7.136**

So, where the defendant fails to attend court, the court—besides having the power to continue with the original proceedings—will normally issue a warrant (a 'bench warrant') for his arrest and the defendant will then be brought to court in custody (Bail Act 1976, s 7(1) and (2)). However, warrants may be 'backed for bail' authorizing the defendant's release from custody after arrest, but with a duty to attend court.[284] Indeed, the court has the power instead, and where there is good reason, to enlarge the defendant's bail.[285] **7.137**

At the hearing of the case[286] the defendant must be given the opportunity to put forward any defence.[287] If found guilty, the maximum sentence is three months' prison and/or a fine not exceeding level 5. The failure to attend court may also be treated as a contempt of court, carrying a maximum sentence of twelve months and/or a fine (Bail Act 1976, s 6(7)).[288] Bail conditions for the original offence may also be strengthened and bail may even be refused.[289] **7.138**

Impact on sentencing of commission of offence while on bail

The fact that an offence has been committed while on bail for another offence is an aggravating feature when the defendant comes to be sentenced for that later offence.[290] Indeed, even before sentencing, the defendant's right to bail in the later proceedings may also be affected (see below). **7.139**

---

[281] *R v Rowland*,14 February 1991, CA; *R v Ashley* [2004] 1 WLR 2057, CA.

[282] See Practice Direction (Bail: Failure to Surrender) [2004] 1 WLR 589.

[283] See *Laidlaw v Atkinson*, The Times, 2 August 1986; *R v Scott* (2008) 172 JP 149, CA.

[284] Magistrates' Courts Act 1980, s 117 and Supreme Court Act 1981, s 81(4).

[285] Magistrates' Courts Act 1980, s 129(1) and (3).

[286] The procedure to be followed is set out in the Consolidated Criminal Practice Direction 2002, para I.13.

[287] *R v Davis* (1986) 8 Cr App R (S) 64; *R v Boyle* [1993] Crim LR 40, CA; *R v How* [1993] Crim LR 201, CA; *R v Hourigan* (2003) 147 SJLB 901, [2003] EWCA Crim 2306.

[288] See Sentencing Guidelines Council Guidelines for sentencing for 'Fail to Surrender' on the SGC website, <http://www.sentencing-guidelines.gov.uk>, to be found under 'guidelines', 'Sentencing Guidelines Council guidelines', 'Final Guidelines', entitled 'Definitive Sentencing Guideline – Fail to surrender to bail', dated 29 November 2007.

[289] See para 3 of guidance by Thomas LJ, 5 May 2006, at <http://www.judiciary.gov.uk/docs/judgments_guidance/protocols/bail_trials_absence.pdf> (last accessed 19 September 2009). See 7.144, et seq, the right to bail.

[290] Criminal Justice Act 2003, s 143(3). See Sentencing Guidelines Council Guidelines for sentencing for 'Overarching Principles: Seriousness', para 1.22 on the SGC website, <http://www.sentencing-guidelines. gov.uk>, to be found under 'guidelines', 'Sentencing Guidelines Council guidelines', 'Final Guidelines', entitled 'Overarching Principles: Seriousness', dated 16 December 2004. See for example *R v Povey* (2009) 1 Cr App R (S) 42.

Refusing bail

7.140 The right to bail is of course not absolute. Both the police after charge and the court have the power to refuse bail. The police have no power to refuse bail pre-charge—their powers to detain pre-charge and to release a suspect on bail on condition to return to the police station are dealt with above.

The police's power to refuse bail

7.141 After charge, the custody officer has the power to refuse the defendant bail. According to s 38 of PACE the custody officer must release a defendant on bail unless, among other things

- his name or address cannot be ascertained or the custody sergeant has reasonable grounds for doubting whether the details given are real;
- the custody sergeant has reasonable grounds for believing that the defendant will fail to appear in court;
- in the case of an imprisonable offence, the custody officer has reasonable grounds for believing that the defendant's detention is necessary to prevent the defendant from committing an offence;
- in the case of a non-imprisonable offence, the custody officer has reasonable grounds for believing that the defendant's detention is necessary to prevent the defendant causing physical injury to any other person or from causing loss or damage to property (when considering this factor, custody officers should take into account the suspect's intentions, behaviour, and prior record [291]);
- the custody officer has reasonable grounds for believing that the defendant's detention is necessary to prevent the defendant from interfering with the administration of justice or with the investigation of offences; or
- the custody officer has reasonable grounds for believing that detention is necessary for the person's own protection.

7.142 When making many of these decisions the custody officer (by virtue of PACE, s 38(2A)[292]) shall have regard to the same exceptions and considerations which a court must take into account when deciding whether to grant bail. These are set out below.[293]

7.143 If a person has been charged and refused bail, he will be produced in court as soon as is practicable and in any event not later than the first sitting after he is charged with the offence (PACE, s 46(2)).[294]

---

[291] Home Office Circular 111/1992.
[292] Inserted by the Criminal Justice and Public Order Act 1994, s 28(3).
[293] See Bail Act 1976, Sch 1, Part I, para 2(1) considered at 7.152 et seq and para 9 considered at 7.147 et seq. Note that these provisions do not apply where the custody officer's concerns are about the suspect's name and address, or what is required for their own protection.
[294] See *R (Nikonovs) v Governor of Brixton Prison* [2006] 1 WLR 1518, DC, para 21.

The courts' power to refuse bail

The courts' approach

Section 4 of the Bail Act 1976 provides a statutory right to bail: a presumption that a defen- **7.144**
dant should be granted bail unless one of a number of stated reasons for the refusal of bail
is made out. The burden is on the State to establish the facts relevant to bail and justify
detention.[295] There should be equality of arms between the prosecution and the defence,
certainly on the issue of disclosure.[296] The presumption is consolidated by judicial comments that a defendant should only be remanded in custody if it is necessary, a high threshold required by both the Bail Act and Article 5.[297]

However, in two particular situations, applicable only to those charged with imprisonable, **7.145**
non-summary offences (within Bail Act 1976, Schedule 1, Part I, see 7.152) the presumption in favour of bail is, in effect, reversed[298] even though the European Court disapproves
of presumptions against bail as they are inconsistent with Article 5(3).[299] Firstly, by virtue
of paragraph 2A of Part I, a defendant[300] 'need not' be granted bail[301] if it appears to the
court that he was on bail on the date of the alleged offence. Secondly, by virtue of paragraph 6 of Part I, a defendant[302] 'need not' be granted bail[303] if having been released on bail,
he has been arrested on suspicion of breach of bail conditions or failing to attend court.[304]
In both circumstances, the court, when deciding whether to grant bail, 'still must bear in
mind the overall principle that bail should only be refused if there is a good reason to refuse
it, and the approach that must remain is that it is in all the circumstances proportionate to
refuse bail'.[305]

Schedule 1 of the Bail Act 1976 sets out the exceptions or grounds which a court should **7.146**
take into account when considering whether to refuse bail in any case. Within Schedule 1
there are three Parts, applicable to offences of different gravity, which contain different
grounds on which bail may be refused. The grounds applicable to these three Parts will be
considered, in turn, below.

---

[295] See European authorities such as *Wemhoff v Germany* (1979–80) 1 EHRR 55, para 12; *Khudobin v
Russia* (2009) 48 EHRR 22, paras 103–5; *Letellier v France* (1992) 14 EHRR 83, para 35; *Neumeister v Austria*
(1979–80) 1 EHRR 91, para 5; *Tomasi v France* (1993) 15 EHRR 1, para 84.
[296] See *Lamy v Belgium* (1989) 11 EHRR 529, para 29; *Nikolova v Bulgaria* (2001) 31 EHRR 3, para 58,
read in the light of *R v DPP ex parte Lee* [1999] 1 WLR 1950, QB.
[297] *R (Fergus) v Southampton Crown Court* [2008] EWHC 3273 (Admin), paras 19 and 20.
[298] Considered in *R (Wiggins) v Harrow Crown Court* [2005] EWHC 882 (Admin), para 24.
[299] See *Shishkov v Bulgaria* ECHR-2003-I, para 59 onwards, and para 65.
[300] Other than a defendant charged with an offence punishable by life imprisonment (such as public nuisance). A later version of para 2A applies to these defendants: see the Criminal Justice Act 2003, s 14 and the
Criminal Justice Act 2003 (Commencement No 14 and Transitional Provision) Order 2006, SI 2006/3217.
[301] The term 'need not' conveys a discretion to grant bail: *R (Wiggins) v Harrow Crown Court* [2005]
EWHC 882 (Admin).
[302] Other than a defendant charged with an offence punishable by life imprisonment (such as public
nuisance). A later version of para 6 applies to these defendants: see the Criminal Justice Act 2003, s 15 and
Criminal Justice Act 2003 (Commencement No 14 and Transitional Provision) Order 2006, SI 2006/3217.
[303] See *Wiggins* above.
[304] See Bail Act 1976, s 7 at 7.134 et seq.
[305] See *R (Wiggins) v Harrow Crown Court*, para 34.

7.147 When considering whether one of these grounds is made out, the court (by virtue of Bail Act 1976, Schedule 1, Part I, paragraph 9), has regard to such of the following reasons as appear to it to be relevant (see also s 114(3)(b) of the Coroners and Justice Act 2009, not in force at time of writing):

- the nature and seriousness of the offence and the probable method of dealing with the defendant for it (but this cannot be the conclusive reason[306]);
- the character, antecedents, associations, and community ties of the defendant;
- the defendant's bail history;
- the strength of the prosecution evidence; and
- any other considerations which appear to be relevant.

Defendants charged with non-imprisonable offences (Part II of Schedule 1)

7.148 Part II of Schedule 1 of the Bail Act, sets out exceptions to the right to bail where a defendant is accused of non-imprisonable offences.[307] These include a number of minor public order offences such as causing harassment, alarm, and distress contrary to s 5 of the Public Order Act 1986.[308]

7.149 The defendant need not be granted bail[309] if among other things

- it appears to the court that, having been previously granted bail, the defendant has failed to surrender to custody and the court believes that if released on bail the defendant would fail to surrender to custody (paragraph 2);
- the defendant should be kept in custody for his own protection (paragraph 3); or
- the defendant has been arrested under s 7 of the Bail Act 1976[310] and the court is satisfied that there are substantial grounds for believing that the defendant, if released on bail would fail to surrender to custody, commit an offence on bail or interfere with witnesses or otherwise obstruct the course of justice (paragraph 5).

Defendants charged with imprisonable summary offences (Part IA of Schedule 1)

7.150 Bail Act 1976, Schedule 1, Part IA[311] sets out exceptions to the right to bail where a defendant is accused of imprisonable summary offences.[312] These include many of the offences which may apply to those alleged to have been involved in public disorder.

7.151 The defendant need not be granted bail[313] if among other things

- it appears to the court that, having been previously granted bail, the defendant has failed to surrender to custody and the court believes that if released on bail the defendant would fail to surrender to custody (paragraph 2);

---

[306] *Hurman v State of Mauritius* [2006] 1 WLR 857, PC.
[307] Sch 1, Part II, para 1.
[308] See Ch 1.
[309] See *Wiggins* above.
[310] See 7.134 et seq.
[311] Inserted by the Criminal Justice and Immigration Act 2008, Sch 12, para 6.
[312] Sch 1, Part IA, para 1, and see also Bail Act 1976, Sch 1, Part I, para 1(2).
[313] See *Wiggins* above.

- it appears to the court that the defendant was on bail in other criminal proceedings on the date of the offence and the court is satisfied that there are substantial grounds for believing that the defendant, if released on bail would commit an offence while on bail (paragraph 3);
- the court is satisfied that there are substantial grounds for believing that the defendant, if released on bail, would commit an offence while on bail by conduct that would cause fear of or actual physical or mental injury to someone else (paragraph 4);
- the defendant should be kept in custody for his own protection (paragraph 5);
- if, the defendant having been arrested under s 7 of the Bail Act 1976[314] the court is satisfied that there are substantial grounds for believing that the defendant, if released on bail, would fail to surrender to custody, commit an offence on bail or interfere with witnesses or otherwise obstruct the course of justice (paragraph 7).[315]

Defendants charged with imprisonable non-summary offences (Part I of Schedule 1)

Bail Act 1976, Schedule 1, Part I, paragraph 2(1) sets out exceptions to the right to bail where a defendant is accused of imprisonable non-summary offences.[316]   **7.152**

The defendant need not be granted bail[317] if the court is satisfied that there are substantial grounds for believing that the defendant, if released on bail (whether subject to conditions or not) would   **7.153**

- fail to surrender to custody;
- commit an offence while on bail; or
- interfere with witnesses or otherwise obstruct the course of justice.

Also the defendant need not be granted bail if the court is satisfied that the defendant should be kept in custody for his own protection (Bail Act 1976, Schedule 1, Part I, paragraph 3). A defendant may be remanded for a short period of time in order to obtain information about him (paragraph 5).   **7.154**

Reviews and challenges to bail decisions

Records of decisions

There are a multiplicity of procedures for a suspect or the prosecution to have bail decisions reviewed. Indeed the court may review them of its own motion.[318] However, the reasons behind all bail decisions must be known in order for these procedures to be effective.[319] The police and courts have an obligation to make and provide records of their decisions and reasons: PACE, s 30B (street bail) and s 38(3) (detention after charge); and   **7.155**

---

[314] See 7.134 et seq.

[315] See also para 8, remands for a short period of time to obtain information about a defendant.

[316] Defined in the Bail Act 1976, Sch 1, Part I, para 1(1) and (2), including criminal damage of value over £5,000.

[317] See *Wiggins* above.

[318] See for example *R (on the application of Fergus) v Southampton Crown Court* [2008] EWHC 3273 (Admin).

[319] *R (on the application of Shergill) v Harrow Crown Court* [2005] EWHC 648 (Admin), para 14; *Neumeister v Austria* (1979–80) 1 EHRR 91, para 5; and *Tomasi v France* (1993) 15 EHRR 1, para 84.

Bail Act 1976, s 5 and s 5A (the police's powers to grant bail and the decision by the courts on bail[320]).

7.156   The reasons given must be tailored to the facts of the case, certainly where bail is refused. In a judicial review of a decision by a Crown Court judge to withdraw bail the Divisional Court stressed that 'any such reason justifying the decision to withdraw bail must be stated by the decision maker explaining why bail should be withdrawn and that reason must relate to the facts. Such a reason must be more than merely reciting that one of the statutory grounds has been made out. The underlying facts have to be put forward'.[321]

Varying bail conditions following street bail

7.157   A suspect on street bail with conditions may request a custody officer at a police station to vary the conditions (PACE, s 30CA(1)[322]). Further requests to vary may be made. However, a custody officers dealing with a further request may only vary bail conditions if the request is based on information which was not available when the previous request was considered (s 30CA(2)).

7.158   A suspect may also apply to a magistrates' court to vary the conditions (s 30CB[323]). The court has the power to vary the conditions if a request has already been made to a custody officer to vary the conditions under s 30CA and it has been refused or not dealt with within forty-eight hours or the conditions have been varied in some way already under s 30CA.

Defence applications to vary bail conditions from the police station

7.159   Both a suspect pre-charge and a defendant post-charge who has not yet appeared in court may apply to another custody officer to vary bail conditions (Bail Act 1976, s 3A(4)[324]). A suspect or defendant can also apply to the court to vary his bail conditions (PACE, s 47(1E),[325] Magistrates' Courts Act 1980, s 43B[326]).

Prosecution applications for reconsideration of bail decision by the police or magistrates

7.160   The prosecution can apply to a magistrates' court for a decision by the police or by a magistrates' court to grant a defendant bail after charge, to be reconsidered (Bail Act 1976, s 5B[327]). This procedure is only available where the defendant is charged with offences triable either way or on indictment. It also only applies where the application is based

---

[320]   See also the Criminal Procedure Rules 2005, rule 19 (for example rule 19.10–19.12) and paras 23–26 of Law Commission 'Guidance for bail decision-takers and their advisers'.

[321]   *R (on the application of Fergus) v Southampton Crown Court*, para 21. See also Law Commission 'Guidance for bail decision-takers and their advisers', para 4. See also para 7.115.

[322]   Inserted by the Police and Justice Act 2006, Sch 6, para 10.

[323]   Ibid.

[324]   Inserted by the Criminal Justice and Public Order Act 1994, s 27.

[325]   Inserted by the Criminal Justice Act 2003, s 28, Sch 2, paras 1, 6.

[326]   Inserted by the Criminal Justice and Public Order Act 1994, Sch 3. For the procedure, see the Criminal Procedure Rules 2005, rule 19.1.

[327]   Amended by the Criminal Justice and Public Order Act 1994, Part II, s 30. For the procedure, see the Criminal Procedure Rules 2005, rule 19.2.

on information which was not available to the police or court which made the original decision. Separately, where a magistrates' court has granted bail to a person charged with an imprisonable offence, and the prosecution opposed bail, the prosecution may then appeal to the Crown Court against the grant of bail (Bail (Amendment) Act 1993, s 1(1)[328]).

Applications to vary bail conditions after first court hearing

Where a defendant has already been granted bail by a court, on an application by either the defence or prosecution, a later court may vary existing bail conditions or impose bail conditions where bail had been granted unconditionally (Bail Act 1976, s 3(8)(a) and (b)). **7.161**

Appeals against bail conditions, from a magistrates' court to the Crown Court

By virtue of s 16 of the Criminal Justice Act 2003 a defendant can appeal to the Crown Court against bail conditions in limited circumstances: **7.162**

- only against certain bail conditions (eg residence, curfew, not to contact someone else, s 16(3));
- at the stages of magistrates' court proceedings specified in s 16(1), which apply mainly to offences triable either way or only on indictment; and
- only after an application to the magistrates' court has already been made, by the defendant (under s 3(8)(a) above) or by the prosecution (s 3(8)(b), above or s 5B(1), above).

Renewed applications for bail to the same court

Where a defendant has been refused bail, under s 4(1) above, the court has a duty to consider, at each subsequent hearing, whether he ought to be granted bail (Bail Act 1976, Schedule 1, Part IIA, paragraphs 1–3[329]). At the first hearing after that at which the court decided not to grant bail, the defendant may support a renewed application for bail with any arguments—as to fact or law—that he desires (whether or not he has advanced that argument previously). At subsequent hearings the court need not hear arguments as to fact or law which it has heard previously. A defendant will therefore need, before the court will entertain a further bail application, to persuade the court that there has been a material change of circumstances or that there are circumstances which had not already been brought to the court's attention.[330] European Convention authority suggests that the mere passage of time requires the court actively to reconsider a defendant's bail position in order to comply with Article 5(3).[331] **7.163**

---

[328] See s 1(4), (5), and (7). For the procedures, see the Criminal Procedure Rules 2005, rules 19.16 and 19.17. See *R v Isleworth Crown Court, ex p Clarke* [1998] 1 Cr App R 257.
[329] Added by the Criminal Justice Act 1988, s 154.
[330] *R v Nottingham Justices ex p Davies* [1981] QB 38, DC; *In re Moles* [1981] Crim LR 170.
[331] *Bezicheri v Italy* (1990) 12 EHRR 210, para 21: 'an interval of one month is not unreasonable'. See also Law Commission 'Guidance for bail decision-takers and their advisers', paras 34–36. Also *Aquilina v Malta* (2000) 29 EHRR 185, para 49.

Appeals against refusals of bail by a magistrates' court to the Crown Court

7.164 A defendant can appeal to the Crown Court against the refusal of bail by a magistrates' court (Supreme Court Act 1981, s 81(1)(g)). This application can only be made if the magistrates' court has issued a full argument certificate under s 5(6A) of the Bail Act 1976[332] (Supreme Court Act 1981, s 81(1J))[333].

Appeals to the High Court

7.165 The inherent power of the High Court to entertain an application for bail from the magistrates' court has been abolished (Criminal Justice Act 2003, s 17(2) and (3)). This does not affect any right a person may have to apply for a writ of habeas corpus or any other prerogative remedy (s 17(6)(b)[334]). Nor does it affect the High Court's power to consider a judicial review of a decision about bail at an early stage of criminal proceedings. But this is a jurisdiction which is limited to a challenge that a refusal of bail or the imposition of conditional bail is unlawful, without jurisdiction or *Wednesbury* unreasonable.[335] In *R (M) v Isleworth CC*, Maurice Kay LJ in the Divisional Court[336] confirmed that these decisions do not fall within the definition of 'matters relating to trial on indictment', which are excluded from judicial review by Supreme Court Act 1981, s 29(3).[337] However, 'it is a jurisdiction which [the court] should exercise very sparingly indeed. It would be ironic and retrograde if, having abolished a relatively short and simple remedy on the basis that it amounted to wasteful duplication, Parliament has, by a side wind, created a more protracted and expensive remedy of common application . . . The test must be on *Wednesbury* principles, but robustly applied.'[338] Arguably, where Convention rights are in play, the principles should be applied less robustly.

---

[332] Inserted by the Criminal Justice Act 1982, s 60(3), subsequently further amended.

[333] Amended by the Criminal Justice Act 1982, s 60(1)(b). See also the Criminal Procedure Rules 2005, rule 19.10, for full argument certificates from magistrates' courts. For the procedures, see rule 19.18. See also, in the Crown Court, Supreme Court Act 1981, s 81(1)(a).

[334] Confirmed in *R (on the application of M) v Isleworth Crown Court* [2005] EWHC 363 (Admin), para 9. For an example of a successful application for habeas corpus see *Remice v HMP Belmarsh* [2007] Crim LR 796 and for the use of habeas corpus to challenge a refusal of bail as an abuse of process, see *R (Hauschildt) v Highbury Corner Magistrates Court* [2009] Crim LR 512.

[335] See the Supreme Court Act 1981, s 31; CPR Part 54. See generally M Fordham, *The Judicial Review Handbook* (2008, 5th edn).

[336] [2005] EWHC 363 (Admin), para 7.

[337] See Ch 9.

[338] *R (M) v Isleworth CC*, paras 11–12.

8

DEFENCES OF EXCUSE AND JUSTIFICATION

A. **Introduction**	8.01	The meaning of property	8.95
B. **General Principles**	8.03	The meaning of 'damage'	8.99
Reasonableness	8.05	Belief in consent	8.103
Burden of proof	8.24	Subjective belief	8.106
C. **The Prevention of Crime**	8.33	Remoteness: 'in order to protect' and	
The use of 'force'	8.36	'immediate need'	8.110
'The prevention of crime'	8.56	E. **Necessity/Duress of Circumstances**	8.124
'Such force as is reasonable in the		A single defence?	8.124
circumstances'	8.64	Duress of circumstances: definition	8.136
Remoteness	8.86	Persons for whom the defendant has	
D. **The Protection of Property**	8.89	responsibility	8.140
The common law	8.89	Mixed test: subjective but reasonable belief	8.148
Lawful excuse: Criminal Damage Act		Death or serious injury	8.158
1971, s 5	8.91	F. **Acting in the Public Interest**	8.161

A. Introduction

This chapter examines the extent to which a person whose conduct would otherwise be **8.01** characterized as criminal may be relieved of liability on the basis of a lawful justification or excuse.[1,2]

We consider in turn the following aspects: **8.02**

B. General Principles
C. The Prevention of Crime
D. The Protection of Property
E. Necessity/Duress of Circumstances
F. Acting in the Public Interest

---

[1] This chapter does not address justifications arising from guaranteed rights under the European Convention on Human Rights. These are considered separately in detail in Ch 10.
[2] There is considerable academic and judicial disagreement as to whether, taken together or individually, the various 'defences' are properly described as justifications or excuses. For ease of reference, we describe them all as 'defences'. (See 8.24 further.)

B. General Principles

8.03 The common law developed rules to accommodate the moral principle that it may be defensible in limited circumstances to do what would otherwise be unlawful in order to prevent a greater 'evil' being caused to oneself, to others, or to property.

8.04 Some of those principles now have statutory embodiment—for example, the use of force in the prevention of crime is governed by s 3 of the Criminal law Act 1967 and the causing of damage in order to protect property is principally governed by s 5 of the Criminal Damage Act 1971; in other respects common law rules continue to evolve as legal works in progress as seen in the development of duress of circumstances or necessity and, rather less certainly, in notions of a public interest defence.

Reasonableness

General

8.05 The pivotal legal condition that tends to determine upon which side of the criminal threshold the conduct falls is the 'reasonableness' of the person's behaviour judged against all the circumstances. It is the common denominator in most of the defences discussed in this chapter. Below we consider the place of 'reasonableness' in the context of each defence in turn.

8.06 A significant exception is the statutory version of the 'defence of property' defence in s 5(2) of the Criminal Law Act 1971. Where a person damages or intends to damage property in order to protect other property, no criminal damage offence is committed if he or she 'believed . . . that the means of protection adopted . . . were or would be reasonable having regard to all the circumstances' (see 8.106 below). It follows that the test here is simply whether the defendant genuinely believed that his or her actions were reasonable in the circumstances and not whether they were, in fact, reasonable.[3]

8.07 That apart, reasonableness is an objective standard to be determined as a matter of fact by the tribunal of fact—in indictable cases, by the jury as a body representing the corporate good sense of the community as a whole and in summary cases, by the magistrates or District Judge.

8.08 There is no statutory definition of 'reasonable'. It is not a term of art and is to be given its ordinary and natural meaning. Nor is there any formulaic legal answer to the question of what is reasonable conduct in a given case. The issue has to be determined with regard to the circumstances which will, in turn, vary considerably from case to case.

8.09 Thus, in relation to the proposed prevention of crime provision in s 3 of the Criminal Law Act 1967 (see 8.33 below), the Criminal Law Revision Committee suggested:

> The court, in considering what was reasonable force, would take into account all the circumstances , including in particular the nature and degree of forced used, the seriousness of the

---

[3] See *Jones* [2003] EWCA Crim 894.

evil to be prevented and the possibility of preventing it by other means; but there is no need to specify in the clause the criteria for deciding the question.[4]

The principal general consideration is proportionality—in other words, a favourable bal- **8.10** ance between the actual or intended consequences of a person's conduct and the seriousness and imminence of the threat or damage that he or she seeks to prevent—'the greater evil'.

Subjective belief in the circumstances

Notwithstanding that the final arbiter of reasonableness is the tribunal of fact (save for the **8.11** defence under s 5 of the Criminal Damage Act 1971), the defendant's own honestly-held beliefs as to the circumstances may be highly relevant. As a proposition of settled legal principle, the phrase 'reasonable in the circumstances' means 'in the circumstances as the defendant genuinely believed them to be' and not 'in the circumstances as they were in fact'.[5] Thus, the circumstances *as the defendant genuinely believed them to be* will tend to set the factual background against which the tribunal of fact has to gauge the reasonableness of the defendant's actions.

Note, however, that, unlike the other defences considered in this chapter, duress of circum- **8.12** stances or necessity, while allowing a defendant to rely upon a mistaken belief, nevertheless requires that the mistaken belief should be reasonable in the circumstances.

Putting this all together, although the general principle applies to all of these defences, its **8.13** precise legal function varies according to the particular ingredients of the defence. The spectrum ranges from the almost complete subjectivity of s 5 of the 1971 Act (where the sole issue is whether or not the defendant believed that his or her actions were reason- able in the circumstances), through s 3 of the Criminal Law Act 1967 (where the issue is whether his or her actions were, in fact, reasonable in the circumstances as he or she believed them to be), to 'the predominantly, but not entirely, objective test'[6] for duress of circum- stances which additionally requires that his or her beliefs in the circumstances were reasonable.

Below we consider in greater detail the function of subjective beliefs in relation to each **8.14** form of defence in turn.

Relevance of the actual circumstances

The subjectivity principle has profound practical implications for the conduct of a trial. **8.15** It is invariably contended by the prosecution that it must follow that, as the only legally relevant circumstances are those genuinely believed by the defendant to exist, then the actual circumstances are irrelevant.

Accordingly, it is argued that defence evidence of the actual circumstances has no relevance **8.16** either. In this respect, there has been no consistent approach in first instance trials—thus, for example, expert scientific evidence of the dangers of GM crops[7] or of the damage caused

---

[4] Cmnd 2659, para 23.
[5] See, for example, *B (a minor) v DPP* [2002] AC 428; *K* [2001] 3 WLR 471.
[6] *Safi* [2004] 1 Cr App R 157.
[7] *Ayliffe et al*, Cardiff CC, September 2005.

by cluster bombs[8] has been excluded, whereas evidence of the local effects of climate change has been admitted where the object of the action had been to prevent carbon discharge into the atmosphere.[9]

8.17 The point has never been fully litigated and there are arguments to the contrary. To take the example of the prevention of crime defence under s 3 of the Criminal Law Act 1967, the section simply requires the force to be 'reasonable in the circumstances'. There is nothing in the language of the section that precludes a defendant from asserting not only that his conduct was reasonable in the circumstances as he believed them to be, but also that his conduct was reasonable as a matter of fact.

8.18 While in many cases that go to trial the sincerity of the defendants' beliefs is so apparent that it is frequently conceded by the prosecution, there is rarely any concession that those beliefs were well-founded in fact and, by definition, it is never conceded that the defendants' actions were a reasonable and proportionate response. This is frequently the central issue in the case and, it is arguable that, in order to make that judgement, the jury must be entitled to consider any objective evidence on the point.

8.19 Similarly, the prosecution may assert that the defendants' actions were merely a 'publicity stunt', thereby challenging the genuineness of the defence claim that they believed that they had no choice but to act as they did. Again, the objective correctness of the defendants' belief in the circumstances may be relevant in establishing the integrity of their actions.

8.20 Conversely, however, this approach comes at a cost to the prosecution because the defendant is, in turn, saved from any legal or evidential need to establish the correctness of his or her beliefs. Nor is the prosecution entitled to call evidence that the circumstances are other than as believed by the defendant—for example, that cluster bombs do *not* cause indiscriminate injuries.

8.21 Thus, assuming that the sincerity of the defendant is not in issue, the jury must be directed that they must approach the reasonableness of his or her actions on the basis that what he or she genuinely believed to have been the circumstances were, in fact, the circumstances.

8.22 Moreover, in establishing the nature and sincerity of his or her beliefs as to the circumstances, a defendant may be entitled to rely upon the hearsay provisions of the Criminal Justice Act 2003 to give evidence of the contents of the information—for example, scientific data or news reports—that led him/her to the belief that the circumstances are as claimed.

8.23 Evidence of the objective circumstances *will* be irrelevant if those circumstances were unknown to the defendant at the material time and did not, therefore, inform his or her belief that a crime was to be committed.

---

[8] *Olditch and Pritchard,* Bristol CC, April 2007.
[9] *Hewke et al,* Maidstone CC, Sept 2008.

Burden of proof

There is no general defence of 'justification' in English law. The various justifications or **8.24** excuses discussed in this chapter do not all proceed from the same legal foundations and classicists can correctly point out that not all of them amount to 'defences' in the strictest technical sense.

In some instances, the wording of the offence itself includes a particular exemption or **8.25** 'excuse' that the prosecution must exclude in order for the offence to be made out. For example, the principal offences under the Criminal Damage Act 1971 all include the requirement that the damage was caused or was to be caused 'without lawful excuse'.

On the other hand, common law concepts such as duress of circumstances/necessity,[10] **8.26** amount to independent, general defences to most criminal offences and do not operate to negative any particular legal ingredient of the charge. As Lord Wilberforce stated in *Director of Public Prosecutions for Northern Ireland v Lynch*[11] (a case of duress by threats): '(Duress) is something which is superimposed upon the other ingredients which would by themselves make up an offence'.

Lastly, the 'defence' may arise naturally out of the general rule that the prosecution carry **8.27** the legal burden of proving all the necessary constituent elements of an offence.[12] By way of illustration, for any assault to be a crime, it must be unlawful and where, for example, lawful self defence or the prevention of crime is relied upon, 'it is quite essential that the jury should understand that the issue is not properly to be regarded as a defence . . . but a matter which the prosecution must disprove as an essential part of their case'.[13]

In *Bayer*[14] it was stated that: **8.28**

> A person will not however commit a crime if he or she was or may have been lawfully justified in acting in the way complained of. Many statutes contain words like 'unlawfully' or 'without lawful excuse' in order to give a warning about the application of this principle. The principle, however, will be applied even if these words are omitted, because the defendant will lack the necessary *mens rea* (except in relation to offences of strict liability).
>
> This was made clear by Lawton LJ in *Renouf* (1986),[15] in which the Court of Appeal ruled that the statutory defence set out in section 3(1) of the Criminal Law Act 1967 ('a person may use such force as is reasonable in the circumstances . . . in effecting or assisting in the lawful arrest of offenders or suspected offenders') was available against a charge of reckless driving. In that case the defendant had used his car to chase some people who had assaulted him and had so manoeuvred his car as to prevent their escape. Lawton LJ said: ' . . . It is no answer for

---

[10] Also now regarded as a legal excuse rather than as a justification: *Hasan (Z)* [2005] AC 2 AC 467 Per Lord Bingham, para 18; For an earlier analysis see: *Hibbert* (1995) 99 CCC (3d) 193; *Attorney General v Whelan* [1934] IR 518, 526; and *Glanville Williams, Criminal Law, The General Part* (1961, 2nd edn) p 755.
[11] [1975] AC 653.
[12] *Woolmington v DPP* [1935] AC 462. Unless a statutory exception (or insanity) applies, in which case the burden lies upon the defence.
[13] *Wheeler* [1967] 3 All ER 829; See also *Lobell* [1957] 1 QB 547, *Abraham* [1973] 1 WLR 1270. In relation to s 3 defences generally see *Cameron* [1973] Crim LR 520; *Khan* [1995] Crim LR 78; *O'Brien* [2004] EWCA Crim 2900.
[14] [2003] EWHC 2567 (Admin).
[15] [1986] 2 All ER 449.

the prosecution to submit, as counsel for the Crown did, that the wording of ss 1 and 2 of the Road Traffic Act 1972 shuts out any possibility of such a defence because they contained no words such as "lawful excuse". Nor does s 20 of the Offences Against the Person Act 1861; but s 3(1) has been used to provide a defence to charges under that section.'[16]

8.29 Whatever the merits of that debate[17] and the correct juridical path, there is one common principle—where these defences, as we term them, are raised, the burden of disproving them to the criminal standard of proof lies on the prosecution throughout.

8.30 It does not follow, however, that in every single case the prosecution must necessarily prove, for example, that there was no duress of circumstances or that any force used was not reasonable in the prevention of crime and so on. As a basic rule, there must at least be *some* evidence supporting the defence before the prosecution have to take up the burden of disproving it. This is described as an 'evidential burden' on the defendant to raise the issue.

8.31 Where there is simply no evidence supporting the defence, the judge is entitled to withdraw the case from the jury.[18] Some dicta go so far as to suggest that in these situations, such a defence can only be raised by the defendant giving evidence:

> Before this defence can leave the ground, it is necessary in our judgement for the defendant to assert in his evidence, and not merely through the mouth of his counsel and not merely through a defence statement, that that was his state of mind.[19]

8.32 However, this is not necessarily so. The general legal rule is that the evidential burden can be discharged by relevant evidence from any admissible source.[20] Thus, admissible out of court statements, including answers made by a defendant in police interviews, may provide sufficient evidence of his or her beliefs and intentions. Sometimes, activists may be in possession of written material that sets out the reasons for their actions. In *Olditch and Pritchard*[21] two men who had attempted to damage American B52 bombers had with them on arrest a videotape in which they expounded their reasons for so doing.

C. The Prevention of Crime

8.33 Section 3(1) of the *Criminal Law Act* 1967 provides that:

> A person may use such force as is reasonable in the circumstances in the prevention of crime, or in effecting or assisting in the lawful arrest of offenders or suspected offenders unlawfully at large.[22]

---

[16] As to the argument that 'unlawful' can be implied as a legal element in all offences, the observations of Hodgson J in *Albert v Lavin* 72 Cr App R 178 ('In defining a criminal offence the word "unlawful" is tautologous and adds nothing to its essential ingredients') have been disapproved in *Kimber* 77 Cr App R 225 and *Williams (G)* 78 Cr App R 276.

[17] 'In the end all classifications are somewhat artificial and are really made for convenience and ease of understanding and exposition': *Blackstone's Criminal Practice* (2009), A3.20.

[18] *Hill* (1988) 89 Cr App R 74; *Pommell* [1995] 2 Cr App R 607.

[19] *Jones* [2003] EWCA Crim 894 per Buxton LJ, para 14.

[20] *Bullard v R* [1957] AC 635, HL.

[21] Bristol CC, April 2007.

[22] The second limb of the section, covering the use of force in the arrest of offenders unlawfully at large, falls outside the scope of this work and is not considered further.

The subsection states a rule of both criminal and civil law. It replaces 'the rules of the common law on the question when force used for a purpose mentioned in the subsection is justified for that purpose' (s 3(2)) (See 8.42 below). **8.34**

The defence is a general one and applies whether or not the offence charged expressly includes terms such as 'unlawfully' or 'without lawful excuse'.[23] **8.35**

The use of 'force'

Taken literally, s 3 excuses only the use of 'force' and there remains some controversy as to whether it can be invoked as a defence where the conduct comprised in the charge does not involve the application of force to the person or to property—for example, where there has been a peaceable trespass or the cutting of a security wire at a military base or the painting of a building. **8.36**

In *Blake v DPP*[24] a clergyman protester against the first Iraq war had written a biblical quotation with a felt pen on a concrete pillar near the Houses of Parliament. Charged with criminal damage, his defence under s 3 failed on the basis, inter alia, that his conduct was 'insufficient to amount to the use of force within the section'. **8.37**

'Force' is not a term of art and is to be given its ordinary and natural meaning in keeping with basic rules of statutory construction. In *Renouf*[25] the defendant had used his car to chase some people who had assaulted him. He edged their car onto a grass verge and manoeuvred his car as to prevent their escape. It was held that s 3 could afford a defence to a charge of reckless driving: 'the word "force" is one of ordinary usage in English and does not require judicial interpretation'. **8.38**

Definitions of 'force' in the *Shorter Oxford English Dictionary* include 'physical strength; strength, impetus, violence or intensity of effort; power or might; physical strength or power exerted upon an object *esp* violence or physical coercion' and, pertinently, 'in relation to law: "unlawful violence offered to persons or things"'. **8.39**

Those definitions, particularly the last, appear wide enough to encompass force applied towards property as well as towards the person. We speak, for example, of 'forcing' a door or window open. **8.40**

Even so, there are obiter remarks in some of the cases that suggest that the section should itself be confined to the use of force to the person because force applied in the protection of property is separately catered for as a 'reasonable excuse' for criminal damage under s 5 of the Criminal Damage Act 1971. Such reasoning is difficult to follow. Firstly, s 5 provides a 'lawful excuse' for causing or planning criminal damage but does not purport to cater for 'force' applied to property which causes no damage. **8.41**

---

[23] See, for example, *Renouf* [1986] 1 WLR 522; *Bayer v DPP* [2003] EWHC 2567 (Admin); *Rothwell* [1993] Crim LR 626.
[24] [1993] Crim LR 586.
[25] [1986] 1 WLR 522.

8.42   Secondly, although the common law rules permitting the use of force grew haphazardly and have been described as 'both complex and uncertain',[26] the common law certainly recognized that reasonable force directed at the person and force applied to property were both permissible in the prevention of crime.[27] Moreover, there is nothing in the language of s 3 that creates any distinction between person and property.

8.43   Even so, in *Hutchinson v Newbury Magistrates' Court*,[28] Buxton LJ understood, without apparently referring to authority, that 'section 3 was introduced to deal with physical force to the person. It does not contemplate damage of the present type.' In that case the veteran campaigner, Jean Hutchinson, had caused £2,500 worth of damage by cutting at the perimeter fence of the Atomic Weapons Establishment, Aldermaston.[29]

8.44   Six years later, in *Jones and Milling*,[30] the House of Lords considered the ambit of s 3 in the context of direct action against the second Iraqi war. The appellants had variously obstructed operations at Marchwood Port, Southampton Water by chaining themselves to gates, painting, and attaching themselves to tanks, and by cutting fences, or interfering with security at RAF Croughton in Northamptonshire, and RAF Fairford in Gloucestershire. Lord Bingham expressed 'some doubt whether s 3 was ever intended to apply to conduct like the appellants' which, although causing damage to property in some cases, was entirely peaceable and involved no violence of any kind to any person' (paragraph 25).

8.45   Lord Hoffmann preferred to 'pass over the question of whether damaging property counts as the use of force within the meaning of section 3 . . . There is much to be said for the view that offences against property have their own provisions for justification, such as "reasonable excuse" as defined in section 5 of the 1971 Act and that "force" in section 3 means force against persons committing crimes . . . But I am willing to assume for the sake of argument that chaining oneself to railings or putting sugar into the petrol tanks of lorries involves the use of force for the purposes of section 3' (paragraph 71).

8.46   However, the point was never formally resolved in *Jones and Milling* as the prosecution had not raised the issue below and 'this question of interpretation was not the subject of appeal and it has not been fully investigated'. Moreover, Lord Bingham also acknowledged that there was some authority that could support an argument that what the appellants did or intended to do amounted to force.

8.47   Those authorities begin with *Robinson*[31] in which a group of squatters had barricaded themselves into premises. However, when the police entered in order to enforce a possession order, 'no sort of physical resistance was offered' and 'possession was obtained without any fighting or use of individual force'. They were charged with 'conspiracy to contravene

---

[26]   D Ormerod, *Smith and Hogan Criminal Law* (2008, 12th edn) p 364.
[27]   See, for example, *Hale, Pleas of the Crown*, Vol 1, Ch 8; *Blackstone, Laws of England*, Book 3, Ch 1; Stephen, *Digest of the Criminal Law*, Art 306; *Hanway v Boultbee* (1830) 1 M and Rob 15; *R v Rose* (1847) 2 Cox 329; *Bayer v DPP* [2003] EWHC 2567 Admin.
[28]   (2000) 122 ILR 499, 508.
[29]   She failed in her stated aim to exceed the £5,000 threshold that would have entitled her to jury trial.
[30]   [2007] 1 AC 136.
[31]   [1970] 3 All ER 369.

the Forcible Entry Act 1429', inter alia, by 'holding the said land and premises in a forcible manner, to wit with a strong hand and with a multitude of people'. The trial judge had directed the jury that if the premises had been 'barricaded up so that it required force to get in, then that would be the use of force—passive force, you may think, but nonetheless force'. That direction was guardedly upheld by the Court of Appeal:[32]

> We would not be prepared to state as a simple and bare proposition of law that any barricading of the premises which caused the true owner to use force in removing the barricades necessarily amounted to the use of force in retention. So much would depend on the facts in each individual case . . . because, if one was not careful, a proposition stated in those words might reach the almost ridiculous conclusion that a tenant who merely turned the key in the lock and thus caused the landlord to break in, breaking down the doors, would himself be using force to retain property from the landlord.

In *Swales v Cox*[33] police officers had chased a suspect to the respondent's house. They tried to **8.48** open the door in order to enter in the purported exercise of their power under s 2(6) of the Criminal Law Act 1967 to 'enter (if need be by force)' for the purpose of making an arrest. Initially, they were prevented from doing so by the suspect who held the door from the inside. He let go and the officers then entered. The Divisional Court held that the word 'force' in the context of the 1967 Act (and, it follows, in the context of s 3) means the application of 'any energy to an obstacle with a view to removing it'. In the case of a door, 'force' was used if the door was open and it was necessary to use energy to open it further or, if the door was closed, and the handle was turned from the outside and the door was eased open.

In *R v Chief Constable of Devon and Cornwall ex p Central Electricity Board*[34] protesters had **8.49** occupied land which the Board wished to survey for the purposes of building a nuclear power station. They acted peaceably but intended to obstruct the survey by prostrating themselves in front of the Board's machinery. The Court of Appeal reviewed the refusal of the Chief Constable to intervene and remove them. In a famous judgment, Lord Denning MR found on those facts that their conduct amounted firstly to a breach of the peace:

> I think that the conduct of these people, their criminal obstruction, is itself a breach of the peace. There is a breach of the peace whenever a person who is lawfully carrying out his work is unlawfully and physically prevented by another from doing it. He is entitled by law peacefully to go on with his work on his lawful occasions. If anyone unlawfully and physically obstructs the worker—by lying down or chaining himself to a rig or the like—he is guilty of a breach of the peace . . . [35]

---

[32] The Court relied upon *Russell on Crime* (1964, 12th edn) vol 1, p 286 and *Milner v Maclean* (1825) 2 C & P 17, 18 : 'In this case there was, it is true, no one assaulted, nor is it necessary that there should be, to constitute a forcible entry; for, if persons either take or keep possession of either house or land, with such number of persons, and show of force, as is calculated to deter the rightful owner from sending them away, and resuming his own possession, that is sufficient in point of law to constitute a forcible entry, or a forcible detainer.'
[33] [1981] QB 849.
[34] [1982] 1 QB 458.
[35] For breach of the peace see 6.125.

8.50 However, Lord Denning went on to hold that their conduct also amounted to an unlawful assembly (as then defined) under common law. The importance of the ruling for present purposes is the clear implication that peaceable obstruction can amount to the use of force:

> The old authorities, going back to Coke, Blackstone, Stephen and Archbold, all say that an unlawful assembly is an assembly of three or more persons *with intent to commit a crime by open force*. I think this case comes within that statement and I think it is still the law. But I need not go into it further, in view of my holding that their conduct is also a breach of the peace.

8.51 Pausing there, it would certainly seem perverse if the defence in the 1967 Act operates only to excuse someone who uses physical force in the prevention of crime but not someone who uses something less than force for the same purpose. It may be that the answer to the paradox lies in the parallel continued existence of common law rules. As noted above, s 3(2) of the 1967 Act abolishes 'the rules of the common law on the question when force used . . . is justified'. By necessary implication, however, the subsection leaves untouched the rules of the common law 'on the question' when something less than force is justified.

8.52 The common law allowed 'a general liberty between strangers to prevent a felony': *Duffy*.[36] It surely follows that, if the common law went so far as to tolerate the use of force in the prevention of crime, modern interpretation would allow proportionate action falling short of force.

8.53 In *Bayer v DPP*[37] the Divisional Court confronted common law principles which, although concerned in that case with the protection of property, would appear to apply equally to the prevention of crime. The defendants had been charged with aggravated trespass.[38] They had attached themselves to a tractor that was drilling GM maize seeds as part of a licensed government trial. They could not rely upon the prevention of crime defence under s 3 of the 1967 Act as the licensed trial did not amount to a crime. Nor could there be any 'lawful excuse' for criminal damage under s 5 of the Criminal Damage Act 1971 as they themselves had caused no damage. Their defence relied instead on the common law and 'the defence of property'—namely, 'nature, crops and domestic animals . . . in close proximity to the site'. They maintained that the test to be applied was whether their actions were 'reasonable in all the circumstances'. They failed because the court held that the common law defence could only arise where the property was threatened by an unlawful or criminal act. However, Brooke LJ stated:

> It is a principle of the common law that a person may use a proportionate degree of force to defend himself, or others, from attack or the threat of imminent attack, or to defend his property or the property of others in the same circumstances . . .
>
> Although no authority directly in point was quoted to us, we are prepared to assume for the purposes of this judgment that when the respondents tied themselves to the tractors in Horselynch Plantation they were using force . . . If in the circumstances as they believed them to be they thought that unlawful damage was being inflicted or was about to be inflicted on

---

[36] [1967] 1 QB 63.
[37] [2003] EWHC 2567 (Admin).
[38] For aggravated trespass see 5.47.

the property of another, then it is hard to understand why the defence should not be available if they prevented the damage by tying themselves to the tractors rather than by attacking the tractor drivers.

The authors suggest (a) that 'force' within the meaning of s 3 includes force applied to **8.54** person or property; (b) that 'force' can include the application of energy to an object; and (c) that the common law may permit reasonable action falling short of force in the prevention of crime.

In practice, prosecutors tend to adopt a flexible approach. In *Ayliffe and Others*,[39] Greenpeace **8.55** activists charged with public nuisance had peaceably boarded a GM cattlefeed tanker and peaceably positioned themselves on the rudder and rigging so that the ship could not safely move. They remained until removed by the police. No point was taken that this was not capable of amounting to force. Similarly, the point was not raised in the trial of *Olditch and Pritchard*[40] where two men had cut through fencing at RAF Fairford—albeit with the intention of damaging B52 bombers if they had been able to reach them.

'The prevention of crime'

A clearer limitation on the operation of the section is that the force must be used only **8.56** 'in the prevention of crime'—that is to prevent a criminal offence punishable under the domestic law of England and Wales.

The preliminary question answered negatively by the House of Lords in *Jones and Milling* **8.57** (above)[41] was whether a war of aggression contrary to International Law is 'capable of being a "crime" within the meaning of section 3 of the Criminal Law Act 1967 and if so is the issue justiciable in a criminal trial?'

The conjoined appeals in *Jones and Milling* all involved direct action aimed at preventing **8.58** the commencement of the invasion of Iraq. In each case, the defendants maintained that their actions were justified under s 3 on the basis that they acted to prevent crime—namely a war of aggression contrary to International Law. While the House accepted that the crimes of planning, preparation, and waging of an aggressive war are established in customary international law, it rejected the argument that they have been assimilated into 'entirely domestic' law and, therefore, that s 3 had any application.

However, certain specified war crimes are triable in the domestic courts, for example, under **8.59** the International Criminal Court Act 2001 and are, therefore, crimes for the purposes of s 3. Grigson J so found in one of the cases below[42] and his finding was not appealed to the House of Lords by the prosecution. In due course in subsequent trials, some of the appellants in *Jones and Milling* were able (successfully) to justify their conduct on the basis that their intention was to prevent such war crimes.

---

[39] Cardiff CC, September 2005.
[40] Bristol CC, April 2007.
[41] [2007] 1 AC 136.
[42] *Olditch and Pritchard*, Bristol CC, 12 May 2004.

8.60 This is because the 2001 Act[43] translated certain war crimes under the Rome Statute of the International Criminal Court (1998) into offences punishable in the domestic courts. These do not include a war of aggression but it is an offence 'for a person to commit genocide, a crime against humanity or a war crime' where the acts are committed in England or Wales or 'outside the UK by a UK national, a UK resident or a person subject to UK service jurisdiction'.[44]

8.61 There are two categories of war crimes under the 2001 Act: 'grave breaches of the Geneva Conventions' and 'other serious violations of the laws and customs applicable in international armed conflict, within the established framework of international law.'[45] A number of prohibited acts are listed:

(a) extensive destruction and appropriation of property, not justified by military necessity and carried out unlawfully and wantonly;

(b) intentionally directing attacks against the civilian population as such or against individual civilians not taking part in hostilities;

(c) intentionally directing attacks against civilian objects, that is, objects which are not military objectives;

(d) intentionally launching an attack in the knowledge that such attack will cause incidental loss of life or injury to civilians, or damage to civilian objects, or widespread, long-term and severe damage to the natural environment which would clearly be excessive in relation to the concrete and direct overall military advantage anticipated;

(e) attacking or bombarding, by whatever means, towns, villages, dwellings or buildings which are undefended and which are not military objectives;

(f) destroying or seizing the enemy's property unless such destruction or seizure be imperatively demanded by the necessities of war.

8.62 Grave breaches of the Geneva Conventions are also punishable in this country under the Geneva Conventions Act 1957; the Geneva Conventions (Amendment) Act 1995; and the Genocide Act 1969.[46]

8.63 However, elsewhere on the spectrum of political protest, the application of s 3 may be severely limited. It would seem, for example, that direct action aimed at properly licensed abortion clinics or properly licensed animal laboratories could not be legally justified under s 3 unless the activities therein could be shown to be otherwise criminal.

'Such force as is reasonable in the circumstances'

The Criminal Justice and Immigration Act 2008

8.64 No doubt in response to the media focus on the perceived shortcomings of the law relating to self-defence following notorious cases such as *Martin (DP)*[47] (in which the defendant

---

[43] The Act came into force on the 1 September 2001 and applies to specified war crimes committed after 1 July 2001 by nationals of the States that have ratified the Rome Statute of the International Criminal Court.

[44] International Criminal Court Act 2001, s 51.

[45] Ibid, Sch 8, s 2.

[46] See also the Criminal Justice Act 1988, War Crimes Act 1991, Merchant Shipping, and Maritime Security Act 1997.

[47] [2000] 2 Cr App R 42.

was initially convicted of the murder of a burglar by shooting), s 76 of the Criminal Justice and Immigration Act 2008 was passed 'to clarify the operation of the existing defences'[48] of both self-defence and the prevention of crime under s 3 of the Criminal Law Act 1967. The section does not appear to have attempted to change the law in any respect. Accordingly, it represents a useful summary of the relevant principles.[49]

It is worth quoting s 76 in full: **8.65**

(1) This section applies where in proceedings for an offence—

   (a) an issue arises as to whether a person charged with the offence ('D') is entitled to rely on a defence within subsection (2), and

   (b) the question arises whether the degree of force used by D against a person ('V') was reasonable in the circumstances.

(2) The defences are—

   (a) the common law defence of self-defence; and

   (b) the defence(s) provided by section 3(1) of the Criminal Law Act 1967 . . .

(3) The question whether the degree of force used by D was reasonable in the circumstances is to be decided by reference to the circumstances as D believed them to be, and subsections (4) to (8) also apply in connection with deciding that question.

(4) If D claims to have held a particular belief as regards the existence of any circumstances—

   (a) the reasonableness or otherwise of that belief is relevant to the question whether D genuinely held it; but

   (b) if it is determined that D did genuinely hold it, D is entitled to rely on it for the purposes of subsection (3), whether or not—

     (i) it was mistaken, or

     (ii) (if it was mistaken) the mistake was a reasonable one to have made.

(5) But subsection (4)(b) does not enable D to rely on any mistaken belief attributable to intoxication that was voluntarily induced.

(6) The degree of force used by D is not to be regarded as having been reasonable in the circumstances as D believed them to be if it was disproportionate in those circumstances.

(7) In deciding the question mentioned in subsection (3) the following considerations are to be taken into account (so far as relevant in the circumstances of the case)—

   (a) that a person acting for a legitimate purpose may not be able to weigh to a nicety the exact measure of any necessary action; and

   (b) that evidence of a person's having only done what the person honestly and instinctively thought was necessary for a legitimate purpose constitutes strong evidence that only reasonable action was taken by that person for that purpose.[50]

---

[48] Criminal Justice and Immigration Act 2008, s 76(9).

[49] Ibid, s 76 came into force on 14 July 2008: Criminal Justice and Immigration Act 2008 (Commencement No 2 and Transitional Savings Provisions) Order 2008, SI 2008/1586. It applies whenever the offence took place but does not apply in relation to any trial on indictment where arraignment took place before that date or to any summary trial which began before that date: s 148(2) and Sch 27, para 27(1) and (2) of the 2008 Act.

[50] The language of subsec (7) reproduces the famous dictum of Lord Morris in *Palmer v R* [1971] AC 814 (approved in *McInnes* (1971) 55 Cr App R 551). The dictum has been incorporated into the Judicial Studies Board model directions and has become a conventional part of summings-up.

(8) Subsection (7) is not to be read as preventing other matters from being taken into account where they are relevant to deciding the question mentioned in subsection (3).

(9) This section is intended to clarify the operation of the existing defences mentioned in subsection (2).

(10) In this section—

    (a) 'legitimate purpose' means—

        (i) the purpose of self-defence under the common law, or

        (ii) the prevention of crime or effecting or assisting in the lawful arrest of persons mentioned in the provisions referred to in subsection (2)(b);

    (b) references to self-defence include acting in defence of another person;

    and

    (c) references to the degree of force used are to the type and amount of force used.

Subjective belief

8.66 The declaration in s 76(3) of the 2008 Act that 'the question whether the degree of force used by D was reasonable in the circumstances is to be decided by reference to the circumstances as D genuinely believed them to be' expresses a basic common law rule—that the relevant circumstances are those which the defendant subjectively believed to exist, not those that actually existed.

8.67 The rule is reflected in a line of authorities beginning with the seminal decision of the House of Lords in *DPP v Morgan*.[51] It is now settled law that a defendant's mistake of fact will result in acquittal for all crimes that require a specific *mens rea*.[52] In other words, a person lacks the necessary intent to commit an offence if he or she has based his or her actions on a genuine, albeit mistaken, belief in the nature of the circumstances. As liability turns on the genuineness of the belief, not its accuracy, it is immaterial that the belief may be unreasonable.

8.68 The *Morgan* principle has since been applied sequentially to particular legal situations— for example, subjective belief as part of self-defence in *Williams (Gladstone)*[53] and *Beckford*,[54] and in kidnapping and criminal damage in *Baker and Wilkins* per Brooke LJ:[55]

> When a court is required to determine objectively what is reasonable conduct it will necessarily apply the common law test of determining what is reasonable given the actual beliefs and state of mind of the person whose conduct is being judged unless Parliament has indicated a different test.

8.69 However, the circumstances as the defendant believed them to be cannot include a mistaken belief as to the law when the law applicable to the facts is otherwise. Accordingly, a defendant's mistaken conclusion that, in the circumstances as he or she believed them to

[51] [1976] AC 182.
[52] See, for example, D Ormerod, *Smith and Hogan Criminal Law* (2008, 12th edn) p 132.
[53] (1984) 78 Cr App R 276.
[54] [1988] AC 130. See also *Oatridge* (1992) 94 Cr App R 367; *Drane* [2008] EWCA Crim 1746.
[55] CA, 17 October 1996, [1997] Crim LR 497.

be, the activity that he or she was seeking to prevent amounted in law to a crime cannot be relied upon. Per Lord Bingham in *Jones and Milling*:

> It is accepted that the reasonableness of the force used must be judged objectively in the circumstances which the defendant believed to exist, but this belief can extend only to facts and not to the legal consequences or implications of those facts.[56]

The place of the basic principle in the context of direct action and, in particular, in the context of s 3 was reviewed by the House of Lords in *Jones and Milling*.[57] Lord Hoffmann referred to the general reasoning in *Baker and Wilkins* and stated at paragraphs 72–73: **8.70**

> . . . the Court of Appeal decided that in considering whether a defendant was entitled to rely upon section 3, it must be assumed that the events which the defendant apprehended were actually going to happen. Provided that his belief was honest, it did not matter that it was unreasonable. If those events would in law constitute a crime, he was entitled to use such force as was reasonable to prevent it.

> My Lords, I have no difficulty with these propositions. I am willing to assume that, in judging whether the defendant acted reasonably, it must be assumed that the facts were as he honestly believed them to be.

The role of the democratic process: Lord Hoffmann

Trial defences which attempt to justify direct action as a reasonable form of crime prevention inevitably invite comparison with lawful alternatives and, in particular, with the avenues of redress of wrongs provided by the democratic process, law enforcement authorities, and the public courts. **8.71**

These are obvious and proper considerations. The tribunal of fact is required to weigh all the circumstances and is plainly entitled to have regard to the existence of lawful means of preventing crime. **8.72**

However, in *Jones and Milling*,[58] Lord Hoffmann devoted the latter part of his speech to what he termed 'the limits of self-help' in an apparent attempt to disengage the tribunal of fact from the process entirely. The conjoined appellants, as frequently noted in this chapter, were all charged with offences arising from direct action at the commencement of the invasion of Iraq. All relied, inter alia, on s 3. **8.73**

Lord Hoffmann purported to conduct a philosophical analysis of the nature and apparatus of the modern democratic process[59] and appears to have concluded that criminal conduct of this sort should never be characterized as reasonable and, therefore, justified in a 'functioning democratic state'. In such a situation, there can be no evidence capable of supporting a defence that the use of force is reasonable and the judge should prevent the issue from going to the jury. **8.74**

> The crucial question, in my opinion, is whether one judges the reasonableness of the defendant's actions as if he was the sheriff in a Western, the only law man in town, or whether it

---

[56] [2007] 1 AC 136.
[57] Ibid.
[58] Lord Mance expressly associated himself with this part of Lord Hoffmann's speech.
[59] Citing Max Weber (*Politics as a Vocation*, 1918) and Hobbes (*Leviathan*, Ch 13).

should be judged in its actual social setting, in a democratic society with its own appointed agents for the enforcement of the law. . . .[at paragraph 74]

The Court must, in judging what is reasonable, take into account the reason why the state claims the monopoly of the legitimate use of physical force. The tight control of the use of force is necessary to prevent society from sliding into anarchy . . . [at paragraph 77]

Civil disobedience on conscientious grounds has a long and honourable history in this country. People who break the law to affirm their belief in the injustice of a law or government action are sometimes vindicated by history. The suffragettes are an example . . . But there are conventions which are generally accepted by the law-breakers on one side and the law-enforcers on the other. The protestors behave with a sense of proportion and do not cause excessive damage or inconvenience. And they vouch the sincerity of their beliefs by accepting the penalties imposed by the law. The police and prosecutors, on the other hand, behave with restraint and the magistrates impose sentences which take the conscientious motives of the protestors into account. . . . [at paragraph 89]

These appeals and similar cases concerned with controversial activities such as animal experiments, fox hunting, genetically modified crops, nuclear weapons and the like, suggest the emergence of a new phenomenon, namely litigation as the continuation of protest by other means. . . . [at paragraph 90]

The practical implications of what I have been saying for the conduct of the trials of direct action protesters are clear. If there is an issue as to whether the defendants were justified in doing acts which would otherwise be criminal, the burden is upon the prosecution to negative that defence. But the issue must first be raised by facts proved or admitted, either by the prosecution or the defence, on which a jury could find that the acts were justified. In a case in which the defence requires that the acts of the defendant should in all the circumstances have been reasonable, his acts must be considered in the context of a functioning state in which legal disputes can be peacefully submitted to the courts and disputes over what should be law or government policy can be submitted to the arbitrament of the democratic process. *In such circumstances, the apprehension, however honest or reasonable, of acts which are thought to be unlawful or contrary to the public interest, cannot justify the commission of criminal acts and the issue of justification should be withdrawn from the jury.* [at paragraph 94] (emphasis added)

8.75 In the context of the case and the issues in the appeal, Lord Hoffmann's remarks are arguably obiter and were certainly tangential to the certified questions of public importance in the appeal which concerned the justiciability of international crimes in domestic courts. Nevertheless, he plainly intended to restrict this type of defence. Insofar as he could be taken as purporting to declare a principle of general application in such cases, we suggest he may have been wrong in law.

8.76 The underlying rule which Lord Hoffmann invokes is not in doubt: where the defendant bears an evidential burden but there is *no* evidence capable of amounting to the defence as a matter of law, the judge should remove it from the jury (*Wang*[60]).

8.77 However, transposed into the context of s 3 of the Criminal Law Act 1967, the removal of the defence from the jury requires a conclusion that, as a matter of law, there is no evidence upon which a reasonable jury could find that the means adopted by a defendant was reasonable in the circumstances as he or she believed them to be. In practice, that seems to imply that the value judgement of a judge should prevail over that of the lay jury.

---

[60] [2005] 2 Cr App R 8.

Pausing there, one can obviously envisage cases where the evidence is simply not capable of supporting a claim to have acted reasonably. However, others may require more difficult judgements on issues such as proportionality—usually whether the consequences of the use of force outweigh the gravity of the crime that it is sought to prevent. **8.78**

What is or is not 'reasonable' is classically a question of fact for the tribunal of fact. There is no statutory definition but, in all its legal usages, the expression is always taken to mean the standard of conduct to be expected from ordinary, rational individuals—in other words, the qualities supposedly embodied in the twelve individuals who comprise the jury—said to represent 'the corporate good sense of the community'. **8.79**

More significantly, Lord Hoffmann's view that the judge may prefer his or her judgement to that of the jury does not sit easily with Lord Diplock's statement of the basic principle in *Attorney General for Northern Ireland's Reference (No 1 of 1975)*,[61] in which the House of Lords construed the identical terms of s 3(1) of the Criminal Law (Northern Ireland) Act 1967: **8.80**

> There are, however, some classes of offences in which one of the constituent elements of the crime is a failure by the accused to conform to standards of care, of self-control, of caution or of reasoning power to be expected of a 'reasonable man'. In criminal cases tried by jury, the jury represent the reasonable man. That is the justification for the jury system. So in this class of crime it is for the jury, not the judge, to determine whether or not the accused has fallen short of the requisite standard and in doing so it is for them to act on their own opinion as to what that standard is.
>
> Where on a trial by jury for an offence of this class an issue is raised whether the conduct of the accused fell short of the standard to be expected of the reasonable man, *it does not seem to me that a decision on that issue can ever be a point of law.* If in the judge's view the evidence that the accused has fallen short of what the judge himself considers to be the requisite standard is so weak that a verdict of guilty would, in his view, be perverse, he is no doubt entitled to direct the jury to acquit. But, in doing this, he is not performing the function of deciding a question of law but is exercising the overriding discretion of the judge in any criminal trial to take whatever steps are necessary to ensure that the innocent are not convicted.
>
> *What amount of force is 'reasonable in the circumstances' for the purpose of preventing crime is, in my view, always a question for the jury in a jury trial, never a 'point of law' for the judge.* (emphasis added)

In the analogous context of self-defence 'it is both good law and good sense that (a defendant) may do, but may only do, what is reasonably necessary. But everything will depend on the particular facts and circumstances. . . . Of all these matters the good sense of the jury will be the arbiter': *Palmer v R*.[62] **8.81**

In *True*,[63] a case of duress, the Court of Appeal explained 'There are a number of circumstances in which a jury may have to decide a question of fact based upon their judgment of what a reasonable person would have done. It is not for the judge to withdraw that question **8.82**

---

[61] [1976] 2 All ER 937, 947C.
[62] [1971] 1 All ER 1077.
[63] [2003] EWCA Crim 2255.

from the jury, unless, in a clear cut case, it is obvious to him that there is simply no relevant evidence to go to the jury.'

8.83   Lord Hoffmann appears prepared to deny the jury such a constitutional role within his 'functioning democratic state'—preferring judicial determination of what is reasonable. The social and political foundation of his approach is that the evolution of the modern state has removed both the necessity and the justification for direct action in the modern age.

8.84   In practice, Lord Hoffmann's personal views do not appear to have made any substantial impact. Most particularly, a cautionary postscript came in the subsequent acquittal at Bristol Crown Court of Olditch and Pritchard, two of the Appellants in *Jones* whose defences would have failed if the judge had chosen to follow the Hoffmann approach. The case is a good illustration of the difficulties in substituting judge for jury. They had conspired to disable American bombers at a British airbase two days before they were to be used in the invasion of Iraq. The defendants believed the bombers would be carrying cluster bombs and depleted uranium weaponry, the indiscriminate use of which would amount to war crimes.

8.85   Lord Hoffmann himself had posed the question: 'What if the sovereign power, when called, will not come?' The Bristol defendants contended that they had to act to prevent crime because the state was itself the criminal offender. Firstly, the High Court had already ruled prior to their action that the lawfulness of the invasion was not justiciable in a domestic court: *R (Campaign for Nuclear Disarmament) v Prime Minister of the UK*.[64] Secondly, a criminal prosecution for war crimes required the consent of the Attorney General who, in their opinion, was not independent. Lastly, they questioned whether, during this period, the State was functioning properly and constitutionally as Parliament and the country had been deliberately misled by ministers and unelected advisers. In those circumstances, they maintained that damaging US bombers was a proportionate and reasonable method of preventing the unlawful infliction of civilian death and destruction by those same bombers. In the event, they were acquitted.

Remoteness

8.86   The action which is said to be taken in prevention of crime must have some direct or circumstantial connection to the crime that it seeks to prevent. In *Ayliffe and Others*[65] (later to be joined in the *Jones and Milling* appeal in the House of Lords) the defendants had, inter alia, painted and chained themselves to tanks and gates at a Ministry of Defence dock where equipment was being loaded for transport to the Iraqi war. They applied to a District Judge for disclosure of government information. Their skeleton arguments referred to 'a strong possibility' that the activities at the naval base constituted the aiding and abetting of war crimes. The application was refused and, on appeal, the Administrative Court gave them short shrift.

8.87   It held that, had it been established that the 'normal activities' of the airbase or port had involved the commission of war crimes or the aiding and abetting of war crimes, then the

---

[64] [2003] 3 LRC 335.
[65] [2005] EWHC 684 (Admin).

charges against them 'must have failed'. However, per Jack J, the written formulation of the defence arguments did not disclose any defence because there was no nexus between what the defendants did or intended to do and the prevention of actual war crimes:

> In addition to the lack of any basis for asserting that any war crime was being committed by anyone, there is simply no nexus or connection between the cutting of the perimeter fence and the speculated possibility. There is furthermore no nexus or connection between writing on a tank and the speculative possibility that the tank might in some circumstances once in Iraq be used to commit a war crime. The purpose of these actions was to effect a protest, not to prevent a war crime.

Analogous remoteness principles have been held to apply to the defences of protection of property and duress of circumstances. For any of these defences to succeed there must be evidence of a nexus between the defendants' actions and the activity that they seek to avoid or prevent. **8.88**

D. The Protection of Property

The common law

Despite numerous judicial pleas for codification, the common law defence of 'protection of property' continues to exist separately from the statutory 'lawful excuse' under s 5(2) of the Criminal Damage Act 1971. On one level the defence is wider than the statutory defence because the latter only arises where the defendant has caused or intended to cause criminal damage contrary to the 1971 Act; whereas the common law defence is capable of applying to the taking of reasonable steps falling short of damage.[66] **8.89**

However, in two other respects, the common law defence is significantly narrower. The first difference is that the infliction of damage which it seeks to prevent must amount to an unlawful or criminal act; this is not a necessary component of the statutory defence.[67] Secondly, the reasonableness of the person's conduct must be objectively judged. As we examine below, s 5(2) focuses purely upon the defendant's honest but subjective beliefs. **8.90**

Lawful excuse: Criminal Damage Act 1971, s 5

The principal criminal damage offences under the 1971 Act each require the defendant to have been acting 'without lawful excuse'. Essentially, s 5(2) provides that a person who causes or intends to cause criminal damage to property[68] has a 'lawful excuse' for so doing where he or she honestly believes (a) that other property was 'in immediate need of protection' and (b) that the means of protection were or would be reasonable having regard to all the circumstances. **8.91**

---

[66] See, for example, *Bayer v DPP* [2003] EWHC 2567 Admin. In its 1993 report the Law Commission recommended (at para 37.6) that the ingredients of the two defences should be reconciled when any statutory restatement of the law was formulated.

[67] See *Cresswell v DPP* [2006] EWCA 3379; *Currie v DPP* 171 JP 233; *Bayer v DPP*.

[68] Or a right or interest in property.

8.92   Section 5(1) applies the defence to causing deliberate or reckless criminal damage (s 1(1)), threatening to damage property (s 2) and possession of 'anything' with intent to use it to commit criminal damage (s 3). It is not available to a defendant on any charge involving either a threat to destroy or damage property in a way which he knows is likely to endanger life or an intent to use or cause or permit to be used anything in his custody or under his control so to destroy or damage property.

8.93   The defence applies equally to attempts and conspiracy charges. Section 1(1)(a) of the Criminal Law Act 1977 criminalizes any agreement which, if carried out as intended, 'will necessarily amount to or involve the commission of any offence or offences by one or more of the parties to the agreement'. It follows that, if the defendants had a lawful excuse, the planned conduct would not amount to the commission of any offence under the Criminal Damage Act.

8.94   The material parts of s 5 are as follows:

> (2) A person charged with an offence to which this section applies shall, whether or not he would be treated for the purposes of this Act as having a lawful excuse apart from this subsection, be treated for those purposes as having a lawful excuse—
>
> > (a) if at the time of the act or acts alleged to constitute the offence he believed that the person or persons whom he believed to be entitled to consent to the destruction or damage to the property . . . had so consented or would have consented to it if he or they had known of the destruction or damage and its circumstances; or
> >
> > (b) if he destroyed or damaged or threatened to destroy or damage the property in question . . . in order to protect property belonging to himself or another or a right or interest in property which was or which he believed to be vested in himself or another, and at the time of the act or acts alleged to constitute the offence he believed—
> >
> > > i. that the property, right or interest was in immediate need of protection; and
> > >
> > > ii. that the means of protection adopted or proposed to be adopted were or would be reasonable having regard to all the circumstances.
>
> (3) For the purposes of this section it is immaterial whether a belief is justified or not if it is honestly held.
>
> (4) . . .
>
> (5) This section shall not be construed as casting doubt on any defence recognised by law as a defence to criminal charges.

The meaning of property

8.95   The defence does not extend to the protection of people: *Baker and Wilkins*.[69] The defendant must believe that he or she is protecting some property interest. The decapitation of a statue of Mrs Thatcher on the basis of a belief that she was responsible for negative developments in world politics could not amount to a belief that the defendant was protecting property: *Kelleher*.[70]

8.96   Section 10(1) states:

> 'In this Act "property" means property of a tangible nature, whether real or personal, including money and—

---

[69] [1997] Crim LR 497.
[70] [2003] EWCA Crim 2486.

(a) including wild creatures which have been tamed or are ordinarily kept in captivity, and any other wild creatures or their carcasses if, but only if, they have been reduced into possession which has not been lost or abandoned or are in the course of being reduced into possession; but

(b) not including mushrooms growing wild on any land or flowers, fruit or foliage of a plant growing wild on any land.

Badgers which had been enticed into traps by the Department for Environment, Food and Rural Affairs (DEFRA), remained wild animals and were not property under s 10. Accordingly, individuals who destroyed badger traps had no defence under s 5: *Cresswell v DPP*.[71] **8.97**

There is no requirement that the property being protected must be situated within the United Kingdom. **8.98**

The meaning of 'damage'

Section 5(2) contemplates actual or potential damage to two respective sets of property: (a) the property which it is sought to protect; and (b) the property which the defendant has damaged or intended to damage in order to protect the former. The damage which it is sought to prevent need not be unlawful or criminal: *Jones*.[72] **8.99**

There is no statutory definition of 'damage'. '[W]hat constitutes criminal damage is a matter of fact and degree and it is for the [tribunal of fact], applying their common sense, to decide whether what occurred was damage or not': *Roe v Kingerlee*.[73] 'Damage' includes not only permanent or temporary physical harm, but also permanent or temporary impairment of value or usefulness.[74] Damage need only be slight[75] and it is certainly not necessary to have rendered the property useless or unable to serve its normal function'.[76] Property can be damaged although nothing is actually broken—for example, by the removal of an integral part.[77] The temporary spoiling of an item which can be restored to its original condition without any real cost or difficulty is capable of amounting to damage. Graffiti is normally considered to cause damage.[78] In *Hardman v Chief Constable of Avon and Somerset Constabulary*[79] it was held that a pavement was damaged by drawings in water soluble paint which could be removed by high-pressure water jets. On the other hand, it has been held that spittle which could be removed with a cloth did not damage a police officer's raincoat: *A(A Juvenile) v R (1978)*.[80] **8.100**

---

[71] [2006] EWHC 3379 (Admin); *Currie v DPP* 171 JP 233.
[72] [2005] QB 259.
[73] [1986] Crim LR 735.
[74] *Morphitis v Salmon* [1990] Crim LR 48; *Whiteley* (1991) 93 Cr App R 25; *Fiak* [2005] EWCA Crim 2381.
[75] Even the trampling of grass: *Gayford v Trouler* [1898] 1 QB 316.
[76] See *Samuels v Stubbs* [1972] 4 SASR 200.
[77] *Tacey* (1821) Russ & Ry 452.
[78] Including the 'whiting out' of National Front slogans: *Fancy* [1980] Crim LR 171.
[79] [1986] Crim LR 330 (HHJ Llewellyn Jones and justices).
[80] [1978] Crim LR 689 (HHJ Streeter and justices).

8.101   Impermanent damage has been considered in the context of computer data. In *Cox v Riley*[81] programmes held on a printed circuit card were erased by pressing 'delete'. It was held that the erasure damaged the card because retrieval required 'time, labour and expense'. In *Whiteley*[82] a computer disk was held to have been damaged by the addition and deletion of files. The interference amounted to 'impairment of the value or usefulness of the disk to the owner'.

8.102   However, since the passing of the Computer Misuse Act 1990, cases such as these are more likely to be prosecuted under the criminal provisions of that Act rather than as criminal damage. Indeed, s 3(6) provides that, for the purposes of the Criminal Damage Act 1971, 'a modification of the contents of a computer shall not be regarded as damaging any computer or computer storage medium unless its effect on that computer or computer storage medium impairs its physical condition'.[83]

Belief in consent

8.103   As set out above, s 5(2)(a) provides a lawful excuse if the defendant honestly believed that the person(s) whom he or she believed to be entitled to consent to the damage had consented or would have consented if they had known of the circumstances. In *Denton*[84] the defendant was entitled to be acquitted of arson to his employer's mill where he believed that the employer had encouraged him to do so (even though the employer was making a fraudulent insurance claim).

8.104   However, the belief of a vicar, 'however powerful, however genuine and however honestly held, that (he) had the consent of God and thence the law of England and that God had the requisite authority' to consent to anti-war graffiti did not 'raise or amount to' a lawful excuse: *Blake v DPP*.[85] The concept of God as a 'person' within the meaning of s 5(2)(a) was also thought to be problematical.

8.105   The role of divine intervention was pragmatically defined by Stephen J in his *History of the Criminal Law* (1883)[86]: 'My own opinion is that if a special divine order were given to a man to commit murder, I should certainly hang him for it, unless I got a special divine order not to hang him.'

Subjective belief

8.106   As stated under General Principles above, the s 5 defence is undoubtedly the broadest of the defences considered in this chapter. 'It is self-evident that this provision, on its face, gives considerable latitude to those who are minded to take direct action in the honestly held belief that in so doing they are protecting the property of others': *Jones*.[87]

---

[81]   (1986) 83 Cr App R 54.
[82]   (1991) 93 Cr App R 25.
[83]   Criminal Damage Act 1971, s 3(6). When it comes into force on a day to be appointed, Sch 14 of the Police and Justice Act 2006 amends the 1971 Act by inserting these words in the shape of a new s 10(5).
[84]   [1981] 1 WLR 1446.
[85]   [1993] Crim LR 586.
[86]   Vol II, 160, n 1.
[87]   [2004] 3 WLR 1362, CA.

The determining feature is the existence or otherwise of the defendant's honest belief. It is **8.107**
the fact that the defendant believed either that he or she had or would have had consent to
the damage (s 5(2)(a)) or that his or her actions were or would be reasonable in all the circumstances (s 5(2)(b)) that provides the defence rather than the fact that they were actually
reasonable.[88]

The single condition that the belief need only be genuine, although unreasonable, is **8.108**
contained in s 5(3): 'it is immaterial whether a belief is justified or not if it is honestly
held'.

Thus, in *Jaggard v Dickinson*[89] the defendant had permission to treat the house of a friend **8.109**
as her own. However, due to intoxication, she broke into the wrong house. The Divisional
Court quashed her conviction, holding, per Mustill J at 531:

> . . . the court is required by s.5(3) to focus on the existence of the belief, not its intellectual
> soundness; and a belief can be just as much honestly held if it is induced by intoxication,
> as if it stems from stupidity, forgetfulness or inattention.

Remoteness: 'in order to protect' and 'immediate need'

Apparently ill at ease with the implications of s 5, the Court of Appeal has endeavoured to **8.110**
dilute its plainly subjective constituents. Firstly, the phrase 'in order to protect property'
has been construed *not* as a reference to the defendant's own purpose or intention but,
instead, as imposing a legal requirement for an objective causal link or nexus between the
defendant's actions and the protection of the property. This construction has been much
criticized. For example, in the opinion of *Smith and Hogan Criminal Law*, 'The insistence
that the test is objective is 'difficult to reconcile with the wording of the statute which suggests a subjective test'.[90]

In *Hunt*[91] the defendant, who assisted his wife as warden of a block of old persons' flats, **8.111**
set fire to some bedding. His stated reason was to demonstrate deficiencies in the fire
alarm system. The Court held that, while this may have been done to draw attention to the
defective fire alarm system, it was not done in order to protect the property.

> The question whether or not a particular act of destruction or damage or threat of destruction or damage was done or made in order to protect property belonging to another must be,
> on the true construction of the statute, an objective test. Therefore we have to ask ourselves
> whether, whatever the state of this man's mind and assuming an honest belief, that which he
> admittedly did was done in order to protect this particular property, namely the old people's
> home in Hertfordshire?

---

[88] See *Jones* [2003] EWCA Crim 894.

[89] [1981] QB 527; see further *DPP v Beyer* [2004] 1 Cr App R 38 in which Brooke LJ noted the disparity with the common law 'defence of property' which requires the defendant's conduct to be objectively reasonable.

[90] D Ormerod, *Smith and Hogan Criminal Law* (2008, 12th edn) p 994; see also Professor Smith's critical commentary on *Johnson v DPP* [1994] Crim LR 673.

[91] (1977) 66 Cr App R 105; see also *Pomell* [1995] 2 Cr App R 607; *Blake v DPP* [1992] Crim LR 586 in which the defendant had written anti-war graffiti with a felt pen. The Court of Appeal held it necessary for the court to take an objective view when considering if, on the facts believed by the defendant, the action taken did protect, or was capable of protecting, foreign property.

> 'If one formulates the question in that way, . . . it admits of only one answer: this was not done in order to protect property; it was done in order to draw attention to the defective state of the fire alarm. It was not an act which in itself did protect or was capable of protecting property.

8.112 In *Hill and Hall*[92] the Court followed *Hunt* and additionally disqualified the defence because the circumstances failed to meet the test of 'immediate need' in s 5(2)(b)(i). The defendants were charged with possessing hacksaw blades which they intended to use to make a 'symbolic' cut in the perimeter fence at an American naval facility. They believed that the purpose of the base was to monitor Russian nuclear submarines and that, if hostilities broke out, the base would be the subject of a devastating Russian attack resulting in the endangerment of their own property and that of their neighbours. If enough people were to cut a strand of the perimeter wire as part of a concerted CND campaign, the Americans might conclude that that the safety and integrity of the base was jeopardized and withdraw from the base. One of the defendants testified: 'I don't expect a nuclear bomb to fall today, or tomorrow, but there is always that possibility that it is going to happen.'

8.113 On that evidence, the trial judge directed the jury to convict. The Court of Appeal agreed, holding that the proposed act, the 'symbolic' cutting of a fence, was too remote from the protection of property from nuclear attack to qualify:

> There are two aspects to this type of question. The first aspect is to decide what it was that the applicant . . . , in her own mind thought. The learned judge assumed, and so do we, for the purposes of this decision, that everything she said about her reasoning was true. . . . Up to that point the test was subjective. In other words one is examining what is going on in the applicant's mind. Having done that, the judges in the present cases . . . turned to the second aspect of the case, and that is this. He had to decide as a matter of law which means objectively, whether it could be said that on those facts as believed by the applicant, snipping the strand of the wire, which she intended to do, could amount to something done to protect either the applicant's own home or the homes of her adjacent friends in Pembrokeshire. He decided, again quite rightly in our view, that that proposed act on her part was far too remote from the eventual aim at which she was targeting her actions to satisfy the test.

8.114 While acknowledging that the final test is the sincerity of the defendant's subjective belief that 'the property . . . was in immediate need of protection', the Court held that, on her evidence quoted above, there could be no basis upon which to find that the need for protection, even as seen by the defendant, was 'immediate'.[93]

8.115 Notwithstanding criticisms of *Hill and Hall*, the decision has been regularly followed. In *Johnson v DPP*[94] a squatter damaged the door frame of a house in the course of changing the locks. The Divisional Court relied upon *Hill and Hall* to support a finding that his purpose in changing the locks was to enable him to use the front door to bring in his furniture and that neither his belongings nor his possession of the house were in need of immediate protection.

---

[92] (1988) 89 Cr App R 74; see also *Ashford and Smith* [1988] Crim LR 682.
[93] The Court in *Hunt* avoided expressing any view on the meaning of 'in immediate need of protection'.
[94] [1994] Crim LR 673.

In *Jones*[95] the defendant had damaged local authority premises in a protest over a grant of planning permission that had reduced the value of his home. The Court held that the defence was not available as there was no 'direct and proximate threat' to his own property. **8.116**

Hunt and *Hill and Hall* were also cited with approval by both the Court of Appeal[96] and the House of Lords[97] in *Jones and Milling* in the context of actions against the invasion of Iraq. In the former, Latham LJ stated: **8.117**

> This (statutory) test requires an answer to the question: 'Could the act done be said to be done in order to protect property? . . . the only objective element which the jury would have to consider is whether it could be said that on the facts, as believed by the defendant, the criminal damage alleged could amount to something done to protect another's property.

While the principle in *Hill and Hall* survives intact , the idea that the judge may and should direct a conviction in those circumstances has not. As a matter of general principle, where there is *no* evidence capable of amounting to a defence in law, the judge should remove it from the jury. However, where there is *some* evidence, however weak, the defence should be left to the jury notwithstanding that an acquittal might be perverse. Even before *Hill and Hall* the principle had been set out plainly by the House of in *DPP v Stonehouse*, per Lord Salmon at 79/80:[98] **8.118**

> Whilst there is no doubt that if a judge is satisfied that there is no evidence before the jury which could justify them in convicting the accused and that it would be perverse for them to do so, it is the judge's duty to direct them to acquit. This rule, which has long been established, is to protect the accused against being wrongly convicted. But there is no converse rule—although there are some who think there should be. . . . If the judge is satisfied that, on the evidence, the jury would not be justified in acquitting the accused and indeed that it would be perverse of them to do so, he has no power to pre-empt the jury's verdict by directing them to convict. The jury alone have the power to decide that the accused is guilty.

However, in *Hunt and Hill* Lord Lane CJ distinguished *Stonehouse*: **8.119**

> The situation here in the instant case was not the same. The judge here was dealing with the defence of lawful excuse. Certainly the prosecution had to destroy that defence, but it was no part of their affirmative case. It bore a similarity to the defence of self-defence, and as in that case, so in this, there was no need for the judge to direct the jury on those matters, unless there was some evidence capable of constituting that defence. In fact there was none.

In *Kelleher*[99] the appellant had decapitated the former Prime Minister Lady Thatcher—at least, in the sense that he removed the head of her recently completed statute whilst it was on display in the Guildhall gallery. Mantell LJ again confirmed the correctness of the 'objective' approach in *Hill*. However, relying on *Stonehouse*, he rejected the notion that in those circumstances a judge is entitled to direct a jury to convict. **8.120**

---

[95] [2003] EWCA Crim 894; see also *Lloyd v DPP* [1992] 1 All ER 982; *Mitchell* [2004] Crim LR 139.
[96] [2004] 3 WLR 1362.
[97] [2007] 1 AC 136.
[98] [1978] AC 55.
[99] [2003] EWCA Crim 3525. See also *Thompson* [1984] 1 WLR 962; *Challinor* (1984) 80 Cr App R 253; *Gordon (Note)* (1987) 92 Cr App R 50; *Gent* (1989) 89 Cr App R 247.

8.121 The extent of the judicial role was finally settled in *Wang*[100] in which the House of Lords reaffirmed *Stonehouse*. Lord Bingham was prepared to state that *Hill and Hall* 'is not easy to reconcile with the majority opinions (in *Stonehouse)*':

> If . . . there was in truth *no* evidence of lawful excuse which the jury could be asked to consider, the trial judges were entitled to withdraw that issue from the jury. But the relevant conclusion appears to have been 'that the causative relationship between the acts which [the defendant] intended to perform and the alleged protection was so tenuous, so nebulous, that the acts could not be said to be done to protect viewed objectively.' . . . this was a question to be left to the jury, however predictable the outcome might reasonably be thought to be. In any event, the jury should not have been directed to convict, as they evidently were.

8.122 If there is evidence that the conduct did amount to the protection of property, it does not matter that the defendant may have an additional purpose in mind. In *Chamberlain v Lindon*[101] a landowner had demolished a neighbouring wall in order to protect a right of way. The Divisional Court held that it made no difference that his self-help had a further purpose, namely to avoid the expense of litigation.

8.123 Each case will have to turn on its own circumstances. However, while *Hunt* and *Hill and Hall* remain good law, it follows that, in direct action cases, the presence or otherwise of a practical connection between the conduct of the defendants and property that they seek to protect may be decisive. One can see, for example, evident differences between the symbolic damage in *Hill and Hall* and those in the facts in *Olditch and Pritchard*.[102] In the latter case, two days before the (by then inevitable) invasion of Iraq, the defendants had also cut the fence at an RAF base which hosted USAF B52 bombers. However, the cutting of a fence had been in pursuance of an intention to reach and then disable bombers which they knew were soon to take off carrying cluster bombs which they believed would be used to cause unnecessary damage to Iraqi property. In those circumstances, therefore, the cutting of the fence had been done 'in order to protect property' as it was a necessary step towards preventing the aircraft from taking off to bomb Iraqi property; their evidence, unlike that in *Hill and Hall*, was that they did believe that the bombing was imminent. The prosecution did not contend otherwise.

E. Necessity/Duress of Circumstances

A single defence?

8.124 Whether or not the common law defences of 'necessity' and (the confusingly named) 'duress of circumstances' are conceptually identical, they represent a sparing acceptance that an individual may be impelled to break the law where he or she honestly and reasonably believes that not to do so would result in death or serious injury to him/herself or others. The broad test is whether a sober person of reasonable firmness would have

---

[100] [2005] 2 Cr App R 8.
[101] [1998] 1 WLR 1252.
[102] Bristol CC, April 2007. See 8.55 above.

responded similarly in the circumstances. Once again, the relevant circumstances are those that the person genuinely believed to exist at the time.

The haphazard evolution of 'duress of circumstances' has divided academic and judicial **8.125** opinion on whether the defence is a legal creature in its own right or whether instead it is should more properly be treated as an extension of the defence of duress by threats and/or as a form of the defence of necessity.

Whatever the legal ingredients, the title is misleading insofar as it includes the word 'duress'. **8.126** One normally tends to associate the term with the bringing of pressure by one person upon another as in the defence of 'duress by threats' rather than with a forced reaction to a set of circumstances.[103] In *Quayle*[104] the Court of Appeal made an attempt to introduce the more felicitous term, 'necessity of circumstances'.

However, as both duress of circumstances and duress by threats essentially share the same **8.127** components, this may amount to little more than a semantic reservation. 'It now seems to be generally accepted that duress and duress of circumstances will be treated as identical by the courts as regards all elements other than the obvious one of the source of the threat'[105]—in other words, whether the compulsion to act stems from threats or from some other external circumstance.

Taking matters a stage further, there is now ample authority for the proposition that both **8.128** types of duress are, in turn, variants of the basic defence of necessity:

> There is, of course, no obvious distinction between duress and necessity as potential defences … duress is only that species of the genus of necessity which is caused by wrongful threats: *Howe* (1987)).[106]

> To admit a defence of 'duress of circumstances' is a logical consequence of the existence of the defence of duress as that term is ordinarily understood, i.e. do this or else. This approach does no more than recognise that duress is an example of necessity. Whether 'duress of circumstances' is called 'duress' or 'necessity' does not matter: *Conway* (1989).[107]

> The distinction between duress of circumstances and necessity has, correctly, been by and large ignored or blurred by the courts: *Shayler* (2001).[108]

> *Abdul-Hussain* (1999)[109] reflects other decisions which have treated the defences of duress and necessity as being part of the same defence and the extended form of the defence (duress of circumstances) as being different labels for essentially the same thing: *S(DM)* (2001).[110]

> Duress of threats and duress of circumstances are probably instances of the potentially wider defence of necessity: *Safi* (2004).[111]

---

103 See *Cole* [1994] Crim LR 582.
104 [2005] EWCA Crim 1415.
105 D Ormerod, *Smith and Hogan Criminal Law* (2008, 12th edn) p 354.
106 [1987] AC 417, 429C per Lord Hailsham.
107 [1989] QB 290.
108 [2001] 1 WLR 2206.
109 [1999] Crim LR 570.
110 [2001] Crim LR 986; see also *Hasan* [2005] UKHL 22; *Martin (Colin)* [1989] 1 All ER 652; *In re A (Conjoined Twins)* [2001] Fam 147, 232 per Brooke LJ.
111 [2004] 1 Cr App R 157.

8.129   Even so, it is not possible to superimpose a single set of principles across the entire spectrum of circumstances to which duress and necessity could potentially apply without exposing a number of apparent inconsistencies. 'Any attempt at a definition of the precise limits of the defence is fraught with difficulty because its development has been closely related to the particular facts of the different cases which have come before the courts': *Shayle*.[112]

8.130   For example, following *Re A (Children)*,[113] the well-known decision allowing the surgical separation of conjoined twins which would result in the death of the weaker twin in order to achieve the survival of the other, it appears possible that necessity may afford a defence to murder, whereas duress classically does not.

8.131   In other medical cases the defence of necessity has been allowed where action has been taken or is to be taken not to avoid death or serious injury but simply to prevent damage to health where the purpose has been, for example, the sterilization of a mental patient, the relief of pain, or to procure an abortion.[114] By distinction, fear of death or serious injury remains a core ingredient of duress of circumstances and the courts have rejected the argument that, by analogy with those decisions, the threshold has been lowered generally.

8.132   For example, in *Quayle*[115] the Court of Appeal suggested that, having regard to the medical cases, the development of 'necessity' was best understood on a case-by-case basis and that no 'overarching principle' applicable to all situations could be derived from such authorities.

8.133   It may be then that these anomalies can be accommodated on the basis that the courts are prepared to countenance different policy considerations when reviewing cases of 'medical necessity' which they would not apply outside the unique world of medical decision making. Thus understood, the existence of these medical cases does not detract from the substantive general similarities between necessity and duress of circumstances.

8.134   Perhaps the best approach for the reader may be to proceed on the basis that the relationship of duress of circumstances to necessity 'has not been settled'.[116] However, as defences to public order offences, it is probably safe to say that for all practical purposes, and certainly for the purposes of this chapter, they are 'essentially the same thing'.

8.135   That being so, and as there is no doubt that 'duress of circumstances' exists as a defence, we do not propose to give additional consideration to 'necessity' as an alternative and different category of defence.

---

[112] [2001] 1 WLR 2206.
[113] [2000] 4 All ER 961.
[114] See *Bourne* [1939] 1 KB 687; *Gillick v West Norfolk and Wisbech Area HA* [1986] 1 AC 142; *In re F (Mental Patient: Sterilisation)* [1990] 2 AC 1.
[115] [2005] EWCA Crim 1415.
[116] D Ormerod, *Smith and Hogan Criminal Law* (2008, 12th edn) p 343.

Duress of circumstances: definition

The earliest developments of the defence of duress of circumstances by that name came in   **8.136**
a series of road traffic cases in the 1980s.[117] In *Pommell*[118] the Court of Appeal confirmed
that the defence applies to all crimes except murder, attempted murder, and some forms of
treason.

The general definition now most commonly cited was provided by Simon Brown J   **8.137**
in *Martin*:[119]

> First, English law does, in extreme circumstances, recognise a defence of necessity. Most
> commonly this defence arises as duress, that is pressure upon an accused's will from the
> wrongful threats or violence of another. Equally, however, it can arise from other objective
> dangers threatening the accused or others. Arising thus it is conveniently called 'duress of
> circumstances'.
>
> Secondly, the defence is available only if, from an objective standpoint, the accused can be
> said to be acting reasonably and proportionately in order to avoid a threat of death or serious
> injury. Thirdly, assuming the defence to be open to the accused on his account of the facts,
> the issue should be left to the jury, who should be directed to determine these two questions:
> first, was the accused, or may he have been, impelled to act as he did because as a result of
> what he reasonably believed to be the situation he had good cause to fear that otherwise death
> or serious physical injury would result? Second, if so, may a sober person of reasonable firm-
> ness, sharing the characteristics of the accused, have responded to the situation as the accused
> acted? If the answer to both these questions was yes then the . . . defence of necessity would
> have been established. (emphasis added)

In *Abdul-Hussain*[120] the Court of Appeal considered duress of circumstances and by threats   **8.138**
in the context of an aircraft hijacking. The appellants were all Shiite Muslims from Southern
Iraq. Most had offended against the laws or regulations of the Saddam Hussein regime,
from which they were fugitives. In the summer of 1996, they were living in Sudan and
feared return to Iraq at the hands of the Sudanese authorities as they were overstayers. They
anticipated torture and execution if returned to Iraq. They hijacked a plane forcing it to fly
to Heathrow.

The trial judge withdrew the defence from the jury holding that 'there was at no time   **8.139**
sufficient connection between the danger feared by the defendants . . . and the criminal act
of hijacking the aircraft . . . of such a close and immediate nature as is established by the
authorities as being required to lay the basis for the defence of necessity'. Their appeal was
allowed. Rose LJ identified a number of propositions which included the following:

(a) unless Parliament provides otherwise, the defence of duress, whether by threats or from
circumstances is generally available in relation to all substantive crimes except murder,
attempted murder, and some forms of treason;

---

[117] See *Willer* (1986) 83 Cr App R 225; *Conway* [1989] QB 290. See also *DPP v Harris* [1995] 1 Cr App
R 170; *Backshall* [1998] 1 WLR 1506.
[118] [1995] 2 Cr App R 607; see also *Shayler*.
[119] [1989] 1 All ER 652.
[120] [1999] Crim LR 570.

(b) the courts have developed the defence on a case-by-case basis and its scope remains imprecise;

(c) imminent peril of death or serious injury to the defendant, or those for whom he has responsibility, is an essential element of both types of duress;

(d) the peril must operate on the mind of the defendant at the time when he commits the otherwise criminal act, so as to overbear his will, and this essentially is a question for the jury;

(e) but the execution of the threat need not be immediately in prospect;

(f) the period of time which elapses between the inception of the peril and the defendant's act, and between that act and execution of the threat, are relevant but not determinative factors;

(g) all the circumstances of the peril including the number, identity, and status of those creating it, and the opportunities (if any) which exist to avoid it are relevant, initially for the judge and, in appropriate cases, for the jury, when assessing whether the defendant's mind was affected as in (d) above;

(h) as to (f) and (g), if Anne Frank had stolen a car to escape from Amsterdam and had been charged with theft, the tenets of English law would not have denied her a defence of duress of circumstances, on the ground that she should have waited for the Gestapo's knock on the door;

(i) there is no reason of principle or authority for distinguishing the two forms of duress in relation to the elements of the defence which have been identified;

(j) the judgment in *R v Martin (Colin)*[121] affords the clearest and most authoritative guide to the relevant principles and appropriate direction in relation to both forms of duress.

Persons for whom the defendant has responsibility

8.140 The person(s) whom the defendant seeks to protect from serious injury must be those for whom he or she 'reasonably regards himself as being responsible'.

8.141 No conceptual difficulty arises where there is a direct relationship. In *Wright*[122] the person threatened was the defendant's boyfriend.

8.142 Responsibility for the safety of the general public was considered by the Court of Appeal in *Shayler*.[123] The defendant had been a member of MI5 from November 1991 to October 1996. In 1997 he disclosed a number of documents relating to security or intelligence matters to a national newspaper. He was later charged with disclosing documents or information without lawful authority, contrary to ss 1 and 4 of the Official Secrets Act 1989. He contended that, as a member of the government secret services, he owed a responsibility to the general public at large. His acts were necessary to protect a yet to be identified group from among the public for whose protection MI5 had responsibilities who would inevitably suffer because of MI5's incompetence.

---

[121] [1989] 1 All ER 652.
[122] [2000] Crim LR 510.
[123] [2001] 1 WLR 2206.

When the House of Lords[124] determined the subsequent appeal Lord Bingham thought **8.143** it 'a little unfortunate' that the Court of Appeal had 'ventured into (the) vexed and uncertain territory' of necessity or duress of circumstances as it had not been raised before the trial judge—the defence put forward being that of 'public interest' (see 8.161 below). Even so the Court of Appeal did review the authorities and Lord Woolf CJ concluded at paragraph 63 that:

> The defence is available when a defendant commits an otherwise criminal act to avoid an imminent peril of danger to life or serious injury to himself or towards somebody for whom he reasonably regards himself as being responsible. That person may not be ascertained and may not be identifiable. However, if it is not possible to name the individuals beforehand, it has at least to be possible to describe the individuals by reference to the action which is threatened would be taken which would make them victims absent avoiding action being taken by the defendant. The defendant has responsibility for them because he is placed in a position where he is required to make a choice whether to take or not to take the action which it is said will avoid them being injured. Thus if the threat is to explode a bomb in a building if defendant does not accede to what is demanded, the defendant owes responsibility to those who would be in the building if the bomb exploded.

Mr Shayler failed because he was 'not in a position to identify any incident which is going **8.144** to create a danger to the members of the public which his actions were designed to avoid. Instead he is blowing the whistle on the past conduct of individual members of and MI5 as a whole.'

It seems then that one test is whether one can define the grouping for which the defendant **8.145** has a legitimate responsibility 'by reference to the action . . . which would (otherwise) make them victims'.

The notion of a general responsibility to the public was considered by the Scottish **8.146** High Court of Judiciary (the equivalent of the High Court) in *Lord Advocate's Reference (No 1 of 2000)*[125] where damage had been caused to a vessel which had a role in carrying Trident missiles. The defence had argued that their actions were a matter of necessity as they were averting the risk posed to the people of the area by the presence of Trident missiles:

> In our opinion there is no acceptable basis for restricting rescue to the protection of persons already known to and having a relationship with the rescuer at the moment of response to the other's danger. . . . the existence of a prior relationship as a pre-condition of necessity has nothing to commend it, in our view. . . . If one had to define 'companion' it would be anyone who could reasonably be foreseen to be in danger of harm if action were not taken to prevent the harmful event. There was considerable discussion whether the defence of necessity could be available where the place and person or persons under threat from the apprehended danger were remote from the locus of the allegedly malicious damage. We can see no reason in principle why the defence should not be so available. In the modern world many industrial processes have inherent in them the potential for mass destruction over a wide area surrounding a given plant. If a person damaged industrial plant to prevent a disaster which he reasonably believed to be imminent but which he could avoid by the actions taken, there is no compelling

---

[124] [2003] 1 AC 247.
[125] [2001] JC 143.

reason for excluding the defence of necessity solely on the grounds that persons at risk were remote from the plant provided that they were within the reasonably foreseeable area of risk.

Compulsion

8.147 It has been said that 'necessity can very easily become simply a mask for anarchy'.[126] As was stressed in *Safi*:[127]

> The courts treat such a defence (as it can conveniently and compendiously be called) with great caution. The authorities stress the need for great and imminent danger and require that the defendant's response to the situation be judged by an objective standard of reasonableness and proportionality. Some authorities speak of the defendant's choice being overborne whereas others speak of an unwilling choice between two alternatives[128] . . . The defences which have evolved to deal with circumstances of necessity encompass such a wide range of circumstances that in some cases the reference to the overbearing of choice may be helpful whereas in other cases, it would be inappropriate. But as the civil division of this court has said:[129]

> 'The defence is available on the basis that, if it is established, the relevant actors have in effect been compelled to act as they did by the pressure of the threats or other circumstances of imminent peril to which they were subject, and it was the impact of that pressure on their freedom to choose their course of action that suffices to excuse them from criminal liability.'

Mixed test: subjective but reasonable belief

Subjective belief

8.148 It has been said that the *Martin* definition 'applies a predominantly, but not entirely, objective test': *Safi*.[130]

8.149 As with the defences previously discussed in this chapter, the subjective element is represented by the rule that the reasonableness of the defendant's actions is to be judged according to the circumstances as he or she genuinely believed them to be rather than as they were in fact.[131]

8.150 In *Safi and ors* (above), the Court of Appeal again considered duress in the context of the hijacking of an Afghan plane in Afghanistan by members of 'The Organisation of Young Intellectuals of Afghanistan' in 2001. They continued to detain crew and passengers and to threaten them with weapons after landing at Stansted airport before surrendering to the British authorities. They claimed they had no other way of escaping death or serious injury from the Taliban regime. Their actions after landing at Stansted continued to be the result of duress, as there came into existence an imminent threat of their being removed by the relevant authorities directly to Afghanistan or indirectly via Pakistan with the risk of death or serious injury because Pakistan would return them to Afghanistan.

---

[126] *Southwark LBC v Williams* [1971] Ch 734, 746.
[127] [2004] 1 Cr App R 157. See 8.148 below.
[128] See Professor KM Smith, 'Duress and Steadfastness : In Pursuit of the Unintelligible' [1999] Crim LR 363, 368–9.
[129] *Re A (Conjoined Twins)* [2001] Fam 147, 235–6 per Brooke LJ with whom Ward LJ agreed at 198A.
[130] [2004] 1 Cr App R 157.
[131] See *Cairns* [1999] 2 Cr App R 137.

The Court quashed their convictions and ordered a re-trial holding that: 'It is clear that **8.151** it is the defendant's reasonable belief in relation to the words or conduct said to constitute the threat for the purpose of the defence of duress that is critical.' Accordingly, the trial judge had been 'incorrect to hold that there must be a threat in fact, rather than something the defendant reasonably believed to be a threat, before the defence of duress can be invoked . . . if there was a threat in fact, it would be superfluous to superimpose a further requirement that the defendant must reasonably believe there to be a threat'.

Reasonable belief

It appears, however, that there is presently a significant difference between duress of **8.152** circumstances/necessity and the prevention of crime and the protection of property defences. For the former to succeed, the defendant's belief as to the circumstances must itself be reasonable when judged objectively. In other words, although the risk of death or serious injury need not exist in fact, the defendant's belief that it did exist must at least be one that it was reasonable to hold.

In *Safi* the court noted the classic jury direction formulated by Lord Lane CJ in *Graham*:[132] **8.153**

> Was the defendant, or may he have been, impelled to act as he did because, as a result of what he *reasonably* believed . . . (the circumstances to be) . . . , he had *good cause* to fear that if he did not so act . . . (another) . . . would kill him or . . . cause him serious physical injury?

The *Graham* direction had earlier been approved as 'entirely correct' by Lord Mackay in the **8.154** House of Lords in *Howe*,[133] had been followed in *Conway*,[134] and was incorporated into the *Martin* definition of duress of circumstances set out above.[135] The expressions 'reasonably believed' and 'good cause to fear' plainly suggest an objective assessment of the reasonableness of the defendant's belief.

However, it should be noted that the court in *Safi* was careful to leave open the question **8.155** whether 'the defendant's belief has to be merely a genuine belief or whether it must not only be a genuine but also a reasonable belief' while simultaneously acknowledging that 'in general, the law that mistake of fact will constitute a defence to a criminal charge, even if it is not a reasonable mistake'.[136]

Pausing there, once it is accepted, in keeping with general principle (see *Morgan* above), **8.156** that the relevant circumstances are those that the defendant genuinely believed to exist, there seems to be no basis in legal logic for insisting upon the additional requirement in duress cases that the belief must be reasonable.[137] If the test is the existence of a genuine belief, as *Safi* holds it to be, whether the belief is reasonable or not is logically irrelevant. It may be that this is a policy requirement having regard to the courts' reluctance to increase

---

[132] [1982] 1 WLR 294.
[133] [1987] AC 417, 459.
[134] [1989] QB 290.
[135] (1989) 88 Cr App R 343; see also *M* [2003] EWCA Crim 1170; *Blake* [2004] EWCA Crim 1238; *Bronson* [2004] EWCA Crim 903.
[136] Citing *B (a Minor) v DPP* [2002] AC 428 and *K* [2001] 3 WLR 471.
[137] See the criticisms in D Ormerod, *Smith and Hogan Criminal Law* (2008, 12th edn) p 331.

the availability of a legal 'mask for anarchy' but it does not seem to follow as a matter of principle.

8.157 Lastly on this aspect, if the reasonableness of the defendant's belief is to remain crucial to the defence, then hearsay evidence of the factual existence of a threat or injurious circumstances, if known to the defendant, may be admissible under the provisions of the Criminal Justice Act 2003:

> In cases of duress it is routinely admissible. In *Subramaniam v Public Prosecutor* (1956)[138] the Privy Council held that what was said to the defendant was admissible to show that he had good reason to fear death or personal injury; there can be no reason to suppose that such evidence could not also be admissible to show the defendant's state of mind in relation to the existence of a threat or other circumstance giving rise to a defence of duress (*Safi*).

Death or serious injury

8.158 As is apparent from the various dicta quoted above, the person must fear that imminent death or serious injury to him/herself or others will result if he or she does not act. Liberalization of this requirement has been resisted save in cases of medical necessity. For example, in *Quayle*[139] the appellants unsuccessfully argued that, in the light of the medical cases, cannabis use for the avoidance of severe pain should be equated with the avoidance of serious injury.[140]

8.159 Much reference herein has been made to the House of Lords decision in *Jones*. Some of the appellants relied upon duress of circumstances arguing that their actions were necessary to prevent death and injury to civilians in the course of the invasion of Iraq. The Court of Appeal had held that the defence was available only to those faced with the commission of a crime that would cause death or serious injury: *Jones*.[141] The point was not subsequently addressed in the House of Lords.

8.160 This appears to confuse the requirements of duress of circumstances with those of the prevention of crime defence under s 3 of the Criminal Law Act 1967. As *Smith and Hogan Criminal Law*[142] points out:

> With respect, that cannot be right. The defence was available in *Martin* when his wife was threatening suicide (not a crime) moreover, one can envisage many circumstances in which D, or those for whom he is responsible, face a threat of death or serious injury by non-criminal means (for example, a rapidly engulfing forest fire leads D to steal a car to escape to safety).

F. Acting in the Public Interest

8.161 There may be an additional and discrete argument that a person who acts unlawfully but reasonably in protection of the 'public interest' commits no offence.

---

[138] [1956] 1 WLR 965.
[139] [2005] EWCA Crim 1415; see also *Brown* [2003] EWCA Crim 2637. cf *Lockwood* [2002] EWCA Crim 60—which the Court in *Quayle* described as a 'slight foundation . . . The question whether it was appropriate to leave any issue of necessity to the jury at all was never argued or before the court in *Lockwood*.'
[140] See also *Brown* [2003] EWCA Crim 2637.
[141] [2004] 3 WLR 1362; [2004] EWCA Crim 1981.
[142] D Ormerod, *Smith and Hogan Criminal Law* (2008, 12th edn) p 345.

In *Shayler*[143] an ex-MI5 agent was prosecuted under the Official Secrets Act 1989 for dis- **8.162**
closing information to a national newspaper. He failed in his argument, based on common
law and Article 10 of the European Convention on Human Rights, that his disclosures
were necessary in the public interest to avert damage to life or limb or serious damage to
property.

> The public interest which Mr Shayler seeks to assert is the right of the public to be provided
> with information which will enable it to assess whether the powers given to the security and
> intelligence services are being abused and whether the services are being run properly. He
> seeks to draw attention to past incidents of misconduct. His point is that, unless the services
> are reformed, they will continue to be operated in a manner which creates a danger to the
> public in respect of life, limb and property.

It was held, as a matter of statutory construction, that a defendant prosecuted under the **8.163**
Official Secrets Act 1989 is not entitled to be acquitted if he shows that it was, or that he
believed that it was, in the public or national interest to make the disclosure in question.
The implication is that, unless the language of the statute that creates the offence so
provides, there is no legal route for importing a defence of 'acting in the public interest'.

It could be said that the decision in *Shayler* should be confined to an interpretation of the **8.164**
1989 Act alone and that a similar argument has yet to be tested under more general criminal provisions. Moreover, its application to common law offences may involve different
principles of construction. For example, public nuisance requires an act or omission that
'obstructs or causes inconvenience or damage to the public'.[144] Conceivably, it might be
argued that this means the public interest in general and that, where the 'victim' of the
offence is the public, a defendant whose actions have served a higher public interest should
be acquitted.

There is some slight support for a public interest defence in principles of liability in civil law **8.165**
and, in particular, that protection of the general interests of the public is capable of overriding
private interests. Therefore, it is argued by analogy, there should be a defence where a
person takes reasonable steps, albeit otherwise criminal, to prevent an activity that, considered objectively, is contrary to the public interest ('a greater evil') such as the importation
of GM crops or the waging of an aggressive war.

Certainly, the argument derives some support in the context of private nuisance from the **8.166**
first instance decision of Buckley J in *Dennis v Ministry of Defence*.[145] The plaintiff, a
landowner, had brought an action for nuisance caused by the noise of Harrier jets from
nearby RAF Wittering in Cambridgeshire. Buckley J thought the case 'raises an important
and problematical point of principle in the law of nuisance. Namely, whether and in what
circumstances a sufficient public interest can amount to a defence to a claim in nuisance.'
He found that nuisance was established but that the public interest, objectively assessed,

---

[143] [2001] 1 WLR 2206, CA; [2003] 1 AC 247, HL.
[144] Stephen, *Digest*, 184.
[145] [2003] EWHC 793, QB.

'as represented by the MOD maintaining a state of the art air strike force and training pilots, provides immunity'.[146]

8.167 However, set alongside *Dennis* has to be the decision of the Court of Appeal in another civil case, *Monsanto v Tilly*[147] (the facts of which are closer to the subject matter of this work). Monsanto were licensed by the Department of the Environment to conduct GM crop growing trials. The defendants, as an unincorporated association, advocated the symbolic destruction of the crops and had taken direct action uprooting plants. Monsanto claimed, inter alia, for trespass to land and goods. The defence pleaded 'that the acts were necessary to protect third parties and their property and/or were in the public interest'. The Court held that these justifications were not capable of affording a defence in law. Stuart-Smith LJ thought, at paragraph 26, that 'a moment's reflection' showed that the issue of public interest:

> . . . is incapable of being tried in a court with our adversarial system of justice. (Counsel for the defendants) submitted that it would be necessary for the court to conduct some form of balancing exercise to see whether the law breaking in question was proportionate to the danger . . . if this really is the law, the law would be setting itself a task which no court could possibly answer.

8.168 There remain significant and unresolved legal issues—not least whether the public interest is a justiciable concept in a criminal trial (Monsanto suggests it is not) and, if so, whether it is to be assessed objectively or according to the circumstances as the defendant believed them to be. Apart from *Shayler*, the authors are not aware of any appellate authority which has addressed public interest as a defence to a criminal charge nor of any trial in which the defence has been advanced successfully.

---

[146] See also *Miller v Jackson* [1977] 1 QB 966 in which the Court of Appeal declined to continue an injunction against a village cricket club to restrain them from playing near a residential area. It held that the public interest of the village as a whole in retaining a cricket team outweighed the hardship to individual adjoining householders. However, this case cannot be elevated to a statement of legal principle and does no more than illustrate the occasional role of public interest considerations in the grant of discretionary remedies such as injunctions. It is also a decision that the Court declined to follow in *Kennaway v Thompson* [1981] 1 QB 88.

[147] [2000] Env LR 313; *Monsanto v Tilly* was cited with approval by Lord Hoffmann in *Jones v Milling*—see 8.44, 8.73 above.

9

PUNISHMENT, APPEALS, AND RESTRICTIVE ORDERS

A. **Sentencing Principles in Protest Cases**	9.01	
Conditional discharge: *R v Jones (Margaret)*	9.03	
Fines	9.13	
Community penalty	9.14	
Mitigation	9.19	
B. **Binding Over**	9.20	
Binding over to keep the peace	9.20	
Binding over to come up for judgment	9.42	
C. **Alternatives to Conviction**	9.47	
Cautions	9.47	
Simple cautions	9.49	
Conditional cautions	9.59	
Juveniles: warnings and reprimands	9.70	
Fixed penalty notices	9.73	
Penalty offences	9.74	
Giving the notice	9.75	
Penalty notices	9.77	
Effect of the penalty notice	9.80	
D. **Appeals**	9.82	
General	9.82	

Appeals from the magistrates' court to the Crown Court		9.83
Appeals by way of case stated: from the magistrates' court and Crown Court to the Divisional Court		9.95
Judicial review		9.105
Appeals from the Crown Court to the Court of Appeal		9.117
Referrals by the Criminal Cases Review Commission		9.153
Appeals from the Court of Appeal and Divisional Court to the Supreme Court		9.157
Petitions to the European Court of Human Rights		9.159
E. **Injunctions**		9.166
Injunctions in Protest Cases		9.170
F. **Anti-social Behaviour Orders (ASBOs)**		9.178
G. **Football Banning Orders**		9.183

A. Sentencing Principles in Protest Cases

This section considers the sentencing exercise to be conducted following conviction in protest cases. Protestors may be convicted of a diverse variety of offences from obstructing a railway engine to criminal damage. However, the fact that they engaged in acts of civil disobedience borne of a genuine and longstanding commitment to a particular cause may require the courts to conduct a special analysis of the sentencing decision and ultimately this may take the case outside the normal range of sentences for those offences. **9.01**

The maximum sentences and the courts approach to sentencing for the public order offences discussed in this book are set alongside those offences in Chapters 1, 2, and 4. **9.02**

It is beyond the scope of this book to undertake a detailed examination of general principles of sentencing in the criminal law.[1]

Conditional discharge: *R v Jones (Margaret)*

9.03 The starting point in protest cases is the 'convention' identified by Lord Hoffmann in *R v Jones (Margaret)*.[2] This is often cited in support of a plea for a lenient sentence by way of a conditional discharge. A conditional discharge is an order by which the offender is released or 'discharged' without any penalty for a specified period, for example twelve months. If he commits no further offence or does not otherwise breach the order he suffers no penalty, and, more significantly, as with an absolute discharge, the conviction is deemed not to be a conviction. If the offender commits a further offence during the period, he may be sentenced for the breach (Powers of Criminal Courts (Sentencing) Act 2000, s 13(6)). A Crown Court dealing with a person conditionally discharged by a magistrates' court is limited to the lower court's powers (Powers of Criminal Courts (Sentencing) Act 2000, s 13(7)).

9.04 In *R v Jones (Margaret)*[3] Lord Hoffmann explained the 'convention' in protest cases as follows:

> . . . civil disobedience on conscientious grounds has a long and honourable history in this country. People who break the law to affirm their belief in the injustice of a law or government action are sometimes vindicated by history. The suffragettes are an example, which comes immediately to mind. It is the mark of a civilised community that it can accommodate protests and demonstrations of this kind. But there are conventions which are generally accepted by the law-breakers on one side and the law-enforcers on the other. The protestors behave with a sense of proportion and do not cause excessive damage or inconvenience. And they vouch the sincerity of their beliefs by accepting the penalties imposed by the law. The police and prosecutors, on the other hand, behave with restraint and the magistrates impose sentences which take the conscientious motives of the protestors into account. The conditional discharges ordered by the magistrates in the cases which came before them exemplifies their sensitivity to these conventions.[4]

9.05 In *R v Jones (Margaret)* anti-war protestors broke into various military air bases and damaged aircraft, fuel tankers, bomb trailers, and runways on the eve of the invasion of Iraq in 2003 by American and British warplanes. They passionately disagreed with the decision of US and UK governments to wage war with Iraq and acted to hamper that war effort and to prevent death and destruction. They were charged with either aggravated trespass or criminal damage and sought to raise the defence of 'prevention of crime' under s 3 of the Criminal Law Act 1967.[5] Ultimately, the House of Lords (Lord Bingham giving the leading opinion) ruled that s 3 applied only to the prevention of crimes in domestic

---

[1] For general principles of sentencing, see *Archbold Criminal Pleading, Evidence and Practice 2009*, Ch 5; Dr David Thomas QC, *Current Sentencing Practice* (2009); Robert Banks, *Banks on Sentence* (2009; 4th edn); and the Sentencing Guidelines Council website at <http://www.sentencing-guidelines.gov.uk/>.

[2] [2006] UKHL 16; [2007] 1 AC 136.

[3] Ibid, para 89.

[4] Ibid, para 89.

[5] See 8.33 et seq 356.

law and that the customary international law crime of waging 'a war of aggression' was not a 'domestic' crime.

However, Lord Hoffmann, in passages under his headings of *The Limits of Self Help* and **9.06** *Civil Disobedience*, specifically sought to curtail 'the emergence of a new phenomenon, namely litigation as the continuation of protest by other means'.[6] In effect, he was saying that civil disobedience is a part of our democracy but such direct action protestors, who for example break into air bases and disable warplanes, should accept that they are breaking the law in order to make their point. They should behave peacefully and, when arrested and their case comes before the court, plead guilty. In return they will be treated with the utmost leniency by the courts, mindful of their genuine and passionate, as opposed to morally blameworthy, motivation. What such protestors should not expect to do is to fight the case and run justification defences of necessity or the prevention of crime and seek to use the trial process to continue their demonstration.

Lord Hoffmann's comments have particular resonance in terms of sentencing principles in **9.07** protest cases. Firstly, his comments suggest that this 'generally accepted convention', including 'accepting the penalties imposed by the law', places civil disobedience protestors in a special category. The sincerity of their beliefs and the possibility that their actions may be vindicated by history means that they are less morally blameworthy than the 'average' offender convicted of an offence such as criminal damage. Accordingly, they merit leniency and should be dealt with by way of a conditional discharge.

Secondly, however, in order to claim such leniency the protestor must abide by the conven- **9.08** tion. According to Lord Hoffmann that means, 'the protestors behave with a sense of proportion and do not cause excessive damage or inconvenience'. To that, one might add, the protestor must not be violent.

Thirdly, and most importantly, it is implicit in Lord Hoffmann's comments that abiding by **9.09** the convention means pleading guilty. So does that mean that a direct action protestor who contests the case and seeks to argue a justification for his actions risks a greater punishment on conviction than a conditional discharge? The general rule is that a defendant who pleads guilty at the first opportunity is entitled to a one-third reduction in the severity of the penalty compared with that which would be imposed upon conviction after a contested trial.[7] Thus, in ordinary criminal cases, a timely guilty plea can make the difference between whether a person is sent to prison or not. Yet the reason for this reduction in sentence for a guilty plea is twofold. Firstly, by pleading guilty the defendant has accepted responsibility for the offence and demonstrated some remorse. Secondly, the offender has saved the court

---

[6] Ibid, para 90.

[7] The Criminal Justice Act 2003, s 144 requires the sentencing court to take account of the stage at which the guilty plea was tendered. The Sentencing Guidelines Council guideline, *Reduction in Sentence for a Guilty Plea* (16 December 2004), states that the level of the reduction will be gauged on a sliding scale ranging from a maximum of one third (where the guilty plea was entered at the first reasonable opportunity in relation to the offence for which sentence is being imposed), reducing to a maximum of one quarter (where a trial date has been set) and to a maximum of one tenth (for a guilty plea entered at the 'door of the court' or after the trial has begun).

the time and expense of a contested trial and, in some cases, spared the 'victim' of the offence the ordeal of testifying at trial. But how do those reasons factor into protest cases?

9.10   The question of accepting responsibility and expressing remorse does not apply to the participant in acts of civil disobedience. For a start, there is often no issue about the identity of the offender or that the actor has done the deed. On the contrary, the civil disobedient will often say, 'Yes of course I chained myself to the railings. But this is why I did it.' Moreover, there will be little expression of remorse. A protestor spurred into acts of civil disobedience to prevent (or draw public attention to) what he perceives to be a greater evil—such as war or climate change—acts from a sense of higher moral purpose. He is unlikely to feel a sense of remorse or wrongdoing for acts of criminal damage or aggravated trespass against military bases or power stations which he perceives to be responsible for such evil.

9.11   The orthodox rationale for obtaining a reduction in sentence for a guilty plea in other criminal cases, such as sparing a vulnerable witness the rigours of giving evidence, does not apply neatly to the protestor case. Lord Hoffmann identifies such defendants as being in a special category—meriting the leniency of a conditional discharge because of the sincerity of their beliefs. It is submitted that such defendants should not forfeit such leniency by virtue of pleading not guilty and advancing their case in a trial.

9.12   It is true that one reason for permitting a reduction in sentence for a guilty plea is that the defendant has saved the court the time and expense of a contested trial. However, rather than inflating the sentence, the court could address that issue by ordering the defendant to pay some of the costs of the prosecution and, if he is subject to a legal aid representation order, to pay the costs of the defence as well. As always, however, the court must have regard to the defendant's means and cannot make a costs order which is disproportionate or oppressive. It should be noted that an order to pay costs is not a sentence in itself, but ancillary to a sentence.

Fines

9.13   In protest cases, a financial penalty (sentence by way of a fine) may often be imposed where the conduct is minor. However, it is unlikely to be imposed where determined and conscientious individuals driven by the moral conviction in the justness of their cause are likely to commit further acts of civil disobedience in the near future. Accordingly, in considering the appropriate penalty the court will want to pass a sentence which has the effect of giving the court some form of future hold or control over the offender. Whereas a fine could be paid in full within a short period and the court would have no continuing sanction over the offender, a conditional discharge requires an offender not to commit further offences within a specified period. If he does so, he breaches the conditional discharge and, in addition to the sentence for the new offence, he can be resentenced for the original offence.

Community penalty

9.14   The propriety of passing a community penalty in direct action protest cases was considered in yet another 'Jones' case, the 'Arms Fair' case: *R v Jones and others*.[8] This case concerned a

---

[8] [2006] EWCA Crim 2942.

group of protestors who pleaded guilty to obstructing a railway engine or carriage contrary to s 36 of the Malicious Damage Act 1861. They had demonstrated against an arms fair held in the London Docklands Excel centre. They staged a number of incidents on the Docklands Light Railway, which services the Excel centre. Some climbed on the roof of a stationary train and refused to move until 'persuaded' down by police officers. Others chained themselves to a door on the train. Some even engaged in a mock fight to serve as a distraction whilst others climbed on the roof. The result was that a number of trains were prevented from moving for prolonged periods and the delays caused frustration and annoyance to passengers.

Almost all the defendants were of exemplary character. For example, one defendant was **9.15** a university don, one of the most outstanding research fellows in applied maths and theoretical physics in the country. Many had given considerable voluntary service to the community, working with the homeless or those with learning difficulties. The original sentencing judge nevertheless passed community orders with the requirement of eighty hours unpaid work and, in addition, anti-social behaviour orders (ASBOs). One defendant received a suspended sentence.

The Court of Appeal quashed community penalties for the majority of the defendants,[9] **9.16** and ASBOs in every case, substituting them with conditional discharges.

Moses LJ said that in this type of case community penalties were not appropriate. He said **9.17** that, 'It should never be forgotten that a community penalty is not a soft option. It originated and still is considered as but one step short of imprisonment and it is a serious penalty that these days, in particular, requires hard and sometimes unpleasant, and certainly boring work.'[10] Most importantly, however, the sentences were excessive because the judge had failed to give sufficient regard to their sincerely held beliefs and motivation. Moses LJ said:

> The judge was careful not to make any comment as to the propriety or otherwise of challenging this country's holding of arms fairs and he was right to do so. But the fact that this was a source of legitimate protest was important in relation to the sort of sentence which ought to have been passed. If a criminal offence is committed in the course of a protest, a political protest, that is clearly a relevant factor in relation to the propriety of the sentence. If one needs authority for that proposition, it is to be found in *R v Jones & Ors* [2006] UKHL 16, in the remarks of Lord Hoffmann, in his speech at paragraph 89. Of course, they do not excuse the criminal offences committed in this case but they are highly relevant to the appropriate punishment. Although the judge acknowledged that these offences were committed in a demonstration, he seems to have paid little heed to the motives with which these offences were committed.[11]

---

[9] Moses LJ did distinguish between defendants of good character or those who had minor but irrelevant past convictions and a defendant who had a number of recent and relevant previous convictions for politically motivated protests. In the case of the latter, the Court upheld community sentences with the requirement to perform unpaid work of eighty hours. Such defendants that had been sentenced by way of a suspended sentence had those quashed and replaced with a community penalty.

[10] [2006] EWCA Crim 2942, Moses LJ at para 26.

[11] Ibid, para 16.

9.18 In relation to the anti-social behaviour orders,[12] the Court of Appeal queried whether the defendants' actions met the test of being activity likely to cause harassment, alarm, or distress.[13] However, the Court of Appeal said that it was plain that the judge had fallen into error when considering the second limb of the act[14]—the necessity of making such an order. Moses LJ said the case of *Boness*[15] teaches that the purpose of the order is not to punish the offender, but to protect persons from further acts of anti-social behaviour by him. The test of necessity was not met here, especially given the character of the defendants. Moreover, said Moses LJ, if any of the defendants sought to commit further offences, the sanctions of the criminal law would be sufficient deterrent. Finally, the ASBOs were objectionable because they were disproportionate.[16]

Mitigation

9.19 Mitigation of sentence for a protestor, who is convicted or pleads guilty, may therefore include some of the following subjects: (a) the sincerity of belief; (b) the length of time it has been held; (c) the lack of damage to property; (d) the lack of injury to the person; (e) the absence of an identifiable victim, particularly a vulnerable one; (f) the age and good character of the defendant; (g) old or irrelevant previous convictions and cautions; and (h) the adverse effect the conviction may have upon the defendant (possible loss of job etc). This is not an exclusive list. Mitigation must be tailored to the individual facts and circumstances of each case and each offender.

B. Binding Over

Binding over to keep the peace

Introduction

9.20 A person before a criminal court, whether a defendant (convicted or not) or a witness or a person merely brought before the court on complaint with a view to being bound over, may be bound over to keep the peace or to be of good behaviour, by requiring him to enter into a recognizance, with or without sureties, and with the power to commit him to prison if he does not comply: s 1(7) of the Justices of the Peace Act 1968. The Justices of the Peace Act 1361, which remains on the statute book in part, enjoins those with the appropriate power to take steps 'to restrain the offenders, rioters, and all other barrators' for the sole purpose of 'keeping of the peace', so as to avoid the peace being 'blemished'.

9.21 A binding over order in these circumstances is neither a conviction nor a penalty. It is an undertaking as to future conduct with or without (often without) any admissions about past behaviour.[17]

---

[12] For a more detailed discussion of ASBOs, see 9.178 et seq below.
[13] Crime and Disorder Act 1998, s 1C(2)(a), as amended.
[14] Ibid, s 1C(2)(b), as amended.
[15] *R v Dean Boness and others* [2005] EWCA Crim 2395, [2006] 1 Cr App R (S) 120.
[16] [2006] EWCA 2942 Crim, paras 33–51.
[17] It should also be noted that breach of the peace is not in itself a criminal offence in England and Wales. It is in Scotland. See 6.139.

Historically, binding over to keep the peace or to be of good behaviour was a simple and in **9.22** many ways effective method of curbing interpersonal violence.[18] It served as a less formal sanction than a conviction and often as an alternative, more immediate, means of controlling anti-social behaviour than criminal trial.[19] Today, much as it was in early modern times, the power to bind over is frequently used as a method of disposal in cases involving minor assaults or minor incidents of public disorder, where the prosecution are prepared not to proceed, provided that the defendant agrees to be bound over to 'keep the peace'.[20]

Preventative justice

The power to bind over to keep the peace is exercisable 'not by reason of any offence having **9.23** been committed, but as a measure of preventative justice, that is to say, where a person's conduct is such as to lead the justice to suspect that there may be a breach of the peace, or that he may misbehave'.[21]

Bind over: how it works

The person bound over is required to enter into a recognizance in an amount which will be **9.24** forfeited if he fails to keep the peace or be of good behaviour for a specified period. 'Recognizance' or 'recognisance' is an acknowledgment, literally a recognizing, of a debt owed to the Crown—a solemn promise not to breach the peace for a specified period and that, in the event of a breach, he is bound to repay that debt or sum. In *Veater*, Lord Lane said, '[T]he essence of a binding over is that the person bound acknowledges his indebtedness to the Queen.'[22]

The power of a magistrates' court to bind over a person arises in two ways: firstly, upon **9.25** complaint. Traditionally, this was by a constable who arrested a person for a breach of the peace and took them before the court. However, a complaint may be made by 'any person' (Magistrates' Court Act 1980, s 115). Secondly, the court may make such an order of its own motion under common law powers and pursuant to the statutes.[23] Whilst an order under s 115 can only be made after a full hearing of the complaint, the court can bind a person over of its own motion at any stage before the conclusion of criminal proceedings. This may be either upon conviction as an alternative to sentence or where the prosecution decides not to proceed,[24] decides to offer no evidence, or even after the acquittal of the defendant[25] or during an adjournment in proceedings. Even a witness before the court may be bound over.[26] All that is required is that the court considers

---

[18] Professor JA Sharpe, *Crime in Early Modern England 1550–1750* (1984) p 36.
[19] Ibid, pp 48 and 90.
[20] Note, a breach of the peace is not a criminal offence. See 6.139.
[21] *Veater v G and Others* [1981] 1 WLR 567, 574, per Lord Lane CJ.
[22] Ibid, 577 per Lord Lane CJ.
[23] Justices of the Peace Act 1361 and Justices of the Peace Act 1968.
[24] *Lincoln Crown Court, ex p Jude* [1998] 1 WLR 24.
[25] *Inner London Crown Court, ex p Benjamin* (1986) 85 Cr App R 267.
[26] *Sheldon v Bromfield Justices* [1964] 2 QB 573. Note, however, that a witness who is not before the court cannot be bound over. So, for example, the victim of an assault who is not a party to proceedings and has not been called to give evidence against the assailant, who pleaded guilty, cannot be bound over: *Swindon Crown Court, ex p Pawitter Singh* [1984] 1 WLR 449. Likewise, a person who is subject to an unconditional witness order, but who is in the event not required to give evidence: *Kingston-upon-Thames Crown Court, ex p Guarino* [1986] Crim LR 325.

that the person's conduct is such that there might be a future breach of the peace occasioned by him.

To be of good behaviour?

9.26 A person may be bound over to keep the peace *or* to be of good behaviour. Clearly, the two are not the same. 'Breaching the peace' connotes potentially violent or harmful conduct.[27] 'Being of good behaviour' is rather more vague and subjective. In *Hughes v Holley*[28] Glidewell LJ explained that '*contra bonos mores* meant contrary to a good way of life which had the property of being wrong rather than right in the judgment of the majority of contemporary citizens'.[29]

9.27 In *Hashman and Harrup v United Kingdom*,[30] the European Court of Human Rights said that 'to be of good behaviour' was insufficiently precise in law to enable a citizen to regulate his conduct. Accordingly, the concept did not qualify as a 'restriction . . . prescribed by law' so as to justify an interference with the right to freedom of expression under Article 10(2). That case concerned hunt saboteurs who blew a hunting horn and engaged in 'hallooing' with the intention of distracting the foxhounds and disrupting the activities of the Portman Hunt in Dorset. A complaint was made to the magistrates, who required the defendants to enter into a recognizance to be of good behaviour in the sum of £100 for twelve months. The defendants appealed to the Crown Court, which found that there had been no violence or threats of violence and the defendants had not committed any breach of the peace and had not been likely to occasion a breach of the peace. Nevertheless, their conduct had been *contra bonos mores* and that concept was wider than breach of the peace. The Crown Court upheld the magistrates' decision, as did the High Court.

9.28 The European Court of Human Rights noted that in the interim, the Law Commission had recommended the abolition of the power to bind over. The Law Commission Report concluded:

> We regard reliance on *contra bonos mores* as certainly, and breach of the peace as very arguably, contrary to elementary notions of . . . natural justice when they are relied on as definitional grounds justifying the making of a binding over order. Because an order binding someone over to be of good behaviour is made in such wide terms, it fails to give sufficient indication to the person bound over of the conduct which he or she must avoid in order to be safe from coercive sanction . . .[31]

---

[27] *R v Howell* [1982] 1QB 416.

[28] (1988) 86 Cr App R 130.

[29] In that case, the appellant had accosted a female plain clothes police officer in a 'red light' district of Leicester and attempted to solicit her for immoral purposes. She laid a complaint that his conduct was such that he should show cause why he should not enter into a recognizance to be of good behaviour. The justices found his behaviour to be offensive and *contra bono mores* and so ordered him to be of good behaviour for twelve months. The Divisional Court upheld the magistrates, holding that before justices could exercise this power, they must have some cause to believe that without a bind over the defendant might repeat his conduct.

[30] (2000) 30 EHRR 241.

[31] Law Com No 222: *Binding Over* (February 1994) para 4.34.

The European Court agreed. It recalled that 'one of the requirements flowing from the   **9.29**
expression 'prescribed by law'[32] is foreseeability. A norm cannot be regarded as a 'law' unless
it is formulated with sufficient precision to enable a citizen to regulate his conduct.'[33] The
Court noted that 'conduct which is "wrong rather than right in the judgment of the majority of contemporary fellow citizens", by contrast, is conduct which is not described at all,
but merely expressed to be "wrong" in the opinion of a majority of citizens.'[34] Accordingly,
the European Court held that *contra bonos mores* did not comply with the requirements of
Article 10(2) and thus there had been a violation of Article 10 of the European
Convention.

The current position in law then seems to be this: s 1(7) of the Justices of the Peace   **9.30**
Act 1968 has not been amended subsequently, so the term 'to be of good behaviour'
remains on the statute books. However, an order binding over a person 'to be of good
behaviour' is open to challenge on the basis that it is insufficiently precise to be a lawful
order.

Procedural requirements

Where a court is contemplating exercising its power to bind a person over, it must give that   **9.31**
person an opportunity to make representations. Where the case arises from a complaint
being laid before the court under s 115 of the Magistrates' Court Act 1980, that presents
no difficulty because the defendant will be summonsed to court for a hearing. But the court
may also bind over any other person before it, of its own motion. Natural justice requires
that they be afforded an opportunity to say why they should not be bound over. The
case of *R v Hendon Justices ex parte Gorchein*[35] illustrates the point. Dr Gorchein was
involved in an everyday incident of 'road rage' with a man called Palache. The aggrieved
Dr Gorchein initiated a private prosecution and took out a summons for assault against
Palache. The matter came before the justices who asked both men whether they would
agree to be bound over to keep the peace. They both refused. The trial proceeded and
Palache was duly convicted of assault. At that stage the justices announced that *both* parties
were to be bound over to keep the peace in the sum of £50 for twelve months. The Divisional
Court quashed the order in respect of Dr Gorshein. Lord Widgery CJ cited the case of
Sheldon v Bromfield Justices,[36] a similar case factually, which concerned a 'mere witness'
before the court. In that case Lord Parker CJ had said, 'I must say I shudder at the idea that
that can be done . . . It seems to me to be elementary justice that, in particular, a mere witness before the justices should, at any rate, be told what is passing through the justices'
minds, and should have an opportunity of dealing with it.'

Similarly, it is good practice to allow an acquitted defendant, whom the court proposes   **9.32**
to bind over, the opportunity to address the court on the matter: *R v Woking Justices*

---

[32] Any interference with the freedom of expression under the European Convention on Human Rights,
Art 10(1), must be justified under Art 10(2) '. . . such formalities, conditions, restrictions or penalties as are
prescribed by law and are necessary in a democratic society for the prevention of disorder or crime . . .'.
[33] (2000) 30 EHRR 241, para 31.
[34] Ibid, para 38.
[35] [1973] 1 WLR 1502.
[36] [1964] 2 QB 573.

ex p Gossage.[37] In that case, the same Lord Widgery CJ did not consider it a breach of natural justice to impose a bind over after acquitting the defendant without an opportunity to address the court. He drew a distinction between witnesses and defendants because the latter had had a trial and the opportunity of counsel, to cross-examine witnesses and call evidence. Nevertheless, he said that it would be 'at least courteous and perhaps wise' for the court to inform the acquitted defendant that it was contemplating a bind over and invite representations.

9.33 In the case of an acquitted defendant the standard of proof is the criminal standard. In *R v Middlesex Crown Court ex p Khan*,[38] the Divisional Court stated that before binding over an acquitted defendant the judge should be satisfied beyond reasonable doubt that the defendant posed a potential threat to others and was a man of violence. A mere belief that an acquitted person might pose such a threat was not enough. That case concerned a man charged with assault occasioning actual bodily harm. His defence was self-defence. He was acquitted by the jury. Nevertheless, the Crown Court Recorder trying the case proposed, despite protests from counsel, to bind over the acquitted defendant to whom it was made clear in stark terms that if he did not consent to be bound over he was going into custody. The Court of Appeal quashed the order. The Court pointed out that the defendant had not been acquitted on a technicality, but on the merits of the trial by a jury. It was 'very unfortunate in those circumstances' that immediately after such a verdict the judge spoke in terms of binding over the defendant. Collins J said, 'it is exceedingly rare that it would be appropriate to bind over a defendant who had been acquitted'. In such circumstances, however, it was particularly important to apply the criminal standard of proof—which had not been applied in this case.

9.34 In the case of a convicted defendant, where the court proposes to bind him over in anything other than a 'trivial sum', his means and other personal circumstances should be investigated and he should be allowed to make representations in respect of them.[39] In *Lincoln Crown Court, ex p Jude*[40] it was held that a sum of £500 was not so trivial as to enable the court to dispense with the requirement of a means inquiry. However, there is no upper limit, save that which is reasonable and proportionate in the circumstances. A person may, therefore, be bound over in a sum which exceeds the maximum fine for the relevant offence.[41]

9.35 Similarly, the period for which the person is bound over is entirely subject to the discretion of the court subject, as always, to the requirements of reasonableness and proportionality.

9.36 The court may only order the person to be bound over to keep the peace.[42] There is no power to insert specific conditions tailored to the situation. In *Randall*[43] the appellant was

---

[37] [1973] QB 448.
[38] (1997) 161 JP 240.
[39] *Central Criminal Court, ex parte Boulding* [1984] QB 813.
[40] [1998] 1 WLR 24.
[41] *Sandbach Justices, ex p Williams* [1935] 2 KB 192.
[42] In the light of *Hashman and Harrup v UK* (2000) 30 EHRR 241 binding over 'to be of good behaviour' lacks sufficient precision and foreseeability to be lawful.
[43] (1986) 8 Cr App R (S) 433.

a man with a history of convictions for indecently assaulting young males. He was sentenced to probation with the condition of psychiatric treatment. Subsequently, he advertised himself in a local newspaper as a tutor for children. Whilst that was clearly of concern, it was not a breach of the terms of his probation order. Accordingly, the judge bound over Mr Randall in the sum of £500 to keep the peace and be of good behaviour and not to teach or seek to teach any person under 18 years of age. The Court of Appeal held that whilst a court has power to attach conditions when an offender is bound over to come up for judgment (see below), there was no power to include a specific condition to a statutory bind over under the Justices of the Peace Act 1361. Accordingly, the bind over was a nullity.

The right of appeal against a bind over imposed by the magistrates' court lies to the Crown **9.37** Court.[44] This is an appeal by way of rehearing and so, if the facts which led to the binding over are not accepted by the appellant, they must be proved to the satisfaction of the Crown Court.[45] Where a bind over is imposed by the Crown Court on sentence, the right of appeal lies to the Court of Appeal.[46]

Refusal to be bound over

A person must consent to be bound over to keep the peace, because the essence of a **9.38** bind over is that the person enters into a recognizance in a sum of money to be forfeited if he fails to do so. Thus, he openly recognizes his indebtedness and promises to keep the peace and be of good behaviour. The sanction available to the magistrates' court for refusing to enter into a recognizance or rather the failure to do so is imprisonment. This may be for a maximum of six months or, if sooner, until the person complies with the bind over.[47] Whilst imprisonment cannot be imposed on a person who is under the age of 21,[48] a person aged between 18 and 20 may be detained[49] in a young offender's institution for refusing to consent to be bound over. The Crown Court may deal with a refusal to be bound over as contempt of court.

In *Steel and others v United Kingdom*[50] the European Court of Human Rights considered **9.39** the position of protestors who refused to be bound over to keep the peace and were committed to prison in default. The Court found in the case of those protestors who had either created a risk of violence or acted in such a way as was 'likely to cause a breach of the peace', that their detention had been lawful and thus there was no breach of Article 5. The Court said that the applicants could reasonably have foreseen that, if they acted in a manner the natural consequence of which would be to provoke others to violence, they might be ordered to be bound over to keep the peace, and if they refused so to be bound over, they might be committed to prison. The national law was sufficiently clear and precise.[51]

---

[44] Magistrates' Courts (Appeals from Binding Over Orders) Act 1956, s 1(1). See 9.94 et seq below.
[45] *Shaw v Hamilton* [1982] 1 WLR 1308.
[46] Criminal Appeal Act 1968, s 50(1).
[47] Magistrates' Court Act 1980, s 115(3).
[48] Powers of Criminal Courts (Sentencing) Act 2000, s 89.
[49] Ibid, s 108.
[50] (1999) 28 EHRR 603.
[51] Ibid, para 75.

Failure to comply and forfeiture

9.40   If a person who has been bound over by the Crown Court is adjudged to have failed to comply with the conditions of the order, the court may forfeit the whole or part of the recognizance in its discretion; allow time for payment; direct payment by instalments; or discharge the recognizance or reduce the amount due under it.[52] However, the Crown Court is not empowered to impose a prison term immediately.[53] Instead, when forfeiting a recognizance, the Crown Court must fix a term of imprisonment or detention, to be served in default.[54] In essence, the Court must give the person time to pay and inform him how long he will serve if he fails to pay by the due date. In the Crown Court, the maximum periods of imprisonment are determined by the sum in question. These are set out in s 139(4) of the Powers of Criminal Courts (Sentencing) Act 2000:

An amount not exceeding £200	7 days
An amount exceeding £200 but not exceeding £500	14 days
An amount exceeding £500 but not exceeding £1,000	28 days
An amount exceeding £1,000 but not exceeding £2,500	45 days
An amount exceeding £2,500 but not exceeding £5,000	3 months
An amount exceeding £5,000 but not exceeding £10,000	6 months
An amount exceeding £10,000 but not exceeding £20,000	12 months
An amount exceeding £20,000 but not exceeding £50,000	18 months
An amount exceeding £50,000 but not exceeding £100,000	2 years
An amount exceeding £100,000 but not exceeding £250,000	3 years
An amount exceeding £250,000 but not exceeding £1 million	5 years
An amount exceeding £1 million	10 years

9.41   In a magistrates' court, the procedure for forfeiture is governed by s 120 of the Magistrates' Court Act 1980. A recognizance can be declared to be forfeit only by way of an order on complaint,[55] by virtue of whichever power the bind over was originally imposed. Such proceedings are civil in character, and require only the civil standard of proof.[56] However, the person concerned should be told the nature of the breach alleged and be given opportunity to present evidence, call witnesses, or give an explanation.[57]

Binding over to come up for judgment

9.42   Quite separately the Crown Court has the common-law power[58] to bind over a defendant when convicted 'to come up for judgment' upon specified conditions.[59]

9.43   It may be exercised in relation to any offence save where the penalty is fixed by law. The effect of the bind over to come up for judgment is as follows: The convicted offender is

---

[52]   Powers of Criminal Courts (Sentencing) Act 2000, s 139(1).
[53]   *Finch* (1962) 47 Cr App R 58.
[54]   Powers of Criminal Courts (Sentencing) Act 2000, s 139(2).
[55]   Magistrates' Court Act 1980, s 120, as amended. The section does not specify who can make the complaint. It is to be assumed that a complaint that the person bound over has breached the order may be made by 'any person'—as per s 115.
[56]   *Marlow Justices, ex parte O'Sullivan* [1984] QB 381, DC.
[57]   *McGregor* [1945] 2 All ER 180.
[58]   *Spratling* [1911] 1 KB 77.
[59]   This power is recognized by the Powers of Criminal Courts (Sentencing) Act 2000, s 1(8)(a).

bound over for a specified period and may be required to enter into a recognizance. In this version of the bind over, the court may attach specific conditions. If he breaches any of those conditions, he will be brought back before the court and sentenced for the offence. If, however, he abides by the conditions of the bind over during the specified period, he will either not be sentenced for the offence or will receive a nominal penalty. In addition to being sentenced, the offender may forfeit his recognizance. Thus, it is a sort of hybrid between a conditional discharge and a deferred sentence (whereby the sentencing judge postponed sentence for a period of up to six months to see whether the offender had changed his ways)—though, in practice, the power is now rarely used.

9.44 A bind over to come up for judgment is not a sentence itself. There is no power to impose it in addition to a sentence for the offence.[60] An offender must consent to the making of the order and acknowledge himself bound by its terms, though consent would not be vitiated by a realistic expectation of a custodial sentence in the alternative.[61] Where the judge proposes to call an offender to come up for judgment, notice shall be given to him.[62]

9.45 The standard of proof to be applied is the criminal standard. So where it is alleged that the offender has breached the terms of the order, the facts against him must be proved beyond reasonable doubt.[63]

9.46 Since a bind over to come up for judgment may only be made by the Crown Court, appeal lies to the Court of Appeal.[64]

C. Alternatives to Conviction

Cautions

9.47 A caution is an alternative to a conviction. It is essentially a formal warning for an adult offender issued by a senior police officer. It is a method of formally disposing of an offence, diverting the offender from a conviction in the formal trial process. It is often used for low level offences committed by those who have little or no previous convictions. It is not a conviction, but it does require a formal admission of guilt. Therefore, it is recorded on a person's criminal record—albeit in a separate section of the record. However, a caution is usually regarded by the courts as much less serious than a conviction.

9.48 There are now two types of caution: simple cautions and conditional cautions.

---

[60] *Ayu* [1958] 1 WLR 1264. This was a case in which a man was sentenced to twelve months' imprisonment and upon the expiration of his term of imprisonment bound over on his own recognizance in the sum of £10 to return to Nigeria and not to return to England for five years. The Court of Appeal (Lord Parker CJ) said that once he had been sentenced the court had no additional power to bind over to come for judgment.
[61] *Williams* [1982] 1 WLR 1398.
[62] *David* (1939) 27 Cr App R 50.
[63] *McGarry* (1945) 30 Cr App R 187.
[64] Criminal Appeal Act 1968, s 50(1). See also *Williams* [1982] 1 WLR 1398.

Simple cautions

9.49   Simple cautions are a non-statutory disposal. Their use is governed by Home Office Circular 16/2008 *Simple Cautioning of Offenders*. Paragraph 8 of the Circular sets out the aims of the simple caution:

(a) to deal quickly and simply with less serious offences where the offender has admitted the offence;

(b) to divert offenders, where appropriate, from appearing in the criminal courts;

(c) to record an individual's criminal conduct for possible reference in future criminal proceedings or relevant security checks; and

(d) to reduce the likelihood of reoffending.

9.50   The decision to offer a person a simple caution is for the police rather than the prosecutor. The decision is often made at the point of charge. The charging officer must always consider whether a caution is the more appropriate disposal. Even after charge, the Crown Prosecutor has an independent duty to consider whether a caution is appropriate. Moreover, in relation to indictable-only charges, only a Crown Prosecutor can make the decision to impose a simple caution for such an offence.[65]

Criteria for a simple caution

9.51   In determining whether a simple caution is appropriate, the Home Office Circular 16/2008 provides that the following matters must be considered:

(a) whether the suspect made a clear and reliable admission of the offence (either verbally or in writing).[66] An admission of the offence which is corroborated by some other evidence will be sufficient to provide a realistic prospect of conviction. This corroboration could be obtained from information in the crime report or obtained during the course of the investigation. A caution will not be appropriate where, for example, intent is denied or there are doubts about their mental health or intellectual capacity, or where a statutory defence is offered.[67] An admission which may be qualified—where, for example, an offender commits an offence while under the influence of alcohol and cannot remember the full circumstances, but evidence of involvement is agreed either through supporting witness evidence or other evidence (such as CCTV)—may be considered a full and frank admission if all evidence is accepted by the offender.[68] If the admission is made outside the context of a formal interview, a written record of it must be made and the person must be invited to sign the record to confirm its accuracy.[69] The admission of guilt must be made before the person can be invited to accept a caution, and the admission must not be induced by the offer of a caution;[70]

(b) whether there is 'a realistic prospect of conviction' were the person to be prosecuted in accordance with the full code test set out in the Code for Crown Prosecutors. For this

---

[65] Home Office Circular 16/2008, paras 4 and 11.

[66] Ibid, para 9.

[67] Ibid, para 16.

[68] Ibid, para 16.

[69] Ibid, para 19.

[70] Ibid, para 18. See also *R (R) v Durham Constabulary* [2005] 1 WLR 1184.

purpose, a clear, reliable admission corroborated by some other 'material and significant evidential fact' will be sufficient;[71]

(c) whether it is in the public interest to use a simple caution as the appropriate means of
disposal;[72]

(d) whether a caution is appropriate to the offence and the offender, having regard to the
gravity of the offence.[73]

A simple caution cannot be imposed on a person who refuses to accept it.[74] And in practice **9.52**
representations can be made as to why the suspect should not receive a caution, but should
instead be released without charge, for example because of his age or good character or the
circumstances of the offence.

If a person has previously received a caution then a further simple caution should not nor- **9.53**
mally be considered. However, if there has been a sufficient lapse of time to suggest that a
previous caution has had a significant deterrent effect (two years or more) then a caution
can be administered. A caution can also still be administered if the current offence is trivial
or unrelated to any previous offences, or as part of a mixed disposal. If the suspect has previously received a reprimand or warning, a period of at least two years should also be allowed
to elapse before it will be appropriate to administer a caution.[75]

If an offender has a previous conviction, the current offence may still be considered for a **9.54**
simple caution as long as the current offence is not related to the offences for which the
previous conviction was received. The decision to proceed with a caution in these circumstances remains at the discretion of the police officer or the CPS, but there should have been
a significant time lapse between the original conviction and any new offence before a caution will be appropriate.[76]

The Circular gives as an example of a mixed disposal a case where a person who is arrested **9.55**
for being drunk and disorderly is found in possession of a set of keys which he admits he
intended to use in order to steal from cars. A fixed penalty notice could be imposed for the
drunk and disorderly offence, and a caution for the 'going equipped' offence.[77]

Administering the caution

A simple caution should be administered by a custody officer or a suitably trained person **9.56**
to whom authority to administer cautions has been delegated. The offender must be asked
to sign a form which sets out details of the offence, and which makes clear the implications
of accepting the caution.[78] Fingerprints and other identification data can be taken and
retained.

---

[71] Home Office Circular 16/2008, para 9.
[72] Ibid, para 9.
[73] Ibid, para 9.
[74] Ibid, para 16.
[75] Ibid, para 23.
[76] Ibid, para 23.
[77] Ibid, paras 15 and 54.
[78] Ibid, para 44.

Consequences of a caution

9.57   As stated above, a caution is not a conviction, but it is recorded on a person's criminal record and stored on the police national computer. If a caution is imposed on a person employed in a 'notifiable occupation'[79] (such as those who work with children, the disabled, or other vulnerable people, or in national security, or in the administration of justice) the police should disclose the caution to the employer.

9.58   A caution imposed for certain offences may also have adverse implications for people who work with children or vulnerable adults.[80] A caution may be cited in any subsequent court proceedings. With effect from 19 December 2008, the Rehabilitation of Offenders Act 1974, has been amended so that cautions will become immediately spent.[81]

Conditional cautions

9.59   The 'conditional caution' is a newly created statutory disposal for offenders who have attained the age of 16.[82] The conditional caution regime is governed by the Criminal Justice Act 2003, Part 3[83] and the Conditional Cautioning Code of Practice.[84] The Director of Public Prosecutions has issued *Guidance on Conditional Cautioning*.[85]

9.60   A conditional caution is defined by s 22(2) of the Criminal Justice Act 2003 as 'a caution which is given in respect of an offence committed by the offender which has conditions attached to it'. In essence, it enables the Crown Prosecutor to attach conditions (such as making financial or other reparation; or to attend an anger management; or drug or alcohol treatment programme). In the event that a person fails to comply with the conditions, without reasonable cause, the offender may be charged and prosecuted for the original offence.

Offences that may be conditionally cautioned

9.61   The DPP's *Guidance on Conditional Cautioning*[86] sets out at Annex A the full list of offences for which a conditional caution may be given, They include all summary offences[87] (for example, assaulting or obstructing a police officer; offences under ss 4, 4A, and 5 of the Public Order Act 1986; drunk and disorderly; obstructing a highway etc), and some

---

[79] See Home Office Circular 6/2006, *The Notifiable Occupations Scheme: Revised Guidance for Police Forces.* This provides guidance as to the type of professions and occupations which might be 'notifiable occupations', rather than an exhaustive list.

[80] Home Office Circular 16/2008, paras 38 and 39.

[81] Criminal Justice and Immigration Act 2008, s 49 and sch 10—in force from 19 December 2008— see SI 2008/3260.

[82] Originally, a conditional caution was only available for those who had attained 18 of age. However, the Criminal Justice and Immigration Act 2008, s 48, extended that to those aged 16 and 17. That section is in force with effect from 1 February 2009—see SI 2009/140.

[83] Criminal Justice Act 2003, ss 22–7.

[84] Issued under ibid, s 25 and see Criminal Justice Act 2003 (Conditional Cautioning Code of Practice) Order 2004, SI 2004/1683.

[85] See <http://www.cps.gov.uk/Publications/directors_guidance/conditional_cautioning.html>.

[86] Ibid.

[87] Other than road traffic offences under the Road Traffic Act 1988 and the Road Traffic Offences Act 1988.

either-way offences (though the only public order related either-way offence in Annex A is criminal damage).

In contrast to a simple caution, the decision to offer a conditional caution is for the Crown **9.62** Prosecutor and not the police. Crown Prosecutors must take into account the factors set out at paragraphs 3.4–3.23 of the DPP's *Guidance on Conditional Cautioning*.

Statutory criteria for a conditional caution

Before a person may be given a conditional caution the five requirements set out in s 23 **9.63** of the Criminal Justice Act 2003 must be satisfied:[88]

(1) The first requirement is that the authorised person has evidence that the offender has committed an offence.
(2) The second requirement is that a relevant prosecutor decides—
    (a) that there is sufficient evidence to charge the offender with the offence, and
    (b) that a conditional caution should be given to the offender in respect of the offence.
(3) The third requirement is that the offender admits to the authorised person that he committed the offence.
(4) The fourth requirement is that the authorised person explains the effect of the conditional caution to the offender and warns him that failure to comply with any of the conditions attached to the caution may result in his being prosecuted for the offence.
(5) The fifth requirement is that the offender signs a document which contains—
    (a) details of the offence,
    (b) an admission by him that he committed the offence,
    (c) his consent to being given the conditional caution, and
    (d) the conditions attached to the caution.

The conditional caution regime requires a full admission of guilt. That is potentially prob- **9.64** lematic. Before the third and fifth requirements can be satisfied, the offender must have made an admission under caution in interview[89] and signed a document which contains the details of the offence and an admission that he committed it—effectively a signed confession. In the event that the person breaches the conditions of the caution and is then prosecuted for the original offence, those oral and written confessions are admissible in evidence.[90] One can easily envisage the scenario of a defendant in those circumstances seeking to argue that he was induced into making a false confession with the offer of a conditional caution. For that reason, the Code of Practice provides that, in order to ensure that the offender gives informed consent, he should be advised of his right to legal advice before he is asked to confirm that he admits committing the offence. The Code of Practice also states that the offer of a conditional caution should not act as an inducement.[91]

Conditions

The attraction of the conditional caution regime is that it allows flexibility and for the **9.65** conditions to be tailored to the circumstances of the offence and offender. Any condition may be imposed by the Crown Prosecutor provided that it has one or more of the following

---

[88] Criminal Justice Act 2003, s 22(1).
[89] Conditional Cautioning Code of Practice, para 4.1(ii).
[90] Criminal Justice Act 2003, s 24(2).
[91] See also *R (R) v Durham Constabulary* [2005] 1 WLR 1184.

purposes of (a) facilitating the rehabilitation of the offender; (b) ensuring the offender makes reparation;[92] and (c) punishing the offender.[93] Thus any number of conditions might fit into those categories—for example, rehabilitation could include attending a drug or alcohol dependency course, whilst reparation could include making good property that had been criminally damaged, and punishment could include a financial penalty. The newly added s 22(3A) of the Criminal Justice Act 2003 permits a condition of a financial penalty of up to one-quarter of that which could have been imposed upon summary conviction or £250 (whichever is the lower), and/or a condition of attendance at a specified place at specified times for up to twenty hours.

9.66 A standard condition to be included is that the offender must not commit any further offences until the other conditions have been completed.

9.67 The conditions must be (a) proportionate; (b) achievable; and (c) appropriate, ie relevant to the offence and the offender.[94]

Effect of a conditional caution

9.68 As with simple cautions, a conditional caution is not a criminal conviction but it will be recorded on a person's criminal record (in a separate section) on the police national computer. The conditional caution now attracts the protection of being immediately spent under the Rehabilitation of Offenders Act 1974.[95]

Failure to comply with conditions

9.69 Failure to comply with any of the conditions imposed under a conditional caution renders a person liable to prosecution for the original offence.[96] The signed admission document and interview under caution in which an oral admission of guilt was made, will be admissible in evidence to prove the charge.[97] A constable who has reasonable grounds to suspect a person has failed, without reasonable cause, to comply with any of the conditions may arrest that person without a warrant.[98]

Juveniles: warnings and reprimands

9.70 Reprimands and final warnings are a statutory disposal governed by the Crime and Disorder Act 1998, ss 65 and 66 for those aged 17 and under. They operate in a similar but not identical way to a simple caution. Extensive guidance on their operation has been issued by the Home Office called *Final Warning Scheme: Guidance for the Police and Youth Offending Teams*.[99]

---

[92] Criminal Justice Act 2003, s 22(3).
[93] The last objective was added by the Police and Justice Act 2006, s 17 (in force 7 July 2009—SI 2009/1679) which amends s 22(3) of the 2003 Act accordingly.
[94] Conditional Cautioning Code of Conduct, para 5.1.
[95] As amended by the Criminal Justice and Immigration Act 2008, s 49 and Sch 10 (as of 19 December 2008—SI 2008/3260).
[96] Criminal Justice Act 2003, s 24(1).
[97] Ibid, s 24(2).
[98] Ibid, s 24A(1).
[99] See <http://www.homeoffice.gov.uk/documents/final-warning-scheme.pdf?view=Binary>.

The criteria for a reprimand or warning is provided in s 65(1) of the Crime and **9.71** Disorder Act 1998 as follows:

(a) a constable has evidence that a child or young person ('the offender') has committed an offence;
(b) the constable considers that the evidence is such that, if the offender were prosecuted for the offence, there would be a realistic prospect of his being convicted;
(c) the offender admits to the constable that he committed the offence;
(d) the offender has not previously been convicted of an offence; and
(e) the constable is satisfied that it would not be in the public interest for the offender to be prosecuted.

Unlike the system of cautioning for adults, the final warning scheme does not require the **9.72** consent of the juvenile or his parent or guardian. Moreover, a reprimand or warning cannot be imposed if the juvenile already has a previous conviction.

Fixed penalty notices

The fixed penalty notice regime is a familiar concept from road traffic offences. It provides **9.73** a cheap and simple alternative to the formal prosecution by way of trial. In essence, a police officer who reasonably suspects a person has committed a 'penalty offence' may issue that person with a penalty notice. The recipient then has a choice whether to pay the penalty charge, thereby discharging their liability or to dispute the matter and insist that the prosecution proves its case in the normal trial process.

Penalty offences

Under the Criminal Justice and Police Act 2001, fixed penalty notices may now be used to **9.74** deal with a wide range of offences, in particular low level public order offences.[100] Those 'penalty offences' include

- behaviour likely to cause harassment, alarm, or distress (Public Order Act 1986, s 5);
- being drunk on a highway, other public place, or licensed premises (Licensing Act 1872, s 12);
- disorderly behaviour while drunk in a public place (Criminal Justice Act 1967, s 91);
- consumption of alcohol in a designated public place (Criminal Justice and Police Act 2001, s 12);
- throwing fireworks in a thoroughfare (Explosives Act 1875, s 80, repealed by the Fireworks Act 2003 when in force);
- trespasing on a railway (British Transport Commission Act 1949, s 55);
- throwing stones etc at trains or other things on railways (British Transport Commission Act 1949, s 56);
- destroying or damaging property (Criminal Damage Act 1971, s 1(1)) (limited by Home Office guidance to damage not exceeding £300, or £500 if public property);
- depositing and leaving litter (Environmental Protection Act 1990, s 87).

---

[100] The full list of 'penalty offences' for which a fixed penalty notice may be given is set out in the Criminal Justice and Police Act 2001, s 1(1). Section 1(2) empowers the Secretary of State to amend or add to the list by way of secondary legislation.

Giving the notice

9.75 Where a police constable has reason to believe that a person aged ten or over has committed a penalty offence, he may give him a penalty notice in respect of the offence.[101] Unless the notice is given in a police station, the constable giving it must be in uniform.[102] At a police station, a penalty notice may be given only by an officer who has been authorized by the chief officer of police for that area to give penalty notices.[103]

9.76 Though the sections of the 2001 Act speak of a 'constable' or 'police officer', the power to issue notices is not confined to police officers. Fixed penalty notices can be issued for certain offences by community support officers.[104]

Penalty notices

9.77 Section 2(4) of the Criminal Justice and Police Act 2001 defines fixed penalty notices as notices that 'offer the opportunity, by paying a penalty, to discharge any liability to be convicted of the offence to which the notice relates'.

9.78 Section 3(3) sets out the requirements to be met for the notice to be valid. It must

(a) be in the prescribed form;[105]
(b) state the alleged offence;
(c) give such particulars of the circumstances alleged to constitute the offence as are necessary to provide reasonable information about it;
(d) specify the suspended enforcement period (see s 5) and explain its effect;
(e) state the amount of the penalty;
(f) state where the penalty may be paid; and
(g) inform the recipient of his right to ask to be tried for the alleged offence and explain how that right may be exercised.

9.79 The Act empowers the Secretary of State to set the amount of the penalty. However, he may not specify an amount which is more than a quarter of the amount of the maximum fine for which a person is liable on conviction of the offence.[106]

Effect of the penalty notice

9.80 A person who receives a penalty notice has twenty-one days[107] either to pay the penalty or to request a trial. Where he asks to be tried for the alleged offence, proceedings *may* be brought against him.[108] Such a request must be made by the recipient in the

---

[101] Ibid, s 2(1).
[102] Ibid, s 2(2).
[103] Ibid, s 2(3).
[104] Police Reform Act 2002, sch 4. See 6.08 et seq.
[105] 'Prescribed' means prescribed by regulations made by the Secretary of State: Criminal Justice and Police Act 2001, s 3(4).
[106] Ibid, s 3(2).
[107] Ibid, s 5.
[108] Ibid, s 4. The 'may' clause allows prosecutors a measure of discretion to decide whether there is sufficient evidence and whether it is in the public interest to proceed to a trial.

manner specified in the penalty notice and before the end of the period of 'suspended enforcement'.[109]

If, by the end of the suspended enforcement period, the penalty has not been paid but the **9.81** recipient has not made a request to be tried, a sum equal to one and a half times the amount of the penalty may be registered under s 8 of the 2001 Act for enforcement against him as a fine.

D. Appeals

General

This section contains a general outline of the principal avenues for the appeal and review of **9.82** criminal convictions and sentences.[110] It covers the following types of appeal:

- appeals from the magistrates' court to the Crown Court;
- appeals from the magistrates' court and Crown Court to the Divisional Court by way of case stated;
- judicial review by the Divisional Court;
- appeals from the Crown Court to the Court of Appeal;
- references by the Criminal Cases Review Commission;
- appeals from the Court of Appeal and the Divisional Court to the House of Lords; and
- appeals to the European Court of Human Rights.

Appeals from the magistrates' court to the Crown Court[111]

Appeals against conviction

Section 108(1)(b) of the Magistrates' Court Act 1980 provides that a person who has been **9.83** convicted following a plea of not guilty may appeal to the Crown Court against conviction. A case which results in a conditional or absolute discharge may be appealed, notwithstanding that these orders may not amount to 'convictions' for other purposes.[112] This amounts to a general right of appeal. There is no requirement that the appellant first obtains leave or permission from either the magistrates' or Crown Court. Note, however, that the right of appeal to the Crown Court ceases if an application is made for the magistrates to 'state a case' for the opinion of the High Court (see below). The Crown Court may dismiss the appeal, quash the conviction or remit the case to the magistrates for rehearing.[113]

Procedure is governed by Part 63 of the Criminal Procedure Rules 2005 (CPR) (as **9.84** amended).[114] Notice of appeal must be given to the clerk of the relevant magistrates' court and to the prosecutor within twenty-one days of sentence or of being otherwise dealt

---

[109] See, ibid, s 5. The 'suspended enforcement' period is twenty-one days.
[110] The section does not cover discrete forms of appeal such as appeals to the Court of Appeal against verdicts of insanity or findings of unfitness to plead under the Criminal Appeal Act 1968, ss 12 to 15.
[111] References to the magistrates' court may be taken to include the youth court unless otherwise stated.
[112] Magistrates' Courts Act 1980, s 1A.
[113] Supreme Court Act 1981, s 48.
[114] SI 2005/384 (as amended by r 14 and Sch 2 of the Criminal Procedure (Amendment) Rules 2008, SI 2008/2076).

with—for example, by committal for sentence to the Crown Court. The Crown Court may grant leave to appeal out of time.[115]

9.85 Exceptionally, the Crown Court may reopen a conviction notwithstanding that a plea of guilty was entered in the court below. This is possible in five situations:

(a) *When a plea is equivocal when made.*
If the Crown Court is satisfied that the guilty plea was equivocal, in other words, ambiguous, at the time it was entered, it may remit the case to the magistrates for a re-hearing.

(b) *When a plea is subsequently shown to be equivocal.*
The Crown Court may also remit the case if it is satisfied that the plea was unambiguous but that material has emerged that undermines the plea—for example, where it indicates a defence to the charge.

(c) *When a plea is entered under duress.*
Again the Crown Court may remit if satisfied that the plea was somehow the product of duress from some source.

(d) *When autrefois convict or acquit arises.*
Where there has been a guilty plea, the Crown Court may nevertheless quash the conviction if one of the special 'pleas in bar' of *autrefois convict or acquit* are made out. In other words, if it is shown that there has effectively been an earlier conviction or acquittal in respect of substantially the same offence.

(e) *When a reference is made by the CCRC.*
The Criminal Cases Review Commission may refer any summary conviction to the Crown Court whether or not a guilty plea had originally been made (Criminal Appeal Act 1995, s 11).

9.86 The appeal before the Crown Court takes the form of a re-hearing *de novo*[116] and essentially follows the procedure of a summary trial. Neither side is restricted to the evidence called below. Reasons must normally be given for the Crown Court's decision—whether to allow or dismiss the appeal.[117]

9.87 Before repeal, the *Legal Aid in Criminal and Care Proceedings (General) Regulations 1989*[118] provided that the solicitor for a legally-aided person was entitled to a copy of the justices' clerk's notes of evidence. However, there is no corresponding provision in the *Criminal Defence Service (General) (No 2) Regulations 2001*.[119] Even so, 'any case notes should be sent to the Crown Court when there is an appeal': *Practice Direction (Criminal Proceedings: Consolidation) 2002*.[120] It remains good practice for the notes to be supplied to the parties to the appeal.

---

[115] A written application with specified grounds must be made CPR r 63.2(6).
[116] Supreme Court Act 1981, s 79(3).
[117] See *Harrow Crown Court ex p Dave* [1994] 1 WLR 98; *ILCC ex p London Borough of Lambeth* [2000] Crim LR 303.
[118] SI 1989/344.
[119] SI 2001/1437.
[120] [2002] 1 WLR 2870, para V.52.2.

Magistrates may grant bail pending an appeal.[121] A person refused bail by the magistrates may apply to the Crown Court.[122] **9.88**

An unsuccessful appellant may be ordered to pay prosecution costs.[123] A successful appellant may be awarded costs.[124] **9.89**

Appeals against sentence

Any person may appeal to the Crown Court against sentence whether imposed on a plea of guilty or following conviction: s 108(1) of the Magistrates' Court Act 1980. Under s 108(3) sentence means 'any order made on conviction by a magistrates' court' which is not expressly exempted by the subsection.[125] Importantly, an order for costs is not a sentence for these purposes. **9.90**

As with appeals against conviction, there is a general right of appeal and no requirement for leave or permission from either the magistrates' or Crown Court. Similarly, bail may be granted by the magistrates or, if refused, by the Crown Court. **9.91**

The function of the Crown Court is not to review the magistrates' decision but it should ask itself what, on the evidence, was the right sentence.[126] A sentence appeal also involves a fresh hearing. It follows that sentence is 'at large'. If the appeal fails, the Crown Court is not restricted to the sentence passed below and may pass any sentence that the magistrates had power to pass.[127] This means that in theory the court can increase the sentence, although in practice this is rare, and the appellant should be given a warning at the hearing if the court is considering it. **9.92**

Costs may be ordered for or against a successful or unsuccessful appellant as with appeals against conviction. **9.93**

Appeals against binding over[128]

Any person who is aggrieved at being bound over by magistrates (whether following a conviction for an offence or otherwise) may appeal: s 1(1) of the Magistrates' Courts (Appeals from Binding Over Orders) Act 1956. The appeal is also by way of a rehearing. If the facts are disputed, they must be proved.[129] **9.94**

---

[121] Magistrates' Courts Act 1980, s 113.

[122] Supreme Court Act 1981, s 81(1).

[123] Prosecution of Offences Act 1985, s 18(1)(b); CPR r 78(1)(2).

[124] Ibid, s 16(3).

[125] These are orders for payment of costs, orders for the destruction of an animal under the Protection of Animals Act 1911, s 2 and orders 'made in pursuance of any enactment under which the court has no discretion as to the making of the order or its terms' (including a declaration of relevance under the Football Spectators Act 1989, s 23).

[126] *R v Swindon Crown Court ex p Murray* (1998) 162 JP 36.

[127] Supreme Court Act 1981, s 48(4).

[128] For bind overs generally, see 9.20 et seq above.

[129] *Shaw v Hamilton* [1982] 1 WLR 1308.

Appeals by way of case stated: from the magistrates' court and Crown Court to the Divisional Court

The magistrates' court

9.95   Any person who was a party to magistrates' court proceedings or who is aggrieved by 'any order, determination or other proceeding of the court' may question the proceeding on the basis that it is 'wrong in law or in excess of jurisdiction'. He may do so by applying to the magistrates to 'state a case' for the opinion of the High Court.[130] Accordingly, either the defendant or the prosecutor may appeal.

9.96   The procedure is available only in relation to errors of law or jurisdiction; it is not a method of challenging findings of fact unless the finding is alleged to be such that no reasonable bench could have properly made such a finding on the evidence.[131] The appeal itself is not a rehearing but consists of a legal review by two or three Court of Appeal or High Court judges. The High Court may 'reverse, affirm or amend' the magistrates' decision or remit the case with its opinion or make any other order as it sees fit.[132]

9.97   The 'case' consists of a statement of the findings of fact and law made by the magistrates which identifies the question of law upon which the opinion of the High Court is sought. It is formally drafted by the justices' clerk in consultation with the magistrates taking into account representations from the parties. In practice, it is frequently drafted by one or both of the parties for formal adoption by the magistrates' court.

9.98   The application to state a case must be made to the magistrates within twenty-one days of the decision. The magistrates may grant bail for a person in custody unless the person has been committed to the Crown Court for sentence.[133] On the making of an application, the right to appeal to the Crown Court ceases.[134] However, where the application for the case to be stated relates only to conviction, the person may appeal to the Crown Court against sentence.[135] Moreover, if, after a successful case stated, the matter is remitted to the magistrates' court, an appeal to the Crown Court would lie against any subsequent conviction or sentence.[136]

9.99   Magistrates may refuse to state a case if they consider the application to be frivolous[137]—in other words, 'futile, misconceived, hopeless or academic'. Refusals should be rare.[138] Where there is a refusal to state a case, the magistrates must provide reasons. A refusal may be challenged by judicial review and the High Court may make a prerogative order (see 9.106 below) requiring the magistrates to state the case.

---

[130]   Magistrates' Courts Act 1980, s 111(1).
[131]   *Bracegirdle v Oxley* [1947] KB 349; *Braintree District Council v Thompson* [2005] EWCA Civ 178.
[132]   Supreme Court Act 1981, s 28A(3).
[133]   Ibid, s 113.
[134]   Magistrates' Court Act 1980, s 111(4).
[135]   *R v Crown Court at Winchester, ex parte Lewington* [1982] 1 WLR 1277; *Sivalingham v DPP* [1975] CLY 2037. There does not appear to be any authority for the converse situation: see commentary in Paul Taylor, *Taylor on Appeals* (2000).
[136]   *R (Drohan) v Waterford JJ* (1990) 2 IR 309.
[137]   Magistrates' Court Act 1980, s 111(5).
[138]   *R v Mildenhall Magistrates' Court ex p Forest Heath District Council* (1997) 161 JP 401.

Procedure is governed by Part 64 of the CPR and Part 52 of the CPR.   **9.100**

Section 111(2) of the Magistrates' Courts Act 1981 provides that the time limit for apply-   **9.101**
ing is twenty-one days from the decision or order appealed against. On the other hand, it
has been held that the proceedings must have been finally decided before an application can
be made.[139] As Sedley LJ pointed out in *Essen v DPP*,[140] this can give rise to unfairness when
an interlocutory decision was made more than twenty-one days before the final determination and he suggested that the authorities 'could usefully be revisited'. There is, however,
also a view that the High Court has no 'case stated' jurisdiction to review magistrates' interlocutory decisions at all.[141]

Bail may be granted by a High Court judge in chambers.[142]   **9.102**

The Crown Court

A similar High Court jurisdiction of case stated exists in relation to orders, judgments, or   **9.103**
other decisions of the Crown Court.[143] Importantly, however, no such appeal is available
from any judgment or other decision 'relating to trial on indictment' (see further 9.110
below) which can only be challenged in the Court of Appeal (see below). Decisions made
by the Crown Court when acting in its own appellate capacity are, however, appealable by
way of case stated. 'Any party to the proceedings' may apply. This distinguishes appeals
from the Crown Court by way of case stated from appeals from the magistrates' court
which may also be brought by 'any person . . . who is aggrieved by the conviction etc'.

Procedure is governed by the CPR rule 64.7 and is similar to that for appeals from the   **9.104**
magistrates' court.

Judicial review

General

Applications for judicial review are heard in the Administrative Court, part of the High   **9.105**
Court. This is the principal means by which the High Court supervises the decision making of a wide range of 'inferior' public bodies and tribunals including magistrates and, in
much more limited circumstances, the Crown Court.

The High Court exercises control and grants relief by means of the discretionary preroga-   **9.106**
tive orders:

(a) quashing orders: used to nullify decisions and orders;
(b) mandatory orders: used to compel the inferior body to comply with its obligations;
    and
(c) prohibiting orders: used to prohibit the inferior body from acting in excess of its
    jurisdiction.

---

[139] *Loade v DPP* [1990] 1 QB 1052.
[140] [2005] EWHC 1077.
[141] *R v Rochford JJ ex p Buck* (1979) 68 Cr App R 114; but cf *R (Watson) v Dartford Magistrates' Court*
[2005] EWHC 905 (Admin).
[142] Supreme Court Act 1981, s 81(1)(d).
[143] Ibid, s 28.

9.107 It is important to grasp, however, that the orders are discretionary and relief may be refused where, for example, the point has, in all the circumstances, become academic or where the lower court would have reached the same conclusion if it had properly directed itself or because of delay.

9.108 A detailed treatment of the principles of judicial review is beyond the scope of this work. However, the principal grounds for review are (a) errors of law, including errors in the exercise of a discretion; (b) excess of jurisdiction; (c) breaches of natural justice; and (d) that the decision is so unreasonable or irrational that no reasonable tribunal which properly directed itself could reach such a decision as a matter of law—'Wednesbury unreasonable'.[144]

9.109 Where human rights are engaged, the court will subject the decision to 'a degree of scrutiny appropriate to the interest to be protected' and, in particular, to the requirement for proportionality.[145]

The Crown Court: trial on indictment

9.110 Importantly, Crown Court decisions 'relating to trial on indictment' are expressly excluded from judicial review, the alternative being an appeal to the Court of Appeal. The phrase has been held to exclude all decisions relating to the conduct of the trial including conviction and sentence. Most, if not all, aspects of a jury trial are not reviewable. In *Smalley*[146] the House of Lords held the test to be whether the decision was one affecting the conduct of a trial or by way of pre-trial directions.

9.111 A considerable body of case law has built up but examples of Crown Court decisions held *not* to relate to trial on indictment and, therefore, reviewable include an order committing an acquitted defendant to prison unless he agreed to be bound over;[147] an order estreating the recognizance of a surety;[148] and a forfeiture order made against the owner of property who was not a defendant.[149]

9.112 Examples of decisions held to relate to trial on indictment include a refusal to order costs following an acquittal,[150] a refusal to grant legal aid,[151] and a refusal to allow a private individual to conduct a prosecution in person.[152]

The magistrates' court and Crown Court appeals

9.113 Some of the aspects of judicial review overlap with the High Court's parallel 'case stated' jurisdiction to set aside decisions of magistrates and, in its appellate capacity, the Crown Court. Distinctions are not always plainly evident. By way of guidance in relation to magistrates' decisions, Collins J has stated that the normal appeal route from magistrates'

---

[144] *Associated Picture Houses v Wednesbury Corporation* [1948] 1 KB 223.
[145] *R (Daly) v Secretary of State for the Home Department* [2001] 2 AC 532.
[146] [1985] AC 622.
[147] *R v Inner London CC ex p Benjamin* (1987) 85 Cr App R 267.
[148] *Re Smalley* op cit.
[149] *R v Maidstone CC ex p Gill* (1987) 84 Cr App R 96.
[150] For example, *Ex p Meredith* (1973) 57 Cr App R 451.
[151] *R v Chichester CC ex p Abodunrin* (1984) 79 Cr App R 293.
[152] *R v Southwark CC ex p Tawfick*, The Times, 1 December 1994.

errors of law is by way of case stated but that judicial review may be appropriate where there is an allegation of unfairness or bias or an issue of fact to be raised which the magistrates did not decide themselves.[153] He added, where a 'stated case' was more appropriate, judicial review should not be used to avoid the more stringent twenty-one day time limit of the former. An acquittal by magistrates is not generally reviewable unless there has been no jurisdiction to acquit.[154] Nor is sentence generally a matter for review unless there is a jurisdictional issue—in which case the court may substitute any lawful sentence.[155]

Where facts emerge after conviction in the magistrates' court, it is said that an appeal to the Crown Court is the appropriate procedure because that court's power to investigate facts is not available to the High Court.[156] Similarly, the court will not set aside a decision merely on the ground that fresh evidence has been discovered.[157] **9.114**

Procedure

Procedure is governed by Part 54 of the Civil Procedure Rules 1998.[158] The leave of the High Court is required to apply for judicial review. This may be granted or refused on the papers by a single judge. An application for leave may be renewed to a full court of two or three judges. An application may be made within three months of the decision to be challenged but, in any event, to succeed it must be 'promptly' made. **9.115**

Where the applicant is in custody, the magistrates have no power to grant bail but application may be made to a High Court judge.[159] The Crown Court may grant bail to any person who has applied for leave to make an application for a quashing order.[160] **9.116**

Appeals from the Crown Court to the Court of Appeal[161]

Interlocutory appeals

Where there has been a preparatory hearing ahead of the trial proper, interlocutory appeals from the Crown Court on points of law may be brought by either party.[162] **9.117**

Preparatory hearings may be held where the Crown Court considers that 'substantial benefits are likely to accrue from a preparatory hearing' in serious or complex fraud cases[163] **9.118**

---

[153] *R (P) v Liverpool City Magistrates* (2006) 170 JP 453.
[154] *R v Dorking JJ ex p Harrington* [1984] AC 743.
[155] Supreme Court Act 1981, s 43.
[156] *R v Huyton JJ ex p Roberts* [1988] COD 43.
[157] *R v Carlisle CC ex p Marcus-Moore*, The Times, 26 October 1981.
[158] SI 1998/3132.
[159] Criminal Justice Act 1948, s 37(1)(d).
[160] Supreme Court Act 1981, s 81(1)(e).
[161] In October 2008 the Registrar published a new *Guide to Commencing Proceedings in the Court of Appeal (Criminal Division)*. The full text is available at <http://www.hmcourts-service.gov.uk/docs/proc_guide.pdf>.
[162] Criminal Procedure and Investigations Act 1996, s 35(1) and Criminal Justice Act 1987, s 9(11), as amended.
[163] Criminal Justice Act 1987, s 7(1).

or, in other complex, lengthy or serious cases,[164] for purposes which include identifying material issues, trial management, or expediting the proceedings before the jury. At a preparatory hearing the judge may decide, inter alia, any questions of the admissibility of evidence or 'any other question of law relating to the case'. Rulings or orders on such questions may be appealed.[165]

9.119 Procedure is governed by Part 65 of the Criminal Procedure Rules 2005 as amended. Leave of the trial judge or the Court of Appeal is required. The court's power to grant leave is exercisable by a single Court of Appeal judge, renewable, if refused, to the full Court of Appeal.

Appeals against conviction

9.120 Anyone convicted of an offence on indictment may appeal to the Criminal Division of the Court of Appeal. Permission is required.[166] An appeal lies only with the leave of the court itself or under a certificate issued within twenty-eight days of conviction from the trial judge that 'the case is fit for appeal'.[167] The power to grant leave is exercisable by a single judge of the Court of Appeal—renewable, if refused, to the full court. The grant of a trial judge's certificate is rare and, in practice, tends to occur only in cases where there is a clearly arguable issue of law.[168]

9.121 Procedure is governed by the relevant sections of the Criminal Appeal Act 1968 and Parts 65–70 and Part 74 of the CPR.

9.122 The Court of Appeal is purely a creature of statute and the only statutory test for quashing a conviction is that the court 'think(s) that the conviction is unsafe'.[169]

9.123 There is a considerable amount of law (and debate) as to how the court should approach this single test which it is beyond the scope of this work to review comprehensively. The short point is that it is capable of wide interpretation according to the circumstances. Thus, if for any reason the court concludes that the appellant was wrongly convicted or is left in doubt (sometimes referred to as 'the lurking doubt test'[170]) as to whether he or she was rightly convicted, it must necessarily quash the conviction. Equally, however, if the court is satisfied that the conviction is safe despite any legal misdirection, irregularity, or fresh evidence, it will dismiss the appeal.

9.124 Almost by definition, an unfair trial is to be treated as unsafe. Equally an unlawful conviction will be unsafe and, if a trial should never have taken place, for example, where

---

[164] Criminal Procedure and Investigation Act 1996, s 29(1). A preliminary hearing was held in the Greenpeace/Drax power station case in order to determine whether the defence of necessity was to be permitted to be put forward.

[165] Re: fraud cases: Criminal Justice Act 1987, s 9(11), as amended; re: other cases: s 35(1).

[166] Criminal Appeal Act 1968, s 1(1) as amended (CAA).

[167] Ibid, s 1(2).

[168] As for the procedure in applying for a certificate, see the Criminal Procedure Rules 2005, SI 2005/384, r 68.4.

[169] Criminal Appeal Act 1968, s 2, as amended.

[170] *Cooper* [1969] 1 QB 267; *Stafford v DPP* [1974] AC 878.

there has been an abuse of process, the conviction will be quashed notwithstanding that there was a plea of guilty.[171]

In a few cases the court is asked to receive evidence which was not called at trial. The court **9.125** has power to receive such evidence 'if they think it necessary or expedient in the interests of justice' having regard in particular to considerations such as whether there is a reasonable explanation for the failure to adduce the evidence at trial and whether the evidence is 'capable of belief'.[172] The court has always resisted the argument that, where fresh evidence is received, the test of its impact on the safety of the conviction should be the likely effect that the evidence would have had on the minds of the jury.[173] The nearest the judges have come to ceding their own assessment to that of a notional jury was the dictum of Lord Bingham in *Pendleton*:[174]

> It will usually be wise for the Court of Appeal, in a case of any difficulty, to test their own provisional view by asking whether the evidence, if given at the trial, might reasonably have affected the decision of the jury to convict. If it might, the conviction must be thought to be unsafe.

With increasing frequency, where the court quashes a conviction, it will order a retrial. The **9.126** test is whether 'it appears to the court that the interests of justice so require'.[175] This is said to be a balance between the public interest and the legitimate interests of the defendant. Relevant considerations include the length of time between the original conviction and appeal, whether the defendant has already had to serve a large part of any sentence that s/he could expect on a further conviction and the availability of witnesses.

Where an appeal is wholly unmeritorious and where, for example, an appellant has ignored **9.127** counsel's advice to that effect, the court may (but rarely does) direct that all or part of the time that an applicant for leave to appeal has spent in custody since the commencement of the appeal proceedings shall not count towards his/her sentence: s 29 of the Criminal Appeal Act 1968.

Where it appears that the jury could on the indictment have found the appellant guilty of **9.128** some other offence and it appears to the court that the jury must have been satisfied of facts which would make him/her guilty of that offence, the court may substitute a conviction for that offence instead of allowing the appeal.[176]

Bail may be granted by the court,[177] although it tends to do so only in exceptional circum- **9.129** stances and only where there is obvious merit in the appeal.

---

[171] *Mullen* [2000] QB 520.
[172] Ibid, s 23.
[173] See *Stafford v DPP*, above.
[174] [2002] 1 WLR 72; see also *Dial* [2005] 1 WLR 1660; *Harris* [2006] 1 Cr App R 55; *George* [2007] EWCA Crim 2722.
[175] Ibid, s 7.
[176] Criminal Appeal Act 1968, s 3.
[177] Ibid, s 19.

Appeals against sentence by the defendant

9.130 It should be noted firstly that there is a 'slip rule' which allows the Crown Court judge to vary or rescind a sentence or other order within fifty-six days of it having been made: s 155(1) of the Powers of Criminal Courts (Sentencing) Act 2000.[178] This is essentially a power to correct procedural or legal errors although it is accepted that it may be relied upon where a judge, on reflection, considers that he or she was too harsh originally. Exceptionally, it may be used to increase the sentence if appropriate.[179]

9.131 Sentences passed by the Crown Court following conviction on indictment or committal for sentence by the magistrates may be appealed to the Court of Appeal. Unless the sentencing judge certifies that the case is fit for appeal, an appeal against sentence requires leave.[180]

9.132 For appeal purposes, the expression 'sentence' includes a wide range of orders including, for example, hospital orders, recommendations for deportation, and confiscation orders under the Proceeds of Crime Act 2002.[181]

9.133 The two most common grounds of appeal are that the sentence was wrong in principle or 'manifestly excessive'. The court may quash a sentence and replace it with any sentence that the Crown Court had power to pass provided that the appellant is 'not more severely dealt with on appeal than he was dealt with by the court below'.[182]

Appeals against sentence by the prosecution

9.134 The Attorney General may refer a sentence for a serious offence to the Court of Appeal if it appears to the Attorney General that the 'sentencing . . . has been unduly lenient': s 36 of the Criminal Justice Act 1988. The test to be applied by the court is whether the sentence was outside the range which the judge, applying his mind to all relevant factors, could reasonably consider appropriate.[183]

9.135 References may only be made in relation to a sentence for an indictable only offence or for an offence specified by order under the Act.[184]

9.136 The leave of the court is required for a reference. The court may quash the sentence and pass in its place 'such sentence as they think appropriate for the case and as the court below had power to pass'. The court determines the appeal on the basis of the material that was before the sentencing judge.[185]

9.137 Procedure is governed by Schedule 3 of the 1988 Act supplemented by Part 70 of the CPR.

---

[178] As amended by the Criminal Justice and Immigration Act 2008, Sch 8.
[179] See, for example, the cases set out in *Blackstone's Criminal Practice* (2009), D19.95.
[180] Criminal Appeal Act 1968. Ibid s 11.
[181] Ibid, s 50.
[182] Ibid, s 11(3).
[183] *AG's Ref (No 4 of 1989)* [1990] 1 WLR 41.
[184] See Criminal Justice Act 1988 (Review of Sentencing) Order 2006, SI 2006/ 1116, Sch 1.
[185] *AG's Ref (No 19 of 2005)* [2006] EWCA Crim 785.

Attorney General's Reference on a point of law following acquittal

Where there has been an acquittal, the Attorney General may refer a point of law to the **9.138**
Court of Appeal for the court to 'give their opinion on it'.[186] Having done so, the court may
further refer the point to the House of Lords if it appears that they ought to consider the
point. Whatever the court's opinion, the acquittal continues to stand. The acquitted person
is nevertheless entitled to participate in the proceedings.

The process is governed by Part 70 of the CPR. **9.139**

Prosecution appeals against rulings

The prosecution can appeal against terminating rulings: Part 9 of the Criminal Justice Act **9.140**
2003 confers prosecution rights of appeal from rulings 'in relation to trial on indictment'
that would effectively result in an acquittal if not reversed.[187] This includes a ruling that
there is no case to answer. An appeal may only be brought with the leave of the Court of
Appeal or of the trial judge.[188]

There is no right of appeal under the Act against a ruling that a jury be discharged or from **9.141**
a ruling appealable under other legislation[189]—for example, a ruling in a preparatory hearing (see 9.117 above).

At or before the point at which the prosecution informs the Crown Court that it intends to **9.142**
appeal, it must inform the court that it agrees that the defendant should be acquitted of the
offence(s) if leave to appeal is not obtained or if the appeal is abandoned.[190] With that
agreement, the ruling becomes a 'terminating ruling' if not overturned. From the point at
which the prosecution informs the Crown Court of its intention to appeal, the ruling has
no effect 'whilst the appeal is pursued'.[191]

The prosecution must either serve notice of appeal or apply orally to the trial judge for leave **9.143**
to appeal. The judge must decide whether or not the appeal should be expedited and, if so,
whether to adjourn the trial in order for the appeal to be determined.[192] If he or she decides
that the appeal need not be expedited, the judge may nevertheless adjourn the trial or
discharge the jury. Proceedings may continue in relation to offences that are unaffected by
the ruling.

The Court of Appeal may (a) confirm the ruling—in which case, it must order an acquittal **9.144**
or (b) reverse or vary the ruling—in which case it may order that the trial resume or order
a fresh trial unless the defendant could no longer receive a fair trial.[193] Procedure is
governed by Part 67 CPR.

---

[186] Criminal Justice Act 1972, s 72.
[187] Criminal Justice Act 2003, s 58.
[188] Ibid, s 57(4).
[189] Ibid, s 57(2).
[190] Ibid, s 58(8).
[191] Ibid, s 58(10).
[192] Ibid, s 59.
[193] Ibid, s 61.

9.145 At the time of writing, the additional provisions of Part 9 of the Criminal Justice Act 2003 giving the prosecution a right to appeal 'qualifying evidentiary rulings' have yet to be brought into force. They are, nevertheless, included here for the purpose of completeness.

9.146 A 'qualifying evidentiary ruling' means an evidentiary ruling in respect of a qualifying offence made in or before a trial on indictment before the opening of the defence case.[194] An evidentiary ruling is one which 'relates to the admissibility or exclusion of any prosecution evidence'. Qualifying offences are those listed in Part 1 of Schedule 4 of the Act. They include, inter alia, serious offences of violence, drugs, sexual offences, and criminal damage.

9.147 Leave is required from the Court of Appeal or trial judge. Leave is not to be granted unless the court is satisfied that the ruling or rulings taken together 'significantly weaken the prosecution case'.[195]

9.148 Provisions relating to expedition, adjournment, and discharge of the jury are similar to those which apply to 'terminating rulings' appeals. There are as yet no procedural rules in place.

Prosecution applications for retrials for serious offences

9.149 Part 10 of the Criminal Justice Act 2003 also permits the prosecution to apply to the Court of Appeal to quash an acquittal for a 'qualifying offence' and direct a retrial where there is 'new and compelling evidence'.[196] The qualifying offences are set out in Schedule 5 and include most serious offences.

9.150 An application requires the personal consent of the Director of Public Prosecutions.

9.151 The court must order a retrial if (a) 'there is new and compelling evidence in the case'[197] and (b) 'it is in the interests of justice for an order to be made'.[198] Evidence is 'new' if it was not adduced at the original trial. Evidence is 'compelling' if it is reliable, substantial, and in the context of the issues, highly probative of the prosecution case.

9.152 As to the interests of justice test, the court must have regard, in particular, to any likelihood of an unfair trial; the passage of time; whether the evidence would have been adduced in the trial but for a prosecution failure to act with due diligence or expedition; and whether, since the trial, the prosecution have failed to act with due diligence or expedition.[199]

Referrals by the Criminal Cases Review Commission

9.153 The Criminal Cases Review Commission (CCRC) was set up in 1995 to investigate alleged miscarriages of justice and, where appropriate, to refer a conviction on indictment or resulting sentence (unless fixed by law) back to the Court of Appeal[200] at any time

---

[194] Ibid, s 62.
[195] Ibid, s 63.
[196] Ibid, ss 75–97.
[197] Ibid, s 78.
[198] Ibid, s 79. See *Dunlop* [2006] EWCA 1354; *Miell* [2008] 1 WLR 627.
[199] Ibid, s 79.
[200] Criminal Appeal Act 1995, s 9. The CCRC may also refer any summary conviction or sentence to the crown court: ibid, s 11. The CCRC's investigative powers are set out in ss 17–21 of the 1995 Act. On average about 70 per cent of cases referred back are successful appeals.

notwithstanding that the court may have previously dismissed an earlier appeal. The reference is the equivalent of leave to appeal granted by the court itself. However, the court is not bound by any other aspect of the reference and determines the appeal in the ordinary way. A reference 'shall be treated for all purposes as an appeal'.[201]

The test which the CCRC is required to apply by statute is whether there is a 'real possibility' that the court will quash the conviction or sentence.[202] Normally, a reference must involve an argument or information not originally available.[203] In exceptional circumstances, there may be a reference without any such development.[204] **9.154**

When the CCRC refers a case, it provides a Statement of Reasons setting out the nature of its investigation, the relevant facts and circumstances, and its approach to the evidence and the applicable law. As stated above, the court is not bound in any way. Grounds of appeal are still required. From that point on, the case proceeds as would a normal appeal in which leave has been granted. In other words, the court approaches the case as it would any other and, for example, receipt of fresh evidence still needs the leave of the court notwithstanding that the CCRC acted upon it.[205] Additional grounds of appeal also need leave to be argued. **9.155**

The court may dismiss an appeal if the only ground for allowing it is that there has been a change in the law and, had the reference not been made, the court would have otherwise refused an application for leave to appeal out of time.[206] **9.156**

Appeals from the Court of Appeal and Divisional Court to the Supreme Court

Appeals to the Supreme Court lie from most substantive decisions of the Court of Appeal[207] and, in 'a criminal cause or matter', direct from the Divisional Court.[208] Either the defendant or the prosecution may appeal. Before 1 October 2009, these appeals had been considered by the Judicial Committee of the House of Lords.[209] **9.157**

An appeal requires a certificate from the Court of Appeal or Divisional Court that a particular point of law of general public importance is involved—'the certified question'. There is no appeal against a refusal to certify a point. An appeal also requires the leave of either the Supreme Court or the lower court. Conventionally, leave is almost always refused by the lower court, which in the past allowed the Judicial Committee itself to decide whether or not to grant leave. There is no reason to believe this practice will change. **9.158**

---

[201] Ibid, s 9(2).
[202] See *R v CCRC ex p Pearson* [2000] 1 Cr App R 141.
[203] Criminal Appeal Act 1995, s 13.
[204] Ibid, s 14.
[205] *Conway* 70 Cr App R 4.
[206] Criminal Appeal Act 1995, s 16C as inserted by the Criminal Justice and Immigration Act 2008, s 42.
[207] Criminal Appeal Act 1968, s 33.
[208] Constitutional Reform Act 2005, s 40.
[209] Administration of Justice Act 1960, s 1(1)(a).

Petitions to the European Court of Human Rights

9.159 The Human Rights Act 1998 was intended 'to give people in the UK opportunities to enforce their rights under the European Convention (of Human Rights) in British courts rather than having to incur the cost and delay of taking a case to . . . Strasbourg'.[210]

9.160 Even so, any person, non-governmental organization, or group of individuals who have exhausted the remedies offered by the domestic courts, and who remain dissatisfied, may still go on to petition the European Court of Human Rights over violations of the rights guaranteed under the Convention.[211]

9.161 In addition, any domestic court or tribunal may, 'if it considers that a decision on the question is necessary to enable it to give judgment', refer an issue for determination to the Court.[212] The lower courts have been firmly discouraged from doing so, it being preferable to seek clarification through the domestic appeal processes.[213]

9.162 An individual applicant must exhaust all local remedies before a complaint becomes admissible—in other words, he or she must have pursued domestic appeal avenues so far as possible.

9.163 Any state found in breach of the Convention can be ordered to make 'just satisfaction' and any state whose law is incompatible with the Convention can be ordered to rectify the discrepancy. A successful applicant may receive modest compensation.

9.164 Legal aid is not available for the drafting and filing of a petition. However, if the Court takes the initial step of referring the application to the relevant government for its observations, then Council of Europe funding is available thereafter, subject to means. The petition must be brought within six months of the final domestic decision.[214] The Court sits in committees of three judges, chambers of seven judges and, exceptionally, in Grand Chambers of seventeen judges in cases that raise a serious question of interpretation or application of the Convention or a serious issue of general importance.

9.165 Once an application is registered, a judge rapporteur is assigned. He or she may refer the case to a committee which may, if unanimous, declare a case inadmissible. If not, the case is referred to a full chamber which decides upon its admissibility and merits. Once the case is declared admissible, the chamber places itself at the disposal of the parties with a view to reaching a friendly settlement. If that is not achieved, the chamber will determine the application. Either party can request a rehearing before the Grand Chamber. The request is determined by a panel of five judges who assess the importance of the issues involved.

---

[210] Prime Minister's preface to the White Paper, 'Bringing Rights Home', Cm 3782.
[211] For a detailed treatment of the legal relationship between protest and the Convention, see Ch 10.
[212] Treaty of Rome, Art 234.
[213] *R v Plymouth JJ ex p Rogers* [1982] QB 863; *Henn* [1981] AC 850.
[214] Treaty of Rome, Art 35.

E. Injunctions

An injunction is a remedy by which the court makes an order addressed to the defendant **9.166**
in civil proceedings requiring him or her to do or not to do a specific act. In the context of
protest, it is available as a final or interim remedy in tort to prevent trespass or nuisance or
intimidation, and within the specific provisions of the Protection from Harassment Act
1997. Undertakings as to future conduct are often given in order to avoid an injunction,
but a breach of an undertaking or of an injunction may be punished as a contempt of court.

Section 1(1) of the Protection from Harassment Act 1997 provides that a person must not **9.167**
pursue a course of conduct amounting to the harassment[215] of another, and which he knew
or ought to have known would do so. Pursuing a course of conduct in breach of s (1)
amounts to a criminal offence.[216] A breach or apprehended breach of s 1(1) can be the
subject of a civil claim by the victim in which damages may be awarded[217] and an injunction[218] granted by the County Court or High Court to restrain the defendant from pursuing the harassment.[219] In the context of protests, it is the injunction, as opposed to damages,
that is often the primary aim of the claimant, as the losses incurred as a result of the activities of protestors usually far outweigh the financial means of the protestor.

Whereas these provisions provide protection from harassment only to individuals,[220] **9.168**
the Serious Organised Crime and Police Act 2005 amended the 1997 Act to include injunctive protection that extends to corporate claimants.[221] The new s 1(1A) provides that a
person must not pursue a course of conduct which involves the harassment of two or
more persons which he knows or ought to know would do so and by which he intends
to persuade any person either not to do something that he is entitled to do, or to do
something that he is not under any obligation to do. Section 2 was amended to make a
breach of s 1(1A) an offence, and thus the offence still relates only to offending against
individuals.

Significantly, however, a new s 3A was inserted to enable any victim of an actual or **9.169**
apprehended breach of s 1(1A), or any person falling within s 1(1A)(c), to apply for an
injunction restraining that person from harassing 'any person or persons mentioned or

---

[215] Harassing a person includes alarming the person or causing the person distress: s 7(1). Harassment is
not further defined.

[216] This criminal offence is a summary only offence punishable with a maximum of six months' imprisonment or a fine not exceeding level 5 on the standard scale, or both: s 2(2) of the Protection from Harassment
Act 1997.

[217] Section 3(2).

[218] A breach of the injunction is a criminal offence, punishable by up to five years' imprisonment: ss 3(6)
and (9).

[219] A claim under s 3 of the 1997 Act is subject to Part 8 procedure, issued on From N208 and automatically allocated to the multi-track: CPR Part 65.28. For extended commentary on interim injunctions, see *The
White Book*, Vol 2, Section 15, *Interim Remedies*.

[220] *DPP v Dziurzynski* [2002] EWHC 1380 at para 33; *Majrowski v Guy's and St Thomas's NHS Trust*
[2007] 1 AC 224 at para 19.

[221] *Smithkline Beecham Plc & others v Greg Avery (representing SHAC) and others* [2009] EWHC 1488
(QB).

described in the injunction'.[222] Whilst the 'person' subject to harassment is limited to an 'individual',[223] the injunction can be sought by the person the harassment is intended to persuade, and this includes corporate claimants.[224]

Injunctions in Protest Cases

9.170 The terms of an injunction can be wide and may include an exclusion zone (for example at Stonehenge or near a factory or laboratory), a ban on megaphones, or a limit on numbers. The approach of the courts is best demonstrated by way of example.

9.171 In *Oxford University and others v Brougton and others*[225] the university sought to extend an interim injunction limiting demonstrations around an animal research laboratory that was being constructed. The existing order had permitted a demonstration of up to fifty people opposite the main entrance each Thursday afternoon (with a megaphone permitted for this hour), but banned protest within an exclusion zone that covered the immediate vicinity of the site and banned the use of video cameras within this zone. On application, the Court extended the exclusion zone[226] on the basis that it sought to counter intimidation and harassment, and could not be justified if its configuration invited angry assemblies outside or close to public entrances. All noise amplification devices were banned within the exclusion zone, save on the occasion of a lawful peaceful assembly conducted in compliance with the Public Order Act 1986. Balancing the interests of protestors concerned to advance a message and the impact of the amplified protest noise upon the captive audience going about their lawful business in the adjoining buildings, the use of the megaphone on hourly occasions for an indefinite period was not said to be justified. The Court refused to reduce the persons permitted at the demonstration from fifty to twelve and removed the ban on the use of video cameras. It did hold that the university was entitled to a restraint on publication of material serving to identify a person protected by the injunction. It is important to note that the court observed that an order reflecting a balance of competing interests inevitably needed subsequent reconsideration from time to time in the light of experience and future developments.[227]

9.172 In *Christopher David Hall and others v Save Newchurch Guinea Pigs (Campaign) and sixteen others*,[228] members of a farming partnership and a local councillor sought injunctive relief under the Protection from Harassment Act 1997 against animal rights activists, restraining them from participating in an alleged campaign of harassment and intimidation aimed at closing down the farm. The campaign admitted that since 1999 it had been conducting a campaign aimed at closing down the guinea pig breeding business. In advance of a planned

---

[222] Section 3(A)(2).
[223] Section 7(5).
[224] See judgment of Jack J in *Smithkline Beecham Plc & others v Greg Avery (representing SHAC) and others* [2009] EWHC 1488 (QB) at para 43.
[225] [2006] EWHC 1233. A very limited part of this judgment was appealed in relation to undertakings given by two of the defendants: see [2006] EWCA Civ 1305.
[226] Considering *Burris v Azadani* [1995] 1 WLR 1372.
[227] For further applications in relation to the order, see *Oxford University and others v Broughton and others* [2008] EWHC 75, QB.
[228] [2005] EWHC 372, QB.

demonstration, the claimants obtained an interim injunction on short notice, restraining 'the protestors' from pursuing a course of conduct which amounted to harassment of the 'protected persons' (including the farmers and contractors). The Court held that it could grant interlocutory injunctive relief in harassment cases under the Supreme Court Act 1981 s 37(1) in wide terms to restrain conduct that was not in itself tortious or otherwise unlawful, if such an order was reasonably necessary for the protection of a claimant's legitimate interests.

To that end the Court concluded that it had power to impose an exclusion zone when   **9.173**
granting a non-molestation injunction restraining harassment of the victim by the defendant, provided no unnecessary restraint was placed on the defendant.[229] The claimants were entitled to injunctive relief against all of the defendants on the basis that there was a good arguable case that unless restrained they would be involved in a continuation of the campaign. However, the defendants were entitled to continue to protest on a weekly basis on Sundays between 12 pm and 3 pm. An exclusion zone of 100 yards would apply to the homes of protected persons and the premises of contractors, subcontractors, and suppliers. There should be no more than twenty-five protestors at each demonstration. That figure was said to represent a fair balance between the proper protection of the claimants and the rights of the defendants to protest.

The sixth claimant who represented the residents of two parishes was not entitled to   **9.174**
an order permitting him to represent the residents of a further five parishes. There was a very substantial body of opinion within the parishes that strongly supported his action, but there were some who did not or who took a neutral position. His representative capacity did not depend upon a majority vote. However, if adequate steps were taken to protect the protected persons from harassment and intimidation, the impact upon the community at large would cease. Thus, the court held the residents of the community at large did not have an interest that required protection beyond that properly to be afforded to the protected persons. The Court refused to impose a wider exclusion zone on the grounds that it had not been demonstrated that the imposition of the proposed 200 square kilometre exclusion zone was reasonably necessary for the protection of the protected persons' rights.

Further illustrations of the scope of injunctions against protestors can be seen in: **9.175**

- *Smithkline Beecham Plc & 11 others v Greg Avery* (representing SHAC) *and Robin Webb* (representing ALF);[230]
- *Heathrow Airport v Garman*[231] (third runway protests at Heathrow)
- *Huntingdon Life Sciences v Stop Huntingdon Animal Cruelty*[232] (animal rights activity);
- *Westminster City Council v Haw*[233] (obstruction of the highway in an anti-war protest);

---

[229] *Burris v Azadani* (1995) 1 WLR 1372 applied.
[230] [2007] EWHC 948, QB and [2009] EWHC 1488 (QB).
[231] [2007] EWHC 1957 QB.
[232] [2007] EWHC 522 where Holland J visited the numerous sites involved.
[233] [2002] EWHC 2073, QB.

- *Silverton v Gravett*[234] (protests against fur retail outlet);
- *RWE Npower v Rev. Malcolm Carrol*[235] (protest camp to stop development); and
- *Monsanto PLC v Tilly and others*[236] (trespass and GM Crops).
- *Novartis Pharmaceuticals UK Limited and others v SHAC and others.*[237]

9.176 CPR 19.6 provides that proceedings can be brought against representative parties, |and therefore injunctions can be binding against those who are not directly party to proceedings. This can only occur if it is shown that all those represented share the same interests. By way of example, in *Heathrow Airport v Garman*,[238] divergence of views within the membership of some protest groups led to the discharge of representative orders, although Swift J did conclude that it was appropriate in the case of the group called Plane Stupid as she was 'entirely satisfied that Plane Stupid fulfils the necessary characteristics of an unincorporated association and that its supporters have identical aims, objectives and interests.' CPR 19.6(4)(b) provides a safeguard in such cases as an injunction cannot be enforced against individuals not named in the injunction without the permission of the court.[239]

9.177 In criminal proceedings anyone convicted or acquitted of any offence, including any public order offence, may since 30 September 2009 (see Domestic Violence, Crime and Victims Act 2004 s12) become the subject of a restraining order under the 1997 Act (see ss 5 and 5A). Such an order may prohibit conduct specified in order to protect a victim or other named person from conduct which amounts to harassment or which will cause a fear of violence.

F. Anti-social Behaviour Orders (ASBOs)

9.178 The Crime and Disorder Act 1998 provides for an anti-social behaviour order to be made prohibiting the person made subject of that order from doing 'anything described in that order'.[240] These orders can be made in 'stand alone' civil applications in the magistrates' court,[241] or following conviction in criminal proceedings.[242] An order can be made in either case if the court is satisfied that the person has acted in an anti-social manner, that is to say in a manner that has caused or was likely to cause harassment alarm or distress to one or more persons not of the same household as himself[243] and that such an order is necessary to protect relevant persons from further anti-social acts by him.[244] Whilst ASBOs were

---

[234] Unreported, 19 October 2001.
[235] [2007] EWHC 947.
[236] [2000] Env LR 313.
[237] [2009] EWHC 2176 (QB) (Arts 8, 10, and 11 ECHR considered).
[238] [2007] EWHC 1957 QB.
[239] Ibid at para 73 and [2007] EWHC 948, QB.
[240] Crime and Disorder Act 1998, s 1(4).
[241] Ibid, s 1.
[242] Ibid, s 1C. For an example of an ASBO imposed on animal rights protestors after convictions, see *R v Avery and others* [2009] EWCA Crim 2670.
[243] Ibid, s 1(1)(a)/1C(2)(a).
[244] Ibid, s 1(1)(b)/1C(2)(b).

introduced to tackle the problem of anti-social behaviour in communities, they are increasingly being used to restrict the activities of protestors.

It is beyond the scope of this work to examine the extensive jurisprudence in relation to **9.179** ASBOs and there are a number of publications that offer comprehensive coverage of the subject.[245] In the context of protest however, it is becoming common for prosecutors to routinely apply for post-conviction ASBOs, and it is these ASBOs—rather than the sentence—that often result in the greatest restriction on the defendant's way of life. To take as a hypothetical example, animal rights activists convicted of offences of interfering with contractual relations contrary to s 145 of Serious Organised Crime and Police Act 2005 as a result of their activities at ABC guinea pig breeding farm. A sentencing hearing is listed at which the judge is to consider not only the appropriate sentence, but also the prosecutor's application for an ASBO containing terms prohibiting the defendant from going within 10 miles of ABC, but also prohibiting the defendant from protesting at any guinea pig breeding establishment in England and Wales or attending any anti-vivisection protest at any animal research facility. The sentence passed may be a short prison sentence or even a suspended sentence of imprisonment, but the implications of an ASBO could be extensive and far longer lasting, as the ASBO imposed can be until further order of the court.

An ASBO can only be made if it is necessary to protect relevant persons from harassment, **9.180** alarm, or distress, and the test of *necessity* is one that the courts have focused upon.[246] In a protest case though, there is a further issue, namely, would such an order unjustifiably infringe the defendant's right to freedoms of expression and assembly protected in Articles 10 and 11 ECHR? An order therefore has to be not only necessary, it also has to be a proportionate interference in the defendant's Convention rights to express legitimate concern about the treatment of animals at such establishments.

What arises is the difficult question as to whether the courts are entitled to restrict the **9.181** defendant's right to protest beyond that already imposed by statute, on the grounds that the defendant has committed a protest related offence? And if the ASBO relates only to *unlawful* protest, then is that not already prohibited by the criminal law?[247] The Court in *W and F*[248] held that the ASBO is there to prevent others from anti-social behaviour by the offender. Therefore, the Court should not impose an order which prohibits an offender from committing specified criminal offences if the sentence which could be passed following conviction (or a guilty plea) for those offences should be a sufficient deterrent.[249]

---

[245] See, for example, Maya Sikand, *ASBOS: A Practitioner's Guide to Defending Anti-Social Behaviour Orders* (2006). See also detailed guidance in the Home Office publication *A Guide to Anti-Social Behaviour Orders* available at <http://www.harassment-law.co.uk/pdf/asbogide.pdf>.

[246] For example, *P(Shane Tony)* [2004] 2 Cr App R (S) 343; *McGrath* [2005] 2 Cr App R (S) 52; *Boness* [2006] 1 Cr App R (S); *W & F* [2007] 1 WLR 339.

[247] For the Courts' rather uncertain approach to whether an ASBO may include a term prohibiting the defendant from committing a specific criminal offence see *R v Kirby* [2006] 1 Cr App R (S) 151; *R v Morrison* [2006] 1 Cr App R (S) 488; *Lamb* [2006] 2 Cr App R (S) 84; *Braxton* [2005] 1 Cr App R (S) 167.

[248] *W and F* [2007] 1 WLR 339.

[249] Ibid, per Aikens J.

9.182 Therefore, whilst outside of the protest context, a person could be excluded from, say, a shopping centre where he has previously committed anti-social behaviour as that would be a proportionate interference in his liberty given that he could do his shopping elsewhere. But it could be argued that the geographical exclusion condition preventing even legitimate protests as part of an authorized procession near the guinea pig farm in the hypothetical example was a disproportionate interference in the defendant's Convention rights. The only condition that could be imposed would be a restriction on unlawful protest, but, given that the maximum sentence for breach of an ASBO and for an offence under s 145 of the 2005 Act is the same, it would be unlawful to impose such a condition as it could not be said to be necessary as it was no more of a deterrent than the criminal offence. As to the more general conditions in the prosecutor's application, the same submissions could be made with even more force.

G. Football Banning Orders

9.183 The Football (Spectators) Act 1989, as amended by the Football (Disorder) Act 2000 and the Violent Crime Reduction Act 2006;[250] makes provision for orders to be made by either a magistrates' court or the Crown Court, banning individuals from attending certain football matches;[251] and requiring them to report to a police station at the time of a football match;[252] to surrender passports at certain times to prevent attendance at overseas matches;[253] and to notify the police of any change in name or address.[254]

9.184 Section 14A of the Football Spectators Act 1989 (as amended) provides that:

(1) This section applies where a person ('the offender') is convicted of a relevant offence.
(2) If the court is satisfied that there are reasonable grounds to believe that making a banning order would help to prevent violence or disorder at or in connection with any regulated football matches, it must make such an order in respect of the offender.
(3) If the court is not so satisfied, it must state in open court that fact and give its reasons.

9.185 An order can be made following conviction of a 'relevant offence'.[255] These include a wide range of offences involving violence; possession of offensive weapons, public disorder,[256] drunkenness, and damage to property; as well as some specifically sporting

---

[250] In force as of 14 March 2007: SI 2007/858. See the Violent Crime Reduction Act 2006, ss 52(1) and 65 and Sch 5, in which certain provisions of the Football (Disorder) Act 2000 were repealed and the 1989 Act subject to the amendments set out in the Violent Crime Reduction Act 2006, Sch 3.

[251] The Football Spectators (Prescription) Order 2004, SI 2004/2409, amending the Football Spectators (Prescription) (Amendment) Order 2006, SI 2006/71. In short, this applies to association football matches if one team belongs to the Premier League, the Football League, or the Football Conference; or if either team is from abroad or if either team represents their country or territory.

[252] Football (Spectators) Act 1989, s 14(4).

[253] Ibid, s 14E(3).

[254] Ibid, s 14E(2B).

[255] Ibid, s 14A, 14(8), and see amended Sch 1 to the 1989 Act.

[256] Whilst the Public Order Act 1986, s 5, is a listed offence, s 4 is not. However, the Court of Appeal has held that an offence under s 4 was a 'relevant offence' provided it had been committed in the relevant circumstances, namely in connection with a football match.

related offences.[257] The 'relevant period' is usually two hours before the match and ending one hour after the match, but in cases involving the use or threat of violence the period is twenty-four hours before kick off and ends twenty-four hours after the end of the match.[258]

The offences must be committed at or in connection with a football match, or when travel-ling to or from a football match. There is no requirement that the person in fact attended the match, but the offending has to be related to the match. For these reasons, the Court of Appeal in *R v Elliot*[259] quashed the banning order made in a case where a group of men had attended a football match and were later involved in violence at a public house that was in no way related to football. This reasoning was followed in *R v Arbery and Mobley*[260] where the violent disorder of which the appellants were convicted was a street fight close to King's Cross railway station in London. The facts are illustrative. The appellants were Northampton Town supporters who had watched their team lose to Crystal Palace. After the game, the appellants and their fellow supporters were in a public house waiting for the next train back to Northampton. A group of Charlton Athletic supporters (who had been watching another match) arrived and directed some racial abuse at one of the Northampton Town support-ers, who left the public house followed by the appellants. The two factions met in the street and, following some verbal altercation, embarked upon a large-scale fight. In making an order, the Recorder ruled that the violence would not have happened if those participants had not been following their respective teams. In overturning the order, the Court of Appeal followed the now well-established principle[261] that a narrow construction of the meaning 'related to a football match' should be adopted. **9.186**

The other procedure is by way of complaint made by the chief officer of police on the grounds that the respondent has at any time caused or contributed to any violence or dis-order in the United Kingdom or elsewhere.[262] **9.187**

Whether applied for following conviction or by way of complaint, the court must only make an order if satisfied that there are reasonable grounds[263] to believe that making a banning order would help to prevent violence or disorder at or in connection with any regulated football matches.[264] **9.188**

The Court of Appeal in *Gough v Chief Constable of Derbyshire*[265] held that banning orders contravened neither European law on free movement of persons nor the European **9.189**

---

[257] Eg an offence under the Football (Offences) Act 1991 or under the Sporting Events (Control of Alcohol etc) Act 1985.
[258] See Sch 1 of the 1989 Act as substituted by the Violent Crime Reduction Act 2006.
[259] [2007] 2 Cr App R (S) 430: see also *R v Beaum*ont [2008] EWHC 523 (Admin).
[260] [2008] EWCA Crim 702.
[261] *R v Smith (Paul Roger)* [2003] EWCA Crim 2480; *R v Elliot (Gregory)* [2007] EWCA Crim 1002; *R v Mabee (Craig)* [2007] EWCA Crim 3230; see also *Football Banning Orders*, Journal of Criminal Law, Vol 72, Part 2, April 2009.
[262] Football (Spectators) Act 1989, s 14B.
[263] See discussion in *R v Smith* [2004] 1 Cr App R (S) 341. A single offence may be sufficient: *R v Hughes* [2006] 1 Cr App R (S) 632.
[264] Football (Spectators) Act 1989, s 14A(2) or 14(B)(4)(b).
[265] [2002] QB 1213.

Convention on Human Rights. While the proceedings were held to be civil, an exacting standard of proof was required:

> It does not follow from this that a mere balance of probabilities suffices to justify the making of an order. Banning orders under section 14(B) fall into the same category as antisocial behaviour orders and sex offenders' orders. While made in civil proceedings they impose serious restraints on freedoms that the citizen normally enjoys. While technically the civil standard of proof applies, that standard is flexible and must reflect the consequences that will follow if the case for a banning order is made out. This should lead the magistrates to apply an exacting standard of proof that will, in practice, be hard to distinguish from the criminal standard.[266]

---

[266] See *B v Chief Constable of Avon and Somerset Constabulary* [2001] 1 WLR 340, 354 and *R (McCann) v Manchester Crown Court* [2001] 1 WLR 1084, 1102, para 90.

10

HUMAN RIGHTS

A. Introduction	10.01	D. Article 8: Right to Respect for		
B. Articles 10 and 11	10.13	Private and Family Life	10.144	
Introduction to Articles 10 and 11	10.15	E. Article 5: Right to Liberty and		
Positive and negative obligations	10.28	Security	10.150	
The scope of Articles 10 and 11	10.39	'Kettling': deprivation of liberty vs		
Limitations on the right to protest	10.77	restriction of movement	10.158	
'Prescribed by law': the requirement		F. Article 6: Right to a		
of legality	10.78	Fair Trial	10.162	
Legitimate aims	10.98	Statutory defences and reverse		
Necessary in a democratic society	10.101	burdens of proof	10.163	
C. Article 9: Freedom of		Legal assistance	10.167	
Thought, Conscience,		Disclosure	10.174	
and Religion	10.122	G. Article 2: Right to Life	10.180	
Manifesting a belief	10.126	H. Article 3: Prohibition of		
Article 9: and Articles 10 and 11	10.131	Torture	10.184	

A. Introduction

The Human Rights Act 1998 incorporates into domestic law the European Convention on **10.01**
Human Rights (ECHR). The approach of the Convention is to give effect to rights, to
make rights 'practical and effective', not 'theoretical and illusory'. The key rights in the
context of public order and protest are Article 10 (freedom of expression) and Article 11
(freedom of assembly and association). This chapter also considers aspects of the following
rights in this context: Article 2 (right to life), Article 3 (prohibition of torture), Article 6
(right to a fair trial), Article 8 (right to respect for family and private life), and Article 9
(freedom of thought, conscience, and religion).

In practice, the introduction of Articles 10 and 11 into English law has been more subtle **10.02**
than dramatic. It has produced a shift in emphasis of the law's approach to controlling
public meetings—moving or static, processions or assemblies—from the old common
law restrictions upon the use of the highway (and other public spaces) to the positive
importance of the right to express views publicly, so long as they are expressed without
violence.

10.03 The introduction of positive rights in this area has been described as a 'constitutional shift' in English law.[1] The common law, prior to the Human Rights Act, was 'hesitant and negative'[2] in its approach to such rights. The orthodox view[3] was that expressed by Dicey:

> At no time has there in England been any proclamation of the right to liberty of thought or to freedom of speech.[4]
> and
> . . . it can hardly be said that our constitution knows of such a thing as any specific right of public meeting.[5]

10.04 So, for example, in *Duncan v Jones*,[6] Lord Hewart CJ, reflecting the views of the time, in a case concerning the right to speak at a public meeting in the street, expressed the view that:

> There have been moments during the argument in this case when it appeared to be suggested that the court had to do with a grave case involving what is called the right of public meeting. I say 'called', because English law does not recognise any special right of public meeting for political or other purposes. The right of Assembly, as Professor Dicey puts it, is nothing more than the view taken by the court of the individual liberty of the subject.

10.05 In *DPP v Jones*,[7] Lord Hope looked back at the observations of Charles J in *R v Graham*[8] as reflecting the traditional view of public assemblies:

> I can find no warrant for telling you that there is a right of public meeting either in Trafalgar Square or any other public thoroughfare. So far as I know the law of England, the use of public thoroughfares is for people to pass and repass along them.

10.06 Although the majority (three to two) in *DPP v Jones* found that the common law had moved on from this restrictive position, their speeches were cast in terms of peaceful assembly being part of the public's 'reasonable use' of the highway (along with stopping to sketch or to tie shoelaces), and then only so long as it did not interfere with the *primary right* to pass and repass along the highway.

10.07 This is a far cry from the fundamental importance attached to the positive right to peaceful assembly guaranteed under the ECHR. This right, together with freedom of expression, is recognized as being of 'special importance'[9] and is repeatedly described by the European Court of Human Rights (ECtHR) as one of the foundations of a democratic society.[10]

---

[1] Sedley LJ in *Redmond-Bate v DPP* [2000] HRLR 249, [1999] EWHC Admin 732.

[2] Lord Bingham, *R(Laporte) v Chief Constable of Gloucestershire Constabulary* [2007] 2 AC 105, para 34.

[3] See, for example, Lord Bingham's analysis in *R (Laporte) v Chief Constable of Gloucestershire Constabulary*, ibid, para 34; and Lord Hewart CJ, *Duncan v Jones* [1936] 1 KB 218, 221–2.

[4] *An Introduction to the Study of the Law of the Constitution* (1959, 10th edn) pp 239–40.

[5] Ibid, p 271.

[6] [1936] 1 KB 218, 221.

[7] [1999] 2 AC 240.

[8] (1888) 16 Cox CC 420, 429–30.

[9] *Ezelin v France* (A/202) (1992) 14 EHRR 36, para 51.

[10] *Makhmudov v Russia*, Application No 35082/04, 26 July 2007, paras 63–4; *Rassemblement Jurassien et Unite Jurassienne v Switzerland*, Application No 8191/78, 17 DR 93, para 119; *Steel v UK* [1998] 5 BHRC 339; *Ziliberberg v Moldova*, Application No 61821/00, admissibility decision 4 May 2004; *Sergey Kuznetsov v Russia*, Application No 10877/04, 23 October 2008, para 39; see also, Lord Hope in *R (Countryside Alliance) v Attorney General* [2007] 3 WLR 922, para 58.

In *Sergey Kuznetsov v Russia*,[11] a case concerning a picket outside the regional courthouse accusing the senior judge of corruption, the ECtHR stated:

> . . . any measures interfering with the freedom of assembly and expression other than in cases of incitement to violence or rejection of democratic principles—however shocking and unacceptable certain views or words used may appear to the authorities—do a disservice to democracy and often even endanger it. In a democratic society based on the rule of law, the ideas which challenge the existing order must be afforded a proper opportunity of expression through the exercise of the right of assembly as well as by other lawful means.[12]

Guidelines produced by the Office for Democratic Institutions and Human Rights (ODIHR)[13] of the Organisation for Security and Co-operation in Europe (OSCE)[14] as a guide to international principles on freedom of peaceful assembly, in particular under the ECHR, emphasize that, contrary to even the majority view in *DPP v Jones*, use of public spaces for peaceful assembly should be regarded as equally legitimate as more conventional uses of such spaces: **10.08**

> Participants in public assemblies have as much claim to use [public places] for a reasonable period as everyone else. Indeed, public protest, and freedom of assembly in general, should be regarded as an equally legitimate use of public space as the more routine purposes for which public space is used (such as pedestrian and vehicular traffic).[15]

The notes to the Guidelines cite with approval the US concept of a right of access to 'public fora'—public places such as parks, squares, streets, avenues, pavements, and footpaths to which everyone has an equal right of access—for the exercise of free speech rights.[16] **10.09**

Although the ODIHR Guidelines are not directly enforceable in domestic law, they have been endorsed by the European Commission for Democracy through Law ('the Venice Commission'[17]—an advisory body to the Council of Europe) and may provide a useful aid to interpreting the content of directly enforceable rights under the ECHR. This view is shared by the Parliamentary Joint Committee on Human Rights (JCHR).[18] **10.10**

---

[11] Application No 10877/04, 23 October 2008.

[12] Ibid, para 45.

[13] The ODIHR is the principal institution of the OSCE (see below) dealing with the 'human dimension' of security. The office, originally named Office for Free Elections, was created in 1990 by the Charter of Paris and established in 1991. The name of the office was changed in 1992 to reflect the broadened mandate it received at the 1992 Helsinki Summit.

[14] The OSCE is the world's largest security orientated inter-governmental organization. It is an ad hoc organization under the United Nations Charter (Ch VIII), and is concerned with early warning, conflict prevention, crisis management, and post-conflict rehabilitation. Its fifty-seven participating States (which includes the UK) are from Europe, the Caucasus, Central Asia, and North America; and cover most of the northern hemisphere. It was created during the Cold War era as an East–West forum.

[15] Guidelines on Freedom of Peaceful Assembly and interpretative notes thereto at p 25, available online at <http://www.venice.coe.int/docs/2008/CDL(2008)062-e.pdf>.

[16] See *Hague v Committee for Industrial Organisation*, 307 US 496 (1939), cited at fn 24 of the ODIHR Guidelines ibid.

[17] The Venice Commission is composed of independent members in the field of constitutional law. All members of the Council of Europe are members and since 2002 non-European states have also become full members.

[18] See Seventh Report of Session 2008–9, Demonstrating respect for rights? A human rights approach to policing protest, vol I, para 24.

10.11 Ironically, at the same time as positive rights to public assembly and freedom of expression have been introduced into domestic law, there have been a plethora of legislative measures restricting and, in some instances criminalizing, otherwise peaceful protest: the Serious and Organised Crime and Police Act 2005 creates new offences of harassment intended to deter lawful activities[19] and harassment of a person in his home;[20] trespassing on designated sites, including nuclear facilities, military and political sites;[21] and introduces a controversial new requirement, backed by criminal sanctions, to seek prior authorization to hold demonstrations in the vicinity of Parliament.[22] Other measures, not ostensibly directed at protest activity, have been increasingly used in that context. Protestors, journalists, academics, and NGOs giving evidence to the Joint Committee on Human Rights[23] identified use of the power to stop and search under the Terrorism Act 2005 without any requirement of reasonable suspicion; the increased use of civil injunctions; anti-social behaviour orders, and dispersal powers as having a restrictive effect on the right to peaceful assembly.

10.12 This chapter considers the jurisprudence of the European Commission and Court of Human Rights in the context of public order and protest and seeks to examine the effect the Convention rights have had, or might yet have, on the domestic law in this area.

B. Articles 10 and 11

10.13 Article 10 states:

(1) Everyone has the right to freedom of expression. This right shall include freedom to hold opinions and to receive and impart information and ideas without interference by public authority and regardless of frontiers. This Article shall not prevent States from requiring the licensing of broadcasting, television or cinema enterprises.

(2) The exercise of these freedoms, since it carries with it duties and responsibilities, may be subject to such formalities, conditions, restrictions or penalties as are prescribed by law and are necessary in a democratic society, in the interests of national security, territorial integrity or public safety, for the prevention of disorder or crime, for the protection of health or morals, for the protection of the reputation or rights of others, for preventing disclosure of information received in confidence, or for maintaining the authority and impartiality of the judiciary.

10.14 Article 11 states:

(1) Everyone has the right to freedom of peaceful assembly and to freedom of association with others, including the right to form and to join trade unions for the protection of his interests.

(2) No restrictions shall be placed on the exercise of these rights other than such as are prescribed by law and are necessary in a democratic society in the interests of national security or public safety, for the prevention of disorder or crime, for the protection of health or morals or for the protection of the rights and freedoms of others. This Article

---

[19] Serious and Organised Crime and Police Act 2005, s 125.
[20] Ibid, s 126, see 3.148.
[21] Ibid, ss 128–131, see 5.46 and 5.140 et seq.
[22] Ibid, ss 132–138, see 3.94 et seq.
[23] See JCHR Seventh Report of Session 2008–9.

shall not prevent the imposition of lawful restrictions on the exercise of these rights by members of the armed forces, of the police or of the administration of the State.

Introduction to Articles 10 and 11

Articles 10 and 11 are not absolute rights, unlike for example Article 2 (the right to life) and Article 3 (prohibition of torture). Articles 10 and 11 are qualified rights, providing less protection than absolute rights. The first paragraph of each sets out the right. The second sets out the restrictions upon the right. According to Convention law and Constitutional law[24] the right must be interpreted 'broadly, purposively'. This is the theory, at least. Also the restrictions must be construed 'strictly and narrowly', and be justified in each case with convincing and compelling reasons. These restrictions permit restraint upon freedom of expression and freedom of assembly only where this (a) is 'prescribed by law'; (b) pursues one of the legitimate aims set out in the second paragraph of the relevant article; and (c) is necessary in a democratic society, that is, it must meet a pressing social need (often the protection of the rights of others) and be proportionate to the legitimate aim pursued. All of these concepts are discussed below.

10.15

In practical terms, once a Convention right is 'engaged' (ie actively applicable to the specific circumstances under consideration), the court in civil or criminal proceedings must consider whether the restrictions imposed upon the right were justified and justly proportionate in all the circumstances. If they were not, a criminal prosecution may fail, or a civil case claiming compensation for interference with that right may succeed.

10.16

In the context of protest cases, Article 11 has been described by the ECtHR as the 'lex specialis' and Article 10 the 'lex generalis'.[25] In practice, the ECtHR and the Commission have found Article 10 to be 'closely linked' to Article 11 in this area and have recognized the 'protection of opinions and the freedom to express them [a]s one of the objectives of the freedoms of assembly and association as enshrined in Article 11'.[26] Further, the ECtHR has observed that:

10.17

> Freedom of thought and opinion and freedom of expression guaranteed by articles 9 and 10 of the Convention respectively, would [. . .] be of very limited scope if they were not accompanied by a guarantee of being able to share one's beliefs or ideas in community with others, particularly through associations of individuals having the same beliefs, ideas or interests.[27]

As a result, the Strasbourg institutions have tended to read Articles 10 and 11 together in their analysis of protest cases, casting any finding of violation under the heading of one and recording a formal finding that it was unnecessary to give separate consideration to the other.[28] For this reason Articles 10 and 11 are considered together below.

10.18

---

[24] See, eg, *Thomas v Baptiste* [2006] AC 1, PC.
[25] *Ezelin v France* (1991) 14 EHRR 362, para 35.
[26] *Christian Democratic People's Party v Moldova*, Application No 28793/02, 14 May 2006, para 62; see also, *Djavit An v Turkey* [2003] Reports of Judgments and Decisions, 2003-III, p 233, para 39; *Ollinger v Austria* App No 76900/01, 29 June 2006, para 38.
[27] *Chassagnou v France* (1999) 29 EHRR 615, para 100.
[28] See, for example *Sergey Kuznetsov v Russia*, Application No 10877/04, 23 October 2008, [23]; *Ezelin v France*, paras 35 and 37; *Rai, Allmond and 'Negotiate Now' v UK* (1995) 19 EHRR CD 93, [1]; *Appleby v UK*

10.19 It is significant that protection for public protest is derived from the rights to freedom of expression and assembly, and also, occasionally, freedom of thought conscience, and religion (Article 9—see below), because, as a result, the focus of the Convention jurisprudence is heavily on protest activity as a means of expression and communication of political, moral or religious ideas.[29] The Court has emphasized that especially strong reasons are required to justify interference with political speech on serious matters of public interest.[30]

10.20 The right to freedom of expression under Article 10 has been held to:

> constitute [. . .] one of the essential foundations of [a democratic] society, one of the basic conditions for its progress and for the development of every man. Subject to Article 10(2), it is applicable not only to 'information' or 'ideas' that are favourably received or regarded as inoffensive or as a matter of indifference, but also to those that offend shock or disturb the state or any sector of the population. Such are the demands of that pluralism, tolerance and broadmindedness without which there is no 'democratic society'.[31]

10.21 The special importance of Article 10 is underlined by s 12 of the Human Rights Act 1998, which provides for particular safeguards where 'a court is considering whether to grant any relief which, if granted, might affect the exercise of the Convention right to freedom of expression.'

Assembly for the purpose of imparting information and ideas

10.22 Article 10 is relevant in the public order context where there is an intention to 'impart information and ideas' in the broadest sense, for example, at a public meeting, assembly, demonstration, march, procession, picket, sit-in, etc. 'Information and ideas' for the purposes of Article 10(1) have been given a very broad interpretation. Political expression, which includes any matter of public interest and concern[32] attracts the strongest protection.[33] However, artistic,[34] scientific,[35] and commercial[36] expression, as well as entertainment[37] have all been held to be protected. Further, Article 10 protects not only the *substance* of the information and ideas imparted, but also the *form and means* by which they are expressed.[38] Thus, the distribution of leaflets; marking of property as a protest against road construction; obstruction of a grouse shoot;[39] display of banners or posters;[40]

(2003) 37 EHRR 783; *Christians Against Racism and Fascism v UK*, Application No 8440/78, 16 July 1980, DR 21, p 138; *Rassemblement Jurassien and Unite Jurassienne v Switzerland*, 10 October 1979, DR 17, p 93.

[29] See Lord Hope in *R (Countryside Alliance) v Attorney General* [2007] 3 WLR 922, [56]–[58].

[30] *Sergey Kuznetsov v Russia*, [47]; see also *Piermont v France* (1995) 20 EHRR 301 [76]; *Karman v Russia*, No 29372/02, §36, 14 December 2006; *Feldek v Slovakia*, No 29032/95, §83, ECHR 2001-VIII, and *Sürek v Turkey (No 1)* [GC], No 26682/95, §61, ECHR 1999-I.

[31] *Handyside v United Kingdom* (1976) 1 EHRR 737, para 49; *Sunday Times v United Kingdom (No 2)* (1992) 14 EHRR 229.

[32] *Thorgeir Thorgeirson Islande v Iceland* (1992) 14 EHRR 843, para 64.

[33] *Lingens v Austria* (1986) 8 EHRR 407, para 42.

[34] *Muller v Austria* (1988) 13 EHRR 51, para 27.

[35] *T v United Kingdom*, (1982) Application No 8231/78, 49 DR 5.

[36] *Markt Intern Verlag GmbH & Klaus Beerman v Germany* (1989) 12 EHRR 161, para 26.

[37] *Groppera Radio AG v Switzerland* (1990) 12 EHRR 321, para 55.

[38] See *Tabernacle v Secretary of State for Defence* [2009] EWHC Civ 23, The Times, 25 February 2009.

[39] *Steel v United Kingdom* (1999) 28 EHRR 603.

[40] *Bogdanov Kandshov v Bulgaria*, Application No 68294/01, 6 November 2008.

cutting of a chainlink fence at an atomic weapons establishment;[41] burning of the US flag;[42] and a peace camp outside an atomic weapons establishment[43] have all been found to engage Article 10. However, freedom of forum is not guaranteed: the ECtHR has to date refused to derive a right of access to private property for the purposes of exercising free expression.[44]

The ECtHR has held that 'the right to freedom of assembly covers both private meetings and meetings on public thoroughfares, as well as static meetings and public processions; this right can be exercised both by individual participants and by those organising the assembly'.[45] Since protection of personal opinions is one of the purposes of freedom of association, Article 11 also includes the right not to join an association or assembly.[46]   **10.23**

However, the right to freedom of assembly is not solely concerned with freedom to convey ideas, as the Panel of Experts on Freedom of Assembly of the ODIHR/OSCE has observed: **10.24**

> peaceful assemblies can serve many purposes, including (but not limited to) the expression of views and the defence of common interests, celebration, commemoration, picketing, and protest. Freedom of peaceful assembly can have both symbolic and instrumental significance, and can be an important strand in the maintenance and development of culture and in the preservation of minority identities. It is complemented by other rights and freedoms such as freedom of association, the right to establish and maintain contacts within the territory of a state, freedom of expression, and freedom of thought, conscience, and religion. As such, freedom of assembly is of fundamental importance for the personal development, dignity, and fulfilment of every individual and the progress and welfare of society.[47]

Article 11 does not, however, guarantee a right to assemble for purely social purposes.[48] In *R (Countryside Alliance) v Attorney General*,[49] Lord Hope referred to the ECtHR's emphasis on Article 11 as a fundamental right in a democracy and, like freedom of expression, one of the foundations of such a society.[50] In light of this emphasis, he rejected the contention that fox hunting with hounds could engage Article 11, expressing the view that: **10.25**

> The situations to which [Article 11] applies must relate to activities that are of that character [ie of fundamental importance in a democratic society], of which the right to form and join

---

[41] *Hutchinson v Newbury Magistrates Court*, The Independent, 20 November 2000; judgment 9 October 2000, para 62.

[42] *Percy v DPP* [2002] Crim LR 835.

[43] *Tabernacle v Secretary of State for Defence*.

[44] See *Appleby v United Kingdom* (2003) 37 EHRR 783, in particular para 47, discussed below.

[45] *Sergey Kuznetsov v Russia*, Application No 10877/04, 23 October 2008, para 35; *Djavit An v Turkey*, Application No 20652/92, para 56, ECHR 2003-III; *Christians against Racism and Fascism v the United Kingdom*, Application No 8440/78, Commission decision of 16 July 1980, 21 DR 138, 148; *Rassemblement Jurassien and Unite Jurassienne v Switzerland*, Application No 8191/78, 10 October 1979, 17 DR 93.

[46] *Young, James and Webster v UK* (1981) 4 EHRR 38; *Chassagnou v France* (1999) 29 EHRR 615, [103].

[47] Guidelines on Freedom of Peaceful Assembly and interpretative notes, op cit, p 11.

[48] *Anderson v UK* [1998] EHRLR 218.

[49] [2008] 1 AC 719.

[50] See *Rassemblement Jurassien et Unite Jurassienne v Switzerland*, Application No 8191/78, 17 DR 93, para 119; *Steel v UK* (1998) 5 BHRC 339; *Ziliberberg v Moldova*, Application No 61821/00, admissibility decision 4 May 2004; *Sergey Kuznetsov v Russia*, Application No 10877/04, 23 October 2008, para 39; see also, Lord Hope in *R (Countryside Alliance) v Attorney General* [2007] 3 WLR 922, para 58.

a trade union which Article 11 refers to is an example. The purpose of the activity provides the key to its application.[51]

10.26   Similarly, Baroness Hale, in the same case, expressed the view that Article 11 must be read in the context of Articles 10 and 9 and as such it protects 'the freedom to meet and band together with others in order to share information and ideas and to give voice to them collectively', but not a right to assemble for recreational purposes such as fox hunting.[52]

10.27   Associations or organizations, as well as individuals, may be the victim of a breach of Convention rights within the meaning of Article 34, but only where they are directly prejudiced by the interference.[53]

Positive and negative obligations

Direct and indirect obstacles to freedom of assembly

10.28   Articles 10 and 11 both impose 'negative obligations' on States not to place disproportionate or unnecessary restrictions on freedom of expression and assembly, either directly, for example, by imposing excessive bans on public assemblies,[54] or indirectly, by placing obstacles in the way of lawful gatherings in order to deter individuals or organizations from participating in them.[55] Examples of indirect obstacles might include overly bureaucratic prior-notification requirements, or financial burdens on non-commercial event organizers, such as a requirement to obtain public liability insurance or to pay for road closures or clean-up costs following the meeting or procession.[56]

10.29   The evidence to the Parliamentary Joint Committee on Human Rights on behalf of the environmental protest group Climate Camp is of note in this regard. They told the Committee that their experience of current policing of protest:

> Is not like Southall in the 1970s where you have got a small group of police becoming very ill-disciplined and beating someone up on the street or killing someone, it is not like that. What you have got is hundreds of really petty incidents which cumulatively make going to a protest extremely unpleasant, potentially frightening or worrying and then the only way to challenge it would be hundreds of really petty complaints about different issues.[57]

---

[51]   *R (Countryside Alliance) v Attorney General*, ibid, para 58.

[52]   Ibid, para 118 (Baroness Hale) and para 56 (Lord Hope).

[53]   *Societatea de Vanatoare 'Mistretful' v Romania*, Application No 33346/96, Decision 4 April 1999; *SEGI v IS States of the EU*, Application Nos 6422/02 and 9916/02, Decision 23 May 2002; *Vatan v Russia*, Application No 47978/99, Decision 7 October 2004.

[54]   See, for example, *Guneri v Turkey*, Application No 42853/98, 12 July 2005.

[55]   See, for example, *Aldemir v Turkey*, Application No 32124/02, 18 December 2007, paras 41–3; and *Oya Ataman v Turkey*, No 74552/01, 5 December 2006, para 16. See also Principle 2 of the ODIHR/OSCE Guidelines on Freedom of Peaceful Assembly.

[56]   Local Authority Guidelines require organizers of peaceful protest in Parliament Square to obtain a minimum of £5 million public liability insurance cover—see Liberty's comments in this regard in their evidence to the JCHR Seventh Report of Session 2008–9, Ev 164, para 30 and their reference to the case of students seeking to protest at the closure of their school who were charged £1,866 by the local council for road closures and associated services at Ev 163, para 29; see also discussion at p 17 of the Guidelines and interpretative notes of the ODIHR/OSCE, ibid.

[57]   Parliamentary Joint Committee on Human Rights report Demonstrating respect for rights? A human rights approach to policing protest, para 54.

Complaints are also frequently made about bail conditions being used as indirect restraints **10.30** on protest. An arrest, followed by bail, may amount to a violation of Article 11, both because of the direct interference with the arrested person's ability to continue his or her participation in the protest, but also because the mere fact of arrest and potential prosecution, even where no criminal proceedings in fact ensue, or proceedings result in acquittal, may have a chilling effect on freedom of assembly.[58]

Securing effective enjoyment of the rights to freedom of expression and assembly

In addition to negative obligations on the State, Articles 10 and 11 also impose *positive* **10.31** *obligations*, requiring States actively to promote the effectiveness of these rights. The ECtHR has explained these duties in the following terms:

> A genuine and effective respect for freedom of association and assembly cannot be reduced to a mere duty on the part of the State not to interfere; a purely negative conception would not be compatible with the purpose of Article 11 nor with that of the Convention in general. There may thus be positive obligations to secure the effective enjoyment of these freedoms . . . This obligation is of particular importance for persons holding unpopular views or belonging to minorities, because they are more vulnerable to victimisation.[59]

The State may be under an obligation to put in place positive measures to secure freedom **10.32** of expression and assembly even in the sphere of relations between private individuals or companies.[60]

In determining whether or not a positive obligation arises, the ECtHR has regard to: **10.33**

> the fair balance that has to be struck between the general interest of the community and the interests of the individual, the search for which is inherent throughout the Convention. The scope of this obligation will inevitably vary, having regard to the diversity of situations obtaining in Contracting States and the choices which must be made in terms of priorities and resources. Nor must such an obligation be interpreted in such a way as to impose an impossible or disproportionate burden on the authorities . . . [61]

Duty to protect against counter-demonstrators

Positive obligations under Article 11 have, for example, been interpreted as imposing a **10.34** duty to protect the rights of demonstrators to protest in safety, free from violence, and interference by counter-demonstrators. In *Plattform 'Ärzte für das Leben' v Austria*,[62] a group of doctors who had sought to demonstrate against abortion complained that the Austrian police had failed adequately to protect their demonstrations from disruption and

---

[58] *Bączkowski and Others v Poland*, Application No 1543/06, 3 May 2007, paras 67–8; *Balcik v Turkey*, Application No 25/02, 29 November 2007, para 41.

[59] *Bączkowski v Poland*, ibid, para 64, see also *Plattform 'Ärzte für das Leben' v Austria* (1988) 13 EHRR 204, para 32.

[60] *Özgür Gündem v Turkey*, Application No 23144/93, ECHR 2000-III, judgment of 16 March 2000, paras 42–6, where the Turkish government were found to be under a positive obligation to take investigative and protective measures where the 'pro-PKK' newspaper, and its journalists, and staff had been victim of a campaign of violence and intimidation; also *Fuentes Bobo v Spain*, Application No 39293/98, judgment of 29 February 2000, para 38, concerning the obligation on the State to protect freedom of expression in the employment context; see also *R (Pro-Life Alliance) v BBC* [2003] 1 AC 185.

[61] *Appleby v United Kingdom* (2003) 37 EHRR 783, para 40; see also 10.72.

[62] (1988) 13 EHRR 204.

threatened violence from pro-abortion groups. Although the ECtHR found no violation on the facts of this case, because it found that the police had taken proportionate steps to protect the doctors' demonstrations, it emphasized that '[i]n a democracy the right to counter-demonstrate cannot extend to inhibiting the exercise of the right to demonstrate'.[63] This reflects the principle in Article 17 of the ECHR, which provides that nothing in the Convention may be interpreted as conveying a right to engage in any activity aimed at the destruction of any of the rights and freedoms guaranteed by the Convention.

10.35 The ECtHR in *Plattform 'Ärzte für das Leben'* also stated that while States are under a duty to 'take reasonable and appropriate measures to enable lawful demonstrations to proceed peacefully, they cannot guarantee this absolutely and they have a wide discretion in the choice of the means to be used'.[64] The obligation 'is an obligation as to measures to be taken and not as to results to be achieved'.[65]

Obligations on the state; no excessive burdens on demonstrators

10.36 The primary responsibility for ensuring the safety of demonstrators, counter-demonstrators and members of the public rests squarely on the State. The Joint Committee on Human Rights reports that it received evidence from a number of witnesses about police imposing conditions on protest organizers requiring them to arrange road closures and police demonstrations themselves.[66] The ODIHR/OSCE Guidelines on Freedom of Peaceful Assembly and interpretative notes provide that:

> Under some circumstances, it may be legitimate to impose on organizers a condition that they arrange a certain level of stewarding for their gathering. However, such a condition should only be imposed as the result of a specific assessment and never by default. Otherwise it would violate the proportionality principle. Any requirement to provide stewarding in no way detracts from the positive obligation of the state to provide adequately resourced policing arrangements. Stewards are not a substitute for the police, and the police still bear overall responsibility for public order.[67]

Further:

> Organizers and stewards have a responsibility to make reasonable efforts to comply with legal requirements and ensure that their assemblies are peaceful, but they should not be held liable for failure to perform their responsibilities if they made reasonable efforts to do so . . . Moreover, if an assembly degenerates into serious public disorder, it is the responsibility of the state, not of the organizer or event stewards, to limit the damage caused. In no circumstances should the organizer of a lawful and peaceful assembly be held liable for disruption caused to others.[68]

Demonstrators vs counter-demonstrators: the balance to be struck

10.37 The State must also take care not to impose excessive measures against counter-demonstrators. In *Öllinger v Austria*[69] the ECtHR found the Austrian authorities to have acted disproportionately, and therefore contrary to Article 11, in banning a Jewish

---

[63] Ibid, para 32.
[64] Ibid, para 34.
[65] Ibid, para 34.
[66] See para 48 of JCHR report, op cit.
[67] Guidelines and interpretative notes, p 72.
[68] Ibid.
[69] Application No 76900/01, 29 June 2006. See also 10.151.

memorial service in Salzburg municipal cemetery planned to coincide with a pre-arranged gathering of a group named 'Comradeship IV' in memory of SS soldiers. Initially the State had sought to justify the ban on grounds of necessity to protect the Comradeship IV gathering. However, before the ECtHR, it relied principally on the rights of other cemetery goers to manifest their religion in peace, free from the 'heated debates' that had occurred when the two groups had met previously. The ECtHR found that the State authorities had placed too much weight on the rights of the cemetery-goers to worship and too little on the applicant's right to 'express an opinion on an issue of public interest'.[70] Further, the Court found that less restrictive measures, such as allowing both gatherings to proceed, but with a police presence to keep the peace, would have been possible. An outright ban on the Jewish memorial service was therefore disproportionate.[71]

Under domestic law, where conflicts between demonstrators and counter-demonstrators **10.38** threaten a breach of the peace, the balance between the positive obligation to protect demonstrators from interference from those who do not like their views and the rights of others to counter-demonstrate is likely to follow the analysis of Lord Rodger in *R (Laporte) v Chief Constable of Gloucestershire Constabulary*[72] at paragraphs 73–81. *Laporte* concerned a judicial review of police action stopping a coach of protestors en route to a demonstration against the Iraq war. Not only did the police stop and search the protestors and their vehicle, but they refused to let them proceed to the demonstration and escorted the coach back to London. The police sought to justify their action as necessary in order to prevent a breach of the peace. Their Lordships held that action to prevent a breach of the peace could only lawfully be taken if the breach was imminent and it was not in this case. The action was therefore unlawful. Lord Rodger's analysis of the circumstances in which preventative action may be taken to prevent imminent violence was therefore strictly obiter. However, it provides an authoritative summary of the key propositions under domestic law:

(a) wherever it is possible to do so, preventative action must be directed at those who resort to or threaten violent action and not at those to whom the violence is directed;[73]

(b) in cases where one group is making deliberately offensive remarks with the intention of provoking violence from others, then they may be ordered to desist under the common law power to prevent a breach of the peace and if they fail to do so, they may be arrested for obstructing a police officer in the execution of his duty;[74]

(c) even where it is not the intention of the provocative group to provoke violence, but nonetheless their behaviour is 'outrageous' in a 'way which is liable to produce such a reaction', then action may lawfully be taken against them if this is *necessary* to prevent a breach of the peace;[75] and

(d) the difficult cases arise where the *only way* to prevent an imminent breach of the peace is to interfere with the Article 10 and 11 rights of entirely innocent third parties who are in no way responsible for the violent reactions of others. This would have been the

---

[70] Ibid, para 44.
[71] For the limited power to ban meetings in England and Wales see Ch 3.
[72] [2007] 2 AC 105. See also 3.04, 4.61, 4.63 et seq, and 6.124.
[73] *Beatty v Gillbanks* (1882) 9 QBD 308.
[74] See, Lord Rodger in *Laporte*, para 74.
[75] *Wise v Dunning* [1902] 1 KB 167; *Albert v Lavin* [1982] AC 546; *Steel v UK* (1998) 5 BHRC 339.

situation in *Laporte* had a breach of the peace been imminent. Lord Rodger, Lord Mance, and Lord Brown considered that there may be exceptional circumstances in which it would be lawful to interfere with the rights of innocent third parties where this was *strictly necessary* to prevent an imminent breach of the peace and no less intrusive means could be used to achieve this end.[76]

The scope of Articles 10 and 11

Activity which shocks, offends, or disturbs

10.39 The Convention does not merely protect expression which is favourably received or regarded as inoffensive or as a matter of indifference, but also that which offends, shocks, or disturbs.[77] However, assessing what this means in practice can be difficult. As discussed in paragraph 10.77 et seq below, Article 10(2) permits restrictions on freedom of expression where this is prescribed by law and necessary in a democratic society for the pursuit of one of the legitimate aims set out. These include, amongst other reasons, the prevention of disorder or crime and the protection of the rights of others. In reality, expression which offends, shocks, or disturbs, although protected under Article 10(1) is often restricted on the claimed basis that this is necessary under Article 10(2) for the protection of the rights of others. The question then arises as to whether this is legitimate and, if so, how the balance is to be struck.

10.40 In this context, the Parliamentary Joint Committee on Human Rights has raised concerns about s 5 of the Public Order Act 1986, which, in certain circumstances, criminalizes 'threatening, abusive or insulting words or behaviour, or disorderly behaviour'.[78] The Committee cited examples, including that of a man who had received a summons issued under s 5 of the Public Order Act 1986 in respect of a sign he had displayed outside the Church of Scientology's London headquarters stating 'Scientology is not a religion, it is a dangerous cult'. The police alleged that the use of the word 'cult' violated s 5, although the prosecution was subsequently discontinued.[79] The JCHR concluded that language or behaviour that is merely insulting should not be criminalized and recommended that 'the Government amend section 5 of the Public Order Act 1986 so that it cannot be used inappropriately to suppress the right to free speech, by deleting the reference to language or behaviour that is merely "insulting"'.[80]

The application of Articles 10 and 11 in English cases: is protection from insult a 'legitimate aim'?

10.41 *Dehal v DPP*,[81] was a case concerning s 4A of the Public Order Act 1986,[82] rather than s 5, but it is nonetheless relevant as it considered the circumstances in which criminal

---

[76] See Lord Rodger at paras 80 and 85; Lord Brown at paras 123–9; Lord Mance at paras 144–51.
[77] *Handyside v United Kingdom*; see also *Redmond-Bate v DPP* [2000] HRLR 249, para 20.
[78] See 1.171 et seq.
[79] JCHR Seventh Report of Session 2008–9, paras 78–85.
[80] Ibid, para 85. In the government response to the JCHR report, an undertaking was given to consider this proposal further—Command paper Cm 7633 pp 4–5.
[81] [2005] EWHC 2154 (Admin).
[82] See 1.206 et seq.

sanctions for 'threatening, abusive or insulting words or behaviour' would be justified. Moses J held that the fundamental feature of the relationship between s 4A POA 1986 and Article 10 is that:

> the criminal law should not be invoked unless and until it is established that the conduct which is the subject of the charge amounts to such a threat to public disorder as to require the invocation of the criminal as opposed to the civil law.
>
> . . .
>
> It is neither desirable nor possible to provide any universal test for that which goes beyond being a matter of legitimate protest, save to stress the importance of providing a justification for invoking the criminal law, namely where there is a threat to public order. The impact of the very words of the statute the 'Public Order' Act should remind the court of the importance of drawing that distinction.[83]

The facts of *Dehal* were that the appellant had been convicted as a result of a poster he had displayed at Luton Guruwarda accusing the President of the Temple of being a hypocrite and a liar as well as a 'proud, mad dog', who had assaulted the appellant and exploited his congregation for his own greed. In the context of this case, Moses J, whilst making clear that he did not condone the appellant's comments, held that: **10.42**

> However insulting, however unjustified what the appellant said about the President of the Temple, a criminal prosecution was unlawful as a result of section 3 of the Human Rights Act and Article 10 unless and until it could be established that such a prosecution was necessary in order to prevent public disorder.[84]

This decision gives significant weight to freedom of expression and requires in return a certain degree of robustness from those who might be insulted: it is only if an insult is such as to provoke public disorder that a criminal prosecution will be justified. **10.43**

The reasoning of the Divisional Court in the earlier case of *Percy v DPP*[85] appears to afford more weight to protection from insult as a legitimate aim in itself. *Percy* concerned an appeal by way of case stated brought by Lindis Percy, a long-standing protestor against weapons of mass destruction and US military policy, who had been convicted under s 5 of the Public Order Act 1986 when she had written 'Stop Star Wars' across a American flag, laid the flag on the ground and stepped on it in front of American service personnel at RAF Feltwell. Ms Percy successfully challenged her conviction on the ground that it amounted to a disproportionate interference with her rights under Article 10. **10.44**

The District Judge who had convicted Ms Percy had found as a matter of fact **10.45**

(a) that her behaviour was 'motivated by strongly held beliefs that the 'Star Wars' project was misguided, posed a danger to international stability and was not in the best interests of the United Kingdom.' But,

(b) that she had been aware of the effect of her conduct on those present and that, in the absence of any explanation other than that it had been 'a spontaneous protest' that her actions were calculated to offend.

---

[83] *Dehal v DPP*, paras 5 and 7.
[84] Ibid, para 12.
[85] [2002] Crim LR 835.

10.46   In these circumstances, the District Judge concluded that Ms Percy's actions were not reasonable and that her prosecution and conviction pursued a legitimate aim, namely the 'pressing social need in a multi-cultural society to prevent the denigration of objects of veneration and symbolic importance for one cultural group.' Further, he found the interference with Ms Percy's right to freedom of expression to be proportionate because she could have conducted her legitimate protest in ways which did not cause insult or distress.

10.47   Hallett J, who gave the lead judgment of the Divisional Court, expressed:

> no difficulty in principle with the concept that there will be circumstances in which citizens of this country and visiting foreign nationals should be protected from intentionally and gratuitously insulting behaviour, causing them alarm or distress. There may well be a pressing social need to protect people from such behaviour. It is, therefore, in my view, a legitimate aim, provided of course that any restrictions on the rights of peaceful protestors are proportionate to the mischief at which they are aimed. Some people will be more robust than others. What one person finds insulting and distressing may be water off a duck's back to another. A civilised society must strike an appropriate balance between the competing rights of those who may be insulted by a particular course of conduct and those who wish to register their protest on an important matter of public interest.

10.48   On the facts of *Percy*, on the issue of competing rights, the Divisional Court found that the District Judge had erred in affording too much weight to his finding that Ms Percy could have conveyed the message of her protest in ways that did not cause insult. As a result, he had erred in his approach to assessing the proportionality of the interference with Ms Percy's Article 10 rights and the conviction fell to be quashed on that basis. However, it is significant that, unlike Moses J in *Dehal*, Hallett J did not find that protection from insult *per se*, (without provocation of public disorder), could never be sufficient to legitimize a criminal charge.

10.49   Prevention of public disorder has been a factor in two further cases in which the higher courts have considered the interplay between s 5 of the Public Order Act 1986 and Article 10.

10.50   In *Hammond v DPP*,[86] the Divisional Court considered an appeal by way of case stated against a conviction under s 5 of the 1986 Act, where a preacher had taken to the streets of Bournemouth carrying a sign displaying the words 'Stop Immorality', 'Stop Homosexuality', and 'Stop Lesbianism'. This action caused a number of the members of the public to feel insulted and distressed and one of the police officers called to the scene decided that Mr Hammond was provoking violence and that it was necessary to arrest him in order to prevent a breach of the peace. He was subsequently charged with an offence under s 5 of the Public Order Act 1986. The Divisional Court in this case, refusing his appeal, confirmed that Article 10 does not provide a defence to a charge under s 5,[87] but suggested that it does play a role in the trial court's determination of

---

[86] [2004] EWHC 69 (Admin), The Times, 28 January 2004. See also 1.202 and 10.139.
[87] Ibid, para 20.

whether, as a matter of fact, particular words are 'insulting'.[88] The Court also held that Article 10 must be brought into play in considering whether the defence of reasonableness provided for in s 5(3)(c) is made out.[89] On the facts of this case, the magistrates had found that the charge under s 5 pursued the legitimate aim of preventing public disorder and the Divisional Court upheld their finding that the appellant's conduct had not been reasonable, notwithstanding the weight to be given to his freedom to exercise his Article 10 rights.

In the earlier case of *Norwood v DPP*,[90] the Divisional Court considered Article 10 in relation to the religiously aggravated offence under s 5 of the Public Order Act 1986 and s 31(1)(c) and 28(1)(b) of the Crime and Disorder Act 1998 (as amended).[91] Mr Norwood, a regional organizer for the British National Party, had been convicted for having displayed a poster in the window of his home bearing the words 'Islam out of Britain', 'Protect the British people', and featuring a picture of one of the twin towers of the World Trade Centre in flames on 11 September 2001; and a Crescent and Star surrounded by a prohibition sign. In that case, the Divisional Court found that the appellant's conviction had been a proportionate response to the pressing social need to protect the rights of others and/or to prevent crime and disorder;[92] and held that the mechanics of Article 10's operation on a prosecution under s 5 POA 1986 'are confined to the objective defence of reasonableness in section 5(3)'.[93] On the facts of this case, the Court observed that, once the District Judge had found that the appellant's poster was intentionally insulting and likely to cause harassment, alarm, and distress, it was difficult to envisage circumstances in which it would nonetheless have been objectively reasonable.[94] **10.51**

This is a somewhat narrower application of Article 10 to the interpretation of s 5 of the Public Order Act 1986 than that identified by the Divisional Court in *Hammond*. However, it seems unlikely on the facts of *Norwood*, that even if the Divisional Court had considered Article 10 in assessing whether the words of the poster were in fact threatening, abusive, or insulting, it would have made any difference to the outcome of the case. In both cases, the prevention of public disorder was at least one of the legitimate aims pursued. **10.52**

The authors suggest that, particularly in light of the views expressed by the Joint Committee on Human Rights, the position expressed by Moses J in *Dehal* is to be preferred to the broader statement of Hallett J in *Percy*. If the criminal law is to be invoked in restricting freedom of expression on grounds of insult, this should be limited to situations in which it is strictly necessary to prevent public disorder. This approach is consonant with the **10.53**

---

[88] Ibid, paras 11 and 21.

[89] Ibid, paras 22 and 23.

[90] [2003] EWHC 1564.

[91] See Ch 2.

[92] *Norwood v DPP*, para 40.

[93] Ibid, para 37.

[94] When this case was considered by the ECtHR (*Norwood v UK*, Application No 23131/03), the Court held that Mr Norwood could not rely on Art 10 rights by virtue of Art 17. Art 17 precludes any Convention right from being interpreted as a 'right to engage in any activity or perform any act aimed at the destruction of any of the rights and freedoms set forth [in the Convention] or at their limitation to a greater extent than is provided for in the Convention'.

jurisprudence of the ECtHR. In *Chorherr v Austria*,[95] for example, a conviction for behaviour 'likely to cause annoyance' was upheld as compatible with Article 10, but seemingly only on the basis that the applicant's actions in handing out anti-military leaflets at a military parade had threatened to result in public disorder.

10.54 Similar concerns to those raised about s 5 of the Public Order Act 1986 have been raised about s 42A of the Criminal Justice and Police Act 2001, as inserted by s 126 of the Serious Organised Crime and Police Act 2005, in that it provides for criminal sanctions in respect of expression which may cause only distress, as opposed to a likelihood of public disorder.[96] This provision is discussed in detail at 3.148.

10.55 It is of note that in relation to expression that is 'insulting' of government institutions, a higher level of tolerance is required. In *Incal v Turkey*,[97] the ECtHR found a breach of Article 10 where the applicant had been convicted of inciting hatred and crime as a result of leaflets he had prepared (but not distributed) containing strongly worded criticism of government policy. In finding the interference with the applicant's Article 10 rights to be disproportionate, the ECtHR observed:

> The limits of permissible criticism are wider with regard to the government than in relation to a private citizen, or even a politician. In a democratic system the actions or omissions of the government must be subject to the close scrutiny not only of the legislative and judicial authorities but also of public opinion. Furthermore, the dominant position which the government occupies makes it necessary for it to display restraint in resorting to criminal proceedings, particularly where other means are available for replying to the unjustified attacks and criticisms of its adversaries. Nevertheless it remains open to the competent State authorities to adopt, in their capacity as guarantors of public order, measures, even of a criminal-law nature, intended to react appropriately and without excess to such remarks.[98]

Disruptive activity (including disruption to traffic)

10.56 The case by case approach of the ECtHR, as opposed to the building upon precedent approach at common law, does not always produce uniform clarity. There are some European cases which in broad terms suggest that protest causing disruption should be tolerated, and therefore not prosecuted, so long as the disruption is peaceful, does not put the safety of the public at risk, is of modest duration, and does not interfere substantially with the rights of others. But there are other cases, tending to suggest, on the contrary, that apparently peaceful disruption, even just sitting down on a public road, may properly lead to prosecution. Some of these cases are now considered.

10.57 The ECtHR has recognized that activity which takes the form of physically impeding the activities of others may still constitute expression of opinion and therefore fall within the scope of Article 10.[99] Indeed, the Court has held that a certain degree of disruption must be tolerated by the authorities if the rights inherent in Articles 10 and 11 are to be

---

[95] (1993) 17 EHRR 358.

[96] See concerns expressed by Justice in its supplementary memorandum to the JCHR, Seventh Report of Session 2008–9, vol II, Ev 153–4.

[97] (2000) 29 EHRR 449.

[98] Ibid, para 54.

[99] *Steel v UK* (1998) 28 EHRR 603, [92].

protected adequately. In *Sergey Kuznetsov v Russia*,[100] the applicant was prosecuted for, amongst other things, causing obstruction to citizens seeking to enter the regional courthouse. The ECtHR found that, on the facts of that case, obstruction of passage to the courthouse was not a 'relevant or sufficient reason' for the interference with his Article 11 rights entailed by his subsequent prosecution. In so finding, the Court observed:

> any demonstration in a public place inevitably causes a certain level of disruption to ordinary life, including disruption of traffic, and [. . .] it is important for the public authorities to show a certain degree of tolerance towards peaceful gatherings if the freedom of assembly guaranteed by Article 11 of the Convention is not to be deprived of all substance.[101]

Similarly, in *Nurettin Aldemir & others v Turkey*,[102] the ECtHR found it likely that the applicants would have 'caused some disruption in a particularly busy square in central Ankara' had their demonstration been allowed to proceed. However, in light of the intended purpose of the demonstration, which had been to draw attention to a sensitive bill proposed in Parliament and the fact that the rally was initially peaceful, the forceful intervention of the police to disperse the assembly and the subsequent prosecution of the applicant was disproportionate and in breach of Article 11. Similar conclusions were reached by the ECtHR in *Oya Ataman v Turkey*[103] and in *Balcik v Turkey*.[104]   **10.58**

This is an apparently more tolerant approach on the part of the ECtHR than that exhibited, for example, in the case of *Lucas v UK*.[105] *Lucas* concerned a peaceful protest outside Faslane naval base in Scotland, during which Mrs Lucas and a number of other protestors sat down in the middle of a public road. The protestors were warned by police that if they did not move they would be arrested for breach of the peace, which is an offence in Scotland.[106] Mrs Lucas refused to move and was duly arrested. She was subsequently convicted of breaching the peace. Under Scottish law a charge of breach of the peace requires proof that the accused's conduct would be 'genuinely alarming or disturbing, in its context, to any reasonable person.[107] The Justice of the Peace who tried Mrs Lucas found that her intentional disruption of traffic could reasonably have been expected to cause any reasonable person who observed it, including car drivers, to be alarmed, upset, or annoyed and provoke a disturbance. Mrs Lucas applied to the ECtHR on the basis, amongst other complaints, that her prosecution and conviction did not pursue a legitimate aim as required by Articles 10(2) and 11(2) and/or amounted to a disproportionate interference with her   **10.59**

---

[100] Application No 10877/04, 23 October 2008.
[101] Ibid, para 44; see also, *Patyi & Others v Hungary*, Application No 5529/05, 7 October 2008; *Galstyan v Armenia*, Application No 26986/03, 15 November 2007, paras 116–17; *Bukta v Hungary*, Application No 25691/04, 17 July 2007, para 37; and *Oya Ataman* Application No 74552/01, 5 December 2006, paras 38–42.
[102] Application Nos 32124/02, 32126/02, 32129/02, 32133/02, 32137/02, 32138/02, 18 December 2007.
[103] Op cit.
[104] Application No 25/02, 29 November 2007.
[105] Application No 39013/02, 18 March 2003.
[106] For breach of the peace, see 6.125 et seq.
[107] *Smith v Donnelly* [2001] SCCR 800.

rights under Articles 10(1) and 11(1). The ECtHR dismissed her application as manifestly unfounded and expressed itself as seeing:

> no reason to doubt the assessment of the national courts that the applicant's actions in sitting in a public road could be alarming or disturbing to a reasonable person. The applicant's conduct either did or could have caused disruption to traffic on the road and could have posed a threat to the safety of the protestors and other road users.

The ECtHR went on to conclude that:

> the arrest, detention and conviction of the applicant may be regarded as pursuing the interests of public safety and/or the prevention of disorder and therefore, that the interference with her rights pursued one or more of the aims listed in Article 10 § 2. Finally, the Court finds that the actions of the police in arresting and detaining and of the national court in convicting the applicant were proportionate to the legitimate aim pursued in view of the dangers posed by the applicant's conduct in sitting in a public road and the interest in maintaining public order as well as the relatively minor penalty that was imposed. Therefore . . . any interference with the applicant's rights under Article 10 was justified under the terms of that provision.

The ECtHR reached the same conclusion in respect of Article 11.

10.60 The European Commission on Human Rights had earlier reached the same conclusion in the very similar German 'sit-in' cases of *CS v Germany*,[108] *Schiefer v Germany*,[109]and *W M and HO v Gerrmany*.[110] A similar approach has been adopted in cases concerning prior notification of demonstrations (discussed in paragraphs 10.111 et seq below), holding that objectives at the very mildest end of public order, such as the regulation of traffic, justify some level of interference with Article 10 and Article 11 rights.[111]

10.61 The decisions in *Lucas* and the German cases appear difficult to reconcile with the ECtHR's broad statements of tolerance in the face of minor disruption caused by peaceful protest in *Kuznetsov, Nurettin Aldemir, Oya Ataman,* and *Balcik*. In *Kuznetsov*,[112] the ECtHR cited the following factors as having been 'important' to its finding that the disruption caused was not a 'relevant and sufficient' reason for the interference with the applicant's rights: (a) there had been no complaints from anyone who was affected by the applicant's obstruction of the courthouse; (b) the applicant complied with the police request that he move to a less disruptive location; (c) the obstruction was for an 'extremely short duration'.[113] It may be that the Turkish cases are distinguishable from *Lucas* and the German 'sit-in' cases on the basis that the police had intervened forcefully to disperse the gatherings before the

---

[108] Application No 13858/88, 6 March 1989.

[109] Application No 13389/89, 6 March 1989.

[110] Application No 13235/87, 6 March 1989. See also, *GS v Austria*, Application No 14923/89, 30 November 1992; and the admissibility decisions in *Friedl v Austria*, Application No15225/89, 30 November 1992 and *G and E and Norway*, Application Nos 9278/81 and 9415/81, 3 October 1983.

[111] *Andersson v Sweden*, Application No 12781/87, 13 December 1987; *JK v Netherlands*, Application No 15928/89, 13 May 1992. However, cf *Galstyan v Armenia*, Application No 26986/03, 18 October 2007, in which a criminal conviction for obstructing traffic and 'making a loud noise' was found to be a disproportionate interference with Art 11.

[112] Application No 10877/04, 23 October 2008.

[113] On the facts this appears to have been about thirty minutes. Compare *G v Germany*, Application No 13079/87, 6 March 1989.

protestors had in fact caused any disruption; the disruption had merely been a reasonably foreseeable consequence of the protest and it was the forceful intervention of the police that the ECtHR found to be disproportionate.

It is also fair to say that the ECtHR has been far more robust in finding violations of **10.62** Articles 10 and 11 in cases where there has been no interference by the applicants with the rights of others.[114] Indeed, a comprehensive survey of Strasbourg jurisprudence on protest cases found only one finding of a violation in circumstances where the protest had involved direct action, ie where there was deliberate interference with the activity against which the protest was directed.[115]

It remains to be seen whether the decisions in *Kuznetsov, Nurettin Aldemir,* and *Oya Ataman* **10.63** represent a shift in the balance struck by the ECtHR in favour of freedom of expression and assembly where only minor disruption is caused, for example to free flow of traffic, or whether those decisions are confined to their own facts.

It is of note in this regard that the recent Guidelines on Peaceful Assembly drawn up by **10.64** the ODIHR/OSCE[116] emphasize that 'even conduct that deliberately impedes or obstructs the activities of third parties' should be included within the definition of 'peaceful assembly'.[117]

It is also of note that the European Court of Justice has recognized that protection of the **10.65** rights to freedom of expression and assembly may justify a measure of disruption to the lawful activities of others, even when this amounts to a substantial restriction on the EC Treaty right to free movement of goods. In *Schmidberger v Republik Österreich*[118] the European Court of Justice held that the refusal of the Austrian authorities to ban an environmental demonstration blocking the Brenner motorway between Germany and Italy for approximately thirty hours constituted 'a measure of equivalent effect to a quantitative restriction' on free movement of goods. However, in the circumstances of this case, Austria had been entitled to conclude that permitting the demonstration to take place was the least restrictive measure compatible with the legitimate aim of upholding rights under Articles 10 and 11 of the ECHR. Therefore, there was no breach of the EC Treaty, notwithstanding the interference with free movement of goods.[119]

---

[114] See discussion in *Drieman v Norway*, Application No 33678/96, 4 May 2000.

[115] See David Mead, 'The Right to Peaceful Protest Under The European Convention on Human Rights— A Content Study of Strasbourg Case Law' [2007] EHRLR 345. The case in which the sole finding of a violation in a direct action case occurred was *Hashman and Harrup v UK* (2000) 30 EHRR 241, discussed below at 10.89.

[116] Referred to at 10.08 above.

[117] The Guidelines, dated 4 June 2008 are available online at <http://www.venice.coe.int/docs/2008/CDL(2008)062-e.pdf>.

[118] Case C-112/00 ECJ 12 June 2003.

[119] A similar challenge was brought in the domestic courts by International Trader's Ferry Ltd (ITF) against the decision of the Chief Constable of Sussex not to provide policing at a level sufficient to safeguard every shipment made by ITF from violent attack by demonstrators protesting against the company's live animal exports. However, the analysis in this case did not focus on the balance drawn by the Chief Constable between ITF and the rights of those who wished to protest peacefully (although this was a factor), but rather on a range of issues, principally the disproportionate financial cost of providing the level of policing that would have been required to guarantee all shipments: *R v Chief Constable, ex p ITF Ltd* [1999] 2 AC 418.

10.66 In reaching this conclusion, the European Court of Justice emphasized that both established case law and the preamble to the Single European Act and subsequently Article F.2 of the Treaty on European Union require Member States to respect the fundamental rights guaranteed by the ECHR. The Court also noted that States enjoy a wide margin of discretion in determining whether a fair balance has been struck between the competing interests of ECHR rights and EC Treaty rights.

Violent activity

10.67 It is clearly established that Articles 10 and 11 do not protect demonstrations where the organizers and participants have violent intentions which result in public disorder.[120] However, the ECtHR has held that peaceful demonstrators who were simply present when violence was perpetrated by others are protected.[121] For example, in *Ezelin v France*,[122] the applicant (a lawyer) sought to challenge a disciplinary penalty imposed on him for taking part in a demonstration that had involved violence and public disorder on the part of some of the other demonstrators. It was common ground that Mr Ezelin had not himself engaged in any violent or anti-social behaviour. However, the French authorities sought to justify the interference with Mr Ezelin's Article 10 and 11 rights on the basis that he had not disassociated himself from the unruly incidents. This argument was rejected by the Court and a breach of Article 11 was found. In *Ziliberberg v Moldova*,[123] the ECtHR, citing with approval the European Commission in *Ezelin v France*,[124] observed that:

> an individual does not cease to enjoy the right to peaceful assembly as a result of sporadic violence or other punishable acts committed by others in the course of the demonstration, if the individual in question remains peaceful in his or her own intentions or behaviour.[125]

10.68 However, in *R (Parminder Singh and another) v Chief Constable of the West Midlands Police*,[126] concerning a demonstration by members of the Sikh community against a theatre performance they considered to be offensive to their religion, the Court of Appeal, held that police dispersal powers under s 30 of the Anti-social Behaviour Act 2003 may lawfully be used to disband groups of protestors *en masse* when the conditions of the section are met. In so doing, the Court accepted a reading of s 30(7) which entailed that an officer seeking to use powers under s 30(4) 'was entitled to consider the presence or behaviour of "any one or more of the persons in the group" to be the presence or behaviour of the group' and to give a direction to the whole group accordingly.[127] On its face this reasoning would suggest that the rights of peaceful protestors could be overridden on the strength of the presence or behaviour of just one individual within the group. But Hallett

---

[120] *G v Germany* (1989) 60 DR 256; *CS v Germany*, Application No 13858/88, 6 March 1989; *Christians Against Racism and Fascism v UK*, Application No 8440/78, 16 July 1980, 21 DR 138; *Cisse v France*, Application No 51346/99, 9 April 2002.

[121] *Ciraklar v Turkey*, Application No 19601/92; 80-A/B(E) DR 46 at 52; *Ezelin v France*; *Ziliberberg v Moldova*, Application No 61821/00, admissibility decision 4 May 2004.

[122] (A/202) (1992) 14 EHRR 36.

[123] Application No 61821/00, admissibility decision 4 May 2004.

[124] Op cit.

[125] Op cit.

[126] [2006] 1 WLR 3374.

[127] Ibid, para 112.

LJ, with whom the other members of the Court agreed, sought to emphasize that it is the behaviour of the group as a whole that should be considered:

> Whether or not a group's behaviour on any particular occasion warrants a dispersal direction will depend on the circumstances. Police officers must act proportionately and sensibly . . .

> . . . it is only when the behaviour of a group of people moves beyond legitimate protest and into the realms of behaviour that causes actual or likely intimidation, harassment, alarm and distress that an officer can use an authorisation to direct them to disperse.[128]

The difficulties that arise in leaving protection of fundamental democratic rights down to the proportionality assessment of individual police officers in the heat of the moment, and the problems this raises in terms of legal certainty, are discussed in paragraphs 10.82 et seq below. **10.69**

In respect of restrictions imposed on protest activity in *advance* of the planned activity, the ECtHR has held that prior restrictions on the basis of the possibility of minor incidents of violence are likely to be disproportionate, and any isolated outbreak of violence should be dealt with by way of subsequent arrest and prosecution rather than prior restraint.[129] **10.70**

Illegality

The ECtHR has held that the fact that an assembly is illegal does not preclude reliance on Article 11.[130] For example, in *Oya Ataman v Turkey*,[131] the applicant had participated in a demonstration in Sultanahmet Square in Istanbul against a particular type of prison. Advance notice of the demonstration was required under Turkish law, but none had been given. The demonstration was therefore unlawful. The ECtHR nonetheless found that the police action in dispersing the demonstration with tear gas and arresting the applicant had violated her Article 11 rights, because it was a disproportionate reaction, notwithstanding the illegality of the demonstration. On the other hand, in other cases, for example, *Ziliberberg v Moldova*,[132] the ECtHR has upheld criminal sanctions for failure to comply with administrative requirements for the conduct of lawful assemblies, for example requirements to give prior notification.[133] *Ziliberberg* was recently followed by the ECtHR in the case of *Rai and Evans v UK*[133a] in the context of the requirement for prior authorization of demonstrations in the vicinity of Parliament Square contained in s. 134(2) and s. 132(1)(a) of the Seniors Organised Crime and Police Act 2005. **10.71**

Private property

In *Appleby v UK*[134] the ECtHR considered the case of three individuals and an environmental group 'Washington First Forum', who had sought to collect signatures for a petition **10.72**

---

[128] Ibid, paras 89 and 92.
[129] *Stankov v Bulgaria*, Application No 29221/95, 2 October 2001.
[130] *Cisse v France*, Application No 51346/99, 9 April 2002, para 50; *Oya Ataman v Turkey*, para 39; *Nurettin Aldemir v Turkey. Samut Karabulat v Turkey Application* No 16999/04, 27 January 2009 paras 35–8.
[131] Application No 74552/01, 5 December 2006.
[132] Application No 61821/00, admissibility decision 4 May 2004.
[133] See also, *Andersson v Sweden*, Application No 12781/87, 13 December 1987.
[133a] Applications Nos. 26258/07 and 26255/07, 17 November 2009; see further discussions of this case at 10.111–10.121 below.
[134] [2003] 37 EHRR 38. See also 5.13.

in the privately owned town centre of Washington, Tyne and Wear. The company which owned the shopping mall comprising the town centre refused the applicants permission to set up a stand within its precincts or to collect signatures. The applicants complained to the ECtHR that the United Kingdom was in breach of its positive obligation to secure the applicants' rights under Articles 10 and 11, particularly where, as here, the town centre had been publicly owned land prior to its sale to private owners and the local authority, which had been responsible for the sale could, by virtue of s 35 of the Highways Act 1980, have required the purchasers to have entered into a 'walkways agreement'. This would have guaranteed public rights of access and would have given the local council the power to issue by-laws regulating use of those rights. The applicants pointed out that the shopping mall in question was labelled as the 'town centre' on maps and either contained, or was in close proximity to, public services and facilities. They argued that it should therefore be regarded as 'quasi-public' space, in which Article 10 and 11 rights should be protected.

10.73 The ECtHR observed that the Article 1, Protocol 1 property rights of the landowners were also in play and concluded that:

> notwithstanding the acknowledged importance of freedom of expression, [Article 10] does not bestow any freedom of forum for the exercise of that right. While it is true that demographic, social, economic and technological developments are changing the ways in which people move around and come into contact with each other, the Court is not persuaded that this requires the automatic creation of rights of entry to private property, or even, necessarily, to all publicly owned property (government offices and ministries, for instance). Where, however, the bar on access to property has the effect of preventing any effective exercise of freedom of expression or it can be said that the essence of the right has been destroyed, the Court would not exclude that a positive obligation could arise for the State to protect the enjoyment of the Convention rights by regulating property rights. A corporate town where the entire municipality is controlled by a private body might be an example (see *Marsh v Alabama*, [(326 US 501, 66 S Ct 276, 90 L Ed 265 (1946)]).[135]

10.74 On the facts of *Appleby*, the ECtHR found that there were many other outlets open to the applicants for the exercise of their expression rights, for example, they could campaign on the streets leading to the shopping mall; as well as in the old town centre; via the local media; or by door-to-door canvassing. In these circumstances, the prohibition on the applicants campaigning from the shopping mall itself did not 'destroy the essence' of their rights under Article 10 or 11. There was therefore no breach of these rights.

10.75 In the earlier case of *Anderson v United Kingdom*,[136] the European Commission of Human Rights had considered a claim brought on behalf of a group of individuals who had been excluded altogether from a privately owned shopping mall which covered most of the area of Wellingborough town centre on the grounds of their alleged misconduct and disorderly behaviour. Unlike the case of *Appleby*, *Anderson* did not raise any issue under Article 10 as the applicants had not sought to conduct any form of protest or campaign in the shopping mall, they has simply used the mall for social purposes and sought to complain under Article 11 in respect of their exclusion. Their application was dismissed as being manifestly

---

[135] Ibid, para 47.
[136] [1998] EHRLR 218.

unfounded on the basis that there was 'no indication [in the Strasbourg jurisprudence] that freedom of assembly is intended to guarantee a right to pass and repass in public places, or to assemble for purely social purposes anywhere one wishes'.[137]

In practical terms, the ECtHR's decision in *Appleby* has considerable significance for protestors, because a significant amount of contemporary protest takes place on private property.[138] Both the organizations Liberty and Justice have argued for development of the domestic law to afford greater protection for expressive activities on privately owned land, such as shopping centres, precincts, and parks, which are open to the public and would traditionally have been public spaces.[139]   **10.76**

Limitations on the right to protest

As indicated above, Article 10 and Article 11 are not absolute, but qualified rights. The rights of freedom of expression and freedom of assembly may therefore be restricted, but only in so far as those restrictions   **10.77**

(a) are prescribed by law;
(b) pursue one of the legitimate aims specified;
(c) are necessary in a democratic society.

The term 'restriction' 'must be interpreted as including both measures taken before or during the public assembly, and those, such as punitive measures, taken after the meeting'.[140]

'Prescribed by law': the requirement of legality

'Prescribed by law' has an autonomous Convention meaning. For a restriction to be 'prescribed by law', it must have a basis in, and comply with, domestic law; this includes the common law[141] and rules of procedure[142] as well as statute and secondary legislation. However, the fact that a particular provision is 'lawful' as a matter of domestic law is not determinative of whether it is 'prescribed by law' for the purposes of the Convention.   **10.78**

In *R (Gillan) v Metropolitan Police Commissioner*,[143] Lord Bingham considered the requirement of legality in the following terms: **10.79**

> The lawfulness requirement in the convention addresses supremely important features of the rule of law. The exercise of power by public officials, as it affects members of the public, must

---

[137] See *CIN Properties Ltd v Rawlins* [1995] 2 EGLR 130 for the consideration of this case in the Court of Appeal.

[138] See, for example, the evidence to the JCHR of Phil McLeish on behalf of Climate Camp at Seventh Report of Session 2008–9, vol II, Ev 29–31.

[139] Supplementary memorandum submitted by Justice, Seventh Report of Session 2008–9, vol II, Ev 154–5; supplementary memorandum submitted by Liberty, op cit. For further discussion of protest rights and private land see Jacob Rowbottom, 'Property and Participation: A Right of Access for Expressive Activities' [2005] 2 EHRLR 186–202; Kevin Gray and Susan Gray, 'Civil Rights, Civil Wrongs and Quasi-Public Space' [1999] EHRLR 45; B Fitzpatrick and N Taylor, 'Trespassers Might be Prosecuted: The European Convention and Restrictions on the Right to Assemble' [1998] EHRLR 292.

[140] *Ezelin v France*, judgment of 26 April 1991, Series A No 202, para 39.

[141] *Sunday Times v UK* (1979–80) 2 EHRR 245, para 47.

[142] *Barthold v Germany* (1985) 7 EHRR 383.

[143] [2006] 2 AC 307. See also 4.84 et seq and 6.87 et seq.

be governed by clear and publicly-accessible rules of law. The public must not be vulnerable to interference by public officials acting on a personal whim, caprice, malice, predilection or purpose other than that for which the power was conferred. This is what, in this context, is meant by arbitrariness, which is the antithesis of legality. This is the test which any interference with or derogation from a convention right must meet if a violation is to be avoided.[144]

10.80 Thus in *R (Laporte) v Chief Constable of Gloucestershire Constabulary*,[145] the House of Lords found a breach of the appellant's rights under Articles 10 and 11, because the action taken by the police, in diverting the appellant's coach back to London in order to prevent her and her fellow passengers from participating in a planned demonstration at RAF Fairford, was unlawful as a matter of domestic law. The common law powers to prevent an anticipated breach of the peace, on which the police sought to rely, required a reasonable apprehension of an *imminent* breach of the peace. There had been no such apprehension in this case. Rather, the police had anticipated that a breach of the peace might occur at some future point had the coach been permitted to proceed to Fairford. In these circumstances the police action failed to meet the requirements of legality.

Accessible

10.81 It is a further requirement that the legal basis for any restriction on fundamental rights must be accessible, normally in the sense that it is readily available for inspection, either in the form of a written law, or in case reports if it is a principle of common law. What matters is that 'the citizen must be able to have an indication that is adequate in the circumstances of the legal rules applicable to a given case'.[146] This means that, for example, internal police policy and guidelines are unlikely to meet the requirement of legality unless they are published.[147] However, in *R (Gillan) v Metropolitan Police Commissioner*,[148] the House of Lords held that the fact that police authorizations to stop and search under s 44 of the Terrorism Act 2000 are not published does not render them unlawful on this basis.[149]

Not arbitrary, not uncertain

10.82 What is required is that the legal provision or rule governing the restriction on fundamental rights must be 'formulated with sufficient precision to enable the citizen—if need be, with appropriate advice—to foresee, to a degree that is reasonable in the circumstances, the consequences which a given action may entail'.[150] Otherwise it will be found to be arbitrary.

10.83 Further, the House of Lords has emphasized that where Parliament legislates for restrictions on fundamental rights, it must do so expressly or by necessary implication:

> . . . the principle of legality means that Parliament must squarely confront what it is doing and accept the political cost. Fundamental rights cannot be overridden by general

---

144 Ibid, para 34.
145 [2007] 2 AC 105. For the facts of *Laporte* see 10.38 above.
146 *Sunday Times v UK (No 1)* (1979) 2 EHRR 245 para 49.
147 *Govell v UK*, Application No 27237/95, 26 February 1995.
148 [2006] 2 AC 307. See fn 143 above.
149 See paras 31–5 and 52–7.
150 *Ezelin v France*, para 45.

or ambiguous words. This is because there is too great a risk that the full implications of their unqualified meaning may have passed unnoticed in the democratic process. In the absence of express language or necessary implication to the contrary, the courts therefore presume that even the most general words were intended to be subject to the basic rights of the individual.[151]

However, the ECtHR has recognized that whilst legal certainty is desirable, laws must be **10.84** sufficiently flexible to adapt to changing circumstances and thus it has acknowledged that 'many laws are inevitably couched in terms which, to a greater or lesser extent, are vague and whose interpretation and application are questions of practice'.[152] The concept of legal certainty does not preclude the existing elements of an offence being 'clarified and adapted to new circumstances which can reasonably be brought under the original concept of the offence'.[153]

The degree of precision required will depend on 'the content of the instrument in question, **10.85** the field it is designed to cover and the number and the status of those to whom it is addressed'.[154] Where the law affords a discretion on public authorities, it must:

> indicate the scope of any such discretion conferred on the competent authorities and the manner of its exercise with sufficient clarity, having regard to the legitimate aim of the measure in question, to give the individual adequate protection against arbitrary interference.[155]

In *Rai, Allmond and 'Negotiate Now' v UK*,[156] the European Commission of Human Rights **10.86** considered an extremely broad statutory discretion conferred on the then Secretary of State for National Heritage to regulate demonstrations in Trafalgar Square. Although the statutory provision in question and the regulations made thereunder conferred an entirely unfettered discretion on the Minister to grant or refuse permission to demonstrate, the applicants' challenge to the legality of the provision was rejected as 'manifestly unfounded'. The Commission found that 'executive or administrative statements' made in the House of Commons explaining how the discretion would be exercised were adequate to enable citizens to regulate their conduct and thus to ensure that the provisions were sufficiently foreseeable to meet the requirement of legality.

In *R (Gillan) v Metropolitan Police Commissioner*,[157] the House of Lords assessed the extent **10.87** to which the statutory discretion conferred on the police under s 44 of the Terrorism Act 2000 to stop and search for articles of a kind which could be used in connection with terrorism, without the requirement of any grounds for suspecting the presence of such articles, could be reconciled with the prohibition on arbitrariness and/or discrimination. The appellants were a student and a journalist who had been present at a peaceful

---

[151] *R v Home Secretary, ex parte Simm* [2000] 2 AC 115, 131.
[152] *Sunday Times v UK* (1979) 2 EHRR 245, para 49; see also, *Bronda v Italy* (1998) 33 EHRR 81, para 54; *Kuijper v Netherlands*, Application No 64848/01, 3 March 2005; *Larissis and Others v Greece*, judgment of 24 February 1998, *Reports* 1998-I, p 377, para 34.
[153] *CS v Germany*, Application No 13858/88, 6 March 1989.
[154] *Hashman Harrup v UK* (2000) 30 EHRR 241, para 31.
[155] *Malone v UK* (1984) 7 EHRR 14.
[156] (1995) 19 EHRR CD 93.
[157] [2006] 2 AC 307. See fn 143 above.

demonstration against an arms fair. Their complaints in respect of the statutory power to stop and search were twofold:

(a) first, they made the generic complaint, which formed the focus of the appeal, that without any requirement for reasonable suspicion, the statutory power was arbitrary, and thus unlawful, because it lacked any sufficient safeguards to prevent misuse of the power, given that no particular grounds are required for its apparently lawful exercise. In respect of this complaint their Lordships held that, although the decision to exercise a stop and search in any individual case might lawfully be based on no more than a police officer's 'hunch' or a 'professional's intuition', nonetheless, the statutory framework, read with the code of practice issued under s 66 of the Police and Criminal Evidence Act 1984, gives the requisite degree of certainty against which individual instances of the power can be tested;[157a] and

(b) the appellants' second complaint was that the power to stop and search had been exercised unlawfully on the particular facts of their cases, because, they alleged, it was used not for the purpose specified in the statute, namely to search for articles connected with terrorism, but to inhibit their participation in lawful protest. In the *Gillan* appeal, this issue was left to be resolved in subsequent litigation.

10.88 Legality has been an issue in many of the protest cases brought against the United Kingdom. In particular, the concepts of 'breach of the peace' and being 'bound over to keep the peace' or to be of 'good behaviour' have been challenged for lack of clarity and certainty.

10.89 *Hashman Harrup v UK*,[158] concerned complaints by two hunt saboteurs that a bind over order imposed on them under the Justices of the Peace Act 1361 to 'keep the peace and be of good behaviour' was an unlawful interference with their right to freedom of expression under Article 10 of the ECHR. The applicants had blown a horn and shouted during the course of a hunt with the intention of distracting the hounds from the chase. They were not prosecuted with any offence, and indeed on the facts found by the domestic court they had not perpetrated any breach of the peace. However, the domestic court found that no such finding was necessary for the lawful imposition of a bind over. The Strasbourg court held that in these circumstances, where the imposition of the bind over was purely prospective, ie it had no element of sanction or punishment for past action, the requirement to be of 'good behaviour' or to refrain from acting '*contra bonos mores*' failed to meet the requirement of legality. The term, without reference to past behaviour, was insufficiently clear to enable the applicants to know what it was they were being required to refrain from doing.

10.90 By contrast, in the earlier case of *Steel v UK*,[159] two of the applicants were found by the domestic courts to have caused breaches of the peace by virtue of their protest activity. In this context, although the ECtHR noted that the requirement not to act '*contra bonos*

[157a] At the time of going to press, the European Court of Human Rights has decided, contrary to the view of the House of Lords, that the scope of the discretion conferred by ss.44–47 of the 2000 Act is too broad to meet the requirement of legality, both in terms of the authorization of the power to stop and search and its application in practice. See *Gillan and Quinton v UK Application* no. 4158/05, 12 January 2010 paras. 76–87. For a commentary on this decision see 6.87 et seq.

[158] (2000) 30 EHRR 241.

[159] (1998) 5 BHRC 339.

mores' was 'very vague', it held that the bind over orders imposed were sufficiently certain and the conduct they proscribed sufficiently foreseeable to meet the requirement of legality. The orders were to be interpreted as prohibiting further breaches of the peace similar to those the applicants had been found to have caused in the past.[160]

Likewise, in the later cases of *Lucas v UK*,[161] *McBride v UK*,[162] and *Nicol and Selvanayagam v UK*,[163] the ECtHR again upheld, respectively, a conviction[164] for breach of the peace, an arrest for breach of the peace, and a committal to prison for refusing to be bound over to keep the peace. In all three cases, the Court followed its decision in *Steel* in finding the definition of breach of the peace, both in Scottish and English law, to be sufficiently certain to meet the requirement of legality. **10.91**

In *Chorherr v Austria*,[165] the ECtHR found that a law making it a criminal offence to cause a 'breach of the peace by conduct likely to cause annoyance' was sufficiently clear and precise to meet the requirement of legality. **10.92**

In the UK context, concern has been expressed by campaigning organizations about a number of recent legislative developments which provide for criminal sanctions in respect of broad and ill-defined categories of behaviour, which are increasingly being used to restrain protest activity. **10.93**

For example, s 125(2) of the Serious Organised Crime and Police Act 2005[166] extends the scope of the criminal offence of harassment to proscribe harassment of two or more persons which is intended to persuade them to do or to refrain from doing something they are entitled to do or not to do. This provision was passed with animal protestors and animal research organizations in mind. Given the already broad scope of harassment in the Protection from Harassment Act 1997, which includes causing alarm or distress, this has the potential to cover a significant amount of protest activity. The non-governmental organization Justice, in its Parliamentary briefing when the Serious Organised Crime and Police Act was at the Bill stage, pointed out that: **10.94**

> Many types of legitimate speech and other types of expression cause alarm or distress; handing out leaflets with a distressing picture of a human or animal rights abuse, for example, would qualify.[167]

Although the explanatory notes to the Serious Organised Crime and Police Act state that s 125(2) is not intended to encompass 'lawful lobbying', it is arguable that the scope of the offence is too broad and indiscriminate to meet the requirement of legality. **10.95**

---

[160] Ibid, para 76.
[161] Application No 39013/02, 18 March 2003.
[162] Application No 27786/95, 5 July 2001.
[163] Application No 32213/96, 11 January 2001.
[164] This was a Scottish case. Unlike in England, breach of the peace is a criminal offence in Scotland.
[165] (1993) 17 EHRR 358.
[166] See fn 19 above.
[167] Justice Briefing for House of Lords Second Reading of the Serious Organised Crime and Police Bill, March 2005, para 29. See also Peacerights, *The Right to Protest Under UK Law: A Civil Liberty in Decline?* March 2007, pp 21–2.

10.96   The observations of Swift J in *Heathrow Airport & Others v Garman & 6 Others*[168] highlight the difficulty of predicting in advance whether or not particular action (in that case proposed protest at Heathrow Airport against the development of a third runway) would be caught by the provisions of the Protection from Harassment Act 1997, as amended:

> In particular, having regard to the contrast between the offences created by section 2 and section 4 of the 1997 Act, 'harassment' cannot, in the context of that Act, be confined to conduct which would place the victim in fear of violence. Neither in my view can it be right that harassment is confined just to conduct that will cause alarm and distress. Quite where the line is to be drawn and whether a particular type of conduct can properly be considered to amount to harassment will depend on the particular facts and circumstances of the incident in question. It is not a matter that can—save in a clear case—be predicted in advance. All I am able to say at this stage is that the fact that the actions of protestors will or may cause annoyance and inconvenience to the travelling public (whether by a blockade or any other form of action) does not necessarily mean that their conduct will amount to harassment. It may do. It may not.[169]

10.97   Legal certainty is an area about which the Parliamentary Joint Committee on Human Rights expressed considerable concern in its report 'Demonstrating a respect for rights? A human rights approach to policing protest'.[170] The JCHR referred to complaints from a number of those from whom it received evidence of 'a bewildering array of [overlapping] powers and offences in relation to protest activities which decreases the foreseeability and predictability of the law'.[171] The JCHR concluded that there is a need for 'greater clarity about how broad police powers are used' and that 'the better approach is to draft legislation itself in sufficiently precise terms so as to constrain and guide police discretion, rather than to rely on decision makers to exercise a broad discretion compatibly with human rights'.[172]

Legitimate aims

10.98   Articles 10(2) and 11(2) set out the 'legitimate aims' which may justify interference with the rights to freedom of expression, assembly, and association. The ECtHR has held that the aims listed in Articles 10(2) and 11(2) are exhaustive and has stated that they are to be narrowly construed.[173] However, in practice, the Court has adopted a notably inclusive approach to its interpretation of what constitutes, in particular, 'public safety', 'the prevention of disorder or crime' and 'the protection of the rights and freedoms of others'. For example, in *Lucas v UK*,[174] despite the applicant's entirely peaceful protest, the ECtHR held that her prosecution had pursued the legitimate aims of protecting public safety

---

[168] [2007] EWHC 1957 (QB), unreported, 6 August 2007.

[169] Ibid, para 99(c). NB Although the ECtHR considered, inter alia, the Protection from Harassment Act 1997, s 2, in *Selvanayagam v UK*, Application No 57981/00, 12 December 2002, it was not asked to consider in that case whether the offence of harassment itself was sufficiently clearly circumscribed as to meet the requirement of legality. The case was also before the Serious Organised Crime and Police Act.

[170] JCHR Seventh report of Session 2008–9.

[171] Citing from Justice's memorandum to the JCHR at para 71 of vol I. The Justice memorandum is at vol II, Ev 149.

[172] JCHR Seventh report of Session 2008–9 vol I, para 76. This view is borne out by the ECtHR finding in *Gillan and Quinton v UK* Application no. 4158/05, 12 January 2010. See 6.87 et seq.

[173] *Sidiropoulos v Greece* (1998) 27 EHRR 633, para 40; *Ashughyan v Armenia*, Application No 33268/03, 17 July 2008, para 89.

[174] Op cit, see 10.59, above.

and/or preventing disorder. Likewise, in *Andersson v Sweden*,[175] the Commission held that the aim of 'properly regulating traffic and otherwise maintaining order in public places' fell within the legitimate aims contained in Article 10(2) such as to justify the requirement to obtain a permit to demonstrate.[176]

Even the protection of 'territorial integrity' has been given a broad interpretation by the **10.99** ECtHR in the context of protest activity. In *Piermont v France*,[177] a German member of the European Parliament was expelled from the French dependent territories of French Polynesia and New Caledonia because she expressed the view at a public rally that the activities of the French government and in particular their nuclear testing at Mururoa constituted interference in the affairs of the Polynesians. France sought to argue that her expulsion pursued the legitimate aim of protecting territorial integrity. The ECtHR found that in the particular circumstances of the case this was one of the legitimate aims pursued, albeit that the interference had been disproportionate.[178]

It can be seen from the above that in practice the circumstances in which the justification **10.100** advanced by a State party will be found not to be a legitimate aim are rare indeed. The battleground is far more likely to be whether the interference complained of was necessary in a democratic society in that it pursued a 'pressing social need' and was proportionate to the legitimate aim pursued.

Necessary in a democratic society

The ECtHR has repeatedly held that the only necessity capable of justifying an interference **10.101** with the rights enshrined in Articles 8–12 of the Convention 'is one that may claim to spring from a "democratic society"'.[179] Accordingly:

> States must not only safeguard the right to assemble peacefully but also refrain from applying unreasonable indirect restrictions upon that right. In view of the essential nature of freedom of assembly and its close relationship with democracy there must be convincing and compelling reasons to justify an interference with this right.[180]

The ECtHR has also repeatedly held that: **10.102**

> in assessing the necessity of a given measure a number of principles must be observed. The term 'necessary' does not have the flexibility of such expressions as 'useful' or 'desirable.' In addition, pluralism, tolerance and broadmindedness are hallmarks of a 'democratic society'. Although individual interests must on occasion be subordinated to those of a group, democ-

---

[175] Application No 12781/87, 13 December 1987.
[176] See also, *Patyi & Others v Hungary*, Application No 5529/05, 7 October 2008, where the principle justification advanced for prohibiting a proposed demonstration was that it would 'cause a disproportionate hindrance to the traffic'. NB, however, in *Patyi*, the Court found a breach of Art 11 in that it did not accept the respondent state's evidence that the applicant's actions would in fact have cause sufficient disruption to justify the ban.
[177] (1995) 20 EHRR 301.
[178] Ibid, paras 72 and 77.
[179] *Christian Democratic People's Party v Moldova*, Application No 28793/02, paras 62–3, ECHR 2006; *Djavit An*, Application No 20652/92, 20 February 2003, [56]; *Bączkowski v Poland*, Application No 1543/06, 3 May 2007, para 61.
[180] *Sergey Kuznetsov v Russia*, para 39; *Ouranio Toxo v Greece*, Application No 74989/01, para 36, ECHR 2005-X (extracts); *Adali v Turkey*, Application No 38187/97, 31 March 2005, para 267; domestically, see *Reynolds v Times Newspapers Ltd* [2001] 2 AC 127, 200F.

racy does not simply mean that the views of a majority must always prevail; a balance must be achieved which ensures the fair and proper treatment of minorities and avoids any abuse of a dominant position. Lastly, any restriction imposed on a Convention right must be proportionate to the legitimate aim pursued.[181]

10.103 This was emphasized by Lord Bingham in *R v Shayler*:[182]

'Necessary' has been strongly interpreted: it is not synonymous with 'indispensable', neither has it the flexibility of such expressions as 'admissible', 'ordinary', 'useful', 'reasonable' or 'desirable': *Handyside v United Kingdom* (1976) 1 EHRR 737, 754, para 48. One must consider whether the interference complained of corresponded to a pressing social need, whether it was proportionate to the legitimate aim pursued and whether the reasons given by the national authority to justify it are relevant and sufficient under article 10(2): *The Sunday Times v United Kingdom* (1979) 2 EHRR 245, 277–8, para 62.

10.104 The burden of justifying the interference lies firmly on the State, which must provide 'relevant and sufficient' reasons for the interference.[183]

10.105 The requirement that any interference must be necessary in a democratic society means that the protection afforded by Articles 10 and 11 are 'applicable not only to "information" or "ideas" that are favourably received or regarded as inoffensive or as a matter of indifference, but also to those that offend, shock or disturb. Such are the demands of that pluralism, tolerance and broadmindedness without which there is no "democratic society".'[184]

10.106 In assessing whether a restriction on a fundamental right is proportionate, the ECtHR will scrutinize whether the reasons advanced by the State party seeking to justify the interference are 'relevant and sufficient'.[185] However, this is a sphere in which the contracting States are afforded a margin of appreciation.[186]

10.107 In certain circumstances recent legislative developments may be evidence of what is 'necessary in a democratic society'—see, for example, the discussion of this issue by Lord Bingham, Baroness Hale, and Lord Brown in *R (Countryside Alliance) v Attorney General*.[187]

10.108 The necessity for any restriction on freedom of expression must be 'convincingly established', *a fortiori* in the case of criminal sanctions.[188]

10.109 In *Ezelin v France*[189] the ECtHR emphasized that:

. . . the freedom to take part in a peaceful assembly is of such importance that a person cannot be subjected to a sanction—even one at the lower end of the scale of disciplinary penalties—

---

[181] *Chassagnou v France* (1999) 29 EHRR 615, para 112.
[182] [2003] 1 AC 247, para 23.
[183] *Stankov v Bulgaria*, Application No 29221/95, 2 October 2001, para 87.
[184] *Piermont v France* (1995) 20 EHRR 301, para 76; *Castells v Spain*, 23 April 1992, Series A No 236, p 22, para 42.
[185] Ibid, para 40.
[186] *Patyi & Others v Hungary*, Application No 5529/05, 7 October 2008, para 39; *F v Austria* (1992) 15 EHRR CD68; *Rassemblement Jurassien and Unite Jurassienne v Switzerland*, p 120; *Handyside; Sunday Times (No 1)* (1979) 2 EHRR 245 para 59.
[187] [2008] 1 AC 719, Lord Bingham at para 45; Baroness Hale at paras 124–6; Lord Brown at paras 157–61.
[188] *Sunday Times v UK (No 2)* (1992) 14 EHRR 229.
[189] (A/202) (1992) 14 EHRR 36, para 53; see also, *Sergey Kuznetsov v Russia*, Application No 10877/04, 23 October 2008, para 43.

for participation in a demonstration which has not been prohibited, so long as this person does not himself commit any reprehensible act on such an occasion.

The ODIHR/OSCE Guidelines on Freedom of Peaceful Assembly advocate a test akin to **10.110** the US doctrine of 'clear and present danger' such that restrictions on assembly should only be imposed on public order grounds when participants in the assembly incite imminent lawless action and such action is likely to occur.

Prior authorization

In contrast to the recommendations of the ODIHR/OSCE Guidelines, the Divisional **10.111** Court in *Blum & Others v DPP*[190] held that no individual proportionality assessment was required in respect of prosecutions for failure to comply with the requirement to obtain prior authorization to demonstrate within the designated area under the Serious Organised Crime and Police Act 2005, s 134(2) and s 132(1)(a).[191] Protestors had demonstrated peacefully and in some cases silently against the war in Iraq in Parliament Square and behind railings opposite Downing Street. One of them had told the police verbally in advance. But they had not given written notice as required by the 2005 Act. Their submission that it was entirely unnecessary to arrest and prosecute them because no harm had been done was rejected. The court relied on the decision of the ECtHR in *Ziliberberg v Moldova*.[192]

Although prior restraint on freedom of expression calls for the most careful scrutiny and **10.112** justification,[193] in *Ziliberberg*, the ECtHR held that subjecting meetings in public thoroughfares to a prior authorization procedure:

> does not normally encroach upon the essence of the right. Such a procedure is in keeping with the requirements of Article 11(1), if only in order that the authorities may be in a position to ensure the peaceful nature of a meeting, and accordingly does not as such constitute interference with the exercise of the right.

Further,

> since States have the right to require authorisation, they must be able to apply sanctions to those who participate in demonstrations that do not comply with the requirement. The impossibility to impose such sanctions would render illusory the power of the State to require authorisation. It appears that in the present case, the State imposed a sanction on the applicant strictly for his failure to comply with the prohibition on participation in unauthorised demonstrations.[194]

In reaching its decision in *Blum*, the Divisional Court considered a number of Strasbourg **10.113** authorities (*Plattform 'Ärzte für das Leben' v Austria*,[195] *Ezelin v France*,[196] *G v The Federal*

---

[190] (2007) UKHRR 233. See also 3.117.
[191] See 3.94 et seq.
[192] Application No 61821/00, 4 May 2004.
[193] *Sunday Times Ltd v UK (No 2)* (1992) 14 EHRR 229, para 51.
[194] Op cit. See also 3.119.
[195] (1988) 13 EHRR 204.
[196] (1991) 14 EHRR 362.

Republic of Germany,[197] *Stankov v Bulgaria*,[198] and *Ciraklar v Turkey*[199]), but held that all were distinguishable from *Blum* in that, unlike *Ziliberberg*, none dealt with the question of the proportionality of criminal proceedings brought to enforce an authorization procedure.

10.114 Since *Blum*, the Divisional Court, in *Tucker v DPP*,[200] has confirmed that the prior notification requirements in SOCPA 2005 are in themselves compatible with Articles 10 and 11. The general compatibility of these provisions had been conceded in *Blum*: the appellants in that case had rather sought to challenge the *application* of the provisions to their particular cases. Further, in *Moase v City of Westminster Magistrates Court*,[201] the Divisional Court rejected an argument that the decision in *Ziliberberg*, that prior notification requirements do not normally breach Article 11, was limited to demonstrations on the public thoroughfare. Mr Moase had sought to argue that since his demonstration had taken place entirely on the green of Parliament Square and not on any public thoroughfare, the justifications for prior notification considered in *Ziliberberg* (for example the regulation of traffic) did not apply. This argument was rejected.

10.115 The ECtHR considered the case of *Blum* under the name of *Rai and Evans v UK*.[202] It found the imposition of criminal sanctions on the applicants for failure to comply with the prior authorization requirements to have been lawful and proportionate. There was no breach of Articles 10 or 11.

10.116 In so finding, the ECtHR confirmed that the starting point was its decision in *Ziliberberg* and reiterated the passages of that judgment cited above. It also confirmed that Contracting States have a certain margin of appreciation in making the proportionality assessment, subject to supervision at the Strasbourg level. However, it is of note that the ECtHR did not adopt the same approach as the High Court did in finding that once the compatibility of the statutory prior authorization procedure was established then no individual proportionality assessment was necessary on a case-by-case basis. Rather the ECtHR identified a number of factors which, in its view, made the prosecution of Mr Rai and Ms Evans proportionate. These were

(a) the manner in which the police ended the demonstrations was reasonable and calm—this distinguished it from the cases of *Oya Ataman* and *Balcik*;[203]

(b) the applicant's demonstration had not been an urgent response to a recent or imminent political event meaning that there was no time to comply with the notification requirement, as had been the case in *Bukta v Hungary*;

---

197 Application No 13079/87, 6 March 1989.
198 Application No 29225/95, 2 October 2001.
199 Application No 19601/92, 19 January 1995.
200 [2007] EWHC 3019 (Admin). See also 3.121.
201 [2008] EWHC 2309 (Admin), 27 June 2008.
202 Applications Nos. 26258/07 and 26255/07, 17 November 2009.
203 See also *Samut Karabulut v Turkey* Application No 16999/04, 27 January 2009.

(c) the evidence from the Metropolitan Police Commissioner was that had the notification requirements been complied with, it is unlikely that any conditions would have been imposed on the applicants' demonstration;

(d) the ECtHR was not satisfied that the pre-authorization requirement in fact acted as a deterrent on (lawful) demonstrations generally;

(e) in seeking to end the applicants' demonstration, the police had given an opportunity for the applicants to disband without the imposition of sanctions, but the applicants had refused to comply;

(f) the sanctions in fact imposed on the applicants were not severe (a fine at the lowest end of the statutory scale, a conditional discharge and orders for a contribution to prosecution costs).

A further factor was identified in *Kuznetsov v Russia*,[204] in which the ECtHR considered the proportionality of a prosecution to enforce a prior notification requirement where the applicant had given only eight instead of the requisite ten days' notice of his demonstration. The ECtHR held that 'a merely formal breach of the notification time limit was neither relevant nor a sufficient reason for imposing administrative liability on the applicant'.[205]   **10.117**

It appears, therefore, that the domestic courts will have to look at the circumstances of the particular case before them in assessing whether a particular prosecution for failure to obtain prior-authorization for a demonstration is proportionate, but what *Rai and Evans v UK* shows is that the authorities will be afforded a significant degree of deference, and factors such as the peaceful and non-obstructive nature of the protest, will not save participants from lawful prosecution.   **10.118**

In keeping with the particular limitations on prior restraint in respect of freedom of expression and assembly, the stage at which the authorities intervene to disperse a demonstration may be relevant to questions of proportionality. In *Molnar v Hungary*,[206] the police waited several hours before dispersing an unlawful demonstration against a recent election. The ECtHR found that the applicant in that case had had 'a sufficiently long time to show her solidarity with her co-demonstrators' and that 'the police showed the necessary tolerance towards the demonstration, although they had had no prior knowledge of the event'.[207]   **10.119**

By contrast, in *Balcik v Turkey*,[208] the applicants' public assembly to make a press statement against prison conditions was dispersed, and the applicants arrested, within half an hour.   **10.120**

---

[204] Application No 10877/04, 23 October 2008.
[205] Ibid, para 43.
[206] Application No 10346/05, 7 October 2008.
[207] Ibid, para 43.
[208] Application No 25/02, 29 November 2007.

In that case, the ECtHR was 'particularly struck by the authorities' impatience in seeking to end the demonstration' and found the interference with Article 11 to be disproportionate, notwithstanding the applicants' failure to comply with the requirement of prior notification.[209]

10.121 The authors note that the government has stated its intention to repeal ss 132–138 of the Serious Organised Crime and Police Act 2005.[210]

C. Article 9: Freedom of Thought, Conscience, and Religion

10.122 Article 9 states:

> (1) Everyone has the right to freedom of thought, conscience and religion; this right includes freedom to change his religion or belief and freedom, either alone or in community with others and in public or private, to manifest his religion or belief, in worship, teaching, practice and observance.
> (3) Freedom to manifest one's religion or beliefs shall be subject only to such limitations as are prescribed by law and are necessary in a democratic society in the interests of public safety, for the protection of public order, health or morals, or for the protection of the rights and freedoms of others.

10.123 Like Articles 10 and 11, Article 9 has been described by the ECtHR as 'one of the foundations of a democratic society'.[211] As with Article 10, Article 9 enjoys special protection under the Human Rights Act 1998. Section 13(1) HRA 1998 provides:

> If a court's determination of any question arising under this Act might affect the exercise by a religious organisation (itself or its members collectively) of the Convention right of freedom of thought, conscience and religion, it must have particular regard to the importance of that right.

10.124 The right to freedom of thought, conscience, and religion protects 'atheists, agnostics, sceptics and the unconcerned' as well as the religious.[212] This includes pacifist views,[213] but beliefs will not necessarily be covered simply because they are 'idealistic'.[214] In *R (Williamson) v Secretary of State for Education*,[215] Lord Nicholls observed that, to engage Article 9 rights, a belief must be 'consistent with basic standards of human dignity or integrity' and

> must relate to matters more than merely trivial. It must possess an adequate degree of seriousness and importance. . . . it must be a belief on a fundamental problem. With religious belief

---

[209] Ibid paras 51–4; see also *Samut Karabulut v Turkey* Application No. 16999/04, 27 January 2009 para 37.

[210] *Constitutional Renewal—The Governance of Britain*, White Paper available online at <http://www.justice.gov.uk/docs/constitutional-renewal-white-paper.pdf>. <http://www.justice.gov.uk/docs/constitutional-renewal-white-paper.pdf>. See 3.126.

[211] *Kokkinakis v Greece* (1993) 17 EHRR 397, para 31.

[212] *Buscarini v San Marino* (2000) 30 EHRR 208, para 34.

[213] *Arrowsmith v UK* (1978) 3 EHRR 218.

[214] *Vereniging Rechtswinkels Utrecht v Netherlands*, Application No 11308/84, 13 March 1986; *K v Netherlands*, Application No 15928/89, 13 May 1992.

[215] [2005] 2 AC 246.

this requisite is readily satisfied. The belief must also be coherent in the sense of being intelligible and capable of being understood.

... for its manifestation to be protected by article 9 a non-religious belief must relate to an aspect of human life or behaviour of comparable importance to that normally found with religious beliefs.[216]

A corporate, profit-making body can neither enjoy nor rely on Article 9 rights.[217]   **10.125**

Manifesting a belief

Although Article 9 is primarily directed at private belief and activity, it is relevant in the   **10.126**
public order context, because the ECtHR has recognized that the existence of religious
convictions is bound up with manifesting one's religion, which includes 'bearing witness in
words and deeds':

> According to Article 9, freedom to manifest one's religion is not only exercisable in community with others, 'in public' and within the circle of those whose faith one shares, but can also be asserted 'alone' and 'in private'; furthermore, it includes in principle the right to try to convince one's neighbour, for example through 'teaching', failing which, moreover, 'freedom to change [one's] religion or belief', enshrined in Article 9 (art. 9), would be likely to remain a dead letter.[218]

However, the right to manifest one's beliefs does not amount to a right to act in pursuance   **10.127**
of whatever beliefs one happens to hold. Thus in *Arrowsmith v UK*,[219] the ECtHR
acknowledged that pacifism was a 'belief' within the scope of Article 9, but the applicant's
actions in handing out a leaflet encouraging members of the armed forces to refuse to be
deployed in Northern Ireland was not a 'manifestation' of pacifist beliefs. Likewise in *R v
DPP, ex parte Pretty*[220] the House of Lords held that there was no question of the appellant
manifesting her belief in assisted suicide in seeking a legal assurance that her husband
would not be prosecuted were he to help her to end her own life. In considering this issue,
Lord Steyn gave the example of animal rights activists conducting attacks on places where
animal experiments are carried out as an example of behaviour which, whilst in accordance
with strongly held beliefs, did *not* amount to a manifestation of those beliefs for the purposes of Article 9.[221]

Refusal, on pacifist grounds, to pay taxes that will be used to fund military operations does   **10.128**
not amount to a 'manifestation of belief' within the meaning of Article 9, even where this
is founded on religious belief. In *C v UK*,[222] the European Commission of Human Rights
dismissed as manifestly ill-founded a claim by a Quaker that the legal obligation on him
to pay income tax into a general fund that made no provision to ensure that his monies

---

[216] Ibid, paras 23 and 24.
[217] *X v Switzerland* Application No 7865/77, 27 February 1979.
[218] *Kokkinakis v Greece*, para 31.
[219] (1978) 3 EHRR 218.
[220] [2002] 1 AC 800.
[221] Ibid, para 63.
[222] (1983) 37 DR 142 (Application No 10358/83).

were not spent on military expenditure was a violation of his rights under Article 9. The Commission held that:

> The obligation to pay taxes is a general one which has no specific conscientious implications in itself . . . Furthermore, the power of taxation is expressly recognised by the Convention system and is ascribed to the State by Article 1, First Protocol.[223]

10.129   This decision has been confirmed in a number of subsequent cases[224] and was followed domestically by the Court of Appeal in *R (Boughton) v HM Treasury*.[225]

10.130   Even where a particular action does constitute a 'manifestation of belief', whether or not there has been an *interference* with the right to manifest ones beliefs will depend on a number of factors, including the extent to which, in the circumstances, an individual could reasonably be expected to be at liberty to manifest those beliefs in practice. Interference will not readily be established when a person has voluntarily accepted a role which does not accommodate his right to manifest his religious belief through a particular practice, for example where he has chosen to accept a particular job, knowing that it will require him to behave in a particular way.[226] This is especially the case where there are other means open to that person to practise or observe his beliefs without undue hardship or inconvenience.[227] In *R (Begum) v Governors of Denbigh High School*,[228] the House of Lords rejected a claim by a muslim schoolgirl that her exclusion from a particular high school for insisting on wearing a jilbab violated her right to manifest her religion. The majority of their Lordships held that since the wearing of a jilbab was a sincere manifestation of the claimant's religious belief, Article 9(1) was engaged. However, since Ms Begum's parents had specifically chosen to send her to that particular high school, knowing that the school uniform prohibited the wearing of a jilbab and there were other schools in the area that Ms Begum could attend where she would be permitted to wear a jilbab, there was no interference with her right to manifest her religious beliefs.

Article 9: and Articles 10 and 11

10.131   In practice, it is rare for the ECtHR to analyse a public order case under Article 9. More commonly, the Court will consider Articles 10 and/or 11 first and then declare that the same considerations arise in respect of Article 9 without separate consideration.[229] Even where there is an interference with the right to manifest beliefs, such interference may be justified if it pursues a legitimate aim and is necessary and proportionate in a democratic society. For example, in *Ghai v Newcastle City Council*[230] it was held that the Claimant's

---

[223] Ibid, p 147.
[224] *V v The Netherlands* (1984) 39 DR 267 (Application No 10678/83); *BH & MB v United Kingdom* (18 July 1986) (Application No 11991/86); *Moratilla v Spain* (1992) 72 DR 256, 262 (Application No 17522/90); *Bouessel du Bourg v France* (1993) 16 EHRR CD 49.
[225] [2006] EWCA Civ 504, 4 May 2006.
[226] *X v Denmark* (1976) 5 DR 157; *Ahmad v United Kingdom* (1981) 4 EHRR 126.
[227] *Kjeldsen, Busk Madsen and Pedersen v Denmark* (1976) 1 EHRR 711; *Karaduman v Turkey* (1993) 74 DR 93.
[228] [2007] 1 AC 100.
[229] See, for example, *Incal v Turkey* (2000) 29 EHRR 449 and the cases discussed below.
[230] The Times, May 18 2009; [2009] EWHC 978 (Admin).

wish to be cremated on an open funeral pyre after his death constituted a manifestation of his religious beliefs and the present law banning such a course was an interference with his rights under Article 9. However, the interference was justified under Article 9(2), in the interests of the protection of public morals, and the rights and freedoms of others, whom, it was maintained, would be offended by open air cremations.

In *Pendragon v UK*,[231] the European Commission of Human Rights considered a complaint by the Honoured Pendragon of the Glastonbury Order of Druids that a ban under s 14A of the Public Order Act 1986 prohibiting trespassory assemblies within a 4 mile radius of Stonehenge over the summer solstice violated his rights under Articles 9, 10, 11, and 14. **10.132**

On 21 June 1995, the Honoured Pendragon had sought to conduct a druidic ceremony close to the Hele Stone at Stonehenge. He had conducted similar ceremonies, entirely peacefully, at the spring and autumn equinox and winter solstice for the previous seven years. On this occasion, however, he was arrested and charged with taking part in a prohibited assembly. He was detained until after the solstice had passed but was subsequently acquitted of all charges at trial. He nonetheless complained that his arrest and detention constituted a violation of his rights. The European Commission on Human Rights disagreed. The Commission referred to its earlier decision in the similar case of *Chappell v UK*[232] in which it had dismissed an application under Article 9 concerning druidic access to Stonehenge. However, in *Pendragon's* case, the Commission noted that the powers exercised by the police, namely those arising from s 14A of the Public Order Act 1986 were principally concerned with limitations of certain types of assembly. The Commission therefore chose to 'deal with the case principally under Article 11 of the Convention, whilst having regard to Articles 9 and 10'. Having adopted this approach, the Commission concluded that, in light of the violent disorder that had occurred at Stonehenge in previous years, albeit nothing to do with Mr Pendragon, the ban on all trespassory assemblies over the period of the summer solstice was necessary and proportionate and there had been no violation of the applicant's rights under Articles 9, 10, 11, or 14. **10.133**

This decision is perhaps surprising in light of the uncontested evidence that Mr Pendragon and his fellow worshippers had had nothing to do with any previous violence or disorder at the site, nor was there any reason to suspect that they would engage in such behaviour in the future. However, as the Commission itself acknowledged, this decision is in line with the Commission's earlier decisions upholding blanket bans against protest in a specified location in the cases of *Christians Against Fascism and Racism v UK*[233] and *Rai, Allmond and Negotiate Now v UK*.[234] One explanation for this apparent willingness on the part of the Commission to countenance such broad measures is the importance it attaches to the particular factual context of the case before it. **10.134**

---

[231] Application No 31416/96, 19 October 1998.
[232] Application No 12587/86, 14 December 1997, 53 DR 241.
[233] Application No 8440/78, 16 July 1980, 21 DR 138.
[234] (1995) 19 EHRR CD 93.

10.135   In the *Christians Against Facism and Rascism* case, the Commission upheld a general ban for a period of two months on all public processions, with limited exceptions, within the Metropolitan Police District. The Commission emphasized that '[a] general ban of demonstrations can only be justified if there is a real danger of their resulting in disorder which cannot be prevented by other less stringent means'.[235] However, it found that the particular context in which this ban had been imposed, namely recent and serious riots arising out of public processions by the National Front and related counter-demonstrations, together with the fact that the applicants in this case could have held their procession just two days later than their planned date, meant that the adverse effects of the ban on the applicants' rights were not disproportionate to the legitimate aim pursued.

10.136   In *Rai, Allmond and Negotiate Now*, the Commission upheld a ban on all demonstrations concerning Northern Ireland in Trafalgar Square. It observed that the circumstances of Northern Ireland raised 'sensitive and complex issues' and that in this context a general policy of banning all demonstrations concerning this subject in Trafalgar Square pursued the legitimate aims of preventing disorder, and protecting the rights, and freedoms, of others. Further, the Commission emphasized that there was no prohibition on the applicants holding their rally elsewhere.

10.137   Similarly, in *Pendragon*, the Commission emphasized the fact that Mr Pendragon was not ultimately convicted of any offence and he could, even under the terms of the ban, have conducted his ceremony as and where he wished provided less than twenty people attended.

10.138   This is to be contrasted with the case of *Kokkinakis v Greece*,[236] in which the ECtHR considered the case of a Jehovah's Witness who was convicted of proselytizing (a criminal offence under Greek law). The Greek government sought to justify the conviction on the basis that it was necessary in order to ensure the personal freedoms of others. The ECtHR found that this was a legitimate aim, but that the conviction in this case was not necessary in a democratic society and therefore disproportionate. The ECtHR held that a distinction has to be made between bearing Christian witness and improper proselytism:

> The former corresponds to true evangelism, which a report drawn up in 1956 under the auspices of the World Council of Churches describes as an essential mission and a responsibility of every Christian and every Church. The latter represents a corruption or deformation of it. It may, according to the same report, take the form of activities offering material or social advantages with a view to gaining new members for a Church or exerting improper pressure on people in distress or in need; it may even entail the use of violence or brainwashing; more generally, it is not compatible with respect for the freedom of thought, conscience and religion of others.[237]

---

[235] Op cit, p 150.
[236] (1993) 17 EHRR 397.
[237] Ibid, para 48.

Preacher cases

In the domestic context, convictions for public order offences related to public preaching   **10.139**
were considered in *Hammond v DPP*[238] and *Redmond-Bate v DPP*.[239] The facts of *Hammond*
are set out at 1.20 and 10.50 above. In that case, the Divisional Court adopted much the
same approach as the ECtHR in public order cases involving Article 9 as well as Article 10.
It found Article 10 to be the principal right affected, notwithstanding that the 'freedom of
expression' in question had been public preaching. Thus although Article 9 was held to be
engaged, the court found that it did not add anything to the matters that it had to consider
in relation to Article 10.[240]

In *Redmond-Bate*, the Divisional Court considered the position (after the enactment of the   **10.140**
Human Rights Act 1998, but prior to it coming into force) of a woman convicted of
obstructing a police officer in the execution of his duty after she refused to cease preaching
on the steps of Wakefield Cathedral. The content of her preaching had been such as to
attract a large and hostile crowd. The officer had asked her to stop as he feared a breach of
the peace would ensue. The appellant's appeal by way of case stated was decided in her
favour on the basis of the common law authorities of *Beatty v Gilbanks*[241] and *Duncan v
Jones*,[242] but the Divisional Court nonetheless made observations on what it described as
the 'human rights dimension' of the case. Sedley LJ referred to s 13 of the Human Rights
Act 1998 (Freedom of thought, conscience, and religion) and queried whether 'when the
Act comes into force, Article 9 may become prominent in a case such as the present because
of the presence in the Act of Section 13'. However, he went on to find that since the Act was
not then in force, and therefore s 13 could not be relied upon to 'prioritize' Article 9 rights,
'in a case like the present they do not usefully add to the rights recognised by Article 10'.[243]

Notwithstanding Sedley LJ's speculation about the significance that s 13 of the Human   **10.141**
Rights Act 1998 might obtain, since the coming into force of the 1998 Act, the courts have
continued to analyse public order cases involving Articles 9 and 10 predominantly in terms
of Article 10.[244]

Article 9 will, however, warrant separate consideration where it is in conflict with Article   **10.142**
10 rights. For example, in *Öllinger v Austria*,[245] discussed at 10.37 above, Austria sought to
justify a ban on a demonstration in a public cemetery on grounds that it was necessary to
protect the rights of other cemetery-goers to manifest their religious beliefs in peace. In
these circumstances, a balance must be struck between Article 10 and Article 9.

Where speech or other expression goes so far as to amount to 'such a general, vehement   **10.143**
attack against a religious group [. . . that it] is incompatible with the values proclaimed and

---

[238] [2004] EWHC 69 (Admin), The Times, 28 January 2004.
[239] [2000] HRLR 249; [1999] EWHC Admin 732.
[240] Ibid; see in particular paras 16–8.
[241] (1882) 9 QBD 308.
[242] [1936] 1 KB 218.
[243] [1999] BHRC 375, para 12.
[244] See, for example, *Connolly v DPP* [2007] HRLR 17 and *R (Parminder Singh and another) v Chief Constable of the West Midlands Police* [2006] 1 WLR 3374.
[245] Op cit.

guaranteed by the Convention, notably tolerance, social peace and non-discrimination',[246] the 'speaker' may be precluded from relying on Convention rights altogether by virtue of Article 17. Article 17 specifies that:

> Nothing in this Convention may be interpreted as implying for any State, group or person any right to engage in any activity or perform any act aimed at the destruction of any of the rights and freedoms set forth herein or at their limitation to a greater extent than is provided for in the Convention.

D. Article 8: Right to Respect for Private and Family Life

10.144   Article 8 states:

(1) Everyone has the right to respect for his private and family life, his home and his correspondence.

(2) There shall be no interference by a public authority with the exercise of this right except such as is in accordance with the law and is necessary in a democratic society in the interests of national security, public safety or the economic well-being of the country, for the prevention of disorder or crime, for the protection of health or morals, or for the protection of the rights and freedoms of others.

10.145   Article 8 rights may be engaged in a wide variety of ways in public order cases. For example, the activity may be an integral part of the cultural life of its participants;[247] since Article 8 may be engaged in relation to an individual's professional, or business activities,[248] industrial action may raise issues under this article; surveillance and data recording in respect of those who participate in protest activity engages Article 8;[249] further the Article 8 rights of those not engaged in, but affected by, public order activity will frequently be relevant.

10.146   The concept of 'private life' protected by Article 8 is extremely broad, see, for example, the discussion of 'general principles' by the Grand Chamber of the ECtHR in the case of *Marper v UK*.[250] The right to respect for private life has been described as being 'of such scope as to secure to the individual a sphere within which he can freely pursue the development and fulfilment of his personality'.[251]

10.147   However, the scope of activity which falls within the broad notion of 'personal autonomy' protected by Article 8 is not unlimited. For example, Article 8 does not include a right to pursue particular leisure activities.[252] Further, 'the claim to respect to private life is automatically reduced to the extent that the individual himself brings his private

---

[246] *Norwood v United Kingdom* Application No 23131/03, 16 November 2004.

[247] See, for example, *Gypsy Council of Great Britain v UK*, Application No 00066336/01, 14 May 2002; *Connors v UK* (2005) 40 EHRR 9.

[248] *Niemietz v Germany* (1992) 16 EHRR 97.

[249] *Wood v Commissioner of Police for the Metropolis* [2009] EWCA Civ 414, 21 May 2009; see J Simor and B Emmerson, *Human Rights Practice*, 8.007-8 for discussion of ECHR cases relating to photographs, CCTV, and surveillance generally.

[250] Application Nos 30562/04 and 30566/04, 4 December 2008.

[251] *Bruggemann and Scheuten v Germany* (1977) 3 EHRR 244, para 55.

[252] *Countryside Alliance v Attorney General* [2008] 1 AC 719.

life into contact with public life or into close connection with other protected interests'.[253]

In *Wood v Commissioner of Police for the Metropolis*,[254] a case concerning covert police pho- **10.148** tography of the media coordinator of an organization which campaigns against the arms trade, Laws LJ, who was in the minority, although not on this point, identified three checks on the broad scope of Article 8:

(a) the alleged threat or assault to the individual's personal autonomy must attain 'a certain level of seriousness' if Article 8(1) is to be engaged at all;[255]
(b) the alleged interference with the right must have occurred in circumstances where there was a 'reasonable expectation of privacy', for example in relation to telephone calls made from one's home or place of work,[256] or in respect of access to healthcare services.[257] However, photographs, even when taken overtly in a public place, may nonetheless engage Article 8 depending on the activities photographed, the reason for the photograph, the use to which it is put and whether or not it is stored, published or destroyed;[258] and
(c) the scope of the justifications available to the State pursuant to Article 8(2): in addition to the 'legitimate aims' set out, there is a requirement that the interference be pre-scribed by law and necessary in a democratic society.

In *Wood*, the majority of the Court of Appeal, Laws LJ dissenting, found overt police pho- **10.149** tography and storage of the resulting images to amount to a breach of Article 8. However, the decision is highly fact sensitive. Mr Wood was of good character and had not been involved in any reprehensible activity. He had been photographed by police because he had attended the Annual General Meeting of a company which organized arms fairs and there had been concern there might be unlawful activity there on the part of anti-arms trade protestors. The majority of the Court of Appeal held that the police actions had been disproportionate. Both members of the majority expressly left open the question of whether the taking of the photographs was 'in accordance with the law'. Unless or until express legal provision is made governing the circumstances in which (a) the police may photograph members of the public going about their lawful business and (b) retain the images for future use, it must be arguable that such action does not meet the requirements of legal certainty.

E. Article 5: Right to Liberty and Security

Article 5 guarantees the right to liberty and security of person. Unlike Articles 8, 9, 10, and **10.150** 11, Article 5 is not a qualified right. This means that interference with this right cannot be

---

[253] *Bruggemann and Scheuten v Germany. Ghai v Newcastle City Council* The Times, May 18 2009; [2009] EWHC 978 (Admin).
[254] Op cit.
[255] Op cit, para 22.
[256] *Halford v UK* (1997) 24 EHRR 523.
[257] *Campbell v MGN Ltd* [2004] 2 AC 457.
[258] *Hannover v Germany* (2005) 40 EHRR 1; *Peck v UK* (2003) 36 EHRR 41.

justified on grounds of proportionality. Instead, Article 5(1) specifies the circumstances in which a lawful deprivation of liberty may occur. The circumstances of most relevance to the law of public order and protest are

(1) (a) the lawful detention of a person after conviction by a competent court;
   (b) the lawful arrest or detention of a person for non-compliance with the lawful order of a court or in order to secure the fulfilment of any obligation prescribed by law;
   (c) the lawful arrest or detention of a person effected for the purpose of bringing him before the competent legal authority on reasonable suspicion of having committed an offence or when it is reasonably considered necessary to prevent his committing an offence or fleeing after having done so.

10.151 Article 5(3) states that:

Everyone arrested or detained in accordance with the provisions of paragraph 1(c) of this article shall be brought promptly before a judge or other officer authorised by law to exercise judicial power and shall be entitled to trial within a reasonable time or to release pending trial. Release may be conditioned by guarantees to appear for trial.

10.152 Article 5(4) guarantees the right of those deprived of their liberty to have access to a court so that the lawfulness of their detention may be speedily determined and their release ordered if the detention is not lawful.

10.153 Article 5(5) guarantees an enforceable right to compensation for breaches of any of the other provisions of Article 5.

10.154 The meaning of 'liberty' for the purposes of Article 5 is 'individual liberty in its classic sense, that is to say the physical liberty of the person',[259] or 'classic detention in prison or strict arrest'.[260] In order for Article 5 to be engaged, there must be a deprivation of liberty, which is to be distinguished from and is clearly more serious than mere 'restriction of movement', which in turn is protected under Article 2 of Protocol 4 to the Convention and not one of the 'Convention rights' under the Human Rights Act (HRA) 1998, s 1 and Schedule 1. However, the distinction is not as clear-cut as it might be, 'but merely one of degree or intensity and not one of nature or substance'.[261] '[A]ccount must be taken of a whole range of factors such as the type, duration, effects and manner of execution or implementation of the penalty or measure in question.'[262]

10.155 Until the case of *Austin v Metropolitan Police Commissioner*[263] the boundary between 'deprivation of liberty' and 'restriction of movement' had been analysed by the courts, both domestically and in Strasbourg, by reference to the factors set out above. In one of the leading Strasbourg authorities on this issue, *Guzzardi v Italy*,[264] Judge Matscher, in a dissenting opinion, but in line with the majority on this issue, observed that the concept of 'deprivation of liberty' has a core which could not be the subject of argument but which was

---

[259] *Engel v Netherlands (No 1)* (1976) 1 EHRR 647, para 58.
[260] *Guzzardi v Italy* (1980) 3 EHRR 533, para 95.
[261] Ibid, para 93.
[262] Ibid; *Ashingdane v UK* (1985) 7 EHRR 528; *Amuur v France* (1996) 22 EHRR 533.
[263] [2009] 1 AC 564; see 3.32, 4.67, 4.73 et seq, and 10.158, below.
[264] Op cit.

surrounded by a 'grey zone' where it was extremely difficult to draw the line. In *Secretary of State for the Home Department v JJ*,[265] Lord Hoffmann described the core, or paradigm case in the following terms:

> The prisoner has no freedom of choice about anything. He cannot leave the place to which he has been assigned. He may eat only when and what his gaoler permits. The only human beings he may see or speak to are his gaolers and those whom they allow to visit. He is entirely subject to the will of others.[266]

In *JJ*, the House of Lords conducted a detailed analysis of the extent to which the 'grey zone' extends beyond this paradigm. The issue was whether the restrictions imposed by control orders on six individuals amounted to deprivations of liberty or merely restrictions on movement. The majority held that orders imposing curfews for eighteen hours per day and extensive restrictions on residence, communication, and contact with others amounted to a deprivation of liberty.[267] On the other hand, in a further control order case decided on the same day, an order imposing a fourteen hour per day curfew, electronic tagging, and similar restrictions on access to visitors as in *JJ* was found by the House of Lords not to amount to a deprivation of liberty.[268]   **10.156**

In *R (Gillan) v Metropolitan Police Commissioner*,[269] the exercise of the power to stop and   **10.157**
search under the Terrorism Act 2000 was found not to amount to a deprivation of liberty where the procedure was brief, and no physical restraint such as the use of handcuffs or removal to another location was involved.

'Kettling': deprivation of liberty vs restriction of movement

In *Austin v Metropolitan Police Commissioner*,[270] the House of Lords considered the posi-   **10.158**
tion of a protestor and a member of the public held against their will for approximately seven hours within a police cordon at Oxford Circus on 1 May 2001 in a containment tactic referred to as 'kettling'. The claimants were held without access to food, drink, or toilet facilities. The dilemma which faced their Lordships was that the courts below had found, and this was not challenged in the House of Lords, that the actions of the police had been necessary in order to prevent serious public disorder; and yet none of the justifications for interference with an individual's liberty contained in Article 5(1)(a)–(e) was clearly applicable. Thus, if Article 5(1) were engaged in this situation, there would have been a violation of the appellants' right to liberty notwithstanding that the police had acted proportionately and out of necessity to prevent serious injury to persons and property. The difficulty, as Lord Neuberger expressly acknowledged,[271] was that where a person is confined in a small area against her will in conditions of some discomfort for well over six

---

[265] [2008] 1 AC 385, HL.
[266] Ibid, para 37.
[267] *Engel v Netherlands*; *JJ and ors v SSHD*.
[268] *SSHD v MB* [2008] 1 AC 440.
[269] [2006] 2 AC 307, HL, para 25. The European Court of Human Rights in *Gillan and Quinton v UK* Application No. 4158005, questioned the House of Lords' Finding on this issue, but declined to decide the print, having found a violation of Article 8.
[270] Op cit. See fn 263.
[271] Op cit, para 51.

hours, it is surprising, on a traditional analysis of Article 5(1), if this were not to amount to a deprivation of liberty.[272]

10.159 In the face of this dilemma, their Lordships pointed out that the Strasbourg Court had never been called upon to consider Article 5 in the context of crowd control and asked whether the *purpose* for which an individual is detained can affect whether or not there has been a deprivation of liberty. Their Lordships considered four Strasbourg authorities in which paternalistic motives appear to have played a part in the findings that there had been no deprivation of liberty within the meaning of Article 5(1).[273] They also made reference to the observations of the Strasbourg Court in the cases of *Soering v UK*[274] and *N v UK*[275] to the effect that 'inherent in the whole of the Convention is a search for a fair balance between the demands of the general interest of the community and the requirements of the protection of the individual's fundamental rights'. In the light of this, Lord Hope, with whom the other members of the House agreed, concluded that measures of crowd control which involve a restriction of liberty will not engage Article 5(1) unless they are carried out in bad faith or go beyond what is reasonably required for the purpose for which they were undertaken.

10.160 On its face, this decision represents a considerable inroad into the protection afforded by Article 5 in the context of public order and protest. The practical implications of the *Austin* decision were seen during the policing of the G20 summit in April 2009, where 'kettling' was again used to 'contain' protestors, barely two months after the House of Lords gave judgment. The Parliamentary Joint Committee on Human Rights records evidence from witnesses, including a Member of Parliament who had attended the protest as an observer, of poor communication by the police; use of force against protestors within the cordon; and the application of a blanket policy of refusing any person within the cordon permission to leave, even where they required medical treatment, unless they gave their name, address, and agreed to be photographed.[276]

10.161 The *Austin* decision is to be challenged in the ECtHR and it remains to be seen whether the Strasbourg Court will agree that the cases cited by their Lordships bear the weight that they have been given, particularly in light of the Strasbourg Court's rather different analysis in *HL v United Kingdom*.[277] In the meantime, Lord Walker's note of caution in *Austin* lends support to the view that the decision in that case should be limited to the specific issue of crowd control and that measures such as those deployed against Ms Austin must be limited

---

[272] It was common ground that there had been an 'imprisonment' for the purposes of the tort of false imprisonment, albeit justified by the defence of necessity.

[273] *X v Federal Republic of Germany* (1981) 24 DR 158 (children kept at police station for two hours for questioning rather than arrest); *Guenat v Switzerland* (1995) 81 DR 130 (individual taken to police station for humanitarian reasons due to his strange behaviour); *HM v Switzerland* (2002) 38 EHRR 314 (mentally competent adult placed in nursing home in order to receive necessary medical care); *Nielsen v Denmark* (1988) 11 EHRR 175 (child committed to psychiatric ward at mother's request).

[274] *Soering v United Kingdom* (1989) 11 EHRR 439.

[275] (2008) 47 EHRR 885.

[276] *Demonstrating Respect for Rights? Follow-up.* Twenty-second report of Session 2008–9, 14 July 2009 paras 19 and 20.

[277] (2004) 81 BMLR 131, see in particular paras 93.

to situations where they are strictly necessary for the prevention of serious injury and not extended to benign purposes generally, such as, for example, ensuring the free flow of traffic.

F. Article 6: Right to a Fair Trial

Article 6 covers the right to a fair trial and associated rights. A general exposition of **10.162** Article 6 is beyond the scope of this work.[278] However, there are three specific issues that arise in connection with public order cases which are of note.

Statutory defences and reverse burdens of proof

First, a significant number of public order offences provide for statutory defences, the bur- **10.163** den of proof of which lies on the accused.[279] This may raise issues in respect of the presumption of innocence under Article 6(2). The issue of 'reverse burdens' was comprehensively reviewed by the House of Lords in *Sheldrake v DPP* [280] in the context of the offences of being drunk in charge of a motor vehicle contrary to s 5(1) of the Road Traffic Act 1988 and belonging to a proscribed organization contrary to s 11 of the Terrorism Act 2000. Their Lordships identified the following propositions of general application to all statutory offences imposing a burden of proof on the accused:

(a) placing a legal burden on the accused to prove a defence amounts to an interference with the presumption of innocence in Article 6(2);[281]
(b) however, not every such interference will amount to a breach of Article 6;[282]
(c) it will have to be determined on an offence by offence basis whether the interference with the presumption of innocence in the context of that offence pursues a legitimate aim, is within reasonable limits and proportionate;
(d) the factors to be taken into account in making that assessment include: the opportunity given to the accused to rebut the presumption; that the rights of the defence are maintained; retention by the court of a power to assess the evidence; the potential consequences for the accused; the difficulty the prosecutor may face in the absence of a presumption; and the difficulty the accused may face in proving the defence.[283]

The majority of their Lordships held the imposition of a legal burden on a defendant **10.164** charged with being drunk in charge of a motor vehicle to prove that there was no likelihood of him driving to be justifiable given the legitimate object of preventing death , injury, and damage caused by unfit drivers and because:

---

[278] For detailed discussion of fair trial rights see R Clayton and H Tomlinson, *The Law of Human Rights* (2009, 2nd edn); A Lester, D Pannick, and J Herberg, *Human Rights Law and Practice* (2009, 3rd edn); J Simor and B Emmerson, *Human Rights Practice*.
[279] See, for example, the discussion in Ch 5 at 5.66 et seq of failing to comply with directions to leave land under ss 61, 63, 69, and 77 of the Criminal Justice and Public Order Act 1994.
[280] [2005] 1 AC 264.
[281] Ibid, para 41.
[282] Ibid, para 21.
[283] Ibid, paras 21 and 51.

[t]he defendant has a full opportunity to show that there was no likelihood of his driving, a matter so closely conditioned by his own knowledge and state of mind at the material time as to make it much more appropriate for him to prove on the balance of probabilities that he would not have been likely to drive than for the prosecutor to prove, beyond reasonable doubt, that he would.[284]

10.165 By contrast, in the linked appeal of *Attorney General's Reference (No 4 of 2002)*, heard at the same time as *Sheldrake*, their Lordships held that the burden placed on a defendant under s 11(2) of the Terrorism Act 2000 to show, in relation to the offence of membership of a proscribed terrorist organization, that the organization was not proscribed when he became a member and that he had not taken part in the activities of the organization at any time while it was proscribed, was not justified and so must be read as an evidential burden if it is to be compatible with Article 6.[285]

10.166 The application of these principles to the various public order offences in which reverse burdens of proof arise is discussed in the context of each offence/defence as it is considered throughout this book.

Legal assistance

10.167 The second issue under Article 6 of particular relevance in public order and protest cases is access to legal assistance. This is of especial relevance in prosecutions arising out of protest, where the very common charges of aggravated trespass, criminal damage, obstruction of the highway, etc, are unlikely to result in a custodial sentence and funded legal advice, assistance and representation is frequently refused on this basis.

10.168 Article 6(3)(c) provides for free legal assistance in criminal cases if the accused does not have sufficient means to pay for it and 'the interests of justice require it'.[286] In deciding whether the 'interests of justice' test is met, the following criteria are relevant: the complexity of the proceedings; the capacity of the individual to represent himself; and the severity of the potential sentence.[287] These criteria broadly reflect the factors governing the grant of legal aid in criminal cases set out in Schedule 3 to the Access to Justice Act 1999. Where legal aid is refused on the basis that, if convicted, the accused is unlikely to receive more than a fine or conditional discharge, it is unlikely that Article 6(3)(c) is breached. If, however, the case raises complex issues of law, for example, complicated boundary disputes in an aggravated trespass case, or issues of justification raising points of international law via the International Criminal Court Act 2001,[288] then it is arguable that legal aid is required in order to ensure a fair trial.

10.169 Although Article 6 does not contain an express guarantee of legal assistance in civil cases, such an entitlement may, in certain circumstances be implicit in the right of access to a

---

[284] Ibid, para 41.
[285] Ibid, paras 51 and 52.
[286] This phrase comes from the text of Art 6(3)(c) itself.
[287] *RD v Poland* (2004) 39 EHRR 240; *Quaranta v Switzerland*, Application No 11932/86; *Granger v United Kingdom* (1990) 12 EHRR 469; *Vaudelle v France* (2003) 37 EHRR 397.
[288] However, cf Lord Hoffmann's observations in *Jones v DPP* [2007] 1 AC 136. See 5.56 and 5.127 et seq.

court and the right to a fair hearing. In *Steel and Morris v UK*,[289] the ECtHR found that there had been a breach of Article 6(1) and the principle of 'equality of arms' where two environmental campaigners, who were sued by the McDonalds Corporation for libel, were forced to represent themselves due to lack of funding. The trial had lasted 313 days, had involved complex expert evidence and McDonalds had been represented by leading and junior counsel experienced in libel law.

The ECtHR emphasized that the Convention is intended to guarantee rights that are **10.170** 'practical and effective' and stated that:

> it is central to the concept of a fair trial, in civil as in criminal proceedings, that a litigant is not denied the opportunity to present his or her case effectively before the court . . . and that he or she is able to enjoy equality of arms with the opposing side.[290]

This decision was a marked departure from the ECtHR's previous decisions in respect of **10.171** access to legal aid in defamation cases.[291]

In respect of civil cases more generally, in *R v Legal Services Commission, ex parte Jarrett*[292] **10.172** Burton J endorsed the approach of the ECtHR in *X v UK*[293] to the effect that:

> Only in exceptional circumstances, namely where the withholding of legal aid would make the assertion of a civil claim practically impossible, or where it would lead to an obvious unfairness of the proceedings, can [a right to legal aid in civil proceedings] be invoked by virtue of Article 6(1) of the Convention.[294]

Where other Convention rights are engaged, as was the case with Article 10 in *Steel and* **10.173** *Morris*, adequate protection of those rights may require the provision of funded legal assistance.[295]

Disclosure

The third aspect of fair trial rights of particular note in the context of public order **10.174** and protest is disclosure. The general position in both civil and criminal proceedings is that:

> [the] right to adversarial proceedings . . . means in principle the opportunity for the parties to a criminal or civil trial to have knowledge of and comment on all evidence adduced or observations filed, even by an independent member of the national legal service, with a view to influencing the court's decision.[296]

In the context of criminal proceedings, there is an additional obligation on prosecutors **10.175** to disclose not only the evidence on which the prosecution proposes to rely, but also any

---

[289] (2005) 41 EHRR 22.
[290] Ibid, para 59.
[291] See *McVicar v UK* (2002) 35 EHRR 584.
[292] [2002] ACD 25.
[293] (1984) 6 EHRR 136.
[294] See also *Pine v Law Society* [2002] UKHRR 81.
[295] See, for example, in relation to safeguarding effective participation in an official investigation into a death in custody under Art 2: *Jordan v UK* (2003) 37 EHRR 52; *R v Secretary of State for the Home Department, ex parte Amin* [2004] 1 AC 653.
[296] *Lobo Machado v Portugal* (1996) 23 EHRR 79, para 31.

prosecution material capable of undermining the prosecution case or of assisting the case for the accused,[297] including material which might undermine the credibility of prosecution witnesses.[298] This includes both material in the possession of the police or prosecution and that to which they could reasonably gain access.[299]

10.176 The right to disclosure is not absolute and material may be withheld, on order of a judge, on grounds of public interest immunity.[300] This includes reasons of national security and protection of informers, and police methods of investigation of crime. Any such measures interfering with the right to disclosure must be limited to that which is 'strictly necessary' and any difficulties caused to the defence by a limitation on its rights must be sufficiently counterbalanced by the procedures followed by the judicial authorities.[301]

10.177 It is of note that in *R v Stratford Justices, ex parte Imbert*,[302] the Divisional Court observed obiter, and prior to the coming into force of the Human Rights Act 1998, that neither Article 6(1) nor 6(3)(a) or (b), imposes an absolute obligation on the prosecutor in summary only cases to provide advance disclosure of the evidence on which the prosecution proposes to rely, *provided* that magistrates are alert to the need to grant reasonable adjournments to enable defendants or their representatives to deal with the evidence when it is given.

10.178 It is submitted that, although it may be possible to ensure a fair trial through the granting of adjournments rather than requiring disclosure in advance of trial, this is likely in all but the simplest of cases to result in more expense and delay than if the necessary disclosure had been made in the first place. This is particularly the case in light of the significant reduction in legal aid for summary proceedings, meaning that the many defendants are forced to represent themselves. The observations of the Divisional Court in *ex parte Imbert* appear to be premised on an assumption that advocates dealing with a summary only case will in the main be able to react with sufficient speed to challenge the evidence adequately as and when it is given. Expecting the same of unrepresented defendants, unfamiliar with court procedures, is unlikely to be conducive to a fair trial. Unrepresented defendants in summary proceedings should continue to push for advance disclosure in order to meet the requirements of Article 6(1) and 6(3)(a) and(b).

10.179 Where proceedings engage other Convention rights, such rights themselves may give rise to duties of disclosure to ensure effective participation.[303] In the context of judicial review

---

[297] Criminal Procedure and Investigations Act 1996, s 3(1)(a); *R v H and C* [2004] 2 AC 134, para 14; *Edwards v UK* (2000) 30 EHRR 121; *Rowe and Davis v UK* (2000) 30 EHRR 1; *R v Davis* [1993] 1 WLR 613.

[298] *Edwards v United Kingdom* (1992) 15 EHRR 417, European Commission on Human Rights opinion, at para 50.

[299] *Jespers v Belgium*, Application No 8403/78, 15 October 1980; see also Attorney General's Guidelines on Disclosure.

[300] *R v H and C*; *Rowe and Davis v UK*; *Jasper v UK* (2000) 30 EHRR 411; *Fitt v UK* (2000) 30 EHRR 480.

[301] *R v H and C*; *Rowe and Davis v UK*; *R v Davis*.

[302] [1999] 2 Cr App R 276.

[303] See, for example, *McMichael v UK* (1995) 20 EHRR 205, in which the applicant's Art 8 rights in family proceedings entailed a duty of disclosure sufficient to ensure his effective participation. See also, *Jordan v UK*, re obligations of disclosure under Art 2 in relation to investigations into deaths involving state responsibility.

proceedings, the House of Lords has held that where issues of proportionality arise in respect of interference with Convention rights, more disclosure may be necessary than in ordinary judicial review proceedings.[304]

G. Article 2: Right to Life

Article 2 protects the right to life. It includes a 'negative obligation' on the State not to take **10.180** life intentionally, except in the exceptional circumstances set out in Article 2(2), which include, in the public order context, where fatal force is 'absolutely necessary' for the purpose of quelling a riot or insurrection[305]. The case of *Gulec v Turkey*,[306] in which the ECtHR found a breach of Article 2 where police fired live rounds into a crowd in order to disperse a protest is discussed in Chapter 6.

Article 2 also imposes a 'positive obligation' on the State to take reasonable steps to avoid a **10.181** 'real and immediate risk to life' of which the State knew or ought to have known at the time.[307] There is also a positive obligation on the State to conduct a prompt, independent, and effective investigation into the circumstances of any death for which the state may have been responsible.[308]

Where a death occurs at the hands of the police or other State agent in a public order situation **10.182** there will automatically be a coroner's inquest[309] unless this is overtaken by criminal proceedings against those responsible. If criminal proceedings do not address all aspects of the State's potential liability, a further independent and effective investigation will be required.[310]

The positive obligation to protect life from the criminal acts of third parties may arise **10.183** where public disorder or protest activity presents a real and immediate threat to life. See by way of analogy, the positive obligation under Article 3 to protect individuals from inhuman or degrading treatment as analysed in *E v Chief Constable of the Royal Ulster Constabulary*,[311] discussed below.

H. Article 3: Prohibition of Torture

Article 3 provides for an absolute prohibition on state inflicted torture and inhuman or **10.184** degrading treatment. It also imposes a positive obligation on state parties to:

---

[304] *Tweed v Parades Commission for Northern Ireland* [2007] 1 AC 650.
[305] The other exceptions are where fatal force is 'absolutely necessary' in defence of any person from unlawful violence; or in order to effect a lawful arrest or to prevent the escape of a person lawfully detained.
[306] (1999) 28 EHRR 121.
[307] *Osman v UK* [1999] 1 FLR 193 ECHR; *Kilic v Turkey* (2001) 33 EHRR 1357; *Chief Constable of Herfordshire v Van Colle; Smith v Chief Constable of Sussex* [2008] 3 WLR 593.
[308] *Jordan v UK* (2003) 37 EHRR 52; *Finucan v UK* (2003) 37 EHRR 656; *Savage v South Essex Partnership NHS Trust* [2009] 2 WLR 115.
[309] Coroners Act 1988, s 8.
[310] *R v Secretary of State for the Home Department, ex parte Amin* [2004] 1 AC 653.
[311] [2008] 3 WLR 1208.

take measures designed to ensure that individuals within their jurisdiction are not subjected to torture or inhuman or degrading treatment, including such ill-treatment administered by private individuals . . . These measures should provide effective protection, in particular, of children and other vulnerable persons and include reasonable steps to prevent ill-treatment of which the authorities had or ought to have had knowledge.[312]

10.185 As with Article 2 in respect of the right to life, Article 3 imposes an obligation on the state to instigate a prompt, independent, and effective investigation into allegations of torture or inhuman or degrading treatment.[313]

10.186 Ill-treatment must 'attain a minimum level of severity' before Article 3 is breached.[314] Various factors including the duration of the treatment; its physical or mental effects; and the age, sex, vulnerability, and state of health of the victim are relevant to an assessment of whether the threshold is met.[315]

10.187 Where an individual sustains injuries whilst in the custody of the State, the ECtHR has applied a somewhat lower threshold for inhuman and degrading treatment than in other situations. In *Ribitsch v Austria*,[316] the ECtHR emphasized that 'in respect of a person deprived of his liberty, any recourse to physical force which has not been made strictly necessary by his own conduct diminishes human dignity and is in principle an infringement of the right set forth in Article 3'. However, in *Raninen v Finland*[317] the ECtHR held that the handcuffing of a detainee did not violate Article 3, even where the detention was unlawful and the handcuffing unnecessary.

10.188 In considering a complaint under Article 3, the ECtHR will usually require medical evidence in support of any alleged injuries and the burden is on the applicant to prove 'beyond reasonable doubt' both the existence of the injury and its causation. However, such proof may follow from 'the coexistence of sufficiently strong, clear and concordant inferences or of similar unrebutted presumptions of fact'.[318]

10.189 Once injury and causation have been established, the burden shifts to the state to provide convincing and credible arguments to explain or justify the degree of force used.[319] Where injuries are inflicted by police in dispersing a peaceful protest, the ECtHR has found breaches of Article 3 even where the injuries sustained are apparently fairly minor: in *Balcik v Turkey*,[320] one of the applicants had sustained 'bruises on both arms and swelling on the

---

[312] *Z v UK* (2002) 34 EHRR 3, para 73; *Gldani Congregation of Jehovah's Witnesses v Georgia*, Application No 71156/01, 3 May 2007.

[313] *Aksoy v Turkey* (1997) 23 EHRR 553; *Assenov v Bulgaria* (1998) 28 EHRR 652.

[314] *Ireland v UK* (1979–80) 2 EHRR 25, para 162.

[315] Ibid.

[316] (1996) 21 EHRR 573, para 38.

[317] (1997) 26 EHRR 563.

[318] *Balcik v Turkey*, Application No 25/02, 29 November 2007, para 29; *Saya & Others v Turkey*, Application No 4327/02, 7 October 2008; *Salman v Turkey* [GC], Application No 21986/93, para 100, ECHR 2000-VII.

[319] *Balcik v Turkey*, paras 31–3.

[320] Op cit.

left foot';[321] in *Saya & Others v Turkey*,[322] the applicants suffered from 'tenderness on the back of the right leg' and 'scratches on the back'. In both cases a breach of Article 3 was found. The ECtHR found it relevant to its assessment of the State's justification of the force used that, in both cases, (a) the police had not been called upon to act without prior preparation; (b) there was no evidence that those against whom the force had been directed had posed a threat to public order or had engaged in acts of violence; and (c) there had either been no prosecutions of those individuals, or they had been acquitted of all charges.[323]

The positive obligation to protect individuals from torture, and inhuman, or degrading treatment at the hands of third parties imposes a duty on the State to protect those who may be the target of protest or disorder, or otherwise caught up in it. In *E v Chief Constable of the Royal Ulster Constabulary*,[324] the House of Lords considered the case of a primary school child in Belfast who, with other children at her school, had been subject to violent threats and missile attacks from a hostile crowd of 'loyalist' protestors who had sought to prevent her attending her Roman Catholic school. The applicant (the mother of the child) sought to argue that in failing to make substantial arrests and disperse the protest, the Royal Ulster Constabulary had breached its obligation to protect her daughter and other children from inhuman and degrading treatment. It was common ground that at least some of the actions of the protestors were inhuman or degrading. The House of Lords acknowledged that the police were under a positive Article 3 duty, but on the facts of this case found that this had been discharged as the police had done all that could reasonably be expected of them in the circumstances.

10.190

---

[321] Ibid, para 6.
[322] Op cit.
[323] *Balcik*, para 32; *Saya*, para 21.
[324] Op cit.

INDEX

ABC guinea pig breeding farm 9.179
ACPO (Association of Chief Police Officers)
    6.01, 6.02, 6.06
Aerodromes, licensed, trespassing on 5.176
Affray 1.89–127
    alternative verdicts 1.123
    common law 1.90–1
    cumulative effect 1.121
    definition 1.93–4
    elements 1.96–7
    historical development 1.89–94
    jurisdiction 1.95
    mental element 1.119–20
    person of reasonable firmness 1.108–18
    public/private place 1.122
    sentencing 1.124–7
    threats 1.98–102
    unlawful violence 1.103
    violence towards another 1.104–7
Aggravated trespass 5.47–73
    additional act 5.57
    cycle track defined 5.51
    defences 5.63–5
    elements 5.53–4
    highways defined 5.50
    intention to intimidate, obstruct, or disrupt 5.58
    land defined 5.49
    lawful activity 5.59–62
    in the open air, defined 5.49
    penalty 5.52
    powers to remove persons committing 5.66–73
    restricted byway, defined 5.50
    statutory powers 5.47, 5.66–8
    trespass on land, defined 5.55–6
    use against trespassers 5.48
Aircraft, drunk on 2.177
Alcohol, at sporting events 2.182
Alcohol-related disorder
    see also Drunk and disorderly
    directions to leave 6.57–9
Ancient monuments 3.154
Animal research facilities, protection 2.125–45
    see also Intimidation
    activists' activity 5.03
    criticism of legislation 2.133–5
    injunctions 9.171–7
    interference with contractual relations 2.131
    intimidation of persons 2.132
    legislative intent 2.126–30

offences 2.125
sentencing 2.136–9
    cases 2.140–5
Animal rights activists 5.03, 9.179, 9.182
ANPR (Automatic number plate recognition) 6.04
Anti-social behaviour
    dispersal of groups see under Police powers
    low-level 1.173
    orders (ASBOs) 9.178–82
        conditions 9.182
        necessity 9.180–1
Anti-war protesters 5.60, 9.05
Appeals
    Attorney General's reference on point
        of law 9.138
    autrefois convict/acquis 9.85
    basic types 9.82
    against conviction 9.122–9
    to ECHR see European Court of Human Rights
    from Criminal Cases Review Commission
        9.153–6
    from Crown Court to Court of Appeal 9.117–56
        acquittal, Attorney General's reference on
            point of law 9.138
        against conviction 9.122–9
        against rulings, by prosecution 9.140–8
        against sentence
        by defendant 9.130–3
        by prosecution 9.134–7
    bail 9.129
    fresh evidence 9.125
    interlocutory appeals 9.117–9
    re-trials
        ordering 9.126
        prosecution applications for 9.149–52
    unsafe conviction 9.122–4
    from Crown Court to High Court 9.103–4
        interlocutory appeals 9.117–9
    from magistrates' court to Crown Court
        9.83–94
        against binding over 9.94
        against conviction 9.83–9
        against sentence 9.90–3
        autrefois convict/acquis 9.85
        bail pending 9.88
        costs 9.89
        hearing 9.86
        notes of evidence 9.87
        plea, equivocal/under duress 9.85

449

Appeals (*cont.*)
    from Crown Court to Court of Appeal (*cont.*)
    from magistrates' court to Divisional
        Court 9.95–102
        bail 9.102
        case stated 9.97–8
        grounds 9.96
        refusal by magistrates 9.99
        time limit 9.101
    to Supreme Court 9.157–8
Archbold, JF 2.101
Arms trade campaigns 6.46, 9.14–5
Arrest
    breach of the peace 6.156–9
    caution on 7.44
    citizen's power 7.33–7
    complaints 7.64
    de-arresting 7.26
    definition 7.01
    discretion to 7.18–32
    entry/search of property 7.49–53
    evidence for 7.10–13
    information given on 7.38–44
    instructions to 7.11
    lawful 7.02–6
        unlawfulness, consequences 7.60–4
    necessity test 7.22–6
    offence committed 7.14–7
    police powers 7.02–32
    reasons for 7.19–21
        information given 7.40–3
    record of 7.44
    search after 7.45–8
    security guards/store detectives, power of 7.33
    street bail *see* Street bail
    suspicion 7.07
        reasonable grounds 7.08–17
        unlawfulness, consequences 7.60–4
        Wednesbury reasonableness/*Wednesbury*
            plus 7.27–32
    without warrant 7.04
ASBOs *see under* Anti-social behaviour
Assault and battery 2.04
Assemblies
    advance notice requirement 3.64
    conditions
        failure to comply 3.73
        intimidation 3.68–70
        police imposition 3.65–72
    demonstrations *see* Counter-demonstrators;
        Demonstrators
    disruptive activity 10.56–66
    freedom of expression and assembly *see under*
        European Convention on Human Rights
    historical background 3.53–5
    human rights
        pre-ECHR 10.03–6

        under ECHR 10.07–10
        illegality 10.71, 10.78–80
        insulting behaviour 10.41–55
        intimidation 3.68–70
        legality/illegality *see* legality/illegality of assemblies
        legitimate aims justifying interference 10.98–100
        necessity in a democratic society, as justifying
            interference 10.101–10
        prior authorization 10.111–121
        on private property and 10.72–6
        prohibition 3.74–5
        public assemblies defined 3.56–63
        right to assemble 3.02–6
        shocking, offensive, disturbing activity 10.39–40
        trespassory *see* Trespassory assemblies
        violent activity 10.67–10.70
Association of Chief Police Officers (ACPO)
        6.01, 6.02, 6.06
Atomic Weapons Establishment 5.149
Attorney General, reference on point of law 9.138
Austin case (*Austin v Commissioner of Police
        for the Metropolis*) 3.36, 3.63, 3.74–5, 4.67,
        4.73–4, 6.56, 6.69, 6.81, 6.114, 6.152, 6.163,
        6.166, 6.169–73, 7.33, 10.155, 10.158–61
Austin, Louis 10.158–61
Automatic number plate recognition (ANPR) 6.04

Badger traps 8.97
Bail conditions 7.109–65
see also Street Bail
    background 7.109–11
    court attendance 7.134–8
    from court 7.126–30
        applications to vary 7.162
        common conditions 7.129–30
        necessity 7.126
        renewed applications for bail 7.163
    from police station 7.122–5
        breach 7.132–3
        necessity 7.123
        statutory basis 7.122
        time limits 7.125
        varying conditions 7.159
    High Court appeals 7.165
    human rights and bail 7.112–20
    offence while on bail 7.139
    prosecution applications for reconsideration 7.160
    records of decisions 7.155–6
    refusing bail
        background 7.14
        court's approach 7.144–7
        Crown Court appeals 7.164
        imprisonable non-summary offences 7.152–4
        imprisonable summary offences 7.150–1
        non-imprisonable offences 7.148–9
        police power 7.141–3
        risks justifying 7.113–6

statutory basis of bail 7.121
street bail *see* **Street bail**
Battery 2.04
Belief
  freedom of *see under* **European Convention**
    on Human Rights (Article 9)
  manifestation of 10.126–30
Bennion, F 2.156
Binding over
  to come up for judgment 9.42–6
  to keep the peace 6.127–8, 9.20–41
    appeals 9.37, 9.94
    background 9.20–2
    failure to comply/forfeiture 9.40–1
    good behaviour requirement 9.26–30
    period 9.35
    power of court 9.25
    as preventative justice 9.23
    procedural requirements 9.31–7
    recognizance/recognisance 9.24
    refusal to be bound over 9.38–9
    representations 9.31–2
    specific conditions 9.36
    standard of proof 9.33
    sum stipulated 9.34
Blum case (*Blum v DPP*; **Parliament Square**
  case) 3.103, 6.171, 10.111–7
  see also **Parliament Square**
Bomb hoaxes 2.51–5
  definition 2.51
  sentencing 2.52–5
Breach of the peace 6.125–2
  at common law 6.126
  arrest power 6.156–9
  binding over *see* **Binding over**, to keep
    the peace
  categories 6.131–4
  citizen's right/duty 6.141, 6.153–4
  criminal law and 6.139–40
  definition 6.129–38
  freedom of expression and 6.135
  further breach 6.144–5
  human rights and breach of the peace 162–167,
    6.171–2
  imminent 6.148–51
  innocent third parties 6.168–73
  key issues 6.125
  pickets, limits on 4.61–7, 6.160
  preventative action 6.146–8, 6.152
  private property, police powers 6.161
  reasonableness of actions 6.136–7
  timing of action 6.142–3
British National Party 10.51
Burden of proof
  see also **Reverse burden of proof**
  excuse/justification defences 8.24–8.32
Burglary 5.179–80

By-laws
  highway 4.94–102
  local authority 3.152–5
  open spaces 3.155
  railways, prosecutions 3.154
  trespass 5.149–51

CAAT (Campaign Against the Arms Trade) 6.46
Campaign Against the Arms Trade (CAAT) 6.46
Campers, unauthorized 5.113–125
  statutory powers 5.113
Caravans, trespass with
  defence 5.96
  directions to leave 5.114–8
  failure to leave/re-entering 5.95
  local authority powers 5.120–4
    guidance on 5.125
  relevant caravan site, defined 5.94
  residing in a vehicle 5.115
  statutory defence 5.119
  statutory powers 5.91–2
  trespass/occupier, defined 5.93
  vehicles, powers to seize/remove 5.97
Cautions
  as alternative to conviction 9.47–8
  conditional 9.59–68
    background 9.59–60
    conditions 9.65–7
    effect 9.68
    failure to comply 9.68
    offences 9.61–2
    statutory criteria 9.63–4
  simple 9.49–58
  administering 9.56
  basis 9.49–50
  consequences 9.57–8
  criteria 9.51–5
  mixed disposal 9.53, 9.55
  refusal to accept 9.52
Charging process *see under* **Detention at police station**
Chartists 1.05
Chequers 5.143
Children, removal home (by police) 6.67–8
Circumstances, duress of *see* **Necessity/duress**
  of circumstances defences
CO11 6.04, 6.47–8
Common prostitute 4.111–4
Commons 3.154
Community penalty 9.14–9
Community support officers *see* **Police community**
  support officers
Computer data, misuse 8.101–2
Conditional cautions *see under* **Cautions**
Conditional discharge convention 9.03–12
Conscience, thought, and religion, Freedom
  of *see under* **European Convention on**
  Human Rights

Constable
  see also **Police powers**
  assault on, in the execution of his duty 2.02–11
    definition 2.03
    elements 2.04
    mistaken self-defence 2.10
    offence 2.02
    self-defence 2.07–9
    sentencing 2.11
  execution of duty 2.06, 2.21–30
    outside of duty 2.31–3
  obstruction of, in the execution of his duty 2.12–36
    nature of obstruction 2.12–17
    offence 2.02
    resistance element 2.13
    wilfulness 2.18–9
  office of 2.0, 2.205
Consumer picketing 4.68–71
Contamination or interfering with goods 2.146–53
  elements 2.147–8
  possession with a view to 2.151
  sentencing 2.152–3
  statutory basis 2.146
  threats 2.149–50
Cordons, police 6.69–71
  see also **Kettling**
Counter-demonstrators
  conflict with demonstrators 10.37–8
  duty to protect against 10.34–5
Country parks 3.154
CPS (Crown Prosecution Service) 7.104, 7.105
Criminal Cases Review Commission (CCRC),
  referrals 9.153–6
Criminal damage 2.112–24
  aggravated
  elements 2.120
  possession with intent 2.123
    sentencing 2.121, 2.124
    threats to damage/destroy property 2.122
  courts triable 2.114
  damage defined 2.115
  elements 2.113, 2.120
  lawful excuse defined 2.118
  mens rea 2.117
  offences 2.112
  possession with intent 2.123
  property defined 2.116
  sentencing 2.119, 2.121, 2.124
  threats to damage/destroy property 2.12
Criminal Intelligence (Crimint) 6.04
Crimint 6.04
Crown Court
  see also under **Appeals**
  judicial review appeals 9.113–6
  trial on indictment 9.110–2
Crown Prosecution Service (CPS) 7.104, 7.105
CS gas 6.197
Custody *see* **Detention at police station**

Degrading treatment 10.184–90
Demonstrators
  see also **Counter-demonstrators**
  excessive burdens on 10.36
Detention at police station 7.76–108
  bail *see* **Bail conditions**, from
    police station
  charge
    decision 7.105–8
    options 7.104
    sufficient evidence to 7.103
  custody officer, role 7.66–71
  custody record 7.66, 7.68–71
  deferred bail 7.102
  detainee's rights 7.78–82
  foreign nationals 7.87–8
  formal interview 7.100–1
  further investigations 7.99–102
  interpreters' availability 7.88
  juveniles, under 17 7.86
  legal advice 7.79–82
    delays 7.81
  medical attention 7.93
  personal information
    collection 7.72–6
    retention 7.76–7
  physical conditions 7.89–93
  pre-charge detention 7.95–8
    justification 7.95–6
    time limits 7.98
  right to inform someone 7.83–4
  special groups 7.85
  threshold test 7.103
Disclosure
  duties 10.179
  rights 10.174–8
Disguises, removal 6.33–42
  constable's power 6.40–1
  human rights and 6.42
  inspector's authorization
    6.33–41
  religious offence and 6.40
Disruptive activity 10.56–66
Distance weapons 6.199
Disturbing activity 10.39–40
DNA profiles 7.75–7
Downing Street 5.143
Druidic ceremony 10.132–4
Drunk and disorderly 2.168–7
  see also **Alcohol-related disorder**
  alcohol related offences 2.168–9
  failure to leave 2.175
  offence 2.170–2
  on aircraft 2.177
  public place 2.173–4
    designated 2.176
Duress of circumstances *see* **Necessity/duress**
  of circumstances defences

ECHR *see* European Convention on Human Rights
Election meetings 3.90–3
European Commission for Democracy through
    Law 10.10
European Convention on Human
    Rights (ECHR)
  see also Human rights
  Article 2 (right to life) 10.180–3
    criminal third party acts 10.183
    further investigations 10.182
    negative obligation 10.180
    positive obligation 10.181
  Article 3 (prohibition of torture) 10.184–90
    absolute prohibition 10.184
    custody injuries 10.188–9
    ill-treatment 10.186
    investigations/explanations 10.185, 10.189
    positive obligation 10.190
  Article 5 (right to liberty and security)
    as stated 10.150–3
    deprivation of liberty/restriction of movement,
      distinction 10.155–6
    kettling 10.158–61
    liberty defined 10.154–5
    not a qualified right 10.150
    stop and search, terrorism prevention
      10.155–6, 10.157
  Article 6 (right to a fair trial) 10.162–79
    disclosure *see* Disclosure
    legal assistance 10.167–73
    reverse burden of proof 1.45, 10.163–6
  Article 8 (right to respect for private and
    family life) 10.144–9
    application 10.145
    as stated 10.144
    checks on scope 10.148
    personal autonomy 10.147
    private life concept 10.146
  Article 9 (freedom of thought, conscience,
    and religion)
    and Articles 10 and 11 10.131–8
    as stated 10.122–3
    beliefs/views covered 10.124
    corporate/profit-making body 10.125
    manifestation of belief 10.126–30
    preaching/proselytizing 10.138–43
  Articles 10 and 11 (freedom of expression and
    assembly)
    and Article 9 10.131–8
    as qualified rights 10.15–6
    as stated 10.13–4
    assembly to impart information and
      ideas 10.22–7
    counter-demonstrators *see*
      Counter-demonstrators
    direct/indirect obstacles 10.28–30
    disruptive activity 10.56–66
    excessive burdens on 10.36

    in protest cases 10.17–21
    insulting behaviour 10.41–55
    legality/illegality *see* legality/illegality of
      assemblies
    legitimate aims justifying
      interference 10.98–100
    necessity in a democratic society, as justifying
      interference 10.101–10
    positive obligations 10.31–3
    prior authorization 10.111–21
    private property and 10.72–6
    restrictions 10.77
    shocking, offensive, disturbing activity 10.39–40
    violent activity 10.67–70
  incorporation into UK law 10.01–12
European Court of Human Rights, petitions
    to 9.159–65
  applicants 9.160–62
  just satisfaction 9.163
  procedures 9.164–5
Exclusion zone, failure to leave 5.158
Excuse/justification defences 8.01–4
  burden of proof 8.24–32
Expression, freedom of expression and assembly *see*
    under European Convention on Human Rights

Fair trial, right to *see* European Convention on
    Human Rights (Article 6)
Fairford (RAF) direct action 8.55
Fairs, Pleasure 3.154
Family life, right to respect *see* European Convention
    on Human Rights (Article 8)
Fear or provocation of violence 1.128–70
  definition 1.133–4
  distribute or display elements 1.10–153
  elements 1.136
  historical development 1.128–32
  immediacy 1.162–5
  jurisdiction 1.135
  mental element 1.154–9
  public/private place 1.165–70
  threatening, abusive or insulting elements 1.143–9
  uses towards another 1.137–42
  violence defined 1.60–165
  writing element 1.150, 1.153
Filming, police powers 6.44
Fines 9.13
Fingerprints 6.43, 7.76
Firearm/imitation firearm, trespassing with 5.166
Fireworks, at sporting events 2.182
Fixed penalty notices 9.73–81
  administering 9.75–6
  basic procedure 9.73
  effect 9.80–1
  offences 9.74
  statutory definition 9.77–9
Flint, Caroline 3.99
Foot impressions 7.76

Football related disorder 2.178–82
  alcohol/fireworks at 2.182
  banning orders 2.182, 9.183–9
    reasonable grounds 9.188
    relevant offences/complaints 9.185–7
    standard of proof 9.189
    statutory basis 9.183–4
  context 2.178
  spectator offences 2.179–81
  ticket touting 2.180
Foreign mission's premises, trespassing on 5.167–9
Fox-hunt saboteurs 5.03, 5.53, 5.58, 5.61, 5.71
Freedom of expression and assembly *see under*
  European Convention on Human Rights
  (Articles 10 and 11)
  thought, conscience, and religion *see under*
    European Convention on Human Rights
    (Article 9)

G20 protests 6.07, 6.174, 6.197
Gangs, stop and search 6.77
Gardens (local authority) 3.155
GCHQ premises 5.143
Gillan **case** *(R (Gillan) v Metropolitan Police*
  Commissioner) 4.84, 6.87, 6.90–6.8 *passim*
GM crop protests 8.53, 8.55, 8.167–8
Graffiti 8.100
Guinea pig breeding farm 9.179
Gypsy communities 5.139

Habeas corpus 7.165
Hain, Peter 3.98
Handcuffs 6.196
Harassment, alarm, or distress 1.71–205
  see also **Home, protection at**
  as anti-social behaviour 1.173
  defences 1.195–202
  definition 1.174–6
  disorderly elements 1.181–3
  elements 1.178–9
  harassment, alarm, or distress, as
    alternatives 1.186–90
  historical development 1.171–3
  intentional 1.206–30
    causation 1.211–3
    defences 1.220–3
    definition 1.207
    elements 1.210
    historical development 1.206
    intoxication 1.217
    jurisdiction 1.208
    mental element 1.214–6
    police powers 1.224–6
    proportionality 1.209, 1.223
    public/private place 1.218–9
    sentencing 1.227–30
    specific defences 1.220–23

jurisdiction 1.177
mental element 1.191–92
public/private place 1.193–4
sentencing 1.203–5
  specific defences 1.195–202
threatening, abusive, or insulting elements 1.180
within sight or hearing 1.184–5
Haw, Brian 3.98–9, 3.122–5, 4.46–8
Her Majesty's Inspectorate of Constabulary (HMIC)
  proposals 6.201–4
High Court
  see under **Appeals**
  quasi-military organizations, prohibition 2.49–50
Highway
  background 4.01–2
  bye-laws 4.94–102
  definition 4.03–4
  human rights 4.38–48
  obstruction 4.19–50
    definition 4.24–8
    elements 4.20–2
    lawful authority 4.34
    lawful excuse 4.33–7
    order to remove 4.49–50
    statutory basis 4.19
    wilfulness 4.29–32
    picketing and 4.51
  reasonable use 4.13–8, 4.33–7
    human rights 4.38–48
  road blocks *see* **Road blocks; Road traffic stops**
  to pass and repass right 4.05–12
  traffic, disruption to 10.56–66
  trespassory assemblies 4.09–12, 5.136–5.138
  use 4.05–18
    reasonable 4.13–8, 4.33–7
HMIC (Her Majesty's Inspectorate of Constabulary)
  proposals 6.201–4
Home, protection at 3.142–51
  see also **Harassment, alarm, or distress**
  background 3.142
  harassment offence 3.148–51
  police directions 3.143–7
Homosexuality, public statements against 10.50
Human rights
  see also **European Convention on**
    Human Rights
  bail conditions 7.112–20
  breach of the peace 162–167, 6.171–2
  compliance 3.117–21
  judicial review 9.109
  police information gathering 6.05
  police powers 6.184–94
  pre-Human Rights Act 10.03–6
  restrictive measures 10.11
  stop and search 6.113–7
Hunt saboteurs 5.03, 5.53, 5.58, 5.61, 5.71
Hyde Park 3.135–6

Independent Police Complaints Commission 7.64
Industrial action *see* Watching and besetting
Inhuman or degrading treatment 10.184–90
Injunctions
  basis 9.166
  principles 9.167–9
  in protest cases 9.170–7
    enforcement 9.177
    trespass to land 5.30–3
Insulting behaviour 10.41–5
Intentional harassment, alarm, or distress *see under*
  Harassment, alarm, or distress
Interfering with goods *see* Contamination or
  interfering with goods
Intimidation 2.154–67
  see also Animal research facilities, protection
  animal research facilities 2.132
  animal rights activists 5.03, 9.179, 9.182
    see also animal research facilities, protection
  assemblies *see under* Assemblies
  definition 2.162
  elements 2.159–66
  hiding of tools 2.164
  historical development 2.155–7
  mens rea 2.159, 2.160
  penalties 2.167
  persistently following 2.163
  statutory basis 2.154
  wrongful compulsion 2.161
Iraq invasion protests 8.57, 8.117

Jehovah's Witnesses 10.138
Judicial review 9.105–16
  basic principles 9.105, 9.108
  discretionary powers 9.106–7
  human rights and 9.109
  magistrates' court/Crown Court
    appeals 9.113–6
  procedure 9.115–6
  processions 3.47–52
  trial on indictment 9.110–2
Justification *see* Excuse/justification defences
Juveniles
  detention at police station 7.86
  warnings/reprimands 9.70–2

Kerb crawling *see under* Prostitution, street-based
Kettling 4.02, 4.74, 6.174, 10.158–61
Kingsnorth Power Station, climate camp 6.81
Land *see* Trespass to land

Laporte case (*R (Laporte) v Chief Constable of Gloucester
  Constabulary*) 3.02, 3.60, 4.61, 4.63–7, 4.75,
  5.31, 6.03, 6.28, 6.56, 6.81, 6.114, 6.129–31,
  6.147, 6.150–1, 6.167–73, 7.33, 10.38, 10.80
Legal assistance 10.167–73
Legality/illegality of assemblies 10.71, 10.78–80

accessibility of basis 10.81
arbitrariness/certainty of rules 10.82–97
prescribed by law requirement 10.78–80
Local authority bylaws 3.152–5
Location specific offences
  by-laws 3.152–5
  NHS facilities 3.138–41
  Nuclear bases 3.137
Loitering *see under* Prostitution,
  street-based
Luton Guruwarda 10.42

Magistrates' courts
  appeals *see under* Appeals
  judicial review 9.113–6
Manifestation of belief 10.126–30
Medway River 4.96
Meetings 3.76–93
  election 3.90–3
  open air 3.77
  private 3.78–9
  public
    attempts to break up 3.87
    control 3.84–6
    definition 3.80–3
    police powers to attend 3.88–9
    right 3.76
MI5 agent's disclosures 8.162–4
Military bases 5.143
Miners' strike 7.129
Mitigation of sentence 9.19

National Domestic Extremism Co-ordinator
  (NEDC) 6.01
National Domestic Extremism Team (NDET)
  6.01, 6.04, 6.06
National Extremism and Tactical Co-ordination Unit
  (NECTU) 6.01, 6.04, 6.06
National Intelligence Model 6.01
National parks 3.154
National Public Order Intelligence Unit
  (NPOIU) 6.01, 6.04
Naval facility 8.112–4
NDET (National Domestic Extremism Team)
  6.01, 6.04, 6.06
Necessity/duress of circumstances defences 8.124–60
  as single defences 8.124–35
  compulsion 8.147
  death/serious injury 8.158–60
  defendants, persons for whom
    responsible 8.140–6
  duress of circumstances
    definition 8.136–9
    development 8.125–6
  reasonable belief 8.152–7
  as single defence 8.124–35
  subjective belief 8.148–51

NECTU (National Extremism and Tactical Co-ordination Unit) 6.01, 6.04, 6.06
NEDC (National Domestic Extremism Co-ordinator) 6.01
New age travellers 5.03
Newport Rising 1.05
NHS facilities 3.138–41
Northern Ireland, Trafalgar Square demonstration 10.136
NPOIU (National Public Order Intelligence Unit) 6.01, 6.04
Nuclear bases 3.137
Nuisance *see* Public nuisance
Number plate recognition (automatic) (ANPR) 6.04

ODIHR (Office for Democratic Institutions and Human Rights) Guidelines 10.08–10
Offence
    specific offence
Offensive, disturbing activity 10.39–40
Offensive weapon, trespassing with 5.165–6
Office for Democratic Institutions and Human Rights (ODIHR) Guidelines 10.08–10
Open air meetings 3.77
Open spaces
    see also Parliament Square
    by-laws 3.155
    Hyde Park 3.135–6
    Parliament Square Garden 3.120–34
    Royal Parks 3.135–6
Organisation for Security and Co-operation in Europe (OSCE) 10.08
Ormerod, D 1.68, 1.101, 1.14
OSCE (Organisation for Security and Co-opearation in Europe 10.08

Parks 3.155
Parliament Square 3.94–129
    see also Blum case
    see also Open spaces
    authorities involved 3.95
    authorization 3.107–11
    conditions 3.110
    designated area 3.101–2
    future proposals 3.126–9
    Brian Haw issues 3.98–9, 3.122–5, 4.46–8
    human rights compliance 3.117–21
    offences 3.112–6
    proposals 3.98–9
    Sessional Orders 3.96–7
    statutory basis 3.94, 3.100
    written notice 3.103–6
Parliament Square Garden 3.120–4
Peaceful picketing *see* Watching and besetting
Percy, Lindis 10.44–8
Person of reasonable firmness 1.76–7
Personal information

on detention *see under* Detention at police station
    requirement to give 6.27–32
Photographs *see under* Police powers
Picketing 4.51–71
    see also Watching and besetting
    breach of the peace 4.61–7, 6.160
    consumer 4.68–71
    employment law context 4.53–67
    highway and 4.51
    lawful authority 4.54–7
    numbers 4.58–9
    peaceful 4.53–60
    right 4.52
Pleasure fairs 3.154
PNC (Police National Computer) 6.04
PNICC (Police National Information, and Coordination Centre) 6.04
Poaching 5.178
Police community support officers 6.08–15
    accredited persons, defined 6.15
    codes of practice 6.14
    powers 6.11–3, 6.178
    to detain 6.12, 7.33
    statutory basis 6.09, 6.10
Police National Computer (PNC) 6.04
Police National Information, and Coordination Centre (PNICC) 6.04
Police powers
    see also Constable
    alcohol-related disorder, directions to leave 6.57–9
    arrest 7.02–32
    caution before questioning 6, 22
    children, removal home 6.67–8
    community support officers *see* Police community support officers
    complaints *see* Independent Police Complaints Commission
    consent 6.25
    control of movement 6.55–71
    cordons 6.69–71
    cordons *see* Cordons
    CS gas 6.197
    detention *see* Detention at police station
    disguises *see* Disguises, removal
    dispersal of groups, anti-social behaviour 6.60–8
        authorization criteria 6.60–3
        children, removal home 6.67–8
        constable's direction 6.64–6
    distance weapons 6.199
    distraction tactics 6.200
    filming 6.44
    fingerprints 6.43
    freedom and 6.205
    handcuffs 6.196
    harassment, alarm, or distress, intentional 1.224–6
    HMIC proposals 6.201–4
    home, protection at 3.143–7

human rights *see under* **Human rights**
information gathering 6.01–5
  databases 6.04
  human rights and 6.05
  specialist teams 6.03
kettling *see* **Kettling**
meetings, attendance 3.88–9
name/address/date of birth/personal details,
  requirements to give 6.27–32
photographs 6.44, 7.74, 10.148–9
overt surveillance 6.45–54
private property 6.161
refusing bail 7.141–3
response to protest 6.06–7
road/traffic stops *see* **Road blocks; Road traffic stops**
stop and search *see* **Stop and search powers**
tasers 6.198–9
trespass to land 5.38–9
use of force 6.174–204
  background 6.174
  equipment 6.195–200
  freedom of assembly and 6.194
  human rights and 6.184–94
  loss of life 6.186
  minimum severity requirement 6.187–8
  reasonable force 6.181–3, 6.189
  sources of power 6.175–80
  third party inflictions, prevention 6.191, 10.183
usurpation (quasi-military organizations) 2.45
voluntary encounters, records of 6.23
water canons 6.199
Police station, detention *see* **Detention at police station**
Police support units 6.07
Political uniforms, prohibition 2.37–41
Prevention of crime defence 8.33–88
  prevention issues 8.56–63
  reasonable force 8.64–85
    democratic process and 8.71–.85
    statutory basis 8.64–5
    subjective belief 8.66–70
  remoteness 8.86–8
  statutory basis 8.33
  use of force 8.36–55
    force defined 8.38–42
    peaceful obstruction 8.49–55
    to property 8.43–9
Private and family life, right to respect *see* **European Convention on Human Rights (Article 8)**
Private meetings 3.78–9
Private property
  see also **Protection of property defence**
  assemblies and 10.72–6
Private security guards, power of arrest 7.33
Processions
  advance notice 3.12–27

commonly or customarily held 3.16–9
  defences 3.26
  determined route, absence 3.21
  failure to comply 3.24
  historical background 3.13–4
  immunities 3.27
  nature/delivery 3.22
  organizer 3.25
  practicability 3.20
  statutory provision 3.15–27
banning 3.38–46
banning orders
  basis 3.38
  failure to comply 3.46
  justification 3.45
  procedure in London 3.42
  procedure outside London 3.40–1
  variation/renewal procedures 3.43–4
commonly or customarily held 3.16–9
conditions 3.28–37
  failure to comply 3.37
  historical background 3.29–30
  imposition 3.31–6
determined route, absence 3.21
judicial review 3.47–52
organizer 3.25
procession defined 3.08–9
public place defined 3.10–11
right to process 3.02–6
Prohibited places 5.152–4
Prostitution, street-based 4.103–7
  historical development 4.103–4.106
  kerb crawling 4.125–41
    annoyance or nuisance, as likely to cause 4.132–5
    elements 4.128
    for purpose of prostitution 4.141
    jurisdiction/penalty 4.126
    motor vehicle, immediate vicinity 4.138–40
    offence defined 4.125
    persistence defined 4.129
    persistent soliciting, distinction 4.147
    person committing 4.127
    statutory basis 4.125
    street/public place 4.136–7
  loitering 4.108–24
    common prostitute defined 4.111–4
    elements 4.110
    jurisdiction/penalty 4.109
    loiter or solicit, defined 4.115–8
    statutory basis 4.108
  offences 4.107
  persistent soliciting 4.142–7
    elements 4.145
    for the purpose of prostitution, defined 4.124
    jurisdiction/penalty 4.143

Prostitution, street-based (*cont.*)
persistent soliciting (*cont.*)
kerb crawling, distinction 4.147
person committing 4.144
soliciting defined 4.146
statutory basis 4.142
street or public place, defined 4.119–24, 4.136–7
Protected site, trespass on 5.140–8
designated sites, defined 5.142–3, 5.148
informing the public 5.146
penalties/proceedings 5.147
public access rites and 5.145
site defined 5.141
statutory offence 5.140
time allowance to leave 5.144
Protection of property defence 8.89–123
see also **Private property**
at common law 8.89–90
attempts/conspiracies 8.93
belief in consent 8.103–5
damage defined 8.99–102
lawful excuse 8.91–4
property defined 8.95–8
remoteness 8.110–23
statutory basis 8.94
subjective belief 8.106–9
Protest rights 3.00–1
Provocation of violence *see* **Fear or provocation of violence**
public, Meetings 3.88–9
Public assemblies *see* **Assemblies**
Public interest defence 8.161–8
Public meetings *see under* **Meetings**
Public nuisance 2.99–111
defences 2.110
definition 2.101–5
historical development 2.99–100
mens rea 2.108
private nuisance, distinction 2.106–7
prostitution *see* **Prostitution, street-based**
sentencing 2.111
vicarious liability 2.109
Public place
drunkenness *see under* **Drunk and disorderly**
processions 3.10–1
prostitution *see under* **Prostitution, street-based**

Quasi-military organizations, prohibition 2.42–50
defence 2.48
High Court powers 2.49–50
procedure 2.47
reasonable apprehension 2.46
statutory basis 2.42–4
usurpation of police functions 2.45

Racial and religious hatred 2.56–98
actus reus 2.65

aggravated offences 2.88
hostility requirement 2.93–6
racial/religious groups 2.90–2
sentencing 2.97–8
test 2.89
broadcasting programme 2.78–9
defences 2.82
forfeiture 2.87
hostility requirement 2.93–6
liability of corporations 2.83
mens rea 2.66
public performance of play 2.73–4
racial hatred 2.60–1
racial/religious groups 2.90–2
recording
distributing/showing/playing 2.75–7
possession 2.80–1
religious hatred 2.62–4
sentencing 2.84–6, 2.97–8
sexual orientation 2.58
statutory basis 2.56
stirring up 2.57–9
words, behaviour 2.67–8
written material 2.67–8
possession 2.80–1
publishing/distributing 2.69–72
RAF Fairford direct action 8.55
Railways
prosecutions, bylaws 3.154
trespassing on 5.177
Raves 5.03, 5.98–112
defences 5.105–6
directions to leave land 5.98
definitions 5.99–103
first offence 5.104
second offence 5.107
third offence 5.108
sound equipment
forfeiture 5.110–2
powers to seize/remove 5.109
vehicles, powers to seize/remove 5.109, 5.112
Re-trials *see under* **Appeals**
Reasonableness defence 8.05–23
circumstances
as objective standard 8.07–9
relevance of 8.15–23
subjective belief in 8.11–14
exception 8.06
proportionality 8.10
Religion, Freedom of *see under* **European Convention on Human Rights (Article 9)**
Religious hatred *see* **Racial and religious hatred**
Reprimands, for juveniles 9.70–2
Residential premises, adverse occupation 5.161–4
Reverse burden of proof 1.45, 10.163–6

Right to
fair trial *see* **European Convention on Human Rights** (Article 6)
life *see* **European Convention on Human Rights** (Article 2)
respect for private and family life *see* **European Convention on Human Rights** (Article 8)
Riot 1.01–4, 1.05–55
at common law 1.06–8
common purpose 1.32–5, 1.44
compensation 1.53–5
definition 1.15
elements 1.19
historical development 1.05–14
intoxication 1.42–5
jurisdiction 1.16
mental element 1.37–41
person of reasonable firmness 1.36
present together 1.22–4
prosecution 1.18–9
public/private place 1.24
quorum 1.20–1
reform proposals 1.09–14
secondary liability 1.35
self-defence 1.31–2
sentencing 1.46–52
single/separate offences 1.23
violence defined 1.25–31
Road blocks 4.72–93
at common law 4.73–6
PACE powers 4.77–9
parking prohibition/restriction 4.88–91
stop and search powers 4.80–93
Road traffic stops 6.118–24
authorization 6.120
constable's power 6.121
road checks 6.119
road stops 6.122–6.4
vehicles' stop and seizure 6.118
Roller skating rinks 3.15
Royal Parks 3.135–6
Royal residences 5.143

Sacheverell Riots 1.05
Samples from detainee 7.75–7
Scarman, Lord 3.14
Search *see* **Stop and search powers**
Security guards, power of arrest 7.33
Sentencing principles 9.01–2, 9.01–19
specific offence *see under* **Offence**
Sexual offence, trespass with intent to commit 5.181
Sexual orientation, hatred 2.58
Shocking, offensive, disturbing activity 10.39–40
Simple cautions *see under* **Cautions**
Smith, ATH 2.21
Smith, Sir J 1.102, 1.112
Special Branch 6.01

Spencer, JR 2.101
Sporting events, alcohol/fireworks at 2.182
Squatter damage 8.115–6
Stephen, Sir J 2.102
Stonehenge 10.132–10.4
Stop and search powers 6.72–124
articles searched for 6.74–5
authorization
commander/assistant chief constable's 6.87–92
inspector's 6.82–4
conduct of search 6.103–12
record of search 6.111–2
removal of clothing 6.110
statutory requirements 6.106–7
constable's powers 6.85–6
human rights and 6.113–7
police road blocks 4.80–93
reasonable grounds 6.76–81
statutory basis 6.72, 6.73
terrorism prevention 4.80–91, 6.87–102
commander/assistant chief constable's authorization 6.87–92
constable's power 6.93–102
human rights and 4.80–91, 6.87–102, 10.155–6, 10.157
terrorism defined 6.89
Store detectives, power of arrest 7.33
Street bail 7.54–9
see also **Bail conditions**
conditions 7.58, 7.157–8
breach 7.131
considerations 7.56–7
notice in writing 7.59
Street-based prostitution *see* **Prostitution, street-based**
Supreme Court, appeals 9.157–8

Tasers 6.198–9
Taxes, obligation to pay 10.128
10 Downing Street 5.143
Territorial Support Group (TSG) 6.07
Terrorism prevention
police cordons 6.71
stop and search *see under* **Stop and search powers**
trespass offences 5.03
Thatcher, Lady, statue decapitation 8.95, 8.120
Third party inflictions, prevention 6.191, 10.183, 10.190
Thought, conscience, and religion, Freedom of *see under* **European Convention on Human Rights** (Article 9)
Ticket touting 2.180
Tomlinson, Ian 6.174
Torture 10.184–90
Trade disputes *see* **Picketing; Watching and besetting**
Trafalgar Square 3.120–34, 10.136
Traffic, disruption to 10.56–66
Trespass by encroachment 5.34

Trespass to goods 5.02
Trespass to land
  abatement 5.34–7
  aerodromes, licensed 5.176
  aggravated trespass *see* **Aggravated trespass**
  authorized/justified entry 5.09
  background 5.01–5
  burglary 5.179–80
  bye-laws 5.149–51
  caravans *see* **Caravans, trespass with**
  civil tort 5.06–10
  criminal law development 5.41–6
  damages 5.40
  defences 5.11–5
  definitions 5.01–2
  encroachment 5.34
  enforcement, court officers, obstruction
    of 5.170–5
  entry, violence to secure 5.37, 5.159
  exclusion zone, failure to leave 5.158
  foreign mission's premises 5.167–9
  human rights defence 5.13–5
  injunctions 5.30–3
  intention 5.07
  interim possession orders 5.23–9
    trespass during 5.26–7, 5.160
  necessity defence 5.11–2
  orders for possession 5.18–22
  person suing 5.16–7
  poaching 5.178
  police role 5.38–9
  political/security concerns and 5.03
  possession orders 5.18–22
  prohibited places 5.152–4
  protected sites *see* **Protected site, trespass on**
  public authorities, possession orders 5.21
  public space, privatization 5.04
  raves *see* **Raves**
  residential premises, adverse
    occupation 5.161–4
  residing, as purpose 5.74–90
    defences 5.86
    directions to leave 5.74–7
    failure to leave/re-entering 5.84–5
    home elsewherre 5.83
    human rights issues 5.87–9
    land defined 5.81
    occupier defined 5.79–80
    trespass defined 5.78
    vehicle defined 5.82
    vehicles, power to seize/remove 5.90
  self-help/abatement 5.34–7
  sexual offence, intent to commit 5.181
  vagrancy offences 5.155–7
  violence to secure entry 5.37, 5.159
  with weapon of offence 5.165–6

Trespass to person 5.02
Trespassory assemblies 5.126–39
  banning orders 5.128–39
    geographical reach 5.132–3
    limited, defined 5.130
  concept 5.126–7
  human rights and 5.139
  offences/penalties 5.135
  on highways 5.136–8
Trespassory orders, banning powers, assembly,
  defined 5.131
Trial on indictment 9.110–2
TSG (Territorial Support Group) 6.07

Use of force *see* **Police powers, use of force;**
  Prevention of crime defence, use of force

Vagrancy offences 5.155–7
Vehicles
  powers to seize/remove 5.90, 5.97, 5.109, 5.112
  road traffic stops 6.118
Venice Commission 10.10
Violence
  affray *see under* **Affray**
  assault and battery 2.04
  provocation *see* **Fear or provocation of violence**
  riot and 1.25–31
  to secure entry to land 5.37, 5.159
Violent activity 10.67–70
Violent disorder 1.09, 1.56–88
  alternative verdicts 1.80–1
  as combination 1.65
  cumulative effect 1.74–5
  definition 1.59–61
  elements 1.63–4
  historical development 1.56–8
  jurisdiction 1.62
  mental element 1.78–9
  person of reasonable firmness 1.76–7
  sentencing 1.82–8
  three or more persons 1.65–70
  violence defined 1.71–3

War crimes 8.56–63
Warnings, for juveniles 9.70–2
Watching and besetting 2.154, 2.155, 2.157
  offence 2.158, 2.165–6
Water canons 6.199
Weapon of offence, trespassing with 5.165–6
Wednesbury reasonableness/ *Wednesbury*
  plus 7.27–32
Wolfenden Committee 4.105
Wood, Andrew 6.46, 6.52, 6.54, 10.148–9
Wood case (*Wood v Commissioner of Police for the*
  Metropolis) 6.03, 6.05, 6.45–6, 6.45–54, 6.52,
  6.54, 10.148–9